THE MAMMOTH BOOK OF

True Hauntings

Edited by PETER HAINING

ROBINSON   RUNNING PRESS
PHILADELPHIA · LONDON

Constable & Robinson Ltd
3 The Lanchesters
162 Fulham Palace Road
London W6 9ER
www.constablerobinson.com

First published in the UK by Robinson,
an imprint of Constable & Robinson, 2008

A copy of the British Library Cataloguing in Publication
Data is available from the British Library

UK ISBN 978-1-84529-688-9
3 5 7 9 10 8 6 4 2

First published in the United States in 2008 by
Running Press Book Publishers

9 8 7 6 5 4 3 2 1
Digit on the right indicates the number of this printing

US Library of Congress number: 2008931721
US ISBN 978-0-76243-396-4

Running Press Book Publishers
2300 Chestnut Street
Philadelphia, PA 19103-4371

Visit us on the web!

www.runningpress.com

Printed and bound in the EU

For my son
RICHARD
herein you'll find the result of all those years of *rustling* . . .

"The tea-party question, 'Do you believe in ghosts?' is one of the most ambiguous that can be asked, but if we take it to mean, 'Do you believe that people sometimes experience apparitions?' the answer is that they certainly do."

Professor H H Price, 1953

"Probably every fourth person you talk to has had an experience with a poltergeist or ghost – or knows someone who has."

Steven Spielberg, 1982

Foreword

I am a Researcher of the Supernatural

I have been fascinated by stories of ghosts since my teenage years. First as a newspaper reporter and later as an author I have investigated stories of the supernatural in Britain, Europe, America and even further afield – though never as a member of an organized group or society. This is not because I have an aversion to such organizations – far from it, because many of them have brought a scientific approach to a subject too long treated as superstitious nonsense – but I prefer to plot my own course through the voluminous material that exists on the subject in newspaper files and libraries and make my own enquiries into haunted localities with the people involved. This book, which focuses on the supernatural in the twentieth century, is the result of almost half a century of my research.

I investigated my first ghost story in the winter of 1958 as a reporter on a newspaper in rural Essex and still have the cutting from the *West Essex Gazette*. The story concerned the Holt family who lived in a 500-year-old farmhouse, Brook House Farm in Chigwell, which they claimed was haunted by a ghostly presence they named "The Invisible". Sitting in the living room of the dilapidated wood and plaster house surrounded by bowls and pails to catch the water that dripped from the ceiling whenever there was heavy rain, seventy-five-year-old Henry Holt, a retired works foreman, told me about the events that had been a regular occurrence for many years:

"The ghost paces up and down the Long Room and a tiny passageway beside it. I'm not frightened of what I can't see and it never causes any trouble. My wife and I have often laid awake at night listening to him."

My suggestions that the haunting in the house might be due to creaking timbers or the weather rattling through the rafters were immediately denied by Mr Holt and the three members of his family then living in Brook House. Hilda, one of the couple's seven children, recounted her own experience:

"It was about midnight one winter when I heard these footsteps outside my room. The next morning I asked Dad if he had been in the passage. He said, 'Me? I was asleep at that time. You must have heard *him*'."

The family had become convinced that the ghost was that of a former Vicar of Chigwell who had lived and died in the house in 1525. When I left the family late that evening after having neither heard nor seen anything myself, Mr Holt provided a tantalizing footnote to the haunting.

"We've lived in the house for eighteen years now and the ghost has been heard pretty regularly. But just recently he's stopped pacing about at night. We're all wondering why?"

I did, too. But one thing was certain: the Chigwell haunting certainly whetted my appetite to find out more about the supernatural and the paranormal. Before leaving the *Gazette*, I even had the opportunity to appeal for any ghost stories from readers and was almost overwhelmed by the response. My subsequent article, "Ghosts – West Essex has the Right Spirit for Them" was published in November 1960, and the accounts, which were a mixture of the possible and the improbable, remained in the back of my mind – as well as my expanding files of relevant material – when I moved to London to work on a magazine and, subsequently, enter the world of book publishing. My interest inspired me to publish several books of ghost stories and lead to an introduction to Paul Tabori (1908–74), then a leading authority on the supernatural and editor of the popular *Frontiers of the Unknown* series focusing on the latest developments in psychic knowledge. He was also the executor of the estate of the ghost hunter, Harry Price (1881–1948) and enabled me to gain access to Price's huge library of 15,000 books, newspaper cuttings, documents and photographs that he had bequeathed to the University of London.

My knowledge of the supernatural was increased immeasurably through consulting this archive of material and it proved invaluable when I was later working on several books on the theme. In particular with information about the experiments of the pioneer Victorian "ghost hunters" – especially the members of the Society for Psychical Research – and Price's own National Laboratory of Psychical Research. These men and women had started the search for conclusive answers to supernatural phenomena through investigations into reported hauntings in the late nineteenth and early twentieth century. The statements, cuttings and glass-plate photographs opened a window onto psychic enquiries over a hundred years ago and while exposing many of the spirit mediums to be frauds and their pictures as fakes, there were still a number of eyewitness accounts that defied a logical explanation.

The name of Harry Price is, of course, inextricably linked to Borley Rectory on the Essex/Suffolk border, which for years was known as "The Most Haunted House in England". The verdict on Price's part in this story of the Rectory, its ghostly nun, weird phenomena and ultimate fate when it was burned down in 1939, is still disputed. Some investigators believe that Price, who was a clever amateur magician, created the most striking effects himself, while others have refuted these charges – both groups ensured that the controversy continues. Living near the Rectory myself has caused me to be drawn into the argument on several occasions, in particular when a couple I knew well told me of a horrifying experience they had undergone when visiting the site of the Rectory a few years ago.

Borley Rectory

My expanding knowledge of ghost lore made me the focus of interviews locally and nationally, as well as appearances on several radio and television programmes. An interview on the prestigious BBC radio morning show, *Today*, in 1974, provoked a response that left both the producers and myself amazed. At the time, I was planning an illustrated history of ghosts and hoped to augment the many old engravings, sketches and pictures that I had collected with the addition of a few photographs. If there was anyone listening to the broadcast that had such a thing, I said, I would be very pleased to hear from him or her.

In the next three weeks I received almost one hundred letters, many of them enclosing photographs of varying quality that showed ephemeral figures in all manner of situations from old mansions to modern council flats, from gardens to open countryside. Of these, almost two dozen were clearly *not* fakes and undeniably difficult to explain. They subsequently appeared in my book, *Ghost: The Illustrated History* (1975), which sold very well in Britain and America as well as a number of other countries of the world.

Thereafter, hardly a year has passed without my receiving letters, cuttings and the occasional photograph from readers on the subject of ghosts. Among this correspondence there were some extraordinary stories that I pursued whenever time and other commitments permitted. But amongst them all was one account that still intrigues me today and I propose to share it in print here for the first time.

The letter arrived at my home in November 1976 and was from a Mr Frederick Knaggs of Hull. It was written in a neat hand and enclosed a colour photograph of a floodlit building marked "The Farmhouse". Mr Knaggs introduced himself as a man in his fifties who had served for ten years as an infantryman in combat zones with the Armed Forces and thereafter for several years in the merchant navy before settling down on Humberside. He was a man, he said, who was "accustomed to the hardness and reality of life", so what had occurred to him in 1970 had been an opinion-changing experience. He then went on to describe the events plainly and without any attempt at sensationalism:

"I was employed at Pontin's Holiday Camp at Middleton Towers near Morecambe from 1966 to 1970. While I was there I heard different stories about a ghost, known as 'The White Lady,' who was said to walk at certain times in an area of the camp by an old farmhouse near the castle wall. I heard a story of the head waiter and his wife who had woken up one night to see the ghost bending over their bed – and had left the very next day. Then there were two lady campers who woke up the camp with their screams one night after midnight when they were confronted by 'The White Lady'."

Mr Knaggs was, he said, intrigued by these stories. He was told that the ghost was believed to be that of a woman who had been murdered on her wedding night in the farmhouse over a hundred years earlier. Then he described how he had come face to face with her.

"One night I sat on the grass by the castle wall near the farmhouse from midnight until the early hours. About 2 a.m. something drew my attention and I saw the figure of a lady in an old-fashioned dress. She was pale and appeared smoky white as she walked past the castle wall. At first I couldn't believe it was a ghost. I wasn't really frightened and realized I was seeing 'The White Lady'. I was about ten yards from her. She kept stopping and then walking on until she finally disappeared into the castle tower at the end of the wall. I must have watched the ghost for about five minutes. I have no doubt at all about what I saw."

Mr Knaggs invited me, or anyone else who might be interested, to visit Middleton Towers. He was confident the ghost would be seen again. I replied to my correspondent thanking him for his story and suggested he contacted the Society for Psychical Research or The Ghost Club. At the time of writing, I am still waiting for another sighting of "The White Lady".

When I first began work on this book in the winter of 2006, sifting through a lifetime of newspaper cuttings, personal stories and archival research, I had just the kind of experience that prompts stories of hauntings. My study in Peyton House, the sixteenth-century timber-framed house where I live, is on the top floor of three in an annexe to the main building. The middle floor is my library and, below that, a storeroom. For several days I was conscious every evening of a *tap-tap* sound coming from the library below. Whenever I investigated, though, there was nothing to see.

The mysterious sounds continued and I began to wonder if the house had a *second* ghost. Readers of my earlier book, *The Mammoth Book of Haunted House Stories* (2005) will remember that Peyton House is haunted by a "smoke ghost," which makes its presence felt each June and has been seen recently by my wife, Philippa. We believe it may be the last trace of a man who died in a fire in our outbuildings during the early years of the nineteenth century, and perhaps I can recommend anyone who might be interested in the full story to consult that book.

In any event, for several more days I hurried down from my office using the spiral staircase that links the two floors before the mystery was finally explained. The cause of the sounds was nothing supernatural at all. I caught a fleeting glimpse of a small bird at the window. He tapped the window again with his beak and then, seeing me, flew off. The little creature had obviously been looking at his own reflection in the window and – fearing a rival – was trying to drive *himself* off. My "ghost" was the bird's reflection in the glass.

Despite the everyday explanation for my story, there have been a great many more reports of supernatural phenomena over the past one hundred years that have not been so simply resolved. Indeed, we live in times when at least fifty per cent of the population have some sort of paranormal belief and of these about half have had a paranormal experience. These are not my figures, but those quoted by Dr Caroline Watt, the senior lecturer at the Koestler Parapsychology Unit at the University of Edinburgh. Set up by a bequest from the famous author Arthur Koestler, it investigates such experiences. Dr Watt, who dislikes any reference to herself or her team as "Ghostbuster", is campaigning to make parapsychology a more mainstream area for research and teaching. She explained her reasons in the *Guardian* in August 2007:

"Where I work, parapsychology is defined as the scientific study of the capacity attributed to individuals to interact with their environment by means other than recognized channels. The neutral term 'psi' is used to denote this hypothesized capacity. As yet, most mainstream scientists are not persuaded that replicable evidence of psi phenomena exists. So why research and teach a controversial subject such as parapsychology at higher education institutions? Clearly psychologists and parapsychologists should play a role in trying to understand the beliefs and experiences [of the population]. In many cases, normal mechanisms, such as a need for a sense of control over one's environment or the misjudgement of the likelihood of coincidence, may cause people to (mis)interpret an experience. But there is also the possibility that psi phenomena are genuine. This is a hypothesis that can be put to test under controlled conditions and that is part of what parapsychologists do."

By putting the clock back one hundred years – as I have done in this book through the medium of newspaper reports, personal accounts and extracts – it is possible to see how the first crude attempts by the Victorians to treat ghosts and other supernatural phenomena as a subject worthy of research have developed, been refined and gained momentum in the twentieth century. Accounts of haunted houses and people seeing spirits of the dead, it will be seen, can no longer all be summarily dismissed. As recently as 1978 in his otherwise excellent book, *The Paranormal*, psychologist Stan Gooch declared, "There seems to me to be virtually no valid evidence for the existence of ghosts." In the pages that follow I think the reader will discover, as I have done as a researcher of the supernatural through fifty fascinating, intriguing and often baffling years, that there most certainly *is* the evidence.

                                                    Peter Haining

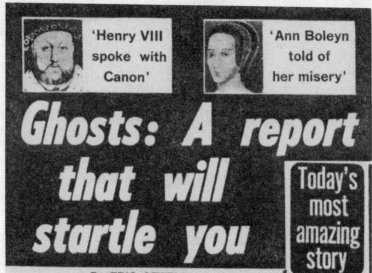

'Henry VIII spoke with Canon'

'Ann Boleyn told of her misery'

Ghosts: A report that will startle you

Today's most amazing story

By ERIC SEWELL

AN astonishing document, claiming supernatural communication with the spirits of the long-dead King Henry the Eighth and members of the Tudor Court, is to be published by an authoritative church council whose honorary vice-presidents include 13 bishops.

Entitled "The Tudor Story," this secret, 60,000-word manuscript reveals startling disclosures of strange psychic phenomena centring on the late Canon W. S. Pakenham-Walsh who died two months ago. Among the amazing claims—supported by leading figures in religious research—are:

That the earthbound spirit or "ghost" of King Henry the Eighth spoke at length with Canon Pakenham-Walsh, who acted as his father-confessor.

That the recalled spirit of Ann Boleyn sought the help of the Church in redeeming the soul of Henry the Eighth, and regarded the canon as her "champion."

That the supernatural signature of this king, who died 400 years ago, was put to a document in a Chelsea garden:

That evidence of survival after death, within the framework of the Christian Church, is clearly established in scripted reports of what took place over 30 years between spirit members of the Tudor Court and the Canon and his witnesses.

DEATH CELL

As I write, I have beside me the Canon's own diary of these incredible events. I have, too, the document purporting to bear the signature of the long-dead Henry.

Last night, Church of England colleagues of the late Canon told me: "We are prepared for fierce controversy over this fantastic and amazing manuscript. But we are also prepared to vouch for its authenticity.

"As a result of its publication, the Church may have to re-assess the whole question of contact between the earthly and the spiritual worlds."

Only their great esteem for Canon Pakenham-Walsh, say these churchmen, has overcome their cautious reluctance to make public this document—which they frankly admit is "beyond the ordinary person's experience."

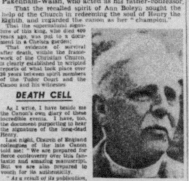

CANON PAKENHAM-WALSH

1900–09

Spectres in the Fog

Source and date: *Daily Graphic*, 5 March 1900

Mr AWC Clayden read a paper before the Royal Meteorological Society on "Spectres in the Fog." He explained that during dense fogs in February, he made a number of experiments with a view to raising his own "spectre" and disproving the validity of ghosts. This he ultimately succeeded in accomplishing by placing a steady limelight a few feet behind his head when his shadow was projected on the fog. If he breathed heavily, so that the condensed vapour drifted across the shadow, fragments of circular globes appeared fringing the head of a larger shadow than that of the fog. If he stood about eight or ten feet from the light, the outlines of the shadow were very distinct, but they became less so as he moved away, until at a distance of about twenty feet not a vestige of shadow could be seen. If a person is in a fog, he must be close to its margin, or the light will not throw a shadow. If he is on the margin, he will see the phenomena to the best advantage. If he is outside it, but not too far away for the details of his shadow to be sharp, he may be able to see the shadows of others. Again, when he is in or upon the margin of the mist, his shadow will appear enlarged and its apparent size will depend upon the density of the mist and the brightness of the light. The poet Coleridge ascended the Brocken Mountains in 1799 to see the most famous of these spectres and later saw one in England which he commemorated in verse.

The Phantom of Lincoln's Inn

Source and date: *Daily Mail*, 13 May 1901

On Saturday night, Sir Max Pemberton, the well-known author and director of this newspaper, accompanied our news editor, Mr

Ralph D Blumenfeld, in an all-night vigil to establish the veracity of claims that a Georgian house in Lincoln's Inn is haunted. It has been claimed that this shadowy corner of the ancient Inns of Court has been the centre of weird manifestations that have forced six or eight tenants to leave in a great hurry in less than two years. The supposedly haunted chambers were entirely empty of furniture beside two chairs and a card table. Alone in the house, the two men shared in the weirdest experience of their lives after making a thorough search of the premises. As Ralph Blumenfeld explains, "Even a black beetle could not have escaped unobserved." The electric lights were left on in each room and powdered chalk was sprinkled to obtain footprints of any person or thing, which might have trodden the floors. At seventeen minutes to one, the door of a small room unlatched itself very audibly and swung open to the fullest extent. At four minutes to one the door of the small room to the left behaved exactly the same. Both were closed and nothing further occurred until just before 2 a.m. when the same procedure was followed. At seven minutes past two both doors again opened in the same manner precluding any possibility that a draught might have caused the mysterious openings. Hastening to the two door-ways, the men found, clearly defined about the middle of each floor, footprints of a bird, three in the room to the left and five in that to the right. Both thought these imprints were such as a bird the size of a turkey might have made. All were sharply delineated. There was no trace of dragging. Whatever manner of thing had bequeathed these footprints to the chalk had done so with remarkable precision. At this point Blumenfeld and Pemberton decided to terminate the sitting and after measuring and sketching the footprints, left the haunted chambers to their ghostly tenant.

Ghost Troubles Village Public House

Source and date: *Illustrated London News,* 24 December 1901

As the Festive Season with its delight in ghost stories approaches, there has been much talk among the customers at *The George* in Newington, near Sittingbourne, Kent, of a spirit that does not come from the bottle. A supernatural figure has, it seems, been frightening the customers, smashing glasses and scattering objects in the bar of the village's ancient public house. According to a legend, the ghost may be that of the Earl of Rochester who was buried alive in the back garden of *The George* as a punishment for seducing a nun from a nearby nunnery [This ghost was again reported to be active in a story in the *Daily Mail*, 6 October 1982.]

Investigation of Haunted Abbey

Source and date: *The Times*, 14 November 1902

A group of members of the Society for Psychical Research are to investigate reports that the ghostly figure of Lady Elizabeth Hoby who is said to haunt the thirteenth-century Bisham Abbey at Marlow in Buckinghamshire has been seen again. Lady Elizabeth who lived in the Abbey during the sixteenth century was a scholar who studied Latin, Greek and French. She devoted a great deal of time to teaching her son, Thomas, but grew impatient when he constantly blotted his copy books with ink. One day she lost her temper and beat the poor youth to death. Following her own death, the ghost of Lady Elizabeth has haunted the Abbey vainly wringing her bloodstained hands. [The *Daily Express* reported on 21 December 1964 that during alterations at Bisham Abbey several children's copybooks full of ink blots had been found beneath the floor of one room lending further credence to the story.]

Ghost of an Elephant at Luna Park

Source and date: *Brooklyn Eagle*, 18 September 1903

Visitors to Luna Park, Coney Island have been hearing stories of the repeated appearance of the ghost of an elephant who died six months ago. Topsy, who was aged 36, was rumoured to have killed a couple of circus trainers in Texas before arriving at Luna Park. Last year, she crushed one Thomas Blount to death when he stupidly fed her a lit cigarette. Then for a time Topsy got on well, doing odd jobs at Coney Island, although she would only ever obey her *mahout*, Willy Alt. Earlier this year, she charged some workmen and it was decided she had to go. Poisoning and shooting were considered too cruel and so on a Sunday in March, Topsy was made to step on metal plates and electrocuted. Since then, according to the keeper of another elephant, Frank Gummis, the ghost of Topsy has returned twice to warn other elephants they should leave Coney Island before they suffer the same fate. Our readers will be interested to know that the press of America has had a field day with our strange story of a ghost elephant.

Phantom Cyclist?

Source and date: *Daily Mirror*, 24 December 1903

Reports have reached us of a "Phantom Cyclist" on the roads around Brighton in Sussex. People have stated that they have been repeatedly struck by "an unknown force or thing" which cannot be explained except as a manifestation of the supernatural.

Fighting Ghost: Midnight Struggle with a Spectre

Source and date: *Evening News*, 26 January 1904

The ghost of Tondu, Glamorganshire has reasserted itself in the most aggressive fashion. According to a correspondent, a respectable resident of the district which the uncanny apparition haunts and terrorizes was proceeding at midnight along a lonely, narrow roadway adjoining the deserted buildings and coke ovens of the abandoned Ynishawdra Colliery – an ideal spot for ghosts – when he was actually attacked by the unnatural monster. The gentleman is muscular, but the sight which suddenly met his gaze at the far end of a tunnel-like bridge made him turn hot and cold. An exceptionally tall, cadaverous figure was standing there, shrouded in white, with a death's-head and eyes like hollow sockets. It clasped him as though in a vice. The man could not grip. There seemed nothing more tangible than air, but he felt himself held as though in the folds of a python. With a frantic effort he clutched again at this supernatural assailant and it was gone. Women and children now creep indoors when nightfall comes and bands of stalwart men sally forth to lay the terror of Tondu.

Ghost Scare in Blyth

Source and date: *Blyth News & Ashington Post*, 14 March 1904

Our correspondent in Blyth has informed us of a "ghost scare" in the town of Blyth. After reports circulated that "something of a ghostly nature" had been reported inside a schoolhouse, large crowds gathered around the building, returning each day in the hope of solving the mystery. Stories of a white figure being seen inside one of the classrooms and a creaking noise heard in a corridor were unconfirmed as we went to press.

Mysterious Falling Stones

Source and date: *Journal of the Society for Psychical Research*, June 1904

Mr W G Grotendieck of Dortrecht, Sumatra has written to us of an experience at one o'clock in the morning last September. He was awakened by the sound of something striking the floor and the sounds continued. "I found that small black stones were falling, very slowly, from the area of the ceiling. They appeared near the inside of the roof and all my efforts to observe the stones as they erupted from the ceiling were met with frustration because they moved with extraordinary slowness." [This account is one of the first in the twentieth century to record the activities of a poltergeist.]

Spectral Visitor at Kirkstall

Source and date: *Daily Mirror*, 9 September 1904

A station porter at Kirkstall, Leeds was pacing the platform at midnight recently when he noticed a spectral figure clad, apparently, in a long grey sheet, down which streamed a long streak of red. A passenger alighting at the station early in the morning a day or two later called the attention of the same porter to a weird figure gesticulating from the roof of one of the wooden sheds which lie behind the station buildings. On another night strange lights were seen flickering around the station and the neighbourhood of the goods shed and again the ghost appeared. This time a party was formed with the object of solving the mystery, but although each one took a different direction, the search was again fruitless.

Dr Butts' Ghost

Source and date: *Occult Review*, March 1905

Last Easter-time an undergraduate at Cambridge University reported seeing a ghost in the Old Lodge of Corpus Christi College. The youth had rooms opposite those said to be haunted. At three o'clock one afternoon he was at work there and became conscious of a curious and apparently causeless sense of uneasiness. He got up and looked out of the window and saw a man with long hair leaning out of an upper window in the opposite set of rooms. Only his head and shoulders were visible and he stood very still and seemed to fix the undergraduate with a long and hostile stare. On enquiry, the young man found the door to the rooms locked and it was quite impossible for anyone to have entered them. The ghost is believed to be that of Dr Butts, Master of the College from 1626 to 1632, who described himself as a "destitute and forsaken man". Butts was found hanging by his garters in the room on Easter Sunday, 1632 and has haunted the college ever since.

Unusual Haunting in Kent

Source and date: *Daily Mail,* 28 May 1906

The stables of Mr J C Playfair at Furnace Mill, Lamberhurst, Kent have been disturbed several times this month by an unseen force. One morning, the horses were found to have been turned the reverse way round in their stalls, their tails in the mangers and their heads in the stalls. One horse was missing and later found in the hay room nearby. A partition had been knocked down to get it out and the door of the hay room was barely wide enough for a man to enter. Other phenomena included the removal of some heavy barrels of lime which were hurled down the wooden stairs; a large water butt too heavy for any human being to move overthrown; and locked and bolted doors found open. Two watchdogs were on guard at all times and had not reacted to the mysterious disturbance in any manner.

A Peculiar Parisian Ghost

Source and date *Daily Mail,* 1 May 1907

An elderly Parisian lady, Mme Blerotti, has called upon the magistrate of the Sainte Marguerite district to investigate the "something" that haunts her flat in the Rue de Montreuil. Whenever she entered her flat, she told him, she was forced onto her hands with her legs in the air. Other members of her family, including her son, had all been impelled to act in the same peculiar way. The concierge of the building told the court, "All that you have heard is true. I thought the tenants had gone mad, but as soon as I entered the room, I found myself on all fours, endeavouring to throw my feet in the air." Our correspondent states that the magistrate has "ordered the rooms to be disinfected".

Ambushing a Ghost

Source and date: *Daily Chronicle,* 19 November 1908

A queer story of a nine-feet-high spook that terrorizes Galway is told by the Dublin correspondent of the *Central News*. It is said that two young men coming into Galway from Newcastle made a short cut by the railway line and when opposite a place called Glanville they observed coming towards them on the lines a dark object which they both agree in relating was of human form and about nine feet in height. When the object came within a few yards of them, they state that it vanished. On coming into Galway, the young men told of the weird occurrence to their friends and accordingly a party was organized to visit the place the following evening and lay an ambush for the ghost. They had not long to wait, for it suddenly appeared straight in front of them whereupon one of the party raised his revolver. But he never fired a shot. The weapon dropped from his hand, which became powerless, and he fell in a swoon into the arms of one of his companions, while the ghost vanished from view. General terror prevailed among the ghost hunters lest the case of their companion might become serious and the hunt for the spectre was forgotten. A year ago several persons stated they had seen a spectre near the scene of the present apparition and there is great terror in the district over its reappearance.

1910–19

The "White Lady" of Hurstmonceaux

Source and date: *Mid-Sussex Times,* 20 December 1910

Colonel Claude Lowther, the owner of Hurstmonceaux, has added to the list of ghostly happenings associated with the famous fifteenth-century castle. One night earlier this year he saw a girl he did not recognize in the courtyard. She seemed very distressed and was wringing her hands, which he noticed were white and shrivelled. He thought she might be a gypsy girl begging, but as he walked towards her, she disappeared. The Colonel now wonders if she was the ghost of a young girl who tried to resist the advances of an earlier owner of the castle by plunging into the moat in a vain attempt to escape. Thereafter Hurstmonceaux was believed to be haunted by the "White Lady". On another occasion, Colonel Lowther says he saw a horseman in breeches and velvet jacket near the old bridge over the moat. He was himself riding at the time, and as he neared the figure it suddenly passed right through his own horse's head and disappeared.

The Bowmen: A Story of the War

Source and date: *London Evening News,* 29 September 1914

First publication of the story by Welsh journalist and author, Arthur Machen, of a company of British Expeditionary Force soldiers in danger of being cut-off by superior German troops at Mons until the intervention of ghostly archers led by Saint George. Although Machen insisted his story was a pure invention, contradictory reports by officers and men serving on the front quickly turned his piece of fiction into a fact that proved impossible to dispel for many years and haunted its creator for the rest of his life.

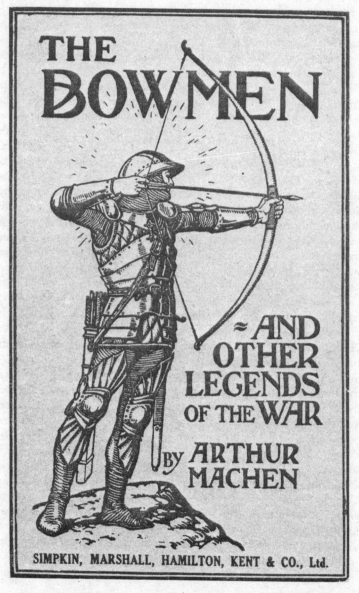

A Ghostly Ring of Angels

Source and date: *Evening News,* 27 May 1915

"There is a scientific reason for the appearance of a ring of ghostly angels round a contingent of Germans, which was reported in the Press on the information of two officers." This statement was made to the *Evening News* by Mr F L Rawson, a well-known authority on occult phenomena. "This case of the apparition which caused the Germans' horses to become unmanageable may easily have been caused through one of the English being a very religious man and believing that this would take place. If it was his particular form of belief that angels would surround a man, then his thought could sufficiently intensify the matter to enable another man who was psychic to see the apparition. That person might not know that he was psychic, but seeing the ring, he would state the fact aloud. The thoughts of those around would intensify the form and all present would see them." Mr Rawson believes that the horses would see the ghosts quite easily as animals are more psychic than human beings and can see finer forms of matter than the ordinary person could possibly see.

The Ghost of "Leathery Colt"

Source and date: *Halifax Courier,* 12 July 1915

One night in the month of January, a man and a woman were returning home about midnight from the house of a sick relative and, just as they reached the spot where the Railway Hotel now stands, there came a gust of wind and "Leathery Colt" and his dreadful horses darted by while they clung to each other in terror. Neither had heard the legend of the traveller named "Leathery Colt" who had been brutally murdered many years before at *The Fleece* in Elland and his body hidden in the cellar. Thereafter, it was said, on certain midnights, a travelling carriage with headless horses and a headless coachman would drive furiously along Westgate, the spectral vision accompanied by a sudden rush of wind and the terrified cries of those who saw it, "There goes Leathery Colt!"

Phantom Vehicle

Source and date: *Kent Messenger,* 12 March 1915

After accounts circulated last week of a phantom vehicle being seen by Colonel Leland of The Clearing, Hawkhurst, and his chauffeur, the Colonel has kindly supplied us with an account of his experience: "I had to go back to the Depot to do some work after dinner, about 9 p.m. My own car, allotted to me by the WD, and my driver, Webber, a soldier, were waiting for me, and I left the house a few minutes after nine. We had gone two or three hundred yards when I noticed a moving light on my left; concluding that it was a horse-driven vehicle coming into our road. I told Webber to slow down and let it come ahead. This was done and the vehicle, which was very indistinct, drew in and turned the way we were going. I told Webber to go up behind it and not pass. He did so and we kept close behind it for about two hundred yards. I could plainly see the back of the vehicle, which was black and appeared to be a hearse; it was moving at a trot. The queer part was I could see no driver and the two panels at the back and the keyhole for locking the doors showed up most distinctly under the rays of our lamps. When he got around a corner, I said to Webber, 'Push on.' We did so and the road before us was empty. We accelerated but there was nothing to be seen and Webber said, 'Lord, sir, what was that?' We went down and around Sunbury but did not see any vehicle. I can assure you that the vehicle, whatever it was, only rounded the corner a few yards ahead of us and there was nowhere it could have gone."

Phonographic Record of Ghosts

Source and date: *Light,* 7 August 1915

In June an experiment was carried out by Dr W J Crawford in which he took phonograph records of the raps, bell-ringing and other sounds produced at the séances for the physical phenomena which he is investigating. On Thursday, Mr Horace Leaf, who has recently visited Ireland, called upon us with one of the records kindly sent by Dr Crawford, and this was tested on a phonograph – the various sounds (with the exception of the bell-ringing, which was very faint) being clearly audible. Dr Crawford has proved to the satisfaction of himself and his fellow-investigators that the noises produced are objective sounds and not the result of collective hallucination – an important matter to the scientific investigator who desires to check his result at every step.

A Ghostly Picture

Source and date: *Sunday Times*, 20 February 1916

A strange story is told concerning the funeral of a Grenadier Guardsman named Jonathan Owen in the mining village of Risea, Monmouthshire. The soldier came home wounded from France and died recently at Harrogate. He was buried in the cemetery of his native village in the same grave as his little daughter who had just predeceased him. After the funeral, the relatives thought they would like a photograph of the grave, which was abundantly embowered in foliage and flowers. Then an amazing thing happened. When the plate was developed the photograph revealed the faces of Owen and his little girl looking out from the foliage. They are both, it is stated, plainly visible and the resemblance is convincing. This mystifying incident has created great excitement throughout the district and is being investigated by spiritualists and those interested in psychical research. [Among those who studied the photograph was Sir Arthur Conan Doyle who wrote later, "I myself investigated this matter and have found the facts to be as stated."]

Fiery Outbreaks at Swanton Rectory

Source and date: *The Times*, 30 August 1919

A series of mysterious disturbances have occurred at the Rectory of Swanton Novers, near Melton Constable, our correspondent writes. These phenomena have included spontaneous outbreaks of fire; petrol, paraffin, methylated spirits, sandalwood oil and water pouring from the ceiling; floorboards torn up and ceilings torn down, etc. The manifestations lasted for days and the fifteen-year-old maidservant was at first suspected of hoaxing the family. However, she denied this and the Rector has ventured the opinion that the disturbances had a supernatural origin. Nevil Maskelyne, the famous illusionist, also visited the Rectory and saw "barrels of oil" pouring through the ceiling. He could not explain the mystery.

1920–29

The Secret of the Skeleton

Source and date: *The Scotsman*, 14 May 1920

The completion of renovations to Fyvie Castle in Aberdeenshire may have lain to rest the famous "Green Lady Ghost" who has haunted the ancient building for centuries. The legend of the ghostly figure claims that she appears in the corridor near the "ghost room" and disappears through the panels of a dark, wainscoted apartment. When a large fungus began to grow recently in the gunroom, Lord Leith put masons and carpenters to work on restoration. During their labours, the men were horrified to discover a complete skeleton. According to reports, this discovery immediately gave rise to a number of psychic disturbances in the castle and the "Green Lady Ghost" was again seen wandering silently. Lord Leith gave instructions for the bones to be re-interred in the wall and the disturbances have ceased, our correspondent has been informed.

Ghostly Evidence of Murder

Source and date: *Daily News Record*, 26 January 1921

A man has been arrested in Philadelphia and charged with murder in consequence of a ghostly vision. Some time ago, a Mr Freeman, an engineer in the city, found one morning the dead body of his daughter lying on a couch in the drawing room. She was shot through the head. There was no clue to the crime. But, last Monday, Mr Freeman was visiting his daughter's grave. The dead girl, he declares, appeared to him in a vision and uttered the words, "Father, go and see Edwin King. He can tell you everything." King was arrested on Tuesday and charged with murder.

Another Dartmoor Phantom?

Source and date: *Western Daily Press,* 9 October 1921

Dartmoor may have a real-life phantom to match the ghostly dog, "The Hound of the Baskervilles" in Sir Arthur Conan Doyle's classic Sherlock Holmes adventure. In June, a medical officer at Dartmoor Prison was riding his motorcycle across a wild moorland road from Two Bridges to Postbridge. He had two children in the sidecar and as he drove down towards the bridge crossing the East Dart he suddenly shouted to the children to jump clear. They managed to scramble clear as the motorcycle swerved off the road and was smashed to pieces. The doctor was killed instantly. Last week, another motorcyclist was riding home on the same road. He arrived in a dazed condition and his motorcycle badly damaged. Requesting that his name was not published but insisting his story was true, the man told our reporter, "As I drove down the hill I felt a pair of rough, hairy hands close over my own on the handlebars. They dragged me off the road. I remember nothing after that until I regained consciousness and found I was lying very close to the spot where the doctor had died." [Since this report there have been several more stories about encounters with the phantom "Hairy Hands" on Dartmoor – including a similar accident to a motorcyclist in the winter of 1974.]

Ghost Moves a Piano

Source and date: *Pall Mall Gazette,* 17 February 1923

The Cambridgeshire village of Gorefield, a few miles from Wisbech, is disturbed by the activities of a ghostly agency in the house of a well-known resident. Accounts circulated of the happenings in the house have brought people from far and near, anxious to get further particulars and test the truth of the reports. It is stated that furniture is moved and ornaments dashed to the ground, and if articles are restored to their right places they are quickly upset again. Since Monday last the house has been in complete disorder, the repetition of the mischievous doings having induced the occupants to take the attitude that it is useless to restore articles to their proper places, as the ghost is thereby incited to greater assiduity in upsetting them.

Heavy articles of furniture, including a piano, have been moved several feet; a gramophone, standing on a small table at one end of the room, was mysteriously moved to a large table in the centre of the apartment; crockery in the pantry has been thrown down and smashed; while a small table in the kitchen has been seen turning round on the floor, and part of a washstand in a bedroom has been seen flying over the bed. The disturbances occur at all hours of the day and night.

The Farm of Spooks

Source and date: *Warwickshire Advertiser*, 14 April 1923

The village of Fenny Compton, near Banbury, has been attracting crowds of curiosity seekers during the past weeks anxious to see the "ghostly lights". They have all been heading for a deserted farm-house which has been nicknamed "The Farm of Spooks". There, it is said, crowds of several hundred have watched with awe on certain evenings as strange lights have danced around the property. The lights are believed to be will-o'-the-wisps, although the reason for their continued appearance has not yet been determined. [In October 1994, the *East Anglian Daily Times* announced that two University of East Anglia scientists, John Green and Peter Brimblecombe, were carrying out experiments to try and photograph these ghostly lights to establish whether burning marsh gases caused them. Dr Green told the paper, "Will-o'-the-wisps were often reported in the old days, but modern reports are few and far between and it may be that people these days are more reticent to talk about them."]

Phantom Ship Off Cape Town

Source and date: *Manchester Guardian*, 19 October 1925

A correspondent has sent us this remarkable account of the sighting of a ghost ship off the coast of South Africa. Mr N K Stone was the 4th Officer on the P&O Liner *SS Barrabool* sailing from Australia to London. On 26 January of this year, after leaving Cape Town, Mr Stone was on watch from midnight assisting 2nd Officer Mr C C West. He told our correspondent: "About 0.15 a.m. we noticed a strange light on the port bow. We looked at this through binoculars and the ship's telescope and made out what appeared to be the hull of a ship, luminous, with two distinct masts carrying bare yards, also luminous. There were no sails visible, but there was a luminous haze between the masts. There were no navigation lights and she appeared to be coming closer to us and at the same speed as ourselves. When first sighted she was about two to three miles away and when within about half a mile of us she suddenly disappeared. There were four witnesses to this spectacle, the 2nd Officer, a cadet, the helmsman and myself. I shall never forget the 2nd Officer's startled expression, "My god, Stone, it's a ghost ship." I drew a sketch of this strange ship afterwards and many people who have seen it wonder if she was the *Flying Dutchman* we saw that night.

The Flying Dutchman by André Castaigne, *Century* Magazine, July 1904.

A Phantom Army

Source and date: *The Times*, 2 August 1926

In a letter to *The Times*, Frances Balfour of Inverary submitted a document written by his father about a "ghostly vision" seen near Glen Aray in June. His father and grandfather were returning home and were nearing Garran Bridge when they were surprised to see a vast number of soldiers coming towards them. "This extraordinary sight, which was wholly unexpected, so much attracted their attention that they stood a considerable time to observe it. The army continued to advance and they counted that it had fifteen or sixteen pairs of colours, and they observed that the men nearest to them were marching upon the road six or seven abreast attended by a number of women and children some of whom were carrying tin cans and other implements of cookery. They were clothed in red and the sun shone so bright that the gleam of their arms consisting of muskets and bayonets dazzled their sight. My grandfather who had served with the Argyllshire Highlanders was mystified by the dress of the army and supposed it had come from Ireland. He observed that only one person was mounted on a grey dragoon horse and considered him the Commander-in-Chief. He had on a gold-laced hat and a blue hussar cloak, with wide-open loose sleeves, all lined in red. Their curiosity now satisfied, the two men thought it high time to provide for their security against being taken along by the force and climbed over a dyke. When they looked back to observe the motions of the army, they found to their astonishment that they were all vanished, not a soul of them was to be seen! No one has been able to explain this vision and no person to whom my father and grandfather told it doubted that they told anything but the truth.

The Poltergeist Girl

Source and date: *Daily News,* 12 October 1926

The news stories that a thirteen-year-old Rumanian girl, Eleanore Zugun, who was the target of attacks by an invisible spirit that had thrown objects at her and bitten her arm, had been brought to London for tests at the National Laboratory of Psychical Research in London, prompted this leading article by a writer who had been present: "If there is one thing about the poltergeist girl that is beyond dispute it is the fact that she is responsible in some way for the uncanny manifestations. Things are wafted away in her presence, she is bitten by unseen teeth, her face becomes scarred and disfigured, stilettos fly across her room. The suggestion that she is possessed of evil spirits is unsatisfactory and certainly unscientific. The temptation to believe that these phenomena are produced by trickery is obvious. Yet it must be remembered that these 'stigmata' have appeared not in a darkened room before the credulous, but in a laboratory of psychical research in South Kensington, before men expert in tracing every form of conscious deception or complex hysteria. The genuine character both of the markings on her flesh and the movement of the articles in her room have survived the most searching tests. Altogether the eccentricities of the poltergeist girl have proved one of the most bewildering problems, both psychical and psychological, of this generation." [Harry Price, who was one of the team who carried out the tests on the girl, claimed later, "It was not until I brought Eleanore Zugun to London in 1926 that the word 'poltergeist' became common in the British Press."]

Ghost of Fred Archer

Source and date: *East Anglian Daily Times,* 12 April 1927

A mother and her daughter walking near Hamilton Stud Lane in Newmarket saw the ghost of the great jockey Fred Archer on one of his famous grey horses at the weekend. Mrs Elsie Jarrett and her teenager daughter, Mary, were out for a walk on Saturday morning when a horse and rider emerged silently from a copse of trees and galloped towards them. Just as the horse neared them, it vanished as mysteriously as it had appeared. Mrs Jarrett, who had seen Archer ride on a number of occasions in Newmarket, saw the features of the rider quite distinctly and was in no doubt that it was the jockey – although he died almost forty years ago. Mary confirmed her mother's story and said she also recognized the face of the man who had won the Derby five times. This is not the first time Archer mounted on a phantom horse has been reported in the Newmarket area. His ghost is said to have been responsible for a number of unexplained mishaps on the Newmarket Course in recent years.

A Living Woman's Ghost

Source and date: *Daily Express*, 21 December 1928

The Shropshire village of Northwood is in a state of excitement over a series of mysterious nightly visitations. Stories are told of a woman's figure, which has been seen by several people, all of whom agreed that she is dressed in sombre clothing, as distinguished from orthodox ghostly habitments; and is the image of a local farmer's wife who lives in the neighbourhood. A farmer named Morris and a workman named Peate were returning homeward one night with a horse and trap when they saw the woman and stopped the horse with the view of giving her a "lift" as they knew her well. She disappeared suddenly and although the men actually got out of the trap and searched for her she was not to be found. Two nights later Mr Morris saw her again. Mr Arthur Ellis, a wireless factor, was driving his car in the same district and distinctly saw the woman, whom he knows well. She was standing in the road and he jammed on the brakes and swerved to avoid her, pulled up, and found – nothing. This story is corroborated in every detail by a boy named George Bach who was in the car at the time. Many of the more adventurous spirits are prowling the roads at night and it seems that those who have deliberately gone out to watch have drawn a blank every time.

Secret of Peel Castle

Source and date: *Westminster Gazette*, 5 June 1929

"Will anything be brought to light about the *Moody dhoe*?" Peel folk are asking uneasily in connection with the excavations now being made at Peel Castle. *Moody dhoe* is Manx for black dog and Peel Castle for centuries has been famed – if for nothing else – for its tradition concerning the apparition of a black dog, which is said to haunt the place. When the castle was used as a soldiers' garrison the black dog was often seen, it is said, and more than one had died from trying to find the creature in the dark passage where it lives. Superstitious folk about Peel believe that it is as well to let sleeping dogs lie and they hope that no effort will be made to pry into the secret of the closed passage.

Ghostly Visitation in Suffolk Rectory

Source and date: *Daily Mirror*, 10 June 1929

Ghostly figures of headless coachmen and a nun, an old-time coach drawn by two bay horses which appears and vanishes mysteriously, and dragging footsteps in empty rooms. All these ingredients of a first-class ghost story are awaiting investigation by psychic experts near Long Melford, Suffolk. The scene of the ghostly visitations is the Rectory at Borley, a few miles from Long Melford. It is a building erected on the part of the site of a great monastery which, in the Middle Ages, was the scene of a gruesome tragedy. The present Rector, Rev G E Smith, and his wife made the Rectory their residence in the face of warnings by previous occupiers. Since their arrival they have been puzzled and startled by a series of peculiar happenings which cannot be explained, and which confirm the rumours they heard before moving in. Mr Smith has heard the sound of slow, dragging feet across the floor of an unoccupied room and a servant girl brought from London suddenly gave notice after two days' work, declaring emphatically that she had seen a nun walking in the wood at the back of the house. Finally, comes the remarkable story of an old-fashioned coach, seen twice on the lawn by a servant, which remained in sight long enough for the girl to distinguish the brown colour of the horses. Mr Smith has explained that the previous Rector of Borley, now dead, often spoke of the remarkable experience he had one night when, walking along the road outside the Rectory, he heard the clatter of hoofs. Looking around, he saw to his horror an old-fashioned coach lumbering along the road, driven by two *headless men*. [This was the first report of the ghosts of Borley Rectory that would soon become known as "The Most Haunted House in England" as well as the most publicized and controversial case of supernatural activity in the twentieth century.]

1930-39

The Ghost of Charles Dickens

Source and date: *Daily Star*, 10 July 1930

Among the many memories of Sir Arthur Conan Doyle who died this week it has been recalled that the creator of Sherlock Holmes claimed to have been in contact with the creator of Scrooge, Charles Dickens. In September 1927, Sir Arthur, whose interest in Spiritualism is well-known, told a public meeting that he had spoken with the spirit of Charles Dickens. At a séance at Sir Arthur's country house in the New Forest, an instrument like a planchette spelled out the word *BOZ*. In a later exchange about the unfinished novel, *Edwin Drood*, Sir Arthur said that the spirit of Dickens had told him, "The poor chap had a hard time. I always hoped you would put Sherlock on his track. I don't know which is better – to solve the mystery in your notebook or let it remain a mystery." [On 4 January, 1977, the *Daily Telegraph* reported that a "Dickensian Ghost" was believed to be haunting BMA House in Tavistock Square, which stands on the site of Tavistock House, Charles Dickens' home. Several cleaners had talked of strange occurrences in the library including a mysterious figure, the opening and closing of doors and "a mysterious swaying of the heavy curtains". The paper added that it was during his stay at Tavistock House that Dickens's marriage broke up and during one of the amateur theatrical performances that the author used to arrange there, he even introduced a fictional ghost as "being redolent of lost love".]

Hotel Bedroom Ghost

Source and date: *Vale of White Horse Gazette,* 18 August 1933

On the night of Sunday the 13th, Miss Ruby Bower, whose uncle and aunt held the licence of the Black Horse Inn in Cirencester, awoke at midnight with a strange feeling. She felt fearful and uneasy before she opened her eyes. This changed to a sensation of terror when she did so because the room was bathed in an unearthly light. A rustling sound in the corner of the room caused her to look up and her horror increased as she beheld an apparition in the shape of a stout old lady with an evil face and a grim expression, gliding slowly across the floor. Despite her fears and the fact that the whole thing could not have lasted more than a fraction of a second, every detail of the scene is indelibly impressed on Miss Bower's memory. She recalls the old-fashioned clothes of the midnight visitor, the long fawn-coloured dress of stiff silk that rustled as the old lady moved, the white apron with its frills, and the white frilly mob cap. Miss Bower sat up in bed, screamed out, "No! No! Don't! Don't!" at which the ghost vanished. The bedroom was later searched and on one of the panes of the window the name "John" had been scratched several times in the form of old-fashioned handwriting. Disbelievers would say that the writing was there before Sunday – but the landlord is confident that it was not there previously. [In the succeeding weeks, a special investigation into the sighting was carried out and on 8 September, the *Gazette* reported that a medium had been called to the Inn and "the Cirencester Ghost has been laid".]

"Ghost Train" in Sweden

Source and date: *Morning Post,* 3 October 1933

A "ghost train" appearing between the Orresta and Tortuna Station on the Vaesteraas Railway in Central Sweden has frightened and mystified the country people of that district. Recently a party of five persons, while walking on the road near the railway, suddenly saw a lighted train at high-speed glide noiselessly along the railway line. It looked exactly like the ordinary train which was due half an hour later, except for the head and tail lanterns, which were unusually bright and powerful. It was clearly seen by the entire company, but no one heard the slightest sound from it. On several previous occasions the same sight has been seen by single persons in exactly the same spot, but no one has been able to account for it or to offer a satisfactory explanation. Some years ago the railway bank caved in at this section of the line and the old people of the district now prophesy some serious accident. A similar sight one or two years ago frightened people in a desolate part of Lapland where a phantom train was seen rushing through the forest in a district where there was no railway at all.

The Ghost of Oscar Wilde

Source and date: *News Chronicle,* 3 February 1934

The ghost of Oscar Wilde – a pale-faced dandy of a ghost in a loose-flowing tie – is reported to be walking again in the rooms he occupied 60 years ago in Magdalen College, Oxford. The present occupant, Mr Tony Kelly, claims to have been visited at midnight this week by his predecessor. Mr Kelly is an Australian and plays ice hockey for the University – not a man given to aesthetic fancies. He said yesterday, "I had gone to bed about half-past eleven, but for some reason I could not get to sleep. Suddenly I had a most extraordinary feeling, a sort of goose flesh, as if someone was in the room. And so there was – standing by the window – a tall man with a long jacket, very old-fashioned with rows of buttons and very short lapels with a loose tie that was tied in a big knot. He began to walk up and down. I spoke to him and he didn't answer. I put out my hand as he came near me and it went straight through where he seemed to be. Finally he walked away into a corner of the room and just faded out of sight. There isn't a door in that corner, either." It was in these rooms that

Wilde wrote the poem, "Ravenna", that won the Newdigate Prize when he was an undergraduate.

Ghost Bus of Kensington

Source and date: *Morning Post*, 16 June 1934

During an inquest at Paddington yesterday, the junction of St Mark's Road and Cambridge Gardens, North Kensington was stated to be the place where local people had reported that a ghost bus was seen. The inquest was on Ian James Beaton, aged twenty-five, metallurgical engineer, of Hamilton Road, Dollis Hill, who died following a collision between the car he was driving and another driven by Mr George Pink, the chauffeur of the Hon Samuel Vestey of Manchester Square. The jury returned a verdict of accidental death and exonerated Mr Pink. Frederick Robinson of Chesterton Road, Kensington, a witness, said the junction was noted for accidents and it was claimed to be where a ghost bus had been seen. A woman resident in Cambridge Gardens said, "The legend of the phantom bus has been going strong for years. The version I heard was that on certain nights, long after the regular bus service has stopped, people have been awakened by the roar of a bus coming down the street. When they have gone to their windows they have seen a brilliantly lighted double-decker bus approaching with neither driver nor passengers. According to this story, the bus goes careering to the corner of Cambridge Gardens and St Mark's Road and then vanishes. A number of accidents have happened at this corner and it has been suggested that the phantom bus has been the cause." Another version is that the bus, which a woman has been told by a conductor to board, "vanished into thin air" when she approached it. [This legend is believed to have been the inspiration for E F Benson's famous ghost short story "The Bus Conductor" ' which was later adapted into an episode in the classic British horror film, *Dead of Night* (1945).]

Girl Typist Saw Ghost Fall

Source and date: *Sunday Pictorial*, 29 July 1934

A London typist on her way home fainted on passing an office building. She was carried into a chemist's shop in Aldwych. On recovering, she declared that she had had the impression as she walked that a girl had fallen from the window of a high building and crashed at her feet. The shock was so great that she collapsed. Exactly eighteen months ago, the tragedy she described actually happened – a girl fell from an upper storey and was killed at the very spot where the typist, who had never heard of the accident, fainted. A famous psychologist told the *Sunday Pictorial* that there are people with such sensitive minds that they can conjure up subconsciously pictures of past events. These people, placed in environments where tragedies have happened, can describe in minutest detail the particulars of the tragedy – and such experiences are by no means uncommon. The psychologist said, "Recently I had a patient who told me she could not pass a certain street corner near her house as she always seemed to see a motor-bus pinned against the wall there. I made enquiries and found that seventeen years previously – during the war and long before she came to the neighbourhood – a bus ran on to the pavement at this spot and seven people were killed."

The Talking Ghost of Saragossa

Source and date: *The Times,* 26 November 1934

The "voice" of a ghost speaking down a stovepipe in a flat in a detached house has caused a sensation throughout Spain and Europe. The house, inhabited by a family named Palazaon in the Calle Gascon de Gotor, Saragossa, has been visited by scores of people, including the police and medical men, who have all heard the "voice". It appears to be that of an intelligent entity, has spoken for hours on end, answered questions and even asked them. All yesterday afternoon the ghost talked almost incessantly and last night on the orders of a local magistrate the police were preparing to evict the family and remain in the building in the hope of laying the "Duenda de Zaragoza" as the ghost has been called. [A further report in *The Times* of 3 December said the ghost had continued to talk until two days ago, "when it said its final piece and vanished – perhaps for ever. The mystery has never been solved."]

Vampire Ghost that Bullets Cannot Harm

Source and date: *Morning Post,* 2 February 1935

Several families living in a village near Gnjilane, in southern Serbia, are living in terror of their lives through the manifestations of a supernatural being believed locally to be a vampire ghost. Invisible and impervious to rifle bullets, the being enters peasants' houses at the dead of night, opens locked chests, levitates logs of wood from the fire, drenches peasants, their wives and children, with jugs of water and drives the cattle in the byres to frenzy. The phantom does not seem to be afraid of the light, for two of the braver peasants ambushed in one of the haunted houses witnessed the efficient imitation of a spiritualist séance and fired on him, upon which he departed giving three final thundering knocks on the door.

Ghostly Submerged Bells Heard

Source and date: *Brecon and Radnor Express*, 19 December 1935

The bells of a cathedral submerged beneath Langorse Pool, Breconshire have been heard again this year, it has been reported. The dull ringing sound is said to be heard at times of great stillness. These accounts remind us of the story of the thieves who stole a bell from the tower of St David's Cathedral and endeavoured to carry it away by sea. The bell, however, was lost when the sacrilegious crew suffered a shipwreck off the Pembroke coast. Seamen along our coast still declare that whenever they hear it chiming on the ocean bed, they know they can expect a spell of wild weather.

Psychic Experiment on the Brocken

Source and date: *The Morning Star*, 18 June 1932

A group of prominent British and German investigators into psychic phenomena ascended last night to the top of "The Brocken", Germany's magic mountain, and, in accordance with ancient rites, attempted to change a billygoat into a young man. As demanded in the *High German Black Book*, the experimenters had the assistance of Miss Gloria Gordon of England, "a maiden pure of heart" and they anointed the billygoat with blood and honey and the scrapings of church bells. They used a proper pine fire and described a circle of the prescribed size and they uttered every one of the Latin incantations stipulated for such goings-on. The goat was led into the magic circle by a silver cord and a white sheet was thrown over it. Then, in a weird monotone, Harry Price, director of the National Laboratory of Psychical Research, boomed, "One" and with the proper pauses counted to ten. The maiden pure in heart whisked off the white sheet – and there stood the billygoat, somewhat the worse for blood and honey and the scraping of church bells, shivering in the cold. The one hundred or so spectators applauded heartily and the investigators said they were satisfied. They had not expected the hocus-pocus to work anyway – it was all a matter of proving, by painstaking experiment, that there was nothing in all this witchcraft business.

The Spectral Mansion

Source and date: *East Anglian Daily Times,* 11 March 1934

In October 1926, Ruth Wynne and a young girl of fourteen, both newcomers to the area, came across a large house of ancient design while walking from Rougham Green to Bradfield St George near Bury St Edmunds. The house was set behind tall, wrought-iron gates and was reached by a driveway through tall trees. The pair gazed at the building through the trees and saw a corner of the roof above a stucco front and some windows that appeared to be of Georgian design before continuing on their way. A few months later, in February or March, taking the same route, Miss Wynne and her friend were astonished to find no trace of this spectral mansion. [This story has strong similarities with the experiences of two academics, Miss Anne Moberley and Miss Elinor Jourdain, when they were walking at Versailles and saw a gathering of some of the most celebrated figures of the court of Louis XVI, including Marie Antoinette. Their account, *An Adventure*, published that same year, has been regularly reprinted, filmed and dramatized without a solution being found for the mystery, although it has been suggested that in both cases, the women slipped momentarily through a time-fault.]

Haunted House Broadcast

Source and date: *The Listener,* 10 March 1936

A successful broadcast was carried out on Saturday night at an old haunted house near Meopham in Kent. The house belonged to a friend of the psychic investigator Harry Price, who arranged the transmission with Mr S J de Lotbiniere, BBC Director of Outside Broadcasts. The broadcast provided listeners with an idea of the techniques used to investigate an alleged haunting. One phenomenon did occur when the sensitive transmitting thermograph which had been operating in the house's "haunted cellar" showed a sudden rise in temperature at 9.45 p.m. during the broadcast. Almost immediately afterwards it fell sharply below what had been measured during the day. Neither Mr Price nor Mr de Lotbiniere could account for this "kick" in any terms of normality. A member of the BBC transmission team who slept in the house after the broadcast said the next morning that he had definitely heard footsteps in the early hours that could not be accounted for.

The "Brown Lady" Photograph

Source and date: *Country Life*, December 1936

The photograph depicting a shadow figure on the stairs of Raynham Hall in Norfolk was taken by Captain Provand who, with his assistant, Mr Indre Shira, were taking pictures of the staircase. While at work, Mr Shira suddenly called out that he could see an apparition and told Provand to take another shot. The photographer obliged, though he did not see the ghost in the viewfinder. Mr Shira bet him five pounds that it would appear on the photographic plate and has won his bet. The negative has been examined by experts who have been unable to find any hint of faking. A portrait of the "Brown Lady" who is believed to be the figure on the staircase hangs in the house. She is Dorothy Walpole, the daughter of Robert Walpole and sister of the famous Sir Robert Walpole. She died in 1726 and a local legend maintains she was found with a broken neck at the foot of the grand staircase at Raynham.

Germany Declares Psychic Research a Science

Source and date: *Occult Review*, March 1937

The German Government has declared that it is prepared to give its blessing to a Department of Parapsychology at Bonn University. After discussions between the German Home Office, Board of Education, the Foreign Office and Ministry of Propaganda, the Third Reich has "authorized the establishment of a *Forschungstelle fur Psychologische Grenzwisswen schaften* – Department for Abnormal Psychology and Parapsychology – to investigate the incidence of supernatural phenomena within Germany and among Germanic peoples." This is of great historical importance as the Third Reich is the first Government officially to place its cachet on psychical research and is the more striking as spiritualism has been suppressed in Germany.

Photographing a Ghost Dog

Source and date: *Daily Mirror*, 13 May 1937

In the column "Reader's Parliament", Edward Lloyd of Swinford, Rugby writes, "Four years ago when visiting the beautiful Welsh village of Beddgelert, I went to see the grave of Gellert, Llewellyn's faithful dog. I took a photograph of the grave, under the tree, whilst my companion stood nearby. We were the only living persons in the field where the grave is found. After the photo was developed, we discovered a third figure on the left of my friend. It was a large dog sitting on its haunches."

The Ghost Club Arises!

Source and date: *Daily Express* 15 March 1938

The Ghost Club, which was founded in 1862 to investigate cases of psychic phenomena and was revived again in 1881, has been given another new lease of life thanks to the efforts of the well-known ghost hunter, Harry Price. The Club will aim to encourage scientific research into ghosts and other supernatural phenomena through public meetings, lectures and organised ghost hunts. The speaker at the inaugural meeting last night was Mr S G Soul of London University who gave a talk on "Snags in ESP".

Ghost-Ridden Rectory Razed

Source and date: *Daily Mail,* 28 February 1939

Borley Rectory, described as the most haunted house in England, has been razed by a mysterious fire. Its new owner, Captain Gregson, was unpacking books in the hallway when he saw an oil lamp crash to the ground of its own free will. According to eyewitnesses, a woman and a man emerged from the flames. Then they disappeared. When Sudbury Fire Brigade arrived they found the front ground-floor rooms and the bedrooms above ablaze, and before they could obtain control, a portion of the roof fell in. The house had been built on the ruins of a convent and legend has it that in the thirteenth century a monk had been caught trying to elope with a young novice. He was hanged and she was walled up alive, condemned to haunt the spot forever.

Roman Ghost on the March

Source and date: London *Evening News,* 24 July 1939

Except for a few psychic research enthusiasts, the East Mersea road from Mersea will be deserted tonight. None of the local folk will use it. Doors and windows will be fastened – because the armour-clad Roman warrior is walking again. Fields near Barrow Hill, a centuries-old mound on Mersea Island, are stated by experts to have been burial grounds of the Roman period. From these fields, say the local folk, the Roman warrior rises by night. Clad in armour, he patrols the Strood, the Roman road leading to East Mersea. Twice during the last few days – after a lapse of many years – the Roman ghost is said to have been seen marching sorrowfully along the road.

1940-49

Revenge of the Veiled Figure

Source and date: *Daily Mirror*, 22 November 1940

A few days ago news spread through the south of Greece that Greek soldiers on a lonely parade on the Athenian front encountered a veiled figure in the darkness who, when challenged, threw aside her veil revealing the face of the Blessed Virgin. To the awe-struck soldiers, the virgin declared, "It is I! I will not forget to revenge myself through my Greek soldiers on my own day." This report is believed to explain the Greek advance against the Italian forces although the vision is regarded in British military circles to be as true as any other vision of angels that has ever been seen. In England, there have been a number of accounts of "Phantom Armies", notably the report by a retired Lieutenant-Colonel in Devon who, while out walking with his dog, saw a misty group of figures marching in the direction of Dartmouth who he was convinced were a troop of soldiers kitted out for embarkation.

Poltergeists and Nazis

Source and date: *Guardian* 25 July 1941

In an article on the Supernatural at War, David Parson is quoted: "There are extraordinarily significant points of resemblance between the records of Poltergeist hauntings and the Nazi movement. Both are manifested in a subconscious uprush of desire for power. Both suck like vampires the energies of adolescents; both issue in noise, destruction, fire and terror. Hitler

speaks best in a state of semi-trance. Whether the uprush of unconscious energy generated through him and sucking into itself the psychophysical forces of German youth is merely the outcome of an unformulated group-desire for power, or whether, like some of the Poltergeist hauntings, it would seem to have another source, is an open question." Mr Sacheverell Sitwell says something similar in his recently published book, *Poltergeists*: "Adolf Hitler is the perfect type of medium if ever there was one. We could readily believe that this remarkable person, did he feel so inclined, could displace objects and move them about in oblique or curving flight; could rap out equivocal answers; or cause lighted matches to drop down from the ceiling."

Slaughter in the Mountains

Source and date: *Scotsman,* 14 October 1941

The celebrated mountaineer, Frank S Smythe, has described a strange encounter while he was travelling across the Highland hills from Morvich to Loch Duich. Although it was a bright, sunlit day, he experienced a sensation of "something sinister" as he entered the defile which led down to Glen Glomach. "A score or more of ragged people, men, women and children, were struggling through the defile," he says. "They appeared very weary, as though they had come a long way. The pitiful procession was in the midst of the defile when all of a sudden from either side concealed men leapt to their feet and, brandishing spears, axes and clubs, rushed down with wild yells on the unfortunates beneath. There was a short fierce struggle, then a horrible massacre. Not one man, woman or child was left alive; the defile was choked with corpses. Moments later everything had vanished. I am not a superstitious person, but it seemed to me that I had been vouchsafed a backward glance into a bloodstained page of Scottish history."

Frendlins Make War on Gremlins!

Source and date: *New York Sun,* 14 July 1943

American squadrons plagued by the misfortunes brought about by Gremlins now have help at hand. Counter-magic is being used in the shape of the Frendlin – created by Walter Frisch – a typical American kid with a big grin, standing on a horseshoe, a lucky wishbone holding up his suspenders, and a four-leaf clover in his hand. Made of brightly coloured papier mâché, the Frendlin has become the mascot of Gremlin-plagued US squadrons wherever they go. They have also gotten around further. The Frendlin now perches on the desks of a score of generals and he goes wherever they go. He is also the official mascot of United Airlines. [A certain RAF Flight-Lieutenant, Roald Dahl, wrote a short book about these phenomena, *The Gremlins* (1943) which was bought for filming by Walt Disney and put him on the road to international fame as an author of horror stories and children's books.]

Poltergeist Upsets Land Girls

Source and date: *South Wales Echo,* 2 August 1943

This summer there has been a great commotion in the hostel of the Women's Land Army at Gill House, Aspatria, Cumberland. There have been weird noises, ghastly smells and strange figures, all of which have disappeared at daybreak. Several of the girls have vowed they have seen a phantom shape "walking through doors" and one girl was awakened "with the feeling that she was being strangled and pulled through the bed". A local clergyman believes that a poltergeist is responsible for the interferences and was asked to exorcize the hostel. But when he and his wife slept there they heard "rappings travelling to and fro along one of the walls" and felt there was something "unearthly" about the place. Two Women's Land Army officers decided to spend a night in the haunted dormitory, but before dawn "left the room pale and haggard".

Ghost Wrecked a Room

Source and date: *Evening Standard,* 8 December 1943

When Madame Aucher and her daughter, Genevieve, aged 16, went to sleep in a house at Frontenay-Rohan near Poitiers, France, they yearned for a little rest during troubled times. During the night, the girl was suddenly lifted up by what is said to be a "supernatural agency" and thrown to the foot of the bed. The bedclothes were raised up to the roof and suspended in mid-air. Plates and ornaments were thrown violently across the room. When the terrified Madame and her daughter tried another room and sat down on some chairs, these were whisked away from under them and then overturned. A priest was called in to exorcize the house and a policeman sent to investigate. According to a sworn statement made later, an oaken dresser moved away from the wall and crashed to the floor, a table nearly crushed Gendarme Pillon, and the marble top of a table was cracked by a violent unseen blow. As neither prayers nor police have been able to stop the phenomenon, the mother and daughter have left the district.

Journalist's Eyewitness to Ghost

Source and date: *Halifax Mail-Star*, 10 January 1944

A *Mail-Star* reporter and photographer have witnessed the activities of a dangerous ghost that began attacking the Halifax home of Mrs Ethel Hilchie on Christmas Eve. The first sign that anything was amiss was a series of knockings which continued over the New Year until, in desperation, Mrs Hilchie informed the police and this newspaper. Our reporter was actually interviewing her when an outhouse door locked itself and a metal hoop came sailing through the air from an unknown source. As Mrs Hilchie continued her story, a pair of scissors on a shelf opened and closed and a kettle of boiling water upset itself on the stove. During our reporter's visit he also saw a bowl of soup spilled into the lap of one of Mrs Hilchie's children, a soap box fly down a flight of stairs and an alarm clock take flight from a dresser. The *Mail-Star* photographer who visited the Hilchie home in the hope of getting some pictures of the poltergeist was also attacked. He said that nothing happened until he was just about to leave, "when a flash bulb jumped out of my bag and smashed itself on the floor".

"Old Mary" Hates Spirits

Source and date: *American Weekly*, 20 February 1944

When night falls over the little town of Boyle in Eire, the folk who live there make sure their houses are secure from possible attack by "Old Mary", a ghost who hates drinkers and bar rooms. For more than fifty years, each February, this teetotal spirit has returned to haunt the place where she was once the wife of a well-known temperance leader, and died in 1919 vowing to "come back and check out Boyle every single winter". One local resident, Mrs Martha Ann Wylder, said she has seen "Old Mary" on at least twenty-two different occasions. Mrs Wylder, a seamstress and church worker, had known Mrs Kelly well, so she could not be mistaken. "She always comes in from the south, brandishing a big, ugly shillelagh, and makes straight for the places that sell liquor." Two Boyle bartenders, Frank L Kennedy and Hobson Moore, insist they have been confronted by "Old Mary" on two different occasions. Kennedy stated that the ghost "came into my place late in the evening last year, or at least I saw a shillelagh sailing through the door because it was closed. I lost two of my last bottles of imported bourbon." Mr Moore added that on the same night and at almost the identical time, "I felt a cold breeze and all of a sudden a good half-dozen quarts of Irish whiskey toppled to the floor!"

Schoolhouse "Bewitched"

Source and date: *Toronto Globe & Mail,* 14 April 1944

On 28 March, R L Swenson, Stark County Superintendent of Schools, called the Marshall's Office to report "strange happenings" at the Wild Plum schoolhouse, twenty miles south of Richardton, which local people believe is "bewitched". State Fire Marshall Charles Schwartz said his investigation disclosed "a remarkable story beyond belief" pieced together from the sworn testimony of officials, pupils and the teacher, Mrs Pauline Rebel. Mrs Rebel and her eight pupils had been amazed when a pail of lignite coal near the stove had begun to stir restlessly without any apparent cause. Lumps of coal started popping out of the pail like Mexican jumping beans, striking the wall and bounding back. Jack Steiner, a pupil, was hit on the head and slightly injured. The coal pail tipped over and the lumps of lignite ignited. Window blinds on all nine windows started smouldering and a bookcase also burst into flames. Marshall Schwartz said the school officials testified that when they arrived the coal was still "reacting to a mysterious force" and pieces actually trembled in their hands. Analysis by the State chemist failed to reveal any chemical which might have caused such action. "We plan to send the pail and a sample of the coal to the F B I in Washington," added Schwartz. School officials have closed the school pending an investigation.

"Angel" Seen in Peckham Raid

Source and date: *South London Times*, 8 September 1944

Stories of the appearance of an angel in the sky – similar to the "Angel of Mons" in the last war – have been reported by a number of people in Peckham, who state that the vision, which took place during a flying-bomb raid on Southern England, lasted for twenty minutes. It happened at 6 a.m. and the apparition was described by Mrs E Halsey, 67 Hornby Road, as an inspiring and impressive sight. "I have never seen anything so wonderful," she told a reporter. "I believe it was the Angel of Peace. It appeared quite plainly in the sky. The figure was perfect, with large outstretched wings, as if guarding something. The arms were held out and the face looking down. It stayed in the sky for about twenty minutes. There was no question it could be a cloud, because clouds were rushing over it." Mrs Halsey was asleep when her husband, who was "spotting", called her to see the figure. "I was rather annoyed at being awakened at 6 a.m. for I had had very little sleep," she remarked. "Afterwards I was glad I did not miss it. It shook us all up and made us think." Mr D L Phillips, 80 Hornby Road, was also "spotting" and saw the figure. "It was early in the morning so no one could say I was not sober. There was a large cloud of dust rising where a bomb had fallen and the figure seemed to turn its head and look in that direction." Other people also say they are sure it was the figure of an angel. [In response to an article, "They Saw Angels" in the *Daily Telegraph* 7 August 1988, a reader, K W G Williamson of Middlesbrough, wrote, "I can claim to have heard an angel singing – once in a Tiger Moth whilst training in South Africa and again while flying a Spitfire over North Africa. I am sure there are other pilots who can testify to having heard these melodious voices."]

The Witch Walks at Scrapfaggot Green

Source and date: *Sunday Pictorial*, 8 October 1944

Queer things are happening in the remote Essex village of Great Leighs – strange things that seem to defy any normal explanation. Among its straggling lanes and among its scattered cottages, the villagers will tell you great stones are moved mysteriously, straw ricks are overturned on windless nights, sheep stray through un-broken hedges and the church bells ring at odd times. At the eerie centre of it all is Scrapfaggot Green where two hundred years ago a witch was burned at the stake. She was buried under the ashes of the fire that burned her and a great stone was placed over her breast to hold her down. For 200 years there she lay, untroubled and untroubling. But when the war swept through the village, the narrow, winding lanes would not take military traffic so a bulldozer widened them and brushed aside the witch's stone. From that moment, strange happenings began in the village and now there is hardly a man or woman who has not a story to tell of things that don't fit in with ordinary common. Harry Price, head of the London University Council for Psychical Investigation, has been told the story and has a theory. The troubles at Scrapfaggot Green, he thinks, may be caused by a noisy, mischievous spirit. "I have heard several stories of poltergeists which have been put down to the influence of witches," he says. "The spirit usually confines itself to one building, but here a whole village has been affected. It is extraordinary."

Evil Apparition in Hampstead

Source and date: *Daily Telegraph*, 3 September 1947

A ghost has finally driven Mr Brian Harvey, the manager of *The Gatehouse* public house in Hampstead Lane out of his premises. Last month ago he was taken to hospital suffering from shock after claiming to have seen a ghost. He later returned to the pub but was forced to leave on the advice of his doctor. A London medium Trixie Allingham has visited *The Gatehouse* and found the gallery "a cold, evil place". She told the owners that during her visit she clearly saw the ghost of a white-haired smuggler who was said to have been murdered on the premises after an argument over money.

Headless Ghost in Pre-fab

Source and date: *Sunday Dispatch,* 28 March 1948

The ghost of a headless man is causing considerable alarm to people living in prefabricated bungalows in Page Road, Bedfont, Middlesex – so much so that the police have been called in. The bungalows, which are detached, were built by the Feltham Council on land which once formed part of the notorious Hounslow Heath, one-time haunt of highwaymen. For weeks past strange "things" have been happening in the house, No 42, occupied by Mr Joseph Wilkinson, a coach driver, his wife Mary, 27, and Patricia, their four-year-old daughter. They have been haunted by a headless figure. One night the little girl screamed to her parents, "There's a man sitting on my bed." Then when the Wilkinsons' dog Dusty went hysterical with fear overnight, the family sought refuge with a neighbour who sent for the police. The family are now thinking of asking psychic research investigators to visit the bungalow.

Ghost Hunter Accused of Fraud

Source and date: *Daily Mail,* 30 March 1948

The ghost hunter Harry Price who died earlier this month has been accused of fraud by another investigator who went with him on several visits to Borley Rectory in Suffolk, "the Most Haunted House in England". Journalist Charles Sutton visited the Rectory in 1929 and believes that Price "fraudulently manufactured phenomena" to support the ghost stories surrounding the house and his books on the subject. Sutton says that during a visit "an apported pebble hit me on the head". He adds, "After much noisy phenomena, I seized Harry and found his pockets full of bricks and pebbles. This was one phenomenon he could not explain." The claim has been supported by Mrs Mabel Smith, who lived in the Rectory with her husband, Reverend G Eric Smith from October 1928 to July 1929. "I was in residence for some time at Borley Rectory and would like to state that neither my husband or myself believed the house haunted by anything else but rats and local superstition."

1950-59

Evil of the Epsom Ghost

Source and date: *Daily Mail*, 17 July 1950

An evil spirit is terrifying the Sargent family of Epsom in Surrey. The ghost has physically attacked Mrs Betty Sargent several times and she is now afraid it is trying to kill her. She says, "One night I felt something trying to strangle me. I woke up my husband and we left the bedroom and went into the lounge to get away from whatever it might be and tried to sleep on the couch. But in a few minutes the thing tried to choke me again." On another night she was struck by a lamp which rose up from a small bedside table, hit her on the head and then landed on Mr Sargent's head. He continued, "One night, Betty was sitting up in bed when something began pulling her shoulders. It dragged her towards the window, lifting her body so that only her legs and thighs were touching the bed. She cried out for help – I grabbed her by the legs. But whatever it was had very great strength. At first I couldn't hold it, I felt myself being pulled towards the window, too. Then all at once it seemed to lose its power and Betty fell." Mrs Sargent said, "If my husband hadn't been there, I could quite easily have been dragged out of the window and it would have been written off as suicide." The ghost has recently taken to disarranging Mrs Sargent's night clothes, upsetting her cosmetics and even removing a pair of nylons from their cellophane packet and leaving them hopelessly laddered. "If ghosts have a sex," says Mrs Sargent, "it makes me think it must be a woman. It was such a catty sort of thing to do!"

Ghostly Monks Walk Again

Source and date: *Daily Graphic*, 14 November 1950

The ghostly monks who have haunted St Duncan's Church in East Acton for centuries have walked again. After reports of the return of the phantoms by the vicar, Rev Hugh Anton-Stevens, a *Daily Graphic* reporter was sent to establish the truth – and reports an astonishing encounter. Rev Anton-Stevens told this paper, "There is no doubt that on many evenings up to a dozen monks can be seen walking in procession up the central aisle and down into the chancel of St Dunstan's. They wear golden brown habits and are hooded. Apart from myself, three other people, unknown to each other, have seen the figures from time to time." *Graphic* reporter Kenneth Mason writes, "I spent some hours in the church in an attempt to establish whether or not the ghostly monks walked. At one point I dropped off to sleep in the quiet of the church but soon found myself awake again – and absolutely certain I was not dreaming. There, walking towards me, were six monks in grey hooded gowns. I stood up to bar their way – and to my astonishment they passed right through me!" Psychic investigators are being called in by Rev Anton-Stevens.

Mystery Figure Slaughters Pigs

Source and date: *Sunday Graphic*, 27 December 1953

A mystery "thing" has systematically killed 53 pedigree pigs belonging to farmer Harold Crowther of Runcorn. The events at the fifteenth-century farmhouse occupied by Mr Crowther and his wife began on 10 August when Mrs Crowther suddenly saw the ghost of her dead father. "He was dressed as usual," she said, "wearing spectacles and smoking a cigarette with a long ash, which was characteristic of him. I saw him very clearly and then he vanished. The next day the first of the pigs died. I saw him again after the last pig had died while I was clearing out one of the sties." Five veterinary surgeons were called in to examine the bodies of the pigs, which all died within a fortnight. The cause remained a mystery – but Mr Crowther himself had an even more frightening experience. He explained, "Two days after the loss of the last pig, I saw a large black cloud about seven feet in height, shapeless except for two prongs sticking out at the back moving about in the yard. The shapeless mass approached me, stopping about four or five feet away. Then it turned in the direction of the pig sties, passed into an outhouse and disappeared." Mrs Crowther believes she has seen the same thing. "It was much smaller and more sprawled out. At no time did I see the prongs. It just travelled like smoke when drawn by suction."

Belief in Ghosts is Dying Out

Source and date: *Evening News,* 9 March 1954

"Belief in ghosts, like belief in the devil, is dying out," Dr Margaret Murray, the well-known writer on the supernatural told a meeting of the Folk Lore Society last night. "This is attributed to our better methods of illumination," she added. Dr Murray was giving her presidential address to the Society. "Ghosts are notoriously fond of darkness, but now every town and most villages have street lamps, houses are lighted by electricity, vehicles have headlamps which illuminate the dark lane, and pedestrians no longer carry a lantern with a flickering rush light, but can flash the ray of an electric torch on any uncanny-looking object they see – or fancy they see." Dr Murray told the *Evening News* after the meeting: "If you think there is something in the room, all you have to do is to put on the bedside light. Either it was all imagination, in which case the light ends one's fears, or else the ghost disappears – because no ghost is seen in the light!"

The Stone-Throwing Ghost

Source and date: *Perth Weekend Mail,* 22 June 1955

Gilbert Smith and his family who live and work for flax farmer Bill Hack at Mayanup have become the talk of Australia this week after mysterious showers of stones fell on his shack for several nights running. Mr Smith, who is part Aboriginal, reported the phenomenon to his employer and asked for help as he, his wife Jean and seven children were terrified of being driven from their home. When local people heard of these occurrences they called and offered assistance. Some thirty men with spotlights and torches hid in the bushes only to be peppered with stones: some falling very gently and others with great force. No one was hurt and for eight days and nights the showers of stones varying in size from the head of a match to a hen's egg continued. Some of these stones have been taken to Perth for examination but no fingerprints have been found. There is a belief amongst Aboriginals that when a person is dying his spirit leaves the body and lingers until he either dies or recovers. Mrs Smith's father collapsed and died while digging a posthole near their house. She saw a small, round, bright light suspended about five feet above the ground during one of the showers of stones. It had then moved away from her and vanished.

The Flying Dutchman Seen Again

Source and date: *Cape Times* 16 May 1955

A Mrs E Peace writing to us on stationery of the mail ship *Cape Town Castle* has seen the Flying Dutchman again off the South African coast. She writes, "On 4 May, Mr Ingle, a fellow passenger and I were sitting on the bench about three o'clock in the afternoon outside the café at the Table Bay Docks, which faces the Breakwater, waiting for a bus to take us into Cape Town when, nearly touching the quay, I saw the most wonderful sight: a brown sailing ship, lying in a white vapour, a sort of mist, brilliantly and very clearly lighted up in a red glow, with all the masts raised but not a sail showing. So lovely was the spectacle, like some stage effect that I cried out 'Look at that beautiful boat.' Mr Ingle looked and then said, 'But it is an *old* boat and there are no men on her.' I had bent my head towards him, to hear what he said, and then looked again at the boat – but in that second it had gone. Together we ran to the end of the pier, our eyes searching the sea in vain in every direction. Returning to the seat, I asked a woman sitting there and a man beside the bench, had they seen the ship? They *had* and hurried with us to scan the water once more. We were joined by another young woman who said she too had seen it while travelling in the bus towards the café. Mr Ingles said, 'We have had an experience which I think we should report to the *Cape Town Press*. I believe we have seen the *Flying Dutchman*.'"

Tapping at the Window

Source and date: *Evening Standard*, 8 July 1955

Mr Frances Cole, groundsman at the Mid-Kent Golf Club, Gravesend, declares that he is being driven out of his home at the Overcliffe, Gravesend, by a poltergeist. There were tappings on his bedroom window and he heard shuffling footsteps. He was unable to sleep at night; doors opened of their own accord; he saw as he sat up, sleepless, in bed, his black cat spitting with fear and fury as the doors of a built-in cupboard began to open and close. The house is reputed to have been the scene of a murder during the nineteenth century.

The Council House of Horrors

Source and date: *The People,* 17 July 1955

The council house that was allocated to Frank Pell and his family in Coxwell Road, Birmingham, looked like the answer to their prayers after years in rented rooms – but proved to be a house of horrors. Soon after the family of seven moved in, their lives were made a misery by banging doors, loud thuds and a strange smell. In June tragedy struck when the Pells' month-old baby was found dead in bed. After the baby's funeral, the noises and smells continued. Then one evening, Alan Pell, 4, said: "Did the baby go with the little white dog?" Frank Pell asked his son, "What dog?" The child replied, "The little white dog that comes and sits on my bed sometimes. I saw him sitting on the baby's face the night baby left us." The Police were alerted, the house searched, but nothing has been found. The Pells have quit the council house and will be rehoused while surveyors of Birmingham Council carry out a full investigation.

Actor's Ghost in the Underground

Source and date: *Sunday Dispatch,* 15 January 1956

The ghost of the famous Victorian actor, William Terriss, has been seen at Covent Garden Underground Station by several members of the station staff. A four-page report has been sent to the London Transport Executive divisional headquarters concerning the statuesque figure of a man wearing a grey suit, old-fashioned collar and white gloves. Foreman Collector Jack Hayden, one of those who saw this tall, distinguished-looking spectre more than once, eventually rang the headquarters in Leicester Square. "We have a ghost here," he told them. Foreman Eric Davey, a spiritualist, was sent down and held a séance in the anteroom. Davey said, "I got the name 'Ter . . .' something and a murder nearby. That evening somebody suggested Terriss." Pictures of the actor were found. They resembled a psychic sketch made by Davey. When Jack Hayden was shown these he said, "That's him!"

I Took a Ghost for a Ride

Source and date: *Sunday Express*, 15 January 1956

A woman said yesterday that she had seen a ghost near Borley Rectory which Harry Price, the famous ghost hunter, claimed was haunted by a nun and a headless coachman. She is Mrs Jean Clarke of Fobbing, Essex, who said, "I never met Mr Price, but I once gave one of his ghosts a lift in my car." Mrs Clarke, who was a British spy in Germany before the war, said she saw the ghost on a winter's night six years ago. "I was driving my shooting-brake alone, except for

Buff, my cocker spaniel, on the Suffolk-Essex border heading for Bury St Edmunds. I got lost and pulled up to look at my map by the light of the dashboard. Suddenly Buff, sitting in the back, began to howl. It was then I saw sitting beside me, a man dressed in a long, out-dated, cloak-collared fawn coat. I thought it strange that I had not seen him or heard him enter the car – but I had been deeply engrossed in the map. The man pointed forward. I thought perhaps he was a simpleton. But I noticed the atmosphere in the car had become very cold. I assumed the man wanted a lift and started off again. I had not gone more than 40 yards when he motioned me to stop. Then he just floated through the door. Shortly afterwards I discovered I was in the village of Borley – though at the time it had no significance to me for I was in Germany before the war when Mr Price was investigating the hauntings."

Bishop Exorcizes Ghost

Source and date: *New Zealand Herald,* 21 March 1957

The "haunting" of Mr and Mrs Norman Dixon began when they saw "something strange and quivering like a vibrating coil of wire" on the wall of their sitting room in Sunderland, Durham. The couple had only been occupants of the house for a fortnight, they told reporters. The first time they had slept in the upstairs bedroom the sheets were suddenly ripped from the bed and Mr Dixon felt fingers being pressed into his chest. A few nights later, both he and his wife felt something clammy on their backs. Leaving the bedroom, they went downstairs where they found an eerie zigzag line on the living room wall. Following several more visitations, the Right Reverend J A Ramsbotham, the Bishop Suffragan of Jarrow, was called in to exorcize the ghost, and so far the exorcizing ceremony has done the job.

Clayton Family Haunted

Source and date: *Los Angeles Examiner,* 28 August 1957

The home of Elmer Gomez and his family at Clayton, CA is being plagued by a poltergeist. Since late July, the family have become accustomed to nerve-wracking events almost every night. Around nine p.m, three sharp knocks have been heard on the back wall of the house – with nothing found to explain the noises. The property has also been subjected to flying objects and breaking windows. Mrs

Gomez's mother was cleaning up in the kitchen one night when a one-pound box of salt flew off the kitchen table and struck her in the back. A fountain pen made a regular habit of dislodging itself from its pocket in the kitchen calendar and flying about the house – its longest flight being 28 feet, to a landing in an adjacent room. After weeks of sitting out the problem, the Gomez family have appealed for help and the local police are also involved. Constable Vic Chapman who has observed the falling stones believes that the house was once owned by a man who was murdered – not in Clayton, though, but San Francisco.

Ghosts Who Always Come Up Roses

Source and date: *News of the World,* 4 March 1958

Researcher Edith Case of Brampford Speke near Exeter is convinced that ghosts often appear in the form of a phantom scent in the air. She advertised for evidence in a magazine and hundreds of people all over the country wrote of their experiences. A woman in Freshwater, Isle of Wight, said she and her daughter caught a smell of roses all over the house as they discussed recent deaths in the family. It was winter and there were no flowers there. The woman called in a medium who gave her a spirit message from her dead husband. Whenever she smelled roses, she would know that he was near her. Another woman wrote that she was amazed that months after her uncle died she could still smell his tobacco, Harris tweed suit and a particular brand of whisky, in their house at Oxford. She brought neighbours in when the house was suddenly invaded by a fragrance of carnations. Then she remembered it was the anniversary of her uncle's death. A mother in Ross-shire said her baby son died after falling into a sheep-dip. At least once a week afterwards the whole house was pervaded by the smell of the chemical dip. Similarly, a Northampton couple reported that they often smelled aviation fuel after their son was killed in an air crash. They complained about it and the smell was replaced by a strong scent of violets, their son's favourite flowers.

The Most Dogged Ghost in Britain

Source and date: *Daily Mail,* 4 May 1958

The Black Dog, otherwise Black Shuck, the Galleytrot, Old Snarleyow, the Hellbeast, the Shug Monkey, the Ghostly Hound of

Dartmoor, the Barguest, Trash, Padfoot, Skriker or Hooter, is the most widely spread country ghost in England, James Wentworth-Day writes. It is derived from the Viking hound of Odin, the mighty dog of war, whose legend came to East Anglia a thousand years ago. Where the Black Dog appeared, the blood of dead men stained the earth. It is probably the most authentic ghost in all England. Learned men, parsons, antiquaries, squires and farmers, inshore fishermen and scared housewives have testified to its haunting presence. I had heard no legend of a Black Dog in Essex until William Fell, who was a gamekeeper on Old Hall Marshes, told me he had seen The Dog, "as big as a calf with eyes like bike lamps" when driving home with another man in a horse and trap from Peldon. The best of the lot is undoubtedly the Black Dog of Blythburgh on the Suffolk coast. I went to see its burned and blackened footprints on the inside of the church door not long ago. This is what happened. On 4 August 1557, the parson was reading the lesson on a bright Sunday morning. Then thunder crashed and a spear of flame struck through the church wall into the chancel. A score of worshippers were struck down and a great bell clanged to the floor, bringing down tons of masonry. In the midst of it all, with smoke in the air, a great black hound bounded through the church, mangling the people with its teeth, and vanished.

The Thing that Screams in the Night

Source and date: *Lancashire Evening Post,* 4 September 1958

A real spine-chiller of a ghost is the talk of Chipping today. At least three local residents have confirmed that strange things are happening in the night. *The Identikit Description:* Large, luminous eyes, large hands and a creature of weird noises in the night. *Location:* Playing fields in Longridge Road and what is known locally as the Old Hive area. *Habits:* Screams in the night, padding along the dark country roads in the early hours and terrifying elderly people and children. Residents of Old Hive have reported things that scream in the night and are keeping their doors and windows tightly locked. Local policeman PC Duncan McPheat has been told of the alarm felt by villagers but so far has failed to encounter any ghostly wanderings. About sixteen months ago another ghost – that of Leagram Hall, now demolished – was alarming residents of Chipping with its nightly wanderings. The area may now have two ghosts to contend with.

1960-69

Ghosts: a Startling Report

Source and date: *Empire News*, 17 July 1960

An astonishing document, claiming supernatural communication with the spirits of the long-dead King Henry the Eighth and members of the Tudor Court, is to be published by an authoritative church council whose honorary vice-presidents include thirteen bishops. Entitled "The Tudor Story", this secret 60,000-word manuscript reveals startling disclosures of strange psychic phenomena centring on the late Canon W S Pakenham-Walsh who died two months ago. Among the amazing claims – supported by leading figures in religious research – are: That the earthbound spirit or "ghost" of King Henry spoke at length with Canon Pakenham-Walsh, who acted as his father-confessor. That the recalled spirit of Ann Boleyn sought the help of the Church in redeeming the soul of Henry and regarded the canon as her champion. That the supernatural signature of the king who died 400 years ago was put on a document in a Chelsea garden. That evidence of survival after death within the framework of the Christian Church is clearly established in scripted reports of what took place over 30 years between spirit members of the Tudor court and the canon and his witnesses. Last night, Church of England colleagues of the late Canon told the *Empire News*, "We are prepared for fierce controversy over this fantastic and amazing manuscript. But we are prepared to vouch for its authenticity. As a result of its publication, the Church may have to reassess the whole question of contact between the earthly and spiritual worlds."

Hunt for the Ghost of No 10

Source and date: *Sunday Dispatch*, 25 December 1960

As they knocked off for Christmas, workmen demolishing the Prime Minister's house in Downing Street were talking about "The Ghost of No 10". For years there has been an off-the-record story that the ghost – thought to be that of a bygone Prime Minister – walks the building. It is a benevolent ghost and has never done anyone harm. It just walks round and those who claim to have seen it cannot agree whether it wears Regency, Victorian or modern dress. But no one is prepared to reject the story of the ghost – not at Christmas time anyway.

The "Noisy Ghost" of Elkader

Source and date: *Omaha World-Herald*, 29 December 1960

A "noisy ghost" has finally succeeded in driving out the occupiers of a farm near Elkader, Iowa. After weeks of enduring strange happenings, 83-year-old William Meyer and his wife have quit their home and moved in with a daughter in Guttenberg, Iowa. The phenomena had lasted for several months and included a refrigerator being tipped over and eggs flung across the kitchen among other things. Clayton County sheriff Forrest Fischer deputized two men and told them to keep a watch on the home. At first, Fischer thought the whole thing was a hoax, but has had second thoughts after seeing a bottle jump out of a box and smash on the floor.

The Spirit that Burns

Source and date: *L'Express*, 13 April 1962

Police and church officials in St Brieuc have joined forces to try and solve the mystery of a ghost with a curious obsession. The spirit is preoccupied with clothing – one man at Landebia was standing in the presence of others in a market place when his clothes were literally pulled off him, giving way at the seams. At Henabihen, large acid-like burns were reported to have appeared on the clothes of a family in that village – while they were wearing them. And what is believed to be the same ghost has slit all the bedsheets belonging to another family.

The Haunted Tomb of "Black Aggie"

Source and date: *Baltimore Sun,* 31 October 1962

The ghost known as "Black Aggie" has been reported again in the Druid Ridge Cemetery at Pikeville, near Baltimore. She is said to emanate from a "haunted tombstone" that marks the grave of newspaper publisher General Felix Angus who died in the 1920s. Upon his death, the family commissioned a well-known monument sculptor to design the tombstone. He designed a stone with a curious-looking small black angel perched on top. Subsequently the monument acquired the name "Black Aggie" after it was claimed that at the stroke of midnight the angel's eyes would glow. The legend grew that all the ghosts in the graveyard would gather around at midnight and any living person who was struck by her glowing gaze would immediately become blind. Pregnant women who passed under shadow – where no grass would grow – would have miscarriages. Earlier this year, one of "Black Aggie's" arms went missing and shortly afterwards a young student believed to be carrying out a dare was found dead by the tombstone one morning. A medical examination determined that he had died of fright. With new reports of "glowing lights" in the cemetery and the arrival of tourists at midnight determined to brave the risk of being blinded, the family of Colonel Angus are increasingly worried about desecration to his grave and plan to seek permission for the removal of "Black Aggie". [After several more sightings of the ghost, "Black Aggie" was finally removed in 1967 and donated to the Smithsonian Institution where she has remained in store ever since.]

Widow Fights Ghost with Beer

Source and date: *Ilford Recorder,* 7 February 1963

Perryman's Farm has long has the reputation of being the most haunted farm in Essex. For the past fifty years, there have been regular outbreaks of poltergeist activity in which china has been broken and pictures dropped from the wall. The present tenant, Mrs Doris Freeman, a resolute lady in her eighties, has no intention of being driven out of her home by the racket, however. She is attempting to placate the ghost. Before she goes to bed each night she always leaves a bottle of beer and a meal on the table. "It may sound odd, but there is an ancient tradition that a ghost that is fed is a contented ghost. I have not been disturbed for weeks now," she said.

The Glamis Castle Ghost Again

Source and date: *The Scotsman,* 2 December 1963

The "grey lady" who has been seen by generations of the Earl of Strathmore's family in Glamis Castle has been seen again. The Earl himself has admitted seeing the grey-garbed spectre when he looked into the castle chapel one evening. The lady was in an attitude of prayer and disappeared after a few moments. Because of the tremendous public interest in Glamis – the place where the Queen Mother spent her childhood and the birthplace of Princess Margaret – the Dowager Countess Glanville, aunt to Lord Strathmore, has replied to press speculation. "I have seen the ghost," she told journalists yesterday, "but I would rather say nothing about it. One thing leads to another. My telephone would never stop ringing."

George the Ghost Exposed

Source and date: *The People,* 10 May 1964

One of the world's most publicized ghosts was unmasked last week. For eighteen months, "George" – as he was known to his fans – has haunted a stone cottage in the old-world village of Stow-on-the-Wold, Gloucestershire. Stories and articles about him appeared all over the world. A TV programme was devoted to his activities. Priests were called in to advise on the best methods of dealing with him. But I can now reveal, says reporter Ken Gardner, that "George" was really fourteen-year-old David Pethrick who lives in the cottage with his parents. The truth came out two nights ago at a séance to which a team of *People* investigators had been invited. As "George" went through his eerie routine, I suddenly shone a torch on young David who was sitting in a corner of their living room. And I caught him doing a daring ventriloquist act behind a handkerchief. David stopped singing immediately and stuffed his handkerchief into his pocket. I took David to one side and he admitted the voice was his. "I don't know why I do it," he said. "Sometimes I feel that a ghost is inside me."

Penitent Ghost Haunts Navy Wives

Source and date: *Daily Express*, 20 October 1964

The Navy has excused a sailor from all night-duty and his two-year-old son is being given sedatives – all because of a ghost which wants to apologise for a stabbing. An officer from twenty-seven-year-old Able Seaman Dave Smith's ship, the aircraft carrier *Ark Royal*, attended a séance in the house that two frightened naval wives say is haunted. In the beachside villa at Seaton, Devon, the ghost said through a medium, "I cannot rest until I find my mistress to apologise. I should not have killed her." Twenty-three years ago, a Scottish maid killed her mistress with a carving knife in the house, which the Navy has converted into married quarters. The haunting began in August with heavy footsteps, doors slamming, windows opened and lights switched on and off. Apart from Able Seaman Smith and his family, the ghost has also been seen by Mrs Isa Cameron who also lived in the house with her three daughters. The spiritualists have been no more successful than the Vicar of Downderry, Rev Robert Lyle, in quietening the restless spirit.

Clairvoyant and the Ghost at the Crown

Source and date: *East Anglian Daily Times*, 25 June 1966

The noted clairvoyant, Tom Corbett, visited the *Crown Inn* in Bildeston, Suffolk last night to try and lay the ghost that is said to have haunted the pub for centuries. Ghostly footsteps, unexplained hammering sounds and supernatural manifestations have been reported – and a few years ago several people complained of being touched by cold, invisible fingers. Mr Corbett, a reporter and photographer visited the *Crown* and though nothing unusual was seen or heard the clairvoyant said he felt there was a "psychic atmosphere" in the inn. When Mr Corbett left, the two newspapermen decided to stay in one of the *Crown's* double rooms. Paul Henshall writes, "During the night we were suddenly awakened by loud, mysterious footsteps in the corridor outside. We ventured out only to find the passage empty. When we nervously returned to the room we both began shivering. There had been a dramatic and unaccountable drop in the temperature. It was very spooky indeed!"

A Double Haunting

Source and date: *The New York Times*, 2 January 1967

The historian Carl Carmer, who lives in a unique octagonal house in Irvington, New York, near the Hudson River, says that his house has *two* ghosts – a previous resident and a ghost he and his wife brought with them when they moved to Irvington from Twelfth Street in New York City. According to Mr Carmer, the resident ghost was the daughter of a Frenchwoman who owned the house and met an untimely death while she was eloping with a young man from a neighbouring estate. She floats up the driveway on moonlit spring nights. The second ghost, who followed the family from the city, apparently showed up a few months later. "She is rather like a homing dog," the historian says, "she signifies her presence by a delicate scene which is fleeting but very flowery."

Phantom Face on TV Screen

Source and date: *Lincolnshire Echo*, 26 September 1967

A Grimsby family have left their council house at Flottergate after a ghost appeared on closed circuit television. For weeks, Ted Barning, his wife and children had been terrified by a phantom that had been creating disturbances in several rooms of the house. Investigators

from the Ghost Club visited the house and an engineer rigged up the
TV apparatus, with a camera in the Barnings' bedroom where the
largest number of disturbances had occurred. After a watch of
several hours, the face of "an old man of hideous appearance"
appeared on the monitor screen downstairs. When one of the party
of six around the monitor rushed upstairs, the face disappeared. The
engineer stated that he had tried every possible test with the apparatus, but could find no possible explanation for the occurrence.

Live Séance on TV Astonishes Viewers

Source and date: *New York Times,* 18 September 1967

Last night, the Right Reverend James A Pike, former Episcopal
Bishop of California, sat in a television studio in Toronto, Canada,
with Arthur Ford, a minister of the Disciples of Christ Church and
one of America's best-known spirit mediums. They were about to
hold a televized séance that had been arranged by Allen Spraggett,
religion editor of the *Toronto Star* and frequent writer on psychic
subjects. Ford put on a blindfold – to protect his eyes from the strong
TV lights, he said – and went into a trance. During the trance Ford's
spirit guide, "Fletcher", delivered messages allegedly from the spirit
of Bishop Pike's son, Jim Jr, who had shot and killed himself in New
York a year earlier. According to Ford, "Fletcher" was the spirit of a
long-dead French Canadian who regularly transmitted messages
from the spirit world. Astonished viewers across the nation heard
"messages" from the "spirit" of James Pike Jr and were assured that
the "communications" were genuine. Bishop Pike admitted himself
"impressed" but acknowledged that much of the information might
have been acquired by normal means. He added, "But I do not think
Ford has done so. I am convinced that during the séance Ford was in
contact with the spirit of my dead son." [This story appeared on the
front page of the *New York Times* – the only time a psychic event has
been given such prominence in the *Times*.]

The Spirit of Conan Doyle

Source and date: *Sunday Express,* 5 May 1968

An intriguing story has come to light at Windlesham Manor, the
former home of Sir Arthur Conan Doyle, creator of Sherlock
Holmes, and a dedicated Spiritualist. The manor – where he wrote

some of his later Holmes stories – is a rambling, thirty-bedroom mansion by Ashdown Forest and now a home for "retired gentle-folk". Explains Mrs Doreen Hancock, the manageress, "The locals say the house is haunted by his ghost. I've been here for less than a year and I haven't seen the ghost – but I do sense an extraordinary atmosphere. Late at night when I go round checking the lights, I sometimes think of this haunting story. But it wouldn't worry me if I met Sir Arthur on the landing. I'm sure he would be a very friendly ghost." This is not, in fact, the first time there has been talk of the ghost of Conan Doyle. Seven years ago it was blamed for playing pranks with the lift of his former London surgery in Devonshire Place. In 1961 the house was shared by seven doctors and the lift, though serviced every month, often stopped inexplicably between the second and third floors. This was next to the rooms where Sir Arthur wrote Sherlock Holmes tales while waiting for patients. Finally, the doctors advised all their patients: "Use the stairs – it's quicker."

Public Survey of Hauntings

Source and date: *Daily Telegraph*, 4 October 1968

The Institute of Psychophysical Records is appealing in the press and media for first-hand accounts of "perceiving apparitions" to cover all of the senses and not just those that are visual. The researchers are hoping to collate the material to find similarities between accounts of "ghost sightings". Their findings will be published in a book. [Three hundred people responded to this appeal, which was followed by a second appeal in 1974, producing over 1,500 reports. From these questionnaires, the first-ever authentic table of true hauntings was released.]

Position re Apparitions

Lying down	38%
Sitting	23%
Standing still	19%
Walking	18%
Riding	1%
Other	1%

Senses and Apparitions

Sight	84%
Hearing	37%
Temperature	18%

Touch	15%
Smell	8%
Other	4%

Distance from Apparitions

3 feet or less	41%
3–6 feet	27%
6–12 feet	16%
12–30 feet	10%
10 yards or more	6%

Ghost Fever Grips Village

Source and date: *Daily Sketch*, 28 August 1968

Ghost fever has gripped a tiny Welsh mining village. Every night hundreds of residents of Cilfynydd near Pontypridd, Glamorgan, rush out to Ewn Valley to watch what they call the "White Lady". One of the eyewitnesses to the phenomenon, Mrs Violet Thomas whose husband manages the local general store, said that she had seen the apparition just two weeks previously at 10 p.m. when "a white figure rose about 50 yards away". She says it had a human shape and those who saw it were "spellbound". Then it disappeared. Those who have viewed the spectre are adamant in their conviction that they were actually viewing a human-shaped ghost of some kind. Mrs Thomas' husband emphatically said, "It was a ghost." This was in response to a touted explanation by George Graham Cox, head green-keeper of the Pontypridd golf course, who says that what the people are seeing are actually *white owls*.

Film Set Haunted by Ghost Aircraft

Source and date: *Daily Express*, 16 March 1968

Filming of the new blockbuster movie, *Battle of Britain,* has taken a turn for the strange with reports of a phantom aircraft being seen at North Weald Airfield in Essex where many of the scenes for the dramatic wartime story starring Michael Caine, Laurence Oliver, Trevor Howard and Kenneth Moore are being filmed. The airfield, which played a major part in the defence of Britain from the German *Luftwaffe*, has been said to be haunted by the ghost of an airman killed there in 1940 – now a phantom Spitfire has joined the cast.

Producer Benny Fisz explained, "During one of the fly-overs of Spitfires there was distinctly *one* more aircraft than there should have been. But nothing showed up on the negative of the film. We can only assume it was a ghost plane."

Phantom Stalks Theatre Rehearsals

Source and date: *Oxford Mail*, 12 September 1969

Rehearsals for an eerie new production of *The Hanging Wood* at the Kenton Theatre, Henley-on-Thames have been interrupted by a number of mysterious incidents, according to the playwright Joan Morgan. The play is based on the true story of local girl Mary Blandy who was hanged in Oxford in 1752 for poisoning her father. The unusual incidents began as soon as rehearsals started, says Miss Morgan. A large mirror "jumped off the wall", lights went on and off and doors mysteriously opened and closed. The figure of a girl was reported at the back of the theatre – though she was never seen to enter or leave the building and when anyone came near she disappeared. Miss Morgan said, "On another occasion when some members of the cast were discussing Mary Blandy, a cup jumped about six inches off a table and smashed on the floor. This is not the first time strange things have happened when this play has been staged. When the trial of Mary Blandy was enacted at Henley Town Hall three years ago, a similar mysterious figure was seen by several people, myself included."

1970-79

GP Says Return of Dead Spouse as Ghost "Common"

Source and date: *The Times,* 19 November 1970

Widows and widowers who sense the presence of their former marriage partner are in no way unusual. Talking to and seeing the ghost is also a common experience according to Dr W Dewi Rees, a Welsh general practitioner. He has found, however, that very few people who have these experiences disclose them even to close relatives. Dr Rees talked to 293 of his patients about their experiences after the death of their spouse and the results of his study are reported in the *British Medical Journal.* Nearly half the patients had had some sensation of the presence of their spouse and in many that had persisted for several years, but overall the tendency was for the sensation to become less frequent. More than ten per cent of those questioned had spoken to or heard the voice of their partner and a similar proportion had seen a hallucination. Widows of the managerial and professional group were the more likely to have illusions. Others more likely to experience this were people with long and happy marriages and parenthood. Dr Rees emphasizes that in most cases the presence of the ghost was comforting, particularly to those who spoke to the dead partner. [A decade later, in June 1983, the *New York Post* reported that a research project at Arizona University which consulted 300 widows in Phoenix found that more than half of them had seen, talked to or felt the touch of their dead husbands. Professor of Human Development, Arthur Christopherson, who headed the research said, "Many of them say that it is in the privacy of the bedroom where they have actually felt their late husbands touch them. Some of the widows have seen their dead husbands up to twenty years after his death and some have made up to five or six contacts."]

The Face on the Floor

Source and date: *ABC Madrid*, 12 January 1971

One of Spain's most mysterious ghost stories has been puzzling experts since it first came to light in a small house in the village of Bélmez de la Moraleda near Córdoba. An old woman was busy in the kitchen preparing the evening meal when her grandchild started to scream. The grandmother turned from the oven and saw a tormented face staring at her from the faded pink tiles of the kitchen floor. When she tried to rub the vision out with a rag, the eyes opened wider, making the expression even more heart-rending. The woman sent for the owner of the house who agreed to have the tiles taken up and replaced with concrete. But three weeks later another face began to form on the floor, even more clearly defined than the first. Soon, other faces began to appear in different parts of the house. Phenomena investigators were called in and their sensitive microphones picked up whimpering, screams and voices arguing. The whole kitchen floor was finally excavated – and the remains of several human corpses who had been buried alive in 1823 were found. This time when the surface was replaced, the faces and the sounds disappeared as mysteriously as they had begun.

Ghost on a Motorbike

Source and date: *Autocar*, 21 December 1972

It is one thing to imagine the hooded and cowled figure of a monk disappearing amid the moonlit ruins of some desolate abbey but how about hearing the full-throttle roar of a motorcycle on the still air

where none is visible. This is what puzzles the residents of Clouds Hill, Dorset, the home of the legendary Lawrence of Arabia who met his death in a motorcycle accident in the 1930s. Since then, it is claimed, the distinctive roar of his big Brough Superior has been heard regularly around Clouds Hill. People who have lived in the area for years say the sounds are unmistakably those of his machine. Earlier this year, a local motorist even claimed to have been passed by a ghostly figure on a motorcycle he was felt sure was the legendary Lawrence.

Increase in Hauntings

Source and date: *News of the World*, 6 May 1973

Canon John Pearce-Higgins, vice-chairman of the Church of England Fellowship for Psychical Studies and former vice-provost of Southwark Cathedral, gets three or four ghost calls a week. "More people are reporting hauntings because we are living in more enlightened times," he says. "Not long ago they would be afraid they would be laughed at. Many of my calls are to modern homes and council houses or flats. I think this is because they are built on the site of ancient happenings and the spirits from the distant past are returning to the scene." What should you do if you have a ghost? The canon advises a friendly blessing. "Simply say, 'Bless you, but please go away.' And if often works quite well," he says.

Ghost in Author's House of Death

Source and date: *News of the World*, 3 February 1974

The house in which royal biographer James Pope-Hennessy was stabbed to death was, it is claimed, haunted by the ghost of a man knifed to death there seventy years ago. The first killing took place on a staircase only yards from where a bound and gagged Mr Pope-Hennessy died. And the author had called in a Catholic priest to exorcize the spirit of the victim. Mr Pope-Hennessy died while his twenty-five-year-old valet, Mr Leslie Smith, fought with the killer. He is recovering from multiple stab wounds. Now friends of the fifty-seven-year-old bachelor writer have told of the phantoms which roamed the house of death in Ladbroke Grove, Notting Hill, London. According to Mrs Dorrit Forte who lived in the house, a "little man always smiling and friendly" was seen sitting on the staircase and a second presence made itself known "roaming clumsily around the upper floors of the house, one shattering a row of shelves nailed to the wall." Mr Pope-Hennessy's curiosity had got the better of him, said Mrs Forte, "and he discovered that a little man, an ostler who looked after horses for a nearby inn had been stabbed to death on that staircase. The description fitted and the evil presence could have been the murderer making his getaway or entering the house." From his hospital bed, Leslie Smith added, "Mr Pope-Hennessey took the spirits seriously and had an exorcism carried out. He was almost psychic and spoke of the murder as if he had been there."

The Baby-Sitter Phantom on 21st Floor

Source and date: *News of the World,* 14 April 1974

Fear of a ghost who is said to be haunting a couple to protect their eight-year-old daughter's life has driven the family from their twenty-first-floor penthouse flat. Now, like an eerie scene from the film *The Exorcist*, mediums and priests have been called in to expel the unwelcome tenant. Steve Raynor, aged 25, his wife Ellen, and their little girl Karen moved to their tower block home last June. Two months later inexplicable incidents began – plates were rattled, lights and taps turned on and off and heavy furniture trundled across the floor. After talking to a medium, Mrs Carmen Rodgers, the Raynors learned they were being haunted by "Arthur", their former landlord who had been dead nearly three years. He used to babysit for Karen and Mrs Rodgers explained that he fears for the little girl's life if she stays in the flat at Old Ford Road, Bow, London, where she could fall out of a window or down the long staircases. The family are now sleeping on the floor of a relative's home a mile away. Mr Raynor said, "Our lives have been made a misery. We won't go back until that thing has gone."

Jumbo the Jet Age Ghost

Source and date: *Evening News,* 22 October 1974

Terrified cleaners at Heathrow Airport have refused to work on their own at night because, they say, a ghost holds them down by their throats and shoulders. An airport official said today, "We have had reports about some strange presence on the Jumbo jet planes and at present it cannot be explained. Some cleaners have said they have been thrown about by something invisible and others that they have been unable to move." A night foreman for the cleaning company, Mr Parson Lal Palmer said, "It all started when we opened the doors one day and there was a strange smell. It went away but came back again later. Then I sat down in a chair and was horrified when I could not get up again. My eyes shut and I could not open them. It was as if someone was holding me down by the shoulders. It was four or five minutes before I was able to move." [The *Sunday People* reported on 6 July 1980 that a "ghost in a light grey suit" had been seen several times in the VIP Suite in Heathrow Terminal One; while on 27 September 2007 across the other side of the world at the new Suvarnabhumi Airport in Bangkok, *The Times* claimed that a "frail old man with a blue face" believed to be the ghost of Poo Ming, once the guardian of a cemetery on the airport land, was now appearing regularly to workers and passengers using the terminal buildings.]

Thumbs Down to Ghostly Hiker

Source and date: *Sunday Express*, 3 April 1975

A police chief in Germany has threatened to prosecute motorists who spread panic by claiming they have seen a ghost. Drivers who repeat the stories face a hefty £200 fine. The wave of hysteria began when a 43-year-old businessman told a local newspaper he was stopped at midnight by someone he took to be a hitchhiker. He said, "She was a weird-looking old woman, dressed in black. So I stopped the car and offered her a lift. She sat next to me and did not answer my questions, but murmured that something evil would happen. When I next looked she had vanished. The shock was so great I almost crashed into another car." Other motorists claimed similar experiences. Some said the woman disappeared when they opened the car door. Others said she sat next to them, silent, and then vanished. An amateur photographer claims to have taken a snapshot of the woman and an enlargement showed an apparently shadowy, bent figure. Captain Siegfried Eismann, head of the local police in Greifnau, near Germany's border with Austria, has dismissed the ghostly stories as malicious rumours. But a team of ghost hunters from Austria, armed with electronic equipment and high-speed cameras, have arrived in the town planning to track down the woman in black.

Actress Dies after "Exorcism" First Night

Source and date: *Daily Telegraph,* 4 April 1975

Mary Ure, 42, the actress, was found dead in her Mayfair flat yesterday only hours after playing the part of a woman possessed in the first night of the West End play, *The Exorcism* by Don Taylor. Her part as a haunted hostess taken over by the spirit of a woman who had died of starvation centuries ago was an emotional and taxing role, but one which an actress of Miss Ure's talent and experience could take in her stride, the company said last night. Asked if there could have been any connection between the play and Miss Ure's death, a spokesman said, "How can anyone answer a question like that? The information I was given was that she had choked on something and suffocated." [The subsequent inquest recorded a verdict of accidental death "caused by barbiturate and alcoholic poisoning".]

My Haunted Love Life

Source and date: *News of the World,* 11 May 1975

Top cabaret singer Tonia Bern-Campbell makes the extraordinary claim that she is haunted by the ghost of her dead husband, speed king Donald Campbell. The 39-year-old beauty, widowed when the world-record-buster crashed on Coniston Water eight years ago, says Donald suddenly materialises to put the chill on her love life if he doesn't think the man is right for her. That he appears in the night to give advice in times of crisis. That his phantom constantly flits about their flat where she still lives in Dolphin Square, London. Blonde Tonia has jet-set suitors lining up to squire her around. "Really I'd like to marry again, but with this happening, how can I? Donald will reappear at the most embarrassing moments. I might be in the embrace with one suitor and I look over his shoulder to stare right at Donald. He just won't leave me alone and I'm sure he won't disappear until I've found someone he totally approves of!"

Dead but Won't Lie Down

Source and date: *Sunday Times,* 24 August 1975

Frank Smyth, a feature writer on the successful part-work, *Man, Myth & Magic,* has confessed that the story he wrote, "The Phantom Vicar of Ratcliffe Wharf" and which has subsequently been featured in several books about ghosts and a TV special, is a hoax. The story of the shady cleric who was supposed to have run a seamen's hostel in Limehouse in the eighteenth century where he robbed drunks and flung their bodies into the Thames caught out authors, columnists and even our own Jilly Cooper who wrote, "Don't go down there – it's haunted. The watermen only go down there in pairs." Frank Smyth has now admitted, "I decided to create a ghost of the old school. It struck me that a place like Ratcliffe Docks with its skeletal cranes and derelict broken warehouses ought to be haunted. After the piece was published I sat back to await developments." The result staggered even him – but, as he has found, ghosts once invented are not so easy to lay. He says, "I met a lighterman in Islington who said he heard about the phantom vicar from his grandfather. I told him that was impossible; I'd invented him entirely. But he wouldn't have it. 'There's a phantom vicar there all right. That's why they used to close the docks there at five every night – no one would work there after dark.'" [Kingsley Amis who also "invented" a ghost for his account, "Kingsley Amis Sees a Ghost" in *The Listener,* 11 January 1973, in which he described some purportedly true psychic adventures after the publication of his supernatural novel, *The Green Man,* also found himself being taken literally and being forced to issue a strong denial.]

Ghost now Standing on Platform Two

Source and date: *Sunday Mirror,* 30 November 1975

The *Great Eastern* pub housed in a converted station at Maldon, Essex is haunted by a spirit known as the "White Lady." Since the station closed and the track was ripped up eleven years ago, there have been scores of sightings – mainly on the adjoining platform two. Barry Anderson, co-owner of the pub said, "The place has an inexplicable atmosphere about it and there is definitely something going on." Mrs Muriel Andrews, whose husband was stationmaster at Maldon for two years, said, "I saw the lady, a white shrouded figure, four times. She glided up the path towards the waiting room. There were also strange noises at night. My husband slept with a shotgun at the bedside just in case." Builder Harry Jones, 48, who helped convert the station, spoke about who the ghost might be: "Under the floorboards where the bar stands we found a mummy-shaped area of damp soil. Each time we tried to shift it, it resumed its spooky shape and the soil seemed damp to the touch . . ."

Mystery of Everest's Snow Ghost

Source and date: *Sunday People*, 18 January 1976

A ghostly "third man" helped Everest heroes Dougal Haston and Doug Scott in the last stages of their climb, it was claimed yesterday. Details of their remarkable experience were revealed by Dr Charles Clark, medical officer of the successful British team last September. There, in the biting cold and thin air on the roof of the world, they felt "a comforting presence at their side." Haston and Scott, first to climb the southwest face, had to survive a night of horror just under the 29,002-foot summit. They had no food and were having trouble with their oxygen supply. "But both men told of a curious sensation that a third person had been sharing the snow-hole in which they bivouacked," said Dr Clark. Doug Scott at home in Nottingham said, "We were on our way to the summit when I became aware of this thing on my left. I would not call it a person – more a comforting presence. It seemed to accompany us in the snow-hole and Dougal actually was speaking to someone." [On 22 October 1978, the *Sunday People* ran a second story, "Ghost That Walked On Everest" in which mountaineer Nick Estcourt claimed to have seen "a figure plodding 200 yards behind me" who vanished as he climbed up to Camp Five at dawn when no one else could possibly have been on the mountain.]

Haunted Park for Princess

Source and date: *Daily Telegraph*, 28 June 1976

Like so many rambling country mansions, Princess Anne's new home in the Cotswolds is reputed to have a ghost in the grounds. Villagers in Avening recalled at the weekend how dozens of people had claimed to have seen an apparition on or near the 730-acre Gatcombe Park, where the Princess and Captain Mark Phillips are expected to take up residence in the autumn. And it could send a chill down the spine of the canine-loving couple since the ghost is said to be a headless dog. Mr Joe Hatherill, 74, a retired builder, who lives at Hampton Fields, the hamlet opposite the park's main entrance, said, "I have seen it four times altogether and it gave me a right fright. It is a big black dog without a head which brushes up against you. I have lived here for five years and I promise I am not lying. Lots of my friends have seen it. Usually the dog is seen limping over the wall of the estate into the main road from Minchinhampton to Avening." He knows of no local legends that could explain the ghostly hound, but the park can be an eerie place.

I Speak to Hitler Every Day

Source and date: *Sunday People,* 12 September 1976

An "after-life" story by Adolph Hitler is being dictated through a ghostwriter. Psychic researcher John Rayner makes the astonishing claim that he is in daily communication with the infamous Nazi leader who killed himself in Berlin thirty-one years ago. Mr Rayner, an electronics consultant who has made a lifetime study of psychic phenomena says that Hitler is dictating to him a book on life after death. He says the spirit of Hitler moved into his life when he was experimenting with "automatic writing – idle doodling with a pen and pad in the hope that some disembodied entity would make contact." The ex-Fuhrer, he says, is living in the afterlife with his mistress Eva Braun and often meets with Goering and Himmler. Mr Raynor says that Hitler expresses no guilt or regret over the war or the mass killings for which he stands guilty. "He explains that this is because there is no guilt and no blame in the after-life."

Ghost Failed to Return

Source and date: *News of the World,* 14 November 1976

A nineteen-year-old Egyptian girl told her family that she would be blessed with supernatural powers. But first she had to die and be brought back to the world as a spirit or ghost. Her sister and three girlfriends held a séance at her flat in Cairo. Then they hanged the girl, Samia, from a chandelier until she was dead. When her ghost failed to appear, they girls panicked and called the police. They have all been charged with murder.

The House of Demons

Source and date: *New York Post,* 18 December 1977

Terror gripped George Lutz of Long Island at the most horrific sight that ever confronted a husband. The woman on their bed had been his attractive blonde wife, Kathy. Now, suddenly, she had been turned into an ugly, unkempt old hag. But this is no ghost story for Christmas but just one episode in the life of the Lutzes, an ordinary family living in a big, six-roomed modern house, 112 Ocean Avenue, in the quiet town of Amityville on Long Island. Their account of twenty-eight days of terror in the house haunted by violent and malicious demons has gripped the nation. If you thought *The Exorcist* was terrifying and *The Omen* gave you nightmares, wait until you see *The Amityville Horror*, soon to be made on the real experiences of the Lutz family. When George and Kathy bought the house on Ocean Avenue there was only one snag, the estate agent confessed. Just a year earlier it had been the scene of a mass murder. A young man, Ronald Defoe, had murdered his parents, two brothers and two sisters – all shot while they slept. At his trial he said he heard voices telling him to kill his family. The Lutzes were not too superstitious – but took the precaution of calling in their family priest to bless the house when they moved in. Then the terror began. A deep masculine voice was heard commanding, "Get out!" This was followed by the continual sound of doors banging, an evil smell like dead rats filled the house, unblinking red eyes seen peering in the windows, swarms of flies, slime oozing out of the ceiling and many other eerie incidents. The Lutzes were now convinced their home was full of evil spirits and after one more night of horror when an invisible "something" climbed into George and Kathy's bed they packed up and moved out. That was on 14 January 1976. Now a new family live at 112 Ocean Avenue. After remaining shuttered for a year the house was bought by Mrs Barbara Cromarty. She says, "I have experienced none of the apparitions that terrified the Lutz family. All that disturbs me is the hundreds of sightseers who drive up and down the street outside my house every week."

Spirited Sex

Source and date: *Daily Mail*, 13 May 1978

Spiritualists in America are now offering a unique new service to clients desperate to make contact with loved ones who have "gone over" to the other side – séances with sex. According to reports being circulated, astral necrophilia is now available from certain spirit mediums. For a fee of a thousand dollars, these mediums offer customers a chance to make love to partners who have died. The experience is claimed to be the ultimate erotic encounter.

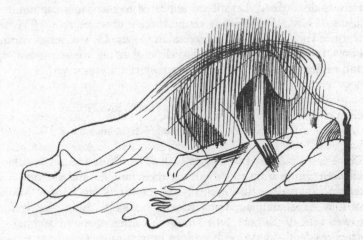

Ghosts of Disaster Flight 401

Source and date: *New York Daily News,* 27 August 1978

International airline crews have reported that the ghosts of a pilot and his flight engineer are haunting a fleet of jets. The phantom fliers are said to give warning of the possible danger and protect planes from crashes. According to author John G Fuller, the ghosts are those of Captain Bob Loft and Flight engineer Don Repo. They were among 99 people killed when the L-1011 TriStar Eastern Airlines Flight 401 from New York to Miami crashed in the Florida Everglades on Friday, 29 December 1972. Mr Fuller, who spent months travelling thousands of miles across the US to interview airline crew and relatives of the two men, says, "Numerous reliable eyewitnesses I spoke to have seen the ghosts appear on the L-1011 jets of Eastern Airlines in the States." He claims that: A stewardess thought she saw smoke coming from a bulkhead wall. She investigated and was confronted by the misty figure of the dead pilot. Cabin crew checking the number of passengers on another flight called the pilot when a man in captain's uniform ignored their questions and just stared in front of him. The pilot recognized Captain Loft – and then the figure vanished. The Captain and two crew of another jet saw the figure of the dead pilot. The flight was cancelled. A Flight engineer arriving at his seat to check the instruments before take-off found the ghost of dead engineer Don Repo seated there. The apparition told him before disappearing, "You don't have to check out the instruments – I've already done that." Don Repo appeared to one flight captain and also told him, "There will never be another crash on an L-1011, we will not let it happen." A spokesman for the United States Airline Pilots' Association said, "If you believe that old country mansions and sailing ships can be haunted – why not a jumbo jet?"

Lincoln's Sad Ghost Haunts White House

Source and date: *Daily Mail*, 1 November 1978

The ghost of Abraham Lincoln walks the White House, knocking on doors, appearing to Presidents, their families and visitors, it is claimed. Theodore Roosevelt said of the wandering spirit, "I think of Lincoln, shambling, homely, with his sad, strong, deeply furrowed face all the time. I see him in the different rooms and halls." The President's ghost has been seen by almost every administration since. Witnesses have included Lady Bird Johnson who was apparently watching a TV special on Lincoln's death when she suddenly realized that someone was compelling her to look towards the mantel. A plaque over it told of the room's significance to Lincoln. And as she read it, she felt "a chill, a draft". Queen Wilhelmina of The Netherlands was supposed to have heard a knock on the door of the Rose Room, where she was staying. She opened it and saw the tall figure of Lincoln. Sir Winston Churchill, uneasy about sleeping in the Lincoln bedroom, would often be found at night in a room across the hall. And Dwight Eisenhower told his Press Secretary, James Haggerty, that he had "often felt Lincoln's presence". [On 16 July 1986, Ronald Reagan was added to the list of Presidents who had seen the ghost in a story in the *Daily Mail*: "President Reagan has been telling dinner guests he has ghosts in the White House Lincoln bedroom and Rex, his dog, barks at the ghost and refuses to enter the room."

Smoking Ghost at Pam's Wedding

Source and date: *Sunday People*, 21 January 1979

The handsome, cigar-smoking guest cut quite a dash at Pamela Eccleston's wedding when she married Australian engineer Arando

Sarraco at St Chad's Church, Romiley, near Stockport, Cheshire. The man, wearing a smart grey suit with a dress shirt and bow tie, attached himself to several groups posing for wedding photographs. But no one knew who he was. Each family thought he was from the other side. Now they are convinced that he really was from the "other side" . . . of the grave. For when the photographs were developed there was no sign of the mysterious stranger – just gaps where he had stood. Pamela, 23, said, "I never really believed in ghosts before. Everybody remembers him because he was so distinguished. When I think back, I saw him puffing away on his cigar – but it never got any smaller."

Ghosts to Entertain Tourists

Source and date: *Daily Mail*, 21 February 1979

Ghosts are being lined up as a tourist attraction in an ancient English city. Parties of foreign visitors to Chester will be ushered round the favourite haunts of some of the city's oldest – and most elusive – inhabitants. Tour manager Peter Beighton said, "The idea of ghost trips came to us because, quite frankly, visitors had complained that Chester was dead at night. Now we'll show them that's what dead doesn't always lie down. The company has traced nine ghosts – including a Roman centurion minus helmet and a four-foot tall phantom who wears a scarlet cloak that trails behind him and has reportedly been seen in *daylight*. [Chester was the first town in Britain to organize conducted ghost tours of the kind that are now so popular throughout Britain, Europe and America.]

The Real-Life Phantom Show

Source and date: *Memphis Commercial Appeal*, 4 April 1979

There was uproar in Memphis today when folk heard the story of Bert Gross and his family watching TV. Their house just went crazy. Insects suddenly filled the room, the TV set crashed to the floor and the fridge started spinning round. Neighbours hurried to catch sight of the commotion. The police came too. They all saw incidents and are now convinced that the Gross home is host to a poltergeist.

Fire-Raising Ghost Brings Terror to Village

Source and date: *Daily Mail,* 11 September 1979

It all began at 5.30 p.m. on 6 August. Madame Gaby Bourdat was coaxing half a dozen cows along a road near the remote French village of Seron when suddenly she smelled smoke. Then she saw it – pouring out of a downstairs window in the abandoned farmhouse belonging to her neighbours, the Lahores. She rushed for help and, with the Lahore family, quickly doused the flames. Within two hours, two other fires mysteriously started – this time in the Lahores' modern four-bedroom house across the courtyard. Since then 90 more fires have broken out in the Lahore home – and nobody knows how or why. Meanwhile the Lahores and their 250 fellow villagers are at their nerves' end. Twenty gendarmes camp permanently at the farm. And the tiny hamlet in the French Pyrenees has been invaded by a succession of exorcists, psychologists, mediums and psychics all of whom have tried unsuccessfully to solve the mystery. Several of the eyewitnesses say each fire starts in the same manner. First comes the smell of smoke. An object is discovered within a circular spot, which is smoking. It bursts into flames. Edouard Lahore, 59, says, "They say it could be the work of a ghost or the rays of the Devil. I just don't know." The fires have also defied the efforts of an investigating judge, the prefect of police and Gregoire Kaplan, head of the Laboratory of Physical Analysis from Pau. Though nearly every conceivable item in the house has been burned – even clothes while they were being worn – lab technicians have been unable to identify a chemical agent. The strange "Affair of Seron" continues to smoulder.

Rich Ghost in Fight for Cash

Source and date: *News of the World,* 4 November 1979

A pretty young London wife claims that the ghost of her wealthy friend has told her to fight the will that does not include her. The friend, Leon Taylor, left his estate of at least £80,000 to his two sons when he died on 14 February. But Mrs Charmaine Edwards says Mr Taylor, 43, promised to cut them out of his will and leave everything to her. She said, "The night after Leon died I woke up with a start to see his form standing at the foot of the bed as real as in life. A few days later I found him sitting in the passenger seat of my car as I drove along. He said, 'You must fight them. Fight the will. We're not going to let them get away with it.' After that I went to various clairvoyants. Each time he spoke through them saying her would help me to fight the will." Mrs Edwards claims she is entitled to the cash because she used thousands of pounds after selling her house to help Mr Taylor when he was short of ready money. She has blocked execution of the will through a High Court order.

1980–89

Paying Ghosts

Source and date: *Jacksonville Journal, Florida,* 6 January 1980

Things began to go bump in the night after a fifty-six-year-old millionaire shot himself in Jim and Corinne Succhi's villa. "The doors opened and shut, water taps started to gush, electric lights flashed on and off, and at midnight we were roused by terrifying screams," said Jim. He and his wife have sued the millionaire's heirs for $50,000 claiming they suffered fear and sleepless nights in the haunted home. The millionaire's lawyer told a court in Palm Springs, Florida, "I've heard of paying guests, but not paying ghosts. Even if it's true that my dead client haunts the house, he has every right to spook where he pleases."

Hanged Man "Speaks"

Source and date: *Sunday People,* 20 January 1980

Four remand prisoners, who tried to raise their spirits in jail by playing with a Ouija board, got more than they bargained for. They say they raised a real spirit – a man hanged 100 years earlier at the same prison in Norwich. "We were scared to death," said thirty-two-year-old Albert Atkins, one of the men who improvized the spirit-raising Ouija board with paper letters. "It spelt out 'Alan Cook was hanged June 8 1879' and added, 'Bless you friend.'" There was little sleep for the four men that night. "All hell broke loose," said Albert. "The table came right across the cell. Our water jug floated on the table. The other blokes stayed in their bunks, scared. The light was on all the time so there could have been no nonsense." A prison officer's check the next day showed that Cook had indeed been hanged at the jail 100 years before for the murder of Charles Stuart and four other people. A surprise sequel comes with a report from East London medium, Mrs Eugenie Dormer, that murderer Alan Cook contacted her during a séance to thank Albert for helping him. She said, "Obviously this was a troubled spirit who had been earthbound and Albert's action released him."

Ghost Keeps Gerald Free

Source and date: *Sunday Mirror*, 2 March 1980

Charlie the ghost has saved Gerald Bell from jail. When magistrates heard how ill his wife was because of Charlie's antics they just couldn't leave her alone in the house with a ghost. So they sentenced Bell, 25, to eighteen hours community service instead. Prison seemed inevitable when Bell, a suspended sentence hanging over him for a previous offence, admitted taking a parcel of clothing from a neighbour's doorstep. Then the court heard about Charlie: the poltergeist made things go bump in the night, caused locked doors to open and threw ornaments about. Bell's nineteen-year-old wife, Lorna, was so scared she often sat up all night rather than go to bed, magistrates at Darwen, Lancashire were told. Mr Peter Turner, defending successfully, appealed to the Bench to allow Bell to stay in the haunted house with his sick wife. After the hearing, the couple said they were putting the house up for sale.

Terror of Moonlight Ghost Clash

Source and date: *News of the World*, 20 April 1980

It was the eerie hour of 2.30 a.m. when Mrs Liz Reeves and her husband got back to their country home one night. Suddenly they found themselves in the middle of a terrifying "ghost battle". As the couple cringed against a wall, they were surrounded by cries and the clash of arms. But in the bright moonlight they could see . . . *nothing*. Mrs Reeves of the Old Smithy, Holme Hale, Norfolk said, "It was frightening. We felt we were in the middle of a battle with people shouting and horses shying." She explained, "The crash of swords did not seem against other swords, but against wood as though they were hitting wooden staves. After a few minutes the sounds moved away and then all the local dogs started howling. We thought about ringing the police, but they wouldn't have believed us." Then came another eerie discovery. Mrs Reeves said, "I did some research and found there was an uprising here by the peasants against the gentry in the 1600s. I never believed in this sort of thing, but I'd like to hear an explanation." A Psychical Research Society spokesman said, "We have been getting reports of almost identical incidents. This is an interesting case which we will investigate."

In the Mood with Glenn's Ghost

Source and date: *Sunday People*, 2 November 1980

Big Band fan John Robinson says he has swinging company when he listens to the music of Ted Heath and Glenn Miller – their ghosts. Heath died in 1969, Miller in 1944 – but according to John they still get a kick out of their old records. "It all started after an amazing experience," said John, a 52-year-old bus driver who lives at Neville Square, Lynemouth, Northumberland. "My wife Jean and I were watching Jack Parnell's band playing Glenn Miller's music on TV. Suddenly I felt there was someone else in the room. I looked at Jean and I could clearly see Glenn Miller's face in front of hers. When the band played his theme, *Moonlight Serenade*, there were tears in his eyes." John went on, "Ted Heath made his appearance in a similar manner. Since then they have come regularly. Always I see their faces in front of Jean's. There is never much conversation between us. They simply ask us to go on playing their music. I'm convinced we have the two band leaders as company."

Friar Held after Apparition

Source and date: *The Times*, 13 October 1981

A Roman Catholic friar in Yugoslavia has been arrested and is awaiting trial after a controversy which followed the alleged appearance of the Virgin Mary, according to the Belgrade newspaper, *Vecernje Novosti*, today. The paper also said eleven people were expelled from the Communist Party and 48 others given Party warnings for visiting the site of the alleged apparition in the southern town of Citluk, where six girls said they saw the Madonna in July. Thousands of people have streamed into Citluk to visit the site, and authorities have claimed that the Roman Catholic Church is trying to use the event for political purposes.

Ghost at the Dentists

Source and date: *Daily Telegraph,* 21 February 1982

Germans love a ghost story. A weird tale that has emerged from mist-shrouded Lower Bavaria has grabbed the Gothic reaches of their imagination with greater force than any other in recent years. For the past eleven months, Dr Kurt Bachseitz, a small-town dentist, has been plagued by a phantom voice which just won't be silenced. The disembodied voice – which answers to the name "Chopper" – first confined itself to Dr Bachseitz's telephone and it was easy to dismiss it as a practical joke. But then it began to issue from various outlets in Dr Bachseitz's surgery which is in a quiet street in the small Bavarian town of Neutraubling. Its staccato, robot-like monotone would issue forth from electric power points, light fittings and pieces of surgical equipment, haranguing Dr Bachseitz and declaring undying love for his pretty seventeen-year-old assistant. When the voice began to disturb Dr Bachseitz as he attended patients – sometimes lecturing to him from the washbasin at the side of the dentist's chair – he called in the police and issued a private summons of harassment against "person or persons unknown". A Post Office team from Darmstadt travelled 150 miles to the town and spent several days and £15,000 investigating the mystery. They left in bewilderment.

Ghost Miner Scares a Pit

Source and date: *Sun,* 18 March 1982

A ghost in a coalmine has scared young pitman Steve Dimbleby, 23, into packing up his £150-a-week job at Silverwood Colliery, Rotherham, Yorkshire. He ran screaming for a mile underground after coming face to face with the frightening phantom miner. Steve, of Sunnyside, Rotherham, described the apparition: "He wore an old-fashioned square pitman's helmet, a waistcoat and grubby shirt. There was a light in the helmet. He bent his head and shone his light in my face. I realized there was something odd. Then when I looked at his face he had no features. It was blank – no eyes, no nose, no mouth." Steve froze with fear when he saw the ghost then ran. "I was ranting and raving and crying. I've hardly slept since it happened on Sunday night. I'd rather go on the dole that down that pit." Coal Board chiefs have now switched Steve to a £100-a-week surface job. They have also confirmed that fourteen years ago, a miner died where the spectre appeared. [In October 1887, another miner, Gary Pine, 19, reported seeing a ghost "in overalls and safety helmet slide through a concrete wall and vanish" in the Cotgrave Colliery in Nottinghamshire. According to the *Sun*, other miners were "refusing to do Gary's job other than in pairs".]

Officialdom Kills Party for Ghosts

Source and date: *Observer*, 6 September 1982

Strange legal action looms in Honking where a religious body has been denied a site for this month's traditional Hungry Ghosts Festival. This is held annually in the seventh month of the lunar year when the doors of Hell are supposed to open and the ghosts are allowed to emerge for temporary release and enjoyment. The festival is organized by the Chinese communities as a hypocritical welcome to the ghosts to prevent them from harassing their living descendants. The main ceremony in Hong Kong has been held for the past eighty-five years and is usually attended by more than 100,000 people. [Despite this threat, the Hungry Ghosts Festival took place in Hong Kong and also Singapore where a threat to some of the street operas or *wayangs* held in side streets and car parks all over the island was averted.]

Sellers Spooks the Pink Panther

Source and date: *News of the World*, 31 October 1982

The ghost of Peter Sellers is haunting the new Pink Panther movie, the producer reckons. A jinx has hit *Trail of the Pink Panther* in which Sellers stars two years after his death. Unused film from the actor's previous Panther movies is being slotted in with newly shot scenes. But producer Tony Adams says that many unexplained incidents have disrupted production. "I think Peter's up there being as mischievous as he usually was down here. Things that shouldn't have happened suddenly did – making it difficult to match new film with the old. Costumes were lost even after they had been checked many times. Sets that worked perfectly suddenly didn't and a lot of scenes were jinxed. We wondered if Peter might be getting at us." Peter Sellers believed he could communicate with the dead and claimed his mother guided his career from the grave.

Halloween – United States 1982

Source and date: *Sunday Times*, 31 October 1982

With detectives still hunting the Tylenol murderer in Chicago and a rash of copycats finding new products to poison, millions of parents across America face an unhappy decision. Do they allow their children to go on the streets gathering sweets from neighbours in the traditional celebration of Halloween? Over the past decade there has been a vague Halloween fear ever since razor blades were found hidden in an apple given to children, mercury poisoned tablets in Denver and insecticides injected into orange juice in Miami. American children look forward to Halloween as English children look forward to Guy Fawkes Night. They dress up as ghosts or ghouls and indulge in "Trick or treat?". But this year some towns across the country are banning trick or treating; others are stepping up police patrols and all are insisting that parents make a thorough check of what their children eat. The combination of genuine grounds for fear plus a degree of hysteria has reached the level where some cities are offering free X-ray services in case you want to check for anything some demented soul might feel like injecting into sweets. Real ghosts had better take heed, too!

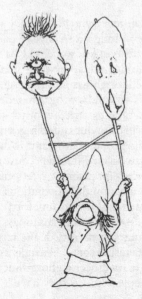

Bargain at Ghost Hotel

Source and date: *Sunday Mirror*, 13 February 1983

Four British holidaymakers believe they have stayed at a phantom hotel in France – as the guests of a group of 80-year-old ghosts. Mystified Len Gisby, his wife Cynthia and Geoff and Pauline Simpson stopped at the quaint little inn near Montelimar during a trip through the country. A number of spine-tingling experiences left them convinced that they were caught up in some strange supernatural experience. Their suspicions were first aroused when they discovered the hotel had no modern amenities and was occupied by people wearing strange early twentieth-century clothing. Stranger still was the bill. It came to 19 francs – about 50p per head – for an evening meal, the bedrooms and breakfast. But the biggest shock came when they decided to find their strange hotel on the way back from holidaying in Spain . . . it had disappeared. Now Len and Cynthia from Dover are travelling back to France in a bid to solve the mystery. Geoff, also from Dover, said, "There's no doubt that this happened to us."

Spectre Inspectors

Source and date: *Radio Times*, 12 March 1983

Good news for ghost hunters who don't fancy spending endless hours in some spooky place waiting for strange things to happen – soon the task of checking out the unknown could be done by a computer. Researchers in Cambridge are adapting a small computer to keep a round-the-clock watch for ghosts and poltergeists. Under laboratory conditions the computer will be programmed to switch on cameras, video equipment and tape recorders if anything out of the ordinary begins to happen. It will print out any changes in temperature to check the old saying among people who claim to have seen a ghost that "suddenly everything went cold". And because many alleged sightings remain unproven due to equipment mysteriously failing to work, the computer will record any unusual fluctuations in the electricity. Tony Cornell, a leading official of the Society for Psychical Research who has spent thirty years investigating hauntings, said "When we investigate we have to conform to very high standards. We started to develop the computer just before Christmas and it could be of great help. Personally, I have never seen a ghost – but I have met hundreds of sane and sensible people who say they have."

John Lennon's Ghost Visits Yoko

Source and date: *Sunday Mirror,* 29 May 1983

John Lennon's ghost is said to be haunting the New York apartment where the ex-Beatle was murdered. Several people claim to have seen his ghostly figure wearing familiar round glasses. Friends of his wife, Yoko Ono, say that John's spirit has spoken to her. Musician Joey Harrow, who lives nearby, is convinced that he saw John's ghost at the entrance to the Dakota building – the spot where he was shot three years ago. "He was surrounded by an eerie light," said Joey. Amanda Mores, a writer who was with Joey at the time, says she also saw Lennon's ghost. "I wanted to go up and talk to him, but something in the way he looked at me said no." Yoko, who still lives in the same block with their son, Sean, claims to have seen John sitting at his white piano and that on one occasion he said, "Don't be afraid – I am still with you." [A year later, on 21 October 1984, *Mirror* reported that Lennon's ghost was also haunting the cellar of the Jacaranda Club in Slater Street where he used to play with Stuart Sutcliffe, the group's original bass player, who died in Hamburg. Licensee Isabel Daley said, "There were two shadowy figures of young men arguing. I recognized one of them as a young John Lennon from photographs I had seen. He said, 'Come on Audrey, that's not right.' I shot up the stairs when I realized they were ghosts." Audrey Reynolds, who was a barmaid in the club in the early 1960s, commented, "It's uncanny. John used to row over everything."]

Charles and the Phychics

Source and date: *Sunday Mirror,* 8 January 1984

A fascination for the mysterious world of the paranormal has earned Prince Charles a new title. It is as though he has become the "Prince of Psychics" following the disclosure that he is backing the University of Wales as it tries to start a course in parapsychology and create Britain's first professor in the subject. Never before has a member of the Royal Family been seen to be so actively involved in the setting up of such a centre which will be devoted to investigating everything from poltergeists and spoon-bending to extra-sensory perception. Prince Charles has always shown an interest in subjects like psychology and alternative medicine and in a letter to Dr Cecil Bevan, the Principal of the University of Wales, about the professorship, Charles asked, "Why don't we have a go at tasking up this scheme?" Inquiries by the *Sunday Mirror* have uncovered details of an astonishing meeting between the prince and Winifred Rushford, one of the world's leading psychotherapists, at her flat in Edinburgh in the spring of 1983. Dr Rushford has since died, but her daughter, Dr Diana Bates, who was present at the meeting, told us what happened; "It was as if the prince and my mother had known each other all their lives. My mother believed there must have been some sort of psychic contact between them already." Dr Bates has refused to reveal whether the prince had voiced any wish to "contact" any relatives who have passed away.

Five-Star Haunts

Source and date: *Daily Mail*, 14 August 1984

If you hear strange noises in the night at your hotel don't tell the plumber – tell the promotions manager. He'll hope your room is haunted. Britain's inns are so proud of their non-paying guests that they now include a ghost write-up in their brochures. Latest to cash in is the huge Trusthouse Forte group which has a new brochure listing its nightly visitors. They include a tragic maid who rustles through rooms at the Berystede Inn, looking for jewels. She died in a fire in the last century, having rushed back into the blazing inn to rescue gifts of jewels given to her over the years. At the White Hart, Lincoln, there is a strange fat man who appears, wringing his hands, and asking about his lost ginger jar. The Dolphin, Southampton has a maid who walks two feet above the floor – the level of the floorboards two centuries ago. One brewery used to employ an official ghost hunter. In those days they wanted to get rid of them. Today the ghosts are good business.

Bishop Saw Ghost of Grandmother

Source and date: *The Times,* 15 August 1984

The Bishop of Salisbury, the Right Rev John Baker, recently appointed as the next head of the Church of England's Doctrine Commission, believes in ghosts and saw one when he was aged four. He discloses in his diocesan newsletter that he saw the ghost of his grandmother shortly after her death. The bishop says he was unaware of her death at the time and told his mother, "I saw Gran last night. She came in and kissed me goodnight and walked around the bed and then she went. But she did look funny. She was wearing a white sheet."

The Ghostbusters in England

Source and date: *Evening Standard,* 16 October 1984

The phenomenal success of *Ghostbusters*, the sixth biggest money-making film in America about three parapsychologists who go into business to combat a plague of poltergeists, has inspired a group of real-life ghostbusters to visit Britain. Lead by "paranormal consultant" to the film, Nonie Fagatt, a healer and psychical researcher, they have been scouring the country looking for spooks. Says Nonie, "The best ghosts are the English ghosts because you look after them so well." Their mission has taken the ghostbusters to some of the best- and least-known haunts with great success and members of the group claim to have seen the ghost of Cardinal Wolsey at Hampton Court, Elizabeth Hobby of Bisham Abbey who spoke through one woman "in strange tongues" and a Roman soldier who kept another female awake all night by "prodding her" at the Francis Hotel in Bath. Nonie, whose last exorcism was televised in America, made a point of visiting the Tower of London, but found it too full of people. She said, "You wouldn't even know it if you saw an Elizabethan ghost in your peripheral vision where most ghosts are seen. And the linoleum floor robs you of your psychic grounding. But you still cannot fail to feel the energy. The place cries out of torture and killings. It makes my chest go tight and then my throat."

Ghostly Gunslinger Leads to Gold

Source and date: *Dallas Morning Herald*, 7 April 1985

Prospector Si Burris of Albuquerque had had another fruitless day searching for gold in southeastern New Mexico. But as the sixty-year-old former rodeo rider set off for home he spotted a young man far off in the distance, down the ravine where he was headed. Hoping for a bit of company, Si hurried along to catch up with him. And when he did he decided that his new companion was not very friendly. Said Si, "He had sandy yellow hair, a gun belt and an insolent sneer. I turned to leave, but he challenged me. He said, 'What's your hurry? You're a prospector looking for gold, right? Go up that rise. There'll be a valley ahead on your right. Go down into it and when you see an old axe handle stuck into a tree dig beneath its trunk.' Then the stranger turned and walked away." Surprised, Si shouted after him to ask who he was. "He looked at me hard and said, 'Friend, call me William Bonney. You'd know me as Billy the Kid.' I figured he must be drunk or joking." Nevertheless, Si hurried off and to his amazement found the tree with the axe handle. He dug down and found his gold. "It was in the rotted remains of a Wells Fargo moneybag. There were old gold and silver coins minted in the 1870s and 1890s." Historians now believe the coins may well be part of the loot Billy the Kid stole during his outlaw career. The $10,000 worth of booty almost matches exactly the description of one of his hold-ups of a Wells Fargo stagecoach.

Voices from a Hitchcock Nightmare

Source and date: *Chicago Daily News*, 25 August 1985

Every day was a nightmare for wealthy eighty-six-year-old Catherine Noordyke of Chicago. Crazy voices would babble in the pre-dawn darkness until in the end she thought she was going insane. Household objects such as cutlery, carpets and rugs would move on their own – as if by unseen hands. Things had begun to go bump in the night after she had married her younger lover, forty-nine-year-old dashing, six-foot tall Neal Faasen. Her once-happy life had become an Alfred Hitchcock nightmare after she began sharing all her worldly goods with her new husband. When Faasen finally dumped Catherine on a relative's doorstep after the five-year marriage, she was penniless – minus a $1,500,000 fortune. "The poor lady was on the verge of cracking up," said lawyer James Zerrenner in Grand Rapids, Michigan. "She really thought she was going mad." In a court action now being brought by Catherine's family, Faasen is accused of fraud. It is claimed that the objects were moved by translucent fishing lines and that Faasen hired people to whisper and laugh outside his wife's bedroom window in a wicked plot to drive her insane.

Haunt of the Dead

Source and date: *Sunday People*, 3 November 1985

The ghost of a man murdered by Tom Fool – who gave his name to the expression "tomfoolery" – has driven a landowner from his castle. Gordon Duff-Pennington is dogged by the footsteps of the murdered carpenter every time he passes the stables on Muncaster Castle, near Ravenglass, Cumbria, at night. Tom Fool Skelton, who managed Muncaster, killed the carpenter for bragging of an affair with the castle's mistress. Mr Duff-Pennington is going to Scotland and leaving the castle to a relative.

Anyone There in the Washing Machine?

Source and date: *Sunday Telegraph*, 24 November 1985

Psychical research at Edinburgh University is to try to find out whether there is anything paranormal at work when some machines work for certain people and refuse to work for others. According to Britain's newly appointed first professor of parapsychology, American, Dr Robert Morris, these machines include television sets, computers, copiers and even telephones. They apparently break down for some people, but immediately work normally when used by others and he will seek to find out if paranormal reactions to machines could exist – and if so what form they might take. The new professorship is being funded by a £500,000 endowment left by the writer Arthur Koestler and his wife who died in 1983. Dr Morris said that he interpreted Koestler's aims as investigating psychical phenomena rather than acting as advocate for them. "I think there is something to be learned, but I am quite sceptical of many claims." He defined psychical experience as anomalous communication between people and their environment, not necessarily limited to telepathy or other well-recognized forms. Other proposed research includes identifying psychic phenomena such as telepathy, clairvoyance and pre-cognition.

Girl Ghost Ends Last Bus Trip

Source and date: *Sunday Express*, 16 February 1986

A Taiwan bus company near Tainan, 200 miles south of Taipei, has been forced to cancel the evening run to an isolated village because of a ghost. Passing through tall, shadowy sugar-cane fields, the driver picked up a young girl passenger, but by the time the bus journey ended the girl had vanished. The company's other frightened drivers insisted a Taoist priest exorcize the haunted vehicle before it was used again.

Verily I Am a Computer Spook

Source and date: *The Mail on Sunday*, 29 December 1985

Complicated modern technology is the latest plaything for ghosts. Or, at least, one very peculiar spirit who calls himself Thomas Harden and haunts the computer of economics teacher Ken Webster, living in the village of Doddleston in Cheshire. Oxford-educated Harden has been dead for more than 400 years, but that does not stop him enjoying a good session on a BBC Micro after a hard day's toll. He calls the gadget a "leems boyste" – light box – or a "scrit devis" in the late Middle English of his time. Ken Webster believes the skills of the man who has haunted his computer for more than a year rather impressive and looks forward to the messages from the past that pop up on his monitor. These are mainly questions about the present day but also offering historical information that has proved interesting and correct. Ken Webster originally thought someone was playing a prank, but after 150 messages and establishing there was a Thomas Harden who was the Dean of Brasenose College Chapel at Oxford, he thinks otherwise. The Dean was apparently expelled for refusing to remove the Pope's name from prayer books during Henry VIII's purge of Roman Catholicism. The Society for Psychical Research has investigated the case no fewer than eight times but remains sceptical. [In July 1988, another computer in Cheshire – an Amstrad PC 1512 in an architect's office in Stockport – was also reported by *The People* to be haunted. A cleaner saw the screen glowing even though it was unplugged, other staff members noticed letters appearing on the screen when it was switched off, and a secretary was terrified when the machine "suddenly started to groan". Experts from *Personal Computer* magazine, called in to investigate the claims, ran tests including focusing a video camera on the spooked machine for three months resulting in very similar effects. Leader Ken Hughes commented "I would not have believed it if I had not seen it myself. I am baffled."]

Trainer Decides Exorcism is Best Bet

Source and date: *The Times,* 10 December 1986

Mr Alex Whiting, a racehorse owner with fourteen horses in training at the St Claud Racing Stables at Costock, Nottinghamshire, could never understand why success had always eluded him at his local racecourse in Nottingham after twenty-four attempts. He had, after all, had winners at Catterick, Newmarket, Wolverhampton and Brighton, so it was unlikely that there was anything fundamentally wrong with the quality of his training. Mr Whiting finally decided that it must be the ghost of his Great Uncle Cyril whose ashes had been scattered on the Nottingham racecourse. The family cannot remember if the scattering was a gesture of celebration or desperation, but they do remember that Great Uncle Cyril, with almost his dying breath, forecast that none of his descendants would ever win at Nottingham. Great Uncle Cyril has proved depressingly right, although Mr Whiting came close last month when his horse, *Taylor's Renovation*, was first past the post. Unfortunately, in the final yards of the sprint, it threw its jockey, Keith Sims, and was disqualified. "I thought the race was won, I couldn't believe it when Sims came off, but there was nothing I could do. Remembering Great Uncle Cyril, it sent a shiver down my spine." So last Friday Great Nephew Alex took decisive action. He asked Father Frank Shanahan, a Roman Catholic priest attached to the parish of the Most Blessed Sacrament in Leicester, to exorcize the ghost of Great Uncle Cyril. Afterwards, Mr Whiting said, "I hope that our troubles are now at an end. The priest carried out a blessing by the finishing post and we are all hoping that it has changed our luck."

Upward Spirits

Source and date: *The Observer,* 10 January 1988

"Channeling" is the new fad among America's Yuppies. At dinner parties from Malibu to New York the talk is about stocks, real estate and then entities. "Channelers" have new consciousness and new

Porches: they are upwardly mobile with spirit guides. And they are not sad spiritualists harassing the beloved dead in suburban front rooms; they are executive class. "Channeling" is contact, usually by trance, with entities in some other cloudy plane – who may be your previous lives, the previous lives of others, or benevolent advisers, a kind of supernatural newsletter. They represent, according to taste, a hidden world, the unused part of the collective mind, or the bits of your own brain you don't quite know. There are hundreds of thousands of these people across America – Shirley MacLaine is among the best known – including Yuppie fundamentalists who have found their own form of spiritualism.

Haunted Wings in the Night

Source and date: *Sunday Express*, 17 July 1988

An astonishing tape-recording of ghostly goings-on aboard a Lincoln bomber that hasn't flown for thirty years is baffling experts. Former pilots who have listened to the tape – made by a radio broadcaster under strict scientific conditions – say it reveals the precise sounds of a Lincoln in flight. Among the noises picked up on the recording are: muffled voices of aircrew; engines droning and changing pitch; morse code blips; clanging hangar doors; switches and levers being operated. Yet bomber RF 398 housed in the museum hangar at RAF Cosford, Shropshire, never saw any active service in the war. Local radio presenter Ivan Spenceley, from Chesterfield, Derbyshire, set up the tape to investigate claims that the aircraft was haunted. He left his machine running in the empty cockpit and staff locked both the bomber and the hangar behind him. He said, "When I played back the recording I shuddered. It was as if the old girl had suddenly taken to the skies. Human voices are clearly audible, but it is impossible to make out what they're saying. It's eerie." Spooky tales have surrounded the bomber ever since it arrived in the hangar to be restored eleven years ago. Some engineers have been too frightened to work on it. Several people have even reported seeing a ghostly airman dressed in battle jacket inside the hangar. The museum's administrator, John Francis, said: "The noises are a mystery. I've got an open mind about it all, but the ghostly stories come from level-headed people who stick by what they have seen and heard."

Liz's Haunted House

Source and date: *The People,* 14 August 1988

Liz Taylor is desperately trying to sell her favourite house in Puerto Vallarta in Mexico because she believes it is haunted by the ghost of Richard Burton. But the creepy goings-on at the palatial mansion with its seven bedrooms and bathrooms, swimming pool and Pacific view have scared off all would-be buyers for almost a year despite dropping the original asking price from almost £1 million to a "silly" £625,000. Liz and Burton bought the mansion as a romantic holiday home after their second marriage thirteen years ago – but now she flatly refuses to go near the place. Maids who worked at the house with Miss Taylor claim that she had at least four chilling encounters in the four years since Burton died. On one occasion she woke in the night to find him lying in bed beside her. She is also said to have seen him sitting in his favourite rocking chair. Another "sighting" allegedly caused her to flee the house weeping, dressed only in a black lace nightie. It is known that she has consulted a spirit medium and there are even claims she has had the house exorcized. She is said to have told a friend, "The joint's haunted. I loved Richard dearly, but I went through enough with him while he was alive without being put through the mixer again now."

The Haunted House of Commons

Source and date: *The People,* 29 January 1989

Down-to-earth Angus Morrison has nicknamed the Commons the Haunted House after grappling with a ghost. Lift operator Angus – all eleven stone of him – was picked up and thrown fifteen feet across a corridor. But there was nobody there. He explained, "I was sitting in the Committee Corridor at 3 a.m. when I began to feel very cold. I was just picked up bodily and thrown about fifteen feet, but I never saw anyone. It really does give me the creeps up there." Now Westminster is buzzing with tales of the unexpected instead of worldly business. Staff have seen a shadowy bearded figure dressed in doublet and hose walking the corridors of power. Labour MP John McWilliam said, "Some people say it's James I. I have been warned about this apparition and the atmosphere can be very eerie." Angus Morrison reckons the Prime Minister should make a new appointment . . . official Ghostbuster.

Putting a Spook in the Wheel

Source and date: *Daily Star,* 31 July 1989

Nervous navvies working in a remote area near Bergen in Norway have put up a road sign to warn motorists of a haunting hazard – "Ghosts Crossing". The red and white triangular sign illustrated with a spook warns drivers of a supernatural danger on a road near a deserted cabin. The decision to erect the sign was made after workers saw mysterious figures and heard weird signs while repairing the highway. A spokesman of Bergen Highway Authority said, "People have experienced so many strange things they swear there are ghosts."

Harriet Gets High Grades as Ghost

Source and date: *Los Angeles Times,* 1 November 1989

The public school in Gorman, California is one of the smallest in the district. But it's become famous in the state by reports of a little girl ghost called Harriet. According to reports by a number of students, she has been seen walking in the corridors of the building on a number of occasions. One pupil had such a close encounter with the ghost that she recognized her. There was no doubt she was the spirit of a popular and high-achieving little girl named Harriet who had been killed accidentally while crossing the street on her way to the school just over a year previously. The school authorities have so far dismissed claims that the stories are pure fantasy invented by the students.

1990–2000

Ghosts in Space?

Source and date: *New York Daily News*, 12 March 1990

Strange sounds and weird lights are said to have been experienced when American scientists secretly sent a human skull known as "The Phantom" on two flights into space to study the effects of radiation. And now they are planning to put a human torso into orbit. The experts from NASA insist there is nothing ghoulish about the experiments which are aimed at learning how much radiation from the sun and stars penetrates the human body and will be vital once the US embarks on ambitious space programmes to build manned stations and send spaceships to Mars. But they were puzzled by stories from crew members of "mysterious experiences" during the first flight last August. The bare cranium of "The Phantom" was packed with 125 radiation detectors and covered with plastic "skin" for the mission. Scientist Dr Richard Bowman said the skull came from an anonymous donor who willed his body to science. He added, "I have no idea whether it even came from an American – I understand skeletons for experimentation often come from other countries."

Going Gazump

Source and date: *The Times*, 5 December 1990

Does the presence of things that go bump in the night enhance or diminish the value of property? And what is the legal position for someone who discovers he has bought a house with a spectral sitting tenant? It depends on the ghost according to an article in *Country Homes and Gardens*. If the spirit is not "of the tiresomely mournful sort that wails, clanks chains or frightens the dogs", it should be good news. Such spooks "can add value and charm to a house which might otherwise just be another victim of the property doldrums". Two alleged haunted houses currently on the market are Rock House in Devon where Rudyard Kipling once lived and Iron Hall in the Lake District. Both make a virtue of their supernatural nature in the estate agents' blurb. Those who do not know they are buying haunted houses and are subsequently upset by creaking stairs and doors apparently have little legal redress. Tony Girling of the Law Society's property committee says, "There is no obligation on a seller to reveal a ghostly presence." Richard Aldington, who is handling the sale of the Kipling house, has his own explanation of its reported otherworldly phenomena. He says, "I think a lot depends on how much one has to drink" – words, surely, that can only come back to haunt him.

Judge Declares House is Haunted

Source and date: *Associated Press*, 20 July 1991

An American appeal court has ruled that a riverfront Victorian house is haunted and a prospective buyer can sue to get his deposit back. The wooden, turreted house overlooks the broad expanse of the

Hudson River, 20 miles upstream from New York, has long been known to house benign ghosts of Revolutionary vintage and is close to the Tappan Zee bridge where the headless horseman once terrified the good people of Sleepy Hollow and Rip Van Winkle lay down to sleep for twenty years. As a matter of law, the house is haunted, the New York state supreme court's appellate division ruled in a majority decision that reversed a lower court decision. The ruling by Justice Israel Rubin means that Jeffrey and Patrice Stambovsky may return to court to try to get back the $32,500 (£20,000) they paid as deposit for the house at Nyack. Mr Stambovsky, 38, a bond trader, said the vendor, Helen Ackley, failed to reveal the Revolutionary war-era ghosts that allegedly inhabit the house when he signed the contract in August 1989. Mrs Ackley, 64, former owner of the house, said her family had been seeing ghosts in the house since they moved in twenty-four years ago. She said, "I feel they are very good friends – it's very comforting to have them around when you are by yourself." One of the spirits is "a cheerful apple-cheeked man" and all of them were "friendly and nice". A judge had ruled last year that *caveat emptor* (let the buyer beware) guides property purchases. But the appeal court declared *caveat emptor* less than all-encompassing and no amount of prudent inspection by the Stambovskys would have revealed the ghosts that are believed to occupy the eighteen-room house. The Stambovskys, who lived in Manhattan's Upper East Side at the time, could not have been expected to know about the house's reputation, Justice Rubin said, writing for the majority. He also said Mrs Ackley could not have delivered a vacant house, since ghosts live there. The Stambovskys now live about a mile from the haunted house.

Tragedy Follows Protests Over Ghost Drama

Source and date: *Mail on Sunday*, 8 November 1992

Ghostwatch, the BBC's controversial Halloween TV spoof, was blamed yesterday for a teenager's suicide. Profoundly disturbed by last Saturday's programme, eighteen-year-old Martin Denham hanged himself from a tree – called The Witch Tree – near his home in Nottingham. A suicide note on Martin's body read, "Dear Mum, please don't worry. If there are ghosts I will be a ghost and I will be with you always as a ghost." The documentary style of the drama starring Michael Parkinson, Sarah Greene and Mike Smith, terrified thousands of viewers who jammed BBC switchboards in protest at its reality and the gory scenes. Yesterday distraught parents April and Percy Denham told how they tried to reassure Martin, who had a mental age of twelve, that it was all make-believe. The BBC point out that the programme was billed as a drama, but Mrs Denham says there should have been a specific warning. Martin had sat transfixed by the programme where the depicted haunted house was, like his own, on a council estate. A BBC spokesman said yesterday that the programme was clearly advertised as fictional drama and added, "Of course, we are very sorry to hear of this tragic event. However, we need to know more about this case before venturing any comment."

Dead Major Returns to Haunt Old Comrades

Source and date: *The Times,* 19 March 1994

Major William Henry Braddell has decided to renew his membership of the Naval and Military Club in Piccadilly more than half a century after being killed by a German bomb. To the delight of psychic investigators and the shock of the staff, the major – who was nicknamed "Perky" – has taken up residence in the Egremont Room. A porter saw the apparition wearing an ankle-length First World War trenchcoat in the small hours gliding slowly from a corner before disappearing. Floodlights outside the London club, which switch off automatically at midnight, came on as the ghostly old soldier appeared at 3.07 a.m. After he faded into a wall they went out, Trevor Newton, the night porter, said. Mr Newton, described by fellow staff yesterday as "a very steady man" who had never heard of Major Braddell, was "rooted to the spot" after his encounter. He has ventured back into the Egremont Room, "but not with any great enthusiasm". The connection was made by Peter Brabbs, a former club steward who knew the "bluff and humorous" Major and recognized the description of his ankle-length trenchcoat. He always wore this and was in the club on 19 May 1941 when a German bomb fell. Major Braddell had left the room to make a telephone call and when he returned his two fellow drinkers were dead. A week later, the Major himself was killed by a bomb in Kensington. Psychic investigators say there has been incredible interest, but there are no plans to exorcize the major's ghost. Peter Brabbs said, "I do not think he has returned to terrify people. The major has probably come back because he was happy here. He's among friends, too; there are quite a few other ghosts." One of these is said to be that of a man who went berserk after visiting the club. "You always know when he's about because there's an icy blast through the rooms. 'Perky' will be company for him and can perhaps cheer him up a bit."

Scientific Spirit Turns to Study of Ghosts

Source and date: *New York Times*, 25 August 1994

Reports of ghostly apparitions cannot be dismissed as the rantings of the insane or the work of hoaxers, a senior clinical psychiatrist said yesterday. Professor Ian Stevenson of the University of Virginia in Charlottesville, who has been studying reports of ghosts in Britain and the United States, said that people to whom the dead appeared had normal, healthy minds. He said there appeared to be an explanation for the sightings, which defied traditional science. "Evidence for these kinds of experiences are too frequent to be dismissed," Professor Stevenson said, citing studies that claim 10–15 per cent of the population had seen apparitions. He has been studying cases dating back forty years in which someone who has died or is about to die appears to a close friend. The professor said that these reports could be checked by scrutinizing death certificates for the time of death and by carefully controlled interviews with the person and family involved. "Studies of the mentally ill show they are not gifted in the same way. They may hear voices and see people, but this is usually related to their illness and their claims cannot be substantiated," said Professor Stevenson.

Ghostly Pulling Power

Source and date: *Northern Echo*, 29 April 1995

"We couldn't believe it," said Pam Scarr, landlady of the *Bonnie Moor Hen* at Stanhope in Weardale. "The pump tap goes down all on its own and enough beer to fill a half-pint glass is pulled and just pours in the drip-tray underneath." Pam and her husband, Joe, are getting used to having a ghost behind the bar at their pub, but there are frightening moments. The pub is next door to a graveyard and while the couple have laughed off locals' stories, "We have heard bloodcurdling screams from the cellar and barrel taps switching themselves off that have changed our minds," says Pam. She adds, "I am frightened – but whenever I go down to the cellar I just sing loudly all the time and keep telling myself the ghost won't harm me."

Phantom Army on the Move

Source and date: *Sunday Times*, 29 June 1997

Some of the weirdest ghosts of the handover of Hong Kong to the rule of China are the hordes of mythical soldiers who have been repeatedly spotted in the centre of the former British colony. Of course, everyone is used to the idea of the People's Liberation Army arriving. But the sight of their green uniforms and red stars is chilling. Rumours that a "phantom army" was on the move last week created an almost hysterical reaction among local people until it was revealed that a newspaper had organized a stunt with two reporters dressed up in uniform to go out asking for money. The two unfortunates returned bruised, their uniforms in shreds. Mythical sightings of foreign troops are now regarded as a classic sign of imminent unrest. During the First World War, ghostly Russian Cossacks were spotted throughout Britain, "with the snow still on their boots". They turned out to be heavily accented Scotsmen from Ross-shire not Russia.

Treat Ghosts Politely!

Source and date: *Village Voice*, 11 August 1998

Archaeologist Alyssa Loorya reckons she has found the way to prevent ghosts in haunted houses from making life difficult for their occupiers. While Ms Loorya and a team of builders were renovating Lott House, one of the few remaining Dutch farmhouses in Brooklyn, NYC, they encountered a number of weird problems. Light bulbs kept burning out soon after they had been replaced, doors were forever slamming although the windows of the Lott House are boarded up, and workers reported a number of strange manifestations. Enquiries revealed that the late owner of the property, Ella Suydam, who had died there in 1989, aged 92, was a stickler for old-fashioned courtesy. "That gave us the clue," says Alyssa Loorya. "All the noise in the house must have upset her ghost. We ring the bell now when we come into the house and even say hello to Ella. It seems to have quietened everything down."

Spooked Spies Go on a Ghost Hunt

Source and date: *Sunday Times*, 20 December 1998

Britain's spies have been spooked. Military intelligence officers may deploy electronic surveillance equipment to hunt for ghosts in the 850-year-old abbey that is their new headquarters. Balls of white light have floated in mid-air in the billiard room in front of one officer. Another member of staff said she had twice seen a figure thought to have been Rosata, a nun who was forced to watch her lover's execution and was then entombed alive in a wall. Other officers have heard children's laughter and seen lights coming from unoccupied rooms. Even animals have been affected: two guard dogs with perfect records for obedience and bravery had to be sent for retraining after they refused to go near the priory. The hauntings were reported over the past few months at Chicksands Priory, near Bedford, which was taken over by the Intelligence and Security Centre, an agency established two years ago by the RAF, army and navy to oversee covert intelligence operations. Its staff ridiculed warnings about the building's history – it is reputed to be haunted by nine spirits including the nun and a suicidal baronet – until they moved in. Brigadier Chris Holton, the centre's director, said, "The ghosts are talking to us. It's ironic that an intelligence organization should be haunted, but the priory is rotten with memories, echoes of the past that are still with us today." Some officers have welcomed the hauntings as a character-forming challenge and have asked for rooms believed to be affected. Holton believes the apparitions are not spirits, but "recordings" of traumatic events imprinted in the fabric of the building and endlessly replayed. Earlier this year military surveillance equipment, including seismic detectors, was used to monitor movement and temperature change. The man operating it heard "strange noises", but the group intend to stay put. Says Brigadier Holton, "What we do here is all about the blurring of barriers. Prejudice is the greatest threat to good intelligence and we must always keep open minds. There is a definite spiritual element to the intelligence business – so this building makes us feel very alert."

US Airman's Ghost

Source and date: *The Times Diary*, 28 June 1999

Spooky sightings at Cirencester Park, the stately pad of Lady Sarah Apsley. The former beauty queen was out walking her dogs when she happened upon a friendly-looking young man in airman's uniform, leaning against the historic 60-foot Queen Anne's Column which towers over the acreage. She says, "The clouds were just breaking up and I glanced at the sky and said, 'It looks as if it's going to brighten up.' When I looked back he had vanished." According to a forest worker, a US airman's ghost has lurked in the park since the Second World War.

The Haunted Supermarket

Source and date: *Daily Mirror,* 2 June 2000

With the dawning of the new century, the last bastion to resist being haunted has fallen. The 24-hour Tesco Superstore in Bury St Edmunds, Suffolk has been plagued by a spectre that has been haunting the store's cafeteria in the small hours. Last month there were also reports of poltergeist phenomena being seen by customers. The supermarket stands near the remains of the mediaeval St Saviour's Hospital, traditionally home for the ghost of a "Grey Lady".

Film Star Moves in with Ghost

Source and date: *Daily Telegraph,* 31 July 2000

Kate Winslet, the twenty-five-year-old star of the twentieth century's biggest grossing movie, *Titanic*, was warned yesterday that she will be sharing the house on the Cornish coast she has just bought with a ghost who appears early in the morning. She has paid a reported £380,000 for the house at Tintagel and is spending thousands renovating the property which has spectacular views over the Atlantic. Miss Winslet will be living in what is reputed to be one of the most haunted parts of Britain. The house is 500 yards from the ruins of Tintagel Castle, said to have been King Arthur's Camelot, and below a hotel that has three ghosts of its own. The actress, who as a child appeared in a film called *A Kid in King Arthur's Court*, already owns a house in west Cornwall, near Angarrack, bought the property privately and is thought not to have known of the ghost. "The secret is now out," said John Mappin, the joint owner of nearby Camelot Castle Hotel. "I know people who have seen the ghost and he is definitely friendly. The house used to be the cottage of the hotel's engineer, who died about seventy years ago, and some people believed it was his ghost that inhabited the house now," said Mr

Mappin. "He has been seen walking from the house to the hotel as if he was going to work. No one has ever been frightened of him and I think he probably adds character to the house." The hotel itself has three ghosts, says Mr Mappin. One throws paintings from the walls if he dislikes them. Another is a nurse who wakes people as if giving them a bed bath late at night. And the third goes through the rubbish bins.

Ghostly Traffic Jam

Source and date: *The Times*, 6 September 2000

A survey published last week claimed that the M6 Motorway is the most haunted road in Britain. Phantom Roman soldiers, a ghostly woman hitchhiker and a spooky lorry are just some of the strange visions that have been reported. Another haunted highway is the A9 in the Scottish Highlands where drivers have reported a ghostly stagecoach with footmen.

Mobile Phones Killing off Ghosts

Source and date: *Sunday Express*, 14 October 2000

Britain's ghosts are being killed off by the mobile phone explosion, according to experts on the paranormal. Haunted tourist attractions across the country could be under threat if the UK's 39 million-plus cell phones continue to grow in number. Paranormal events, which some scientists believe may be caused by unusual electrical activity, could be "drowned out" by intense electromagnetic fields and microwave radiation from mobile calls and text messages. Tony Cornell of the Society for Psychical Research said, "Ghost sightings have remained consistent for centuries. Until three years ago, we'd receive reports of two new ghosts every week. But with the introduction of mobile phones fifteen years ago, ghost sightings began to decline to the point where now we are receiving none. They could be drowning out our ghosts." Experts say the spooky pattern is mirrored in other countries. American researchers running short of their own spirits have begun travelling to the UK – only to find ghosts and ghouls in even shorter supply here. Now the SPR is considering sending ghost hunters to more isolated parts of the world. They hope areas with low mobile phone usage may still have significant ghost populations. Armed with specialist spook-detecting equipment including the prized SpIDER – or Spontaneous Incident Data Electronic Recorder – they hope to stop Britain's ghost stories becoming a dead subject. SpIDER seeks out ghosts by logging temperature changes and fluctuations in magnetic fields and listening for unexplained noises. It then takes infrared photographs and videos. Researchers may also resort to using modified mobile phones in future paranormal investigations. Mr Cornell said, "Perhaps we could use mobile phones with a slightly different frequency – that way we could phone the ghosts up and get some answers."

Ban Sought on Ghost Stories!

Source and date: *Northwest Evening Mail*, 24 December 2000

A Mrs Chen of Taiwan has set a legal first by taking out an injunction against her husband to stop him telling her ghost stories, complaining that he was giving her nightmares, according to the *Apple Daily* Taiwan newspaper. She first filed a complaint with police, and then applied for a personal protection order, which was approved by a district court in Taichung. The couple have been married for twenty years and have two daughters. They separated a few years ago, but have never divorced. Mr Chen found work away from home, at an orchard, but returned every few months to visit his daughters for a few days. His wife claimed he often returned home in the dead of night in a drunken stupor. He would then tell her ghost stories for at least an hour, despite her repeated pleas for him to stop. In his defence, Mr Chen claimed he was only sharing work stories with his wife.

The serious science of ghost hunting – careful and meticulous enquiry into the supernatural – owes a great deal to the pioneer work of two women: the English writer and researcher Catherine Crowe (1790–1872) and the Scottish feminist Eleanor Sidgwick (1845–1936), who became a driving force behind the influential Society for Psychical Research. Both were far removed from the ideal of typically reserved Victorian gentlewomen. Miss Crowe was a painstaking enquirer who braved many haunted houses in order to write her books; while Mrs Sidgwick, the sister of Arthur Balfour, the Prime Minister of Great Britain, was a free-thinker prepared to risk association with "what in the public mind was likely to be regarded as a cranky society" and brought a keen intelligence and critical eye to investigating the stories of the paranormal that were then so fascinating Victorian society

Catherine Crowe came to public attention in 1848 with *The Night Side of Nature*, a groundbreaking investigation into the supernatural based on historical evidence and a variety of contemporary accounts ranging from her native Kent to the Highlands of Scotland. She worked diligently to separate the facts from the gossip, rumours, imaginative exaggerations and even pure deception that embellished many of the ghost stories. In her Introduction, Miss Crowe made a direct appeal to the academic community, urging them that the more credible reports deserved proper scientific investigation:

> "*I avow that in writing this book I have a higher aim than merely to afford amusement. I wish to engage the attention of my readers because I am satisfied that the opinions I am about to advocate, seriously entertained, would produce very beneficial results . . . If I could only induce a few capable persons, instead of laughing at these things, to look at them, my object would be attained and I should consider my time well spent.*"

RAILWAY LIBRARY. TWO SHILLINGS.

THE
NIGHT SIDE OF NATURE
BY MRS CROWE

LONDON: GEORGE ROUTLEDGE & SONS

It was a brave challenge from the feisty little woman who produced several more books on the topic, including *Light and Darkness* (1850) and *Ghosts and Family Legends* (1858) – sadly, though, she did not live long enough to see the "men and women of science" take notice. But a decade later, on 6 January 1882, a group of academics and scientists led by Professor W F Barrett, the Professor of Physics at the Royal College of Science, Dublin, Alfred Russell Wallace, the co-developer of the theory of evolution, and the philosopher Professor Henry Sidgwick, gathered to form a society for the "study of abnormal happenings". The aims of the group were clearly stated in their original manifesto – and embodied the principles that the Society for Psychical Research, as the group named themselves, have followed ever since:

1. *Examination of the nature and extent of any influence which may be exerted by one mind upon another, otherwise than through the recognized sensory channels.*
2. *Inquiry into the alleged phenomena of clairvoyance.*
3. *Investigation of reports of apparitions and auditory and tactile impressions coinciding with some external event (as for instance a death), or giving information previously unknown to the percipient, or being seen by two or more persons independently of each other.*
4. *Examination of alleged communications from the dead, whether through automatic writing, trance-speaking, or otherwise.*
5. *Inquiry into various physical phenomena apparently inexplicable by known laws of nature, and commonly referred by spiritualists to the agency of extra-human intelligences.*
6. *The collection and collation of information and evidence bearing on these subjects.*

The forward-thinking Professor Sidgwick, who had married Eleanor Balfour in 1876 – converting her to feminism in the process – was installed as the first President of the SPR and insisted on the admission of his dark-haired attractive wife, already a gifted mathematician and educator, to serve as the administrator. The partnership was to ensure the establishment and furtherance of the objectives of the society.

Eleanor Sidgwick, in particular, played an important role in the group's activities. She took part in the investigation of several hauntings, sat in at séances with various mediums and generally used her energy, industry and clarity of thought to document the enquiries for the SPR files and edit the Society's *Journal*. Modestly, she refused to put her name on much of this material, anxious that the credit should go to the Society as a whole. In 1920, Eleanor cautiously admitted one significant conclusion she had reached in the third volume of the SPR's *Proceedings*:

> "I can only say that, having made every effort to exercise reasonable scepticism, I yet do not feel equal to the degree of unbelief in human testimony to avoid at least provisionally reaching the conclusion that there are, in a sense, haunted houses, i.e. houses in which similar *quasi*-human apparitions have occurred at different times to different inhabitants, under circumstances which exclude the hypothesis of suggestion or expectation."

Much that has followed in the development of "ghost hunting" can be traced back to the assiduous work of Eleanor Sidgwick – not forgetting, of course, the promptings of Catherine Crow. Writing in The *Observer* of 26 June, 1983 when the Arthur Koestler bequest of £500,000 had just been announced for the "foundation of an institute for the study of paranormal phenomena", Ruth Brandon, author of *The Spiritualists* (1983) paid tribute to the work of the two ladies in bringing science to bear on superstition. In particular, just how far-sighted Miss Crowe had been to push her convictions a century earlier: "One of the most telling weapons in the armoury of believers in the paranormal now is the number of distinguished scientists who have, after investigation, concluded that it is a reality."

ELEANOR SIDGWICK, the formidable first administrator of the Society for Psychical Research, was responsible for supervising many of the group's early investigations and contributed greatly to the gathering of knowledge about paranormal phenomena. Her work led to her being made president in 1908 and "president of honour" in 1930, shortly before her death. Among the many ghost stories she investigated was the "Morton Ghost" described as "one of the best authenticated cases of a haunted house" where four members of a Cheltenham family named Despard repeatedly saw the figure of a "tall lady, dressed in black of a soft woollen material" descending the stairs to their drawing room. The haunting started in 1882 and continued until 1901, the SPR investigation eventually concluding that the ghost was probably that of Mrs Imogen Swinhoe, the unhappy wife of a retired civil servant who had died of drink, aged 41, on 23 September 1878, just four years before the haunting started. In this account compiled by Eleanor Sidgwick and typical of its time, the name and address of the family have been disguised to preserve their anonymity.

MISS MORTON'S GHOST

Location and date:
All Saints Road, Cheltenham, 1901

The house is a commonplace square building, dating from about 1860. Its first tenant was Mr S., whose first wife died in the house (in August, year uncertain). Mr S. married again, but his second marriage was unhappy. Both he and his wife took to drink. In order to prevent his second wife securing his first wife's jewels, he had a secret receptacle constructed for them under the floor of the morning room or study. In that room he died in July 1876, his widow dying in another part of England in September 1878. With the exception of a brief tenancy of six months, terminated by death, the house appears to have remained unoccupied from the summer of 1876 until March 1882, when it was taken by Captain Morton. Neither Captain Morton nor his wife, an invalid, ever saw anything in the house. The eldest sister, Mrs K., an occasional visitor, saw the figure on two or three occasions. Of the four other sisters, three at one time or another saw the ghost; and so did the younger brother. Miss Morton, the chief percipient and the recorder of the case, was aged about nineteen at the time. The first appearance was in June 1882, and is thus described by her:

"I had gone up to my room, but was not yet in bed, when I heard someone at the door, and went to it, thinking it might be my mother. On opening the door, I saw no one; but on going a few steps along the passage, I saw the figure of a tall lady, dressed in black, standing at the head of the stairs. After a few moments she descended the stairs, and I followed for a short distance, feeling curious what it could be. I had only a small piece of candle and it suddenly burnt itself out; and being unable to see more, I went back to my room.

"The figure was that of a tall lady, dressed in black of a soft woollen material, judging from the slight sound in moving. The face was hidden in a handkerchief held in the right hand. This is all I noticed then; but on further occasions when I was able to observe her more closely, I saw

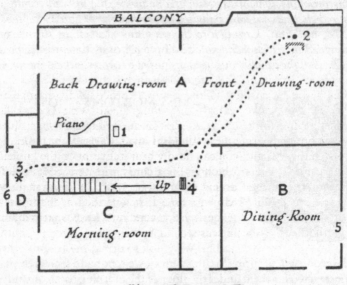

Plan of Ground Floor

the upper part of the left side of the forehead, and a little of the hair above. Her left hand was nearly hidden by her sleeve and a fold of her dress. As she held it down a portion of a widow's cuff was visible on both wrists, so that the whole impression was that of a lady in widow's weeds. There was no cap on the head, but a general effect of blackness suggests a bonnet, with long veil or a hood.

"During the next two years – from 1882 to 1884 – I saw the figure about half a dozen times; at first at long intervals, and afterwards at shorter, but I only mentioned these appearances to one friend, who did not speak of them to anyone.

"After the first time, I followed the figure several times downstairs into the drawing room, where she remained a variable time, generally standing to the right-hand side of the bow window. From the drawing room she went along the passage towards the garden door, where she always disappeared.

"The first time I spoke to her was on the 29th January, 1884. I opened the drawing-room door softly and went in, standing just by it. She came in past me and walked to the sofa and stood still there, so I went up to her and asked her if I could help her. She moved, and I thought she was going to speak, but she only gave a slight gasp and moved towards the door. Just by the door I spoke to her again, but she seemed as if she were quite unable to speak. She walked into the hall, then by the side door she seemed to disappear as before. In May and June 1884, I tried some experiments, fastening strings with marine glue across the stairs at different heights from the ground.

"I also attempted to touch her, but she always eluded me. It was not that there was nothing there to touch, but that she always seemed to be *beyond* me, and if followed into a corner simply disappeared.

"During these two years the only *noises* I heard were those of slight pushes against my bedroom door, accompanied by footsteps; and if I looked out on hearing these sounds, I invariably saw the figure. Her footstep is very light, you can hardly hear it, except on the linoleum, and then only like a person walking softly with thin boots on. The appearances during the next two months – July and August, 1884 – became much more frequent; indeed they were then at their maximum, from which time they seem gradually to have decreased, until now they seem to have ceased."

PROFESSOR WILLIAM FLETCHER BARRETT had been engaged in investigating supernatural phenomena for some years before he helped to found the Society for Psychical Research in 1882. Driven by an academic's interest in every phase of the occult, he led a number of the Society's early investigations into stories of haunted houses. The professor's objective accounts appeared in three important books, Psychical Research *(1911),* On The Threshold of the Unseen *(1918) and* Death-Bed Visions *(1926). In this episode he describes his own experiences at two hauntings, the second in company with Eleanor Sidgwick's husband, Henry.*

A REMARKABLE HAUNTING

Location and date:
Melton Mowbray, Leicestershire, UK, 1902

A remarkable case of haunting occurred some years ago in a manor house in the midland counties of England. I was invited to investigate the case and was offered hospitality. Though the ghost did not appear to me, whilst I slept in the haunted room, yet I heard certain mysterious knockings and some other disturbances which accompanied it; nor could I find any satisfactory explanation of these sounds. The first-hand evidence on behalf of the ghostly figure was, however, abundant and surprising. It was seen in the house independently by nearly a dozen different persons, who at first believing it to be a practical joke, tried to catch it, but it was uncatchable and impalpable; the latter was proved by a young officer, who when staying in the house saw the phantom one night, rose from his bed, followed it and shot through the figure, which moved on unconcerned. The children of my host, from whom the story of the ghost had been carefully concealed, described the same figure, which did not frighten, but rather amused, them, as they said they "could see the wall of the schoolroom through its body."

Another case of haunting investigated by myself and also by Professor Sidgwick occurred not far from my own residence in Kingstown. Here the phantom of a woman wrapped in a grey shawl was seen on the stairs and in a particular bedroom of a house tenanted by a lady and her brother. The figure was seen by different occupants of the room and by a child of five years old, though none were previously aware of the ghostly visitant: the door of the room was locked, yet still the figure made its appearance to the occupier of the room. All attempts at a normal explanation failed and the occupiers had at last to leave the house. Subsequently it was found that some previous tenants of the house had been troubled by inexplicable disturbances of various kinds, details of which they gave.

FRANK PODMORE is remembered as the most sceptical and thorough of the early members of the SPR whose life ended tragically when his investigations of supernatural phenomena were making huge contributions to the group and its status. A government librarian by profession, he was early converted to spiritualism but became disillusioned by the widespread fraud he found among a number of mediums. His books, including Phantasms of the Living *(1886) and* The Nature of the Supernatural *(1908) were groundbreaking treatises in which he advanced thought-provoking theories about the nature of ghosts and poltergeists. In August 1910, he suddenly went missing while on holiday in the Malvern Hills and his body was found in a pool near the local golf course at Malvern. The inquest revealed that there were no marks of injury on the corpse, which had been in the water for three or four days. A verdict of "found drowned" was returned on one of the century's great pioneer ghost hunters. The following extra-*

ordinary story is from an essay "Apparitions and Thought Transference" written in the decade before his death.

THE ROTATING MAN

Location and date:
Bracknell, Berkshire, UK, 1904

I was sitting alone in the library one evening finishing some work after hours, when it suddenly occurred to me that I should miss the last train to H., where I was then living, if I did not make haste. It was then 10.55, and the last train left X. at 11.5. I gathered up some books in one hand, took the lamp in the other, and prepared to leave the librarian's room, which communicated by a passage with the main room of the library. As my lamp illumined this passage, I saw, apparently at the further end of it, a man's face. I instantly thought a thief had got into the library. This was by no means impossible, and the probability of it had occurred to me before. I turned back into my room, put down the books, and took a revolver from the safe, and, holding the lamp cautiously behind me, I made my way along the passage – which had a corner, behind which I thought my thief might be lying in wait – into the main room. Here I saw no one, but the room was large and encumbered with bookcases. I called out loudly to the intruder to show himself several times, more with the hope of attracting a passing policeman than of drawing the intruder. Then I saw a face looking round one of the bookcases. I say looking *round*, but it had an odd appearance, as if the *body* were *in* the bookcase, as the face came so closely to the edge and I could see no body. The face was pallid and hairless, and the orbits of the eyes were very deep. I advanced towards it, and as I did so I saw an old man with high shoulders seem to *rotate* out of the end of the bookcase, and with his back towards me and with a shuffling gait walk rather quickly from the bookcase to the door of a small lavatory, which opened from the library and had no other access. I heard no noise. I followed the man at once into the lavatory, and to my extreme surprise found no one there. I examined the window (about 14 inches by 12 inches), and found it closed and fastened. I opened it and looked out. It opened into a well, the bottom of which, 10 feet below, was a skylight, and the top open to the sky some 20 feet above. It was in the middle of the building, and no one could have dropped into it without smashing the glass, nor climbed out of it without a ladder – but no one was there. Nor had there been anything like time for a man to get out of the window, as I followed the intruder instantly. Completely mystified, I even looked into the little cupboard under the fixed basin. There was nowhere hiding for a child, and I confess I began to experience for the first time what novelists describe as an "eerie" feeling.

I left the library, and found I had missed my train.

Next morning I mentioned what I had seen to a local clergyman, who, on hearing my description, said, "Why, that's old Q." Soon after I saw a photograph (from a drawing) of Q., and the resemblance was certainly striking. Q. had lost all his hair, eyebrows and all, from, I believe, a gunpowder accident. His walk was a peculiar, rapid, high-shouldered shuffle. Later enquiry proved he had died about the time of the year at which I saw the figure.

Sir ARTHUR CONAN DOYLE is, of course, famous for the creation of Sherlock Holmes, though he was also a fine writer of historical and ghost stories. His interest in psychical research began as a young man and as early as 1887, he wrote a letter to Light *magazine about some telepathic experiments he was carrying out. He joined the SPR in 1891 and investigated a number of cases, becoming convinced of survival after death and eventually converting to spiritualism, as he revealed in his books* The New Revelation *(1918),* The Vital Message *(1919) and* The Edge of the Unknown *(1930). Probably the most interesting haunted house case Doyle looked into occurred in Dorsetshire, when he was accompanied by Frank Podmore and a Doctor Scott. The trio bolted the doors and windows, laid worsted thread across the stairs and sat up for two nights. The results did not entirely convince Podmore, but certainly left an impression on Conan Doyle, as he explained when recounting the events in 1916.*

THE CASE OF THE BURIED BONES

Location and date: Charmouth, Dorsetshire, 1907

About this time I had an interesting experience, for I was one of three delegates sent by the Psychical Society to sit up in a haunted house. It was one of these poltergeist cases, where noises and foolish tricks had gone on for some years, very much like the classical case of John Wesley's family at Epworth in

1726, or the case of the Fox family at Hydesville near Rochester in 1848, which was the starting-point of modern spiritualism. Nothing sensational came of our journey, and yet it was not entirely barren.

On the first night nothing occurred. On the second, there were tremendous noises, sounds like someone beating a table with a stick. We had, of course, taken every precaution, and we could not explain the noises; but at the same time we could not swear that some ingenious practical joke had not been played upon us. There the matter ended for the time.

Some years afterwards, however, I met a member of the family who occupied the house, and he told me that after our visit the bones of a child, evidently long buried, had been dug up in the garden. You must admit that this was very remarkable.

Haunted houses are rare, and houses with buried human beings in their gardens are also, we will hope, rare. That they should have both united in one house is surely some argument for the truth of the phenomena. It is interesting to remember that in the case of the Fox family there was also some word of human bones and evidence of murder being found in the cellar, though an actual crime was never established. I have little doubt that if the Wesley family could have got upon speaking terms with their persecutor, they would also have come upon some motive for the persecution. It almost seems as if a life cut suddenly and violently short had some store of unspent vitality which could still manifest itself in a strange, mischievous fashion.

SIR OLIVER LODGE was a close friend of Conan Doyle and like him lost a son during the First World War, which heightened his interest in trying to communicate with the spirits of the dead. A distinguished physicist, who became renowned for his research into electricity and radio, he also devoted a lot of time to researching the life and work of the leading mediums of his time and was President of the SPR in 1904. He created a sensation in 1916 with the publication of Raymond *in which he detailed why he was so convinced of the survival of his son as a result of sittings with two mediums, Mrs Leonard and Vout Peters. Sir Oliver also devised a posthumous test to try and demonstrate his own survival, which later promoted other more sophisticated tests. He conducted a series of fascinating and carefully monitored tests with the famous*

American medium Mrs Leonore Piper and reported on these in Survival of Man (1915).

THE TRANCE REPORTS

Location and date: Liverpool, UK, 1890

At the request of Mr. Myers [of the SPR] I undertook a share in the investigation of a case of apparent clairvoyance.

It is the case of a lady who appears to go off into a trance when she pleases to will it under favourable surroundings, and in that trance to talk volubly, with a manner and voice quite different from her ordinary manner and voice, on details concerning which she has had no information given her.

In this abnormal state her speech has reference mainly to people's relatives and friends, living or deceased, about whom she is able to hold a conversation, and with whom she appears more or less familiar.

By introducing anonymous strangers, and by catechising her myself in various ways, I have satisfied myself that much of the information she possesses in the trance state is not acquired by ordinary commonplace methods, but that she has some unusual means of acquiring information. The facts on which she discourses are usually within the knowledge of some person present, though they are often entirely out of his conscious thought at the time. Occasionally facts have been narrated which have only been verified afterwards, and which are in good faith asserted never to have been known; meaning thereby that they have left no trace on the conscious memory of any person present or in the neighbourhood, and that it is highly improbable that they were ever known to such persons.

She is also in the trance state able to diagnose diseases, and to specify the owners or late owners of portable property, under circumstances which preclude the application of ordinary methods.

In the midst of this lucidity a number of mistaken and confused statements are frequently made, having little or no apparent meaning or application.

Concerning the particular means by which she acquires the different kinds of information, there is no sufficient evidence to make it safe to draw any conclusion. I can only say with certainty that it is by none of the ordinary methods known to Physical Science.

WILLIAM JAMES was one of the first and most influential members of the American Branch of the Society for Physical Research set up in Boston in 1885 under the guidance of William Barrett after the professor had generated great interest in the subject with a series of lectures in the USA and Canada the previous year. The son of the Swedenborgian philosopher Henry James, he had become interested in the supernatural while studying philosophy at Harvard and subsequently contributed essays and reviews to the Boston Daily Advertiser. *He was particularly intrigued by the claims of mediums to be able to contact the dead and sat in on séances all over the continent. Here he describes what occurred at a typical gathering in 1908.*

MESSAGES FROM THE OTHER SIDE

Location and date: Boston, USA, 1908

My own first visit was on Thursday, December 3, 1908. (Thursday is the night on which the circle habitually sits.) Eight persons, counting myself, were present, three women, five men.

We sat at first with our fingers on the solid table beneath the disk, and various tippings came. Then, with our wrists or palms on the ring and our fingers on the disk, various messages were spelt.

Mrs B., whose fifth sitting it was, had her fingers automatically jerked away whenever she placed them on the disk. This had happened previously; and, during the previous lifting of the table on November 19th, she had held her hands in the air some inches above the disk. She kept them in that situation on this present occasion whenever we made attempts to have the table lifted. Such attempts were several times repeated, but with no success.

On the controls then being asked whether they could not *make the disk rotate* without contact, they spelled "no."

Suddenly, while we were sitting with our wrists on the brass ring and our fingers on the disk, which turned and spelled, *we perceived that the ring or rail itself was moving*. It had never done this on any previous evening. The phenomenon was consequently unexpected, and seemed to strike all present with surprise.

Someone immediately suggested that all wrists should be lifted, and then, in brilliant light, and no one's hands in any way in contact with the rail, our fingers, however, resting on the disk, we all distinctly saw the rail or ring *slide slowly and for several inches through the collars, as if spontaneously.*

We then stuck a mark upon the ring to make its motion more obvious, and repeated five or six times the experiment, the same result ensuing, though more slightly each time. It always took the contact of our wrists to start the rail, but *its motion continued when the contact ceased.* This was not from its acquired momentum, for we ascertained that the friction of the collars which held the rail stopped instantly every motion imparted voluntarily by the hand.

On the succeeding Saturday and Sunday evenings, we sat again (one of the ladies being absent), but nothing but that usual tilting of the table and spelling of messages occurred.

So much for the "record," which all present have signed. It will be observed that all the phenomena reported (save the movements of the finger-bowl) were unexpected and startling to the spectators. The explosions and the table's rising seem to have been eminently so, and to have made a great impression.

On December 3rd, when the ring revolved, the conditions of observation were perfect, the light (from an electric chandelier just overhead) being brilliant, and the phenomena being slow enough, and often enough repeated, to leave my own mind in no doubt at the time as to what was witnessed. I was quite convinced that I saw that no hand was on the ring while it was moving. The maximum length of its path under these circumstances was fully six inches. With this conviction that I saw all there was to see, I have to confess that I am surprised that the phenomenon affected me emotionally so little. I may add, as a psychological fact, that now, after four days' interval, my mind seems strongly inclined not to "count" the observation, as if it were too exceptional to have been probable. I have only once before seen an object moved "paradoxically," and then the conditions were unsatisfactory. But I have supposed that if I could once see the same thing "satisfactorily," the levee by which scientific opinion protects nature would be cracked for me, and I should be as one watching an incipient overflow of the Mississippi of the supernatural into the fields of orthodox culture. I find, however, that I look on nature with unaltered eyes today, and that my orthodox habits tend to extrude this would-be levee-breaker. It forms too much of an exception.

PROFESSOR JAMES HERVEY HYSLOP became the chief investigator of American phenomena after the death of William James in 1910. Professor of Logic and Ethics at Columbia University, New York from 1869–1912, he was a prolific writer and researcher as well as a great propagandist for survival, declaring in Life After Death *(1918), "I regard the existence of discarnate spirits as scientifically proved." He also claimed that his predecessor William James "returned" after his death and recounted the events in* Contact With The Other World *(1918). He, too, was alleged to have "returned" according to his secretary, Gertrude Tubby, in* James H Hyslop *(1929). The following story is one of the most unusual cases of a haunting that he encountered.*

THE OLD WOMAN AND THE COFFIN

Location and date: New York, USA, 1906.

I shall refer briefly to one collective case of an apparition as involved three percipients, a lady, her nurse, and a little child, which I investigated. A Mrs Hunter of New York looked into her bedroom one night and to her astonishment saw what looked like a large coffin on the bed. Sitting at the foot of it was "a tall, old women steadfastly regarding it".

When Mrs Hunter spoke of her experience, she was laughed at. Later she went to the nursery and the nurse complained that she "felt so queer". The woman explained that at 7 o'clock she had "seen a tall old woman coming downstairs". This, too, was laughed off.

About half an hour afterwards, Mrs Hunter heard a piercing scream from her little daughter, aged five. This was followed by loud, frightened tones and then she heard the nurse soothing the child.

Next morning the child was full of her wrongs. She said, "A naughty old woman was sitting at the table and staring at me. She made me scream."

When I attended the scene, the nurse told me that she had found the child awake, sitting up in bed. She was pointing at the table and crying out, "Go away, go away, you naughty old woman!" But there was no one there. The nurse had been in bed some time and the door was locked.

A day or two afterwards, a letter reached Mrs Hunter. It was from the son of a Mrs Macfarlane, announcing his mother's death. It said that, "Her last hours were disturbed by anxiety for her husband and family." It transpired that she had left in Mrs Hunter's care a large trunk of valuables.

CAMILLE FLAMMARION, famous as one of the greatest French astronomers, was also a leading figure in investigating paranormal phenomena in the country. He was an enthusiastic supporter of the British SPR and in 1923 was appointed President. Among his relevant books are Mysterious Psychic Forces *(1907),* Death and its Mysteries *(1922) and* Haunted Houses *(1924). In 1918, Flammarion was involved in a very curious case of haunting that was experienced by himself and his wife as well as several others while staying with some friends in Cherbourg.*

THE HAUNTED BED

Location and date: Cherbourg, France, 1918

This little event happened in the night from April 26 to 27, 1918, and the next night, at No. 13, Rue de la Polle, Cherbourg. The house belongs to my friend Dr Bonnefoy, then chief medical officer of the Marine Hospital. I had stayed there in September, 1914, with my wife, my secretary, Mlle Renaudot, and our youthful cook, at the invitation of Madame Bonnefoy, president of the Red Cross and of the *Femmes de France*, who had begged us to leave Paris on the approach of the barbarian armies. After returning to Paris in the following December we had gone back to Cherbourg in April 1918, on a second invitation from Dr Bonnefoy, in consequence of a new German offensive against Paris, and in order to avoid air raids and Berthas.

During this interval between December 1914, and April 1918, Mme Bonnefoy died (October 25, 1916).

There had been a profound affection between us. She had placed in the house a marble plaque recalling my stay there in 1914.

Her husband had placed in a room which he regarded as a sort of oratory her death-bed, the old furniture she loved, her portraits, and her dearest mementoes.

At our return in 1918, this room happened to fall to Mlle Renaudot.

It is in that room that the unexplained noises took place – commotions, movements, sounds of steps. The witnesses are two persons incapable of being influenced by any illusion, and both very sceptical although of different mentalities: Mlle Renaudot, a lady of high scientific culture; and the cook, in conformity with her station, steady and prudent.

I asked them to write down their impressions at once, with the most scrupulous accuracy. They did so on May 7. Let them speak for themselves:

Narrative of Mlle Renaudot

We arrived at Cherbourg, M. and Mme Flammarion, myself, and the cook, on Thursday, April 25. Ever since Dr Bonnefoy's invitation came I had been wondering how we should be lodged in that house, where we had shared the family life more than three years before with charming and most devoted hosts, where we should find ourselves in a very different atmosphere, seeing that the doctor had married again. I had not wished to be given the room and the bed of the departed lady, my old friend, who had shown me so much sympathy, and whom I mourned with a profound sorrow.

It turned out that though I did not get Mme Suzanne Bonnefoy's room I at all events got her bed, taken from the ground floor, where she died, up to a first-floor room which had been her room as a girl. It was a great Breton bed, very old, of carved wood, and surmounted by a canopy hung with tapestry. The whole room was furnished with artistic old wooden furniture, bedside table, hat-rack, ecclesiastical desk. Opposite the bed was a portrait of Mme Bonnefoy – a photographic enlargement of a striking likeness.

I was much impressed with it. The memory of the past came upon me constantly. I saw our friend again, as she seemed so happy in her active and harmonious life devoted entirely to good deeds, and I figured to myself how she must have been on this same bed, which for two days and three nights had been her death-bed.

The first night, April 25 to 26, I did not sleep, thinking of her in the past and the present state of her house. I was also rather indisposed.

Next day, April 26 to 27, I promised myself a good night. About 11 p.m. I went to sleep and put away my old memories.

At 4 a.m. on the 27th a loud noise awakened me. On the left of the bed terrible cracklings were heard in the wall, then went on to the table and round the room. Then there was a slighter sound, repeated several times, as of a person turning in a bed. The wood of my bed also creaked. Finally, I heard a noise of a light step gliding along to the left of the bed, passing round it and entering the drawing-room on the right, where Mme Bonnefoy had been in the habit of listening to her husband playing the organ or the piano, he being an excellent musician.

These sounds impressed me so much that my heart nearly choked me with its beating, and my jaw became stiff.

In my emotion I got up, lighted a candle, and sat down on a basket standing on the landing outside the room. There I tried to account for the noises. They continued with still greater force, but nothing was to be seen.

At 5 a.m., a prey to unreasoned terror and unable to hold out, I went up to the cook, Marie Thionnet, who slept on the third floor. She came down with me. After her arrival we heard nothing more. It may be useful to remark that the cook's character did not at all harmonise with that of Mme Bonnefoy.

At 5.45 a.m. the doctor, on the second floor, got up and went into his dressing-room. The noises he made on getting up and walking about did not in the least resemble those I had heard an hour before.

In the course of the day I sought for an explanation of the phenomenon: cats, rats climbing along the walls. I examined the wall to the left of the bed. It was very thick, covered outside with slates, smooth, and overlooking a yard. It was a bad run for cats or rats, as it was the front wall on the Rue de la Polle. Besides, the noises were very different from those produced by animals.

On Saturday, April 27, I went to bed at 10.45 p.m., disturbed and nervous.

At 11 p.m. the noises started, as in the morning. I at once went upstairs to the cook, in my trepidation. She came down and lay on the bed beside me. We left our candles alight. For half an hour the noises continued, with loud cracks on the wall on the left. Raps sounded on Mme Bonnefoy's portrait or behind it, and the raps were so loud that we feared it would fall. At the same time steps glided through the room. The cook heard all this, too, and was much impressed. She is twenty-six years of age.

At 11.30 p.m. the noises ceased. As these manifestations were very disagreeable, especially as being due to an unknown and incomprehensible cause, I composed myself in the course of the next day, and, supposing that the deceased might be associated with them, since it happened in her house, I begged her to spare me such painful emotion.

We remained in the house until Saturday, May 4. Having heard nothing more, and having calmed down, I then asked the deceased to manifest herself, and to let me know in some way what she might desire.

But I have not observed anything since then, in spite of my wish (mixed with nervousness) to test the phenomena and to obtain, if possible, an explanation of this strange manifestation.

(Sg.) GABRIELLE RENAUDOT.

CHERBOURG, *May* 7, 1918.

The Cook's Account.

On Saturday morning, April 27, 1918, about five o'clock, Mlle Renaudot came for me to witness noises in her room. I went down, but heard nothing.

The following night, April 27, a little after eleven, Mlle Renaudot came again about the same noises, which had returned. I went down with her and heard noises behind the bedside table, as if somebody were scratching the wood. Then I heard as if somebody glided very quickly over the floor from the table to the drawing-room, and also as if somebody had struck sharp blows behind the portrait of Mme Bonnefoy. These noises lasted about half an hour. I acknowledge that I was much afraid, so that my teeth rattled. There were two lighted candles in the room, and we were wide awake, talking about the noises aloud and localising them as they came.

The following night I went down again at Mlle Renaudot's request, as she did not dare to remain alone in the room she was so disturbed, and I slept beside her. I heard some slight further noises, but was much less afraid. We slept very well, and then everything ceased.

It seemed as if my presence interfered with the noises, for they became feebler after I came and then stopped entirely.

Nevertheless, I heard them only too well. They were very impressive and extremely disagreeable to me.

I also slept in Mme Bonnefoy's bed with Mlle Renaudot on the nights of Monday, Tuesday, and Wednesday; but we heard nothing more, fortunately for me, for I should not like to pass again through the half-hour of April 27.

(Sg.) MARIE THIONNET.

CHERBOURG, *May* 7, 1918.

CESARE LOMBROSO was the leading Italian psychic investigator who had been drawn to the paranormal through his admiration for the work of the SPR and in particular that of W F Barrett and William James. Lombroso's books such as After Death – What? *(1908) earned him praise as "a champion of the new trend in human thought in psychiatry". One of his most fascinating enquiries was into the powers of the leading Italian medium, Eusapia Paladino. At one of her séances – as he describes in* Experiments With Eusapia *(1908) – he claimed to have seen the ghost of his mother.*

A DEAD MOTHER'S KISS

Location and date: Genoa, Italy 1903

At the end of Eusapia's séances, especially the more successful ones, true spectral appearances occurred, though much more rarely. Among the more important of these, inasmuch as it was seen by many and was repeated, I note not only the apparition of the deceased son of Vassallo, but also the one first confessed to me personally by Morselli (however put in doubt afterwards) of his mother, who kissed him, dried his eyes, said certain words to him, then again appeared to him, caressed him, and, to prove her personal identity, lifted his hand and placed it on the right eyebrow of the medium ("It is not there," said Morselli), and then placed it on her own forehead, on which, near the eyebrow, was a little blemish.

Morselli was seated at the right of Eusapia, while on the other side was Porro (see below).

DIAGRAM OF TABLE AND SITTERS.

I myself had the opportunity of examining a similar apparition in Genoa in 1903. The medium (Eusapia Paladino) was in a state of semi-intoxication, so that I should have thought that nothing would be forthcoming for us. On being asked by me, before the séance opened, if she would cause a glass inkstand to move in full light, she replied, in that vulgar speech of hers, "And what makes you obstinately stuck on such trifles as that? I can do much more: I can cause you to see your mother. You ought to be thinking of that."

Prompted by that promise, after half an hour of the séance had passed by, I was seized with a very lively desire to see her promise kept. The table at once assented to my thought by means of its usual sign-movements up and down; and soon after (we were then in the semi-obscurity of a red light) I saw detach itself from the curtain a rather short figure like that of my mother, veiled, which made the complete circuit of the table until it came to me, and whispered to me words heard by many, but not by me, who am somewhat hard of hearing. I was almost beside myself with emotion and begged her to repeat her words. She did so, saying, "*Cesar, fio mio!*" (I admit at once that this was not her habitual expression, which was, when she met me, "*mio fiol*"; but the mistakes in expression made by the apparitions of the deceased are well known, and how they borrow from the language of the psychic and of the experimenters), and, removing the veil from her face for a moment, she gave me a kiss.

After that day the shade of my mother (alas! only too truly a shadow) reappeared at least twenty times during Eusapia's séances while the medium was in trance; but her form was enveloped in the curtain of the psychic's cabinet, her head barely appearing while she would say, "My son, my treasure," kissing my head and my lips with her lips, which seemed to me dry and ligneous like her tongue.

ALBERT von SCHRENCK-NOTZING was the most famous German pioneer of psychic investigation and worked on numerous cases in his own country as well as with colleagues in Italy, France and Britain. A physician in Munich specializing in psychiatry, he founded the Gesellschaft fur Metapsychische Forschung *and began a study of telekinesis and teleplastics which made him famous. Among his numerous books were* Phenomena of Materialisation (1920) *in which he claimed to have witnessed a number of genuine physical phenomena and discussed several of the leading mediums of his time including Will Schneider, Eusapia Palladino and Marthe Beraud known as "Eva C". Schrenck-Notzing's rigorous tests of "Eva C" were said to "have convinced Continental savants of the genuineness of the phenomena".*

THE PHENOMENA
OF MATERIALISATION

Location and date: Munich, Germany, 1913

In the sitting of 9th May 1913 the medium Eva C. was completely sewn into a tricot garment in one piece, which only left her hands free. Her head was enveloped in a veil, sewn on to the neck of the garment all round, and her hands remained visible in the light during the whole sitting, and took no part.

The materialisation phenomenon, developed outside this cage, which enclosed her whole body, and could not, therefore, have been produced by rumination, unless we assume that the substance penetrated the veil. Such a penetration could be photographically proved under the same rigid conditions in the case of two different mediums. The process by which the material penetrated through the meshes of the veil has no connection with the act of rumination, and in this, as well as in previous occurrences, other hypotheses must be brought forward for an explanation.

Finally, rumination presupposes an abnormal functioning of the stomach and gullet, as well as the dilatation of the walls of the stomach. In the two mediums with whom the author experimented (girls of twenty-six and nineteen respectively) such pathological peculiarities are not found, nor could they have been hidden from observation for four years. There are no indications pointing in that direction.

It has also been objected that the medium can always prepare herself behind the closed curtain, so that there is always a possibility of making materialisations appear without any apparent participation by the mouth.

This objection also does not apply. Hands and feet remained visible even when the curtain was closed. In a number of sittings the materialisation process even commenced during hypnotisation, and the author had hardly time to open the cameras. In the sitting of 17th May 1910, which also began with an open curtain, the author sat by the medium in the cabinet and observed the evolution out of Eva's mouth of a flocculent substance, which in no way corresponded to the supposed scheme of rumination. The production of complete head images often took place so quickly after hypnosis (e.g., 1st June 1912) that the fraudulent technique required for rumination was rendered impossible owing to the shortness of the time available.

On 1st June 1910 the phenomena were observed with an open curtain. At the sitting of 28th October 1910 the curtain was open from the beginning. Further records of curtains being open will be found in the reports of 3rd November and 28th December 1910, 7th June and 16th August 1911, and 11th September 1912.

Although the above arguments, which could easily be multiplied, dispose of the hypothesis of the rumination of swallowed objects, that hypothesis was further investigated in a sitting on 26th November 1913 in Paris. The initial and final examination of the medium (mouth, nose, and hair, as well as a gynaecological examination), of the séance costume and the cabinet, conducted by the Paris physician Dr Bourbon, and the author, were negative. M. Bourdet and Mme Bisson were also present. Eva C. dined at seven o'clock. The sitting commenced at 8.45 p.m. in a feeble white light. Hands and knees were visibly inactive during the whole sitting. The medium did not leave her chair in the cabinet for a moment. The curtains were open while the phenomenon took place.

Between 9 p.m. and 9.10 p.m. without the help of the hands or knees, a flowing white substance emerged from the medium's mouth, which was inclined towards the left. It was about 20 inches long and 8 inches broad. It lay on the breast of the dress, spread out, and formed a white head-like disk, with a face profile turned to the right, and of life size. Even after the flashlight was ignited the curtain remained wide open. At the same moment the author illuminated the structure with an electric torch, and found that it formed a folded strip, which receded slowly into the medium's mouth, and remained visible until the sitting closed at 9.20 p.m.

While in the state of hypnosis, the medium rose from her chair and took an emetic tendered to her by the author (1 gramme ipecacuanha and ½ gramme tartar emetic), was completely undressed while standing half in and half out of the cabinet, and examined in detail by the author and Dr Bourbon, who took charge of the séance costume, and also examined it carefully. The final examination of the cabinet and chair gave no result. Dressed in a dressing-gown, Eva C. was then laid on a couch in the room, and was not left unobserved for a moment.

After two further doses of the same strength, vomiting set in at 9.30 p.m., which brought up the contents of the stomach. The quantity was about a pint, and was taken charge of by the author, who did not give it out of his hands until he handed it over to the Masselin Laboratory in Paris for analysis. The vomit was brown in colour, and besides the wafers taken with the powders there was no trace of any white substance such as observed by us. The detailed report of the Laboratory in question, dated 29th November 1913, closes with the words:

"The final result of the examination shows that the vomit consisted exclusively of food products and the emetics, and contained fragments of meat, fruit, and vegetables, probably mushrooms, which were found in pieces of considerable size. The rest of the contents consisted of food in an advanced state of digestion. There was not the slightest trace of a body whose appearance or histological structure gave the impression of a foreign body, or of a substance not used for nutrition, and, in particular, there was no trace of paper or chiffon."

ERIC JOHN DINGWALL, anthropologist and author, was for many years the Chief Research Officer of the British and American Societies for Psychical Research and claimed to have investigated over 3,000 cases, some of the more unusual of which he described in How To Go To A Medium *(1927). Of these, he maintained that except for five ghosts, there was a logical explanation for every one he hunted. Only one case left him completely baffled, the events he witnessed while investigating a young English girl of extraordinary powers in 1923. He recounted the story later for* Weekend Magazine.

THE MYSTERY OF STELLA C

Location and date: London, UK, 1923

I believe that 95 per cent of all supernatural mysteries have a natural explanation. Perhaps I have been lucky to solve all but five of the 3,000 cases I have handled. But those remaining five have me completely baffled.

I have attended thousands of Spiritualist séances, and spent months in America with

Houdini, the greatest magician of them all, finding out how fake mediums work the tricks of their trade. But a 21-year-old English girl, Stella C., gave a performance that left me stumped.

This was not the usual messages from the other side, the turning tables and blaring trumpets. This was far more uncanny.

I arrived late at the meeting – too late to get a seat in the circle of chairs, so I sat outside it.

Stella C. sat at a table beneath which a series of small objects had been placed on the floor. The idea was to see if a spirit force could be persuaded to move them.

The red beam of a lantern threw the shadows of the objects on to a screen in such a way that if any material thing moved them, *its* shadow would also be projected on to the screen, which we could all see.

When the main light was turned out I crawled to the table to see what was going on under it.

There, slithering over the carpet towards the objects, was something so fantastic that I could hardly credit the evidence of my own senses. I can only describe the thing as looking like a small pigeon's egg, attached to what seemed like a thick neck of macaroni. As the "thing" came into the beam of the lantern it stopped, gave a shudder and shot away into the darkness. But it threw no shadow.

To this day I have no idea what it was. And remember, nobody knew that I was on the floor looking under that table.

HARRY HOUDINI (born Erich Weiss), the most famous escapologist in history, was also fascinated by the supernatural and investigated a number of hauntings as well as numerous fake mediums, reporting the best of these in A Magician Among The Spirits (1924). *In 1926 he also lent his name to a Bill going through Congress to outlaw all forms of fortune telling. On his death bed, Houdini promised to send a message from the "other world" and for half a century a group of followers met each year in the hospital room in Detroit where he died hoping in vain for a sign. Two years earlier, in April 1924 in a series of articles about his enquiries, Houdini related the following story of the remarkable events that occurred while he was attempting to expose what he called "yet another shabby fraud".*

THE HOAX OF THE SPIRIT LOVER

Location and date: Montana, USA, 1920

One of the most remarkable instances of coincidence that ever came under my observation took place some years ago, in Montana, a coincidence so remarkable that if a story or a novel were built around it the incident would be considered so highly improbable that the yarn would be entirely unconvincing.

The incident occurred quite unexpectedly during my attempt to expose a charlatan medium. It made my attempt unnecessary. The medium himself was a victim of the improbable coincidence and his boasted powers of materializing spirits were proved a shabby fraud.

Three men came to my hotel room in the town in Montana, and asked me to aid them in exposing a medium whose powers seemed so miraculous as to admit of no explanation except supernatural aid. One of the three men was a minister of the gospel. All had tried to pick flaws in the medium's powers, and had attended one of his séances without succeeding.

One of the men, a lawyer, declared that he was about convinced of the reality of the medium's pretended spiritualistic powers.

"Were it not that to admit spiritualism opens the door for a wave of superstition and charlatanry," he said, "I would quit right now and acknowledge myself convinced. The three of us attended a séance last night, in the third story of an office building. We locked the door, locked the window, examined the room carefully, examined the medium's portable cabinet, and then the lights were extinguished, and spirit materializations took place. There was no possible chance for the medium to have confederates enter the room, nor is there any explanation of the materializations except that given by the medium."

I smiled, and agreed to do whatever I could to learn what deception the medium was practising in his séances.

"It sounds very convincing," I said. "But there must be some plausible, natural explanation. If, in my study of spiritualistic phenomena, I had accepted defeat every time I was baffled by something that I could not explain, then I would not have got very far with my investigations. Instead of saying that there is no explanation except an acceptence of spiritualism, I have said to myself merely, 'I have not yet found the true explanation.' It may be that I shall absolutely fail to pierce the methods of this charlatan who has tricked you. My failure would not prove that the medium had power to call spirits into materialisation. There is no reason we should accept spiritualism, which is contrary to all our natural experiences, unless we have absolute proof of it. Failure to disprove spiritualism is far from being positive proof of the reality of spiritualism. I am as open-minded as anybody else on this subject, but I want positive proof. Mere failure to prove fraud in any given ease is not a proof of spiritualism. It is simply an indication that the true explanation of the medium's phenomena has not yet been fathomed."

It was the following might that I was to assist my friends in attempting to show up the medium. The more I pondered the deeception played on them, the more inexplicable seemed the materialization. I was certain that the alleged materialization was nothing more nor less than a flesh and blood human being in the employ of the medium. There must be some way of entry to the room. My friends had locked the door and the window. It occurred to me that the medium or his confederate might have had a pass key, or he might have made his way over the transom, or the lock on the window might be broken. I have had too much experience in opening locks to believe very strongly in their power to keep people out of rooms.

We met, late at night, in the third story of an office building, the minister, the lawyer, and myself. The medium and several men and women were already there. The third of the trio who had called on me arrived a little later. He was a grocer or confectioner – I do not remember which. The medium remarked that there were certain psychic influences in the room that worked against any spiritualistic manifestations, and looked pointedly, as he spoke, at the grocer, who was a small man with cold, skeptical gray eyes and rather a determined chin. I had been introduced to the medium as Mr Koehler, and evidently he did not suspect me.

My eyes traveled around the room. There was but one window, and the door was secured by a Yale lock. It could be opened from inside. Immediately it flashed through my mind that the medium had a confederate in the room, who would open the door and admit the materialization, but the grocer pointed out to me that this could not be done, because there was a light burning in the hall, and this would be visible to those in the room if the door were opened. I answered, rather curtly, that it should be a comparatively easy matter to extinguish the light in the hall, and my friend merely shrugged his shoulders in reply.

There were about a dozen in the room besides the medium when the séance began. Seven of these were women, although the usual proportion of women at a spiritualistic séance is much higher. The medium aroused my suspicions immediately by throwing a double curtain over the window, "to keep out the light," as he explained. The night was dark, and only a very little light could enter the room from outside. One black curtain would be sufficient. When the medium used two, I felt sure that he wished to conceal the entrance of someone through the window after the room should be plunged in darkness. I had examined the window carefully before the curtains were put up, and satisfied myself that there was no means of getting to the window from outside, as there was a drop of two stories to the ground, and no fire escape near, but the action of the medium in arranging a double curtain over the window caused me to revise my theories.

We were required to join hands in a circle around a central table. The lights were put out at the wall switch, and also individually, to prevent any skeptical person in the circle suddenly arising and flashing them on. The grocer, however, at my advice, had brought a strong pocket flashlight, so we were prepared.

The séance was opened by the company singing a hymn. Then there was silence for a space, and more singing, while the medium, tied up in a black bag, went into a trance. The proceedings were directed by a woman who, I think, was a sincere believer in spiritualism, and wanted to make all psychic conditions right for opening spirit communications.

I noticed that the singing was loud enough to deaden any sounds a person might make by entering the room either by the door or through the window, and I knew that if the medium had unlocked the window while he was putting up the drapes, it could be opened very easily without being heard above the noise of the singing. I was uneasy, however, and feared that I was on the wrong track, because I saw no way by which an outsider could gain access to the window, which was too far above ground to be reached by ladder.

Finally the spirit manifestations began. There were table rappings, twanging of mandolins, movements of the speaking trumpet, ghostly touches in the dark – all the old claptrap of spiritualistic séances. Then the messages began, the spirit control being ostensibly an Irishman named Mike, who talked in a thick brogue and cracked numerous jokes, even banging the grocer sharply over the head with the mandolin to cool his skepticism. The medium, during all this excitement, was supposed to be in a deep trance, with his hands made useless by being sealed into the black bag, which in its turn was covered with postage stamps on which everyone present had placed marks by which we should know that the medium had not emerged from the bag. This also is a time-worn device of spiritualistic charlatans. It does not hamper the medium's movements as much as might be expected.

Mike, the spirit control, then asked every person in the circle to think very hard of some departed friend or relative whom they wished to see, for the psychic conditions were right for a materialization. The room was very hot and close, but an almost imperceptible breath of air fanned my cheek, and I knew that the window had been opened. The medium, of course, had unlocked it when he was putting up the curtains.

I moved my chair back, out of the circle, and the grocer, who was on my left, moved in a little to take up part of the space I had occupied. I freed my left hand carefully, and substituted the grocer's hand in the hand of the woman on my left, who must have thought that I sat on her right, still holding her hand. My purpose in leaving the circle was to make an investigation. I wanted a look at that window.

A phosphorescent glow emerging from the cabinet now showed vaguely a human face, whether of man or woman I could not say. But the grocer and lawyer were there to attend to the materialization. It was my purpose to learn how the materialization had gained access to the room. I wormed my way down into the cabinet, and through an opening in the back I reached the window very easily. The double curtain bulged out with a slight breeze, and I knew that *the window was open*.

I poked my head out, and was amazed at what I found. To the left of the window a ladder was hanging from the roof above my head. It was a fireman's extendible hooking ladder, about fifteen feet long, which had been thrust out of the window above, and attached to the top of the building so that the medium's "materialization" could climb down from the window in the third story.

Behind me a scream arose, which I did not take time to investigate. It was a girl's scream, and the name "Marion" was repeated several times.

I tried to push the hooking ladder off from the roof, but I could not dislodge it. The ladder was in two sections, and the lower section, being loose, merely slid upward in its grooves. The upper part of the hooking ladder was securely attached to the roof, and could not be lifted out unless I could raise the rigid upper part of the ladder. So I climbed out, and went up to the window in the story above. Behind me still arose the girl's scream: "Marion! Marion! Oh, God, it's Marion!"

I found the window in the fourth story open. I sat on the sill, lifted the booking ladder from its position and shoved it in the room. The escape of the medium's materialization was cut off, and my own return by the window was also blocked. I found the door locked from the inside. Evidently the "materialization" wished to make himself secure from intruders while he waited for the singing to tell him that the time had come for him to put out his ladder, attach it to the roof, and descend to take his part in the séance.

I made my way quickly through the corridor and down the stairs to the room of the séance, and found everything in turmoil. I had missed the unmasking of the fraud, but I had prevented the escape of the "spirit." What happened while I was going out of the window and removing the ladder, if told in fiction, would seem like stretching the long arm of coincidence so far that it would break under the strain. That is why I said, at the beginning of this article, that the story would be unconvincing if told by a novelist, because of its improbability.

I had wormed my way into the cabinet and was approaching the window when the grocer flashed his pocket light upon the supposed materialization. A woman's scream split the darkness, and the flashlight was violently knocked from the grocer's hand, but the young woman had thrown her arms around the ghost and was covering his face with kisses, screaming "Marion, Marion! It's you! For God's sake, speak to me, Marion!"

While some tried to find the switch, only to find the lights turned off at the chandelier too, someone probably the medium, was striking the girl's hands with a blackjack, endeavoring to break her hold, and the ghost was muttering in great fright: "Frances, let go of me; you're smothering me, Frances," and fighting to free himself.

The combined efforts of the medium and the ghost finally freed him
from the girl's hysterical embrace, but the means of escape was cut
off by my removing of the ladder. The ghost was a real flesh and
blood one, and could not dematerialize into the world of shadows.

The girl, Frances, whose surname I will not mention here, as she is
still living, had attended the séance in good faith, and when the spirit
control asked everyone present to hold in mind the image of a dear
departed one, so that the spirit might be aided in showing itself, she
concentrated her thoughts on her fiancé, who had died a little less
than a year before.

Out of the cabinet, dimly seen by a phosphorescent glow from the
features of the ghost, stepped the materialization. The girl stared,
hoping that this was indeed her fiancé, trying to believe, her heart
beating between skepticism and faith, when the grocer's flashlight lit
up the features distinctly. It was only for an instant, for the flashlight
was knocked from the grocer's hand almost immediately, but that
instant was enough.

The ghost that had emerged from the cabinet was the man she had
been engaged to marry, the man whom she had seen laid away in his
coffin and buried in the earth:

Is it any wonder that the poor girl became hysterical? Is it any
wonder that she threw her arms about her beloved dead, and sought
to hold him in the land of the living? Possessed for the moment of an
unnatural strength, she held him tight, screaming her love at him,
until the struggles of the ghost and the cruel blackjack of the medium
had broken her hold.

The materialization, of course, was a paid employee of the
medium. And he really was the girl's fiancé!

It transpired that the man, who lived in Chicago, had a twin
brother in Wyoming, who was slowly dying of consumption and had
gone west to work on a ranch in hope that the high altitude would
help him. Frances knew of the existence of this twin brother, but she
had never seen him. Marion, realizing that the end was near for his
brother, had himself heavily insured in his brother's name. He sent
for the brother, who came to Chicago while Frances was in Montana
with relatives. In Chicago Marion changed lodgings to break contact
with those who knew him, and he took his brother's name, and gave
his own name to his brother. The brother died in a Chicago hospital
under the name of Marion, but Marion was speeding west to
Wyoming when the end came. Letters from Frances in Montana

were found in the pockets of the dead man, and a telegram brought the heart-broken girl back to Chicago to attend the funeral of her fiancé, as she supposed. Marion, by this fraud, was able to collect the insurance on his own death.

The money did him very little good, however, for he squandered it in mining stocks and gambling and other means, and was soon penniless. He then obtained employment as assistant to the charlatan medium, and did materializations for him, with his face smeared with phosphorescent paint that gave a pale, unearthly radiance to his features in the dark, and yet did not light them up enough so that anyone could certainly recognize his face. It was the flashlight of the grocer that accomplished that.

The strangest part of the whole occurrence is that the girl and the man should meet in this strange way. He had not the slightest notion in the world that his fiancée was in that room, while she, of course, believed him dead.

The insurance company prosecuted the man for fraud, but the medium who employed him departed suddenly, and may still be preying, under another name, upon the credulities of those who want to communicate with their beloved dead. He was a clever magician, and under whatever name he perpetrates his fraudulent tricks, he should be very successful. It is much more lucrative to be a charlatan medium than an honest magician, for rich dupes pay well, whereas the amount of money that can be made by parlor magic is relatively small.

The girl, Frances, refused to have anything to do with her fiancé thereafter, for the fraud he practised both on her and on the insurance company killed her love. She went to the hospital, suffering from a nervous collapse, after her hysteria at the séance, but she recovered, and afterward returned to Chicago.

SHANE LESLIE (John Randolph Shane Leslie, Third Baronet Leslie) devoted much of his life to investigating unexplained phenomena, particularly in his native Ireland where he played a key role in a number of SPR cases. A larger-than-life character who travelled a great deal – especially in Russia where he became a friend of Tolstoy – Leslie wrote one of the most authentic studies, Ghost Book *in 1955, and drew on his own experiences as a ghost hunter for*

various collections of short stories, in particular the curious tale of A
Ghost in the Isle of Wight (1929). *Leslie had a particular fascination
with poltergeists: probably because of his own experience as a young
man as he relates here.*

THE IRISH POLTERGEIST

Location and date: Donegal, Ireland, 1910

In June 1910 I performed the Pilgrimage to
Lough Derg with two young Catholic students,
Mr Smyth and Mr Moynagh. We did the
pilgrimage with fervour and returned walking
from the lake to the village of Pettigo in Donegal. As the village was on family property, I
suggested we should sleep the first night (after
two without much sleep on the Island of St Patrick's Purgatory) in the
Agency. Here I slept as I had often slept in the past the sleep of the
just. But my companions, who had deserved every consideration
from Morpheus, were troubled and tossed and torn by a ghost who
stripped the bedclothes from them.

By the morning they had not slept a wink. They were considerate
enough to avoid telling their host, but they confided the night's work
to Mr Flood, a reputable publican, who was certain that they had
encountered the Protestant spirit of Mr James McCullagh, who had
long been Agent but had died two years previously. Poor James's
feelings can be understood at finding Catholic pilgrims in his beds.
But the Parish Priest at home told me that, before they parted for ever
in this world, the old Agent (who had a compassionate record in the
1879 Famine) had asked him to do his best for him in the next world.
Smyth felt the bedclothes stretched over him and then a foot which
descended between him and the bed. Moynagh said the clothes had
been rolled up over him like the drop-curtain in a theatre.

*VIOLET TWEEDALE was a woman cast in the same mould as
Eleanor Sidgwick – resourceful, self-sufficient and fascinated by the
supernatural. An energetic traveller, she was forever on the search for
material to use in her novels and to bolster her conviction about the
paranormal. A convinced spiritualist, she attended séances with Lord
Haldane and WE Gladstone and was a powerful witness when the*

trance speaker, Meurig Morris, sued the Daily Mail *for libel in 1932. Her friend Sir Arthur Conan Doyle wrote a foreword to her book* Phantoms of the Dawn *(1938). This next strange account is from the most interesting of Tweedale's reminiscences,* Ghosts I Have Seen & Other Psychic Experiences *published in 1920.*

THE INVISIBLE HANDS

Location and date: London, UK, 1908

I was sitting near the library window, reading, in the fading light of a quiet November afternoon. It was one of those utterly still, mournful days, with a grey, brooding sky, save where, in the west, a pale primrose sunset was bathing the horizon in light. I was reading "Man and the Universe," by Sir Oliver Lodge, and had arrived at page 137, which ends Chapter VI.

In those days (the year was 1908) I always tried to arrange at least one week of perfect quiet for the study of a new book which I had just ordered. I would calculate on which day the post would bring it to my country home, and I would arrange my life accordingly. This may sound rather ridiculous, but the truth is that a book such as "Man and the Universe" is such a pure intellectual treat to me, that I like to gloat over it, to taste it slowly, and imbibe it gradually. I try to spin out the joy of it as long as possible by reading slowly, and thinking over the problems presented.

At last I put the book down on a table by my side. I was in no hurry. It lay on its back, open, the pages uppermost; just where I had stopped reading. I fell to wondering on the words I had just read:

"A reformer must not be in haste. The kingdom cometh not by observation, but by secret working as of leaven. Nor must he advocate any compromise repugnant to an enlightened conscience. Bigotry must die, but it must die a natural, not a violent death. Would that the leaders in Church and State had always been able to receive an impatient enthusiast in the spirit of the lines—

'Dreamer of dreams! no taunt is in our sadness,
    Whate'er our fears our hearts are with your cause.
God's mills grind slow; and thoughtless haste were madness,
    To gain Heaven's ends we dare not break Heaven's laws.'"

I must have sat thinking for quite ten minutes when my attention was suddenly attracted by a sound – the sound of paper leaves being rustled. The room was so dead still that the faintest sound would have called my attention, but this sound was by no means faint. I turned my head and looked at the book I had been reading, because, from it, unmistakably the noise proceeded.

I beheld a most enthralling phenomenon. Unseen hands were turning over the pages.

A thrill of intense excitement ran through me, and I stared at the book in breathless interest. The hands seemed to be searching for some particular passage. The number of the page upon which the passage was printed was not, apparently, known to the searcher. I will try to describe what actually happened.

Several leaves of the book were turned over rather rapidly, each leaf making the usual sound which accompanies such an ordinary physical action. Then, as if fearing that the passage required had been overlooked or passed by, several leaves were turned back again.

This manifestation continued for at least ten minutes, and I could see nothing but the pages of the book being turned quite methodically, as by a human hand.

At moments there was rather a long pause in the search, and at the first pause I thought the demonstration might be over, but once again the invisible entity resumed the search, and I found myself saying, "He found something there that interested him. That is why he stopped." For no reason I can give I felt certain my visitor was a male spirit.

On the second pause in the search occurring I had no doubt that again he had found something that interested him. The whole manifestation was very leisurely and wonderfully human. As I sat watching the book being manipulated by unseen fingers, every smallest action suggested design. One could not doubt as to what was taking place. At length there came a pause longer than usual. The book lay flat on its back wide open. There was now no quiver of the leaves. The invisible entity had found what he wanted and gone.

I curbed my curiosity for five minutes more, then feeling convinced that I was again alone I stretched out my hand, took the book and, rising, carried it close to the window.

There was still enough light to read by, and the leaves were open at pages 172–173.

I had only read as far as page 137.

I scanned them eagerly, and at once discovered that a mark had been made on the margin of page 172. A long cross had been placed against a paragraph. The mark was such as might have been made by a sharp finger-nail. The words marked were—

"I want to make the distinct assertion that a really existing thing never perishes, but only changes its form."

Today the mark is as clearly visible on the page as on the day it was made. I can form no conjecture as to who the entity was, but he certainly knew the contents of the book. No one watching the search could doubt that, or that he was desirous of impressing upon the readers of the book a certain fact stated therein, which must have previously attracted his attention.

THOMAS CHARLES LETHBRIDGE developed his interest in the paranormal while he was a student at Cambridge University. Here he took part in several antiquarian expeditions and later became "Official Excavator" to the Cambridge Antiquarian Society from 1925 to 1956. His fascination with the relics that were unearthed drew him into tales of the restless dead and his later publications revealed an objective mind forever seeking explanations for old supernatural traditions. His enquiries led to several important books, notably Ghost and Ghoul (1961) *and* Ghost and Diving Rod (1963), *which offered his theories about the nature of such phenomena. Lethbridge admitted that one cause of his obsession could be traced back to the day at University when he saw a ghost – which he describes here.*

THE GHOST IN THE TOP HAT

Location and date: Cambridge, UK, 1922

The incident happened in 1922, in New Court, Trinity, Cambridge. I had rooms in the block which faces the Backs and my stair was the first on the left of the gateway as you go out towards the river. On the next stair to mine, again on the left, a friend of mine, G.W., had his rooms, two floors up. They were a set of rooms which were said to have been occupied by generations of Buxtons, but, as there were no Buxtons in the college at the time,

G.W. had them. The rooms were on the left of the stair. I am putting in these details in case any later occupant of the rooms has had the same experience.

G.W. and I had not been model undergraduates. I regret to say that we thought far more about shooting, fishing, sailing and the like, than about cutting up dog-fish or wading through text-books. Later in the same year, G. W. was one of the party on the Shiant Islands. We were, I suppose, about the last batch of young men who went to a university simply to finish their education and make friends. I was actually diverted from the Army and sent up to Cambridge at the end of the Kaiser's war, because everyone thought there would never be a war again and training for it was useless. I did not even know you were supposed to get a degree until I got up to the place. A good degree was no lure to us at all. In fact lectures were a bore after years of school.

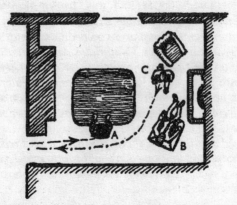

Diagram of occurrence in New Court, Trinity, Cambridge, in 1922. Not to scale.
(A) Unknown man in top hat.
(B) G.W., still seated by the fire.
(C) Myself, going back to my own rooms.
There were more chairs in the room and the bookcase may not be in the right place.

I was sitting rather late one evening in G.W.'s rooms. We were discussing this and that in a desultory sort of way, one on each side of the fire. I was in the chair nearest the window, which looked over the court. Between me and the door in the opposite corner of the room was a square dining-table. Noticing that it was nearly midnight, I got up from my chair and was about to go back to bed. As I got up, and before I had said good night to G.W., the door opened and a man came into the room. G.W. remained sitting in his chair. The man, who had a top hat on, came only a few steps into the room and there stopped, resting both his hands on the table. I thought he was a college porter who wanted to say something to G.W. I said, "Well, good night, G.W." and "Good evening" to the other man, who did not reply. Then I walked round behind the figure standing at the table, through the door, and down the stairs into the court. I went up the next stair to my own rooms and into bed without giving the incident another thought.

Next morning, I met G. W. in Trinity Street. Remembering the visitor of the night before, I said, "Hello, G. W. Why did the porter come in last night? We weren't making a row or anything." "Nobody came in," he replied. I found this statement quite impossible to believe and we argued a bit in the street. But G. W. had not seen the man and I had and that was all that could be said about it. When I had time to think it over, I found I could remember the man's appearance in considerable detail. He was not very tall and he was slight. His face was rather pointed. He did not resemble any of our porters I could remember. Then I thought of something else: he had on a top hat. Our porters wore top hats, but they only wore them on Sundays. That evening had not been a Sunday. More than that, I found I could distinctly remember that he had something white at his throat and not a black tie. Then I got it. This was a man in hunting kit. G. W. had not seen him at all. He was a ghost.

But that does not postulate that he was a visitor from another world. He could have been a thought projection from any unknown source. G. W. may have projected him. Someone may have projected himself while sitting sleepily in a chair in a London club. He may have been one of the countless Buxtons. Anything may have caused him to be there; but I happened to be on the right wave-length to receive the picture. It was just like a television picture without the sound. There was no colour and it was as utterly without feeling as a television shot. But it was full size. There was nothing, of course, about a man dressed in black and white to show as colour. Nevertheless, I do not think there was any colour in his face.

HARRY PRICE is probably one of the best-known and certainly most controversial figures in the history of twentieth-century ghost hunting. Famous – or notorious – for his studies of Borley Rectory

"The Most Haunted House in England," his psychic research into a variety of spirit mediums including the German Willi Schneider and the jailed Mrs Helen Duncan, plus his investigations into supernatural phenomena such as the Indian Rope Trick and the "talking mongoose" of the Isle of Man, Price was often embroiled in controversy and attracted admirers and detractions in almost equal numbers. An excellent amateur magician, he was also an influential figure in the SPR, The Ghost Club and the formation of the first laboratory to scientifically test the paranormal in London. His most extraordinary investigation undoubtedly concerned a little Romanian girl who, in the 1920s, was the victim of what the popular newspapers of the day referred to as a "vampire-like poltergeist".

THE TELEKINETIC GIRL

Location and date: Vienna, Austria, 1926

It is a maxim that in *Poltergeist* cases, one practically never witnesses the displaced objects in flight, or the beginning of the telekinetic movements which are a feature of these cases. A classic exception to the above rule was Eleonore Zugun, a little Roumanian girl, accounts of whose telekinetic or *Poltergeist* phenomena filled the psychic and lay Press during the years 1926–7.

Eleonore was born in Talpa, Roumania, on May 13, 1913, and was first studied by Fritz Grunewald. His friend the Countess Wassilko-Serecki then removed the child from her rather unsuitable home surroundings and adopted her. She resided with the Countess at her flat in the Josefstadterstrasse, Vienna. Soon after her arrival in Vienna, Professor Hans Thirring, of Vienna University, wrote and informed me of the alleged amazing phenomena which the girl was producing, and invited me to investigate.

My first séance with Eleonore was at 5.15 p.m. on May 1, 1926, in the Countess's study-bedroom, fifteen feet square. The sun was shining, and the large French windows flooded the room with light. Both windows and door were fastened. Only the Countess, Eleonore and myself were present. The apartment was simply furnished with a couch, chairs, table, etc., on one side of the room, which was divided longitudinally by means of a matchboard partition, six feet high, with an opening in it at one end. On the far side of the partition were the usual bed, toilet table, chairs, etc.

I had brought Eleonore a toy spring-gun, firing a celluloid ball which was caught in a wire basket attached to the gun. The Countess and I sat on the couch watching the child play with her toy. In a few minutes, the ball had divided into its component halves and the child ran to us with a request that we should mend it. The Countess and I rose and while she was holding one half of the ball, and Eleonore the other, a long steel stiletto paper-knife shot across the room *from behind me*, just missing my head, and fell against the door. I was intently watching the Countess and her *protégée* attending to the toy and can swear that neither touched the stiletto, whose normal resting-place was on a writing-table near the French windows, which were closed and fastened. I was between the table and my hostess, and whatever projected the stiletto *must* have been behind me. But there was no tangible being behind me, and the paper-knife could not have been thrown normally. A further and minute search of the apartment threw no light on the phenomenon, which occurred at 5.43.

The flight of the stiletto was the first of many telekinetic phenomena. At 5.58 a small hand mirror was thrown *over the partition* from the bed side of the room, while the Countess, Eleonore and I were by the couch in the study portion. At 6.15 a metal cap was thrown from the bedroom side of the partition and fell at our feet. At 6.32 a large stuffed cloth dog was thrown *from our side* of the partition and fell on the coal-scuttle near the bed. I had just previously noticed the toy dog on a chair to the right of me; the Countess and Eleonore were on my *left*: neither could have touched it. It is interesting to note that after each phenomenon, the child's pulse-rate increased. Her normal rate was 75; after a minor telekinetic displacement it rose to 95; after the "flight" of the dog it had increased to 126 with some palpitation of the heart.

Soon after the toy dog incident I was watching Eleonore scribbling on a piece of paper. Between the child and me was a chair on which rested a large square cushion. Both girl and cushion were in my line of vision, and the child was five and a half feet away from the chair. The Countess was on the other side of me. At 6.33, as I gazed at it, the cushion slowly slid off the chair. There was no vibration in the room. After each phenomenon I searched the double apartment, and found nothing that could account for these most convincing manifestations, a detailed account of which should be read.

I was so impressed with Eleonore that I persuaded the Countess to bring her to London. They arrived on September 30, 1926, and left on the following October 24. Under much better conditions, and in my own laboratory, numerous telekinetic movements of objects were recorded. Especially striking were the experiments arranged by the late Dr R. J. Tillyard, F.R.S., and myself in which coins placed on the lintel of our séance-room door, six feet, ten and three-quarter inches from the ground, were supra-normally displaced under perfect control conditions. An attempt to induce phenomena while the girl was being hypnotized by Professor McDougall produced no results.

A curious feature of Eleonore's telekinetic phenomena was the accompanying stigmata. Just before, during, or immediately after a phenomenon, red weals would spontaneously appear on various parts of the girl's body. They would gradually turn white, and slowly disappear. A prolonged study of the stigmata suggested that they were really due to physiological causes induced by the mental excitement of the telekinetic phenomena. It is interesting to note that the phenomena, both telekinetic and stigmatic, ceased abruptly after the first appearance of the menses. Eleonore, now aged 26, manages her own hairdressing business in Czernowitz, Roumania.

PROFESSOR CYRIL EDWIN MITCHINSON JOAD was a friend of Harry Price and participated with him in a number of investigations into the paranormal. An outgoing and charismatic head of philosophy at Birkbeck College in London he was for years a member of the panel of the BBC Radio weekly radio programme, The Brains Trust, *answering pressing questions of the day from members of the public. His opening reply to virtually every question of, "Well, it all depends what you mean by . . ." became something of a catch phrase. Joad was Chairman of the University of London Council for Psychical Research and among his enquiries with Price were testing a haunted bed in Chiswick, an attempt to raise the devil on the Brocken Mountains in Germany and discovering a submerged lake in Hyde Park, London using a dowser's wooden bobbin. He also shared Price's fascination with the hauntings at Borley Rectory and wrote the following report for* Harper's Monthly Magazine *in June 1938. The Professor's reputation suffered from attacks by the philosopher Bertrand Russell and Winston Churchill and was ruined when he was successfully prosecuted for failing to buy a ticket for a train journey.*

THE PUZZLE OF BORLEY RECTORY

Location and date:
Borley, Suffolk, England, 1938

Recently a curious outbreak of poltergeist phenomena has come to my notice at a rectory in Suffolk. The rectory is a typical haunted house. Surrounded with evergreens, it stands sombre and gloomy in a large neglected garden. Like many English rectories, it was far too large for the stipend of the rector or the needs of the parish, which contains, if I remember correctly, only one hundred and twenty souls. The cost of the upkeep of the place must have been considerable – there were, I think, seven or eight bedrooms; there was a large stable and a huddle of outhouses – and the parson's stipend was as small as the place was large. The house had a long troubled history, which went back to some conventional story of a nun found guilty of unchastity, and being walled up somewhere in the basement to die of starvation. Whatever may be the truth of this story, accounts of poltergeist phenomena at the rectory had been reaching us at the Laboratory for a number of years. Bells were pulled, pieces of crockery flew unexpectedly through the air, dogs whined, servants refused to stay, and so on. A number of visits had intrigued without satisfying the curiosity of investigators. On one occasion the visitors had been fairly convinced that a genuine phenomenon had occurred; on another, their view was that the young wife of an elderly rector, bored with life in so dull and remote a place, had decided to exploit the house's ghostly history by staging a few phenomena on her own account, thus providing amusement for herself, discomfort for her husband, and bewilderment for investigators. Within the space of a few years three rectors came and went, alleging, in each case, as their reason for departure the disconcerting happenings in the house. Finally the bishop decided to leave the rectory empty and to amalgamate the parish with the next one, letting the incumbent of the neighbouring parish attend to the needs of both. The house, being empty, was leased for a number of months to the University of London Council for Psychical Investigation; observers were asked for, and a number of people volunteered.

The only phenomenon of note that had been observed was the appearance of miscellaneous pencil marks upon the inside walls of the house. A few of these were in the form of messages, but the majority were meaningless squiggles. The walls were whitewashed, so that it was comparatively easy to distinguish the marks, and in order that there might be no doubt which and where they were, each mark had been ringed by a circle drawn in thick blue pencil.

On the evening on which I visited the house one observer had been staying there for some little time, sleeping on a camp bed, and cooking his meals on an oil stove in one of the empty rooms. We were alone in the house, and after carefully examining the garden, we had assured ourselves that there was nobody there. We came in, made a tour of all the pencil marks visible on the whitewashed walls, and carefully noted their date and position. It was my first visit and I was considerably intrigued by the mysterious marks. At seven o'clock we retired to the room with the camp bed and the oil stove, securely locking all the doors and windows before we did so, cooked some sausages and made some tea. We were together in this room for the whole of the ensuing hour, and I am positive that neither of us left it. I am also positive that if anybody had entered the house we should have heard him or her moving about; for the house, being empty, acted as a kind of sounding board, and every noise echoed and re-echoed all over it. About eight o'clock we went out again, and on the wall in the passage immediately outside the room in which we had been eating there was another pencil squiggle. I feel reasonably certain that that squiggle had not been there before; it was, indeed, inconceivable that we should have missed it. I am also reasonably certain that it was not made by the other observer, who was in my company during the whole of the period within which the mark must have been made. I am sure that I did not make it myself and, as I have already said, I do not see how anybody could have entered the house without being heard.

On the other hand, the hypothesis that poltergeists materialize lead pencils and fingers to use them seems to me to be totally incredible; and the question of "why" seems to be hardly less difficult to answer than the question of "how." As so frequently occurs when one is investigating so-called abnormal phenomena, one finds it equally impossible to withhold credence from the facts or to credit any possible explanation of the facts. Either the facts did not occur or, if they did, the universe must in some important respects be totally other than what one is accustomed to suppose. In this particular case my inclination is to doubt the facts; and yet, having reflected long and carefully upon that squiggle, I did not and do not see how it could have been made by normal means.

JAMES REYNOLDS was born in County Tipperary, but made his reputation as a writer and ghost hunter in the United States. He was just twelve years old when he saw his first ghost – "a tall, hollow-eyed, cadaverous creature in a tattered black military cloak who more closely resembled a huge bat than any man out of Gaelic history", he later wrote. Thereafter Reynolds began to collect stories of the supernatural whenever and wherever he came across them and, later publishing a series of very popular collections of true hauntings, notably Ghosts in Irish Houses (1947) *of which the* New York Times *reviewer wrote, "Should sceptics come across this book, it will either convert them or turn them to stone"; and the equally well-reviewed,* Ghosts in American Houses (1956). *In this story, Reynolds describes a chilling encounter with a ghostly barge off the coast of Galway.*

THE PHANTOM SHIP

Location and date: Galway, Ireland, 1932

Crossing the Atlantic between New York and Galway in the late spring of 1932, I was standing at the rail of the steamer a little after dawn on the morning of the day we were to arrive at Galway. A fine, brilliant morning it was, I remember, the ocean in a calmer frame of mind than is usual along this North Atlantic sea lane.

At the first crack of sunrise, I had come up to the top deck, for we were just passing the Headland of Mallin More in County Donegal. Ireland spread its burning green mountains on our left, and I had a very special reason for my early vigil. The night before, as we were off Rathlin Island Light, which guards the northeast extremity of Ireland, I had seen, moving silently along the starlit horizon, slightly ahead of our own ship, a ghostly escort – the Bridal Barge of Aran Roe.

This was the third time I had seen the ghostly barge. Once before, during a midwinter crossing, the cold clear night had seemed to open its indigo portals and in almost the same place, near Rathlin Light, the Bridal Barge had appeared, pursued its unhurried way slightly ahead of my ship, and disappeared again into the night, leaving no wake.

Always at night I had seen the Barge, for the second time was a night in August. A full moon bathed all Clew Bay in Connaught in luminous light. Suddenly I stood spellbound, for into my line of vision, about a mile out to sea, sped the dazzling gold and red of the Bridal Barge. For only a moment, the moon pointed up the gilded shields on the prow and turned into fiery streamers the crimson pall flung across the bier high upon the stern; then, silently gliding into the middle-mist whence it had come, the phantom ship passed into the night.

Many people tell of having seen the Bridal Barge in full daylight. Fishermen gathering their catch off the rocks of Erris Head and Inishmurray say the Barge sometimes looms out of the sea spray or early morning mist, so close that it seems almost to scrape the sides of their small fishing curraghs; so close that the gaping fishermen clearly see the set faces of the fifty golden warriors who forever guard the corpse of Aran Roe.

Realizing the morning was ripening into breakfast time, and since I'd seen no sign of the Barge on either side of the ship, I started down to have coffee. Standing at the inshore rail on the deck below was a man who turned as he heard my footsteps on the companionway and came towards me. "Mr Reynolds, let me introduce myself," he said. "I am Charles Tyrell, professor of history at Notre Dame. I am on sabbatical year. Mostly I shall be at Trinity College doing research on Gaelic legends. I wonder if you would answer a question for me." He paused, seemed undecided, then smiled, "Well, here goes. Did you ever hear of the Bridal Barge of Aran Roe?"

I looked at the man for a moment; then, without batting an eyelash, replied, "But of course. I saw the Barge last night off Rathlin Light."

For a moment the professor looked around, up and down the deck, out to sea, bewildered. Sitting down on the foot-rest of an open deck chair he said, "So it's true. I saw it as well, last night, all red and gold, just the way I had heard about it. I've been told I'd see plenty of ghosts in Ireland; now, even before I set foot on the sod, I see the phantom Barge of Aran Roe."

Here, I realized, was a perfect listener, and, what was even better, a believer. I suggested we ring for a steward, order breakfast brought us there on deck, drink our coffee slowly in the freshness of the lovely morning, and then I would tell him the story of Aran Roe.

Sometime in the early part of the eleventh century there lived on Rathlin Island, an expanse of craggy, barren rock off the Antrim coast, a young warrior prince. Men called him Aran Roe, Aran of the Red Hood, partly because of the scarlet hood of heavy wool which Aran wore thrown back from his brow, but more, perhaps, because of the dark red of his long hair, worn, as was the manner of the time, hanging to his shoulder blades in a thick mane. In front it was cut across in a line with his eyebrows.

The people of Rathlin were vastly proud of their handsome young prince, for he was fearless in battle, could sail a ship unfalteringly among the perilous channels along the coast, which only Rathlin men knew, and was of happy disposition into the bargain. The day he became king would be a fine, wide day.

At this time Arghan, King of Rathlin Island, was nearing the end of his coil. He sat the day's length in front of a roaring fire, for his bones were always cold. Wasted and brooding, he pondered upon his long reign, a masterpiece of ill-fortune. It would not be long before the Old Woman of Gonn would beckon to the king. Then young Aran Roe would take the helm and Rathlin would again prosper.

In a measure the wish of the Rathlin men came to pass. One wild night, surely, the Old Gray Woman of Gonn rode into the bed-chamber of King Arghan and flew away with him on her back.

The next morning the day broke bright and clear. Arghan's death was discovered. Aran Roe donned his scarlet-hooded cape and fastened it on one shoulder with a heavy gold and bronze lunula. He put studded bands of gold upon his arms. Grasping the great Sword of Rathlin in his right hand and a square shield of gilded oxhide in his left, he strode through the halls of Castle Roe.

In the wide courtyard before the Sea-Wall Gate, Aran was proclaimed King of Rathlin. Every man on the island cheered until his throat cracked.

On the day the men of Rathlin Island were cracking their throats with joy over the young king, a barge with twenty-four oars was setting out from Sligo Bay. It was the marriage barge of Mourne O'Glanny, one of the most beautiful and powerful women in the West of Ireland. The O'Glanny were an ancient clan, even in 1115. Soldiers of fortune, they had pirated most of their wealth, raiding lonely castles along the coasts of Ireland and Scotland and plundering Spanish merchantmen. The O'Glanny coffers had been greatly swelled by the dowry brought to Nial O'Glanny by a rich woman from the Glen of Mourne in County Down. This probably explains the first name given to Nial's daughter, Mourne.

A year before this story opens, the Battle of Clontarf had taken place, the great battle in which Brian Boru drove the Danes out of the South of Ireland. O'Glannys appeared in great array at the Battle of Clontarf, and with their spoils they next appear as lords of Sligo Rock in County Sligo. Just why Sligo Rock continued for centuries to arouse men's greed remains a mystery. A vast, ungainly barracks of a house, it has never had a shred of architectural elegance, and is not impregnable, for it has changed hands, time out of mind.

Sligo Rock dominates a formidable seacoast position and over-looks a fine small harbour. Its iron-spiked walls and steep stone staircases have run with so much blood, down the centuries, it is small wonder that, like ancient Castle Swords at the mouth of the Liffey River in County Dublin, it reeks of treachery. Its walls exude a stench of dried and clotted blood of saint and sinner alike.

From this perfidious house set out Mourne O'Glanny in her wedding barge, painted purple, green, and gold, loaded with wines, spices, richly dyed stuffs, beaten gold gorgets, and sharp bronze spearheads. The finest gift of all, she thought, were bales of softly tanned hides, to wear under armour, and thick animal skins, shaggy with warm fur, for cold stone Antrim floors.

In Ireland in the days of Aran Roe and Mourne O'Glanny, marriage customs were as rigid as they were flamboyant. Every move made by the man and woman, once they were betrothed, was according to tradition. Woe to the one who broke it.

The ceremony of the Bridal Barge took months, even years, of preparation.

In eleventh-century Ireland the procedure ran thus. The betrothed woman loaded a barge with her household gear, as well as with splendid presents for her future husband and his family. Naturally this display must be as fine as she could afford. On an appointed day the woman set out from a point of her own choosing. Halfway to the place where her future husband lived, her barge was to halt and await his arrival in a magnificent ship with an imposing display of men-at-arms. The woman joined him at this stage. They then returned to his castle, her well-laden barge following behind. These barges were carved and painted in brilliant colours. Ancient Gaelic runes were embroidered on ribbon-like banners which streamed out behind. Manned by twenty to forty oars, these craft attained a fair speed and moved over the water silently. A high platform was erected in the stern and richly coloured cloths were flung over it. Couches were arranged on the dais. Bards and minstrels grouped themselves about the deck. Lutes and harps made music. It was a veritable *Tristan und Isolde* tableau.

For two days, through cool, golden weather, the purple barge of Mourne O'Glanny noiselessly split the waves in the direction of Rathlin Island. It had been arranged that Aran Roe should proceed from his castle to Dunaff Head, put in at the walled village of Dunaff, and await Mourne O'Glanny at Ballyliffin Castle in Donegal.

Three days out on her journey, when they were off Dungloe, Mourne awoke to broad daylight and a clamour. Voices rose in confusion in the prow of the barge. Looking away over the sea Mourne saw small, swift sailing curraghs, the kind that have red latteen sails and dart among the rocky inlets of County Antrim. When she asked what this was all about, a pageboy ran toward her. She hastily took the rolled parchment from his hand and, spreading it on the broad handrail, she read:

> Fair Mourne O'Glanny—
> Come no further towards Ballyliffin.
> Turn and make with all speed to Sligo
> Rock. The O'Flaherty are abroad again,
> pillaging the North Coast. In a battle
> on the mainland at Dunluce Castle I
> was wounded. Soon I will come to Sligo.
> > Aran Roe

Springing from warrior stock, Mourne first thought to continue on her journey. If she encountered the Black O'Flaherty she would engage them. She had hundreds of spears and small arms in the barge, and thirty men-at-arms. When her mind calmed, she realized it would be useless. She could never overcome the O'Flaherty with her small force. Sadly, and in black anger at this bitter turn of fate, she ordered the barge turned round. As the sun sank in a riot of flaming clouds behind the Bloody Foreland, her oarsmen pulled all out for the protection of Sligo Rock.

Day after day and far into the nights, Mourne O'Glanny paced the spray-wet stones on the battlements of Sligo Rock. Always her eyes searched the miles of dun-grey Atlantic for some sign of Aran Roe. No messenger had come, either by sea or land. It was autumn now; high winds prevailed, and storms attacked the coast, scattering driftwood and cordage from wrecked ships along the beaches.

After waiting for weeks, with no word, Mourne had sent couriers by inland roads and secret goat tracks to try and find what was happening in the North. Two couriers never returned; a third was sent back to Sligo Rock, mutilated and gibbering, the O'Flaherty cattle brand of a black spearhead burned into his cheek.

As months strung out, and no word came, Mourne O'Glanny became desperate with anxiety. When finally snatches of news came to her lonely house, it was bad news, surely.

The O'Flaherty had sacked the Castles of Dunluce, Armoy, and Carnlough. O'Flaherty himself, with his savage men-at-arms, had holed up for the winter in a glen in County Down, near the smoking ruins of Portglenone. Still no news of Aran Roe.

The long winter dragged on, a winter of iron cold. Few men walked the roads and no ships were seen in the bay. Even the gulls were frozen stiff on the pinnacles of Renvyle. Mostly, during these drear days, Mourne O'Glanny sat huddled in a cloak before a leaping fire. Flames and sparks roared up the flues; her thoughts soared with them, speeding on to Castle Roe.

One night Mourne O'Glanny barred the doors of The Rock, as the fishermen thereabouts called the castle, took a flaming oak-knot from the banked fire, and mounted the stairs to her chamber. She had chosen this room, bitterly cold as it was, because from its one great window she could look away to Rathlin Island, hidden behind the Dunamanagh Mountains. She lay staring into the shadowed vaultings of the room for a while, then fitfully she slept. Often during the night the clash of wind wakened her, the sound of bumping, and the drag of chains rasping against rock. "Wreckage," she murmured to the night, and sank into sleep. Before dawn, she wakened sharply and rose from her bed. That bumping again. Pulling aside an oxhide curtain which hung across a window in the wall facing the sea, she looked down. Dawn had not cracked yet. In the foggy darkness she saw a storm-driven hulk, with lines of chains dragging away from it, bumping against the ramp of Sligo Rock. Some hapless ship sucked in by the strong currents. Well, when morning came the men-at-arms could deal with it.

When morning came there was more than a hapless ship to deal with. After a disturbed night, Mourne slept soundly. She stirred, slowly wakened, hearing the sound of clamour, just like that morning last summer when her wedding barge lay off Dungloe and a messenger from Aran Roe had come aboard. This time the clamour seemed more intense, with loud shouting and the sound of many running feet. As she lay listening, there were hurrying feet on the stairs and in the passage, and then the door was flung wide. Garda, her serving woman, stood there, her eyes wide with fear, one hand clutching her mouth to stifle tearing sobs.

Mourne O'Glanny leaped from her bed, flung a cloak across her shoulders. "Garda!" she cried. "What is it – where?" Garda only moaned, pointing outside towards the sea, "Aran Roe – Aran Roe."

Mourne O'Glanny stood motionless on the top step of the water gate, looking down. Thud, thud, bump, bump, in the ebb and flow of the ocean swell, this she had heard all night, a broken barge dragging seaweed-crusted chains.

Servants and men-at-arms crowded below her on the steps and looked hard at Mourne O'Glanny. Not a sound came from their lips. They watched to see what she would do.

Tall, she seemed, in her dark red cloak, lifted like wings in the morning wind. Tall, straight, and very fair. Tawny, the bards called her, with golden eyes. Some said she was more beautiful than Maeve. Who could tell? Mourne of the Fair Girdle. Her body was as a young tree in a wood, round and sweet with sap.

Mourne O'Glanny came to the landing stage. Alone she stepped aboard the barge and walked to the shattered dais where, bound round and round with heavy chains that cut cruelly into his flesh, lay the naked body of Aran Roe. Between his empty eyesockets and on his broad breast, burned black and deep, was the spearhead brand of O'Flaherty. Plundered bridal chests lay heaped in the prow, and the red hooded cloak by which all men knew Aran Roe lay soaked in blood across his mangled feet.

Mourne O'Glanny, with a face as bleak as the Rocks of Moher, walked twice round the ship. Blood, blood everywhere. Each chain ended in the drowned body of a man, Aran Roe's guard of honour numbering fifty men. Fifty chains, fifty men. Standing in the centre of the barge Mourne O'Glanny called to her men-at-arms. "Wrap the body of Aran Roe in my cloak, bear him gently to my house, follow me."

For seven days Mourne O'Glanny kept silent vigil at the bier of Aran Roe. Washed and anointed with the oil of olive from Spain, rubbed dry with pungent herbs found in the glens of Finncairn, she wrapped him in a cloak of scarlet wool cut in full circle. She had dyed the wool and fashioned the cloak herself for their wedding day. Now she drew the hood well down to hide the despicable spearhead brand. The barge she had had repaired, well caulked, and painted scarlet, with white antlers at the prow, the device of Arghan, the name of his house.

Then with much ceremony did Mourne O'Glanny prepare what she had to do. The fifty Rathlin men who were slain with Aran Roe and bound in chains to the gunwales of his ship were wrapped in shrounds of heavy linen, only their faces exposed. An old Warn Woman from out beyond the Kyles of Rah in Mayo mixed a brew. This mixture was rubbed upon the faces of the fifty Rathlin men, and on the face and body of Aran Roe. Then they were gilded with the dust of mountain gold. Nor time nor weather would destroy their look of youth. Age or decay would touch them never.

When this was done, Mourne O'Glanny opened her bridal chests; forth she drew bolts of cloth and mantles, red and gold and white damask, threaded through with copper, gold, and yellow. These she threw across the dais high in the stern of the barge. On this dais, wrapped in his bridal cloak, was laid the body of Aran Roe. A bronze shield and the great sword of the O'Glanny were placed upon his breast, flagons of spiced wine, oaten bread, and fruits piled at his feet. The fifty gilded Rathlin men were bound upright in the prow, holding their spears at ease. They would gaze always to the chosen course, would guard forever Aran Roe.

When all was ready, Mourne O'Glanny called to her servants and her men-at-arms: "Fetch to the battlements of the castle bundles of wood and dry rushes; erect there a bier, cover it with the purple mantle in my marriage chest, then wait upon my orders. When the new moon shows in the sky tonight, I will light my bridegroom on his way, for Aran Roe starts out upon a journey – a journey that will never end."

Dark descended. The new moon appeared, a pale saffron crescent in the sky. As the moon appeared, so came Mourne O'Glanny from her chamber, robed for her Viking funeral. Tawny hair hung in ropes, crossed with beaten gold and copper. On her brow sat a wide crown fashioned of golden alder leaves and flying birds. Beneath her purple mantle showed a habit of emerald damask heavily sewn in gold and copper threads. Many chains of carnelian, green matrix, and the ruby called "pigeon's blood" swung from her white throat. Her arms were circled with jewelled golden bands. All about Mourne O'Glanny gleamed, save her eyes. Her eyes were dull.

Unhurried, Mourne O'Glanny walked to the parapet. Looking down, she called, "Cut the ropes, send forth my bridegroom's barge." Mounting the dais, Mourne O'Glanny took a cup filled with wine which stood upon the last step. Holding it high, she drank, long and deeply. For a few moments she watched the scarlet barge ride out of the bay, breast the little phosphorescent waves, shudder slightly as it passed the sand bar, then take gracefully to the open sea.

Mourne O'Glanny raised high her cup of wine, hurled it far out. It hung suspended for a moment like the moon, then fell into the bay.

"A portent to you, Aran Roe! Sail ever through the years, a symbol of my everlasting love, and to the Black O'Flaherty the curses of all women ring with mine, the women you have robbed of all they love."

Mourne O'Glanny paused. The strongly poisoned wine would soon rob her of speech. Looking down at the weeping women and the sombre men, she said, "Light the pyre. I am ready. And go you far from here." Lying down upon the bier, she closed her eyes.

It is doubtful if the O'Flaherty suffered greatly, if at all, from Mourne O'Glanny's curse. Individually they were forever reviled, but the accumulated blanket of curses may easily have helped in the downfall of the tribe. It is a fact that soon after this occurrence (the massacre of Aran Roe and his men in 1115) the O'Flaherty black star plunged hellward in rapid flight. The Tribe O'Scanlon overcame them at the battle of the Lifford Glen, and in 1203 they were routed at Connellan Castle by the Tribe O'Haggerty and fled to the Lakes of Menlo. Today their last stronghold, Castle Blake on the river Corrib in County Galway, is a ruin, and has been for two hundred years. Visit the ruin of Blake on a moonlight night, a "soft" Galway night; it has a brand of magic I have never encountered elsewhere, the haunted beauty of the lost and damned.

Any attempt to recount the various hauntings accredited to gaunt old Sligo Rock would be nearly endless. Down its long and bloody history legends have clung to its wall thick as barnacles on a tramper's hull. Shrieks and moans of torture are often heard, the crashing of chains and the sound of men in combat, and pools of blood eternally drip down the stone stairs. There is a tale told in the pubs in Portacloy, in County Sligo, of a sailor who once appeared at the fishing village of Kilglass, near The Rock. He said he was of the Tribe O'Flaherty and would sleep in his own castle "the night." He did. For months thereafter a half-demented man coursed up and down the roads, from village to village. Always he was run out of whatever clutch of houses he entered; for the night the man had slept at Sligo Rock he had fallen in the slippery pool of blood on the stairs. He bore a great spot of this blood on the side of his face in the rough shape of a spearhead. At last, no longer able to endure the shame of this flaming brand, which no rubbing or washing could erase, the sailor drowned himself off the breakwater at Portacloy.

When Mourne O'Glanny set the gilded body of Aran Roe adrift in his scarlet Bridal Barge, a timeless argosy, a symbol of their deathless love, she set the torch to a pyre high among the battlements of her castle and was burned to ashes. People say that often on calm nights spirals of blue-grey smoke swirl upward from the ramparts of The Rock as if to signal the ghostly barge. After this smoke is seen, sometime during the night, a fisherman hauling in his nets, the captain of a transatlantic liner, or a woman walking along the Sea Wall Road will watch in silent wonder, for on the horizon, seeming to skim the surface of the sea, lonely and serene, sails the gleaming Bridal Barge of Aran Roe.

ELLIOTT O'DONNELL has been described as the "doyen of twentieth-century ghost hunters" and certainly no other writer of the time can match the number of hauntings he claimed to have experienced. Born by his own account in County Limerick to one of the oldest families in Ireland, he witnessed his first ghost – "something dark and sinister that grabbed me by the throat" – while he was a student in Dublin. The traumatic experience made him decide on ghost hunting as a profession and in the succeeding years he wrote dozens of books, including Twenty Years' Experience as a Ghost Hunter (1916), Confessions of a Ghost Hunter (1928) *and the posthumous* Casebook of Ghosts (1969), *as well as lecturing on the supernatural and occasionally organizing ghost hunts. The following account describes one such haunt – but with a very unexpected climax.*

ALL HALLOWS EVE HAUNT

Location and date:
Hitchin, Hertfordshire, UK, 1939

A few miles from Hitchin, in a wood on the summit of a hill, are the ruins of Minsden church, at one time a chapel of ease, said to have given shelter to many a passing pilgrim.

Tradition associates it with Alice Perrers, mistress of Edward III and Lady of Hitchin Manor, who is credited with stealing her royal lover's rings when he was on his death-bed and powerless to prevent her. In the seventeenth century it witnessed the marriage of Sir John Barrington, Bart., to Susan Draper.

After that time nothing of any note seems to have happened there, and, about 1738, it became so dilapidated that pieces of masonry and plaster not infrequently fell on the clergy and congregation, to the consternation of both.

Probably, soon after that date it was abandoned, some say on account of widespread rumours of its being haunted by the ghost of a nun, alleged to have been murdered during the reign of Henry VIII, when a convent was either attached to the church or occupied its site.

I first heard of the reputed haunting through a photographer living in the neighbourhood of Minsden, who sent me a photograph taken, he said, in broad daylight at the ruins. The chief interest in the photograph lay in what resembled the shadowy form of a nun. The photographer did not claim he had photographed a ghost, he merely called my attention to the shadowy form and implied he could not account for it. He referred to a local belief in the haunting of the spot by the phantom of a murdered nun, and suggested that we should visit the ruins; he would ask a few of his friends to accompany us and I could invite a few of mine. It was October, and, at my suggestion, we chose for the date of our visit to the ruins All Hallows E'en, that being one of the nights in the year when denizens of the spirit world are popularly believed to be in closest touch with the material inhabitants of this plane. Also, since All Hallows E'en is one of the occasions when the working of certain spells is deemed likely to produce interesting results, I asked a lady, who is well versed in such things, to be one of the party. Others I invited were H. V. Morton, the well-known author, Wyndham Lewis, "Beachcomber," and R. Blumenfelt, son of the Editor of the *Daily Express*.

When I arrived at King's Cross I saw a crowd of people collected in front of the Ladies' Waiting Room. Intuition warned me of the reason, and when I cautiously elbowed my way through the gaping throng, I perceived, as I had anticipated, my mediumistic friend, clad – and this I had not anticipated – in orthodox witch's costume, namely, high cap, cloak, gown covered with demons and black cats and, of course, in one hand, a broomstick. The picture was startling enough, and the expressions on the faces of the spectators were a study. While some showed wonder and others amusement, a few looked positively scared; probably they thought she was the escaped inmate of some home for the mentally defective.

Of my three friends, Morton, Wyndham Lewis and Blumenfelt there was not a sign. Indeed, I did not see them till I had bundled the witch into a third-class compartment, much to the consternation of a female occupant, who at once flew out of it. I then caught sight of them stealing surreptitiously into a first-class compartment, as far away from us as possible.

The Hitchin photographer lived with two very proper, elderly female relatives, and when they caught sight of the witch, standing beside me in the doorway, they were immeasurably shocked. "Who is this person?" they demanded. "She must not enter this house." And when I endeavoured to explain why she had come, their indignation grew. "Tom," one of them exclaimed, turning to the photographer, who cowered against the wall, looking extremely sheepish and uncomfortable, "Tom, you never told us a person dressed like this was coming. It's a scandal. What would your dear father, aye, and grandfather say? Why, they never missed a Sunday at chapel in their lives. The mere thought of a woman in such an attire as this," pointing at the witch, who maintained an imperturbability that suggested she was not altogether unaccustomed to such harangues, "coming to the house is enough to make them turn in their graves. Tell her to go away at once." Tom making no response, I had to intervene, and after much pleading obtained permission for the witch to sit with us in Tom's studio till it was time for us to go to the haunted ruins, on the condition, however, that, after leaving the house then, she was never to set foot in it again.

The ruins were several miles distant, and it was well-nigh midnight when we arrived there. As we drew near to the wood, there was a ghostly rustling of leaves, which made the more nervous of the party clutch hold of one another, followed by a buzzing and whirling, as a number of birds, scared at our approach, left their homes in the ivy-clad ruins of the church and flew frantically away.

I had brought with me a variety of articles necessary for the working of the spells, and I proposed that, while the witch muttered appropriate incantations, Messrs Morton, Wyndham Lewis and Blumenfelt should try their luck with hempseed and apples.

Most All Hallow E'en keepers know the hempseed spell. Walking alone in the dark one has to scatter hempseed over the left shoulder, drawing mould over it afterwards with a hoe or other instrument, and repeating, as one does so, these words:

Hempseed I sow, yes, hempseed I hoe;
Oh, those who's to meet me come after me and mow.

And then, if the Powers that govern the Unknown ordain it, one hears footsteps in one's rear and, on turning fearfully around, sees the immaterial counterpart of whoever is to come into one's life within the next twelve months and affect it most. If you are destined to die during that period, you see a skeleton. All this may sound just fanciful and old world, superstitious tripe: but, nevertheless, I have known occasion when something quite unexpected and unquestionably superphysical has happened. On this particular occasion, when asked if they would separate and, alone, amid the gloom and shadows of the trees, put the spell to the test, Messrs Morton, Wyndham Lewis and Blumenfelt answered in the negative, a very decided negative; they much preferred remaining together. The witch did her best to persuade the ghost to manifest itself. Seated on the damp soil she crooned, and incanted, and moaned, there was a note of occasional real misery in the last; but the other world remained obdurate, it would not come at her calling, and perhaps it was just as well, because some of the party might, I think, have been more than a wee bit startled; at least I gathered so from their close proximity to one another and from what, every now and then, sounded suspiciously like the chattering of teeth, though the cold – and out there it was cold – might have had something to do with the last.

Our pulses gave a sudden jump when one of the party exclaimed: "What's that?" We looked, and for a few seconds I thought that the witch's endeavours had at last succeeded in bringing the superphysical, but investigation proved it was only the ghostly effect of the moonlight on one of the ivy-clad ruin arches. We were discussing our disappointment, "professed" disappointment, I fancy, on the part of several, when from afar came a sound like the report of a firearm. "A strange hour and season for anyone to be out shooting," someone observed, and we thought no more about it.

As it was now about four o'clock, the chance of the ghost appearing seemed so remote that we set out on our homeward journey.

And now came our only real thrill. It was a still, grey, chilly morning. There had been a slight fog rising from the damp ground during the night, and it was now so thick that those of our party who were in front, myself among them, could not see the witch and photographer, who were trudging along some little distance in the rear. Through the mist the black shades of trees and hedges stood out faintly. We were hastening, thinking longingly of breakfast and a cheery fire, when suddenly dark figures sprang out from seemingly nowhere, and peremptory tones commanded us to halt. They were policemen, four of them, who in the mist – my eyes, no doubt, were strained by hours of high nerve tension vigil – appeared magnified into giants. They asked what we were doing, tramping a lonely highway at that unearthly hour, and when I said: "Looking for a ghost," the leader of them responded nastily: "That's a good 'un.

You don't expect us to swallow that." He went on to inform us that the booking office at Welwyn railway station had been broken into during the night and the official in charge of it fired at, which explained the report of firearms we had heard.

He was about to search us, and I was feeling somewhat anxious, because one of our party had, I knew, a revolver on him, when I was seized with a sudden inspiration. "Do you know Mr. —?" I said, naming the local photographer.

"Very well," the Sergeant replied, "but he's not here."

"No," I answered, "but he's following with a lady, clad as a witch, and one or two other people. Do you not know last night was All Hallow's E'en, when the dead from crossroads and cemeteries are permitted to mingle once more with the living? We came hoping to see the ghost of the nun that rumour alleges haunts the ruins of Minsden church. Haven't you heard of her?"

"Now I come to think of it," the Sergeant said, "I 'ave 'eard of the party, but I don't pay any attention to tales of that sort. You'll all 'ave to come along to the Police Station and answer such questions as may be put to you."

Grunts and ejaculations of dismay came from Morton, Wyndham Lewis and Blumenfelt, who had hitherto been dumb, too overcome, so I imagined, with the horror of the situation to speak.

Now the appalling thoughts of not getting to their respective newspaper headquarters in time loosened their tongue strings, nor did I feel too happy, for I was cold and shivering and wanted a hot drink very badly.

To my infinite relief, however, at this very critical moment, there loomed into view the witch, photographer and the rest of the party, who were all local. On hearing them corroborate my story, the Police Sergeant capitulated, and all ended well, at least so far as concerned that little incident; but there was some bother when we got back to the photographer's house and tried to smuggle in the witch. One of Tom's elderly relatives hearing us, and making sure we were burglars, or the house was on fire, started to scream, and it took desperate efforts on Tom's part to calm her. Fortunately, she was far too frightened to come out of her bedroom, or she must have seen the witch.

Our train back to London did not arrive for nearly two hours, and all that time we sat huddled together in the dreary room, in momentary dread of one or other of Tom's aged relatives descending on us. To render the situation more embarrassing and alarming, the witch, doubtless affected by sitting on the cold ground for so long, had to retire with sudden haste to the toilet which, as bad luck would have it, was upstairs, next to one of the aged relative's bedrooms. She contrived to get there without attracting attention but, on leaving the place, in her anxiety to catch the train, she slipped, and descending amid an avalanche of paper parcels, landed on the floor with a terrific crash. This was altogether too much for Messrs Morton, Wyndham Lewis and Blumenfelt. They decamped pell-mell, meanly leaving me to grab hold of the witch and drag her and her many parcels to the station.

So ended my first visit to the haunted church of Minsden.

I went there twice afterwards and on the last occasion, when I was alone, I heard sounds of very sweet and plaintive music, and thought, just for a moment, I saw a female figure in white standing in one of the archways. It was gone almost at once, and may possibly have been due to a trick of the moonlight.

EILEEN GARRETT grew up in County Meath with vivid memories of two "invisible children" who played with her in the fields of the idyllic Irish countryside. Her interest in the supernatural grew with every passing year and she was soon acknowledged with possessing exceptional powers of clairvoyance, precognition and trance-mediumship. She became famous in October 1930 when she made spirit contact with Flight-Lieutenant H C Irwin, the doomed captain of the airship that had just crashed in flames, and learned what had happened. During her lifetime, Eileen Garrett took part in innumerable séances in Britain and America and her memoirs, Adventures in the Supernormal *(1968) – from which the following eerie wartime episode is taken – helped to earn her the reputation of being "probably the best-known and reliable psychic in the world".*

A VISION OF TOMORROW

Location & date: South of France, 1940

I was in the south of France in the most desperate early days of the war in Europe, after Munich, and during the evacuation of Dunkirk. Britain had stretched her very life across the Channel and made her offer of national unity with France. The southern country was already crowded with refugees of all types, and a few who had been living there and still stayed on had opened a *foyer du soldat* and soup kitchen. Throughout the whole of France, resentment against England moved like a plague; she was secretly collaborating with Hitler; she had sold France out; she would fight to the last drop of French blood. I knew that this wild hatred of England had been hatched in Germany, and that it was being propagated by German agents who moved through the French countryside and the French cities, dropping hints, making vague suggestions, asking endless questions barbed with poisonous innuendo. I watched France swallow this bait, submit to this deception, and I saw the national morale going to pieces day by day. I thought in my heart: could this be possible in France, where the life of the people and the life of the sea and the soil were one life? If this were possible, was this then the beginning of the end of the world, of the reversion of mankind to savagery, of the extinction of the human race? Humanity seemed to be moving toward madness – a madness destined to end in self-destruction. All about one, people were fleeing from an annihilating force that followed, as those other people, long ago, had fled before the rising water till there was no longer any land to flee to, and the deluge destroyed them utterly.

I kept myself as busy as possible, but in the privacy of my own room and my own spirit I brought the situation to an issue, demanding some sign that would enable me to verify my faith in England and justify my hopes for a world of honorable peace. I saw a large room with high windows, like a turret, and a man sitting in a chair in a mustard-coloured uniform from which shoulder straps, buttons and all insignia had been cut away. The man was unmistakably Hitler. He was fatter than most pictures had made him appear, and tears were running down his soiled and bloated face. As the picture cleared to my perception, another man went out of the room through a doorway. I saw only the back of this second man – a "von Stroheim" back, with cropped hair and the thick crease of flesh above the collar. This man was no dignitary; he was dressed in a rusty black suit, and I had an impression of him as some kind of artisan – maybe a concierge. He did not look back as he went out, but his hand cast back into the room a knife with a short wooden handle and a curved blade. My sight followed the knife as it slid across the floor, and I had the impression of thinking, "That's the Russian sickle." But a voice said, "No, not Russian. That's an Afghan knife."

I looked again at "Hitler"; he sat immobile in his chair, his shorn uniform awry, while tears ran slowly down his cheeks. Then and there I was filled with a transcendent pity too deep and poignant for any words – pity for that life spent in senseless and futile war against its own kind and against the time to which it belonged. Shorn of his flimsy honours, power had gone out from him completely, leaving him a foolish, lonely human creature, to the slow, perhaps eternal, realization of the crimes he had committed against humanity, against the life and peace of the world.

For me, that vision was the key to the assurance that I needed. Through it, I knew within myself, deeper than all desire or hope or reasoning, that Germany would never win the war. Through all the ups and downs of success and disaster that filled the years that followed, I suffered with my kind for the base and heartless cruelties of the war, but never for a moment did I fail to know that *in the end*, and whatever the cost, the United Nations would be victorious. At times, my family and friends lost patience with me when I tried to ease their anger and their agony over Coventry or Lidice by reminding them of the end. I would mourn over the disasters and loss of life, but within myself I knew with a constant and steady assurance that Germany was destined to defeat.

There is one phase in this experience which I have never been able to translate into understandable terms for my own satisfaction. I do not yet know the meaning of the statement: "No, not Russian. That's an Afghan knife." As the war ended in Europe, with Russia's occupation of Berlin, one could easily find a connection between my impression of "the Russian sickle" and the final downfall of Hitler's Nazi dictatorship – but one will be wise not to make one's own acceptances and rejections among the symbols of such an experience, and it may be that the fate of Germany is bound up with the fate of Asia in some future too far ahead for our minds to penetrate.

AIR CHIEF MARSHAL HUGH DOWDING was an unlikely man to have had an abiding fascination with the paranormal, becoming one of the great advocates of spiritualism in his later life. Born in Scotland, he served in the Royal Flying Corps in the First World War and in 1936 was appointed commander-in-chief of RAF Fighter Command, organizing the defence of Britain against the Nazis four years later and triumphing in the Battle of Britain. Amidst the trauma of war, he became a "regular communicator with the spirit world", and in May and June 1943, relayed a series of messages he had received from "the other side" to an enthralled readership of the Sunday Pictorial. *The series is said to have given great comfort to many parents who had lost sons in aerial combat.*

ONE OF OUR BOYS

Location and date: The Ruhr, Germany, 1943

The next episode is the awakening of a Bomber crew, shot down over the Ruhr. The pilot is brought to us by James – James is one of my principal co-operators on the other side. He was commanding a Night Fighting Squadron during the Battle of Britain. He was then, and is now, a very dear friend of mine.

L.L. "Here is a young RAF boy quite unaware of us. Tall, very slim and dark, with big flying boots. James and others are all around him but he can't see them either. Two Guides, one on each side, are directing streams of light on to him from their fingers.

"Now he is beginning to see us. He says he wants to sit down, he is rather tired. He sits down in an armchair. His leg is aching, he takes off one of his flying boots. He says that he 'baled out' and landed badly." (James says No, he never left the machine, but he *thinks* he did.) He speaks:

" 'Sorry, I can't just make it out. Where am I?' I tell him that he has been brought to me because he can believe what I say. I show him a photograph to establish my identity. I tell him that we are in Wimbledon.

" 'Thank God Sir! The last I can remember was that we were over the Ruhr. How did they manage to bring me here?' (He thinks it has been done by the underground organization and is much impressed by its efficiency.)

"I ask him when he left England, and he says Sunday. I tell him this is Thursday. I say that while he has been unconscious he has been brought across a number of frontiers, between Germany and Holland, and between Holland and England, and furthermore that he has crossed the greatest Frontier of all. I hope that this will make him realize what has happened; but not a bit of it, I must try again.

"He asks why he has been brought to *me* specially; and I say I suppose because I love the boys so much. I never see or hear a big formation going over without saying 'God Bless you and bring you back safe.'

"He says 'Well, *we* got back safe all right.' And I say 'Safe. Yes. Do you know Rupert Brooke's poem called 'Safety'? Let's see if I can remember the last four lines,

> " 'War knows no power. Safe shall be my going,
> Secretly armed against all death's endeavour;
> Safe though all safety's lost; safe where men fall;
> And if these poor limbs die, safest of all.'

"He said 'By Jove Sir, that's fine. But anyway *I'm* safe.' So I said to him very gently, 'Yes. Safest of all.' That brought it home to him at last. He said 'D'you mean to say you're trying to tell me that I'm dead?' Then he said 'Why can't you keep still? Why do you keep jumping about?' I replied, 'I have already told you that you will see us looking less and less real, and then you will see your friends who have come to meet you. Look round now and tell me if you can see anyone.'

"Then he said, 'Hallo. There's Clockie – but how can *he* be here. Clockie's dead.' I said, 'He is no more and no less dead than you are.' Then he called out 'Harry!' and added 'Good Lord there's even old Ginger! I must have stumbled into an RAF Camp. I see – I don't mind being dead if this is it. It's a mighty fine piece of work.' Then (answering one of his friends) 'Of *course* I'm coming. You just try to stop me.' "

James: "Thank you Sir. That was well done. He went out from one of the Stations in the South. He was one of *our* boys. Although you only spoke to one there were six others watching and listening-in. He was the most stable. That was why we chose him as spokesman. His quiet acceptance helped the others. They're a fine lot of boys and we're mighty glad to get them over here; but we think what a poor place Earth is going to be without them."

JOHN HARRIES was a specialist travel writer who became intrigued by the supernatural after his wartime service in the RAF. His journeys around the British Isles gathering material brought him into contact with a number of contemporary haunt-

ings which he investigated with a close attention to detail and proven facts. His collection, The Ghost Hunter's Road Book (1974) is a particularly good example of his research – and one story of a personal encounter in 1945 with a terrifying animal ghost in a remote corner of East Anglia is probably as strange as anything to be found in this book.

THE SPECTRAL DOG

Location and date: Dereham, Norfolk, 1945

The practical explanation of the East Anglian Black Shucks, Fen Hounds, and monkeys would no doubt be that they are relics of folk memory from the times of the Viking invaders when these terrifying warriors brought with them both the religious accounts of their god Odin's hounds and also used dogs to hunt animals and human enemies. But science makes little headway with folk who have themselves seen, or imagined, these nocturnal beasts.

A personal experience may be justified in their defence. After the end of the Second World War the writer was awaiting demobilization at the RAF station of Swanton Morley, near Norwich. As was usual for Air Force personnel stationed in remote areas, everyone was issued with a bicycle. The nearest "centre of civilization" was East Dereham, some five miles away on B1147. A network of minor lanes connecting farms made it possible to cut this distance a little – and they were useful when cycling by night without lamps, as was usually the case.

Shortly before midnight in November 1945, when there was a moon screened by light cloud, I set off from Dereham for the RAF station. A premonition made me glance back towards a sharp curve I had just passed. A dog like a black Alsatian or Labrador was loping along the middle of the road. I rode on, imagining that the animal would turn into a farm or cottage. A mile farther I again looked back along a stretch clear of hedges and trees so that the road was quite visible in the weak moonlight. The animal was still coming along.

Dogs have a habit of attaching themselves to troops, possibly because of plentiful food and companionship. Not wanting to tempt someone's pet to follow me from its presumed home in East Dereham I turned the cycle and told the dog to go home. It stood motionless. I could see its jaws were open and its tongue lolling out – but there was no sound of panting. I frankly admit that, lover of dogs as I am, and confident that any indication of fear is the one certain way of turning a friendly animal into an attacker, I was unwilling to approach closer. I cycled on, turning frequently. The dog was always behind, loping easily along the centre of the road. I increased my speed, and on the flat roads of Norfolk on a windless night it is easy to reach twenty miles per hour. The dog kept precisely the same distance from me. I slowed down; so did the dog. I stopped and faced it once more. The animal merely stood motionless.

The approach road outside the RAF station had been widened and straightened to enable fuel tankers and articulated vehicles to use it. Consequently the half mile to the guard room was without concealment. I slowed down and glanced back yet again as I neared the chainlink fencing. The dog was still coming at its easy lope. Then, in a darker patch where a clump of trees bordered the road, it disappeared. I went back and looked. There was nothing to be seen either on the grass verge, below the trees, or in the bare fields beyond the fence – as far as I could see into the gloom. Subsequently, out of interest, I inquired at the farms and cottages on the road if they owned a black Alsatian-type dog or a Labrador. None did. One old woman in a cottage on the outskirts of East Dereham stared at me and then banged the door in my face. From her horrified glance I suspect that she believed, as many Norfolk folk would do today, that she was seeing someone who had the mark of death on him from seeing Black Shuck.

If anyone wishes for circumstantial evidence of this spectral animal's existence – and powers to transform itself into solid flesh – he has only to go to Bungay. Curious scratches on the door of the parish church were reputedly made by Black Shuck when he tried to pursue a victim who had taken sanctuary in the church.

DENNIS BARDENS had what he liked to call a "haunted life" having seen his first ghost as a child living in Southsea, been "pestered" by another when he was a young reporter living in Highgate and then living for a time in a haunted flat in Kensington with his wife and young son. These and other supernatural experiences prompted Bardens into a career as an investigator and he subsequently edited and wrote hundreds of factual programmes for radio and television. Among his most significant books were Mysterious Worlds (1960) and Ghosts and Hauntings (1965) in which he related his encounters with varying spirits from poltergeists to nautical ghosts. This particular experience counts as one of the most bizarre and frightening of all.

MURDERED BY THE NAZIS

Location and date: Prague, 1945

I shall not easily forget my own encounter with a ghost in January, 1946. It was a ghost which I neither saw nor heard, but it remained a terrifying experience.

It was in Prague, and the war had been over only a month or so. The streets were scarred by battle, and the sidewalks decked with patriotic ribbons and a treasured photograph, in memory of some freedom fighter who had fallen there. There was a scarcity of everything; sugar and butter and meat were unheard-of luxuries.

I was sitting in my room at the Esplanade Hotel, working out what my day's routine was to be. As special correspondent of the *Sunday Dispatch* and *Illustrated* – then a thriving illustrated weekly – and a "stringer" for a national daily newspaper, life was interesting enough. Czechoslovakia was gradually returning to normal, although no constitutionally elected government yet existed and the provisional government, with its mixture of Communists, Catholics, Social Democrats and exiles returned from London, had no real mandate from anybody. A quarter of a million Russian soldiers were in the country, and strategic places such as the uranium mines at Yachimov, Ruzin Airport at Prague, and the National Bank, were under Russian control.

The morning's post, as I sipped my ersatz coffee, had little of interest. A few dreary, badly-stencilled handouts combining the jargon of the civil service with the clichés of propaganda – and one postcard, from a friend in Sevenoaks:

" . . . don't go to inordinate trouble in the matter, but as you happen to be in Prague, could you find out what's happened to Mrs Lillian H? The last address I have is c/o Mrs X., number . . . Husinecka, Prague . . ."

It seemed little to ask, so I consulted my street map and found that Husinecka was quite near. Even so, the name of both Mrs H and Mrs

X had a Jewish – and therefore an ominous – ring. In the holocaust and contagion of organised hate unleashed by the Nazis, only a pitiful remnant of Europe's Jewish population remained. Men, women and children, irrespective of age or infirmity, had been subject to every imaginable and unimaginable cruelty and indignity before being granted protracted release of death.

The address proved to be a box-like block of flats starved of paint and void of character. There was no life, and the stairs were unlit and crowded with prams, garbage cans and empty bottles. I had to strike a match to find the number of the flat I sought, and only after incessant ringing was the door opened – by only a few inches. In the half-light I could see an elderly woman; I don't know why, but her face seemed familiar to me. Yes, she said, she was a friend of Mrs H. But the joyless way in which she said this, and her general nervousness, terror almost, made me fear the worst. She asked me into a dingy sitting-room and broke out into such an uncontrolled volley of talk that I wondered if she were mad. On second thoughts I realised that her general demeanour was understandable when one considered the effects of cumulative nervous strain. After all, she was a German Jewess. Somehow, she had escaped the gas ovens, but she must have lived in fear through those long years, concealing her Jewishness, terrified lest it should leak out; and now, with feeling running so high against Germans, Nazi or non-Nazi, even Germans who had been settled in Czechoslovakia for more than 200 years, she was likely to be the victim of violence because of her origins.

I let the stream of talk spend itself, then in answer to my questions, the story of her friend, Mrs H emerged. She was a humble sewing-woman, sixty-two years old and a widow, living alone in a bed-sitting room in Prague when the Germans invaded. She eked out a bare living by odd scraps of sewing and mending. A few family photographs, one or two threadbare dresses of poor quality, and some treasured books were her only possessions. But with the Germans came the reign of terror. Her passport was stamped with the letter "J" and she was not allowed to work, nor to draw rations. Every Jew knew that the process of attrition was only a half-way house to terror.

In despair, she decided to go underground, to pretend to disappear in such a way that it would be inferred by the authorities that she had committed suicide. Accordingly, she left her passport, identity papers and a few odds and ends, together with a suicide note in her room. She filled a humble fibre suitcase with a few garments and left it with her friend in Husinecka. Then, under an assumed name, she joined a convent on the outskirts of Prague. I felt pretty certain that the nuns must have known she was not a Catholic, but had shielded her for humanitarian reasons.

Mrs X, as she told me all this, also said that she made a practice of visiting Mrs H regularly at the convent. This was well meant, but was almost certainly a mistake. Nuns do not receive regular visitors, and the fact may well have been noticed. At any rate, Mrs H enjoyed immunity until 1944 when, for some reason, the convent was raided by the Gestapo. All the sisters were arrested and never heard of again. And Mrs H's true identity was detected. Two pitiful postcards told the remainder of the story: one, from Terezin in Czechoslovakia asked for a dress and some spectacles; the other, from Oświecim in Poland, said simply "I am well." This would be all she would have been allowed to say, and even this meagre concession by the Germans was unusual. But Mrs X knew what it meant; it meant "goodbye," for Oświecim was an extermination camp where hundreds of thousands of Jews went to the gas chambers, besides meeting death by hanging and ill-treatment. And Terezin had an evil enough reputation as it was a transit camp, where prisoners were sorted, by a mere glance, into two classes – those who were to live, and those condemned to slave labour.

While reading the postcard I had a curious feeling of being watched, and a "tingly" feeling in the spine. I gave it no more thought, however. Nor did I tell Mrs X that she might have, unwittingly, encompassed the death of her friend by her visits. She had had troubles enough. I thanked her for her help, and made arrangements to visit Terezin to see what evidence I could find of Mrs H having been there in transit to Oświecim.

It all seems unreal now – that grim red-brick fortress built by the Empress Maria Theresa as a munitions dump. Even at Terezin, the cremation ovens had been busy, and when the American Red Cross had neared the premises sacks of human ash had been dumped into the stream. Over sixty thousand Jews were done to death there, and thousands of cardboard boxes each containing the calcified remains of a human being, abandoned – the Germans had retreated so fast that there had been no time to jettison them. They had kept these remains as a kind of grim "tally" in support of the returns of slaughter made to Berlin.

Typhus had been raging there when the Russians arrived. The sleeping sheds, void of blankets or linen, mere wooden slats or racks on which human beings were crammed in conditions worse than that of cattle, were separated only by a brick wall from the swimming pool constructed by Czech students, who were afterwards murdered, at an execution yard with gallows and three machine-gun emplacements. The wall opposite was pitted with bullet holes.

Certain inmates were conceded a temporary immunity by keeping a card-index of the prisoners. It was in no sense a complete record. Mrs H. was probably there no more than a day or so, and nobody had bothered to record her fate. I was certain she was dead, because her few pitiful belongings had been returned to the Jewish community in Prague – a procedure occasionally utilised in order further to demoralise and terrorise such Jews as remained.

I returned to the hotel in Prague and retired to bed. My third-floor room was large and comfortable, with a hall and bathroom attached. The furnishings were modern – a large wardrobe, dressing-table and double bed with satinwood headboard. There was a bedside table with a reading lamp on it, and there was a large, handsome chandelier, too bright for general use.

At two o'clock in the morning I was awakened *instantly* by what I can only describe as a noise like a pistol shot in my head. In that instant my attention was directed to a particular part of that room, just near the door, in the hall or alcove that led to the door of the apartment. I could see nothing, yet *knew* with every instinct I possessed that something was there. I could even tell its height. Further, I knew – how I don't know – that it was Mrs H. She was trying to tell me something. The room seemed flooded, pervaded by an overpowering atmosphere of sadness charged with menace.

In a sweat of fear, and only by a considerable effort of will, for I felt almost paralysed, I reached for the reading lamp switch. The room, centrally-heated, was inordinately cold. The light seemed to dispel the supercharged tension and gradually the fear and horror lifted. I could feel the presence becoming weaker and weaker, until at last the room, except for myself, was empty – a sad, desolate sort of emptiness, a vestigial remnant of the sadness which had flooded the room in that strange way.

It will be said, I suppose, that my sad mission to Terezin had made some impression on my imagination. I can only say that the experience was very real – a sense of something indescribable but tangible. That incredible, almost electrical tension in the air; that all-pervading sadness tinged with menace . . . I do not think this was a synthetic product of strained nerves. The experience of visiting Terezin, sad as it was with its remainders of mass slaughter, and of crude and needless inhumanity, was not at that time unusual. In one night's air raid on London over six hundred people were killed and many thousands of men, women and children injured, but I have never heard of a place haunted by the spectre of an air-raid victim. Violence in itself, as I have said before, does not produce these phenomena. There are other factors, perhaps some concatenation of circumstances favouring the "registration" of strong emotion. But even if one accepts that vague hypothesis, there remains a greater puzzle. It might explain ghosts which hark back to the past, treading their old familiar paths and making an endless ritual of once transient acts, but how would it explain an active manifestation of some kind of intelligence *after* death?

ALASDAIR ALPIN MACGREGOR was an extraordinary Scotsman of many talents – singer, orator, actor, traveller and writer, once described as "the Last of the Knight Errants" – who wrote books on a wide variety of subjects from biographies to topography and the supernatural. He found his experiences in the trenches of the First World War deeply traumatic and this excited his interest in the supernatural. MacGregor's books on the subject, including The Haunted Isles *(1933),* The Ghost Book: Strange Happenings in Britain *(1955) and* Phantom Footsteps: A Second Ghost Book *(1959) are all models of objective research. This next episode also occurred in the immediate aftermath of the Second World War.*

THE HAUNTED FARMHOUSE

Location and date: Glen Duror, Argyllshire, 1946

Few with any appreciable knowledge of Scotland have not heard of Glen Duror, that steep and comparatively short valley running inland from the roadside at Duror of Appin to terminate in a bowl of mountain. On a rushy and nettly spot at the head of this Argyllshire glen may still be seen the ruins of the humble homestead from which James Stewart – James of the Glen, as history denotes him – was evicted in the middle of the eighteenth century; and farther down one comes upon Acharn, the small farm of which James was tenant when the authorities arrested him on the charge of being accessory to the murder of Colin Campbell of Glenure, factor for the forfeited estates of Mamore and Ardsheal at the time of the Jacobite Rebellion, and known in Highland history as the Red Fox.

In the fall of 1752, James of the Glen – James of Glen Duror – dangled from the gibbet on the knoll overlooking the Ballachulish ferry, but half a dozen miles away – "executed on this spot, Nov., 8th, 1752, for a crime of which he was not guilty".

Adjoining the present farmhouse of Acharn, lying in a fertile hollow close by the Duror river, is the old house in which James was living with his wife and family when a shot, fired by *someone*, brought down the Red Fox by the shorelands of the Lettermore, and in so doing bequeathed to Scotland one of the most fascinating of her historical mysteries. Today, James's old house, now roofed with rusting corrugated iron, forms part of the farm-steading at Acharn.

On the hillside, within a few hundred yards of Acharn, and on the opposite side of the river, stand the farmhouse and steading of Achnadarroch, behind which Ben Vair rises steeply, its lower flanks thickly planted with conifers by the Forestry Commission. Indeed, the whole of Glen Duror has been planted in this wise in recent years, and now presents a thriving, prospering nursery.

The farmhouse is one of the oldest dwellings in the district. It is said to have been built by one of the Stewarts of Ardsheal, an ancient Appin property, the loftier parts of which are to be seen from its windows. At the time Achnadarroch was built, it would certainly have been regarded as a mansion. The old house, whitewashed, and conspicuous against its background of dark-green pines, can be seen when, in passing along that inland strip of the Appin road between Kentallen Bay and Cuil Bay, one looks eastward up Glen Duror. Adjoining the house are not inconsiderable farm-steadings. Immediately behind it, but invisible from the approaches, lies a cottage which, in the days when Achnadarroch was extensively and profitably worked as a sheep-farm, would have been the bothy occupied by the farm-labourers and shepherds. The cottage is inhabited by a man and his wife, who tenant Achnadarroch, but who had sub-let the old farmhouse itself to my friend, Seumas Stewart, of whom you shall hear more anon, and to whom we shall refer hereinafter as Seumas, this being the Gaelic for James, and also the name by which he is now known in Appin – a new *Seumas a' Ghlinne*, as it were: a twentieth-century James of the Glen.

Achnadarroch is a house of many apartments. The more spacious of these are distributed on two floors. There is a series of long, narrow attic bedrooms aloft. With the exception of the Haunted Room (so called because it happens to be a little more ghostly than the rest), which opens off the dining-room, those on the ground floor are large. They are all low-ceilinged, however. The Haunted Room, now used as a bedroom, was once the general storeroom of the house. One cannot but notice the enormous thickness not only of Achnadarroch's outer walls, but also of those separating its various apartments. The living room, formerly the farm kitchen, is panelled in pinewood. The large, square tiles covering its floor are old, and lie very unevenly. Scarcely two of them are in juxtaposition at the same level. They all tend to slope toward the fireplace. The passing of the feet of centuries has worn them hollow in places, especially in front of the fire, and at the three doorways and passages leading into and out of this quaint apartment.

The house possesses nothing in the way of gas or electric lighting: oil-lamps and candles are still the order at Achnadarroch.

At this juncture, one ought to mention that Achnadarroch and the immediate neighbourhood are haunted by one to whom the Appin folks allude as the Maid of Glen Duror. The Maid is often seen in and about the house itself. She appears at the windows on the ground floor, in the adjoining farm-steading, and also in the lonelier parts of Glen Duror. A little, old woman is frequently seen peering in through the lower windows. Among the commonest of her haunts out of doors are the lower slopes of Ben Vair, just behind the farmhouse. Long ago, it seems, she was employed at Achnadarroch by its original Stewart owners, possibly as dairymaid. In any case, she was often to be seen herding the Achnadarroch cattle in that part of Glen Duror now so completely planted; and there is a local tradition that she was thus engaged when a terrific cloudburst swept the glen, carrying her and her cattle down to Cuil Bay, and out into Loch Linnhe.

Originally the Maid, as she is spoken of in the district, was a MacColl, one of a clan still fairly numerous in this neighbourhood, since the MacColls, in former times, were standard-bearers to the Stewarts of Appin. Indeed, MacColls have been associated with the five merk lands of Achnadarroch for some centuries. These lands once formed part of the lands of Duror, which were included in the Lordship of the Isles, and which were granted by the King in 1500 to Duncan Stewart of Appin. MacColls were certainly plentiful at Achnadarroch at the time of the Appin Murder. More than half of the twenty-one persons resident there in 1752, and summoned as witnesses in connection with James Stewart's trial, were MacColls.

I am told by Mrs Cameron, who now lives at Duror Station, but who once resided at Achnadarroch, that the Maid, in "ghostie" form, has always been kindly disposed toward the Appin Stewarts, and toward their followers, the MacColls. Mrs Cameron herself is a MacColl by birth. During her twenty years at Achnadarroch, she frequently saw the grey wraith of the Maid at dusk, and heard things go bump in the night.

Of the Maid, several anecdotes are recounted in Appin. On one occasion, a native was walking up the glen, when he met her, to be informed by her that he must leave the district and travel to Australia where, she assured him, he would prosper. She mentioned one other matter which, on no account, was he to divulge. Anyhow, he did go to Australia, where he certainly prospered.

More recently, an Irishman employed in the locality on fencing some fields, which he did at piece-time rates, was working on a Sunday when he noticed an old woman ascend Ben Vair at a speed which astonished him. She was wearing a green cloak and hood, he said. Enquiring who this aged, yet agile, person might be, he was assured that it could have been none other than the Maid of Glen Duror. This affected him so much that never again did he work on a Sunday, and shortly afterwards felt constrained to leave the locality.

In the autumn of 1945, I went on a few days' visit to Achnadarroch. One morning, while shaving in the bathroom upstairs, I heard what I thought was a terrific crash of dishes downstairs, where Seumas meanwhile was preparing breakfast. I paused in my shaving, and went to the head of the stairs.

"Have you had an awful smash, Seumas?" I asked, leaning sympathetically over the banister.

"Did you hear something just then, Alasdair?" he responded.

I replied that I had heard him knock over some dishes, which sounded as though they had fallen to fragments on the scullery floor.

"When you've lived at Achnadarroch as long as I have," said Seumas, "you'll pay no attention to that kind of thing. It's just the Maid of Glen Duror at her antics."

A night or two later, Seumas and I were seated in the living room of the old farmhouse, refuelling the fire with logs every now and again, as is the custom during those prolonged sessions for which the late-rising Highlanders are noted. Suddenly we stopped speaking, and looked at each other in astonishment, if not also in apprehension. A steam train seemed to be charging along at the back of the old farmhouse. Its noise increased to deafening proportions as it approached, and diminished as it receded. The house definitely shook under its thundering sway. The clock on the mantelshelf stood at 3 a.m. There could be no train passing through Appin at *that* hour; and, in any case, the Oban-Ballachulish line (the only one in the district) ran through the valley in *front* of the house, half a mile ahead, and was completely free of traffic approximately between the hours of 7 p.m. and 9 a.m.

With palpitating resolution, we rose and went to the door. We opened it to find a night of incredible stillness, hung with stars. The ghost train had passed away into the deep silence.

FRED ARCHER was for almost a quarter of a century a very significant figure as a writer, columnist and editor of Psychic News, *the world's leading newspaper on psychic subjects. He conducted innumerable enquiries into spiritualism and psychic subjects, always maintaining on open mind and sense of independence when reporting phenomena. Apart from making the subject accessible to the layman, Archer revealed the occult experiences of a number of famous people, notably George Bernard Shaw – who once told him, "I am three-quarters of a ghost" – and Sir Winston Churchill who admitted to a "psychic hunch" during the Second World War which probably saved the lives of members of his staff. This story concerns the actress, Thora Hird, and the events that occurred while she was starring as Emmie Slee in* The Queen Came By, *the tale of a drama in a draper's shop set during Queen Victoria's Jubilee Year.*

GHOSTS WALK ON FRIDAYS

Location and date:
Duke of York's Theatre, London, 1948

One of Jack London's most exciting stories had as its central character a "lifer" who was made to spend long periods of confinement in a straitjacket. Unexpectedly, the prisoner found that he could alleviate the bodily torture by practising some form of dissociation that enabled him to mentally travel through time and space and relive the adventures of past incarnations. The book was called *The Jacket*.

The story I now relate is Jack London's *Jacket* turned inside out, so to speak. For this jacket in no sense liberated. It squeezed tightly and in some cases literally began to choke those who wore it. Yet the garment did not have a forbidding appearance; nor did it conjure to mind the unpleasant associations of a straitjacket.

It was a woman's jacket, a short-backed velvet garment, not unlike a bolero. The style had been fashionable in Victorian times, when it was popularly known as a "monkey-jacket." (The name derived from the similar short coats worn by the monkeys who accompanied Italian organ-grinders around the streets of London at that period.) This particular piece of Victorian finery had survived for more than half a century. Perhaps the events I shall record will explain why no owner had ever worn it to rags.

When clothes were needed to fit out the cast of a play whose action was set at the turn of the century, the time of Queen Victoria's Jubilee, the jacket was found on an old clothes stall in a street market. It seemed just the right thing to be worn by the hard-worked seamstress who was to be played by the leading lady, Thora Hird – who, incidentally, is the mother of Broadway and London star, Janette Scott.

There seemed to be ample room in the coat when Thora Hird first put it on. But after she had worn it awhile she began to feel an unpleasant tightness about the arms and chest. For a time she said nothing, attempting to dismiss the sensation as being due to her own imagination. It persisted, however, and grew even worse.

There came a night when Thora Hird was unable to appear and her understudy, Erica Foyle, had to play the part. It was the first time she had worn the jacket. And she had exactly the same sensation of increasing tightness which, unknown to her then, had been felt by Thora Hird. Something else happened also: that night Erica Foyle saw the apparition of a young woman – and the apparition was wearing the monkey jacket.

It was when Erica Foyle mentioned her strange experience that others in the company became aware that something unusual was taking place. The stage manager, Marjorie Page, heard Erica Foyle's account of her sensations, then later a similar story from Thora Hird. She decided to try the coat herself. It affected her in the same way as it had the two actresses.

The director of the play, Frederick Piffard, was the next person to be told of these bizarre happenings. His wife put on the jacket. For some time she sat with it on and felt no discomfort. It seemed that she at least was immune. But when she took it off those with her were horrified to see that red weals had risen on Mrs Piffard's throat – marks such as might have been made by human fingers attempting to strangle her.

It was at this juncture that I was brought into the story. Freddie Piffard, with whom I had a slight acquaintance, telephoned to see if I could help to solve the mystery. After hearing the personal accounts of their experiences given by the people concerned, I arranged to hold a séance on the stage of the theatre – the Duke of York's in St Martin's Lane – where the play was being presented.

Late evening, after the performance, seemed to be the best time to bring together all the people involved. It was turning the last hour to midnight before we were ready to begin. Those assembled included the cast of the play, the stage manager, the director and his wife – and three mediums.

The mediums had been told nothing of the events leading up to the séance. Each in turn was given the jacket to psychometrize. The first medium was unable to obtain any distinct psychic impressions. The second said he had the feeling that it had originally belonged to a *young* woman but could say nothing further than that.

The coat was then handed to the third medium. He held it for a few moments and then began to describe a dramatic vision. There was a young girl, he said, about eighteen to twenty years of age. She had a sense of guilt about something. In some way she had provoked anger akin to madness in a man who, nevertheless, was not essentially evil. The medium said he could see a pair of hands, the rough hands of a workman, tearing at the girl's clothing. The two struggled violently until suddenly the girl fell backwards and there was a splashing as she was forced into a butt of water.

The assailant then dragged her body from the water and carried it up a flight of stairs into a room, squalid and bare save for two pieces of furniture. There he wrapped the body in a blanket, then carried it downstairs again, still wet and dripping. At that point the visions faded.

There was an immediate, still more dramatic, sequel. From the auditorium, where she had been listening breathlessly, Marjorie Page rushed onto the stage. She said, in great excitement, that the medium's account of events tallied exactly with a vision that had come to her when she wore the jacket. It had seemed so fantastic at the time that she had not spoken about it to anyone.

The members of the company had by now become so excited that it was difficult to continue. It seemed unlikely that the mediums would get much farther in such an atmosphere, so we brought the séance to a close. Most of the people left the theatre, but a few of us went backstage to Thora Hird's dressing room to carry on the experiment in quieter conditions.

After some discussion, Mrs Piffard put on the jacket. She immediately began to breathe heavily and to wrench at the coat, complaining of its growing tightness. So distressed did she become that when her husband entered the dressing room she did not recognize him. But no clearly defined marks, such as were said to have appeared when she wore the jacket a few days previously, could be seen on her throat.

A man who had come along as a friend of Miss Hird and her husband then asked if he might try the jacket. He was well built, which made the coat naturally tight to his physique. Less naturally, he fainted into complete unconsciousness as soon as he had put it on.

Ivan Staff, an actor in the play, was next to try the experiment. He wore the jacket without in any way being affected.

By this time such excitement had been engendered that one had to consider how big a part suggestion was beginning to play. The original experiences that had started the investigation – those of Miss Hird and Miss Foyle – had been individual and independent, according to their testimony. Thora Hird is a down-to-earth north-country woman, and Erica Foyle seemed a sensible and reliable witness.

The story of the girl being murdered as described by the medium and confirmed by Miss Page as matching her own vision fitted in with the fingerlike weals stated to have appeared on Mrs Piffard's throat. But events had now reached the stage where everyone present knew of what had gone before. However honest they might be, if they were at all susceptible to suggestion – and mediums and theatrical folk react more sensitively than most – any additional phenomena were likely to be self-induced rather than revelatory.

Fresh minds, not emotionally involved and having no inkling of what had already happened, were needed if the experiment was to continue. Where to find them at that hour of the morning was the difficulty, for it was now well past midnight and even the West End of London can be almost deserted at that time.

Another newspaperman and myself decided to take a long chance. We would go out and invite the first passers-by we happened to meet. They would be just ordinary members of the public who could have no connection with any of the people already involved – actors, mediums, and press. We walked down St Martin's Lane without meeting anyone. We reached Trafalgar Square, empty save for Nelson and the sleeping pigeons brooding high on his column.

Then across the square, coming towards us, we saw two people. The couple were in their twenties, we guessed as they neared us, a boy and girl apparently on their way home after an evening in town. We explained to them that we were newspapermen working on a story. We needed the help of two members of the public. Would they assist us by coming along to the Duke of York's Theatre, where some other people were already assembled? That was all they were told. It says something for public confidence in the press, or perhaps for our honest faces, that they agreed to follow us down the dark alleyway – an ideal place for a holdup – that leads to the stage door of the theatre.

Nor was any further explanation given after we had taken them into Thora Hird's dressing room. We simply stated that the people present were conducting an experiment and invited the young lady to put on the monkey jacket. They looked mystified but anxious to please. The girl donned the jacket, and everybody watched her carefully while trying to avoid giving the impression of undue interest.

Smiling round on us, obviously wondering what the fuss was about, the girl showed no signs of discomfort. After a while, feeling that the experiment was a flop, we asked her if she felt any particular sensation that she could describe. Her answer was that she felt perfectly normal.

The young man was then asked to just touch the sleeve of the jacket. He put his right hand on the girl's arm. As he did so a queer expression crossed his face. Asked what was wrong, he said he had the feeling of wanting to grip the arm tightly. He placed his left hand on the other sleeve of the jacket, then moved both hands higher. The nearer they came to the girl's throat, he said, the more the impulse grew upon him. Suddenly he wrenched himself away, dropping his arms to his sides.

It appeared that the boy rather than the girl might possess some kind of sensitive powers. When she took off the jacket we asked him if he would wear it. Amid mounting tension he put it on.

Straightaway he appeared to be having difficulty with his breathing. After a few moments he gasped out: "There is something sinister – like death. It feels as if someone were trying to kill me. But in a *just* way."

The young man was now in a state of distress. As he was a volunteer who had been told nothing of what he was being asked to do, we felt that we could demand no more of him.

In a just way. It was a curious phrase to use. As he was being helped out of the jacket I asked him why he had chosen those words. He said he had no idea and could not understand what they meant. I recalled the description given by the medium much earlier that evening: "a girl who had a sense of guilt . . . who had provoked a man who was not essentially evil." Killed in a just way. The two accounts fitted together. A coherent picture had been built up though it was far from complete.

And there we had to leave it. The jacket, whatever the full story of its associations, must have exerted an unusually powerful psychic influence to so strangely affect so many people. Yet to my mind the most remarkable factor of all was that the person who had been most visibly affected, whose reactions probed most deeply into the mystery, was the young man selected by chance from all the millions who might have been abroad in London that night.

And when I questioned him later – his name was Edward Fosbrook and he lived in north-west London – to find out how he reacted to his unsought and, most people would consider, bizarre experience, he added a final coincidental touch to the story.

He and his girl friend had for some time been interested in Spiritualism. There again the odds must have been pretty high against finding two young people who had the experience to be neither shocked nor afraid by the events of that evening.

HEREWARD CARRINGTON was one of the United States' leading psychical researchers for many years as well as the founder of the American Psychical Institute. He was a highly trained amateur conjuror and shrewd observer which enabled him to expose a number of fake hauntings and several fraudulent mediums in his numerous books such as The Story of Psychic Research *(1930),* Psychical Phenomena and the War *(1945) and* The Invisible World *(1947). Carrington travelled extensively in America and Europe for his research, though some of his best and most authentic cases appeared close to home – like this account of a haunted house in New York State to which he took his wife and two "men-about-town" who, he explains, seem more interested in*

the spirits to be found in bottles than a rather violent ghost
troubling a holiday house.

UNDER THE INFLUENCE

Location and date: New York State, USA, 1937

On the night of August 13, 1937, a party of
seven of us spent the night in a reputed
"haunted house," situated some fifty miles
from New York City. I had heard of the house
from a friend of mine who knew the summer
tenant. He had merely told me that the latter
had been compelled to move back to the city in
the middle of July because neither he nor his wife could secure
uninterrupted nights of sleep, and that their servants had all left in
consequence of the haunting. (He had rented the house until the first
of October. He thus abandoned it some two and a half months
before he had been obliged to.) We knew nothing more about the
house than this, except that "noises" had been repeatedly heard.

Our party of seven visited the house on the night in question. The
group consisted of the former occupant, two of his friends, two
friends of our own, my wife and myself. We also brought with us a
dog which had lived in the house while it was occupied, and which,
according to reports, had behaved in an extraordinary manner on
several occasions.

Arriving at the house, we found it dark and locked-up. The tenant
had some difficulty in entering and turning on the lights. This he
finally succeeded in doing, however, and we could then see that the
house was spacious and well-appointed, and that everything had
been left intact.

I suggested to the owner that, before hearing anything about the
house and its history, it would be a good idea to explore it first of all
from cellar to attic, to see that no practical jokers were hidden
anywhere, and that no cats, bats, rats, mice, or what-not were
present to account for the disturbances. To this he readily consented,
and lighted the house from top to bottom.

Examination of the cellar and the ground floor revealed nothing
unusual. On the second floor, however, two or three of us sensed
something strange in one of the middle bedrooms. This feeling was
quite intangible, but was definitely present, and seemed to be
associated with an old bureau standing against one wall. (The noises

had been heard by Mr X and his wife from the large bedroom on the side of the house.)

Walking along the hall, we came to a door which had escaped our attention the first time we had passed it.

"Where does this lead?" I asked.

"To the servants' quarters," Mr X replied. "Would you like to go up there?"

"By all means," I said, opening the door.

Glancing up, I could see that the top floor was brilliantly lighted, and that a steep flight of stairs lay just ahead of me. Leading the way, with the others close behind me, I ascended the stairs, and made a sharp turn to the right, finding myself confronted by a series of small rooms.

The instant I did so, I felt as though a vital blow had been delivered to my solar plexus. My forehead broke out into profuse perspiration, my head swam, and I had difficulty in swallowing. It was a most extraordinary sensation, definitely physiological, and unlike anything I had ever experienced before. A feeling of terror and panic seized me, and for the moment I had the utmost difficulty in preventing myself from turning and fleeing down the stairs! Vaguely I remember saying aloud:

"Very powerful! Very powerful!"

My wife, who was just behind me, had taken a step or two forward. She was just exclaiming, "Oh, what cute little rooms!" when the next moment she was crying, "No! No!" and raced down the steep flight of stairs like a scared rabbit! (She had not run up or down stairs for more than two years because of an injury to her back, but she flew down the stairs and past those coming up after her without even seeing or touching them!)

May I say, just here, that both my wife and myself are old-time investigators, quite unemotional and thoroughly accustomed to psychic manifestations of all kinds? My wife is a keen, cautious observer, who has sat with many mediums and exposed many frauds. I myself have done the same, and also participated in the Palladino séances, where I believed genuine phenomena were occurring, remaining quite unperturbed when "materialized" hands were pulling me about, passing their fingers through my hair, and so forth. All that time I was dictating to the stenographer precisely how I was controlling the medium – how her hands, feet and legs were being held – as our report on these sittings will show. I remained throughout quite calm and cool, as I have at innumerable séances and investigations since. But in the present instance the reaction was most intense, and almost more physiological than psychological. It was distinctly a bodily and emotional reaction – accompanied, I must confess, by a momentary mental panic and sensation of terror such as I have never known before.

Two or three of those following me had by this time reached the upper floor, and I called out a few times to my wife. Hearing no response I descended the stairs to the lower floor, to see if she had fainted or was ill. I found her sitting on the porch, breathing deeply and slowly collecting her scattered faculties. She assured me that she was all right, and would come up again in a few moments. Her first reaction had been to get into the fresh air.

Leaving her, I ascended the stairs and found the others filing down from the upper floor. Every one of them had experienced the same sensation to a greater or lesser degree. My friend G. B. had likewise experienced the utmost difficulty in swallowing, and tears were running down his face as though he were weeping copiously. All the others were similarly affected.

Having no professional medium with us, we decided to sit for a time in the front bedroom on the second floor, to see if any sounds could be heard, or phenomena of any kind noted. We accordingly arranged ourselves in a sort of circle, prepared the camera and flashlight bulbs, and turned out the lights.

We sat thus for perhaps an hour, during which time nothing visible manifested itself, and (apart from some dubious thumps on the ground floor) nothing unusual was heard. The distinct feeling of a presence was, however, sensed by two or three of the party. (Personally I did not feel this.)

I should say here that the two friends of the late tenant – men-about-town – had looked upon the whole expedition as a sort of lark, and had brought with them a bottle of Scotch and a bottle of gin, intending to have an amusing evening. Every half-hour or so they would go down to the kitchen and mix themselves a stiff drink. It is interesting to note that these cynics experienced the same sensations as the others, and that they also reported difficulty in swallowing, tears running from their eyes, cold perspiration on the forehead, and other physical symptoms as did the rest of the circle.

After sitting for an hour or so with no concrete results, we decided to sit in the upper room, where the original powerful "influence" had been felt. Accordingly, we ascended the stairs – but this time not a sensation of any kind was to be felt! The room seemed absolutely clear of all influences, clean, pure and normal. It felt just like any of the other rooms. What I had previously described as a heavy, malign gas instead of a normal atmosphere was no longer there. Nothing unusual was to be sensed by any of us, and a brief sitting in the room produced no results or untoward sensations whatever.

After our original inspection of the house, and our first violent reactions, the former tenant had told us its history, disclosing for the first time the fact that a suicide had actually been committed on the upper floor, and that these rooms were thought to be the "seat" of the haunting. We had known nothing of this on our first trip, purposely asking for no information concerning the history of the house until we had explored it.

The dog, which on the first occasion had positively refused to go with us into the upper storey, ran up the stairs quite naturally the second time, wagging his tail, prying into all the corners and behaving as any normal dog would. When we had tried to coax him upstairs the first time, he had growled, planted his feet before him, and refused to go forward a step. The hair on his back had stood up like that on a cat; and he behaved, in short, very much as dogs are supposed to behave in the presence of ghostly phenomena. In the present instance, however, it was factual, and I saw it with my own eyes.

It was by this time past five o'clock and getting light, so we decided to call a halt and return on another occasion, bringing with us a medium, as well as apparatus for recording possible sounds, for testing the air in the upper rooms, and so forth. Unfortunately, "the best-laid plans. . . ." One of the friends of the tenant "talked," and a brief note appeared in the papers a day or so later, which the owner of the house saw and read. As a result, he positively refused to allow us to visit the house again, and our most persuasive powers proved of no avail.

One of the most curious cases of a haunted house I have come across was one which I investigated some years ago, in Astoria, Long Island. It is a long story, which I must summarize briefly.

One morning a young man called upon me in a very excited state of mind. He told me that he was living in a house in Astoria, and that he had not only heard footsteps stamping up and down the stairs at night, but that he had, on several occasions, seen a white figure, which had even lain down on the bed beside him, so that he could feel its weight, and also the springs of the bed tremble. When he had turned up the light, however, there was nothing there.

In addition to this, he had received a series of alleged "communications" from the spirit of an old man, who had lived in that house about half a century before, as well as from other visitants. These communications stated that there was gold (valued at several million dollars) buried under the house!

Greatly excited by this, my young friend had begun to dig, and, when my wife and I went over to visit him, we found the cellar filled with earth and rocks, which he had dug up, and a hole more than thirty feet deep which he had excavated. So far no treasure had been discovered, but he was anxious to know if I could help him in any way – particularly in solving the mystery of the ghost.

I spent several nights in the haunted house, but saw and heard nothing of interest during my visits there. In order to check his story, however, I took with me, on three occasions, amateur and professional mediums, to see what their impressions would be. Needless to say they were told nothing as to the house, or its history.

The mediums were never permitted to go downstairs until *after* the sitting, and they knew nothing of any digging operations. I had rather come to the conclusion that the buried treasure was a pure fantasy, and rather hoped that these mediums would say, "There is no treasure here; stop your digging!"

Instead of this, however, they one and all agreed that there *was* a treasure buried under the house, and two of them drew diagrams of an alleged tunnel, near which the buried treasure lay, which had led, many years before, to an old Dutch church, about a quarter of a mile away. This was curious, since none of these mediums knew one another, and no one knew of any such tunnel.

This seeming confirmation naturally stimulated the owner of the house to more intense efforts, so that he spent nearly all his waking hours, both day and night, digging. The entire cellar was filled with rocks and earth which he had excavated. He entirely neglected his business, and worked frantically.

The upshot of this bizarre story is something of an anti-climax. After weeks of digging, no treasure had been found, and the authorities somehow got wind of his activities. One morning they visited the house, and stated that he was endangering its foundations. The poor man was compelled to fill in the immense hole he had so laboriously dug, and all ghostly manifestations ceased. Soon after this, I understand, he moved from the house, and I have heard nothing from him since.

One strange occurrence, however, *did* develop. Inquiries revealed the fact that an old Dutch church had actually stood upon the spot indicated, but that it had been demolished in 1883. This our young friend (an uneducated Sicilian) certainly had no means of knowing. Much of the information given by the mediums was certainly supernormal, inasmuch as they had made statements which were subsequently verified, and had drawn almost identical diagrams of passages, excavations, rooms, and so forth, which they had never seen, but which subsequent measurements proved to be correct!

JOSEPH BRADDOCK, a life-long enthusiast of the weird and the mysterious, was present at a number of the Society for Psychical Research investigations and wrote numerous essays about the supernatural as well as a bestselling book on Haunted Houses *(1956). The book is notable for the investigations Braddock made into photography and ghosts – examining hundreds of examples from the crude Victorian fakes with superimposed portraits to contemporary photographs revealing unexpected people and faces on the negatives. Here Braddock describes one of his most unusual enquiries at a haunted house in 1955.*

PHOTOGRAPHING A GHOST

Location and date: Abthorpe, Northampton, 1955

On October 27, 1955, I received a letter from Calverton Rectory, Wolverton, Bucks, the relevant part of which read as follows: "I am proposing to go with a professional photographer to take night photographs at the old haunted Manor House at Abthorpe, of which we told you and sent you some snaps. We are making this expedition on Monday, 31 of October (*Hallowe'en*). Would you be able to manage to join us? If so, will you make for this address on Monday next. The Rector says he will be very pleased if you will stay at the Rectory for the night." The two gentlemen concerned make a charming pair, an old man and a young man, the Rev. R. Bathurst Ravenscroft and Mr L. E. Stotesbury-Leeson, whose bond, besides friendship, is the Ministry and their common devoted interest in Genealogical researches. Unfortunately, I was lecturing in Bournemouth on the evening of October 31. I let them know my disappointment. The date was considerably changed for me, and I motored to Calverton Rectory on All Saints' Day, November 1.

Mr Stotesbury-Leeson is a direct descendant of the Leeson family of Abthorpe, springing from those of Whitfield and Sulgrave which

appear in the Heraldic Visitations of Northants as far back as the
time of Edward I. Not until after the Reformation was the house –
called Abthorpe Vicarage for very nearly the past two hundred years,
but still to this day known to many as "Leeson Manor" – purchased
by the Leeson family from the Ouseleys of Courteenhall near Northampton. It has remained part of the Jane Leeson trust from 1648,
when "Mistress Jane Leeson died April ye 1st" as the simple record
of the parish register runs. Little is known of "Mistress Jane,"
beyond the facts that she built the village school, which bears under
one of its gables the inscriptions FEARE GOD AND HONOUR Y KING
and JANE LEESON HATH BUILDED THIS HOUS FOR A FREE SCHOOL
FOR EVER. 1642; made an endowment to the church to help provide a
clergyman; left a charitable trust consisting of various annual be-
quests to a number of neighbouring parishes, and died a spinster. The
payments began in 1649 and have continued regularly, the trustees
meeting, until recent times, in the council chamber, as desired by Jane
Leeson in her will.

This pre-Elizabethan Manor, empty and derelict, had fallen into
a sad state of disrepair. On pushing open the warped gates, one
stepped into a wilderness of undergrowth, the drive over-sha-
dowed by yews. Neglected lawns ran up to the worn stone walls;
and, as one entered through the low Tudor doorway, one saw the
long hallway, with dust-strewn rooms to left and right. The right-
hand wing consisted of the Monastic Grange, the oldest part of the
house. Here, in the council chamber Mr Stotesbury-Leeson discovered in 1954 through the crumbling of the inner wall from
damp, a curious chamber or cavity reaching down to the ground-
floor, which looked like a "priest hole." From an attic a collapsed
wall gave another view of the "priest hole" and the false wattled
wall of the council chamber. Certainly the space within the wall
could have concealed a man and might have been used, in times of
religious persecution, as a refuge. The council chamber has its own
eerie atmosphere. In this room there has been seen by one of the
trustees and by others, the apparition of a Franciscan Friar. He is
generally seated, reading a book; but on being disturbed, he glides
across the chamber and disappears into the wall near the "priest
hole."

Mr Stotesbury-Leeson told me that very few of the villagers cared
to pass by the house after sunset. On Sunday, October 31st, 1954,
Mr Bathurst Ravenscroft and he had taken some photographs of the
outside of Leeson Manor in the middle of the afternoon. They made a
tour of the house, ascending a narrow oak staircase to obtain a view

of the "priest hole" concealed within the thickness of the walls. Mr Stotesbury-Leeson writes:

"While I was investigating the inside of the 'priest hole' my companion, who was standing behind me, experienced the chill of some unseen presence, which passed off in a few moments but gave him the feeling that 'it' was there.

"We descended the stairs to the hall and went into the garden, intending later to return and make a further search of the house. Taking up positions on the lawn for photographing the exterior, I clearly sensed that something flashed past me, which quite startled me; and turning my head, I exclaimed 'What was that!' After about a minute (the front door being open) a door within the house, previously closed, opened and closed again with great violence. We sensed a feeling of psychic strain, so much so that we refrained from returning to the house. The sale of the property is in question and we had been discussing this topic.

"As the first member of the Leeson family to enter the house for three hundred years, I was photographed by Mr Ravenscroft in the Tudor doorway. On having the photographs developed, a figure is clearly to be seen standing on my left-hand side, partly in the shadow and partly with the sun shining through it upon the stone lintel. I have three of the photographs in front of me. The first was taken at approximately 3 p.m. and shows the doorway quite clear. The second, taken at 3.10, reveals a figure on the right of the print, half on the sun-lit stonework, half in shadow. In the third photograph, taken a few minutes later from further away, the figure has moved a little more to the left but is not very distinct."

When I reached Calverton Rectory on the night of November 1, 1955, the first thing I learnt was that the professional photographer had been prevented from coming, or perhaps had thought better of the expedition! However, he had lent his up-to-date camera and photographic equipment to Mr Stotesbury-Leeson, who used an Ilford H.P.S. film, with a flash gun fitted to the camera. After supper we drove some fifteen freezing miles in brilliant moonlight to Abthorpe. Altogether we spent three full hours, from 9.15 p.m. until almost 12.30 a.m., making our investigation in the derelict, abandoned, yet not wholly forsaken, Manor House.

I may as well say at once that the photographs were a failure and revealed nothing paranormal. But Mr Stotesbury-Leeson makes this comment: "Curiously enough the long exposures are mysteriously blotted out, in spite of the special film, the clear moonlight night, and the great care we took to adjust the camera each time we used it.

These are the ones on which we set our hopes, and even now I feel that had the stills taken of the Tudor doorway been successful, you would have had at least one good photograph of a spectre."

"Not wholly forsaken" – because we both heard quite unaccountable sounds. There had been a full moon the night before: from a bitter cold clear sky, that brilliant dead world of dry terrible mountain-peaks looked down on us. As to the possibility of movement and any consequent noise, the air was as still as it could be. I am certain that there was not a breath, not a twig; and, no, not a rat nor a mouse stirring.

Mr Stotesbury-Leeson heard more than I did, but this was probably my lack or defect. I felt no psychic chill or sense of unease when I crossed the threshold and entered the first room on the left of the hall. Neither did I feel fear nor discomfort in any other part of the house, only a detached but intense curiosity about what might happen next. I was hoping for proof; to see something.

My companion walked to the door and stood outside. I shone my torch, though the moonlight coming through the broken windows made this almost unnecessary. Suddenly I heard a noise, like a thump or muffled bark; but Mr Stotesbury-Leeson, who heard it also, has described it as a "sort of scraping rushing sound." For a long time we heard nothing more, except the loud clang of a row of rusty bells that my friend set jangling with his walking stick!

Now we went upstairs into the Leeson council chamber where all seemed peaceful as we took several photographs, the camera pointing towards the "priest hole." We invoked Mistress Jane to reveal herself, with no result whatever. We then made separate circuits of the house, shining our torches everywhere, finding nothing unusual. But afterwards, on account of the noises each of our movements produced, we decided to keep together.

It was in a small room in the north-west corner of the first floor that we both heard the oddest sounds of all. I stood by the dusty mantelpiece, Mr Stotesbury-Leeson closer to a half-open window of diamonded glass. It was bitterly cold and we drew our scarves and greatcoats tighter round us. Moonlight broke upon the diamond panes, faintly adulterating the room's darkness, light and shadow shafting down on walls and floor. We stood, for perhaps fifteen minutes, calm, transfixed, neither of us speaking or wanting to speak. The moments seemed long and it is difficult to be positively certain of what one heard. My ears, of course, may have built up imaginary noises, but I don't think they did. Whenever we had stopped talking, the silences could almost be heard. Then a sibilant sound came to me, like a small lisp, a lament, the whimper of water. A strange feeling tingled through the nerves of my skin.

Mr Stotesbury-Leeson heard this, too, and something more; but he shall speak for himself: "I became aware of a noise like a dull groan with a roar, similar to a strong wind blowing through a small hole, which seemed to come from under my feet. The room below was the one where I had heard the first scraping rushing sound. I went downstairs, but now had the impression of hearing the same sound above me. I returned to the small north-west room upstairs and resumed my old position. After I had requested whatever spirits there might be to make themselves known, I noticed a faint sound as of running water which gradually increased in volume and seemed to come closer. It was only afterwards that I remembered that Mistress Jane Leeson had stated that she hoped her Charity would last 'For as long as the sun shines *and the water flows*,' a play on the family coat of arms." Mr Stotesbury-Leeson thinks that his after-thought and theory about the water hits the nail on the head. Could that faint approaching Presence, if she was trying to make herself known to us by the sound of flowing water, have been his ancestor, Jane Leeson? As in so many occult matters we should be content to say we do not know. We must begin and end with a question mark, while we go on seeking.

But now it is time to set a term to our small inquiry about ghosts, which could be extended indefinitely. Maybe the strictly scientific lines upon which the S.P.R. today is working, with its praiseworthy aim of making psychical research respectable by drawing it into the laboratory, will prove most fruitful for man's advance into the Unknown. We live in a universe far more wonderful than any of us can fully contemplate, and the next stage of man's evolutionary development might well be – like wing from chrysalis – that of his psychical unfolding. Wise scientists have always recognised the limitations of science: in a subject so linked with spiritual, not to mention diabolical, knowledge we need not neglect other direct approaches, such as the mystical and the religious. If we are studying the whole of Reality, surely there need be no antithesis between spiritual and material existences, for they may interpenetrate. The scientific approach to these profound mysteries, though most valuable, is not the only one.

*CORAL LORENZEN owes her fascination with the unknown –
and her career as a writer and investigator of the occult – to a high
school teacher who sensing her interests, urged her, "If you're
curious, Coral – inquire!" Later, while studying journalism and
English, she was encouraged to read the books of Charles Forte
and realized there was nothing so weird it was not worth careful
investigation. Lorenzen's numerous books have ranged across a wide
variety of subjects from Unidentified Flying Objects to Monsters of
the Deep and any number of American ghost stories. However
objective she tried to remain in the face of the inexplicable, Coral
Lorenzen could still be surprised as she reveals in this episode from
The Shadow of the Unknown (1970).*

THE BREAK-IN FROM BEYOND

Location and date: New Mexico, USA, 1958

Although I have been extremely interested in
poltergeists for the greater part of my life, I had
always rationalized the intriguing stories of
flying bottles, stones, rappings and tappings,
and was not really firmly convinced of the
reality of the phenomena until I myself had
an unnerving experience. It happened this way.

A summer evening in 1958 ended as usual. We were living in our
home at 1712 Van Court, Alamogordo, New Mexico. The weather
was very hot and, although the desert in that area cools considerably
at night, a house does not lose its heat until the early hours of the
morning. The house, only two years old, had a large evaporative
cooler on the roof which sent damp cooling air through the house.
The heat from the roof, however, made sleep difficult.

We had been in bed for some time and, trying to get even a little
more breeze, I pushed the sheet down and pulled up my pajama top
to let the air blow across my midsection. I was going through a
mental exercise to hasten sleep, as our waking time was six a.m. and
it was drawing close to midnight, when I felt icy fingers pass across
my stomach. Immediately thinking my husband Jim was trying to
play a joke on me, I turned toward him. But he was lying in his usual
place, his back toward me and, if he was not asleep, he was at least
quiet.

It didn't take long for me to chalk the whole thing up to my
imagination; I pulled up the sheet, turned on my side and took up my

sleep-inducing exercise again. Then a sharp sound startled me. It was as though someone had dropped a very thin china piece on a hard cement floor. There was the initial sound of the object striking the floor, then a tinkling sound as the pieces apparently came to rest.

Thinking that one of the children (we had two – a boy of 8 and a girl of 13) had gotten up and broken something in one of the bathrooms, I slipped my feet into my slippers and set out to investigate. The bathroom shared by the children was dark and empty; I turned on the light and looked around anyway. There was nothing to account for what I had heard. I then went to the children's rooms where I found them both asleep, and nothing amiss. Deciding at this point that perhaps something had somehow fallen in our private bathroom I investigated there too but nothing was wrong; everything was in its place.

By this time I was extremely curious and set about a methodical tour of the house and even the patio, turning on lights as I went. I even examined the children's rooms, and they didn't stir. The patio was as devoid of any broken china as was the house and eventually I decided that the whole thing had been my imagination, as had the incident with the "icy fingers," and went back to bed.

The next morning I arose as usual, made my husband's breakfast and sat down with him to have my first cup of coffee. All thoughts of the events of the previous night had completely left my mind, so when Jim looked up from his eggs and said, "Did you find what broke last night?" I almost jumped out of my shoes. I asked him how he knew that something had broken and he said that he had heard it also. Not believing that I couldn't find the cause, he himself made an inspection of the house and grounds before he left for work, but he found nothing. The final disposition of the affair was a curious look between us because we both knew that something outside our understanding had taken place.

At about this time, both my husband and I had been indulging our curiosity about psychology and had been reading extensively from the works of Carl Jung. We found that Jung had formulated a theory to account for such things and had, like some other psychic researchers, found that when poltergeist phenomena are manifested, there is usually an adolescent child in the affected house. Jung felt that an "autonomous particle system" exists, wherein a part of a developing child's personality splits off during puberty and becomes an independent spirit for a while, retaining a form of "psychokinetic energy" capable of the many feats attributed to "noisy ghosts." In other words, the energy causing the poltergeist problems actually originates from a splinter of personality in an adolescent child.

This type of explanation appealed to both my husband and me, not so much because it came from Jung, for whom we had the greatest respect, but because it was reasonable, and certainly fit the facts – the strange noise had occurred in the presence (whether sleeping or awake) of adolescent children.

NANDOR FODOR was born in Hungary, studied law, but on a visit to America in 1926 became intrigued by all the research going on into the supernatural – in particular cases of poltergeists and the theories of Freud and the poltergeist powers of Jung. In his pursuit of information, Fodor travelled extensively and for time worked as a journalist in Britain where he compiled an Encyclopaedia of Psychic Science (1934). *His investigations led to him being appointed Research Officer of the International Institute for Psychical Research and resulted in several classic works, in particular* On The Trail of the Poltergeist (1958) *about the famous Thornton Heath poltergeist in England. Another not dissimilar case two years later in America excited his interest and resulted in this report published in* Fate *in 1964.*

THE BALTIMORE POLTERGEIST

Location and date:
Meridan Drive, Baltimore, USA, January 1960

On January 14, 1960, at the house of Mr Edgar J. Jones at 1448 Meridan Drive in Baltimore, Md., a typical poltergeist outbreak was reported in the local press the mental background of which promised to be rewarding for psychoanalytical inquiry.

I left for Baltimore on Wednesday January 20, and arrived shortly after midnight. On the train, from the meagre information in my possession, I tried to form a picture of the motives that could have activated this poltergeist. I was told of a young boy of 17 who was not a Jones but went under the name of Ted Pauls. It was not clear to me that he was a grandson and, pardonably, I derived the wrong impression that he had given up his family name.

The assumption that he was trying to escape from his family by a change of name was erroneous. But I was informed that he was an ardent science fiction fan and devoted all his time to this particular interest. It seemed to conform to my first impression of escapism. Basically, science fiction serves well for an escape from mundane limitations. In the case of a writer of science fiction there would be a sublimation of the need of escape by turning it into creative channels through story-telling of the magnificence of far-off worlds whirling in the depth of space. In the reader, however, the relaxation and entertainment found in such fantasies may well be a screen for the archaic yearning of returning into the prenatal state. A distinct planet, in the womb of space, is an excellent substitute for the "fetal island" (the child being in its own universe) where earthly (postnatal) ties had not yet existed. One would be hard put to find a better escape from reality than a journey into space.

Ted Pauls did not write science fiction. He was satisfied with editing a multigraphed discussion sheet called *Fanjack*. I thought that this might bear on the escape motive. Then it occurred to me that interstellar space and the worlds scattered in it are also the habitat, in science fiction stories, of nonhuman life. There is a corresponding facet to that in embryonic evolution antecedent to the fetal stage. The thought intrigued me because the linguistic equation of Ted Pauls with tadpole does take back to the nonhuman stage. What is in a name? Shakespeare had asked the question but did not answer it, at least not to the satisfaction of psychoanalysis. I have dealt with the problem in a comprehensive manner in an essay entitled *Nomen est Omen*. Could Ted Pauls have fallen under the spell of his name? (I found out afterwards that his father did pronounce his name as Poles instead of Pauls.) An impish thought followed and I began to chuckle: it would be funny if he had long legs like a frog to leap off into space. As a science fiction fan he would be acquainted with Abraham Merritt's *The Moon Pool*, an outstanding classic in which giant frogmen from Lemurian times stalk the earth in underground caverns.

On my arrival, this fantasy was nurtured by local information. Ted Pauls had long legs; moreover, he walked like a frog with widespread feet and when sitting in his favourite rocking chair, the chandelier, set swinging by the poltergeist, always moved from North to South. This seemed to be a secret signature as North and South are determined by the poles. Ted Pauls? The rocking, of course, hinted at cradle days or at the undulating movements of the maternal body during the period of gestation. I was told he assumed the rocking position automatically and seemed to derive a great deal of pleasure from it.

There it was then, a wonderful fantasy of escapism, which turned out to be entirely my own fancy. Observations in the haunted house quickly pushed it into the background. The chandelier could well act in unison with his rocking as the living room, where the rocking chair was, was longitudinal to the dining room in which the chandelier was hung. Hence, North and South was a natural direction. The kitchen was latitudinal, but it was not a place for continued stay. It was therefore unnecessary to connect the swinging chandelier with rocking memories. The topographical situation was sufficient to account for the preferred movement.

Moreover, Ted Pauls' interest in science fiction was not devoid of a creative and sublimatory element (to which I shall presently return). I brought up the question of Merritt's *The Moon Pool* in a discussion of science fiction books. He could not have had any idea that the question was baited. He answered that he had never read the book. (I inspected his library later. There was one book by Merritt in it, but it was definitely not *The Moon Pool*. The reality situation soon disposed of the fancy that Ted Pauls was a frog. The natural narcissism we have for our names must have completely blinded him to the tadpole interpretation.

So my fancy did not expose him. It only exposed myself as a fantasy fan of strong mystical inclinations. And that was precisely the approach I used with Ted Pauls.

I took with me to Baltimore a science fiction book: Asimov's *Nine Tomorrows*, and inscribed it to him "as from one science fiction fan to another." It was a first and fortunate meeting point between us. For, as I found out, by this time Ted Pauls was getting bitter and hostile to publicity, to the presence of a crowd of journalists and to the nuisance he and his family were exposed to. One frustrated journalist demanded that he should confess to a conscious responsibility for the flight of objects and for the explosive manifestations that accompanied it. He was roused and wrote a letter of angry protest to his editor, a protest very well composed and completely ignored. There was a distinct possibility that the situation would become further aggravated unless a face-saving was presented to the baffled journalists.

My appearance on the scene as a "poltergeist expert" fulfilled this need. They did not have to have an opinion of their own. They could quote me and hang everything on my statements.

So I had an ideal opportunity to release the pressure in both camps. The journalists were easy. They were courteous and respectful. The problem was Ted Pauls. Could I win his full confidence?

Frankly, I did not know. I was floundering in a sea of uncertainties. While I had not witnessed any disturbance, I accepted the record. It was carefully compiled by a fellow researcher, Douglas Dean. He examined every witness and arranged for a number of scientific tests to rule out the recondite physical factors that people like to fall back on. A prima facie case was established for poltergeist activity. Hence, the key to the mystery had to lie in the psyche of Ted Pauls. He was above the pubertal age but things had been happening in the house before, at Christmas time, for instance. Twice in the preceding years the decorative blue balls on the Christmas tree exploded with no known reason. I thought he must have had a strong grievance against Christmas. His birthday was on December 16th, but his grandfather assured me that they never pooled his birthday and Christmas gifts. Christmas is a universal birthday symbol. His own birth preceded it by nine days (the term of gestation in months), but I was assured that his birth was normal, and that he had suffered no injuries during delivery, hence the existence of a trauma of birth could only have been proven from Ted Pauls' dreams. He did not have any to tell me.

Nevertheless, the Christmas mystery cannot be dismissed too easily. Birth can be a crippling experience. It survives in the unconscious as such. It may strongly reinforce other feelings of imperfection and provide, through a rebellion against Fate, an unconscious motive for poltergeist activity. As far as I was able to find out, Ted Pauls had no physical defect, just little peculiarities like his walk, his pixie looks and the odd slant of one of his eyes, making him appear slightly Chinese. I had no time to consult his family doctor or his school psychiatrist (a job with which Douglas Dean had charged himself), but I did find out, from a careful conversation, that he was not crippled in his sexual development. While he had no girlfriend, he did have fantasies about girls and only his shyness kept him away from their company. His sexual development was apparently quite normal, hence the cripple motive could be disregarded.

But before more is said of his motivation, let us place emphasis on the fact that the pubertal disturbance might have been responsible for the poltergeist activity, restrained as it was, at Christmas time. It is an important stage of transition, that well may have mobilized the unconscious imprint of the greatest transition we ever make until death; the entrance into postnatal life. No doubt an explanation could be found for the dormancy period, but I did not have the time to pursue this line of investigation.

The question is often raised why such disturbances should be confined to one person in the household only. Could not there be a contribution from other sources; a kind of pooling of paranormal talent?

We can safely rule out the grandparents because of their age. (At seventy or more one has no vitality to waste.) We can also rule out the parents because they are away during the day. Could we consider the dog?

Hardly. There are no polterdogs. Kristy, the three-year-old female Schnauzer was not an agent but a victim of the poltergeist. She cowered and tried to hide before the phenomena took place. She crouched at the door and scratched frantically in order to be let out. This used to happen a few seconds or minutes before something flew or exploded. Her behaviour was the best evidence that something spooky was going on in the house.

Had I told Ted Pauls that the poltergeist activity was due to a projection of his repressed aggressions against someone in the house (parents or grandparents) he would have turned indignantly against me and would have withdrawn into a shell. It is a delicate matter to tell somebody that he is guilty of something he knows nothing about. However, it is not enough to speak of aggressivity in general terms. Specific reasons should be found. He was not a chronic bed-wetter or sleep-walker in childhood. He had not been exposed to humiliation on either account. But his toilet training could have been over-severe. I know at least of one instance within my clinical experience in which a psychotic disposition developed on this basis alone. His mother was not available for an interview and Ted knew too little about himself. He was not a loquacious young man. He had no friends and lived in his room like a monk in his cell. And there was nothing visible to indicate a disturbed relationship with his parents or grandparents beyond the fact that they did not approve of his quitting school at sixteen and living for science fiction alone.

Grandfather was a retired fireman of 70. He served the Fire Department for 37 years. No doubt he must have regaled his grandson with plenty of stories of his exploits. Like a war horse ready for the bugle, his short-wave radio was going all day to receive signals of fire. He had an easy way to become a hero ideal for his grandson. Proof of it could be seen in Ted's extraordinary interest in fires. This interest caused me anxiety when told about it on my arrival. The thought occurred to me that he may be studying for arson. There have been incendiary poltergeists in the past. Spontaneous combustion is a far more dangerous phenomenon than the hurling or smashing of objects. It could easily result in loss of life in a gutted house. But I found that his interest in fires was open and above board. It was most unlikely to become an idea for the poltergeist. While it is true that in one case a can of fruit dislodged from a shelf full on grandfather's head, this single incident was not enough to suggest that his aggression was directed at the old man. But the old man owned the house and the house was shared by Ted's parents. Any destruction in the house would hit both parents and grand-parents. Against this stands the fact that material damage was slight. More valuable items were avoided and when removed to a safer place were not singled out for destruction.

Before discussing further the problem of motivation, let us con-sider the question of the mechanics of poltergeist activities. This is the central mystery. It is not enough to say that the poltergeist is a bundle of projected repression. We should want an answer as to how this projection takes place. What is the nature of the energy involved? Is it muscular, nervous, electric or electronic? How does it work?

We do not know. Therefore, the best we can do is speculative approach. I would call the poltergeist manifestation the result of somatic and psychic dissociation. Somatic dissociation is something new. It has never been postulated before. It means that the human body is capable of releasing energy in a manner similar to atomic bombardments. The electron shot out of its orbits round the proton is like a bolt of lightning. It can be photographed streaking through the air in a cloud chamber. It is a purely mechanical energy. The atom, as such, has no power to impart direction to it. A human being has. It appears that under strong emotions not only does such a discharge (happily without chain reaction) take place but that the energy thus released is under control. A poltergeist-thrown object can travel slowly or fast, it can change course as if part of the psyche of the projector would travel with it, as if the somatic dissociation that releases it would not free it from mental control. But even that hypothesis leaves a great deal unexplained. The explosive effect may be due to pressure in the unconscious, it may partly release it or it may act as a S.O.S. calling for help. But in the Baltimore case the force was apparently able to enter Coca Cola and soda bottles that had not been uncapped and burst them from within. In one instance, a flower pot of plastic material, wide open at the top, was cracked on both sides by an explosion within that left the plant in the middle undisturbed and the pot itself standing. It indicated that the bilateral explosion was exceed-ingly well balanced. It hinted at brain activity similar to that of an electronic computing machine.

So much for the physical aspect, the elucidation of which fell within the range of Douglas Dean's investigation. My job was to find motives and then decide on a course of action.

The theory of projected aggression could not be dismissed just because the cause of it was not apparent. An unconscious storm may well rage behind conscious compliance with an existing situation. Ted Pauls *was* subjected to too much pushing around. He was not suffered to have a goal of life of his own choosing. The fact that he had no friends strongly suggested that the relationship between himself and his schoolmates was not a good one. He might have been subjected to too much teasing and name calling. There was his walk, his pixie looks, his tendency of withdrawal and his intellectual superiority. (He claimed that the school could no longer teach him anything. This was not due to a swollen head because school authorities describe him as a brilliant boy.) Bitter against his schoolmates, smouldering for not being understood at home, tension must have been growing deep within. He was a well-mannered boy, exceedingly courteous and careful to preserve appearances and not lacking in courage if he was provoked.

When I first saw him, he faced a crowd that he hated, but he faced it and the only sign of the tension in him was the whiteness of his knuckles as he gripped the arms of the rocking chair. To tell him that he was a monster inside would have been considered a preposterous accusation. I just did not know what to do until, out of the blue, a key was presented by the reading of a page of his editorial writing found in the cellar near the multigraphing machine. To my utter amazement I found that this young boy had a great talent for writing. At seventeen he was an accomplished journalist. His vocabulary had left nothing behind and his editorial handling of *Fanjack* showed a rare maturity. He was bursting with a rage for writing and no one in his immediate surroundings understood or appreciated him. They considered his preoccupation nonsensical and drove against it with all their might. Was it, I queried, that the poltergeist activity arose from his frustrated creative rage?

At this thought I began to breathe easily. I found a therapeutic approach to the problem of the poltergeist. The boy had talent that clamoured for expression. Playing the editor was the only balm for his crushed ego. It elevated him above his readers. If then a depressed ego was hiding behind the poltergeist rebellion, raising of his self-feelings to a higher level would stop the release of his creative channels into abnormal channels. If frustrated creativity was responsible for the explosive manifestations, increasing self-confidence and acceptance of his personality by people around him would cancel the poltergeist. He would be lifted to the heights instead of sinking into the depths.

I explained this to Ted, and he drank in the explanation with relief. But I realized that I had yet to prove my sincerity. He may have had his mental reservations about me. So I went out on a limb and stated on television and on radio that I had discovered a boy-wonder who had surprising literary gifts and that recognition of his talent would seal the breach in his psyche and stop the poltergeist for good. I suggested that he should be commissioned to write the story of the poltergeist and give his own treatment to the subject. It would be not only a worthwhile document but also one of scientific value. His unusual somatic talent was not necessarily evidence of madness; on the contrary it may have heralded a gift that the race may possess in the future.

One thing I was certain of, that what I did was good therapy. That was more important to me than to be too scientific. I know I was taking considerable risks. I could not be sure that I was right and that the poltergeist phenomena would stop, but I knew that my publicly expressed confidence in him would pay dividends.

It did. I became an angel of the Lord for Ted Pauls. He was walking on air, beaming with happiness and basking in the sudden change of parental and grandparental attitude. Suddenly they were proud of him and respected him. He was no longer an irresponsible boy of seventeen. He was a man with a great future ahead. He became the pride of his family.

No room could be left for the poltergeist with such an uplifting of the ego. His psychic energies could no longer explode downwards. He was out to reach the heights. However, I had failed to take into consideration that Ted Pauls might not willingly consent to my departure at such a short notice, that he may well stage a tantrum through Poltergeist activity against the severance of the important emotional tie formed with me.

The result was that the poltergeist activity did not immediately cease, rather it reached a crescendo of rage and frustration. Psycho-analytically, this was part of the working-through process. While it appeared to go against my therapeutic approach, actually it did not do so. The protest from Ted Pauls' unconscious level was not maintained too long. It gradually died.

The case is important because accidentally I tumbled on a novel cure of the poltergeist psychosis. (So described by me in my book, *Haunted People*.) It is as simple as the egg of Columbus. Find the frustrated creative gift, lift up a crushed ego, give love and confidence and the poltergeist will cease to be. After that you can still proceed with psychoanalysis, release the unconscious conflicts, but whether you do it or not, a creative self-expression will result in a miraculous transformation.

SUSY SMITH earned an enviable reputation during her long life as an investigator of parapsychology and the supernatural in America, travelling across the length and breadth of the continent to prove that as many inexplicable events occur in the States as in Europe. Among her most popular books were ESP: The Uncanny World of Extrasensory Perception (1962), Reincarnation (1967) *and* Prominent American Ghosts (1968) *for which she visited many old houses and, she says, "met a few of the ghosts – but I'm not sure." There does not seem to be much doubt about her visit to a school, though, as she recalled in this report written in 1967.*

THE BURNLEY SCHOOL SPOOK

Location and date:
Seattle, Washington, USA, 1965

In doing research for my work I have made it a practice never to visit ghost houses with mediums. If a psychic person has happened to be along, I have noted his impressions; but it has not been my purpose to attempt to communicate with the alleged entities who haunt the houses I have visited.

Once, though, I found myself in a haunted school in the company of four mediums, and it was an experience I'll never forget. This is what happened.

The Burnley School of Professional Art, at 905 East Pine Street in Seattle, Washington, had loud creaky footsteps on the stairs and locked doors that opened in the night for about six years, until they abated somewhat in the spring of 1965. I made an appointment on 4 October 1965 with Jess Cauthorn, the owner-director of the school and one of the Pacific Northwest's best-known watercolorists, to visit his school and interview several of the students who had heard unexplained activity in the building. Since I was in Seattle also to study the manifestations of the medium Keith Milton Rhinehart, we decided to ask him to join us later and see what psychic impressions he received there.

The Burnley School is on the corner of Broadway and Pine Street, across from a very old public school now known as Edison Tech. The Franklin Savings & Loan Association occupies the street-level offices of the building, and the art school takes up the two top floors. The structure was originally designed to be a cultural and art center; and it had studios for ballet and piano and a large auditorium on the second floor to be used for special events. Its first official function was a reception for President William Howard Taft when he visited Seattle to open the Alaska-Yukon-Pacific Exposition of 1909. For some years a dancing club known as "Entre Nous" used to rent Christiansen's Dance Studio in the auditorium, for student affairs which were the big social events of Broadway High School each season.

There was a period when the auditorium was used as a temporary school gymnasium for the overflow from across the street; but the ceilings were so low that basketball players had to invent trick shots – such as banking the ball off the ceiling. When the dancing teacher complained that the noise was disturbing his classes, wrestling mats were brought and placed against the gym walls to muffle the noise.

In 1946, Edwin Burnley, a well-known Seattle artist, opened art classes there and taught many budding painters, including Jess Cauthorn, who now owns the school. The big gym has been turned into a classroom full of adjustable wooden desks at which students work during the day, and which the ghost apparently resents exceedingly. He makes noises at night as if he were moving the desks around – great scraping and scrunching sounds as if he were trying to drag them out of there. He is better in the audio department than the material or physical, for nothing is ever actually disturbed in the morning – except the people who had to listen to the noises the night before.

Jess Cauthorn told me that he, himself, has heard these manifestations. He had never believed in ghosts until that time. He isn't really sure that he does now, and yet . . .

"I'm a realistic person," Cauthorn said, "but there are some things you just can't ignore – like the sound of desks being moved in an empty room behind locked doors."

Jess thought that perhaps the ghost had been more active in recent years because, "We've had to enlarge the school to accommodate more students. This meant going into strange nooks and crannies, opening up heretofore unused rooms and employing the long-locked-up back stairway in order to get to new classrooms. That's probably what disturbed the ghost, who, apparently had not been too active up until then."

John R. Nelson, a tall young student, illustrated for me the sound the ghost made on the stairs. He went down and clomped up the wide flight leading from the first floor to the third. The steps are very creaky, and each footstep squeaked in its own specific way. There was no possible doubt that the sound was just that – a footstep on a stair. John said that, when he had been working on a big art project and didn't want to stop, he had sometimes painted most of the night. When he was all alone in the building, and knew he was all alone, he would hear, at any moment between eleven o'clock at night and three o'clock in the morning, footsteps mounting those stairs. He would naturally go to see who was arriving, but nobody was there. At least, no physical presence was there.

"I was scared to death at first," said John.

"Can you ever get used to a thing like that?" I asked.

"Not really," he replied. "You just learn not to work here alone at night."

"You wouldn't get me here alone, even without a ghost," I said, being somewhat of a sissy about big, empty places.

"New students don't believe it, of course," John went on. "But after they've been here some of them work late at night and then they hear it. Jennie Miller . . ." and John nodded toward a girl who had just come into the room, "didn't believe it at first. And she even stayed in the building several nights and didn't hear anything . . ."

"But when I finally did," Jennie interrupted him, "I went bellowing down the hall. I was all alone here and I wanted to run out, but I was scared to go down the stairs."

The students got together and devised tests to catch the haunt. With masking tape they fastened thread across doorways about three feet off the floor. The next day, when they were sure that they had been the last ones out at night and the first ones in in the morning, they found some of the threads broken. On another occasion they stretched the thread across the stairway. Then they turned out the lights and waited upstairs. Some time later, they heard the steps come up both flights; but on examination the thread, which a living being would either have broken or knocked down, was intact.

Lest it be suspected that the noises heard on the stairs were just the normal creakings of old buildings, the students ask how that accounts for the fact that when they hear someone climbing, the creaks are sequential in order from bottom to top.

Cauthorn did not want his students alone there at night if there was any possible danger that a robber could be getting into the place in such a clever way that no one could catch him at it. So he had an insurance investigator check over the building carefully. When the place was pronounced perfectly safe, with all the locks and doors and windows secure against intruders, Jennie again worked late in her studio.

"While I was concentrating hard on my sketches," she told me, "I heard a bang, and then a creak, and then the sound of somebody walking. Naturally I had all the lights on, and I hurried out into the hall to see who it was. Nobody was there." Later that night she heard a key go into the lock of the front door and the squeaking sound of the door opening. "I rushed out and looked down the stairs," she said, "but the door was not open and not a soul had come in."

Jennie's friend, Ellen Pearce, had a studio on the third floor, and they worked there sometimes at night. The main light switch for that floor is on the inside of a room, and you have to grope your way across in the dark to find it. One night the girls heard a moan behind the door of that room, like a human being in great agony. Wondering who could possibly have gotten in there, and what could be happening, they fumbled their way across to the light switch, almost petrified with fright.

"But can you imagine our state when we got the light on and looked behind the door and no one was there?" asked Ellen.

I could. But I said I'd rather not.

Another student, Robert B. Theriault of Seattle, found a certain small room, used by the students for resting and coffee breaks, to be the most sinister of all. Once, when the lights were on in there, he was standing outside the door, but he knew someone was inside because he heard sounds as if magazine pages were being turned, and other movements. However, when he started to enter the room, the rustling stopped, and there was no one in there.

Henry Bennett is a commercial artist who had an apartment on the third floor while he was a student at the Burnley School around 1959–60. Cauthorn told me, "Hank was responsible for the security of the building at night. But often in the morning I would find the front door, or the fire door, wide open, or at least they would be unlocked when I arrived. Sometimes I really chewed Hank out, but he always insisted he had locked the doors and checked the place over the night before. I didn't know what to think."

Bennett confirmed to me that he always carefully locked the building each night. But the doors were often unlocked the next morning, and sometimes even open. "Many curious things happened while I was living there," he said. "You would swear someone was walking up the stairs or moving furniture in some room, or some unseen person was doing construction work on the building. But when I'd turn on the lights, nobody was ever there." Henry Bennett said that the ghost had not scared him; but he was talking from a distance of five years from the time of the events in which he had been involved.

I was to get close to events within a very short time – for the mediums were gathering. Clyde Beck, a member of the American Society for Psychical Research and an individual who believes in attempting to work with all the equipment of a modern technician, had arrived first, loaded down with movie cameras and tape recorders – none of which were usable when things got interesting. By then we were all in the dark, and he had been unable to secure infrared lights and film. After Clyde, came several of the younger mediums of Rhinehart's church – the Aquarian Foundation. Then came the feature attraction of the evening – Dr Keith Milton Rhinehart, himself.

Actually an intelligent young man of twenty-nine, Keith was at that time affecting a mustache and goatee and a loud sports jacket – and he looked more like a beatnik guitar player than the pastor of a church. He brought a few more people with him; so it turned out to be altogether a much larger group than we had anticipated.

Since many people know little about mediums except the reputation some of them have for being fraudulent, I think perhaps I should take a moment here to discuss the subject. Extrasensory perception (or ESP) is not uncommon. Those who have a great amount of it are known as mediums, or "sensitives," or "psychics." They may be born with the natural talent in large degree, or they may have some slight ability and decide to improve it, by sitting for development in classes at which a trained medium presides.

I have sat in a number of development groups myself, and have begun to exhibit an interesting amount of telepathy – I can sometimes see a picture clearly in my mind of something another person is at that moment thinking. I have on one or two occasions gone into a trancelike state. I was not then completely unconscious, but my mind was "withdrawn" to the extent that I was not consciously instigating the words that were spoken through my mouth, words that purported to come from a deceased entity. Whether or not what I said came from my subconscious, I cannot state. I am only sure that certain information was given through me which I did not consciously know, and had not acquired normally.

Because of my own personal experience with this, I am aware that the material mediums produce may be genuine. I also know the effort, the countless hours sitting in classes, which many sensitives spend in order that their psychic talents may be developed as fully as possible. For this reason I must say definitely and firmly that all mediums are not fraudulent.

Yet I know that, just as there are quack doctors and shyster lawyers, there are phoney mediums. I have seen some who put on such sham acts that it was disgusting; and I have been furious, not only with them but with the gullible public who allowed themselves to be taken in by such trickery.

Keith Rhinehart is a natural-born medium who also spent years improving his native capabilities, beginning when he was in junior high school. When he is in good form, his powers are excellent. I have seen much evidence that, when he is entranced, genuine information has been given through him that he could have no possible normal way of knowing. This is usually referred to as "mental" mediumship. Although extremely adequate as a mental medium, Keith prefers to be known as a "physical" medium – one in whose presence curious physical phenomena occur.

One of his special abilities, it is claimed, is the production of "apports" – objects that are said to have been dematerialized from somewhere else on earth and then rematerialized inside the seance room. If the room has been thoroughly searched beforehand, the possibility of trap doors and secret compartments and false arms and bottoms to chairs, etc., eliminated, and the medium has been stripped and examined by a doctor, and *then* apports appear during the seance – it is hard not to consider their appearance as a supernormal manifestation. In the history of psychical research there is evidence for the appearance of apports, under conditions that have been so controlled as to give no opportunity for fraud.

I have seen apports appear in a lighted room under what I considered to be controlled conditions; but still I am reluctant to declare firmly once and for all that the phenomena were genuine. Many investigators much more highly trained than I have also hesitated to commit themselves. This is because there are some mediums who are so adept at prestidigitation that it is difficult for anyone ever to guarantee absolutely that he might not have in some way been hoodwinked.

I am going into this in such detail because of the events which followed at the Burnley School. I want it understood that I do not point an accusation of fraud at anybody for what occurred on the evening I am about to describe. And yet there is no possible way for me to be certain that there was not at least some lighthearted trickery involved. Then again, maybe there wasn't. After all, we were in a building with a reputation for being haunted.

The members of Keith's organization who came with him to the Burnley School that night had trained themselves very carefully, sitting hour after hour in dark rooms letting their natural mediumistic talents develop. I felt, and still feel, that they are sincere workers at their trade. In this group were Judith Crane, a very pretty, well-educated young woman who has gained considerable prominence as a medium, and her fiancé, Donald Ballard, whom she has since married. Don is not a medium and is only a follower of psychic interests insofar as they affect Judy. I can't help but believe that Don would have been furious if he had observed in Judy or her associates anything he thought was in any way dishonest – yet he was with the Aquarian Foundation members all the time that evening. The two other Aquarians present were Kenneth Bower and Helen Lester. The rest of the crowd that began to tour the haunted school included Jess Cauthorn, his students John Nelson and Jennie Miller, Clyde Beck, and me.

As we moved through the building I took notes on the impressions each sensitive expressed. Some were interesting in the light of the history of the school: It was sensed that there had been dancing and basketball in the big auditorium and that there had been exercise mats there at one time. But all this had been published in various newspaper accounts of the haunting which had appeared over the years, one as recent as June 1965, so the mediums could be given no special credit for their successes even if they were genuine "hits." There is always the chance that they may have read the articles.

Several persons stated that a young man had been killed in or near the building long ago, and that he still hangs around and wants to dance and play basketball and have fun as he used to. (Unfortunately for the veracity of the tale, checks with the police since then have revealed no record of a killing in or near the school. An Associated Press reporter made a serious effort to track down verification of a murder, but with no results).

We first decided to try to hold a seance in an area of the basement that had an unpaved dirt floor and old boards and boxes stacked in the corners. There we turned off the lights and sat at first with only one small candle. After a moment, we put that out and sat in the dank dark. Fortunately for my peace of mind, after later developments, some of the girls decided that there might be rats down there, and so we adjourned upstairs. At that time, none of us was in the least afraid of the ghost.

We finally chose a small room on the second floor, just large enough to hold the ten of us, and we put opaque screens over the windows and turned out all the lights. Just enough glow came in around the edge of the screens from the streetlight outside so that we could dimly see those closest to us. Keith and I sat on a short couch, and the others milled about in the dark for a while.

In order to learn if there might be any spirit about who wanted to make an effort to communicate, all those in the room except Keith and me put their fingers on the top of a tall stool. Almost at once it began to move around, so fast that they kept up with it only with difficulty. The stool banged itself with great force against the floor and the wall. It was asked to answer questions in code, with one rap for "Yes" and two for "No"; and it did give some answers this way to a few questions. But whatever was propelling the stool had no interest in such attempts to talk. It preferred to show off its great force by banging itself senselessly against the wall.

Keith and I got monstrously bored watching this – it is very routine in mediumistic circles. Catching me yawning, he asked if we should call it all off and go home.

"In a few minutes," I said, "if nothing else happens."

Soon the game with the stool palled on the participants, and they all settled down quietly, pulling their chairs into a circle facing Keith and me. After a few moments of extreme silence, when the full impact of the darkness crept over us, I glanced toward Keith – and suddenly realized that he was staring at me fixedly with the most malevolent expression I have ever had directed my way. He kept it up, not moving, for at least three minutes. The way he looked, with his dark hair, glittering eyes, mustache, and goatee, one could almost suspect that the devil himself had become incarnate in our midst. Not being quite unsophisticated enough to believe *that*, I decided instead that the medium must have been taken over into trance, and prepared myself for a discussion with some spirit entity who was obviously "earthbound" and must be convinced that he should stop haunting this school. I began racking my brain for suitable phrases from those who had published their experiences involving other such delicate situations.

"Who are you?" erupted suddenly and loudly from the medium.

I jumped a foot and a half into the air and started to shake. "We're here to help you," I quavered. Then I began to explain to him that he had passed through the experience called death and that he must adjust himself to that fact and go away and stop bothering the people at this school – that there were helpful spirits around him who would give him advice and assistance if he would but listen to them. . . .

"I'm not dead," he shrieked, interrupting me. Then he lunged at me, waving his arms, and shouted, "Get out! Get out, all of you!" And no matter how much I talked to him he kept repeating this refrain with the appropriate motions. It was coming to my attention that the techniques that may have worked for those glib writers who had calmed obstreperous entities with a few well-chosen words were not likely to be so successful in my case. I started on a new tack.

"Did you know it is the year 1965?" I asked.

Keith almost leaped out of his seat. 'No, no," he cried. Then apparently taking a second to estimate, he added, "That would make me sixty years old. I'm not old. I'm young!" Yet, as if the idea of his death were beginning to penetrate after all, he began to mutter about blood and a knife. "Blood all over everything," he said, and then such things as: "He got me in the back. I just wanted to stay here and play games and dance but John did me in. He did it; blood, blood, it spurted! The knife dripped blood! John did it. He always hated me." Then, as if taking me for his false friend John he leaned toward me once again, with a look of utter viciousness, and shouted into my face, "Get out, all of you. Go away and leave me alone."

As this dialogue is now written, from notes made the day after the episode, I am appalled by how silly it all was. Even as I sat there participating in this drama, the realization was very present that it was overplayed and amateurish. In retrospect the whole evening seems a trivial travesty of a bad movie or a television turkey.

But while the events were going on and I was participating in them, it was rather necessary to take them at face value, which was not in the least comfortable when the entranced medium kept jumping my way threateningly from time to time. Finally, he lunged and waved his arms in my direction just once too often and I got up and moved over to a bench just opposite the couch. The Thing, whoever it was, by then was muttering irresponsibly to himself, and I saw him glance down at my expensive camera which was on the floor beside where my feet had been. Lest he be inspired to break it, I reached over and picked it up.

As I did so, the maniacal look on Keith's face made me think, "Oh, if I could just get a picture of this for the book." I began to sight the camera at him. Fortunately, I did not have time to flash the bulb – for if it is true, as I have since learned that all spiritualists believe, that any flash of light or sudden shock might kill an entranced medium, it might have been I instead of a ghost who was the villain of this piece.

When the camera went up to my eye, Keith cried, "What are you doing?" and made a leap for me.

I shouted, "Don't you touch me!" and kicked him. It was just a little kick – and it barely connected with his leg; but he plummeted to the floor as if I had landed a rock on his skull. I didn't do anything then for a minute but sit and quiver. Then I began to worry for fear the medium was badly injured, because he was lying there prone, breathing as if each gasp might be his last. I had not more than touched him, but it was evidently enough to have caused the entity to lose his hold.

All of us sat with eyes glued on him, to see if he would come out of it; finally, we heaved sighs of relief as we heard the deep sonorous tones of the medium's special "spirit guide," who acts as his "control" and takes care of him, saying through him, "This is Dr. Robert John Kensington, and we have things in hand." Keith, still entranced, but now by his proper control, got up and sat back on the couch, Dr. Kensington apologizing all the while for having allowed him to be taken over by such an irresponsible entity. He said that he had not realized that the spirit was actually insane until he had gotten into Keith's body; and that the number of mediums present acted as a battery that gave the entity more power.

Keith then came out of his trance, asked for a drink of water, and sat holding his head, complaining of a violent headache. He asked what had happened, and somebody began to tell him. I was doing a lot of thinking, very negatively. If this had all been an act, it was such an overdone performance that it was hardly worthy of Keith's histrionic ability . . . yet if it had not been put on – Good Heavens! I'd been in real danger! I turned and said, perhaps a bit sarcastically: "How did it happen, may I ask, that all of you sat there so calmly while I was being attacked by a maniac?"

The Aquarian Foundation members told me that they knew that touching the medium when he was in such a state would have injured him.

"But what if I had been injured?"

"You didn't have a thing to worry about," they assured me. "We were surrounding everyone with protective thoughts, so everything was completely under control." Under control? I almost had a camera wrapped around my head!

Keith had nearly been clobbered, too, Jess Cauthorn told me later. When we had a long retrospective chat about the evening's experiences he said that he and John Nelson had been sitting on the edges of their chairs, signaling each other, and ready to spring if the medium got one inch closer to me. They had been considering the entire thing to be a clumsy hoax; but they wondered why, if it was a hoax, Keith had not known he was going too far and would be in danger from them if he got the least bit rough. This was part of the whole big mystery. If he was putting on an act, why did he not realize the possibility of being physically restrained by those two men so much larger than he? There were many mysteries about this evening that have never been resolved; and this was one of them. Yet the biggest mystery of all occurred after we left the seance room. It put a slightly different light on the whole performance. But it did not solve anything. It only made the confusion worse.

Rather depressed by the episode that had just taken place, I had gathered my nerve, my wits, and my camera and walked out of the seance room to try to get another picture or two of the school building. I was accompanied by Keith and Clyde Beck. The others remained in the room and then spread out, eventually going downstairs. The three of us walked back down the hall and into the auditorium, around a corner and about fifty feet from the seance room. After discussing the possibility of getting a photo of the large room, and deciding it would be useless to try with my equipment, I started to walk back up the hall. Hearing a funny sound from Keith, I turned to look at him. His eyes were getting that glassy, glittery look again, and he began to mumble, "I told you there was something I could do you couldn't" and other phrases that weren't particularly intelligible. He approached me menacingly.

"It's got him again," I shrieked, rushing up the hall away from him. "Clyde, *do* something!" Clyde did something; he watched to see what was going to happen next. I moved on as quickly as possible, hollering to the people downstairs. Aquarians came bounding up, and as they did the medium began to speak once more in the deep tones of his control. "This is Dr Robert John Kensington," he said. "The entity got back in once again because there was something he insisted on saying. Will you please call the owner of the building?"

Jess Cauthorn was just arriving up the stairs on a run, and he said breathlessly, "I'm here."

"Do you recall if there was a rock about the size of a brick in that room where the seance was held?" Dr Kensington asked.

"No, I don't think so," answered Jess. "I'm almost sure there was not."

"Well, the entity was trying to say that he had the power to bring apports," the voice went on. "Now if you will go into the seance room you will find a rock there close to where Miss Smith was sitting."

We all rushed into the room, and sure enough, right where my feet had been when I sat on the end of the bench, there was now a smooth, oval rock as large as a brick. It could not have been there when my feet were cringing in that spot a few minutes before.

The next day, at my suggestion, students went into the basement of the school building and reported that they found a hole the exact size, into which the rock fit neatly. It was in an area of the dirt where there were a few other similar stones scattered about. They immediately decided that this was the proof they needed that the whole thing had been a hoax. But it really wasn't necessarily that convincing. Even if the rock had come from there, this would not prove it wasn't an apport, because an apport has to come from somewhere; and the spirit would not in that brief interval have gone wandering afar to dig one up. He was said to be haunting *this* place. If he had decided he wanted a rock to heave at me, would he have thought of looking anywhere else for it?

As can be imagined, we all did a great deal of arguing and conjecturing for days afterward. All except Keith Milton Rhinehart, who went home with a terrible headache and was said to have been confined to his bed. As we thought about the apport and tried to explain it, we realized that the medium, being a rather slight man, could not possibly have hidden so large a rock on his person in order to bring it up from the basement without being observed. If one of the women members of the Aquarian Foundation had managed to secrete it somewhere (in some oversize handbag?) how did Keith, down the hall with me, know about it?

The only answer, except one really dealing with ghosts and apports and other supernormal things, is that the whole event was an extravaganza put on by the entire group of mediums in collaboration, to show the visiting author a good time and give her something to write about. But Keith and all the others knew that I was prepared to write scathingly about them if I discovered them in anything fraudulent, or even in anything particularly suspicious looking. They were aware, moreover, that they had much more at stake than a haunted school, for I was in Seattle investigating whether or not the phenomena of all Keith's services and seances were genuine; and I had a magazine contact that they knew was eager for the story. Why, under those circumstances, would they play stupid games with me? Why also would Keith have run the risk of being injured when he leaped at me, knowing full well that the non-Aquarians in the group would certainly have defended me?

Although my experience at the Burnley School was effective enough to scare me temporarily out of my wits, it could not have been permanently convincing. Of all the questions raised by this incident, the biggest that remains is this: If the Aquarians *had* decided to put on an act, why wasn't it a *better* act? These were intelligent adults, not children; they couldn't have been stupid enough to have produced such an overblown, overacted melodrama and expected it to be believed.

But an old, earthbound spirit so dumb as to hang around a school for sixty years without knowing it was time to graduate – he might have acted just the way he did that night. After all, we *were* in a building in which a great many genuinely unexplainable manifestations had already occurred.

I came out of this whole adventure with only one conclusion: You'd better keep your cool if you're going to fool with an old school ghoul.

HANS HOLZER is probably the best-known ghost hunter in America. Director of the New York Committee for the Investigation of Parapsychology and Psychic Research, he has investigated countless hauntings, written over 150 books and made numerous radio and television appearances. He is a scientifically trained archaeologist and historian, which has given an added dimension of authenticity to his most popular works such as Ghost Hunter (1963) *and* The Great British Ghost Hunt (1975). *Holzer has written of several personal encounters with the supernatural of which this story from his own neighbourhood of New York is one of the eeriest.*

THE MAN IN THE UNIFORM

Location and date:
Riverside Drive, New York, 1963

"Please help me find out what this is all about," pleaded the stranger on the telephone. "I'm being attacked by a ghost!" The caller turned out to be a young jeweler, Edward Karalanian of Paris, now living in an old apartment building on Riverside Drive. For the past two years, he had lived there with his mother; occasionally he had heard footsteps where no one could have walked. Five or six times he would wake up in the middle of the night to find several strangers in his room. They seemed to him people in conversation, and disappeared as he challenged them on fully awakening.

In one case, he saw a man coming toward him, and threw a pillow at the invader. To his horror, the pillow did not go through the ghostly form, but slid off it and fell to the floor, as the spook vanished!

The man obviously wanted to attack him; there was murder in his eyes – and Mr Karalanian was frightened by it all. Although his mother could see nothing, he was able to describe the intruder as a man wearing a white "uniform" like a cook, with a hat like a cook, and that his face was mean and cruel.

On 9 March, I organized a seance at the apartment, at which a teacher at Adelphi College, Mr Dersarkissian, and three young ladies were also present; Mrs Ethel Meyers was the medium.

Although she knew nothing of the case, Mrs Meyers immediately described a man and woman arguing in the apartment and said there were structural changes, which Mr Karalanian confirmed.

"Someone is being strangled . . . the man goes away . . . now a woman falls and her head is crushed . . . they want to hide something from the family." Mrs Meyers then stated that someone had gone out through the twelfth-floor window, after being strangled, and that the year was about 1910.

In trance, the discarnate victim, Lizzy, took over her voice and cried pitifully for help. Albert, Mrs Meyers' control, added that this was a maid who had been killed by a hired man on the wife's orders. Apparently, the girl had had an affair with the husband, named Henry. The murderer was a laborer working in a butcher's shop, by the name of Maggio. The family's name was Brady, or O'Brady; the wife was Anne.

After the seance, I investigated these data, and found to my amazement that the 1812 *City Directory* listed an "A. Maggio, poultry," and both an Anne Brady and Anne O'Grady. The first name was listed as living only one block away from the house! Oh, yes – Mr Karalanian found out that a young girl, accused of stealing, had killed herself by jumping from that very room!

MARC ALEXANDER claims that his interest in the supernatural began as a child when he was given a book of stories by Algernon

Blackwood, one of the great ghost story writers of the twentieth century, who, he learned had based a number of his fictions on events that occurred to him in places as varied as the backwoods of Canada, the heart of New York City and the rural English countryside. Alexander began collecting and investigating stories of hauntings in the 1950s and published a series of collections during the next thirty years. Despite his intense research, he admitted to never having seen a ghost – although this had done nothing to dampen his enthusiasm – although he did have one very unnerving experience in the late 1950s that left an indelible impression on him as he recounted in Phantom Britain *(1975).*

THE STEPS IN THE STAIRWELL

Location and date:
Strand, London, UK, 1959

When it is known that I have written books and articles about hauntings, I am invariably asked if I have ever seen a ghost. I have to confess that, although I have slept in quite a few haunted bedrooms, I have never yet glimpsed one, perhaps because I am not psychically developed enough. But I certainly have sensed things and experienced some odd happenings when going about Britain in search of material, and on one occasion I believe I heard a ghost. I know to *hear* a ghost does not sound particularly exciting in comparison to other hauntings described in this book, yet when I realised what it was, I experienced a brief but memorable feeling of sheer terror and I can confirm that the hair on the back of your head does rise.

The story goes back to the autumn of 1959 when three journalist friends of mine invited me to join them in a publishing venture. The idea was to publish a weekly trade magazine for the television industry which we called *Television Mail*. It was an exciting adventure and we plunged in with the confidence that comes through lack of experience. After the euphoria of seeing the first issue come off the printing presses, we suddenly realised that we had to produce another magazine for the following Friday and so on. Our financial resources were pitiful and for our editorial and advertising offices we could only afford two small rooms on the third floor at 408 The Strand, one of the oldest buildings in the street.

My experience occurred one Wednesday, which was the day before we went to press. This meant that, because of our lack of staff, I would be working very late sub-editing material. At that time our reporter was a friend named David Wisely, with whom I had worked on a New Zealand newspaper. He kindly said that, although he had to go out that evening, he would return about midnight to help me finish the final copy.

At twelve o'clock I heard footsteps echoing in the stairwell which rose from landing to landing of offices similar to ours. The steps were extremely slow and laboured, and I thought that Mr Wisely, having perhaps looked upon the wine when it was red, would probably not be in a condition to be very helpful.

The heavy steps continued to resound in the stairwell and then paused at the landing outside my door. I looked up, expecting it to open and for Dave to wander in with a typically cynical remark about the trade press and *Television Mail* in particular. To my surprise I heard the footsteps suddenly continue, slow and measured, up the final staircase which led to an accountants' office above us.

It was obvious someone from that firm was going up to burn some midnight oil. At the time I did not think it was a burglar because one would expect somebody following that profession to be suitably light-footed. It seemed as though the person whose footsteps they were had all the cares of the world on his shoulders. I carried on with my work, envying the absent Mr Wisely who had presumably found something better to do. Three or four minutes later I heard the steps again, just as slow and measured. They came down the stairs, paused outside my door and then continued down the stairway.

This time a nagging voice at the back of my mind told me I ought to investigate. I knew it was unlikely to be a prowler as the front door was always heavily locked. Yet for some reason I remember a certain reluctance to do so. Summoning up my determination, I went to my door, flung it open and stepped out on to the landing to find it in complete darkness.

Whoever had been coming up and down had not needed the lights which were placed on every landing. The steps were still sounding on the stairs as I pressed the switch which illuminated the stairwell from top to bottom. As the yellowish lights came on it seemed that the footsteps faded away, and as I gazed over the banisters, I realised with that feeling of shock that I was alone in the building. The stairwell was deserted, the lights shone on the blank doors of locked offices. I went down the stairs and tested each office door and the front door. It was securely locked. I returned to my desk with mixed feelings, rather like the little boy who saw an elephant for the first time and declared: "I don't believe it."

I thought of the usual things: was it the creaking of old woodwork, had my ears been playing tricks? But no, the memory of those footsteps was too vivid and detailed.

The next day I went up to the office above in the hope of finding some explanation. Speaking to one of the accountants I inquired if his office had been burgled or if there were signs of anything unusual having taken place. He said he had found the door locked when he came that morning and nothing had been disturbed.

"Have you been hearing things?" he asked. I replied that I certainly had and told him about the footsteps.

"Oh, you're not the first to hear those," he said. "I can't explain what they are but I think in some way they are related to an incident which took place a few years ago – a man committed suicide here in the attic . . ."

PETER UNDERWOOD is as well known as a ghost hunter in Britain as Hans Holzer is in America. A member of the SPR for many years, he served as President of The Ghost Club and was once described as having heard "probably more first-hand ghost stories than any man alive". He has investigated scores of haunted houses and from his comprehensive files produced a number of highly regarded volumes including Gazetteer of British Ghosts (1971), The Ghosts of Borley (1973) *and his autobiography,* No Common Task (1983). *For all his diligence, Underwood admits he has not experienced as many ghosts as he hoped, but remains convinced that some "thing" or force does exist.*

THE FEN MYSTERY

Location and date:
Wicken, Cambridgeshire, UK, 1971

In the heart of the Fen country and only a mile from Wicken Fen, the stretch of land that has remained unchanged since the days of Hereward the Wake, there stands an isolated collection of buildings grouped round an imposing farmhouse known as Spinney Abbey.

The name was derived from the ancient priory which formerly occupied the site. Ghostly singing monks, mysterious lights and strange figures have been reported here.

The original Spinney Abbey was for the last fourteen years of his life the home of Oliver Cromwell's distinguished son, Henry, who settled here after he had lost his lands with the return of the Stuarts. It was here that the reputed "stable-fork incident" took place. King Charles II, returning from Newmarket with his retinue, visited farmer Henry Cromwell, and found him farming contentedly. A member of the King's party thought it a fine jest to take up a pitch-fork and carry it before Cromwell, parodying the fact that the farmer had been mace-bearer when he was Lord Lieutenant of Ireland. The mortal remains of this well-loved son of the Protector rest in the little village church where a brass plate tells us that he was the best of Cromwell's sons. Carlyle once said that had *he* been named Protector, English history would have taken a different turn in the seventeenth century.

Now the occupants are the Fuller family and I remember that one of the first things Tom Fuller showed me were some fragmentary ruins of the old building, built in the twelfth century. Part of it was now a piggery and I was told that the pigs, although contented enough elsewhere, are often seen to be fighting whenever they occupy that part of their enclosure. I remember, too, examining the cellars, remnants of the old building with reputed secret tunnels, and seeing the remains of a grating and the attachments for primitive handcuffs showing that the cellars were used as dungeons.

One of the most frequent unexplained happenings here was a mysterious twinkling light which was often seen between the house and Spinney Bank, about a mile away. The lights have been observed within a hundred yards of Spinney Abbey and once a local man saw a light move away from him and illuminate a mill almost a mile distant. Witnesses never seemed to be able to get near the lights for as soon as they are approached, they drift away and when the observer stops, the lights seem to stop too. Such lights are often *Ignis Fatuus* (from the Latin: foolish fire), usually seen in the vicinity of marshy places and churchyards and are sometimes known as "Will-o'-the-Wisp" and "Jack-a-Lantern". They are generally accepted as being a natural although incompletely understood luminosity, due perhaps to the spontaneous combustion of decomposed vegetable matter. At all events, the Fullers told me that local people will go a long way round to avoid Spinney Bank at night.

Outside the room where I learned of the many strange happenings at Spinney Abbey, Tom Fuller told me of the figure of a monk that he had seen glide slowly along the garden path and disappear at an angle of the house. The hood of the clothing which the figure wore covered its face so that no features were discernible but Mr Fuller wondered whether the ghostly monk had any connection with the murder of an abbot at the original Spinney Abbey in 1406. Other people, too, have seen a ghost friar here and sometimes ghostly footsteps, slow and measured, sound and resound about this quiet house.

One Sunday morning unexplained chanting was heard in the west part of the house by six people, including three of the children of old Robert Fuller, who were now telling me about the strange happenings they had encountered over the years. Music, faint but distinct, accompanied the Latin chanting. The whole thing was over in a few seconds but all the six people in the room at the time heard and agreed upon the unmistakable sounds. Robert Fuller himself had heard the same sounds some years before but he heard them in the stack-yard and they appeared to come from fourteen feet above the ground. "Clear as a bell," he said; "pure and sweet, all in Latin; and just where the old Chapel of the Abbey used to stand."

Mr Fuller's daughter Unis and her husband told me that they had heard something they had never been able to explain. It was a curious, uneven, rolling sound, like a coconut being rolled over the floor. After a while it ceased; then it began again and it was heard intermittently throughout that one evening, never before and never afterwards.

During the course of a night I spent in the grounds of Spinney Abbey I placed delicate thermometers at strategic spots: in the piggery where the pigs always fought, the place where the chanting had been heard, another spot where an unexplained female figure had been seen on one occasion and finally where the monk walked. Readings were carefully recorded every ten minutes throughout the night. No thermometer showed any abnormality – except one. Each of them steadily declining from around 31°F at midnight to 24°F at six a.m. But the thermometer placed where the ghost monk walked showed a sudden and inexplicable drop in temperature of seven degrees! This occurred at two-ten a.m. and was verified by my two companions; yet the other thermometers showed no similar drop. This one was no more exposed than the others and in any case ten minutes later, this thermometer showed the temperature back to normal and in line with the others. I have thought of many possible explanations but none that I can accept as probable. It is interesting to note that some horses stabled nearby were quiet throughout the night except at the exact time at which this sudden and unexplained drop in temperature occurred. At exactly two-ten a.m. the horses suddenly made a terrific noise in their stable, kicking their stalls, whinneying and neighing loudly. Gradually they quietened down and by the time the thermometer showed a normal reading at two-twenty a.m. the horses were quiet again. Horses, like cats and dogs, are believed to be supersensitive, so perhaps some shade of a ghost passed near to me that night.

ANDREW GREEN as a member of the SPR and Ghost Club devoted his life to investigating cases of hauntings and his book, Our Haunted Kingdom (1973) *is one of the most comprehensive collections of over 350 reports of paranormal activity ever published, while his* Ghost Hunting: A Practical Guide (1974), *is one of the most instructive. Green founded the Ealing Psychical Research Society and apart from conducting numerous ghost hunts, lectured widely on psychic phenomena and appeared regularly on television. In April 1996 he was famously called upon by the Administrators of the Royal Albert Hall to investigate alleged supernatural phenomena in the building. Appropriately, Green lived in a haunted house, as he describes here.*

THE WOMAN IN WHITE

Location and date: Robertsbridge, Sussex, 1972

My home in Robertsbridge, Sussex, is haunted. Built about 1725 as a pair of tied farm cottages on the Egerton estate, this rather attractive cottage was practically rebuilt in 1971 when the conversion was made into a single building. A rear wall built with stones from the mediaeval villa known as Glottenham Castle, the site of which is about two miles away, had to be removed and reconstructed with modern brick. The stones, however, have been retained in the garden.

Within three feet of the pair of privies in the back garden a copper powder flask was found which suggests that at some time flintlocks were used to defend the privacy of the occupier, though part of a Roman glass bottle was also found in the area.

Whilst working in the garden early in 1972, I felt that I was being watched by a pair of "old characters" standing on what had been, up to 1934, a public footpath leading across the fields to Brown's Farm. On another occasion a vague shape like a white dress hurriedly "flitted" past a hall window.

Three local residents have stated that the property was haunted by a "woman in white". Experienced by visitors, however, is the occasional smell of strong pipe tobacco which wafts around the dining room, close to the inglenook fireplace.

The building had been derelict from 1968 to 1970 and neither the owner nor any of the visitors since it has been re-occupied smokes a pipe, but the phenomenon suggests that someone there did once.

ENA TWIGG was for many years regarded as one of the most respected mediums in the world and in 1968 was named "Spiritualist of the Year". A good-natured and matter-of-fact lady, she was praised by Psychic News *for her "outstanding contribution to modern spiritualism and to a better public understanding of its values". Claiming that paranormal "things" had been happening to her for much of her life, Ena Twigg was consulted on a wide variety of cases, but few more unusual than the hauntings described here.*

THE PYROMANIAC GHOST

Location and date:
Old Kent Road, London, UK, 1973

I have been involved in a number of interesting hauntings. One of the funniest stories involved a theatre, although I did not know that I was being taken to one for this adventure.

When we started, I was picked up, taken to a car, and blindfolded. All I was told was that we were going to a place that was having some trouble – and they thought a haunting might be involved. I was driven round and round, and eventually we arrived at the destination. Our escorts said that we were too early, so we had to drive around once more.

Finally, we stopped. They helped me out of the car. Harry was with me, fortunately. Then they took my arm and guided me while I stumbled along. They took off the blindfold, and there I was on a stage, surrounded by a bevy of girls with next to nothing on. We were in a theatre. The performance was over, but the cast lingered on, curious to see what was going to happen.

I thought, Goodness, what am I doing here in this strange place with these half-naked girls?

The girls all thought it was rather weird – and so did I, for that matter. Finally the girls went off. Then I was supposed to discover what was wrong with the theatre. Everybody insisted that there was something wrong on the stage.

I was quite sure that it wasn't on the stage at all. So I asked them to let me wander around the place, and then I would tell them where the trouble was coming from. When I got up into the gallery, I knew immediately that I had found the place.

"Oh, it's here. There's a spirit of a man sitting here, and he doesn't know he is dead!" I called out. The man had died sitting in that seat in the theatre and didn't know he was dead. He'd frightened the life out of the whole staff. So my job then was to explain to him that the show was finished and he'd just as well get on with his new life.

On another haunting case, I was asked to go to a house with the press. When we arrived at the place, miles from home. I was taken into a room. As I sat down on the settee, I saw a man. He said, "I have been swindled out of this house."

I asked, "What is the matter?"

"They've twisted me out of the price of this house," he replied.

"But you don't need this house now," I pointed out to him. "You are in another world."

Then I relayed to the people in the room what I was hearing. I patiently explained to the poor spirit that he was creating an awful lot of disturbance and distress to the people – they couldn't live in the house because of his activities.

"The thing that has really made me angry," he replied, "is that they've ripped out my oak bookcase that I built with my own hands – they've ripped it out and thrown it away out in the garden."

Now, I was a complete stranger to that house and family. I had never seen either before. So I asked the family if what he was telling me about the bookcase was true. They said it was.

So I began reasoning with the unhappy spirit. "Why raise such a fuss about the bookcase? They don't need it, and you don't need it, so what are you mad about?"

As for being twisted out of the money, the present occupants were only renting the house, they didn't own it. Besides, the spirit didn't need or want the house or money or anything else in this world. Finally he was convinced, and he departed.

The terrible part about this story is that the haunting had been so bad and the spirit had been so determined to make someone pay attention that he had overshadowed the son of the family renting the house, who had committed a violence on his own mother and who had to be put in a mental institution. He was a long time getting well. After I talked with the spirit, the haunting stopped and never occurred again.

Another time I was asked to go to a house off the Old Kent Road. It was a particularly horrible night – pouring with rain, dark, and incredibly dreary.

There was a young couple there, absolutely terrified. The man was a professional photographer. They told me that spontaneous fires were breaking out all over – beds, chairs, rugs, would suddenly catch fire. "Well, we'll be sitting in a room, and a fire will start on the settee, or the chair will start to burn, the beds, the curtains, anything; but nobody has been burnt. Come and have a look at the place."

I had never seen anything like it in my life. The press people were there, and even they were surprised. The windowsills in the children's bedrooms had been seared with fire, but miraculously no one had been burned or injured. It was really terrifying.

So all of us sat down in the living room, and I heard a young man's voice say, "I'm Jimmy."

"Who are you?" I asked.

"I'm her brother [referring to the woman]. I died as a result of a fire when I was three years old."

Then I asked him, "Why are you terrorizing these people like this if you are indeed the one causing the disturbance?"

"It's my only means of making them wake up to the fact that what is happening in the family is too dreadful for words."

I asked him what was going on in the family that had disturbed him so, and he told me the whole story. It is confidential, but it did involve a family quarrel resulting in members not talking to each other. He said, "I will continue to do this until amends have been made and peace has been restored in the family."

"Will you promise me that if I ask the folks here to put this right, you will then get on with your life in the other world and leave them in peace?"

"I promise you that if they make peace with the rest of the family there will be no more disturbance," he said. And there were no more fires.

CANON JOHN PEARCE-HIGGINS, the minister of Southwark Cathedral, became probably the best-known of a trio of exorcists much in demand in the 1970s. A former lecturer and parish priest, he had a deep interest in spiritualism and subsequently worked on a number of cases with the leading mediums of the time. He also delivered lectures in Britain and America and was involved in a number of cases of possession on both sides of the Atlantic. His book, Life, Death and Psychical Rsearch (1973) *was a groundbreaking work about the paranormal. In the following account, the Canon describes a unique case on which he worked with Ena Twigg.*

THE GHOST WHO KNEW HE WAS DEAD

Location and date:
Southwark, London, UK, 1970

The whirligig of time has somehow brought it about that I am now continually being approached by people in trouble who want either themselves or their houses "exorcized". In the case of the former the majority of them are not genuine cases of possession (about 1 in 6), but are schizophrenic or hysterical psychopathological problems, which are rendered infinitely worse and more intolerable if, as is usual, they have first consulted mediums who have told them that they have one or several evil spirits around them. When, as inevitably happens, since there is nothing there except figments of their own imagination or hallucinations, the medium fails to produce any amelioration of the condition, the last state of that person is worse than before. One well-known medium had told a woman who came to me in despair that she was possessed by 36 spirits! She claimed to have got rid of 25 of them (at £3 a time!) but was unable to clear the rest! In the case of haunted houses also there are very few mediums today who are capable of dealing with them successfully. Here again about 1 in 5 are genuine cases.

Since this problem presented itself to me in a pastoral manner, and since I am not psychic, I naturally initially had to have recourse to mediums, and in one of the first cases I dealt with I invoked the aid of Mrs Ena Twigg. This was in a vicarage where the young new incumbent, with a wife and four children, urgently invoked my help to get rid of the terrible atmosphere of depression in the house; there were also footsteps going up and down the stairs, and the eldest boy flatly refused to sleep in the late vicar's bedroom. Mrs Twigg came with her husband and together with the vicar and his wife we sat one evening while Mrs Twigg relayed to us what she said she saw and heard, correctly describing this sad unhappy middle-aged bachelor, who said he was tied to the place by the sense of what he had left undone. We tried to comfort him. We also told him he was upsetting the children. "But", he said, "I come for the children, I am fond of them, children were the only people I could really communicate with when alive." (This was a somewhat rare case where the ghost appeared to realise he was dead.) Through Mrs Twigg he then correctly described alterations in the vicarage itself and in the church – into neither of which places either she or I had ever set foot before. Finally we told the poor man that he must go on and up into the Light. "But", he said, "I don't know where to go." Then we were told that he had dissolved into tears, which seemed to clear the atmosphere somewhat. He then began to thank us for coming, and said we had set him free. "Now I can arise and go to my Father," he said. He then blessed the vicar and his wife, and thanked us for coming, and in particular Mrs Twigg to whom he said, "Had I known you when alive I would have said you were of the devil"! He then asked us to pray for him, which we did.

The vicar reported the house quite clear, but a fortnight later rang me and said they were having disturbances in the choir vestry. Mrs Twigg was unable to come and I invited a male trance medium, who declared the house clear.

On this occasion the Bishop of Southwark was with us, and so we went over to the church where the medium was taken into trance, and in the vestry was controlled by the former incumbent who asked forgiveness for his errors and failures and was absolved by the Bishop. From that time on there has been no more trouble.

After this I used this medium for such cases and we had some quite remarkable successes in clearing all sorts of places, other haunted vicarages, ordinary council houses, usually built on the site of older houses, houses of the rich and of the poor. In many of these the haunter was simply stuck – he did not realise he was dead and so hung about his old home – these were easy to clear. About this time the medium's guide advised me that it would greatly help if I took a Service of Holy Communion before the medium went into trance, and I have made this my practice ever since.

In this way we cleared, after several visits, an ex-vicarage in the Midlands apparently haunted by two Tudor monks from the local priory, which had been dissolved at the Reformation. They were clearly a bad lot, one had made an Irish maid-servant pregnant; and the other had taken away and killed her baby. The girl herself through the medium also spoke to us, pitifully saying, "Mistress Longhurst will not let me go out any more." Apparently Mistress Longhurst was her employer, and the house had been used as a guest house by the Priory. The girl had been locked in an attic and finally poisoned after her baby had been despatched. She was still looking for her baby, unaware of its death and of the passage of time. The monks also had continued to perform their daily offices and although the Priory had been dissolved in 1536, still imagined themselves to be carrying out the daily monastic routine in field and church. I had a most interesting time trying to persuade them that they were dead, which they found it hard to believe since they expected to sleep until the last trump and then, in virtue of their vows, to go straight to paradise or heaven. They could not understand at all where they were. We also had to deal with the dead husband of the lady of the house who had become a chronic alcoholic during his last years and had treated his wife badly. He came begging for, and received, her forgiveness. All this had been previously accompanied by a long story of over five years, from time to time, of heavy thumps in the attic, footsteps on the stairs, doors and drawers paranormally opening and shutting, lights swinging to and fro; on two occasions eerie wailing cries, and the lady's dressing table shaking up and down in the middle of the night. Also there was often a heavy smell of pipe-smoking, though no one in the house smoked. This was later found to be due to the presence of some old (spirit) tramps who had lived in the house while it was for some years derelict. Eventually the place was completely cleared.

In another case a wealthy mother, who had died disinheriting her daughter with whom she had been on poor terms, caused remarkable phenomena, pictures fell off the walls, coat-hangers were found on the roof, footsteps were heard. Much worse, the daughter herself, who was certainly very psychic, on several occasions appeared to be "possessed" by her mother, went into trance and once attacked her husband (whom the dead lady had disliked) with a hammer and indulged in slanging matches quite foreign to her nature. The marriage began to be in jeopardy. Naturally the Will, which left all the money to a charity, was being contested and after our first Holy Communion or Requiem, the lady came through greatly enraged that her Will was being flouted. The medium correctly described her as a tall, proud foreign lady with Edwardian picture hats, handsome and vain. He gave her nationality correctly.

At a second visit she was in a much chastened mood since apparently the spirit helpers had been working on her, and she controlled the medium, went up to her daughter and stretched out her hands and said "Forgive me". Subsequently she came through to me a number of times in the medium's sanctuary and correctly reported to me the progress of the litigation going on, of which I was quite unaware; but checked up subsequently and found the information correct in the main. (*Note.* I have this and many other cases on tape.) I should add that all phenomena ceased from the date of our first visit, and this is commonly the case, unless it happens to be a house in which there are quite a number of haunting entities, which is not uncommon in old houses, and which sometimes take more than one visit to clear. I consider this to be an extraordinarily evidential case, both because of the immediate cessation of the phenomena and also because of the veridical information conveyed . . . excellent ESP at least.

The case of Jim Pike (jun.) who after committing suicide in a New York hotel caused many paranormal phenomena in his father's flat in Cambridge within a few weeks of his death, as recorded by Bishop Pike in *The other side*, is another extremely evidential case. At the sitting with Mrs Twigg at which I was present, the boy came through, and apologised for the annoyance caused and said "I had to find a voice". He promised there would be no more phenomena, and these in fact ceased at once. (From my notes at the sitting.)

I had a very similar case in a garage where the deceased proprietor caused some astonishing phenomena in the manager's office, and when contacted through a trance medium explained his reason for causing the disturbance as being due to anxiety about his widow. These are typical cases of "purposive" hauntings, by persons who are aware that they have died. But in the majority of cases it appears that the haunters are unaware of their condition, and only cause disturbances in order to draw attention to their presence, from the desire to be set free from their frustration.

Thus in yet one more case, a five-year-old child complained of an old lady sitting on her bed. We contacted a poor old spinster who had lived in a cottage before it had been pulled down when the modern flats were erected, and who asked plaintively, "Have the horse-trams come to the top of Putney Hill yet?" and who gave the date as 1901! (My tape.)

All I can say is that in this way during the past few years some 100 or so houses have been cleared of their unwanted visitors. Many of these have spoken to me at length after being removed from the house in question, through the entranced medium in his sanctuary, where I have had to work hard to enlighten them, much after the manner of Carl Wickland, to the fact that they were dead.

With more cases coming in, occasionally urgent, it happened that sometimes the medium was not available, and after consultation with his guide, I was told to go and take the service and cleanse the house alone. Thus on receiving an urgent call from a newly and happily married young bride, who was aware of dangerous suicidal influences around her, I went next day. The lady's clairvoyant sister, who had spent two nights in the flat, had seen a distressed girl wringing her hands in despair and saying "He has let me down, what shall I do, shall I take an overdose, or cut my wrists?" (It appears she did the latter.) The condition immediately disappeared after the service. In this way I evolved what seems an effective form of service (Requiem), invoking the ministry of angels, and which can be used without the presence of a medium.

Some of these cases received a good deal of publicity and presently clergy began to write to me for help. As I cannot deal with even all the ghosts in Southwark let alone other parts of England(!), I now send them the form of service, with instructions as to how to set about cleansing the house. They report back to me in the majority of cases that it has worked and that the phenomena have ceased. From this it seems fairly clear that, when invoked in all sincerity, the power of God through Jesus Christ and the Ministry of Angels can and does work – of course, we have His promise that if sincerely invoked it will. It would seem therefore that the presence of a medium is not essential, although it helps, and of course it enables one to know what has been dealt with. But since the main object of the exercise is to clear the place, this is perhaps a luxury – although it is also a procedure which if I had not started with mediums in the first place, I would never have known how to set in motion. I have to acknowledge my indebtedness to the "sensitives".

BISHOP JAMES PIKE of New York was at the centre of one of the century's most sensational stories about spiritualism, which also involved Ena Twigg and Canon Pearce-Higgins. On 4 February 1966, Pike's son, Jim, committed suicide in a New York hotel room. Although the former lawyer and Naval Intelligence officer referred to himself as "suspicious by nature" he was determined to try and contact his dead son. A year later the opportunity was offered to him by the two British spiritualists. What happened at Ena Twigg's home, on the anniversary of the death, was later described by Pike on US TV and generated a storm of controversy in the press and the media, as he later recalled in his book, From The Other Side (1967).

SÉANCE WITH A SON

Location and date:
East Acton, London, UK, 1967

The sitting room was quite small and was modestly furnished. But I was not unhappy about that. My fear had been of the opposite – heavy drapes, fringed silk lampshades, exotic ornaments, cluttered semi-darkness. What un-examined assumptions we make about the unfamiliar! The furnishings were in fact so undistinguished that I cannot recall them. I do remember that the light was simply that which came through a window – flat and silver-grey, appropriate to a London afternoon in February.

"Do you happen to have something of your son's?" Mrs Twigg asked me quietly as we all sat down. She smiled, with tenderness, as she waited for the answer – which was simply my reaching into a jacket pocket for Jim's passport, the original one he had left in Cambridge. I had brought it along because of Canon Pearce-Higgins' suggestion. But it was clear from the way she asked the question that having something of my son's was not essential. Her comment when I showed it to her was, "It will help."

We all fell silent. Though the idea was not suggested as appro-priate, I felt prayerful; my head bowed some. The feeling – or *sensing* – was like what a Roman Catholic or Anglican generally feels when sitting or kneeling in a chapel where the Sacrament is reserved in a tabernacle or aumbry. He doesn't grasp the how of what is called "the Real Presence"; further, God is obviously present *everywhere*; yet . . .

Now Mrs Twigg began to show some signs of discomfort and distress. "He's here," she said. "He's working hard to get through." She did not close her eyes nor did her posture or countenance change in any radical way. It was almost as if she were continuing our conversation of a few moments before.

"He was normally a boisterous and happy boy," she commented. Then she seemed to be speaking as if for another. "I failed the test, I can't face you, can't face life. I'm confused. Very sudden passing – have had to do this – couldn't find anyone. God, I didn't know what I was doing. But when I got here I found I wasn't such a failure as I thought. My nervous system failed."

Again – or should I say still – I sensed Jim's presence. In fact, I had a direct impression that he was standing behind and to the right of Mrs Twigg, though I could see nothing. I listened intensely, sensing something of the suffering which seemed to be expressed. Mrs Twigg went on, as if reporting someone else's words.

"I am not in purgatory – but something like hell, here," Jim seemed to say. "Yet nobody blames me here."

I puzzled over the words. What could this mean? Suffering, but not being blamed . . .

Then, "I hope nobody blames me *there*."

"I've met my grandmother," was the next remark. That's not right, I thought to myself. (Both of his grandmothers were – and are – alive.) But I said nothing.

"You were under pressure at the same time. I was worried about you, Dad, because they were kicking you around."

Jim had called me "Dad" – that was characteristic – and we had, indeed, both been under pressure. Just how much I was under I was not able fully to acknowledge then – or until nearly two and a half years later when the time of troubles I had actually gone through seemed finally to have passed.

"I came to your room, I moved books, I knocked on the door – came to your bedside – you dreamt about me and spoke to me," Mrs Twigg's voice went on rapidly – speaking, it would seem, for Jim. The words rang true to our experience of the past two weeks even if the exact items did not match. I had not, for example, heard any knocks on the door. Yet the essence of our experience was certainly being articulated.

"I love you very much," the medium's voice went on. "So much love and no means of giving it." How true, I thought, how true. True in one sense now, true in another sense before he died. He was a loving person, yet he seemed incapable of breaking free to express his love. He had come to be able to express his love for me in words now and again during the last three or four months. But still I had the feeling he was blocked – generally not able to tell to anyone freely what he really felt.

Mrs Twigg went on, still quoting in the first person. "I'm tied to my regrets. Yet they are showing me the way out, and we must make progress together. I have to live my way and you yours."

DOM ROBERT PETITPIERRE was the second of the leading exorcists in the Church of England during the later part of the twentieth century. A diminutive little man with a gentle style that belied his ferocious determination, he took a science degree before entering the church and performed over a thousand exorcisms. "Real ghosts have human minds," he declared in 1976, "but demons are an army and their general is Satan." In a career lasting over half a century, Dom Robert took on a remarkable variety of cases and here records one of the strangest.

THE HOUSE OF ILL-FAME

Location and date: East End, London, UK, 1975

The startling sex lives of the young girls in the new home that had been opened for them in the East End of London was worrying everybody connected with the place. Each of the girl had "gone off the rails" within a few weeks of arriving and there seemed to be no way of stopping them.

The trouble continued for five years and then the parish priest discovered that the premises had once been a brothel. He decided that the girls were under evil influences left behind from the days when prostitution flourished in the building and it had to be exorcized.

The priest called me in and told me what was happening in the girls' home. It seemed to me to be a case of human sin leaving a heritage of evil to haunt and disturb those who lived on the site thereafter.

We agreed to call in a Roman Catholic Bishop to exorcize the place. He had two shots at it, but broke down twice. He couldn't get through. So we decided on an exorcism with the Bishop and twelve clergy including myself – which is the Roman Catholic ritual way – and that cleared the mess up. The home was all right afterwards.

Trouble often arises from a house which has been the site of sexual misbehaviour. In the countryside this would apply to the site of an ancient fertility cult. Or it could come from the offices of a company devoted to greed or domination.

I have seen just one ghost – also in the East End of London, in a church. It was one Good Friday and I saw the figure of a priest standing in the nave under the gallery clock.

There should have been no one in the church and after a few seconds I realized it was a ghost. I mentioned it later to the church warden and he said, "Ah, six o'clock – that's about the right time for him to appear."

I believe that a ghost is someone who, after death, has remained "stuck" because he or she was too tied to earthly things like home, garden, or place of work. They remain until released by exorcism – and the best exorcism is prayer.

REVEREND DONALD OMAND also performed immumerable exorcisms in Britain during a thirty-year-long career which took him as far afield as Devon, the Highlands of Scotland and even the notorious Bermuda Triangle. Raised in Scotland where he began the study of the supernatural and perfecting methods of casting-out rituals, he was later called upon by numerous doctors and psychiatrists dealing with "possessed" patients. In June 1973, he carried out undoubtedly the most bizarre case of all – to exorcize the spirit of the Loch Ness Monster – which has understandably earned him a position of some notoriety in the annals of psychic research.

THE GHOST OF NESSIE

Location and date:
Castle Urquhart, Scotland, 1973

The whole business really started in Sweden. I work with an international group of psychiatrists and others who believe in possession. One of them had discovered that round a lake in Sweden there appeared to be a sinister influence on people. There was a more-than-usual percentage of mental cases and broken marriages, while people of high character become demoralized. The doctor found that this lake had a very similar legend to Loch Ness.

Further inquiries showed that there are other lochs in Scotland, lakes in Ireland and two fjords in Norway with the same thing. We made a survey of these places and most of all Loch Ness, and while I don't want to offend the people living round there, we found sufficient evidence to indicate the same pattern as had been first observed in north Sweden.

So we decided when our group met in Oslo last year that I should exorcize Loch Ness. We chose it because it is the biggest, and if I succeeded there I could probably succeed everywhere else.

I must point out that I did not propose to exorcize the monster itself, but the evil that surrounded it. I have always believed that Nessie is a spectre and not a zoological specimen. For one thing, I do not see how it would get on for food if it was a real creature; certainly there would be no fish left in Loch Ness and it is very full of salmon and trout and everything else. I don't doubt the word of people who have seen something there, but I think it is a spectre they have seen. I have seen one in Norway, and when four of us went to Loch Ness last June we thought we saw it.

So I performed a ceremony of exorcism, and reports that we have had so far indicate it was successful. This does not mean that Nessie will no longer be spotted there, it just means that the evil which concentrated about her will have gone.

ARTHUR GUIRDHAM was a resident psychiatrist at Bathford Nursing Home just outside Bath who became convinced after years of research that a great deal of mental illness was a form of "haunting by spirits." He believed that that earth was permeated with a variety of forces and energies that were not recognized by science and had been forced to make room for a "supernatural explanation" by recurrent experiences. Guirdham enjoyed considerable success with several of his books, including A Foot In Both Worlds: A Doctor's Autobiography of Psychic Experience (1973) *from which the following chilling and unnerving episode is taken.*

THE HAUNTED PLACE

Location and date: Otmoor, Oxford, UK, 1933

Otmoor was strange and haunted and out of this world, a sunken plain with low hills around it. The grass was knee high where you crossed its centre, and where there were hedges they were thick like screens and the inwoven roses were utterly static, like flowers in an old mosaic. The moor was crossed by a Roman causeway. There was always a silence of something beautiful and evil about it. It was flooded in the first months of the year. In

February it was a desolation. It was numbed by the cold and the mist that hung above it. Even in summer, with the roses blooming, there was about it the memory of an old evil. I could feel its presence in the grey-green silence of the heavy vegetation.

I stayed a night at the inn at Beckley during the summer vacation. I was due to do my examination in pharmacology. I found the subject easy and interesting. I had worked hard and had no qualms about the result. I returned to Oxford two days before the examination.

When I went to bed that night I began to shiver violently. My rigors were coarse and repeated and beyond my control. The springs of the bed whined continuously with the violence of my movements. My teeth chattered harshly. Even the sound of their detonation was excruciating. I felt deathly cold. I staggered from my bed and took up the mats and carpets from my room as extra covering. On this summer night they had no effect. Next day I felt shrunken with cold and horribly ill. I was jaundiced, and nauseated by the sight of food. I had been living simply and the amount of alcohol I had taken was negligible. I felt so ill that I sent for a doctor. He was an old, impressive and kindly figure. He diagnosed a chill on the liver. At least he got the organ right. I was jaundiced and in the condition from which I was really suffering the organ is vulnerable. He was a kindly old man and no doctor could have been expected to make the diagnosis. He asked me if I was ready for the examination. He came of that vintage of doctors which did not inevitably regard patients as malingerers. I had no doubt he would have written a certificate for my tutor had I pressed him to do so. I assured him I was well prepared.

I recovered in two days. The ice thawed from my muscles and my limbs and jaw were no longer convulsed by coarse tremors. The yellow tinge departed from my skin and eyeballs. I turned up for the examination shaken but competent and passed with ease.

What was the diagnosis? Was it hysteria? I do not know what I had to be hysterical about. Was it an unconscious evasion designed to avoid the examination by dramatic and obvious symptoms? There was no real audience for the display of my suffering. It was during the vacation. I was practically alone in the college, and nobody knew about it except the old doctor. And as I say I knew my work backwards. When it came to the test I passed with ease.

It was years afterwards before I knew that Otmoor was one of the last resorts of malaria in England. I could well understand it. Even in my day there was a sodden luxuriance about it. It was a pool of tropical fetor sunk in the bucolic innocence of the English countryside. I learnt that well after the Middle Ages the yellow men of Otmoor were traditional. For a couple of days I had assumed their affliction. I did not feel this at the time. I only felt desperately ill as one does with malaria even though one may recover quickly from it. Only that, and the feeling that the countryside I loved was beautiful and evil. I have no such feeling about any other region in Britain. People talk about the atmosphere of Glencoe but to me this is fantasy. It is no more horrifying than the frowning majesty of Dunmail Raise with the rain clouds gathering. It is so easy to suggest oneself into a state where every place which has known horrors has a bad atmosphere. The recognition of many bad atmospheres depends on acute imagination plus the reading of history in a state of excitable romanticism.

JOAN FORMAN is another writer fascinated by people and places haunted by evil. Born in Lincolnshire, she spent her early career in education before turning to writing and producing invaluable and well-researched historical works such as the popular Haunted East Anglia (1974) *which revealed the area to be the location of some very extraordinary tales. Few ghost hunters have persisted as determinedly as Joan Forman to solve this next supernatural mystery.*

WRAITH OF A MURDER

Location and date:
Cawthorpe, Lincolnshire, UK, 1974

I have known the stretch of road from the Louth-Legbourne corner to the commencement of Cawthorpe village proper since I was a child. Halfway down the plantation side lies a gateway, with a rutted cart track leading into it, and a clearing with a decrepit shed lying beyond. All round stand the sentinel trees, conifers mainly, with a sprinkling of deciduous wood.

At no matter what time of year one passes that gateway, there is always a scarf of mist stretching out from it, lying inert across the roadway, like a barrier. On days of brilliant sunshine, on mornings of sparkling frost, that mist-barrier is there, always at the same point, lying still and unwavering across the path.

My father, when a young man and long before he met my mother, was engaged to the miller's daughter at Legbourne Mill. He was in the habit when his day's work was over, of cycling out to Legbourne via Cawthorpe, taking the route by the plantation and then through Watery Lane to the Mill.

He possessed a reasonably modern bicycle as cycling was one of his hobbies, but in those days modernity did not extend to battery-powered lamps. Both front and rear lights were acetylene-powered and the lamps had to be lit by hand.

On one particular night, dark, with a moon about to rise but not yet risen, my father rode on his usual journey to the Mill. He had turned into the plantation stretch which leads to Cawthorpe, and was passing the gateway when the front lamp of his bicycle went out. He dismounted and re-lit the lamp, climbed back on the bicycle and was about to move, when the rear lamp of the cycle went out. He got off the machine again, re-lit the rear lamp and once more prepared to ride off. At that point both front and rear lamps were extinguished together.

The young man was now thoroughly alarmed and disconcerted. As far as he could see, there was no earthly reason why even one lamp, still less both, should go out. One more he re-lit both lights, and thereupon jumped on the bike, and pedalled hell-for-leather down the lane. Once out of the mysterious gateway, both lamps remained alight. He came home by the main road through Legbourne village, and for several weeks gave the plantation road a wide berth.

Forty years later when I went to live in Cawthorpe, the plantation road still held its scarf of mist, and not only I, but many of the village's inhabitants, felt a sense of unease when passing the place.

I asked Harry Borrill to tell me of its history and he raised his bushy eyebrows in surprise that I should not know the story. It came in two parts and he told me the latter half first.

On a Christmas morning several years ago, a local man was walking from Cawthorpe to the pub, in Legbourne village, intent on a friendly drink with his cronies to celebrate the season. As he drew level with the plantation gateway, he heard the sound of footsteps approaching behind him. Feeling sociable, he slowed down to enable the man to catch him up, thinking to have a pleasant chat along the road to the inn. The steps came nearer, drew level and then passed him, but *there was no person to be seen*. Immediately following this unpleasant discovery, a herd of pigs dashed past him and he was forced to leap aside to avoid them. When he regained his balance enough to look around, there were no pigs in sight.

As soon as he reached the pub, he told a friend of his experience. He half-expected to be greeted by laughter or disbelief, but surprisingly his friend nodded.

"Aye," he said, "when I was ditching there a few years ago, a lady in a car stopped and asked me about yon place. Said there was a stone nearby to commemorate a murder. It seems that some time in the 1800s, a drover had taken his stock to Louth market and came back with a herd of pigs he'd bought and a pocket full of money from the sale of his own stock. Somebody was lying in wait for him in that gateway, jumped out on him and cut his throat. The stone the lady spoke about had been taken away by the soldiers in the last war. Don't know what became of it."

It seems the scarf of mist has replaced the stone as a *memento mori* in that particular place.

MATTHEW MANNING is well-known for his psychic abilities and power as a healer – all of which stemmed from a childhood encounter with a ghost. From the age of sixteen, he and his family living in Cambridge were subjected to a series of poltergeist-like disturbances, which particularly fascinated the youngster. Later, Matthew discovered that he had a talent for Automatic Writing and his paranormal capabilities were subjected to intensive scrutiny by the Cambridge Psychical Research Society. Here he describes the extraordinary ghostly phenomena that occurred in his seventeenth-century home that changed the course of his life.

THE FIGURE FROM THE PAST

Location and date:
Linton, Cambridgeshire, UK, 1971

I was sixteen years old when I first encountered the ghost that was to have such a profound effect on my life. The year was 1971 and the place was our family home in the village of Linton in Cambridgeshire. It was a meeting that was to lead to me developing psychic powers and guide me into a life affected by the supernatural, the paranormal and the bizarre.

I first saw the shadowy figure on the staircase of our seventeenth-century home. To begin with, I thought it was a burglar. Then I realised it was a ghost. When I looked at him, I thought he was completely solid. He was wearing a green frock coat with frilled cuffs and a cream cravat. He spoke to me and said, "I must offer you my most humble apology for giving you so much fright, but I must walk for my blessed legs."

I grabbed an old envelope and pencil and sketched him where he stood. A few moments later he turned, walked up the stairs and disappeared.

In the months that followed, the ghost appeared again several times and played tricks on both my family and me. Strange antique objects appeared on the stairs and the bed in my parents' bedroom was often found with the covers thrown back and the pillows dented as though someone had been resting his head on them.

We also became aware of the sudden smell of strong pipe tobacco – although no one smoked – and the sound of heavy footsteps in empty rooms. Sometimes we would hear the sound of a bell ringing in the hallway although there was no such bell in the house. On other occasions, a candle was found lit on the cloakroom floor.

While all this was going on, I discovered I had the power of automatic writing – that is when a writer lets his hand and pen be guided by another mind. In that way, I exchanged messages with the ghost and discovered who he was. His name was Robert Webbe and he had been born in the house in 1678. I found out that the style of his clothes was from the 1730s and he had to use two sticks because of his "troublesome legs." He had died in the house in 1733.

I was able to exchange messages with Webbe and check the historical accuracy of the things he said. Then he began writing messages on the walls of my bedroom – though no one ever saw him doing it. Over a six-day period in July 1971, more than 500 pencilled names and dates appeared on the wall. They were in a variety of styles of handwriting and were the names of Webbe, his family and other families who had lived in the area.

When I asked Webbe about these strange things, he admitted he was responsible, but said it was *his* house and he could do whatever he wanted in it. Once when I reached out to try to shake his hand, mine went straight through his. At that moment I experienced an eerie feeling of timelessness.

My meetings with the ghost were an amazing experience and affected my life. It seems that Robert Webbe had been a grain trader and was very proud of the house, which he had enlarged but did not live long enough to enjoy. He wanted to take the house with him. I think that is why he was going round and round in a strange sort of time loop, trapped by his own will in infinity. Then from time to time, someone in the house provided him with enough psychic energy to allow him to make contact.

I remember asking him during my research into local history why the house was haunted. He replied he did not believe in ghosts – and, in any case, there were none in the house!

PROFESSOR JOHN HASTED had worked all his life in Atomic and Molecular Physics, but in the 1970s when he was Head of Experimental Physics at Birkbeck College in London became fascinated by the case of Uri Geller. Already the extraordinary Israeli-British performer had become a celebrity with demonstrations of his psychic powers, in particular his ability to bend spoons, describe hidden drawings and affect the working of watches. His appearances on television intrigued Professor Hasted whose subsequent enquiries inspired him to unite The Metal-Benders *in 1981. In this article written in 1976, he describes how he invited Geller to his home – and a poltergeist came, too.*

URI GELLER'S UNEXPECTED GUEST

Location and date:
Sunningdale, Berkshire, UK, 1974

In the autumn of 1974, I was studying the physics of Uri Geller's metal bending and invited him to my home. During the time he was with us we had a couple of unforgettable teleportations – objects would appear in one room having disappeared from a different place.

Geller was talking to my wife, Lyn, in the kitchen and I was standing in the kitchen doorway when the first occurred. Lyn offered Geller a drink and said, "It's very nice to have you here, but I must tell you I'm a great sceptic and don't believe in any of these things."

Well, at that moment a small ivory statue appeared and fell on the floor. The statue had been in the living room. Geller didn't throw it. His hands were in full view of me the entire time.

While we were photographing the statue, the large key of our clock suddenly appeared in the air and dropped to the floor in front of us. Again there was no way in which Geller could have been responsible for this incident.

After he left us that night, Uri Geller went off to record a television show which was screened the following Monday. I was at work at the time. My wife watched the show with a neighbour and phoned me afterwards. She was very agitated. She said that the clock key had "flown" again – not once, but twice.

When I got home I found the key on the floor. I picked it up – and the clock, which had not gone since the days of the Second World War with its hands standing at ten past six, suddenly struck five.

Lyn and I found that each time we picked the key up, the clock would chime. We subsequently repeated this eighty times for psychical and scientific researchers with exactly the same result. It baffled everyone.

We discovered, though, that as long as we were playing with the clock, we got fewer other things flying about the house. But still in the subsequent months about fifty other objects flew about the house – including the Christmas turkey liver, which "escaped" from a security plastic bag, wired shut. We became convinced we were being haunted by a poltergeist.

To have a poltergeist means you must have strong emotional or psychological problems. My wife had lost her job and was quite upset that winter. She also had events happen in the car, several miles from the house. I had occasional teleportations in my office, too. I think this was all triggered off by Uri Geller's visit to our home.

The clock ritual would quieten things down for long periods, but we finally got rid of our "visitor" after three months by simply not talking about it. We have never had anything like it since.

PROFESSOR ARCHIE ROY of the University of Glasgow is one of the world's leading astronomers – he has an asteroid named after him – and combines a passion for interplanetary worlds with psychic studies. A former President of the SPR, founder-president of the Scottish Society for Psychical Research and a patron of the Churches Fellowship for Psychical and Spiritual Studies, he has conducted numerous enquiries into modern haunting and written more that seventy scientific papers and articles. One of the most interesting and authentic cases Professor Roy investigated concerned a family living not far away from the university which he reported in the News of the World *in June 1978.*

THE COUNCIL HOUSE ROWDY

Location and date:
Balornock, Glasgow, Scotland, 1975

What became known as "The Case of the Council House Rowdy" began when David Grieve, his wife, Elizabeth, their two sons, Derek (14) and Jeffrey (11) and their 80-year-old grandmother, Ann Anderson, claimed they were under attack by a poltergeist at Balornock, Glasgow.

These attacks had been going on for three years when Rev. Max Magee of the Church of Scotland and I became involved. We were called into the case after the family, neighbours, nurses and police had all heard typical poltergeist phenomena.

There had been bangs, raps and what we came to call the sledge-hammer sound. The whole house shook.

There had been movement of furniture, pictures falling off walls, bedclothes stripped off beds, and toys stuffed down the lavatory.

At one stage the family fled to a relative's house about a mile away. The phenomena went with them and started up in the relative's house.

When the family went back to their own house, it started up there and continued in the relative's house. It was as if the relative's place had been psychically infected.

There were two teenage boys in this family and this was typical of poltergeist cases.

Very often there is a teenager who seems to be the focus. The teenager always seems to be around when the phenomena occurs.

He or she is not manipulating the furniture or the pictures or anything like that – but is present and is as scared as anyone else.

There was some trouble in this household, too. They were having a disagreement with the family downstairs.

I didn't see any objects move, but Max and I heard the phenomena under conditions where we had to rule out fraud.

We would have the family together in one room and the other rooms would be sealed when we heard the noises.

In a way, we could even turn it on and off. Max would say, "We are going to beat this thing," whereupon there would immediately be a rattle of raps and bangs as if to say, "Oh, no you won't."

The evidence seemed to point to the older boy as the focus.

He was sent to his grandparents, north of Inverness, whereupon the strange happenings ceased in the family home and started up on a minor scale in his grandparents' home.

We left him there for several weeks. The phenomena began to die out up there and we allowed him to come back.

They did not begin again in the family house, except that about a year later they restarted in the sense that small electrical fires kept breaking out all over.

Then they died away and up to the present there have been no more.

There was no certain event that we could point to as heralding the end of the happenings.

In many cases, it's as if the focus, in this case the adolescent, having grown a little, has changed the status of the whole thing and therefore there is no longer any trigger to start off the phenomena.

Several things convinced us of the genuineness of this case.

First of all there were the reports of the police, the family doctor and the relatives to whom the family fled and who were themselves infested by the poltergeist.

Then there was the total dependence of the family on us, plus our observation of their state of health.

They had lost weight and were in a state of nervous exhaustion.

They congregated and slept in the same room and never had the light out at night for months on end.

Also, we got the sound of the phenomena on tape several times.

DOCTOR ALAN GAULD and TONY CORNELL working together have earned a reputation of being among the most erudite ghost hunters of the late twentieth century. Gauld, a senior lecturer in psychology at Nottingham University and Cornell, president of the Cambridge University Society for Psychical Research, built their reputation on scrupulously detailed enquiry and being the most "hi-tech" of researchers – having designed a sophisticated "ghostbusting" apparatus complete with video camera and computer which they employ at haunts. Gauld and Cornell have written numerous articles and a major survey of hauntings, Poltergeists, *published in*

1979. In this they recount the very curious case of which they themselves may have been the cause . . .

WERE WE THE GHOSTS?

Location and date:
Wisbech, Cambridge, UK, 1957

The case in question took place at Hannath Hall, an attractive but dilapidated Tudor house in Tydd St Mary near Wisbech, Cambridgeshire. The tenants of the house at that time were the family of Mr Derek Page, now Lord Whaddon, then Labour candidate, later MP, for the constituency of Wisbech and the Isle of Ely. Mr Page's family consisted of himself and his wife; two children, aged at that time three and five; and Mrs Page's mother. They had moved into Hannath Hall in August 1957, and during the next few months were frequently disturbed by inexplicable happenings – mostly thumps on doors and raps, but occasionally footsteps and groans, and once a violent jolt imparted to a bed. A local journalist learned of these strange happenings, and contacted the SPR. In consequence of his action, ADC and AG visited Hannath Hall on the evening of 16 November 1957. We were accompanied by Mr D. J. Murray, secretary of the Cambridge University SPR, and Mr (now the Rev.) J. M. Brotherton, a member of the same society; and also by the journalist and two of his friends, who met us at Wisbech to guide us to the house.

We arrived about 10.30 p.m., and during the next hour and a quarter we interviewed the members of the family (apart of course from the children), and carefully examined both the outside and the inside of the house. Hannath Hall has only two floors, and all the rooms on the upper floor open from a single large gallery. The phenomena reported had all taken place on the upper floor, though they were not confined to any particular part of it. The bedroom at the northern end of the gallery had been christened "the haunted room", but seemingly for no better reason than that a nineteenth-century owner of the house was reputed to have left the body of his deceased wife lying there for several weeks, and to have had meals sent up to her.

At about 11.45 p.m. ADC organized a ouija board (i.e. glass and alphabet) séance in the living room downstairs, chiefly to ensure that all the hands in the house were in plain view; whilst AG stationed himself in the gallery upstairs, which was somewhat dimly lit by a single bulb. At 12.08 a.m. he heard a sharp snap from the haunted room; he set this down to a drop in temperature, and did not investigate. At 12.10 he thought he heard quiet footsteps on the stairs. The steps ceased before they reached the gallery. AG went to the head of the staircase and found there was no one on the stairs. He concluded he had probably misinterpreted some noises from below. At 12.32 he was driven downstairs by the cold; during his vigil the temperature in the gallery had dropped from 60°F to 52°F.

At 1.25 a.m., whilst the others continued the séance downstairs, ADC and AG went into the haunted room upstairs with a view to settling down there for the night. The room had no electricity, and we searched it again by the light of our torches. It was used as a storeroom for unwanted furniture and oddments. Across the floor lay two mattresses end to end, and on these we settled down feet to feet, with one blanket over our legs. The thermometer had by now sunk to 49°F, at which it remained during the ensuing events. We extinguished our torches.

A few minutes later we heard gentle taps coming from the floor on AG's left and ADC's right at a point roughly equidistant from both of us and about three feet from the mattresses. Our torches showed nothing but bare boards in the region concerned. We found that we could get specific numbers of raps at request. The raps became louder and moved nearer to the wall of the room. This meant that they came from a position about three feet from ADC's right shoulder. We questioned them by means of a simple code, and found that they would answer leading questions readily, but could not spell out coherent messages. The rapper claimed to be a woman who had been murdered in the house in 1906 – a claim which we have not been able to substantiate. After a while we heard a series of six or seven knocks, growing in loudness, from the position in which the rappings had begun. The last one was of such intensity that AG flashed his torch in its direction. The raps ceased instantly, and there was nothing but bare floor in the place from which they had seemed to come.

Meanwhile the séance downstairs had broken up, and the reporter and his two friends had departed. Messrs Murray and Brotherton came up to the gallery, and heard the rappings. Mr Brotherton ran downstairs, leaving Mr Murray outside the door of the haunted room. He found the Page family sitting round the table in the living room, and then rejoined Mr Murray, who informed him that the raps had continued throughout his absence. Both then at once went downstairs and searched the room immediately below the haunted bedroom.

These activities caused a certain amount of noise, and we decided to leave the haunted room to ask the others to keep quieter. AG went to the door and ADC followed. As AG was passing through the doorway we heard a noise behind us, and found that a wooden dining-room chair, which had been stacked about five feet from the mattresses, was now lying on top of them. AG then left the room whilst ADC replaced the chair. He turned to follow AG and heard the chair drop behind him again. This time it had simply fallen down. He replaced it more firmly and left the room.

We returned to the haunted room about ten minutes later. Mr Murray went with Mrs Page into the room underneath it, and Mr Brotherton and Mr Page stood in the gallery. This left Mrs Page's mother on her own in the living room. We soon heard loud raps, but this time from a position on the other side of the mattresses and about three feet from them; that is, on AG's right and ADC's left, and again about equidistant from us. Mr Murray and Mrs Page in the room below could also hear the raps, and noted down some of the sequences. The raps confirmed, though still in reply to leading questions, some of the information previously given. We then asked the month of the supposed communicator's death, and heard eleven raps. We asked the day of the month. There commenced a series of raps which moved along the floor towards ADC's head. The sixteenth rap seemed to him to come from the air behind his head. He switched on his torch, and the raps ceased immediately. He put out his torch, and we asked the rapper to begin again after ten. The raps were much fainter, and continued up to eighteen. We then made some not very successful attempts to ascertain the rapper's age at death. The raps quite soon died away altogether, and after a few minutes we returned downstairs. It was then quarter to three.

Meanwhile, not long after we returned to the haunted room, the journalist and his two friends had come back to the house. They said that their car had broken down. Mr Page took them to Wisbech in his own car, and did not return until 2.50 a.m.

We returned to the haunted room at 3.34 a.m., this time with Mr Murray. AG walked into the room first, Mr Murray second and ADC last. ADC slammed the door, and we heard a sharp rattle. We turned, and saw by the light of our torches that a brass toasting fork with three prongs had been thrust behind the metal plate to which the door bolt was attached. One of its prongs was inserted through the staple into which the bolt normally ran, thus "bolting" us into the room from the inside.

There were no subsequent phenomena of much interest. On our second visit (21–22 November 1957) we heard some further rappings, faint and distant-sounding, but under conditions of good "control". Altogether we paid between us some twenty visits to the house. On 25–26 April 1959 we brought a non-professional medium to the house, and held a séance in the haunted bedroom. A lady calling herself Eliza Cullen or Culler came through and said she had made the raps. She said she had buried her baby in the garden. But we could not trace any person of that name.

On 22 April 1959, and again in July 1959, Mrs Page, in the living room, twice thought she saw the figure of a small, fair-haired boy peering at her round the boxroom door when she was certain that there was no one there.

It is worth asking how an out-and-out sceptic might set about demolishing this case. He could hardly claim that the memories of the investigators present had retrospectively magnified the events of the evening, because all four of us wrote preliminary notes on the phenomena within a few minutes of their occurrence. These notes were shortly amplified into fuller statements (copies of all relevant documents have been deposited with the SPR). A sceptic could, however, point to various discrepancies between the statements of the different witnesses. In particular, the times of events, despite the fact that we synchronized our watches at the start of the investigation, are very imperfectly recorded, and different witnesses' guesses sometimes conflict with each other. This makes it, of course, very difficult to say with certainty whether the journalist and his friends were or were not under observation during any given set of phenomena, which is obviously an important flaw in the evidence.

Can these discrepancies be said to invalidate the case for the paranormality of the raps? We think not. It seems quite certain that the journalist and his friends left and also returned to the house while the rappings were still in progress, and so were actually observed at a critical period. In any case there are arguments against the possibility of fraud which do not depend upon showing that any given persons were under observation at a particular time.

Let us consider the hypothesis that there was a practical joker concealed somewhere in the house. Of course we measured the whole house inside and out and could detect no place where a trickster could have lurked; but even if there *had* been such a person, he would still have needed to install rapping machinery under the floor of the haunted bedroom. Accordingly we removed all furniture from the room and examined every inch of the floorboards with a magnifying glass. The boards were tongue-and-grooved together. We could detect no tool marks or splintering, and are convinced that no floorboards had ever been taken up. We removed a board that ran through the positions where we had first heard the rappings, but could see nothing suspicious under it or under the neighbouring boards. We then likewise examined the ceiling of the room below, which was also made of boards tongue-and-grooved together, and reached a similar conclusion. After examining the structure of the floor we were convinced that rapping machinery could have been installed under the floor only by removing boards from the floor of the haunted bedroom or from the ceiling of the room below; and that no boards had been removed from either of those places. It therefore does not seem that the case for the paranormality of the raps leans very heavily on proving that certain persons were under observation at given times.

Another possibility which a sceptic might explore would be that of illusions of the sense of hearing. He might suggest, for instance, that the rappings were really quite random, and produced by subsidence of the house. We were in a state of nervous expectancy due to being in a reputedly haunted house, and interpreted these random noises as intelligent responses to questions. Or else he might suppose that a practical joker was outside the house tapping on the window sills with a stick – and certainly in the still hours of the night noises in the haunted room could be clearly heard from outside the house, and of course the flashing of torches could be seen through the uncurtained windows. None the less we do not think there is much to be said in favour of either of these possibilities. All four investigators heard the raps; and all agreed they were answers to the questions. In general they did not occur whilst we were asking questions. They came in an even tempo, at a rate of one a second or somewhat faster. Immediately a question had been put, answering raps began. They were appropriate in number to the questions asked, for example one for "Yes", eleven for "November"; and once a question had received an appropriate answer there was nearly always silence until the next question had been posed. Nor does there seem the slightest reason for supposing that we mistook raps made by a mischief-maker on the walls, windows or window sills of the haunted room for raps made inside it. Auditory localization is an ordinary room (as distinct from localization out of doors or in an anechoic chamber) is more accurate than is commonly supposed; and we conducted extensive experiments in the haunted bedroom to ascertain whether or not we were liable to confuse rappings made from the outside of the house with rappings made inside the room itself. The answer was unequivocally that we were not.

The only remaining possibility for a sceptic to put forward is that of fraud by a member or members of the family or by the investigators themselves.

It is certainly possible that the toasting fork incident was fraudulently produced. We found that if we pushed the toasting fork behind the metal plate so that its prongs just shaved the staple when we closed the door, and then slammed the door, the fork would jump a little and "bolt" us into the room. Almost anyone in the house could have placed the fork in position while we were absent from the room between 2.45 a.m. and 3.34 a.m. – although we should add that the journalist and his friends were definitely absent from the house during this period, and that the members of the family, apart from the children, all signed statements that they were in no way concerned in the production of the phenomena. Incidentally we are convinced that the two children were too young to have been responsible for any of the phenomena; and in any case while phenomena were actually in progress we several times checked up that they were safely asleep.

There is, we fear, no escaping the conclusion that the only persons who could have faked the remaining phenomena were ourselves. In our statements we each considered the possibility that the other had produced the phenomena fraudulently, and, while there is no doubt that ADC could have tipped over the chair without AG seeing him, we neither of us thought that the other could have faked the various series of rappings. When the rappings began we each suspected the other, and in consequence we watched each other like hawks. There were no curtains on the windows of the haunted room and so we were each able to keep a fair check on the other's position. We switched our torches on and off without warning, several times interrupting series of raps, and each of us is prepared to assert quite definitely that if the other had been making the noises with his hand or with a reaching rod he would have been detected. We are left only with the possibility that we conspired together to produce the phenomena fraudulently. To this we must confess that we cannot find a ready answer. No sceptic worth his salt would accept our avowals of honesty, even if supported by evidence as to our moral characters, as refuting the hypothesis of fraud, for he could always conceive of overriding motives which might have impelled us to throw our habitual scruples to the winds – the desire for publicity, for instance, or the sheer joy of deceiving other people. To such dedicated disbelief there is in the last resort no answer.

DORIS STOKES undoubtedly helped to raise the profile of spiritualism in the later part of the last century with her public performances, television appearances and memoirs. She claimed to have developed her psychic abilities as a child when she saw groups of spirit figures and began to hear disembodied voices. Although attacked by several church authorities, Doris Stokes became the resident medium of the Spiritualist Association of Great Britain in 1975 and certainly promoted a new resurgence of interest in psychic phenomena. A story she liked to tell concerned an experience she had as a WRAF when – just for once – she actually ran away from some ghostly figures.

NO SUCH THING AS SPOOKS?

Location and date: Port Talbot, Wales, 1943

It was a stormy night. The rain had stopped, but a wind had sprung up and it was getting stronger every minute. Everything was in motion. Tattered clouds were flying across the moon, great black branches tossed against the sky, dead leaves whirled along the gutter and the six of we WRAFs, brave because we were in a group, decided to take the short cut home through the churchyard.

We joked nervously as we approached the path. Beneath wildly plunging trees the silent gravestones stood in rows, now in moonlight, now in shadow. Wet twigs slapped against our hair, strange dark shapes bobbed by the fence and our skirts tangled round our legs making it difficult to walk. The six of us huddled closer together, yet each voice grew a little louder, a little more daring.

"Bet you wouldn't walk across one of those graves!"

"I would too."

"The spooks'd get you."

"Spooks!" Molly's voice rose in derision. "Don't tell me you believe in spooks."

"Bet you wouldn't stay here all night."

"No. I've got more sense. I'd freeze to death."

I listened to them and laughed. You wouldn't have got me staying there all night either and not because of the cold. I wasn't going to let on but the place gave me the creeps. All those gloomy tombstones. They made me shudder. I glanced across at the church, a pretty stone building in daylight, but now just a black hulk against the sky, and as the moon came out again I stopped in surprise. There were people standing outside the church door. A whole family by the look of it; a man, a woman and two children, just standing there, patiently waiting. What in the world could they be doing? Surely the vicar hadn't arranged to meet them at this time of night.

"I wonder what those people are doing on a night like this," I said to the other girls.

"What people?" asked Molly.

"Those people over there."

They looked vaguely up and down the path. "Where?"

"Over there," I said pointing impatiently. "Look, standing by the church door. A whole family."

They peered in the direction I indicated, and then looked back at me. There was an odd pause and then suddenly, without a word being spoken, they all turned round and ran. Bewildered, I stared after them. What had I said? I glanced back at the family, still waiting, their clothes strangely unruffled in the gale. And then my heart lurched violently. Before my eyes they disappeared. They didn't walk away, they just went out like flames in the wind. For perhaps two seconds I just stood there, my mouth open, staring at the empty space and then I hitched up my skirt and ran as fast as my sensible shoes would allow me.

ARTHUR KOESTLER, whose unorthodox books on political, scientific and literary subjects made him one of the towering intellects of the twentieth century, was also deeply interested in psychic powers and helped to promote their study by leaving a bequest to establish, as the Sunday Mirror *put it: "the first professional ghostbuster". His 1983 will left £500,000 to endow a professorship of psychic research at Edinburgh University – a post subsequently filled by the American parapsychologist, Robert L Morris. Koestler, who worked as a foreign correspondent, served in the Spanish Civil War and came to England in 1940, where his lifetime interest in the supernatural was evident in many of his books right up until the time of his sudden and unexpected decision to die by suicide. What follows is one of Koestler's most striking accounts of the paranormal at work.*

THE HOUSE ON THE LAKE

Location and date: Caslano, Switzerland, 1935

The house stood in the village of Caslano, on a wooded slope, overlooking the Lake. It belonged to a rich, middle-aged woman, the widow of the famous German film-actor, Eugen Kloepfer. Maria Kloepfer was a benefactress of impecunious Communist writers whom she invited to her house, one at a time, for a month or two. Among those who had enjoyed her hospitality were Johannes R Becher, Ludwig Renn, and my brother-in-law, Peter. She also contributed generously to the various committees and front organisations of the Party.

On our first evening in her house, she explained to me that she was attracted by Communism as a new way of social life, but equally by Buddhism and Theosophy as ways of spiritual life, and that she regarded psychoanalysis as a bridge between the two. This might have sounded like the gushings of a frustrated society woman who feels the change of life approaching, but Maria was not that type. She was just the opposite.

I remember her best in her white bathing suit. She was tall, with a lean, sinewy body, with small breasts and long limbs, her skin the colour of baked clay from constant swimming and sunbathing. Stretched out in the grass, she looked like a stranded, ageing mermaid, waiting for the flood to call her back. The only discordant feature was her teeth, held together by conspicuous metal braces.

During the second week of my stay with Maria, we went for a walk in the woods. Ricky, the old mongrel, was ambling a few yards ahead of us. Suddenly Ricky stopped, rooted to the mossy ground, and gave out a growl which then changed into a plaintive, long-drawn howl. Maria also stopped and grabbed my arm – that alone gave me a start, for she normally avoided, and shrank away from, any physical touch or contact. Her face had changed colour in the undefinably painful manner of a person growing pale under a sunburnt skin, and the braces on her beeth became very visible. The wailing dog's hair was actually bristling, and the whole scene was so eerie that I felt suspended between horror and the giggles. Maria turned on her heel and hurried back along the narrow forest path towards the house, striding so fast on her long legs that I could hardly keep up behind her; yet I could see that she needed all her grim determination not to break into a run. The dog now kept running at her side, now and then licking her hand as if to comfort her. When we got home, Maria said curtly: "Don't leave me alone, please." I followed her to a balcony which she rarely used, and which opened on the back of the house, overlooking the woods from which we had come. Mary, the maid, brought up a carafe with *grappa*, giving her mistress a suspicious look, but left us again without saying a word. Maria drank a couple of small glasses, and I asked stupidly: "What happened?" She was not yet quite herself and said unguardedly with a shrug: "Ricky saw the uncle approaching us. He sometimes sees him first, and warns me." On that afternoon, I learnt part of Maria's story.

From time to time, Maria had a hallucination. She saw an uncle, who had died of *dementia praecox* when she was three, advancing on her simultaneously from three directions, from the right, left and front. The frontal image was slightly over life-size, the two lateral images were smaller. Before he could reach her, she was usually seized by a fit. "Don't get frightened," she said, "if you see me rolling on the floor and grinding my teeth – just leave me and call Mary. I don't like people to see it." When the hallucination started, Ricky always behaved as he had today. But sometimes the dog sensed the approach of the uncle before she saw him, and warned her. He had not turned up for the last few weeks, and she had already hoped that she had got rid of him for good. Now she was no longer sure. Anyway, something was bound to happen during the next few days – a sign. – What sort of sign? – Oh, nothing frightening. Just a sign. I would see.

After dinner I learnt more of the story. Maria had suffered one or two nervous breakdowns earlier in her life. She had been for a long period under psychoanalytical treatment. The analyst was a well-known orthodox Freudian whose name was at the time familiar to me, but I have mercifully forgotten it since. He had brought back to her the memory of a previously repressed and forgotten, early traumatic shock. As an infant between the age of two and three, she had been left alone for a few minutes with the deranged uncle, who had committed a sexual assault on her. But the revival of this memory did not cure Maria. On the contrary: it was after the conjuring up of the uncle's ghost that the hallucinations started.

Before that she had not even known that the uncle had ever existed, for he had never been mentioned by her parents. She had then broken off the treatment, against the analyst's warning, for fear that if she continued with it she would go insane. About the same time she divorced her husband, who seems to have treated her abominably. The analyst was the last link with her former world. When that link snapped she had retired to the house on the lake. She wanted no more grave-diggers to work in her brain. She knew everything that lay interred there, even the symbolic meaning of the trinity in her hallucination: the two pocket-editions of the uncle on either side, the large erect one in the centre, advancing upon her. But the knowledge did not help, and she wanted to know no more. She wanted to swim in the lake and get cleaned and tanned by the sun through skin and flesh down to the bones – an ageing, psychic mermaid, stranded upon "the tedious shore of Lethe".

While Maria was talking, first on the balcony overlooking the woods, and then on the terrace facing the sea, I had a strong feeling of listening to the *langage du destin*, as Malraux calls it. That demented uncle seemed to have stepped straight out of the book on Perversions that I had just finished. At moments, an absent look of Maria's reminded me of Attila watching a match burn down between his fingers. There was also that third parallel: the fatal breaking-off of a treatment, which Attila had also done – escaping from the operating table with only a hand pressed against the open gash. I had a feeling of being under a spell, experienced by the spiritual viscerae, as it were. Serial coincidences of this kind had often pursued me when I was passing through a crisis; gradually I have come to regard them as a warning in the symbolic code of the "language of destiny" – see the closing pages of *Arrow in the Blue*.

At some point during that evening, I said to Maria, attempting to joke, that in the matter of being "sore and kicked about" she certainly took precedence over me. She repeated, unsmiling, what she had said before, that the worst kick was still in store for me, and that it would be coming soon.

After that evening, the "uncle" was never again mentioned between us. But the next day, or the day after that, another incident occurred. While we were sitting at lunch, there was a sudden loud crash. A large, heavily-framed picture which, an instant before, had been peacefully hanging on the wall that I was facing, had crashed down on to the sideboard that stood beneath it. It made me jump, whereas Maria, who sat with her back to the picture, did not move a muscle. On the sideboard had stood a row of tumblers filled with milk in various stages of curdling into yoghourt. Maria had a hobby of making her own yoghourt; every morning two glasses of fresh milk were added to the left end of the row, and two glasses of finished yoghourt were taken off the right end. Now most of the glasses were broken; the row looked like a line of soldiers in whose middle a grenade had exploded, and half-curdled milk was splashed all over the sideboard and the floor.

"How on earth did that happen?" I asked, walking over to the battlefield. Maria shrugged, and said nothing. I looked at the back of the picture: the wire was not broken, and the two picture-hooks were still in the wall, solid and undamaged. In fact, I was able to hang the picture back in its former place, where it came again to rest as firmly and innocently as if it had always stayed there. Maria rang the bell, and Mary the maid came shuffling in to clear up the mess. "What happened?" she asked. Maria said quietly:

"*Es spuckt.*"

"*Schon wieder?*" said Mary. "Now Ma'am will have to go without yoghourt for a whole week."

When we had settled down again, Maria said gently, as if talking to a child: "Was the wire broken?"

"No," I said, "but *please* don't ask me to believe in miracles."

"There is no reason to get irritated," said Maria, "but I told you something of the kind would happen."

"What does it mean?" I asked, even more irritated.

"It is a sign," she said, again shrugging.

"A sign of what?"

"I don't know. Please let us drop the subject."

Maria rarely used the rhetorical "please". When she did, it had a strangely helpless, pathetic ring – it carried an echo of a frightened child saying "please" to a maniac with whom she had been left alone in a room.

D SCOTT ROGO was an American writer widely respected for his enquiries into parapsychology who, like Arthur Koestler, died tragically – his body being found stabbed to death in his home in North Carolina in August 1990. Like Koestler he developed an interest in the supernatural while in his teens and aside from contributing to a number of scientific journals also relayed the results of his research in books such as An Experience of Phantoms (1974), On The Track of the Poltergeist (1986) *and* Beyond Reality (1990). *Among the many*

studious reports, his tale of a haunted house written for the UFO
Annual *in 1975 is both revealing and vivid.*

THE PSYCHIC FORCE OF EVIL

Location: Los Angeles, California, USA, 1972

In 1972, I was fortunate enough to move into a
bona fide haunted house and make it my home.
It was an old, small, Spanish-style house originally built in the 1920s and was located in
one of the many outlying suburbs of Los
Angeles. This move was the opportunity of a
lifetime, and for two years I was able to keep a
month-to-month chronicle of a wide assortment of phenomena – from
mysterious phantom footsteps to disembodied voices – which occurred there. It was a fascinating as well as educational experience, and
one I wouldn't trade for the world. But even though I fully enjoyed my
two-year stay, on one occasion I did have a very disturbing experience
in the house . . . so disturbing, in fact, that afterwards it made me think
twice about ever sleeping in the house again.

It happened one night in 1973. By that time, I had already lived in the
house for well over a year and a half, so I certainly wasn't nervous
about being there. But this night was different from any other. I had
gone to sleep about one o'clock in the morning, which was about usual
for me, but woke up with a start within a couple of hours. And as I
awoke, I was overcome by a feeling that there was something evil and
horrid in the room with me. I could even sense from exactly what part
of the room the influence was emanating. It seemed to be coming
directly from the wall right next to my bed. It was an awful sensation
and, before I even knew what was happening to me, I catapulted out of
bed and made a beeline for the door. The only thing on my mind was
that I had to escape from the room at any expense. I was in a state of
stark panic so there was no compromising. I couldn't even get hold of
myself enough to analyze my thoughts. My only concern during those
few brief moments after I awoke was to get the hell out of the room, and
away from the evil I felt there, just as quickly as I could.

By the time I realized what was going on, I was standing in the
middle of the den, into which my bedroom opened. My heart was
pumping madly, but somehow I felt relieved just to be away from my
room and whatever was in there. I just stood there, naked and
stunned, and slowly tried to get a grip on myself. On one hand,

I realized that my actions were totally irrational. But, at the same time, I also knew that something very real and powerful had manifested itself in my room and that my panic was a direct response to it. So, I just stood there and waited to see what would happen next.

Slowly but surely, my heart stopped doing flip-flops and my nerves calmed down a bit. I even began to snicker at myself for getting so scared, but, nonetheless, I still felt a bit nervous about re-entering the bedroom. It took several more minutes before I was able to summon up my courage and sneak back into bed. The room "felt" perfectly normal when I re-entered it. Whatever evil had saturated the room was now gone.

This experience was the most vivid I ever had in the house. I never experienced anything like it again during the remaining year I lived there. But I'll never forget that experience as long as I live and, frankly, I hope I never have a similar experience again.

EDDIE BURKS has been described as the busiest ghost hunter in Britain. Although he experienced a "tunnel vision" of a magic garden at the age of five, the paranormal played no more part in his life while he was employed for many years as the Civil Service's Principal Scientific Officer. The day after the death of his wife in 1970, however, he sensed her presence and realized he had the ability to communicate with spirits. Since then he has investigated several hundred hauntings which have ranged from the ghost of a young man killed during the Civil War to an American pilot shot down over Germany who materialized to Eddie in Lincolnshire. His most famous enquiry as a "ghostbuster" occurred when he was asked to tackle a spirit haunting a London bank, as he told the Independent *in January 1994.*

THE COUTTS BANK REVENANT

Location and date:
Strand, London, UK, 1993

Coutts Bank had been having a lot of problems with the lighting and computers at their London headquarters in the Strand during the winter of 1993. The engineers were baffled and the staff was feeling very uneasy about things. Matters came to a head when a headless apparition was sighted. That was when I was called in to investigate.

As I usually do, I walked up and down the area where people had reported the ghost. When I sense a spirit, my level of consciousness changes. Not unlike the way you feel when someone is standing behind you. Then it develops into communication: a sort of inner voice. The process is not verbal. I suppose that my subconscious turns their messages into words. I certainly don't know who the spirits are at first.

I sensed a very unhappy spirit in the Coutts' building and he began communicating about his life. He said, "I have been waiting a long time. I practised the Law. I would not bend to the Queen's command conveyed to me through her servant, who held the great seal, so a case of treason was trumped up. I was beheaded not far from here, on a summer's day, which made me loath to depart."

By this time I could see a figure. He was tall and slim, with a thin face and aquiline nose, dressed in Elizabethan finery. I described out loud what I could see and the ghost replied, "That is a fair description, but you have not mentioned my ornaments."

He showed me the rings on his hand and the chain and medallion around his neck. He explained, "At my execution I took off my doublet and ruff for I did not wish them to be spoilt. They were to be given to my son. I put around my shoulders the black mantle which was part of my accoutrement in Law. I did not mind if this were stained, for it was stained already through this injustice."

The ghost believed I could help him. He said, "My hope is growing. If you can get me from this place, I shall be much obliged. I wait upon you."

At that moment I saw a woman dressed in Elizabethan costume, all in white. She took the man's hand and led him towards the clear light behind them. He looked back and thanked me and the others for helping him.

My help is to hold the person steady, because they release an enormous amount of emotional energy. There are other spirits helping them, too – whose identities I don't know – and they bring the person who will take them to the light once they are released. I don't think they are always the same, but I sense there is someone among them who has sympathy for the person.

After releasing the man, I left it to Coutts' archivist to try to find out who he was, on the few facts available. Father Francis Edwards, who is a member of the Royal Historical Association, read about the haunting in a newspaper and identified the phantom as Thomas Howard, the Fourth Duke of Norfolk, through his mention of practising the Law, the trumped-up charge and his execution in 1572 by order of Elizabeth I.

The Duke was one of the few people to get "stuck" when he died – the vast majority go through to the other life without trouble. He was beheaded at Tower Hill, two miles away from Coutts, but his family owned property in the Strand area. Sometimes ghosts follow a particular person, which can be very troublesome, but in cases like his they remain in a particular place.

Through Father Edwards, I met Lady Mary Mumford, a descendant of Thomas Howard, who organized a memorial service for her ancestor. On the evening after this I received a communication from the Duke. It said:

"You pleased me greatly with the honour you did me yesterday. Put aside any doubts which you may have entertained concerning the true value of the service, for it has truly relieved me of the vestiges of my sadness and now I feel free to step forward into the greater light. I owe you all a debt which I can only repay in the coinage of love whose quality is raised by my greater awareness of the presence of our God. Therefore accept my love and, when you can and when you will, reflect upon me and send me a token of your love. You may think that a gulf of time does separate us, but it is a moment only, and to me you are my brothers and sisters forever united and bound in the love of God. Remember me in your prayers as I will remember you until the blessed day when we meet in joy. Thank you and I bid you farewell."

MIA DORAN has become familiar to the British viewing public as the psychic on the TV series, Haunted House, *arguably the best of the spate of "ghost hunting" programmes screened in recent years. She saw her first ghost as a child of twelve and by the time she reached her early twenties had become a medium sought after to solve paranormal mysteries. Reports of her successes in the media led to the creation of the popular television series. Despite the painful emotional experience of losing her son, Shane, when he was 25, Mia now believes that some of the best psychics have been through similar traumas, a fact which enables them to be more "open" to the spirits of the departed. In February 2007 she talked about her life and experiences to the* Sunday Times Magazine.

SENSING GHOSTS

Location and date: Minster, Kent, UK, 1974

I was sensitive as a child. If somebody was upset, I would hurt for them. I didn't like arguments. If my mum and dad had a row – though they hardly ever did – I'd get very tense about it. I had a real need for harmony, and still do.

All my mates wanted to come round our house because my parents were so laid-back and open, especially my mum. My brothers' friends used to call her Mrs D and send her Christmas cards, and they treated her with great respect.

The nun was the first time I saw a ghost. She was standing under what used to be the old wishing-well gate at the abbey. I was looking at her, but I was more interested in my bag of chips. Then she disappeared. I said to Dad: "I've just seen a ghost!" He said: "Don't be silly." My friends wouldn't believe me either. The only person who took it seriously was my mum. But she made no big deal about it. I think that helped me be matter-of-fact too. Even though she believes, she looks for the logical first.

I know Mum is gifted. Years ago she told me she could see me in a big white house with a horseshoe drive and a pond. I was in a horrible place at the time, struggling. But by sheer luck, I came to have that house. I know she could do what I do, but she can't do it to order, like me. And she's shy. First time she watched me on TV she did it with a pillow over her face. She won't come to see me at a show in case she puts me off. But if we have a sad or a puzzling case I might tell her about it, because she has great empathy with people.

I see the ability, this heightened awareness, in all my family. In our house we often have ashtrays spinning and doors opening all on their own. Nobody freaks out. We often get ghosts here, but they're not hauntings. If you do a lot of readings in a place, I think you create a doorway – until you go back and close it.

I've never been scared of ghosts. I just feel this is something I'm meant to do. When I help people with hauntings, they have often had priests in, all sorts, and they're terrified by the time I arrive. I get angry. I think: "How dare it frighten these people?" If I can sort it out, I have to. I was brought up a Catholic, a religion that preaches there's no such thing as ghosts, yet trains priests in exorcism. I used to think it was hypocritical. Then I found out if you denounce ghosts you weaken them, so it's quite a clever move.

It's wonderful to find a ghost because it's quite rare. On the Isle of Sheppey, which is 9 miles by 12, there might be 30. Some are good, some bad. Very rarely are ghosts evil, but I had a nasty one on the last TV series. It unnerved me, but you mustn't have fear. That's something my spirit guide, Eric, taught me. Eric's always telling me off, in a nice way. "Take it more seriously." Or "Go in again, you're missing something."

If I'm looking for a ghost, I will sense it in my mind rather than see it with my eyes. I was in a bar in Kent when I saw this woman walk past. I knew she was a ghost because she shimmered. First she tapped me on the shoulder. Then she shoved me so hard I shot off my stool. I went storming into the ladies, having a row with a ghost: "What the hell is your problem?" She said it was not her friend who killed her, and I had to sort it out.

The worst place I've walked around was Canterbury Cathedral. It's supposed to be a holy place but the atmosphere of oppression was terrible. Most hauntings are attached to the location. Rarely will something attach itself to you: if you are strong enough psychically, you won't allow it. Ouija boards are an invitation and they're dangerous: I don't want teenagers playing around with them.

3

Phantoms in the Sky

Ghostly Pilots, Aircraft and Haunted Airfields

The twentieth century saw the appearance of a new type of ghost after centuries of tales about phantom soldiers and supernatural armadas. The rapid development of the "aeroplane" after the Wright Brothers had taken to the skies in the first heavier-than-air machine on 17 December 1903 was soon followed by sightings of phantom aircraft as well as ghostly pilots and haunted airfields. The carnage of two world wars was obviously a major factor in these and other similar sightings that have been reported during the past 100 years – some undoubtedly authentic, others rather dubious but a number worthy of serious consideration.

In the early years of the new century, superstitious people understandably likened the first reports of "mysterious shapes" in the skies over Britain, Europe and America to ghosts. It was, in fact, all too easy to mistake the pioneer "flying machines" for the supernatural figures that had haunted the minds of previous generations. No-one had, of course, seen anything like them before: and those fed on the latest novels of Jules Verne and H G Wells were easily stimulated by the sight of flimsy, weaving experimental aircraft. One example of how such perceptions could be exploited is linked to the legend of the "Angels of Mons" in the First World War. This story of supernatural bowmen coming to the aid of beleaguered British troops was widely believed to be true – despite protestations to the contrary by the creator, journalist and fiction writer, Arthur Machen. Indeed, there were even people seemingly ready to be taken in by a very bizarre "explanation" of the phenomenon a decade later.

In February 1930, stories appeared in the American and British press that a former member of the German Intelligence Service, Colonel Friedrich Herzenwirth, claimed to know the truth about the appearance of the "angels" at the height of the conflict. The Colonel gave an interview to the New York Mirror in which he said that the figures were actually "motion pictures" projected onto "screens of foggy white cloudbanks" over Flanders. They were projected by "cinematographic machines" with powerful Zeiss lenses mounted on German aeroplanes hovering above the British lines. In Herzenwirth's statement – to which authenticity was added by an explanatory diagram – he said the object of the visions had been to "create superstitious terror in the Allied ranks calculated to cause panic and a refusal to fight". But the Germans had miscalculated, he explained to the *Mirror*:

"What we had not expected was the English would turn the vision to their own benefit. This was a magnificent bit of counter-propaganda, for some of the English must have been fully aware of the mechanism of our trick. Their interpretation of our angels as protectors of their own troops turned the scales completely upon us. Had the British command contented itself with simply issuing an Army order unmasking our trickery, it would not have been half as effective."

The convincing Colonel said the Germans had been more successful with their "ghostly motion pictures" on the Russian front in 1915. There the Virgin Mary had been projected onto snow clouds with an uplifted hand as if she was motioning to stop the murderous enemy night attacks. As in France, Herzenwirth said, the German aircraft had flown overhead and "caused entire regiments who had beheld the vision to fall upon their knees in terror". He added:

"The trick was repeated several times and was invariably successful. We knew from prisoners we took that in some cases companies actually killed their officers and flung their rifles away, shouting that they would be guilty of firing upon an Army over which the Mother of God hovered in protection."

The Colonel's "explanation" of the famous phenomenon was recycled around the world by the media during the next few days, but it took a British paper, the *Daily News*, to discover the extraordinary truth. The paper's Berlin correspondent was dispatched to talk to those in authority and reported on 18 February:

"A prominent member of the War Intelligence Department in the present German Ministry declares that the story is a hoax. There are no records in the official archives dealing with the war that make any reference to the use of a projecting machine from aircraft to mislead enemy soldiers. Herzenwirth himself is a myth. It is officially stated that there is no such person."

A frantic search in New York to find the mysterious Colonel soon established that he had vanished as completely as the vision he had described. His claims were a ghost *story* in every sense of the word . . .

A rather more plausible account of a "vision" was reported in September 1916 by Flight-Lieutenant Ronald Jacoby who was stationed with his squadron at Pulham, one of the early English air bases in Norfolk. At just after 5 p.m. while he was on a training flight over the Norfolk Broads and was crossing the glistening 130 acres of Barton Broad, he happened to glance down and got a shock that remained with him for the rest of his life.

"As I looked down from my cockpit, I saw the face of a beautiful girl mirrored as it were in the water beneath. I could scarcely believe my eyes, especially as the face turned in my direction as I passed over it. She was even more beautiful than the 'Lady of Shalott'. I was so impressed that the following day I took up my squadron-leader to have a look."

Neither Jacoby nor his senior officer saw anything on that second September day – but such was the Flight-Lieutenant's conviction about the ghostly figure that he had seen that he began to research the local history for any kind of clues. It was not long before he discovered that there *had* been reports by other pilots, which indicated that the face was only visible from between 450–600 feet up and in the minutes just before the sun dipped into the west. The story had also been a tradition since long before the invention of flight.

From local people Jacoby learned that Barton Broad was a place they would avoid after sundown because a beautiful young girl had been murdered there hundreds of years ago and every so often, reappeared briefly from the waters at sunset looking for her lover. According to William Storer, a local boatman, the girl had been trying to escape from her father in a boat with her lover when the old man had shot at them both with his crossbow. The pair had drowned in the lake. Historian Charles Sampson, author of *Ghost of the Broads* (1931), says the ethereal girl had also been seen leaving the water at sunrise and occasionally moving sorrowfully around the edge whenever a mist settled over Barton Broad.

That same month of September 1916 saw the first ghost of an airman reported at one of the new airbases at Montrose in Scotland. The events that created the haunting had occurred two years earlier on the morning of 27 May 1913 when a pilot stationed at Montrose had crashed. The man was Lieutenant Desmond Arthur of Number 2 Squadron, Royal Flying Corps (later to become the RAF). He had been flying his BE2 biplane and was in the process of making an approach to landing at a height of about 4,000 feet when his starboard wing suddenly collapsed, causing the aircraft to dip into a steep dive. As the BE2 fell, Lieutenant Arthur's seatbelt snapped and he was pitched out of the cockpit. With no parachute to save him, the hapless aviator fell to his death in front of his horrified ground crew waiting for him to land.

Officers from the Royal Aero Club who subsequently investigated the tragedy pinpointed the possible cause as one of the BE2's wings on which a broken spar had been repaired with a crude splice. They debated whether the accident was the result of a botched service – or perhaps a deliberate attempt to kill the young Irish aviator. The argument went as far as the House of Commons where answers were demanded by several MPs with vested interests in the future of flying.

Three years later, with no conclusion having been reached, strange things began to happen at the Montrose airbase. They were noticed by a number of the airman, as historian Thomas Fletcher wrote in an article about the strange episode for *The Scotsman* in June 1956:

"The events began in September 1916. One of the officers twice followed a figure in full flying kit approaching the mess, only to see him vanish before reaching the door. On another night, a flying instructor woke to find a strange man sitting beside the fire in his bedroom. When he challenged the intruder, the chair was suddenly empty. On a further night, two other men woke simultaneously convinced that there was *someone* in their room. Major Cyril Foggin, one of the senior officers, also claimed to have seen the figure no less than five times. All of them were convinced Lieutenant Arthur had 'returned' to get the mystery surrounding his death resolved."

Finally, just before Christmas, the chairman of the investigators, Sir Charles Bright, released the findings of his team: "It appears probable that the machine had been damaged accidentally and that the man (or men) responsible for the damage had repaired it as best he (or they) could to avoid detection and punishment."

The ghost of Lieutenant Desmond Arthur was reported just once more in January 1917. The figure was now said to be happier. Indeed, the legend has persisted that the dead pilot seemed to sense that he had been cleared of causing the crash and could rest in peace.*

One of the twentieth century's earliest authenticated sightings of a ghost aircraft occurred in 1934 on the Wirral peninsula of Lancashire. A bus driver approaching the town of Hoylake on the coast was suddenly aware of an aircraft above him that seemed to be in difficulties. He pulled up the vehicle and calling his conductor, pointed to the drama going on overhead. The two men watched in horror as the plane "swooped down to the sea and disappeared beneath the waves", to quote the driver's own words to the *Liverpool Echo* which ran the story.

According to the *Echo*, the two men immediately reported the accident and a lifeboat was despatched from Wallasey to the spot where the plane had vanished. Not a trace of the machine could be found. Even two RAF aircraft that were called to fly over the area

---

* In 1940 a ghostly biplane described as "looking like a Tiger Moth" was seen by a number of airmen on the Montrose airfield narrowly avoiding a Hawker Hurricane that was making a night landing. Two years later, a Flight-Lieutenant who was said to have been very unpopular with his men crashed and died within moments of taking off from the base. In 1946, a guard on duty at Montrose saw a figure emerging from one of the hangars and ran to challenge him. The man was horrified to be confronted by an airman with "a dead-white face, wearing goggles, helmet and flying suit", who immediately vanished. Later the guard learned that the hangar had been used as a morgue to hold the body of the despised Flight-Lieutenant until he could be removed for burial.

were unable to find anything. After two days of fruitless searching – and not a trace of any wreckage coming to the surface – the hunt was called off. There the episode might have been forgotten, wrote G P J L Estrange in *Prediction* magazine in June 1942, if a similar accident had not been reported in the same neighbourhood less than a year later. He explains:

"Once again a prolonged search took place without result. The same thing also happened when, a few months afterwards, a woman informed the police that she had seen an aeroplane fall into the sea at that very same spot. Is it possible that all the people who reported this occurrence were witnesses of the 'etheric reflection' of an air disaster which had certainly taken place in that district a few years previously?"

The question remains unresolved – though ghost hunters have regularly returned to the beautiful Wirral headland in the hope of seeing the phantom once again fly into oblivion.

A story with striking similarities was also told by Elliott O'Donnell in that same year of 1942. The ghost hunter said that a rumour reported in the national press in January of a phantom aeroplane very like a Nazi Messerschmidt ME2 that had been seen and heard to crash in a field close to an aerodrome in a south-east county of which nothing could be found, had reminded him of an experience he had undergone less than a year earlier in the Thames Valley. He was returning to a hotel on a cloudless night after visiting some friends. Everything was so peaceful, O'Donnell said, that it was difficult to believe the country was at war. Then he heard the unmistakable sound of an aircraft.

"It sounded to me like one of our planes. Searchlights were sweeping the sky all round, but there was no alert. The droning rapidly increased in volume. I looked up into the moonlit sky and saw a plane coming, very low, towards me. There were fields on either side of the road and I wondered if it was going to land on one of them. Getting lower as it flew, it passed almost immediately above me. When it had gone a little way it suddenly nosed downwards and I realized to my consternation it was out of control and falling. There was a whirring and a spluttering as it shot towards the earth and then a crash, curiously hollow-sounding and reverberating. I started running towards the place where it lay, but when I was a few yards from it, it vanished abruptly and inexplicably. I was looking at it one moment and the next staring in wide-eyed amazement into space. The plane – *or whatever it was* – was no longer there and a stillness that was uncanny in its intensity succeeded the terrible crash."

O'Donnell, the man who had seen many strange and inexplicable things in his life, admitted he walked the rest of the way to his hotel "a little jarred and much puzzled". The following day, though, he was determined to discover if there was any explanation for the events he had experienced. The answer was not without surprises:

"As a result of my enquiries, I was informed that about ten years previously a Captain Schofield, when flying towards an aerodrome not very far from Shepperton, had crashed in the very spot where I had seen the phantom plane crash, and been killed. Periodically, at about midnight, ever since then a ghost plane, believed to be that of Schofield and his companion, had haunted the Thames Valley in the neighbourhood of Shepperton. Many people have seen it. I was the latest."

There was another brush with the supernatural for the crew of an RAF bomber a couple of months after this. According to historian Nigel Doughty, a badly shot-up Lancaster was struggling back to base after a mass raid on Germany, which had already seen the loss of a number of planes. Several of the bomber's crew had been killed in the raid and the pilot was badly wounded. To make matters worse, most of the navigating instruments were malfunctioning and the radio was all but useless. Just as the bomber was nearing the coast of England, lumbering through a dense fog, something totally unto-ward happened, as Doughty describes:

"Suddenly, the air-gunner, who had had to take over, saw a light flashing ahead. It was spelling out the identification letters of the flight commander. The delighted air-gunner followed the 'light of salvation' through the swirling fog. After a while, it started to drop gradually down. He followed it. The cloud broke – and there they were lined straight up on their home airfield runway. Scrambling out, the gunner called a cheery greeting to the ground staff, 'Thank God the flight commander led us back!' "

In relating the story, the gunner said that he noticed the little group were looking at him oddly. One of the men finally shook his head and whispered with a puzzled frown, "The flight commander was shot down in flames over the target."

Perhaps, though, the most curious haunting of that traumatic year occurred at RAF Fairlop in Essex. One night in November 1942, the airbase was suddenly put on alert when a report from control said that an unidentified aircraft had been seen approaching the base. As all the Spitfires of No. 603 Squadron were on the ground and accounted for, it had to be a German raider. When a dark shape hove into sight, searchlights raked the sky and the ack-ack battery beside the camp buildings opened fire.

Moments later, a mystified RAF officer was shouting to his men to cease-fire. The fingers of light had revealed what was unmistakably an ancient bi-plane that seemed to be flying completely unscathed through the hail of gunfire. According to the station log, the aircraft remained in view of the officer and gun crew for several moments before disappearing as mysteriously as it had appeared. No one in the unit was in any doubt that the plane was of a type unseen for almost a quarter of a century – a Sopwith Camel fighter, one of the most successful planes flown during the First World War.

A subsequent enquiry into the mystery established that a squadron of Camels had been based at Hainault Farm – the earlier name of RAF Fairlop – some 25 years before to counter the attacks of German Zeppelins and Gotha aircraft. A total of 1,294 enemy aircraft had been destroyed by these sturdy little fighters between the summer of 1917 and the Armistice on 11 November 1918.

In particular, several of these Camels had been converted for night fighter use – curiously referred to as Sopwith "Comics" – and had proved very effective. One of the leading pilots of this group had been Lieutenant George Craig of 44 Squadron. The description of the mystery plane in 1942 with its relocated cockpit, petrol tank under the centre wing section and guns mounted above the upper wing section that were attached to a separate Foster rail-mounting, matched that of Lieutenant Craig's "Kite" precisely. The story of the "return" of the First World War ace soon became a legend in the RAF and it has been retold several times, notably in *Ripley's Believe It or Not* series as a True Ghost Story, "The Winged Phantom" in 1969.

Another of the famous aircraft of the early part of the twentieth century, a Tiger Moth, also made an ethereal appearance not long after the end of the war. This story concerns a Royal Navy pilot who undertook his basic training at Plymouth. Flying a de Havilland Chipmunk, the man's navigation exercises took him along the coast as far west as Lands End, before he turned for home across country to base. Later, insisting on anonymity, the pilot recounted his strange story of what happened to him on one particular fight to *Chilling Tales* (2001).

He was on the return leg to Plymouth and was just about to cross Bodmin Moor when he saw a great mass of dark clouds ahead of him. Calling up the control tower, it was suggested that he change his flight plan to an alternative airport. But the thought of trying to land on an unfamiliar runway filled him with anxiety, as he explained:

"By now I was flying above the cloud which stretched in three directions as far as I could see. I was about to begin the turn towards my new landing site when, about 200 metres ahead, a yellow-painted Tiger Moth emerged from the enveloping cloud-base. I could plainly see the leather-helmeted and goggled pilot as he turned in his open cockpit, first giving me a 'thumbs up' then an unmistakable downward jab that indicated I should follow him."

Startled, but deciding to follow the instructions of the Tiger Moth pilot, he flew down through the swirling cloud on the tail of the yellow aircraft. Suddenly he found himself breaking out of the cloud and perfectly positioned for a landing. There was no sign of his rescuer, however. He touched down with a mixture of relief and bewilderment. His explanation for returning to base rather than seeking the alternative landing spot was not taken well by his instructors – who barked at him in disbelief that no Tiger Moth had flown in this part of the country since the Second World War.

There are several other stories of veterans of the war being seen long after the last examples of their kind had become museum pieces. In 1985, for example, Molly Baker was returning from a holiday with her daughter and son-in-law who lived in Italy on a British Airways jet from Bergamo to Gatwick. As the plane was crossing Germany, it ran into an electric storm and Mrs Baker suddenly found herself being reminded of her husband, Harry who, forty years earlier, had flown a Lancaster in the Pathfinder Force providing lighting for bombing raids on the Nazis. When the lights on the aircraft suddenly went out and there was a distinct smell of burning, she had an inkling of what it must have been like for her late husband. Unbeknown to her, the jet had suffered damage to several of its navigation instruments, which was going to make the homeward journey and landing difficult. As she sat anxiously in her seat, Mary Baker happened to glance out of the little window beside her. What she saw made her wonder if her eyes were playing tricks, she later told the *Sunday Express* of 22 December 1985:

"There was something to the left and a little ahead. Another plane, silhouetted black against the whiteness, flying swift and straight below. It was like a Pathfinder and suddenly I felt Harry was near me. I knew that Harry was down there in his Lancaster and would see us home safely."

Later the pilot, Captain Alan Toland, would also admit to the *Express* that he, too, was suddenly aware of another aircraft as they neared Gatwick. The paper describes his emotions at this critical moment:

"As he braced himself for the touch-down he saw it clearly just for a second, silhouetted against the lights: a big black bomber flying 500 feet in front of him, the rear-gun turret canopy gleaming between the twin tail fins. He saw the great wings rock in a gesture of farewell. And then it was gone and he felt the tyres kiss the runway."

Captain Toland said he tried to convince himself he had imagined the whole incident, so concerned was he for his damaged aircraft. He knew that no Lancaster could possibly match the speed of a modern jet. But when he heard the story of his passenger, Mary Baker, and her Pathfinder husband, he realized like many pilots before him that not everything in flying could be explained by the rational or the normal. . .

The mountainous and picturesque Peak District is an area of the British Isles that has a particular reputation for the sighting of ghost planes. Here, in an area bounded by Sheffield to the east, Glossop to the west and Buxton to the south, over 300 people have lost their lives in more than fifty crashes during and since the Second World War.

Typical of these sightings was the one experienced by David and Helen Shaw in October 1982 when they saw a Lancaster bomber fly overhead while they were visiting Ladybower Reservoir. Enquiries revealed that a Royal Canadian Lancaster bomber had crashed in the nearby Bleaklow Mountains on 18 March 1945 killing the entire crew of six.

In the same area on a sunny afternoon in May 1995, a man walking his dog saw a Second World War Dakota flying very low and about to crash although it was making no sound. Tony Ingle hurried to the field where the plane had appeared to go down but could find nothing. His dog Ben reacted badly as soon as the pair reached the field and refused to go anywhere near it. Here again research established that the plane could have been the ghost of a USAF Dakota that had crashed on 24 July 1945 resulting in the death of the five-man crew and two passengers. The site was less than fifty yards from where the Lancaster had fallen.

Stranger still was the experience of crash investigator Gerald Scarrett while he was up on a 2,000-foot shelf known as James' Thorn in 1995. He was showing a group of aircraft archaeologists the site where a US Superfortress had crashed during a routine flight on 3 November 1948. He was also investigating claims that a ghost plane had been seen flying overhead. According to a subsequent report of what happened in the *Sheffield Star*, the visitors spotted a man in flying gear:

"He was standing behind Mr Scarrett and they asked who he was. When Scarrett turned round, there was no one there. Could it have been the apparition of Captain Landon P Tanner, the pilot of the doomed Superfortress?"

The first ghost of an airman to be rigorously investigated by the Society for Psychical Research took place in 1918. The apparition was that of RAF Lieutenant David E McConnel who was killed in a flying accident on 7 December and seen by one of his fellow officers, Lieutenant James J Larkin. The facts were sent to the SPR by the dead man's father, Mr D R McConnell, who explained that his son had been flying a Sopwith Camel from Scampton airfield near Lincoln to Tadcaster just over 60 miles away. He had left at 11.35 a.m. accompanied by an Avro plane – a two-seater – which was to bring him back after delivering the Camel to the base.

Nearing Doncaster the two planes ran into fog, at the sight of which the pilot of the two-seater decided to make an emergency landing. Lieutenant McConnel opted to go on to Tadcaster. The fog grew increasingly thick and it is believed the young pilot was near to exhaustion when he finally neared his destination at around 3.30 p.m. McConnel senior explained:

"As he at last approached the Tadcaster Aerodrome, the machine was seen approaching by a man in the road about a quarter of a mile distant from the camp, who reported the fog to be extremely dense. During the evidence at the inquest a girl, or young woman, said she was watching the plane and saw it apparently sideslip then right itself. It flew steadily for a minute or two, then mounted and suddenly and immediately nose-dived and crashed. The girl ran to the spot and found the officer dead."

However, a letter to Mr McConnel after the crash from Lieutenant Larkin turned the tragedy of his son's death into another extraordinary example of the intervention of the supernatural in human life. Larkin described his experience in carefully measured words:

"I was sitting in front of the fire at Scampton when I heard someone walking up the passage. The door opened with the usual noise and clatter that David always made. I heard his, 'Hello, boy' and I turned half-round in my chair and saw him standing in the doorway, half-in and half-out of the room, holding the door knob in his hand. He was dressed in his full flying clothes and he was smiling as he always was. In reply to his greeting I remarked, 'Hullo, back already?' He replied, 'Yes, got there all right, had a good trip.' He then said, 'Well, cheerio!' closed the door noisily and went out. I went on with my reading."

According to Larkin, the time was between a quarter and half-past three. Shortly afterwards a Lieutenant Garner-Smith entered the room and asked what time McConnel was due back as "they were going into Lincoln that evening." The seated man replied, "He *is* back, he was in the room a few minutes ago." Larkin himself went into the city that evening – and walked into the biggest surprise of his life.

"In the smoking room of the Albion Hotel I heard a group of officers talking and overheard their conversation and the words 'crashed' and 'McConnel'. I joined them and they told me that just before they had left Scampton, word had come through that McConnel had crashed and had been killed taking the Camel to Tadcaster. As you can understand, Mr McConnel, I was at a loss to solve the problem. There was no disputing the fact that he *had* been killed whilst flying to Tadcaster, presumably at 3.25, as we ascertained afterwards that his watch had stopped at that time. I tried to persuade myself that I had not seen him or spoken to him in my room, but I could not make myself believe otherwise as I was undeniably awake and his appearance, voice and manner had all been so natural."

Another "moment of death apparition" – as they have become categorized by the SPR – took place in 1942 to Flight-Lieutenant

Francis J Pain while he was stationed with a fighter squadron in the Western Desert. He later described the events to Michael Duball in *Life Beyond The Grave* (1957):

"On the morning of 3 July, my squadron took off to intercept a wave of Stuka dive-bombers, with a top cover of ME 109 fighters high above them. After the squadron was separated over a large area of sky, we made our way back to base in ones and twos. I landed and strolled over to the mess tent about a hundred yards away. Flight-Lieutenant Ginger Turner came towards me from my right. 'Some party, Derna,' he said. 'I never saw them until they hit us.'

Flight-Lieutenant Pain says that "Derna" was a nickname that only Turner used for him. He then offered his colleague a cigarette:

"For the first time since I had known him, he refused, saying, 'No thanks, old boy, I don't need one now.' He branched off to his tent, which was ten or twelve yards away on our right. I continued to the mess. Squadron-Leader James came into the bar and said to us, 'Bad show about Ginger. They cut him to pieces as he pulled out from under the tail of a Stuka.'"

The supernatural intervened in an equally extraordinary way in the life of Joseph D Westheimer, a navigator in the US Army Air Force stationed at Haifa in 1944, who would later become famous for his Second World War novel and film, *Von Ryan's Express* (1964). He was based at a small airfield at Ramat David, in what was then Palestine. It was so small, he would recall later, that it did not even have its own radio transmitter. Planes flying missions over the Mediterranean had to find their own landmarks when they returned – which could be difficult at night.

After one particular night bombing operation, Leroy Williams, the pilot of Westheimer's B-24, found himself in low cloud and unable to spot any landmark that would enable them to reach the base. Instead, Williams followed the normal emergency procedure and made contact with Lydda Field near Tel Aviv and asked for a directional bearing to Lydda. Westheimer explained:

"We knew how long it would take to fly from Lydda to Ramat David and when we'd been in the air that long we dropped down to look for the field's lights. But there was no field, only rugged mountains, which would have made it impossible for a big bomber to land. So Leroy decided to try again and we headed back to Lydda to repeat the whole procedure."

By now, though, the B-24 was running low on fuel. Leroy Williams made a quick decision and informed the crew he was going to land at Lydda, where they could refuel and return to Ramat David the next morning. Instead, though, something inexplicable happened, as Westheimer recalled:

"We homed in on the Lydda signal and made a safe landing. But we weren't where we were supposed to be at all. We had landed at Ramat David – the field without a radio. We had followed a signal, no doubt about that – even though there was no signal to follow. *Something* had brought us back to safety, but we never found out *what.*"

Another celebrity who served in the Second World War and had several brushes with the unknown was Michael Bentine, one of the founders of the legendary Goons radio show, who talked about this side of his life to Mark Kahn of the *Sunday Mirror* in August 1981. Bentine had, in fact, been fascinated by the paranormal since he was a child, as his father had been a medium and spirit healer. The older man conducted many experiments in his quest to prove that a parallel form of life existed and Michael had been present at a number of these, witnessing examples of levitation and ectoplasm. Turning to the war years he explained:

"During the war I was an RAF Intelligence Officer and one of my jobs was briefing bomber crews before they set off on missions. I already knew I had the gift of ESP and could sense when people were going to die. Again and again I would see the faces of one or another of these people turn into a skull in front of my eyes and I knew they would die that night. There were times when I prayed that this gift would be taken away from me."

Bentine survived the war, but was reluctant to use his psychic powers. However, in 1984 he took part in a twelve-part series about psychical and spiritual powers for Channel Four and was haunted by his wartime memories once again. He explained:

"We went to this airfield which had been used during the war by Polish airmen. The place was abandoned and deserted and they asked me to see if there were any psychic forces still there. I was very nervous and not sure I should do it. But I did manage to make contact with several of the dead flyers and I was relieved to find they were at peace. In a way it helped me to exorcize those faces I had seen over forty years before."

Not all ghostly airmen have been benign, however. In his exhaustive *Gazetteer of British Ghosts* (1971), Peter Underwood tells the story of an airman who was charged with murdering a woman and child in a house next door to a derelict hall in Ealing, Middlesex and hanged for the crime in 1943. A few years after the war, a photographer who rented the hall and restored it as a studio found his work being disturbed by supernatural occurrences. Underwood writes:

"Lamps hanging from the ceiling swung in unison, footsteps sounded on the unfrequented floor, people were touched, voices were heard. Convinced that the place was indeed haunted, the photographer and his staff held séances at which a dead airman purported to communicate, spoke of an aircraft which at the relevant date was on the secret list and insisted that he had not been guilty of the crime for which he had been hanged."

Underwood found the story convincing. He believed the photographer – who had been a young boy at the time of the events – could not have had any direct knowledge of either the murder, which was described in some detail, or the secret aircraft.

In 1978, a young Surrey couple approached the SPR to complain that the ghost of an RAF pilot dressed in a Second World War leather jacket, helmet and oxygen mask was plaguing their home in Croydon. Four times he had materialized in the house and – poltergeistlike – tossed around a number of Second World War souvenirs. When investigator Brian Nisbet visited the property he discovered that the husband was a collector of military regalia and it was a tailor's dummy dressed in an SS uniform and several other Nazi souvenirs that had been subjected to the spirit's wrath.

It seemed to Nisbet that the ghost was angry at finding reminders of the enemy in the house. Following this piece of intuition, the SPR established that the house was on the site of the old Croydon Airport, which had been operational during the war. Still, though, Brian Nisbet remained puzzled by the haunting, concluding his report: "I have not been able to explain any of the things that have happened to these people."

An evil wartime spirit was also believed to have been the cause of disturbances at another house built on an airfield at Great Waldingfield in Suffolk, used by both British and American aircraft. Richard and Angie Richardson, who lived there in the 1980s, said their nights were regularly disturbed by rattling and banging sounds and an "evil-looking shadow" that would flit across their bedroom. Angela explained:

"There was a story that a plane had crashed on returning from a raid over Germany and the pilot had been incinerated in the blaze. After that people crossing the spot were said to get the impression of an eerie presence and the locals avoided the area at all times. Some of them were very surprised when the airfield was developed after the war. In the end we decided to sell up and leave. It was not a happy time for us – and probably not for that tormented ghost either."

In contrast, the *News of the World* reported a phantom airman who seemed anything but tormented in 1979. He was apparently known as "Fred" and was to be found in the aircraft museum at Cosford in Shropshire. A retired RAF engineer, John Small, who looked after a Lincoln bomber in the collection, has seen him on several occasions. Small said the figure wore a blue battledress and a white polo-necked sweater. He explained:

"The first time I saw him I was speechless. He was sitting on a toolbox inside the Lincoln. Then he vanished. I've seen him again in the plane or in the hangar and so have most of the staff. He doesn't look eerie, though, but quite normal. We think he was a wartime flier."

There are several more haunted wartime airfields that are worth a mention here. Bircham Newton Aerodrome on the empty wastes of East Anglia, for example, made national news in 1972 when the strange events happening there were featured on Jack de Manio's morning radio show and BBC TV's news programme, *Nationwide*. Originally constructed in 1914, the airfield had been abandoned in the inter-war years and then brought back into active service in 1939 as a base for RAF, Australian and Canadian pilots. Following the end of hostilities the base was converted into a hotel – and the haunting began in an area that had been turned into a squash court. Players suddenly became aware of being watched by a man in RAF uniform who disappeared through the walls as soon as he was approached.

After being disturbed by several appearances of the ghostly pilot, they decided to leave a tape recorder in the court overnight. The following morning the tape was found full of weird sounds including a strange, groaning voice and the drone of aircraft. When Jack de Manio replayed the recording on his programme it caused a sensation – and generated numerous ideas about the cause. It was suggested a man named Wiley who had committed suicide in the Officers' Mess during the war could cause the haunting. Alternatively, the figure might have been one of the victims of an Anson that crashed on a nearby church, killing the three-man crew, Pat Sullivan, Gerry Arnold and "Dusty" Miller, all of whom were said to have been keen squash players. When a TV crew set up their cameras to try and film the mysterious figure, they were subjected to a number of unnerving noisy incidents and the sound of hurrying footsteps. Andrew Green investigated the story for his book, *Our Haunted Kingdom* (1973) and relates one particularly fascinating incident:

"During the height of the investigation, a BBC woman interviewer from the *Nationwide* programme decided she would stay the night in the 'haunted court' with a tape recorder and was, at her request, locked in. She described later the intense feeling of cold, the sounds of banging doors opening and closing and the peculiar fact that the recorder stopped without any reason at 12.30. It was only when she returned to the studio that she was able to get the machine going again. No fault was found with it. The hotel was demolished later in 1972 leaving the mystery of the haunted squash court so far unanswered."

Another phantom airman with the ability to walk through solid objects was first reported in 1965 at the new Teesside International Airport, built on what had been a military airfield until the previous year. One winter's evening a young apprentice was suddenly disturbed by a man dressed unmistakably in the uniform of a Second World War fighter pilot. When the youngster asked, "Can I help you, sir?" – a later account in the *Ripon Gazette and Observer* reported – the figure walked straight through a corrugated sheet wall. On a second occasion, the figure disappeared through a solid wall, causing the newspaper to speculate that the ghost "is believed to have been an airman of 264 Squadron stationed at RAF Leeming during the war."

Although ghosts in general have a tendency to be solitary, several distinctive figures believed to be wartime pilots have been observed at Martlesham Heath in Suffolk, which was a major base and is now occupied by Suffolk Police Headquarters and a shopping mall. Since 1978, several police officers have reported weird happenings and the owners of one of the shops have claimed to have seen a "detached human shadow" outside their building. At the former RAF base at Metheringham near Lincoln the ghost seen wandering around the perimeter track is undoubtedly that of a woman. She was a local girl, Catherine Bystock, who was killed in a motorcycle accident during the war. She apparently returns at around 10 a.m. to flag down motorists on the road and ask them to help her boyfriend who is lying injured nearby. She vanishes as soon as any vehicle stops, though. Also in Lincolnshire at RAF Manby near Louth a Second World War pilot wearing flying gear and a long coat regularly returns to his old stamping ground. Several reports during the 1980s have added the information that his appearances have sometimes coincided with the droning sound of aircraft engines on the old runway.

In fact, tales of "phantom engine noises" are by no means uncommon, according to Bruce Halfpenny, a former RAF policeman who has spent years investigating stories of haunted airfields. He has carried out research at a number of old bases throughout the country where unearthly sounds have been reported, he explained to David Gordon of the *News of the World*:

"One of the most interesting cases was at an old airfield, Kelstern, in Lincolnshire where I heard the sound of engines approaching the overgrown concrete runway at dusk several times. I can recognize old bombers from their noise, so I knew it was a Lancaster. It sounded as if it was limping back to base. Then the engines suddenly stopped as if something had happened to the plane. It was uncanny."

Bruce also told the reporter he had felt a "chilling presence" at an old base near Middleton St George in Durham where Canadian fliers were stationed during the war. They were known as "The Ghost Squadron", he said, because of their "death's head" badge. Many of them died and the ghost hunter is sure that some are still haunting the airfield.

A far more unusual and unnerving figure is associated with RAF Mildenhall on the remote Norfolk Breckland. Known as "Old Roger", he is dressed in a fluttering cloak, his long hair streaming in the breeze and playing an ancient flute. It is claimed he has the power to "whistle up" a sandstorm and did this twice during the Second World War to protect the airbase from German raiders. Herbert E Wiseman told the story in the October 1960 issue of *East Anglian Magazine*:

"'Old Roger' was on the spot on two occasions when he was most urgently needed by the RAF. Had he not whistled up his sandstorms the base might have been badly plastered with incendiaries and high explosives. On the first occasion in 1941 when the aerodrome was attacked, the old fellow was distinctly seen playing his pipe and a few moments afterwards up went whirling pillars of sand all around. The raiding planes couldn't find the target so they turned tail and fled and the wind and sand subsided and all was quite and normal again."

The second appearance of "Old Roger" occurred on a March evening two years later. This time it was a single dive bomber that had found its way through the coastal defences. Says Wiseman:

"The lone plane was seen approaching when the whistle started again and a great roaring pillar of sand swept the sky. A few moments later there was not a trace of sand and not a sign of the plane. Anyone who might have concluded that the whole thing was a hallucination or the raider was a 'ghost plane' was quickly proved wrong when the wreckage of the raider was found a few miles away on the East Coast."

But the story did not quite end there. For the investigators who examined the plane found it difficult to understand *why* the German had crashed and killed every member of the crew. Wiseman explains the eerie finale:

"The experts were baffled. They discovered that sand had penetrated the mechanism of the plane at every point. The wreck looked as if sand had been shovelled into it. Some suggested that the raider had flown into a sandstorm. But a soil expert would have none of this. 'Sandstorm!' he is reputed to have said, 'they do not occur in England – at least not sandstorm of such heaviness and violence!' Those who were familiar with the legend of 'Old Roger' knew exactly *who* was responsible for coming to his country's aid . . .'"

In 1968, the famous old Second World War fighter base at North Weald was used for location filming of the multi-million pound epic, *Battle of Britain*, starring Laurence Oliver, Kenneth More, Michael Caine and many more big stars of the time. The station, where the legendary "tin legs" pilot, Douglas Bader, had led the fight against the might of the *Luftwaffe* was refurbished to recreate the atmosphere of those critical days in the war. The work was done so well, it seems, that during the filming the ghost of a pilot was seen in one of the hangars.

Benny Fisz, the producer of the film, gave a conducted tour of the location and introduced a group of journalists to the cast, in between shooting a sequence in which enemy fighters attacked the base. After watching a flyover and the exploding of carefully controlled explosives, Benny told the journalists that all the upheaval seemed to have disturbed a former resident. He explained:

"A couple of times while we've been here there have been some strange occurrences. One of the security staff spotted a chap in RAF uniform walking past a hut long after the actors had stopped filming for the day. When he ran after the man, he vanished completely."

Benny Fisz said during the flyover of Spitfires he and the other members of the cast and crew were startled to see *seven* planes rather than six.

"There couldn't be any doubt about the number as we'd only been able to hire six. But there definitely seemed to be one more as the fighters flew overhead. A lot of people saw it. But the strange thing was once the negative of the film was developed there were just six planes as there should have been."

Air Marshal Sir Victor Goddard experienced a similar optical mystery when he was a young RAF pilot in 1937. Flying over East Anglia, the man destined to play a major role in the Air Force's victory over Germany happened to look out of his cockpit and was totally surprised at what lay below him. In his account, "The Phantom Airfield" published in 1978 he explained:

"Below me was an airfield and hangars and aircraft. What surprised me was that the place was not recorded on any maps or charts I had seen. When I got back to base I reported the sighting and left it at that. Five years later I saw the place again. It had only just been built, I was told, exactly where I had seen it, as part of the RAF's front line against the *Luftwaffe*."

The same area came under the scrutiny of ghost hunter Joan Forman when she was writing her book, *Haunted East Anglia*, in 1974. She, too, found an intriguing tale of a phantom airman. The locality was a house in Bishop's Stortford and the figure was a tall man in a grey-green uniform who had been seen from time to time moving fleetingly around the property. Joan Forman learned that a visitor who also saw the figure in the garden had finally solved the mystery. This lady had identified the figure from a photograph hanging in one of the rooms. She told her host the description matched an airman in the picture who had been killed in an early morning raid. Forman later wrote:

"It seems that airmen from the nearby base at North Weald had been in the habit of dropping in to see the family, treating the place as a welcome home-from-home while posted in England. It was common practice for the boys to drop by in the morning to greet their friends after an early raid. The man in the photograph had been particularly fond of the house and its owners. As can be imagined, both hostess and visitor were deeply disturbed and moved by the occurrence."

The resourceful Eddie Burks was also called on to solve the problem of a haunted RAF station at Linton-on-Ouse near York in 1989. He was asked to sit out a vigil on the roof of the control tower in the hope of solving the haunting said to be caused by a Warrant Officer Walter Hodgson who had "returned" to the training base where he had served until 1943. Three women air traffic controllers had apparently first spotted the ghostly figure in August 1987 – although subsequent sightings had given rise to some dispute as to whether he had been correctly identified.

Eddie Burks was approached to investigate the haunting by the BBC. In order to remove any suspicion that he might have done any prior research in the locality, he was not told about his destination in Linton-on-Ouse until the day he went, 2 March 1989. The following day he told the *Sunday Mirror*:

"I sat on the stairs of the tower. In moments the ghost was with me and I went through his death experience with him. I saw him being carried on a stretcher. I knew it was not wartime. It was several years later and he was an aircraftsman who had been knocked down by a vehicle. I was able to release his spirit into the afterlife."

The verdict of Eddie Burks was once again proved correct when further research into local records established that an aircraftman had indeed died on the base after being hit by a petrol tanker in 1950.

I have just two further stories to add – and both are about what I can only describe as "Spectral Spitfires". The famous fighter plane, which is often credited with winning the Battle of Britain though it should share the credit with the equally proficient Hawker Hurricane, features in two extraordinary supernatural tales. The *Kent Messenger* reported the first of these in 1994:

"People living near the famous Battle of Britain airfield at Biggin Hill, Kent, have often reported the sound of a wartime Spitfire returning from a sortie. Occasionally the plane has actually been seen, screaming low towards the landing strip, then turning into a victory roll before disappearing as mysteriously as it has appeared."

The second, even more bizarre tale, appeared in *The Spectator* magazine in 2003. It claimed that every 24 October a lone Spitfire flew across a cemetery in Chingford, Essex where the bodies of the notorious Kray twins, Ronald and Reggie, were buried. The idea of a flypast to honour the two criminals was amazing in itself – but the idea of a phantom aircraft carrying out this strange annual ritual seemed even stranger. The *Spectator* explained:

"Every year at about 11.30 on the anniversary of the twins' birth, a group of balding villains arrive in hired cars, stamp out their cigarettes on the kerb and wander down the dank lanes to a far corner of the Chingford cemetery. At about 11.40, a lone Spitfire takes off from Old Warden in Kent and flies northwest across the Essex marshes, arriving 300 feet above the grave. As they listen to the sound of the Merlin engines fading away, the old boys pull up the collars of their camel-hair coats around their necks, before setting off to an Italian restaurant in Borough High Street for a meal and a chat about old times."

The problem with this story is that no Spitfire has flown from Old Warden in many years. The airfield is actually in Bedfordshire not Kent and by flying northwest from there an aircraft would fly over Leicester not Essex. Any such flight would, of course, have to be reported to the Civil Aviation Authority and recorded by Air Traffic Control. And there is no such evidence. So *if* a Spitfire does cross the sky over Essex at the appointed time it has to be a spectre. And the only way to find *that* out is to go to the cemetery just before midday on any 24 October and look up – as people have been doing to spy phantoms for over a hundred years now . . .

4

Encounters With The Unknown

Eyewitness Stories by Journalists

M·N·THOMAS

The twentieth century has witnessed numerous investigations into accounts of ghosts and hauntings by organizations such as the Society for Psychical Research, The Ghost Club and the American Psychical Institute. But the pursuit of the truth about such encounters has also attracted the interest of a considerable number of strong-nerved reporters and journalists on both sides of the Atlantic. Some were following up an initial report; others stumbled into supernatural events for which there were no simple or logical explanations. In this section I have assembled a number of such reports that have interested and intrigued me – as well as inspiring admiration for those writers involved.

The reporter who effectively started this tradition over a hundred years ago is, sadly, unknown, although he worked for the *Daily Mail* and the price of telling the story nearly cost him his job and, initially, cost the newspaper a not inconsiderable sum for publishing it. It is a story that begins with a well-known literary figure of the turn of the last century, Stephen Phillips (1868–1915). The accounts of his troubled days in a haunted house in Egham, near Windsor, which he recounted to the *Mail*'s reporter in 1904 were to have repercussions that neither man – nor the newspaper – could have imagined. The owner of the property, in fact, became so upset by the story that he sued both Phillips and the *Daily Mail*.

Phillips was an interesting figure of his time. The son of a churchman, he had toured for six years with Sir Frank Benson's Shakespearean Company, then turned to writing and edited the prestigious *Poetry Review*. He was enjoying what would prove to be a transitory success with his poems, *Christ in Hades* (1896) and blank verse plays, notably *Paolo and Francesca* (1899), when he decided in the spring of 1904 to rent the house in Egham to finish one of his plays. No one had warned him, he later told the reporter from the *Daily Mail*, that the property was reputed to be haunted. He then told his story:

"I had hardly established myself with my family when the most incomprehensible noises began to disturb me. I heard in the night, and sometimes even in the evening, raps, scratchings, the sound of steps, both heavy and light, slow and fast. Cries were added to these noises – choking and despairing cries – as of a person mad with terror or on the point of being strangled.

"That was not all. We saw, even in broad daylight, the doors open, though no hand was visible. Every time I sat down at my desk and started work I was disturbed, as if somebody had entered and had walked in the room. I turned round, I *saw the door opening*, moved by an invisible force, and I heard as usual the steps coming closer and receding in turn.

"I was never afraid of anything, but these phenomena finally annoyed and impressed me. The quiet I had desired was not given to me. And as for work, I could not think of it.

"I was not alone in hearing these noises. My family and servants were more disturbed than I. One evening my little daughter called out and said she had seen in the garden a little old fellow, a sort of dwarf, who had quickly disappeared."

According to the *Mail* reporter, Phillips suffered one sleepless night after another because of the disturbances. Not knowing much about the area, he made enquiries concerning the house and whether anyone knew its history. He learned that on the site, fifty years before, an atrocious crime had been committed. A passing tramp had one night strangled a woman and child.

Stephen Phillips told the reporter that as soon as the people in his household heard the facts they acted immediately. The servants all left his employment early one morning without even taking their belongings. He added that it was only when he was deciding to leave himself that he learned that all the previous tenants had been victims and left precisely as he was doing.

"I believe I am not a poor-spirited person," he added, "and I should like to hear of an explanation. Meanwhile, I have given up the house."

The poet's account of the disturbances caught the attention of the SPR who promptly instituted an enquiry. The investigators concluded the haunting was genuine, but could not offer an explanation. In the interim, the story – to quote one source – "made much stir in England". Phillips gave several more interviews in which he repeated his story word for word.

Within a short while of quitting the house, however, the owner, a Mr Arthur Barrett, angrily contacted Stephen Phillips. He had found it impossible to relet the building and was proposing to bring an action against him and the *Daily Mail*. The case was heard in London and the newspaper was ordered to pay the plaintiff £90. There the episode might have ended unhappily if the *Daily Mail* had not decided to fight the award against them. A subsequent report in the newspaper states:

"The *Daily Mail* appealed against this judgement as making the position of the Press very difficult in such matters. The higher court now decided in favour of the paper, in consideration of the fact that the house was commonly held to be haunted *before* the publication of the story. The press had a right to collect facts of this kind if it did so 'in good faith and without any intention of damaging anybody.'"

If Mr Barrett imagined his attempt to muzzle the press from reporting cases of haunted houses might prove influential on others, the overturning of the award against the *Mail* had quite the opposite effect. Indeed, as the earlier section "A Century of Hauntings" demonstrates, reports like that of Stephen Phillips' haunted house have been popular with editors and readers ever since. Journalists, too, like the anonymous scribe who recorded the case, have had their own encounters with the unknown – sometimes unintentionally – while in pursuit of the facts. This section contains a selection of the best of their stories . . .

A VISIT TO THE DEVIL'S CASTLE

By W T Stead

The Editor of Pall Mall Gazette, *Stead became famous in 1885 when he received a three-month jail sentence for buying a girl child in order to expose the vice trade in Britain. He was also fascinated by ghost stories, encouraged his readers to write of their experiences, and investigated a number of instances himself before publishing his groundbreaking collection* Real Ghost Stories *in 1906.*

There is a certain uncanny fascination about haunted houses, but it is one of which it may emphatically be said that distance lends enchantment to the view. There is something much more thrilling in looking at a haunted house from the outside and reading of it at a distance of many miles, than spending a sleepless night within its walls. It has never been my good fortune to sleep in a haunted house, but on one occasion I went to sleep in the ruins of a haunted castle, and was awakened with a shuddering horror that I shall never forget as long as I live.

It was in Hermitage Castle, Hermitage, that grim old border stronghold which stood in Liddesdale, not many miles from Riccarton, that most desolate of railway junctions. I visited it when I was just out of my teens, with a mind saturated with legendary lore of the Scotch border. I made a pilgrimage to Brankesome Hall, taking Hermitage on my way. I write this, not to maintain the objectivity of any ghostly haunting of Hermitage Castle, but to show that although it may all have been the merest delusion of a subjective character, I have at least gone through an experience which enables me to understand what it feels like to be in a haunted house.

Lord Soulis, the evil hero of Hermitage, made a compact with the devil, who appeared to him, so runs the legend, in the shape of a spirit wearing a red cap, which gained its hue from the blood of human victims in which it was steeped. Lord Soulis sold himself to the demon, and in return he could summon his familiar whenever he chose to rap thrice on an iron chest, on condition that he never looked in the direction of the spirit. Once, however, he forgot or ignored this condition, and his doom was sealed. But even then the foul fiend kept the letter of his compact. Lord Soulis was protected by an unholy charm against any injury from rope or steel; hence cords could not bind him and steel would not slay him. When, at last, he was delivered over to his enemies, it was found necessary to adopt the ingenious and effective expedient of rolling him up in a sheet of lead and boiling him to death.

That was the end of Lord Soulis's body, but his spirit still lingers superfluous on the scene. Once every seven years he keeps tryst with Red Cap on the scene of his former devilries:

When I visited Hermitage Castle I was all alone, with my memory teeming with associations of the past. I unlocked the door with the key, which I brought with me from the keeper's cottage, at a little distance down the valley. As it creaked on its hinges and I felt the chill air of the ruin, I was almost afraid to enter. Mustering my courage, however, I went in and explored the castle, then lying down on the mossy bank I gave myself up to the glamour of the past. I must have been there an hour or more when suddenly, while the blood seemed to freeze down my back, I was startled by a loud prolonged screech, over my head, followed by a noise which I could only compare to the trampling of a multitude of iron-shod feet through the stone-paved doorway. This was alarming enough, but it was nothing to the horror which filled me when I heard the heavy gate swing on its hinges with a clang which for the moment seemed like the closing of a vault in which I was entombed alive. I could almost hear the beating of my heart. The rusty hinges, the creaking of the door, the melancholy and unearthly nature of the noise, and the clanging of the gate, made me shudder and shiver as I lay motionless, not daring to move, and so utterly crushed by the terror that had fallen upon me that I felt as if I were on the very verge of death. If the evil one had appeared at that moment and carried me off I should have but regarded it as the natural corollary to what I had already heard. Fortunately no sulphureous visitant darkened the blue sky that stretched overhead with his unwelcome presence, and after a few minutes, when I had recovered from my fright, I ventured into the echoing doorway to see whether or not I was really a prisoner. The door was shut, and I can remember to this day the tremour which I experienced when I laid my hand upon the door and tried whether or not it was locked. It yielded to my hand, and I have seldom felt a sensation of more profound relief than when I stepped across the threshold and felt that I was free once more. For a moment it was as if I had been delivered from the grave itself which had already closed over my head. Of course, looking back upon this after a number of years, it is easy to say that the whole thing was purely subjective. An overwrought fancy, a gust of wind whistling through the crannies and banging the door closed were quite sufficient to account for my fright, especially as it is not at all improbable that I had gone to sleep in the midst of the haunted ruins.

So I reasoned at the moment, and came back and stayed another hour in the castle, if only to convince myself that I was not afraid. But neither before nor after that alarm did any gust of wind howl round the battlements with anything approaching to the clamour which gave me such a fright. One thing amuses me in looking back at a letter which I wrote at the time, describing my alarm. I say, "Superstition, sneer you? It may be. I rejoiced that I was capable of superstition; I thought it was dried out of me by high pressure civilisation." I am afraid that some of my critics will be inclined to remark that my capacities in that direction stand in need of a great deal of drying up.

HAUNTED BY A SHADOW

By Shaw Desmond

Irish-born journalist and supernatural investigator, Desmond
founded the International Institute for Psychical Research and
wrote My Adventures in the Occult *(1956). A protégé of W T*
Stead, he had a foreboding of the older man's death on the Titanic
while the two men were walking in London in April 1912
discussing Stead's forthcoming trip on the new liner: "There came
to me for the first time in my life, but not for the last, the
conviction of impending death – in this case, that the man at
my side would die within a very short time." The following
concerns one of the many true hauntings Shaw Desmond inves-
tigated.

The "haunt" was one of the queerest in my experience. We have
often heard of a man being haunted by a shadow-man – but who has
heard of a man being haunted by a shadow alone?

In some ways, this was one of the weirdest of my occult experiences and, for the moment, did bring about the psycho-physiological
happening of "making my blood run cold". For such is no figment of
the imagination and many have experienced it.

This great pile had innumerable bedrooms and little drawing-rooms
and "attics". I could quite believe the owner who said that even now
only a part of these innumerable rooms and attics, some of them
packed with costly furniture, had been explored. Even the owner had
not seen them all! I know that when I myself went on a voyage of
discovery alone, I found myself in such vastnesses and such lonely
places that my heart misgave me. Often it would seem to me that this
was no palace of stone and mortar but a palace of dreamland.

I had come out of one of the marble-flagged bathrooms – a room
which itself might house a small family! – when I saw on the white
marble at my feet a shadow. Standing there with my towel, I looked
idly at it, believing it was a shadow from myself and due to the strong
electric lights behind me. Then I noticed a curious thing.

First of all that the shadow gradually assumed a spheroid shape
and that it seemed *to be mounting about my legs*. The other
disturbing thing was that I saw a strong electric light hung *before*
me and therefore that no shadow could be cast.

The effect of this discovery was quietly disturbing. Perhaps it was
the eeriness of this particular part of the building, where even at

noonday I had felt an icy clamminess. Perhaps it was all "hallucination".

Standing as though I were tied there, I saw the shadow gradually build itself up about my legs, mount my body, and then slowly detach itself, and I watched it move away before me down one of the endless dimly lighted corridors, to disappear.

This shadow was quite inchoate. Not like the human form. It just *was*.

The only comparable happening was that of the Richmond Park ghost-keeper of whom a friend and myself asked the way in broad day and who gradually melted away before our eyes.

I know that this does not seem much to set down in black and white, but the thing itself was nerve-shaking. But I freely admit that by this time rather frenetic imagination may have played its part.

I do not think I can be called a timid or apprehensive man. I have, at times, had unique experience in psychical research. I have encountered strangely inimical phenomena without quavering. I have felt and spoken with visitants of the spirit world of every sort and description from saints to devils. But I must affirm that never anywhere have I felt *quite* the eerie and "suggestive" atmosphere of this affrighting place. Again, I may have been peculiarly susceptible to its vibrations, and I have known those who have never seen or felt anything uncanny within its walls. But some people can never feel or see the invisible. They are to be pitied! for contact with the invisible worlds is essential to education and to progress.

Without contact with the spiritual, the people perish.

Within that dwelling, there were three magnificent halls the walls of which, almost Westminster Abbey-like in their imposing proportions, bore priceless paintings, some of the people in which seemed more living than those who looked at them. There they hung, to stare contemptuously or ironically at the staggered guest, and there were moments, especially towards the dusk of evening, when one expected them to come down from their frames to walk among living men, much as the famous Tankerville Castle picture was said to do.

If this be thought far-fetched, I, who as a youngster knew the then earl, can vouch that he told me of even stranger happenings in that home of the famous "Chillingham herd". What I was told by the then Countess of Warwick, about Warwick Castle, when, in the old days, I visited it, was even more remarkable than anything I have set down here.

In one of these halls there was a hand-painted grand piano of superb tone, on which I would play. Here is a note made at the time:

"The massive halls were terrifying in their suggestion. In broad daylight I went to the grand piano in the biggest hall – itself like a cathedral nave – but it took much more courage to find my way to the instrument in the twilight or dark." And as I played, I *know* that my fingers evoked through the music spirit-visitants, who would steal out from their hiding-holes in order to look and listen.

Some of these visitants I would feel to be kindly and beautiful. Others, saturnine and menacing. But even the darker beings, it would seem to me, yielded themselves as I played and found, perhaps, an hour of release from their "hells" on the Other Side. These visitants I did not see with the human eye, for I was rarely clairvoyant in that way. I felt them – but they were all the more real for that, as I have invariably found that materialization destroys, rather than encourages, the sense of reality, much as the advent of the "talkies" left out a good deal of the power of suggestion of the silent film.

Once, in my peregrinations, I happed upon a room which I found was called the "King Edward Room" and which was filled with the most luxurious suite of golden furniture I have seen. There was the golden bed in which the genial bearded monarch had lain – that king who was "of the earth earthy". And yet, though it was daylight, there crept to me the feeling which I always had in that "House" – the feeling that *I was not alone*.

Who was looking at me? Who was asking: "What right has this stranger to my room?" Perhaps it was the dead king himself. Perhaps it was some other. In that place, even when nothing *did* happen, one always expected something *to* happen.

THEY WALK THE BATTLEFIELDS

By James Wentworth Day.

The Editor of The Field *and a regular contributor to* Country Life *and* Daily Mail, *Day specialized in stories of East Anglia where his family had owned property for hundreds of years. He became particularly interested in the supernatural after an extraordinary experience while serving in the British Army in France in 1918 which he relates here.*

The guns in Flanders were dead. In that last month of the grey winter of 1918 an eerie stillness dwelt on the battlefields of France and Belgium. Dead lay unburied in fields and sodden trenches. Guns and rifles, shells and Mills bombs lay rusting. Warneton Ridge was a wilderness of mud and crawling wire, shell-pocked and lonely as the wind. Mont Kemmel, "The Gibraltar of Northern France", alone with its dead and its torn trees, loomed above the grey plains that have been Europe's cockpit for centuries.

By day carrion crows croaked deathlike from shattered trees, travesties of nature whose bare trunks were bullet-scarred and shell-splintered. Moated farms and straggling villages lay ruined, roofless, and gaping-walled – if they stood at all.

By night the winter moon looked on the twisted dead, the corn-fields and roofless farms with white dispassion. Frost mantled the trees and whitened the tents where No. 298 Prisoners of War Company crouched by the gaunt ruins of Bailleul, the town which was blown to atoms in twenty-four hours.

No longer was the night horizon lit by the fantastic spears and flashes of gunfire, the ghostly aurora borealis of the front line, no longer pin-pointed by star shells or shuddering with the thunder of guns.

In our tents and shacks outside the great barbed-wire cages which prisoned 450 Germans, newly-taken, we, the guards, shivered with cold. In their prison tents the Germans slept like sardines for warmth's sake. We were new to the ruins of that spectral town, we and our prisoners, who a month before had been fighting us. The Arctic cold smote English and German alike.

So when at the railhead to pick up post and rations, I heard by chance words of a great country *auberge* – an old posting inn of the eighteenth century – whose stables and ruined rooms were full of abandoned Queen stoves, that perfect little camp cooker, I determined to impound the lot.

Next day, late in the afternoon, after a morning of sudden thaw, I took Corporal Barr, that minute but unquenchable fighting man, and set off along a rutted road from Bailleul to the east. Flooded fields lay on either side. Rotted crops stained the soil. The smell of dead men, cold and oily, that smell which strikes to the pit of the stomach like the smell of a dead snake, was heavy on the air.

Ahead, in the afternoon sun, the road gleamed with sudden splashes and shields of light where water lay. Two kilometres, near enough three, and we came to the standing archway of the *auberge*. The yellow walls of what had been a fine old Flemish inn stood windowless, gazing like dead eyes over the fields of the dead. Bullets had sieved its walls. Shells had shattered the roof where rafters and roof tree stood stark as the ribs of a skeleton.

Under the great arch which had echoed to the clatter of coach wheels and rung with the guttural cries of Walloon and Flamande farmers, the courtyard, with its mighty midden, showed a four-square array of stables, sheds, barns, cartsheds and coach-houses. Doors sagged on broken hinges and sandbags filled empty windows.

Within were wooden bunks, the black ashes of long-cold fires, rusty dixies and mouldy webbing, mildewed bully and Maconochie tins – and Queen stoves!

We found at least a score – enough to warm our pitiful shacks and spare one or two for the prisoners. I told Corporal Barr to bring a party of prisoners next day and remove the lot.

That dour and unimpressionable little man with the square, short body, the beetling black eyebrows and steady eyes – a soldier among the best of them – said "Aye". He was being loquacious.

Then we started back. It was, maybe, four to four-thirty and far from dark. In the sunset the sky had cleared to a wide band of apple-green fading into pink. Overhead high clouds caught a sudden ethereal sheen of crimson and flamingo. The heavens were alight above the stricken earth. On our left fields lay waterlogged and gleaming – lake beyond miniature lake.

On the right a low upland swept up to a torn, fantastic wood of larch and birch. The thin trees were twisted into grotesque shapes by shell blast. It was a Hans Andersen wood of Arthur Rackham trees through whose sun-reddened trunks we could see cloud masses lit with a Cuyp-like glow.

Suddenly, as we splashed through the sunset pools of that deserted road, German cavalry swept out of the wood. Crouching low over their horses' withers, lance-tips gleaming, red pennants flying, they charged out of that spectral wood – a dozen or more German Uhlans in those queer high-topped hats which they had worn in the dead days of 1914. I saw horses, men, lances, and flickering pennons clear and sharp in the level sun.

And up the slope to meet them galloped French dragoons – brass cuirasses flashing, sabres upswung, heavy horsetail plumes dancing from huge brass helmets. Fierce-moustached and red-faced, they charged with flashing sabres on heavy Flemish chargers to meet that flying posse of grey-faced men who swept down with slender lances on flying horses – the hurricane meeting the winter wind.

Then the vision passed. There was no clash of mounted men – no mêlée of shivering lance and down-smashing sabre, no sickening unhorsing of men or uprearing of chargers – only empty upland and a thin and ghostly wood, silver in the setting sun. The earth was empty. I felt suddenly cold.

I am no spiritualist, but to the truth of this vision I will swear.

I glanced at Corporal Barr. He looked white and uneasy.

"Did you see anything?" I asked.

"Aye – something mighty queer," said that non-committal little Glasgow baker. "Ssst! look! What's that?" he gasped. His rifle bolt clicked back, a cartridge snapped in the breech and the butt leapt to his shoulder. In a gap in the hedge on the left two baleful eyes glared at us from a dim, crouching shape. At the click of the rifle bolt it sprang to its feet – a wolf in shape and size – and loped into a sudden burst of speed.

Two rifles cracked almost as one as the grey beast splashed through the shallow floods. Bullets spurted up sudden fountains as it raced away. Not one touched it. Yet the day before I had killed a running hare with my .303 and Barr could pick a crow off a tree at a hundred yards.

The beast raced belly-low into the sunset, leaving a trail of flying water. Bullet after bullet cracked after it, missed by yards. We were both off our shooting.

No wolf was that half-starved ghoul of a beast, but one of the lost, masterless Alsatian sheep-dogs of the dead farmers, pariahs of the battlefield who ravished the flesh of the staring dead.

We reached camp, shaken and oddly shy of talking too much.

Next day, at Neuve Eglise, that skeleton of a village on the spine of the Ravelsberg, I drank a glass or two of *vin rouge* at the *estaminet* of the one and only Marie, a kilometre up the road from the Armentières Road *douane*.

I asked her of the wood and the *auberge*. And Marie, forty-five and peasant-wise, said: "Ah! M'sieu, that wood is sad. It is on the frontier. A wood of dead men. In the wars of Napoleon, in the war of 1870 – in this war in 1914 – always the cavalry of France and Germany have met and fought by that wood. If you will go beyond the *auberge* half a kilometre only, you will find a *petite église*. There you will see the graves of the cavalry of all these wars. It is true, I tell you."

I went. In the tiny churchyard were the graves. And the headstones told the brief and bloody tales of gallant horsemen in frontier skirmishes which had played prelude to three mighty wars. And since I love a horse and revere a good rider, whether he is an Uhlan or a Gascon under Murat, a turbaned Mahratta or a red-coated foxhunter, I stood in homage for a frightened minute.

A PHOTOGRAPHIC SEANCE

By James Malcolm Bird

Bird was Associate Editor of Scientific American, *and his investigations in the USA and Europe did much to explain the mysteries of psychic research to the prestigious magazine's large readership on both sides of the Atlantic. In 1922, the publication offered a prize of $2,500 for the first person who could produce "a spirit photograph under laboratory conditions". Bird here recounts his experiences with one of the first challengers, William Hope, described as "the most famous photographic medium of his time" – though ultimately revealed as a fraud.*

During the late summer of 1922, a test séance was given by William Hope, the photographic medium, before officers of the British Society for Psychical Research. A package of plates was brought in, presumably in the original seals as obtained from the manufacturers; but by special and secret arrangement, the makers had marked these plates, either before wrapping, or with X-rays after wrapping. Several plates were exposed; one of them on development showed a psychic extra; and this plate failed to show the secret mark. The investigators claimed to have actually observed the act of substitution; Hope and his defenders agree that the result shows substitution to have been effected. But with this agreement ceases.

Hope's defenders have brought several different arguments to bear, but always they accuse the investigators, or somebody connected with them, of the substitution. The investigators, in attempting to clear themselves, have given a history of the package of plates, which shows that it was in their hands an unnecessarily long time, and that it was passed about from one custody to another in a very unsatisfactory fashion while they had it. Equally, neither side made adequate attempts to protect the wrapper which had been removed from the package, so that when the claim was advanced, several months too late, that this showed marks of tampering, no defense could be made to this charge. The people, in England and America, who feel that psychic photography is not possible, are entirely satisfied that Hope has been shown up as a fraud. Those who accept psychic photography as within the possibilities are entirely satisfied that he has entered an adequate defense, and that the researchers have been convicted of sharp practice through too great anxiety to "expose" him at any cost. There the matter rests, and the circumstances are such that no arbitration is now possible.

This incident has really nothing to do with my story. But I set it forth here, simply to make it clear, to those who may have known of the charges against Hope and not of his defense, that he *has* entered a defense, and one that does not suffer greatly in comparison with the case for the prosecution. Were this not the fact, were he with any degree of certainty a convicted even if not a confessed fraud, I should still, I think, have sat with him when opportunity offered, merely to see whether I too could catch him. As things stood, it did not seem necessary to apologize to myself even to this extent for sitting with him; it would be unfair to regard him as under any more suspicion than any other physical medium. So when an engagement was made for me to sit with him at the British College on Tuesday, March 13th., the eve of my departure for my Continental jaunt, I arranged to go, as a matter of course.

Hope, when he sits at the College, enjoys quarters specially reserved for him. This includes two small rooms on the top floor, one serving as the studio and one as the dark-room. The only entrance to the suite is through the studio. This room has one window, opening out of doors. It is furnished with a bare table, a few chairs, and the oldest, most disreputable camera in the world. As Mrs McKenzie very pertinently says: "you mention the meagre furnishing of the studio. We purposely do this, for if we had other cameras about, or any appliances, we should immediately be suspect." The general effect upon me was well in line with the psychology of this remark; I looked about the room, and asked myself how in the world fraud could be committed here.

The camera, by the way, is Hope's property rather than that of the College. It was given him by Archdeacon Colley, years ago, and he always uses it. Quoting Mrs McKenzie again, "he has another camera provided by a group of friends, but as some feel happier with a special pen or a favorite old smoking jacket, he likes his old camera." Whether he uses the same box at Crewe, and brings it to London with him, I do not know.

The dark-room is even more startling in its poverty than the studio. There is a single large washing basin, part of the plumbing; there are three developing trays, three jars of chemicals on a wooden shelf, one glass beaker, and three wooden plate-holders; and there is a red lamp on either side of the room. That is literally all. Sir Arthur's habit is to refer to this equipment and to Hope himself with the phrase that Hope is "unquestionably the worst professional or semiprofessional photographer in the world." He is certainly the worst equipped, and I suspect that the plain adjective is not unmerited.

His recent imbroglio with the organized researchers has made Hope realize that test conditions of some sort are his only protection. Hence he sits, now, only with control substantially as found in my session with him. In particular, he insists that all plates used be brought in, in the original seals, by the sitter. I had been advised of this, and, on the morning of the séance, I purchased at the Westminster Photographic Exchange, in Victoria St, a package of a dozen rapid quarter-plates, the size used by Hope's camera. This store, I might say, was neither dictated nor suggested to me; I found it in the classified telephone book, and selected it as the nearest to my hotel of the supply stores there listed. After getting the plates, I dropped the package in my pocket, and carried it about with me until I reached the séance room. From the time it was selected until the time it was used it was not out of my possession, save as detailed below; and never was it out of my sight.

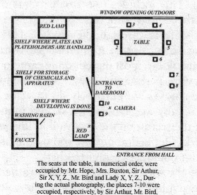

The seats at the table, in numerical order, were occupied by Mr. Hope, Mrs. Buxton, Sir Arthur, Sir X, Y, Z., Mr. Bird and Lady X, Y, Z., During the actual photography, the places 7-10 were occupied, respectively, by Sir Arthur, Mr. Bird, Mr. Hope and Mrs. Buxton.

Arrangement of the rooms and the sitters at the photographic seance with William Hope

There were to be present Sir Arthur and myself, and two friends of the Doyles, Sir X Y Z and Lady Z. The two mediums – Hope and Mrs Buxton – made six in the party in the studio. The four "sitters" taxied out to Holland Park together after luncheon in Sir X Y Z's apartment. Sir Arthur was very perturbed by the muggy weather. It appears that of all plates exposed by Hope, about one in seven shows a psychic extra. One never knows whether one will draw a blank or not; and damp weather is supposed greatly to interfere with the exercise of any mediumistic powers.

The Zs were introduced to the mediums by name; so was I, without mention of my identity or even of my profession. Examination of the premises was first in order, with the general result noted above. I gave my detailed attention to the camera and the other tools of the photographer's profession that were to be used. I am not a professional photographer, but I believe I know what to look for in examining a camera for evidences of trickery. Both box and lens were gone over carefully, without result; but the reservation ought to be made that a pin hole in the bellows, capable of admitting enough light to affect the plate moderately, could perhaps not have been found with the eye. As far as any actual extraneous apparatus inside the box or on the lens is concerned, there wasn't any.

Hope uses no shutter, nor even a lens cap; he makes his exposures by covering and uncovering the camera with the black focussing cloth, after the removal of the dark slide. This struck me as rather curious technique, and I accordingly examined the cloth in question with even more care than I should ordinarily have employed. I found nothing suspicious.

The three plate-holders were handed me, and I was asked to select one. Having done so, I examined this holder with extreme care. It had been thoroughly marked by numerous previous sitters, so that substitution could not profitably have been attempted. Having been examined, it went into my pocket and stayed there until it was needed in the dark-room.

The door was now locked, and the six sitters drew up to the table. The package of plates, still with its original wrapper intact, was transferred from my pocket to the center of the table. The six of us joined hands about the table, and hymns were sung, without music, to the best of our miserable collective ability. Once or twice Hope or Mrs Buxton interpolated a prayer. Presently Mrs Buxton took the package between her hands; Hope added his hands outside hers; and the rest of us, one at a time, followed suit. The package remained above the table and in plain sight here, in its nest of hands. The pose was held for several minutes while Mrs Buxton, apparently in silent prayer, "influenced" the plates. Nobody knows, least of all the mediums, if their claims are valid, in just what this process consists. The procedure is an empirical one, and the nearest one can come to rational explanation is some rather loose statements about harmonious currents and harmonious vibrations.

While the plates were having the spell placed upon them, it was explained again that we might draw a blank, and speculation was indulged in whether this would be the issue. At a word from Hope, the preliminaries were ended; I regained, identified and pocketed the package of plates and Hope and I adjourned to the dark room. During the "influencing" Mrs Buxton gave a convulsive little shudder, like a man with a fly in his ear; this Sir Arthur announced, on the basis of previous experience, to be an almost certain sign that we should have results.

In the dark-room, Hope did not once touch the plates. I was quite aware of the fact that if he did touch them, nothing that might be found on them would be of the slightest significance; therefore it may be taken for granted that whatever else I may have missed, I watched effectively for this. He stood at my shoulder, superintending my manipulation of the glasses and occasionally offering a suggestion; but he did not at any time, under cover of this, attempt to put his hands upon them.

I took the package from my pocket and broke the wrappings. Before I got past the outer one, Hope reminded me that the plates were in pairs, hinged together by a flap of the emulsion; and he suggested that I decide, now, which ones I should use. Whether this was suspicious I am not quite sure. It certainly made it impossible, thereafter, for him to force any particular plate upon me; it also, if he had means for exposing the plates to an extra image in the dark-room, enabled him to know what plates thus to expose, without waiting until I had actually got them in my hands en route to the holder.

I chose the bottom plate of the first pair, and the top plate of the second pair. When I had got the four topmost plates separated from their common inner wrapper, I broke the second away from the first and the third away from the fourth with considerable difficulty. In doing this I was rather inclined to think that I might have touched the emulsion side of one of them, with the ball of my thumb, but said nothing of this. As I got each of the desired plates free, I laid it on the table before me, emulsion side up, and traced my name on it with a blunt lead pencil. I then rewrapped the remaining ten plates and replaced them in my pocket, since it was necessary to keep them under control against the subsequent use of two more of them; and only when I had them thus out of sight and mind did I get the plateholder out of my other pocket. It was of a type unfamiliar to me, and Hope had to tell me what to do; but he scrupulously refrained from pointing or making any other false moves. There was a glass slide outside of each plate, and these I signed as I had signed the plates, to insure against substitution of the entire ensemble or of the slides alone. I finally got the plates, the glass slides and the dark slides in place, latched the holder, and restored it to my pocket. Then we returned to the studio, where the others awaited us.

Sir Arthur and I were to sit together for the first exposure, I alone for the second. Hope focussed the camera upon the two empty chairs, and called me to verify the range and direction. He shifted the hood to the front of the camera; I placed the holder in its seat and removed the dark slide. Sir Arthur by this time was in his seat; I went to mine. Hope raised the hood, held it clear of the camera for about fifteen seconds, and dropped it back into place. During this time he and Mrs Buxton stood at either side of the camera and slightly behind it, with hands joined above it, Hope's free hand holding the cloth, and Mrs Buxton's free member resting lightly upon the box, in plain view.

The exposure terminated, I rose to replace the dark slide and remove the plate-holder. In writing up the sitting in the June issue of the *Scientific American*, I indicated that I replaced it, reversed, immediately. This was obviously an error; the camera would have to be focussed, first, upon the single chair which I was to occupy in the second exposure. My notes indicate that the camera was not disturbed, but that focussing was accomplished by moving the chair. My recollection would contradict this. The point is of some importance, since in the one case we can insist that the camera was in exactly the same condition for both exposures and in the other we cannot. In any event, I have a very distinct remembrance that focussing was accomplished while I stood beside the camera with the plate-holder assembly in my hand, in order to be sure that this should be properly reversed. I glanced through the instrument to verify the focussing with Sir Arthur in my chair, and then replaced the plate-holder in its grooves. The exposure was made as before, and again I accompanied the medium into the dark-room.

If I were having a series of test sittings, I should insist that, part of the time at least, the medium stay out of the dark-room. His presence there, no matter how strongly one may insist upon his inaction, will always be attacked, and the very pertinent question proposed: "What was he doing there, anyhow; why couldn't he stay outside during loading and development?" In a single sitting like mine, this question is easily answered; he didn't stay outside because he was as much privileged to regard me with suspicion as I, him.

Hope got down his beaker and his two jars, and mixed his developer. He was ready with it before I was ready with the plates; to keep him busy I managed to knock it over with my elbow and he had to mix it afresh. The precaution was doubtless superfluous, but certainly harmless. When he was ready again, I had my plates out of the holder and waiting for him in the developing tray. The latter, by the way, I had scratched across with my thumb-nail quite thoroughly, so that it might at least be hoped that if there were the makings of an extraneous image on it, I should effect recognizable damage thereon. I poured the contents of the beaker in, and proceeded with the rocking of the plates. The images came out slowly; but in a couple of minutes it became obvious that the plate with the single portrait on it, at least, was going to show some extras. In a moment or two more the other one was sufficiently developed to make sure that it would be normal.

Development completed, the negatives were placed in the fixing bath, and a report made to those in the studio. All waited in great tension until the fixing was complete; and were then disappointed to find that, as is usually the case, one could not say from the negative whether one recognized the extra or not. Prints would not be ready until next day, and I was obliged to leave for Paris that evening. It was arranged that prints should go to Sir Arthur, who would hand them to me on board the *Olympic*; and, as a very special concession on the part of the College, quite opposed to their ordinary routine and seldom if ever made before, it was agreed that I might have the negative too. I examined the negative very carefully before leaving it, and again on getting it back on the ocean. It had not been altered in any respect.

The prints have been carefully examined by all four sitters and both mediums, and the clear extra has not been recognized – it is not necessary to make this statement of the other mark, between the good extra and my own head, which might by a liberal exercise of the imagination be a human face but by no stretch an identifiable one. This result is not at all unusual; in only a minority of cases is the "psychic extra" recognizable as pertaining to one of the sitters.

Sir X Y Z and his Lady next sat twice, together each time, with Sir X Y Z playing the rôle in the dark-room which I had played during my half of the sitting. They used plates from the second four of my package. They got no extras, nor any extraneous mark of any description whatever.

The photograph is either the product of fraud, or a genuine psychic phenomenon – not necessarily spirit, but merely psychic, supernormal. One who takes it to be a fraud must make a plausible showing as to how it could have been produced, under the conditions described. Substitution of plates or pre-preparation of a plate absolutely will not do. Whatever else Hope may have put over on me, he certainly did not put that over.

Admittedly, photography is peculiarly susceptible to tricks which are difficult of discovery. There is no thought of presenting a complete catalog of these, but some of the types of fraud which might be attempted by a fake psychic photographer may well be considered in the present connection. A member of the faculty of the College of the City of New York, who sat some time ago with Hope, with a result similar to mine, puts forward one suggestion involving nothing more elaborate than ordinary sleight of hand. Working from the obvious fact that the extra image could be obtained by slipping a thin celluloid transparency, showing the face clear on a slightly opaque ground, into the camera with the plate-holder and immediately in front of the latter, he catalogs the following suspicious circumstances:

Hope wore a coat considerably too large for him, with loose sleeves and large pockets. He used an old camera with very loosely fitting plate-holders. He used, not a lens-cap or a shutter, but the dark cloth, and this hung down in front of the camera in such a way as to hide it and part of Hope's body. He posed the subject against a plain background which was dull but not black. All this gave, in the case of the gentleman who puts forward the suggestion, ample opportunity for the clandestine insertion of such a transparency as is described above, and this gentleman has since then got an amateur conjurer to play the trick upon an intelligent audience with complete success. All his suspicious details were repeated at my sitting.

If such a transparency were used, the plate that was exposed through it would have to stay longer in the camera, or else would be much slower in developing. The exposures were not timed, but to my best judgment were of approximately equal duration. I am quite certain that both came out substantially with equal speed in the developer. I have a rather distinct recollection that the four hands of the two mediums were in plain sight throughout the exposure; whether one of them took a brief trip under the black cloth while I was seating myself would of course be much harder for me to say. If the transparency were in front of the plateholder, it could easily be of such size that there would be no danger of my bringing it out with the latter. It would have been used on my *second* exposure; and the mediums would have had opportunity to recover it, during the examination of my negative and before Sir X Y Z sat.

Such a transparency represents only one of a large number of ways in which the plate could have been surreptitiously exposed to an extra of some sort. Perhaps the most dangerous possibility lies in the very curious type of plateholder used. Not alone in its fashion of opening with a hinge does this depart from standard American practice, but the use of a glass screen over each plate is apparently quite superfluous and certainly very suspicious. There are no grooves sufficient to hold the plate in place after the removal of the dark slide; instead of being slipped in from one edge, the plate is laid in the open holder, the glass slide laid in over it, and the frame shut down upon the latter – or perhaps the glass slide is an integral part of the frame, I am not sure which. In any event, it is abundantly clear that an image could be stencilled upon the glass screen and thereby impressed upon the plate. Such an image might be actually radio-active, or it might be a chemical substance that would sufficiently affect the passage of light to make an impression upon the plate, without being visible to the eye. In the latter event, the slide would presumably be treated as the transparency of the previous suggestion.

Another possibility which was in my mind at the time of the séance, and which has been put forward by several correspondents in response to my *Scientific American* article describing this sitting, is that a radio-active image was upon Mrs Buxton's palm while she was influencing the plates in their package. At the time, I was under the impression that this was sufficiently guarded against by the fact that Sir X Y Z's two plates, from my package, showed no extra. But on giving more careful consideration to the matter, it appears that this is not quite the case.

Sir X Y Z did not use my two plates, left over from the package of four at the top of my dozen. Had he done so, I should have been completely protected, since no radio-active or X-rayed image could have reached either of my plates without penetrating, and leaving an impression upon, one of his. But both of his were below both of mine in the package. If this trick were played, my plate that shows the extra must have been the second in the pile; and after the paper wrappings, the rays carrying the extraneous image would have had to penetrate only the glass and the film of the first plate to reach the film of this one. To reach the film of the next one, however, they would have to penetrate the film of the second, and the glass of both second and third – one more film and two more glasses. (The first and second plates are packed with their film sides together, as are the third and fourth.) It seems barely possible, though not at all probable, that rays strong enough to go through one glass and make so marked an impression as my best extra, would be cut down by two further glasses below the point where they would make any visible impression at all. The glasses rather than the films are the critical element here, because whatever of opacity may have been present was in them and not in the films. Had I realized the absence of absolute proof here, at the time of the sitting, I should have developed the two idle plates. If they showed no extras it would be proved that the package, as such, was not tampered with.

I made an attempt to spoil any image which might have been stencilled upon the developing tray, but such an image might have been capable of resisting my scratches. But I am quite sure that the plates moved too much to make possible the one rather clean-cut face; and at the same time too little to justify the assumption that all the extras represent different exposures to the same image on the tray. The probabilities of successful fraud of this type I think are negligible.

Another suggestion places the ever-present radio-active image inside the dark slide. This correspondent writes: "I believe that a clever workman could slit the dark slide of the plateholder, paint on the inner side a face in radium paint (or insert a thin piece of paper, etc., carrying such a face), and fasten the slide together in such a fashion that detection would be impossible." Hope's dark slide was a thin sheet of metal, and I think would not have permitted this technique, but in any event, such an image on either slide should have affected both plates.

The suggestion that there was a pin-hole in the bellows, through which Hope exposed the plate to the extra image, I think need not be taken too seriously. This procedure would have called for a nicety of sleight-of-hand manipulation, under the focussing cloth, for which I am sure he had no opportunity. Most suggestions which have been put forward for apparatus inside the camera would call for a lay-out of such complexity as to insure its discovery when I examined the camera; and most such suggestions fail to indicate how one plate caught the extra and the other missed it.

All these suggestions involve the use of fraud with reference to some part of the apparatus, or of the medium's hands, which might conceivably be subjected to a betraying search. If fraud were practiced, I should think it more likely to lie in some direction to which it might be anticipated that examination would not extend. Now Hope's person is one such direction; he was not to be searched, and he knew this. At any time in the dark-room, could he have exposed the plate to the extra, by straightforward sleight of hand, without my detection? The plate was a fast one, to be sure; but in a room receiving fair light from outdoors, and equipped with several ordinary incandescent lamps, a 15-second exposure was not excessive. Some of the marks on the plate could be called flashes, but at least one of the extras is far beyond any such characterization. Moreover such trickery would have to bargain on movement of the plate as I worked with it. On all these grounds a pretty intense luminous effect would have to be used, if ordinary light were the agent; or a radioactive effect of considerable power. But Hope's dark-room is very dark indeed, and the probability seems small that he could have used anything of sufficient intensity and duration to impress the plate, without impressing my eye at the same time. It must be remembered that if he exposes the plate to the extra in the dark-room, he voluntarily gives up all the advantage of the radioactive class of tricks, for in the dark-room I can see an object so painted or coated.

We may, I think, abandon the notion that actual X-rays were used in the studio. An X-ray machine is far too expensive, and with it, the expectation that both my plates would show anything shown by either, would be far more acute.

In the face of all this, fairness demands that I quote the opinion of a photographer of long experience, who has handled the plate and several reproductions in the course of making the half-tones for magazine and book use. He insists that the extras are luminous finger prints; the better one being from a finger on which a crude face had been painted. One or two of the marks near the corner I think are probably finger prints – though not luminous ones; I have already expressed the belief that I touched the emulsion side of one plate in separating them. But as regards the good extra under this suggestion, I leave it to the gentleman who advances it to explain how this came upon the plate – reiterating merely that Hope never touched the glass.

Another admission that ought to be made is this: Under repeated reproduction, the extras show a decided tendency toward grain, which my own face escapes. Sir Arthur has a lantern slide, made from a print from the original negative. From this slide, a new glass negative has been made, by photography with transmitted light; and in prints from this the best extra looks like the coarsest sort of a newspaper half-tone, the grain being its predominating feature. Examining the original under magnification in the light of this, one realizes that on it, too, the best extra is not so free from grain as the rest of the picture. This may or may not be significant; supporters of the picture's genuineness will attribute it to the fact that the process of getting the extra upon the plate is, in some respects at least, admittedly and necessarily different from the process of normal photography to which the balance of the plate is due, and that some divergence in appearance ought to occur.

Of all the suggestions for fraudulent production, the one which in my judgment is least improbable, from the mechanical side alone, is that by some secret and well-concealed optical arrangement, an extraneous image was projected along with the normal image of me, through the camera's eye and upon the plate. There was no apparatus inside the camera by which such an image, coming in obliquely, could have been turned along the lens axis; the trick image would have had to come straight into the camera, from in front. The wall behind me was quite dark, and apparently unsuitable as a screen from which to reflect such an image. At the same time the completed picture shows marks which, along with the poorer extra, might be interpreted as an image of the path, in the suspended atmospheric dust, of a light beam thrown upon the wall behind me, from a corner of the room. A New York photographer insists that if this beam were of ultra-violet light, rather than the visible kind, the dark wall could have been chemically treated so as to act as a reflecting screen, without any effect visible to the eye; and as regards the light-track on the plate, ultraviolet would presumably be as freely scattered by the dust as visible wave-lengths.

If this suggestion is plausible mechanically, it suffers greatly when we consider it from the human side. The apparatus would be far too expensive for Hope, and presumably for the College, even. Besides, all the indications are that if Hope is a fraud, the College is a dupe rather than a collaborator. Even if the McKenzies were inclined to be conspirators, I doubt that they could get the apparatus from any firm of such low standing as to make the transaction a safe one.

One mechanical difficulty inherent in this or any other use of the ultra-violet part of the spectrum would be the difficulty of finding a source of the ultra-violet that is sufficiently free from the visible wave-lengths. Indeed, I am by no means convinced that such a source exists.

If the thing is a fraud, I am inclined, on mechanical and psychological grounds combined, to believe that it is a comparatively simple one. I think that the average person of some scientific knowledge is far too prone to look for elaborate scientific tricks, and to pass clean over some absurdly simple little home-made artifice which goes under his feet rather than over his head. But if Hope is a fraud, of this or any other sort, it is pretty certain that he has more than one bow to his string. For if he is a fraud, he has certainly substituted plates or plate-holders with other sitters, and this is one thing which he certainly did not do with me.

THE RACKET OF THE POLTERGEIST

By Arthur Machen

Machen, now recognized as one of the leading writers of horror fiction, began his working life as a journalist in London contributing to magazines and daily newspapers, including the Evening News *and* The Referee. *His legendary short story "The Bowmen" which was believed to be fact when published in the* Evening News *in September 1914, unfortunately caused doubts to be cast over his later work, including this story for* The Referee *in January 1928.*

The Battersea Poltergeist – or Racket-spirit – certainly looked promising when it first came to our notice a few days ago. Potatoes, lumps of coal and soda, and a moderate number of pennies were thrown and sown broadcast.

People who kept watch at night in a garden near the afflicted house heard stones pattering about them. One man declared that heavy stones were thrown in his direction with remarkable vigour and accuracy.

Glass doors were smashed, heavy furniture was treated lightly: in fact, the classical programme of the poltergeist was carried out in a thorough and whole-hearted manner. I had hoped a great deal from this troublesome devil of Battersea; but now it seems that there are suggestions of a purely natural explanation – that issue of all most odious to the investigator of secret things.

Setting on one side, then, the Battersea business as probably nonsignificant, we may say that the poltergeist trick – if it be a trick – is both ancient and widely diffused.

The Wesley family were terribly troubled by it in the eighteenth century, and six years ago Dr Weston, then Bishop of Zanzibar, gave a lively account of rackety doings in his dark diocese. The Bishop was summoned to a native mudhut which was disintegrating, not slowly, by the work of time and weather, but violently and after the manner of a volcano. Before the bishop's eyes, as he went in, a portion of wall burst from its place and flung itself into the centre of the hut. A lump of roof fell on Dr Weston's head.

He cleared the hut of its inhabitants and set a cordon of men about it; still it disintegrated. Then the bishop began to exorcize, and the trouble ceased.

Here, then, is the remarkable point. Things are inexplicably thrown and dashed about in England – a case gets into the newspapers once in every three or four years – and things are inexplicably thrown and dashed about in Africa. In most cases, it is just to observe, there is a young person, a boy or girl between ten and fifteen, in the house vexed by these uncouth demonstrations. Are we, then, to conclude that there is a world-wide tradition of this particular kind of mischief handed down amongst the children of the whole earth from remote ages?

This seems difficult and improbable, and all the more so when we consider the handing-down part of the business. You have, let us say, a lonely farmhouse with a boy of twelve or a girl of fifteen amongst its inhabitants. The coals begin to fly, the crockery to smash, the plates to leap off the dresser. You cannot see how it is done, but you say the boy (or the girl) did it.

It may be so; but who taught the young person his tiresome trick? Not the boy or girl at the next farm, since the poltergeist is not a sporadic, but a solitary manifestation. It is not catching, and it doesn't spread. And the secret of the racket is certainly not imparted by the elder members of the family. About nine years ago there were some extraordinary manifestations of this kind in a northern suburb of London. I saw something of the matter, and I remember very vividly the annoyance and distress of the elder members of the family. Their possessions were broken – perhaps three or four pounds' worth of damage was done – and their house was besieged night after night by a noisy mob. They were far indeed, from enjoying the notoriety that the poltergeist had brought them.

There is, of course, the spiritualist hypothesis, though I think that many professed Spiritualists are disinclined to accept this explanation. The manifestations are utterly purposeless; one is inclined to ask with Dickens why a ghost should make such a fool of himself. There is not the faintest evidence of a directing mind behind the phenomena of smashed china and broken glass. Though, by the way, there may possibly be a link between the bangs of the poltergeist and the raps which were a prominent feature in the Cock-lane ghost imposture and in the earlier days of Spiritualism.

Then there is another explanation: the racket is said to be caused by Elemental Earth Spirits, presumably gnomes. I do not think we need trouble to discuss gnomes.

Of course, in spite of all difficulties, the whole business may be the work of mischievous and mystifying children. There may be something in certain cases – in comparatively few cases – of adolescence which urges the human boy or girl to play these puzzling and outrageous tricks; some secret, morbid, and obscure instinct which is as powerful in Africa as in a London suburb. If this be so, then the actions performed, the insensate throwing about of stones, coals, plates, and pots and pans are done consciously, but yet in obedience to an irresistible impulse, closely allied to the impulses of acute mania.

Or, perhaps – it is, I confess, a wild hypothesis – the ferment of the change from childhood to manhood or womanhood, affecting profoundly the whole being, physical, mental, spiritual, may generate a force which transcends all our capacity of definition or explanation, which acts as blindly, with as little sense of direction, as the lightning flash.

And, it is barely possible; the "medium" of the Spiritualists may be a poltergeist child who has grown up.

EDGAR WALLACE RETURNS

By Maurice Barbanell

A London journalist and devoted psychic investigator, Barbanell founded and edited the long-running Psychic News *in 1932 to investigate and debate the supernatural and paranormal world. Among his many contributions to the paper was this story, published in the autumn of its inaugural year and some nine months after the death of the famous novelist on 10 February 1932.*

I did not expect that a controversy would ensue from what seemed a routine newspaper happening. It began when I had engaged a new reporter named A. W. Austen. Dissatisfied with his predecessor, I telephoned the National Union of Journalists with a request to send a suitable applicant for the post. Austen came for an interview.

He was a young man in his early twenties whose previous journalistic experience had been confined to a local newspaper. He knew nothing at firsthand about Spiritualism or psychic phenomena. So far as religion was concerned, he was an agnostic by outlook. Only once had he attended a public demonstration of clairvoyance, but it had been some years earlier and he could not recall the impression it had made.

He seemed to possess the necessary qualities for a reporter, particularly as he was an expert shorthand writer. His scepticism of psychic matters, which was natural to an agnostic, appeared to me a desirable rather than an undesirable qualification, for he would bring to his work an unbiased mind that could not be accused of credulity or incredulity.

In the course of his labours he interviewed mediums and edited reports of psychic happenings that reached us through the post. But he lacked personal experience, which rightly he considered essential before he could form any opinion.

A few weeks after Austen's appointment, I suggested that he should participate in a "friendly test" with Myers, who at the time was getting an average of two or three extras on every six plates that he exposed. As part of the conditions, it was agreed that Austen would buy a packet of half-a-dozen quarter-plates at a branch of a well-known chain of chemists.

The plates remained in Austen's possession all the evening, except when they were loaded into slides in his presence, when they were exposed in the camera and, later, when they were developed in the darkroom while he watched. To make the test complete, I signed each plate as it was loaded into its slide.

Austen's report revealed that he regarded the proceedings with no little apprehension. The thought that there might be a spirit form standing next to him, perhaps even touching him, was, he said, rather frightening.

The proceedings began with Myers offering a prayer. After that, the plates, still in their unopened packet, were passed round to the group, which numbered ten, to be "magnetized." There is a prevailing belief that each individual possesses some quantity of psychic power and that mediums are mediums because they have it in a larger degree. Every sitter held the packet for a few seconds before passing it on to his neighbour.

Next some sacred music was played on a gramophone, again as part of a belief that this helps the conditions needed to obtain psychic results. Presently Myers, Austen and I retired to the darkroom and loaded the slides with the plates while I signed each one to make identification certain, and to answer sceptics who might later say that they were substituted for others.

The three of us returned to the room in Myers' house where the remainder of the group were waiting. Throughout, the room was brightly lit by two powerful electric lamps, a fact which surprised Austen, as he had erroneously believed that all such tests were held in the dark.

During the exposure of the first plate nothing happened. Austen began to feel that he had been frightened for no reason, but his composure disappeared during the second exposure when Myers went into a semitrance state in which he wandered about the room apparently aimlessly. In this state he transmitted spirit messages or made references to what would appear on the plates.

The thing which struck Austen as extraordinary was that two of the plates were exposed to the light for so long that he expected them to be blacked out completely when developed. But the medium's psychic power countered what should normally have happened and produced sharp images on these overexposed plates.

During one exposure Myers, still in his trancelike state, said that a man, who had been known to me before his passing, was present and that he had a message: "Keep the flag flying. We are still in the melting pot." After that Myers said: "It is Israel Zangwill. Do you know him?"

"Yes," I replied, "I know him." I had met him when he lectured for a literary society of which I was secretary. The significance of one part of his message was that Zangwill, who earned fame with his novels depicting Jewish life, called one of his plays, *The Melting Pot*.

The three of us returned to the darkroom to develop the plates. There, to Austen's surprise, but not to mine, on the plate previously indicated by Myers was a perfect extra of Zangwill, much larger than the faces of any of the other sitters shown in the photograph. The extra was, as usual, within a surround of what Austen described as "a whitish substance," but is, of course, ectoplasm, the substance used in making that which is spiritual material.

This result gave Austen's scepticism a mortal blow, for there was no normal explanation as to how Zangwill's face could have appeared on the plate. The plates which he had bought had never been out of his sight except while they were in the camera, from the time he took them from the assistant in the shop until they were developed in the darkroom.

"How could this extra have got there except by Zangwill being present in the room?" asked Austen. It was a fair question.

The sequel, however, was astonishing. A few days after I published the extra in *Psychic News*, I had a letter from the Press Portrait Bureau, a Fleet Street photographic agency, asking me to pay a reproduction fee. They claimed that the Zangwill extra bore a marked resemblance to one of their photographs, and by my publishing it they were entitled to the normal reproduction fee payable by newspapers in such cases.

I replied that I could not admit their claim because it would be tantamount to saying that the extra had been fraudulently produced. Moreover it was not an exact copy. I invited them to discuss the matter in all its implications. There followed a visit of two of their representatives, who had previously asked to inspect the negative. Myers met them in my office and produced this plate. I reiterated the test conditions under which this séance had taken place, which meant that any suggestion of trickery was completely out of the question. The photographers examined the negative and were obviously puzzled. In their long experience they had never encountered such a happening.

As a result of this conversation, Myers agreed to give them a test sitting with their own plates. The conditions were arranged. They were to buy the plates, be present when they were loaded in the slides, sign the plates and watch them being developed. They also promised to sign a report at the end of the test.

The next day Myers telephoned me to say, "I have a strong impression that Edgar Wallace will come on one of the plates at this sitting. Will you ask Swaffer to be present?"

This remark needs some explanation. A few days earlier in Swaffer's flat, Myers had taken some photographs. While he was exposing one plate, he gave clairvoyance, a frequent occurrence, and said: "Edgar Wallace is here. He says he will not come on the plates tonight. He will appear soon in dramatic circumstances."

Wallace, one of the greatest thriller writers of his time, and Swaffer had been journalistically associated for many years, for they worked sometimes for the same newspapers. Wallace was also a playwright and Swaffer a dramatic critic, with a reputation for devastating frankness. Thus Edgar was not unnaturally displeased when Swaffer adversely criticized one of his plays. This resulted in a breach in their friendship, which fortunately was healed not long before Edgar's passing.

It so happened that soon after I had published in *Psychic News* the account by Austen of Myers' mediumship, I received a manuscript in automatic writing that claimed to have emanated from Wallace. This package arrived a few minutes before I was due to call on Swaffer.

I had no time to read the whole of it, but I noticed that it was dedicated to Swaffer. Knowing their intimate friendship, I took the manuscript with me. When I arrived I said somewhat sceptically to Swaffer, "Here is a manuscript that purports to describe by Wallace his life in the spirit world, starting with his passing."

I had expected Swaffer to dismiss it with a peremptory shrug. It is a frequent occurrence, after famous people pass on, for self-styled mediums to believe that they receive communications from them. Alas, I have been plagued with far too many of such "messages."

To my surprise, however, Swaffer opened the parcel and began to read the contents. He went on reading and reading. Soon he looked up and said: "I do not know whether Edgar wrote this, but it is certainly a trained reporter's description of circumstances confronting him in another world. You should not publish it without confirmation."

But how could such confirmation be obtained? Suddenly the answer occurred to me. At the time I was a regular attendant at remarkable direct-voice séances with Estelle Roberts, one of the world's most famous mediums. It was quite usual at each séance for spirit communicators to speak, often reproducing their earthly voices, and to give unassailable evidence of their identity to relatives or friends.

The presiding spirit genius at these seances was Estelle's guide, Red Cloud, obviously an evolved being, who always radiated love, wisdom and compassion. He was particularly expert in training would-be communicators so that when they learned the ropes and managed to speak they always produced what was clearly proof of their individuality.

Having received excellent evidence myself from relatives and friends at these séances, I decided to enlist Red Cloud's help. "I have a manuscript that claims to emanate from Edgar Wallace," I said to this guide. "Is it possible for you to find out whether he is responsible?"

His answer was direct: "I will ask him. Do nothing until I give you his reply." This was good enough for me. A fortnight later, at the next voice circle, Red Cloud said to me: "I have asked Wallace. He says he is responsible for the automatic writings."

With this assurance I published the manuscript in *Psychic News* under the title, "My Life After Death, by Edgar Wallace." It caused a sensation. It was attacked by all sorts of people who questioned its authenticity. I merely smiled. I had received the confirmation I wanted.

It was therefore not without significance that Wallace had promised, through Myers, to produce his psychic photograph. Swaffer and I, together with the two representatives from Press Portrait Bureau, went to Myers' house. Here these professional photographers produced the plates they had bought.

The test conditions were fulfilled in regard to loading the slides, developing the negatives and taking the pictures. I did not learn until later that they introduced another "safeguard." Without mentioning it, when loading the plates, they marked each one with a cutting instrument, in addition to their being signed. This meant that substitution was virtually impossible.

During the exposure of the second plate, Myers, in semitrance, referred to Wallace. Pointing to Swaffer he said, "Edgar is here." There followed a message referring to the publication of the automatic writing manuscript.

Then Myers turned to the photographers and said that, while it was difficult, Wallace was going to make the supreme effort to put a likeness of himself on the plate. Edgar's message was, "if my picture does come it will be unlike any in existence."

When the plates were developed, there was a perfect likeness of Wallace. Naturally, I published it and caused another sensation. I challenged the whole of Fleet Street and Wallace's relatives and friends to produce a similar picture taken during his lifetime. Nobody could do so nor has since done so. This completely destroyed the idea that there was a photograph like it in existence. Thus its authenticity was assured.

The two professional photographers, as arranged, signed a statement immediately after the test in which they stated their satisfaction that there had been no substitution of plates. The perfect spirit test had been accomplished.

MY TALKS WITH THE DEAD

By Hannen Swaffer

Swaffer was credited with inventing the gossip column with "Mr Gossip" in the Daily Sketch *in 1913, followed by "Mr London" for the* Daily Graphic. *Born Frederic Charles Swaffer, he adopted his mother's maiden name "Hannen" for his journalistic work, effecting the Glaswegian rhyming slang for "gaffer". He helped to develop the* Daily Mirror *into a major newspaper, edited* The People, *and championed spiritualism in many articles and pamphlet including* My Talks With The Dead, *in the mid-1900s.*

It all began, as did so many other things in my life, with Lord Northcliffe. Had he really survived death, as a Spiritualist friend told me? Was it true that he could still communicate with this world, and was doing so?

As an Agnostic, I sneered at the idea. As a cynic to whom Spiritualism was a delusion, I mocked.

Yet, being a journalist used to probing things, however apparently fantastic they might seem at first hearing, I set out on an enquiry.

Being an honest journalist, I recorded what happened, produced my evidence at a crowded Queen's Hall meeting, from which thousands were turned away and which was followed by ironical leading articles slating me in the "Morning Post," the "Star" and "Truth," and published "Northcliffe's Return." in which the full story was told.

Spiritualism was true, I was soon convinced. So, being a lifelong crusader, I championed its cause, in the Press and on platforms throughout the length and breadth of Britain, in various parts of the United States, and in Germany, Scandinavia and North Africa.

In Berlin, I addressed a thronged gathering in the Prussian Parliament House, where Germans eagerly demanded to know what the Northcliffe whom they accused of having made them lose the war by his propaganda for Britain had to say about world affairs of the day.

That adventure began in 1924, two years after Northcliffe's passing. Through medium after medium, my old Chief proved the survival of a personality unmistakable to his intimates but incredibly contradictory to those who had not known the man behind the machine, the fascinating humorist behind the iron will that was all that casual acquaintances saw, the baffling paradox that was all things, to all men and women, in different moods.

No, he was not lying peaceably in a grave in North London, as the materialists thought. Nor was he lying there temporarily, waiting for the Last Trump, as the Fundamentalists believed. It was not his destiny to play a harp on a cloud, or sing hymns continuously beside a Throne.

So early as the night of his passing in August, 1922, Northcliffe showed his determination to prove to the world that he was not "dead." He tried to communicate at a circle led by a former Baptist minister in South Norwood. Instead, the very next morning, the correspondence department of the "Daily Mail" received a letter, saying so! It was torn up, no doubt, with contempt.

A fortnight later, he criticised, at the same circle, a weekly Spiritualist journal that its leader edited: "Third column on Page Two should be improved. The leading article of a paper should always be most attractive."

Two years after that, a greatly changed man, he was looking on the Fleet Street in which he had spent his earth life with strangely new eyes.

"Avoid the Press," he warned the South Norwood circle, then his only means of contact. "Day after day, my eyes are opened wider and wider to this fact. I have seen what a curse the opinions of a few journalists may be to the world – and when I see what is printed I wonder how men with intellect can read it."

"I have learned to murder my old self," was another burst of self-revelation. "I have taken my old self and put it from me. I have been born anew, so that my real self can come through. I have been as dead as a doornail in the past. I realise that now."

He had passed from one life to another – just as your "dead" friends have done – the same individual that he was on earth, continuing a life somewhat similar to that which enthralled him here. He was still a journalist, still an organiser, still an enthusiastic propagandist for truth as he saw it.

And so, mellowed though by new experiences and broadened by wider knowledge, he persists today. Every time I sit in a mediumistic circle, he is present. Often he butts into the conversation with a new joke entirely in keeping with the irrepressible humours of his earth life. He sneers at Fleet Street just as he did when he was its master journalist, its one real genius and its most vital propagandist.

And, whether you believe it or not, he still occasionally issues "communiqués" criticising newspapers – in the "Daily Mail" office, when he was its Chief, the arrival of his daily "communiqué" was awaited with anxiety and even dread – although nowadays the only detailed ones point out the faults in "Psychic News," which he helped to found. Years after he "died," he persists in criticising its leading articles, its make-up and its policy. For that policy he is largely responsible.

When it prints something good, he claims the credit for it, just as, in the old days, he claimed all the credit for what was right in the "Daily Mail," whether it had been his idea or not. When it is not "hot" enough, to use his own phrase, the editor is blamed. That was what his editors had to suffer in Carmelite House, Fleetway House and in Printing House Square before his control passed into other hands.

Northcliffe has changed politically since his passing. As a sign of that he always refers to the "Daily Herald" as "the pink paper," meaning it is not red enough for him. "It wants a blood transfusion," was one phrase.

But, then, most newspapers come under the lash of his tongue at various times.

When, because the marketing to readers of cheap sets of Dickens sent up the sale of the "Daily Herald" by perhaps 300,000 in a day, the "Daily Mail," the "Daily Express" and the "News Chronicle" followed suit, so that four of the most largely circulated newspapers in the world were selling Dickens, at the same time, Northcliffe waxed sarcastic.

"There's an awful row amongst the other dead authors," he said. "They ask 'Hasn't any editor heard of us?' They are all jealous of Dickens!"

A recent sneer about a former rival was his remark, made to me in my present home circle: "Whenever I see the 'Daily Express,' I ask it, 'Is your journey really necessary?'"

Generally, his attitude towards Fleet Street is summarised in the biting phrase, "They have poisoned the wells of Truth."

His early purgatory was the realisation that, although the vast newspaper machine of his own creation was being used for purposes out of harmony with his newfound convictions, he could do nothing to change its policy.

For, in his own way, he wanted to save the world – or to show it, rather, how it could save itself. Yet he could not. Mankind was blundering into new catastrophes, and he was unable to warn it. Surely that is a more logical result of earth blunders and misdeeds than a lake of eternal fire!

"I often go along to the 'Daily Mail' conference," he once told me, "and shout 'You're all wrong.' But they can't hear me. And although I am standing there while they plan and plot, they can't see me. Sorrowfully, I come away, helpless. That is my punishment."

"My God, Beaverbrook, if only you knew how difficult it is," he shouted at a sitting, with Evan Powell as the medium, to which I had invited Lord Beaverbrook so that he could get a message from Bonar Law, who wanted to advise his executor about his will. "This is the new revelation. Don't you understand? This is the great reality."

The phase of Northcliffe's self-condemnation is now past. In a higher sphere of activity, he is a propagandist for Spiritualism, for world peace and for universal betterment, ever busy, always working.

Yet his irrepressible humour persists. So does his zest for the journalism his unceasing energy did so much to evolve.

"I'm running the 'St Peter's Gazette'," Northcliffe chuckled, in one of his merry moods. This was a joke, not only about the St Peter who is supposed to guard the Gate, but the fact, which I had at the time forgotten, that he lived at St Peter's, in Thanet.

Northcliffe, as of yore, thinks little of statesmen and their doings.

His former colleagues – slaves and friends at the same time – will recall his frequent gibes about politicians and his wittily-expressed impatience with public men.

Even in the height of our present Prime Minister's popularity, he gave us, from the spirit world, a warning about the world's adulation of a man it had ignored during his long years in the wilderness.

"Why is Churchill worship a national religion?" he asked. "Wasn't the Church ill enough before that?"

Northcliffe's comments on the first number of "Psychic News" were characteristic. Page One, which contained "A Challenge to the 'Daily Mail'," he said was "very good." Of Page Two he said "Dull." Page Three was "nearly right," Page Four a "mix-up," Page Five "very good" and Page Six "wrong."

Of Page Seven, for which I had written an article, "Thou Shalt Not Suffer a Witch to Live," he said, "I will pass that," while two pages devoted to a weekly debate on Spiritualism were "nearly right." "But the paper wants more humour," he added. "It's not hot enough," is his constant advice. "Attack! Attack!"

The spirit guide through whom Northcliffe spoke said, "He calls himself 'the all-watching one'."

"He used to say 'the all-seeing one'," I replied, remembering the humorous postcards he sent his staff when he was away.

"That is what he means," said the guide. "He also says, 'I am the omniscient one.' I do not myself like that phrase. He is not God."

Well, that is Northcliffe as he is today.

"If I were in Fleet Street now," he insists, "I would start a new kind of journalism. People want the truth. Don't editors know it?

"I now call it Flight Street. It always runs away from the facts."

Orthodox people brought up on the old harp-playing and shining-thrones idea may not like to know it. But people, in the other world, change only gradually.

When, on another plane, you again meet your lost ones, they will be the lost ones that you know. Time will have tempered their faults. Broader experiences will have developed them.

But, despite the hymns and the creeds and the litanies and the prayers, they will be working out their own redemption.

It is to a world of eternal progress that Northcliffe welcomes one by one his former colleagues – yes, and all journalists as they pass into the realms to which he went before them.

"Another has joined my band," he says, whenever this happens. He is still "the Chief."

In that world, one day, your friends will greet you. And in it you will enter a sphere for which your attainments, your character and your degree of self-development have suited you. This is as inevitable as the law of gravity, which, without a mediator or a judge, sends a stone to the bottom of a pond, lets a piece of heavy wood go somewhere near the surface and decrees that a cork shall float on top of the water.

SPIRITS SPEAK FOR THE RECORD

By John Gay Stevens

Stevens was an American newspaper reporter and advertising agency copywriter who later became a producer-writer of local and regional radio and television shows in Los Angeles. With a life-long interest in the supernatural, he joined the American Society for Psychic Research and was involved in a number of major investigations for over thirty years. Here he describes one of the strangest phenomena he ever encountered in 1933 for Fate *magazine.*

Because it is customary these days to refer all phenomena, psychic, psychological and physical, to the "Scientific Establishment" for evaluation those of us interested in parapsychology face a frustrating dilemma. Science has no organized program for the investigation of this type of phenomena and its opinion, therefore, must be classed as armchair expertise.

On the other hand, the reality of psychic phenomena always has been clouded by the question of the credibility of its witnesses and investigators. But if you happen to have credentials acceptable in the scientific community you can investigate and report on this sort of thing only at your peril.

However, the critical issue is the matter of immediacy. The average man, faced with the threat of instant global demolition, is getting anxious to learn the answers to life and survival *now*.

And so, while we wait for science to become scientific (to investigate without prejudice) it has been reassuring to me to have had a personal experience that has done a great deal to convince me of the reality of discarnate entities and of survival.

On April 23, 1933, in New York City, a group of us from the American Society for Psychic Research, of which I was a member, recorded a spirit voice séance that left all of us, including four erstwhile cynical sound engineers, convinced of the reality of the spirit voices we recorded.

This was before the work of the Society became limited to the study of statistical, or quantitative research into man's extrasensory powers. At that time, and for the previous half-century, both British and American Societies of Psychical Research had maintained a continuing study of mediumship and spontaneous phenomena.

Mrs Helen T. Bigelow, then secretary of the Society, Mr Bigelow, Dr Hereward Carrington, lifelong psychic investigator*, Chester Grady, Louis Anspacher, and myself were members assigned to investigate and report on mediums producing this type of phenomena. All seances were held at the headquarters of the Society, on lower Lexington Avenue, in Manhattan.

Recording a "voice" séance was not part of our scheduled activities for that year but Dr Frank Black, one of the owners of World Broadcasting Company (now Decca Records), a leading producer-director of many top musical shows in radio at the time, and later musical director of NBC, having an intelligent layman's interest in psychic phenomena, offered to record a voice séance at the World Broadcasting Studios, providing it was supervised by the Society. He then planned to donate the records to the Society for reference and study. The idea was not received with enthusiasm by the Society. All mediumistic phenomena staged in an environment not controlled by trained investigators may be thought to lack evidential value. It was finally decided that the thing was worth doing, however, simply because it never had been done before. This was years before the advent of the wire or tape recorder.

The whole affair was planned by the Society with about as much scientific care as a dinner party. As it turned out, the recording engineers at World Broadcasting Company, led by Charles Lauda, now head recording engineer for Decca Records, took care of the scientific side of the project. They did so well, in fact, that this recording session produced some of the most convincing evidence of the reality of spirit voices we ever had.

Naturally, proving the genuineness of the voices was not their intention. They asked if there was any objection to trying to prove that any purported spirit voices were fraudulent. We welcomed the idea. To a man these engineers were certain there was no such thing as a spirit voice and they regarded this as a heaven-sent chance to prove it all in their own studio under their own recording conditions.

* and frequent contributor to FATE before his death in December, 1958.

At the time, the Western Electric Company, through its ERPI Division (Electrical Research Products Institute), were installing their latest sound recording equipment at World Broadcasting Company. When they heard of this proposed recording of ghost voices some of these Western Electric engineers joined the World engineers to help unmask the voice makers. Collectively they probably made up the most formidable array of sound engineering talent ever organized to debunk a spirit voice.

We (there were perhaps a dozen of us from the Society) engaged the medium, William Cartheuser, for the occasion as we were satisfied he had produced direct or disembodied voices in our own investigations, working under our controls at our headquarters.

The recording studio at 50 West 57th Street was a big, 40-foot-long, windowless, sound-proofed room, two stories high. A dozen chairs were arranged in a circle around a stand microphone in the middle of the floor. Two additional mikes hung close to the ceiling in diagonally opposite corners of the room.

One of the engineers pointed out that the mike on the floor, about head high when we sat down, was mike No. 1. All voices in the circle would be recorded on that mike, he said. The two mikes at the ceiling corners were No. 2 and No. 3. These ceiling mikes, he explained, had such a short range of sensitivity they would not record any voices from the floor. He indicated the control room window that had been covered to keep the light in the control room out of the studio and said he would be talking to us over the speaker recessed in the wall directly over the window. As an afterthought he added they had stationed an engineer at the only exit door to see that no one left or entered the studio.

With so little information we didn't understand the "test". Evidently they had no plan to put controls on the medium so he could not move or speak, a procedure we frequently used. We had no way of knowing that the engineers, after a week or so of conferring, had hit on a very simple plan that covered all possibilities. They concluded that, no matter what tricks the voice maker used, he *had* to work on the floor. If the voices were authentic spirit voices then they need have no such limitation in space. They should be able to speak from anywhere in the room – not only at floor level.

The answer was simple. They would hang mikes at the ceiling where they would not register voices from the floor. If voices could manage to speak close enough to a ceiling mike to be recorded over that mike those voices would have to be supernatural or spirit voices.

By the same token, if the voices only could be heard on mike No. 1 on the floor they must be suspect as normal and fraudulent.

Their test, therefore, was an open and shut matter, based strictly on position-in-space considerations, without regard to the nature of the voices or the content of any messages. They had decided they were not qualified to judge evidence in any field other than their own, and had based their entire case on the placement of those ceiling mikes – 20 feet away from the sitters and 20 feet in the air.

Regardless of the skill of the medium in vocal deception, regardless of his dexterity in eluding controls in the dark, *he had to stay on the floor*. They had removed all extra chairs, piano and bench, music stands, draperies, etc. No voice could be recorded on either of those high mikes unless the speaker was within 12 inches or so of the mike face. Furthermore, the mikes were of the old-fashioned carbon type that were not only very limited in range but also highly directional. And both of them had been carefully turned at right angles to the circle of sitters.

Each mike had been rigged with its own line into the control room. All lines converged at the cutting head of the recording machine. The line from mike No. 1 on the floor went through the monitoring console as usual. But the lines from mikes No. 2 and 3 at the ceiling bypassed the console and were set up with their own DB dial, speaker and power amplifier. The lines from mikes No. 2 and 3 were set at zero and could not be monitored. This means the engineers could tell precisely which mike was bringing in each voice by listening to the individual speaker and by watching the individual dial on each of the three separate lines.

In the studio, since we had no special instruction from the engineers, we went ahead as if at a conventional direct voice setting. In the dark, waiting for the psychic power to build up, we carried on a casual conversation and we wondered what those fellows in the control room were up to. Finally, someone said, "The trumpet is up."

The trumpet, a familiar accessory of voice mediums, is a slim, elongated, collapsible version of a megaphone. It was made of light aluminum and carried a band of luminous paint so it could be seen in the dark. Discarnate personalities are supposed to use it when they are not able to make themselves heard without it. It had been resting on the floor in the middle of our circle of sitters ever since we gathered around the floor mike.

Now the phosphorescent ring of the trumpet was clearly visible a couple of feet above our heads circling the group. It tapped each sitter lightly on the head as if in greeting.

We called roll to see that everyone was in his or her chair and that the hands of all sitters were held by the person on either side to be sure that no one – particularly the medium – left his seat.

Voices gradually built up through the trumpet. These voices identified themselves as some late relative or close friend. Sometimes they were recognized, sometimes not. Now and then we suggested to a voice that it speak into the mike in front of us on the floor – No. 1. It never occurred to us to send them to the ceiling mikes since we had no idea of their significance. After we had sent several trumpet voices to the floor mike the speaker from the control room sounded. "Are these what you call 'spirit' voices?" the engineer asked. There were overtones of cynicism in the question.

The circling trumpet finally clattered to the floor in the middle of the circle. Several minutes of oppressive silence followed. Then the full-blown resonant voice of a man seemed to pop out of space in front of us, directly above mike No. 1. This time the phosphorescent ring of the trumpet was still visible on the floor at our feet. This new voice was brisk and businesslike; we recognized it instantly as a "direct" voice – a voice coming, literally, out of thin air.

After a greeting it said, "We are very interested in the experiment you people are putting on tonight and we would like to help."

We asked, "What experiment is that?"

"I'm talking about your friends the engineers there in the back room," he explained. "We think they have worked out a very interesting testing procedure for us on their equipment."

This new voice brought a query from the control room. "Who is that speaking – the one talking about our test."

"We don't know," we answered. "It's just a voice."

The personality behind the new voice moved in close to mike No. 1. "I'm the one you heard talking to these people in here," he said. "I speak to you directly without the use of any intermediaries or equipment of any kind.

"I'm an engineer over here on this side and, with a couple of my colleagues, would like to collaborate with you in making this test recording. We think what you are doing is important.

"We have a definite plan in mind for your tests. We are perfectly willing to meet any conditions you set up, or make any demonstration you have in mind . . . if it is within our power. Just let us know what you would like to have me do."

"Just a moment," the control room speaker said. There was a pause while the group apparently went into a huddle. Finally the engineer spoke again, "Do you think you could speak to us over one of those microphones located up at the ceiling?"

Instantly, right on the heels of the last syllable of his words, the engineer in the control room heard the voice come into the room over mike No. 2 at the ceiling. "How's this?" it asked. "Does it make any difference to you which microphone I use up here?"

Nothing could have made much difference to those control room engineers at that particular moment. They later admitted they had sat stunned, staring at the No. 2 speaker.

"Is this all right?" the voice insisted from No. 2. This time it was as loud as a bull-horn.

This sparked the control room into action; the man at the console finally found his voice. "Yes . . . yes. That's fine. Would you mind lowering your voice a little? We have no volume control on that line."

"I'm sorry," the voice replied. "I assume this is a test to satisfy yourselves that we are what we claim to be by proving that we can speak to you from any point in space." The voice was now at a normal speaking level.

As the engineers watched intently the needle in the dial face on the line to mike No. 2 flickered in perfect coordination with the sound of the voice from the speaker on that line. There was no doubt they agreed, that voice was speaking within inches of mike No. 2. Moreover, they were almost as much impressed by the speed of the voice's switch from mike No. 1 on the floor to mike No. 2 at the ceiling as they were by the fact that it actually spoke at the ceiling mike.

The engineer now asked, "Would you try that other mike at the ceiling, there across the room from you?"

Again, before the engineer could complete his request, the voice was answering from within inches of mike No. 3. It had traveled through space in a matter of a second.

There was a brief exchange between the two engineers, the one *Here* and the one *There*. This was followed by a long pause. Our control room engineers had nothing more to say.

Those of us in the studio had been listening to all of this in puzzled silence. Finally we spoke up. "Are you ready with your experiment?"

The speaker on the wall said, "It's all over – as far as we're concerned."

We all started talking at once. But the voice broke in, now down at mike No. 1, and still addressing the control room, "If you don't have any other tests we have a demonstration or two we would like to show you."

Without waiting for an answer the voice explained that he was going to make a complete circuit of all three mikes while making a short simple statement about what he was doing. He warned the engineers to keep a sharp eye on their dials and a sharp ear on the speakers so they could follow his fast moves from mike to mike. "When you are ready," he said, "give me a signal."

After an interval of only seconds the control room barked, "Go!"

Speaking at a normal conversational pace the voice said, "I am now making a complete circuit of all three microphones and am now back at No. 1." That voice, speaking without a break, had zoomed up, circled the ceiling and dived back down to mike No. 1 like a toy airplane.

The control room engineers reported they had followed its progress around the speakers and dials. As revealed by the records later, that voice had moved at such incredible speed between mikes it sounded as if it had been recorded on one mike.

At this point the voice introduced a colleague whom he described as a "one-time eminent research engineer in the science of sound when he was back there with you."

The new voice came in on No. 1 mike. He began in a contemplative voice, "We think we have given you some clear evidence. At least you should know by now that our voices are not human voices . . . as you originally thought. We are what we claim to be, surviving personalities speaking to you from another dimension – and not impersonations. We have given you this evidence on your own terms and on your own equipment."

This obviously was meant for the engineering group in the control room.

Then, as if turning to us, he continued, "In those demonstrations it was our intent to prove to you the super-physical nature of our voices by showing you what one of our voices can do in terms of time and motion. Now I am going to show you what one of our voices can do in terms of vocal production – a vocal sound performance that is impossible for the human voice. This should be of particular interest to your recording engineers, since I will produce my voice throughout the entire range of sound audible to the human ear."

None of us had heard of such a thing before and Cartheuser, when questioned later, could not remember anything like this.

The voice said, "I am now speaking to you at the normal level of the human male voice . . . around 300 cycles. If you listen carefully you will notice that I am slowly moving my voice up the scale of sound frequencies in an unbroken flow of sound."

We were fascinated by the sound of that voice gliding smoothly up in perfect pitch like the glissando of a musical instrument, from a resonant baritone to a bright tenor, to a soprano. Through it all he never stopped talking.

"My voice is now at the 1100 cycle point," he said. "This is approximately at the highest point where the human speaking voice can articulate – frame words – that are understandable to you there. From this point I will increase the cycle frequency of my voice until it is beyond the range of your hearing and, you will note, I can articulate clearly and understandably until it disappears."

Even as he spoke, giving frequency levels, 3,000, 5,000, and relevant comments, his voice climbed to the twittering of a small bird, yet every word could be understood. Finally the words become only a fine thread of sound like an incredibly distant radio signal . . . then there was silence.

We sat immobile. There was not the slightest doubt among us that such a thing could be done only by a discarnate entity. The speaker on the wall broke the silence, "We know that none of you could have done that," the control room said.

This started conversation around our circle, including comment from Cartheuser, who never had left his seat. Our chatter was cut off, however, by the readvent of the voice. He told us he would now take his voice *down* through the frequency cycles below the level of the human voice.

He started down, again from the 300 cycle point. His enunciation became slower as his voice deepened to a bass-profundo and on down to the lowest reaches of an orchestral string bass. He paused to explain that this was 100 cycles below where the human voice could frame recognizable words. Still speaking clearly the voice sounded like that of a giant mumbling at the bottom of a well. Still sinking, it faded into a swishing sound that suggested the lowest note on the longest pipe in a giant pipe organ. Then it vanished.

Again there was silence, this time broken by the original spokesman for the spirit engineers.

"Well, there you have it," he announced. "We hope you and your engineers have found our collaboration helpful. We want to thank you people and your medium for making it possible for us to demonstrate and record evidence that our voices are not fraudulently impersonated in this, and many other cases. The power is failing and we must go. But remember, we will be back to collaborate with you on any such experiment you choose to hold in the future."

The entire séance had lasted two hours and 15 minutes and had been recorded on nine 15-minute $33^{1}/_{3}$ rpm LPs. Within a month of the recording date all records, with the masters, were turned over to the Society by Frank Black.

This séance and its records made little if any impression in official circles. Only the engineers in the control room were in a position to testify to the reality of the discarnate voices. But they, like so many others, were not about to go on record officially. So, one of the technically best test cases for the reality of "spirit voice" phenomena went officially unconfirmed. The whole affair, along with the recordings, turned out to be just what it started out to be – no more than an interesting documentary in the archives of the Society.

There was one important result. Those of us who were there came away with the unshakable conviction that, as far as proving survival is concerned, that séance will do very well; the spirits did, indeed, speak for the record.

THE WARNING

By Robert Thurston Hopkins

Hopkins was a photographer/journalist with a special interest in ghosts who wrote features for the Press Association and Reuters, the London Evening News *and* Sunday Express, *plus* Picture Post *for whom he took a series of remarkable pictures of Borley Rectory in 1955, including one of a "dark shadow" bearing a distinct likeness to a nun. Here he describes another equally strange and sinister moment that occurred to him in 1943.*

I am sometimes surprised when I hear people talking of whether they believe in ghosts or not. Believe in them? I have been meeting them, off and on, most of my life. They come and go of their own accord and seem to be occupied solely with their own business. But one ghost did his best to "communicate" with me and he possibly saved my life. I was living in an ancient manor house near Billinghurst in Sussex from 1940 to 1943 and the house was set in deep oak woods and reached by private roads. One night, during a sharp raid by German bombers, I decided to walk over a footpath to the local inn. I went into the hall to pick up my hat. Suddenly I heard a man coughing and muttering outside, and I opened a side door where he seemed to be. There was nobody in sight. I went to the front door. There was nobody there, either. I looked up and down the pathways;

nothing was to be seen – nothing but falling snow. I returned to the hall and felt very uneasy, as German airmen from wrecked planes had several times been found hiding in the adjacent woods, and a few days before I had assisted the local policeman to carry an injured German pilot to my house to await a phone call for the ambulance.

I decided to put off my visit to the local. A little later I again heard "somebody" coughing and muttering outside my window. I felt that he – whoever he was – seemed very anxious to talk to me . . . had an urgent message to deliver, but his voice and presence did not seem quite strong enough to reach me. Returning to the footpaths around my house. I examined the snow-covered ground where whoever or whatever had been muttering and standing. The snow was a thick blanket but there were no tracks – none coming, none going.

When I returned to my room I got a clue to the mystery. My cocker spaniel Duster lay quite still before the log fire, alert, agitated and silent.

If any *human being* had been outside, he would have rushed from door to door barking furiously. But he lay with his nose between his paws, watching me, waiting for me to understand what kind of a person our visitor had been. He had sensed what "it" was all along.

I said: "I guess you are right," and the old spaniel relaxed and sighed.

A minute later there was a terrific explosion a short distance from my house. Later I discovered that a German bomb had fallen across the footpath which ran to our local inn. The explosion had made a crater large enough to hide a couple of houses comfortably.

I then realised that my visitor had possibly prevented me from walking straight into that shattering explosion.

After that, I could not help thinking about that German pilot who had rested for a while in my house. I had watched him as he was carried into the ambulance and he had waved to me, smiled and once more thanked me for some cigarettes I had given to him. I heard that he had died in the hospital a few days later.

AN EMINENT VICTORIAN IN WARTIME LONDON

By Alan Dent

Dent, an eminent journalist, book reviewer and biographer, also had an extraordinary encounter during the war while London was being subjected to a blitzkrieg by German bombers. It was to be almost a quarter of a century before he related the episode in the

Christmas 1967 number of The Illustrated London News – *and only after he had discussed his experience with a relative of the ghost, "who told me that mine was by no means the first intimation that the baroness had been seen walking about London".*

On a sunny June morning during the Second World War I was walking down the north side of the Strand. The sky was blue and serene, but the atmosphere was sinister and chilling because, since there had been heavy air-raids the night before, there came from every direction the singular, sharp noise of broken window-glass being swept, shovelled, and carted away in large quantities. Apart from the LCC workmen doing this job there were very few people about, and very little traffic.

Just after I had passed the Adelphi Theatre I became aware of an elderly lady walking, not so much slowly as with a kind of deliberation, in front of me. My first thought was that I had seen her once or twice before, walking in front of me in just such a way – once, as I remembered, in the middle of Long Acre, and once again, as I more vaguely remembered, in that part of Oxford Street that affords a view of Denby House. As on those occasions she again struck me as a very singular old lady, but I had no impression that she was a hallucination or anything other-worldly.

This time I resolved to have a better view of her, a face-to-face view if possible. I decided to pass her swiftly, walk 20 yards or so on, look into a shop window for a second, and then turn back slowly to get a full front view. From behind and while passing I could see that she was, as on the previous occasions, dressed in a black satin walking-costume of a very old-fashioned style, that she had a good deal of white or yellow lace around her neck, glittering ear-rings of what appeared to be diamonds, and a high bone-supported collarette of a kind I had not seen since my earliest infancy. I could see, too, that she was of an ashen-pale complexion – possibly powdered, but with no lipstick on her mouth, which had a slight but good-natured pout. So far as I could note and remember, she wore a small black hat of some feathery substance, and black leather shoes with what in my childhood were called Cuban heels. I had the impression, too, that the longish skirt of her costume was swathed rather than straight-cut. I tried to see her hands but they were both of them hidden in a black or dark-brown fur muff – which was, again, both out of fashion and out of season.

I passed her just after the point where Agar Street and King William Street debouch together into the Strand – just before reaching the façade of Coutts's Bank, in fact. After briskly walking the length of the bank, which is at least 36 of my strides, I halted. The first shop beyond the bank – now a passport-photographer's – was then a tobacconist's. Stopping at this window, I glanced into it for not more than a second, then turned to walk back and discover, without staring, what this singular lady looked like full face. Let it be understood that I had lost sight of her for rather less than 30 seconds.

To my profound surprise I found, on looking round and turning back, that she had utterly vanished. There was not a soul in front of me for the whole length of the bank. She was not crossing the Strand, and there was no one in the least like her on the opposite side. It was just – but barely – possible that she had suddenly hailed a taxi and driven off in it. But no taxi or car was in sight, in either direction. Why then, she must have gone into the bank – which again was possible, since she ought to have been very close to the bank's front door at the moment when I had turned round to have a good look! It was just on the stroke of 10 o'clock, the bank's opening time. When I reached the front door a commissionaire was in process of throwing the doors open. Much perplexed if not exactly astonished, I said to him: "Good morning, has a lady dressed in black just come in?" He smiled and said: "How could she, sir, I have this second opened the door?" There was nothing to do except to thank him and to come away mystified and far from satisfied. But I still thought of my old lady as an inexplicable, and not as a ghostly, apparition.

Less than a week later I found myself describing this experience to the landlord of a tavern in Long Acre, next door to which, at No 20, I used to live. He was a shrewd old Welshman named Arthur Powell with bushy grey eyebrows and a notable resemblance to the late Lord Beaverbrook. I had not quite finished telling him my story when he interrupted me. He had been listening intently, watching me closely and gravely and without the usual sceptical smile of a listener who suspects one to be spinning a yarn. He said: "I know who it was you think you saw. It was the Baroness Burdett-Coutts. I recognize her from your description of her. You saw her walking into her own bank." I gasped and expostulated. Surely the Baroness died 40 years ago at least? And in any case how did Arthur Powell recognize such a person from my description? He said: "Of course I recognized her. I saw her quite often in the old days. You see, my father was one of her coachmen!"

At this point some customers came into the tavern, and the spell was temporarily suspended. But it was not completely broken, and it remained intact through several subsequent conversations in which this old Welshman repeated his conviction that it was the Baroness I had seen, or that I thought I had seen.

At this time I knew very little about the Baroness Burdett-Coutts – not even that she was directly connected with Coutts's Bank. As a Dickensian I knew that she was a great friend of Dickens in her middle-age, and as a drama critic and theatre-lover I knew that she was a helpful friend of Henry Irving in her old age, that she was reported to have financed some of his last theatrical ventures, and that she lent her large house in Piccadilly for the great actor's lying-in-state. Sir Henry Irving died in October, 1905 (and it is not entirely irrelevant to add here that I myself was born in January the same year).

In 1953 a biography of the Baroness was published by John Murray, called *Angela Burdett-Coutts and the Victorians* by Clara Burdett Patterson, the Baroness's great-great-niece. It need hardly be said that I read this book eagerly, and also reviewed it. Before I had read a word, however, I studied closely the portraits of the Baroness at various ages which illustrate the book. The first is a head-and-shoulders portrait of the girl, Angela Burdett (born 1814), whose earliest recollection was of having a very old lady pointed out to her at Brighton as being Mrs Piozzi, formerly Mrs Thrale. If my ghost is genuine I have more than once beheld a lady who as a child glimpsed Mrs Thrale, who had been one of Dr Johnson's very dearest woman-friends! The second portrait is of Angela Burdett-Coutts in her earliest 30s, a most elegant full-length and full-dress likeness, a watercolour painting on ivory by W. C. Ross. This, the more I look at it, is the one most uncannily like my apparition. The face is in three-quarter profile. The third portrait of the Baroness Burdett-Coutts, again full-length and in full court dress, was painted by Edwin Long and now hangs in the Burdett-Coutts Schools in Westminster. It emphasises the lady's height, a feature which I especially noted in her apparition – her height, and her corresponding leanness.

The last picture, once again full-length, is a drawing of the Baroness as a bride, on the arm of her bridegroom and with an officiating clergyman in the background between the heads of the old-young couple. Her wedding shocked Queen Victoria, who had until then been a friend of the Baroness, and had often sat on her balcony watching the endless traffic in Piccadilly. Only there – she would say – could she watch London traffic without it stopping on her account. But after the wedding the royal visits were discontinued, and the Baroness was invited to Buckingham Palace only on formal occasions.

This is not the place or the occasion to give more than a sketch of this remarkable lady's career. But her family history is of quite exceptional interest even before she was born, in the year before the Battle of Waterloo. Her grandfather, the banker Thomas Coutts, married his brother's servant-maid, and by her had three daughters all of whom made brilliant matches. The eldest, Fanny, married the Marquess of Bute; the second, Susan, married Lord Guilford; and the third, Sophia, married Sir Francis Burdett. For four years before her death Coutts's first wife suffered from mental collapse and ceased to be in any sense a companion to him. Before her death the old man, now over 70, had fallen in love with the actress, Harriot Mellon, then about 40; and in 1815 he married Harriot exactly a fortnight after his wife's death. The three titled daughters were now torn between love of their father and extreme dislike of his marriage to a woman they deemed a vulgarian. After much family quarrelling and disagreement, the old man – who seems to have had a dash of Lear about him as well as a dash of Balzac's Goriot – came to live with his youngest daughter and her husband in the Piccadilly mansion.

When Thomas Coutts died in 1822 it was found that he had left the whole of his great fortune to his wife Harriot. There was much adverse comment on this, but his three daughters had been well provided for already. Harriot Coutts remained a widow for five years, and at the end of that period married William Aubrey de Vere, the ninth Duke of St Albans, who was some 25 years her junior. He had to ask her three times before she consented.

After her marriage the Duchess of St Albans wrote an admirable letter to Sir Walter Scott in answer to one of his which has not been preserved: "Thanks, many thanks for all your kind congratulations. I am a Duchess at last, that is certain, but whether I am the better for it remains to be proved. The Duke is very amiable, gentle and well-disposed, and I am sure he has taken pains enough to accomplish what he says has been the first wish of his heart for the last three years. All this is very flattering to an old lady, and we lived so long in friendship with each other that I was afraid I should be unhappy if I did not say I *will* – yet the name of Coutts – and a right good one it is – is, and ever will be, dear to my heart."

She goes on rather touchingly to comment on her own career, with a slight misquotation to indicate that she had once been Ophelia in her play-acting days: "What a strange, eventful life mine has been, from a poor little player child, with just food and clothes to cover me, dependent on a very precarious profession, without talent or a friend in the world 'to have seen what I have seen, seeing what I see.' Is it not wonderful? Is it true? Can I believe it? – first the wife of the best, the most perfect being that ever breathed, his immense fortune so honourably acquired by his own industry, all at my command . . . and now the wife of a Duke. You must write my life; the History of Tom Thumb, Jack the Giant Killer, and Goody Two Shoes will *sink* compared with my true history written by the author of *Waverley*; and that you may do it well I have sent you an inkstand. Pray give it a place on your table in kind remembrance of your affectionate friend." To this day the Duchess of St Albans's inkstand is still to be gazed upon at Abbotsford.

She died in the year 1837, and to universal astonishment left the whole of the huge Coutts fortune to her husband's granddaughter, Angela Burdett. Here I quote Mrs Patterson: "It appeared that Harriot had taken a great fancy to Angela, who, as is sometimes the way of children of a younger generation, had ignored the family differences and had found pleasure in the kind company of the woman who, after all, must have possessed many endearing attributes." The Duke, her husband, had died leaving her childless, and she made the young girl her regular travelling companion. Incidentally the Duchess travelled in very great state, usually in a cavalcade of coaches with a small army of servants and couriers, with two doctors in attendance (in case one of them fell ill), and with two chambermaids (one for day and one for night) for the extremely interesting reason that she was afraid of ghosts and could not bear to be alone at any time.

The Duchess's will was signed only a fortnight before her death, and young Angela Burdett found herself in the possession of an income of approximately £80,000 a year! Simultaneously she became a national celebrity, a popular byword for good fortune, and got a complimentary mention in the Rev Thomas Barham's *Ingoldsby Legends* which first appeared in volume form in 1840. Again one quotes her biographer: "I think that during the long talks which Angela probably had with her step-grandmother, especially on their interminable drives, the old lady, who herself had no easy youth, must have instilled into her husband's youngest granddaughter a deep concern for the trials and sufferings of others; or at all events she must have discovered in Angela a sympathy and large-heartedness which could easily be encouraged . . ."

Almost from the start she encouraged it in herself: "Angela was occupied at first with her social life, entertaining and being entertained; and gradually, as time went on, more and more with her charities and with business affairs, as she had inherited some of the shrewdness and far-seeing qualities of her grandfather Thomas Coutts. She was one of the first to perceive that the day of private banking firms was over, and the fact that the great business of Coutts was turned into an unlimited private joint stock company was chiefly due to her foresight and influence."

From the start she was naturally besieged with suitors. With the aid of her regular maid-companion, Miss Meredith, she learned how to dispose of these: "Miss Meredith became quite expert at seeing that a proposal was coming, and on these occasions retired to the adjoining room, leaving the door open. When the proposal had taken place, Angela would give a cough, and Miss Meredith would at once return to relieve an awkward situation. Lord Houghton once said that he believed Miss Coutts liked him because he had never proposed to her."

Miss Meredith, in short, acted as Nerissa to this Portia, this "lady richly left." But she was a Portia who, in spite of her sense of fun, retained her dignity.

Her achievements were chiefly philanthropic. Few wealthy persons have ever put their wealth to so much good use, or used so much imaginative foresight in so doing. I have already mentioned Charles Dickens and Henry Irving as being two close friends who taught her to conserve her wealth even while she distributed a large amount of it in charity. An earlier and even closer friend was the great Duke of Wellington. At one time it was commonly stated that she was going to marry him, though he was old enough to be her grandfather. They gave up the idea of marriage early in the year 1847, when Angela was 33 and the Duke was nearly 78. In a letter which survives he advises her not to throw herself away upon a man so much her senior, and she accepted the advice. She lived for another 60 years after this letter was written, pestered by a crowd of beggars and a handful of blackmailers, but untouched by scandal.

In 1871 the State acknowledged her manifold charities by giving her a peerage – the first woman in England to be so honoured for her own deeds and merits. In the following year she was given the freedom of the City of London. The Baroness was married at the age of 67 – to a young man of 27. He was an American and had been her secretary, William Ashmead Bartlett, and the marriage threw a bombshell into English society. Queen Victoria was so little amused that she called the Baroness "a silly old woman" but the biographer writes from her own experience: "I only knew them both when she was an aged woman and he was a man between forty and fifty with greying hair, but she still adored him. As far as one can tell, she, at any rate, was happy during the twenty-six years of their married life. She always addressed him with the utmost affection. Once at Holly Lodge I saw her remove her wedding-ring from her finger for some reason. Presently she turned to her husband and said, 'No one but you shall put it on again, Ashmead,' and he replaced it on her finger with the courtesy with which I always saw him treat her."

The amazing marriage took place at Christ Church, Down Street, Piccadilly in 1881, a church which the Baroness herself had endowed. Her biographer notes: "Just as in the case of many a younger woman, marriage softened the Baroness, gave her a wider and a more understanding outlook with regard to individual relationships, attributes which so far had been reserved mostly for humanity as a whole." In 1882 the bridegroom assumed the bride's name, and the following year he stood for Parliament and was elected Conservative member for Westminster. He predeceased the Baroness, dying in 1902.

Sir Henry Irving, as I have said, died in October 1905, and the Baroness, knowing that his flat in Stratton Street was much too small for the purpose, placed her house at the disposal of his kindred. The great actor lay in state in her large dining-room. Over his heart was laid a cross of flowers from Queen Victoria, and on a table before the coffin was a wreath from Ellen Terry. A procession of mourners moved round the coffin all the day from dawn till dusk.

The Baroness followed Irving to Westminster Abbey little more than a year later. She died at the great age of 92 on December 30, 1906. King Edward VII said of her that she was "after my mother the most remarkable woman in the kingdom." The amount of good that she did with her great fortune is incalculable.

And now here am I, born in the year of Irving's death, fully convinced that I have seen the tangible spirit of Baroness Burdett-Coutts, who died and was buried in the Abbey when I was a two-year-old. I have nowhere told my true story before. I gave a hint of it in a review of a book concerning extra-sensory perception. Shortly after this I had a letter from Mrs Patterson's daughter, Mrs Betty Coxon, who asked me to lunch with her and her husband at the Berkeley Grill. I told them my tale much as I have told it above, without elaboration or adornment. They had no sceptical look in their eyes as I told it. They said, in fact, that it was by no means the first rumour they had heard of their distinguished ancestor being seen on an unattended walk in London. She had been reported as having been seen not only in the West End, but also in the East End, where she endowed a market and a block of model dwelling-houses in Bethnal Green.

Shall I encounter her again? I fervently hope so, and never walk up or down the Strand – which I do at least three days a week – without thinking of her and seeing her again vividly, but, alas, only in the mind's eye. And next time the apparition does meet my actual gaze I shall "cross it though it blast me" as Horatio said of the ghost of Hamlet's father. I shall say "Good morning, Baroness" and see what happens.

MY DOMESTIC GHOSTS

By Mary Carter Roberts

This well-known postwar American journalist and critic contributed to a number of the leading US publications including the prestigious New Yorker. *Like Alan Dent, she finally told the full story of her experiences years after they had occurred, in the December 1950 issue of the magazine. Roberts said she "seemed to possess a personal lodestone" for the supernatural and had been the focus of some quite extraordinary ghosts ever since childhood.*

The first time I was conscious of the ghost my family christened "Kelly", was one afternoon in late winter when I was in the house alone. I was in my room upstairs, dressing, and was expecting my sister Dorothy to arrive any minute.

While I was dressing, I heard someone walk across the front porch and open the front door. It was her step; I consciously recognized it. Then I heard the door close. It had a trick of catching on the last inch or so of the sill when it was being shut, so that we of the household who knew the fault always gave it that extra pressure needed to bring it to.

Whatever came in that day gave that extra shove. I not only heard the door close firmly – I also felt its familiar jar when it caught and had to be pushed hard. Then I heard steps in the downstairs hall.

I called out, "I'll be down in a minute." There was no answer.

When I came downstairs, I found nobody. The house was empty. Dorothy arrived about five minutes later. She had not been there before and no other member of the family had been there, either.

Another afternoon – this was in the summer – my sister Anne and I were sitting in the living room of that same house, happily consuming a healthily, girlish snack, which had been laid out on the tea wagon.

The only other person at home was our mother who, half an hour before, had told us she was going to take a nap. That meant she had retired to her bedroom, which was on the third floor.

Then "Kelly", with flagrant sound effects, came down the two flights of stairs. What is more she imitated Mother's step all the way. She was heavy and slightly lame and when she descended the staircase, she always leaned hard on the banisters and proceeded slowly, making frequent pauses – "Kelly" did just *that*.

Anne and I heard him on the upper flight. We looked at one another, a little surprised and one of us said, "Mother's gotten up."

We went on eating our snack, supposing that she was merely coming down to the second floor to get something she wanted. When, however, her steps began to descend the lower flight, we paid attention, wondering what had made her change her mind about a nap.

When mother should have been halfway down, I went into the hall to meet her. She was not there. Nobody was there. But the sound of her feet kept right on descending, the stairs and the banister creaking all the while. On the bottom tread, there was an extra-loud creak – and then silence.

I turned and found Anne standing beside me. She had heard it all, just as it had sounded to me. We both went upstairs then to the third floor, exchanging looks rather frequently and tiptoed into Mother's room. She was asleep on her bed.

Our "Kelly" was never visible and he was not always audible. Sometimes he would come into a room and, without a sound, sit down in a rocking chair. At least we assumed that he was sitting in the chair, although he may have just given it a push. What happened over and over again was that the rocking chair began incontinently to rock.

My brother, who was of a scientific mind, said that the phenomenon could have been caused by a change in temperature. But the catch in this theory was that none of us could ever detect that there had been a change in temperature when a chair began to move.

Chairs rocked in summer with the windows open; chairs rocked in winter with the furnace on. We had one period piece of fumed oak and black leather – a regular antediluvian monster – wide enough for two sitters and almost as heavy as a piano. It was quite a sight to see that thing, quite empty, start off gaily swinging to and fro with no discernible propulsion.

There were two very nice things about "Kelly". He never did any spectacular haunting when we had company. We used to hear him prowling around sometimes when we were entertaining guests, but he made only off-stage noises and never in a way to attract a stranger's attention. And he was strictly a daylight host; there was never a sound out of him at night.

Later in my life, I acquired what you might call a personal ghost – one that not only lived with me, but also followed me around. I had this one in three different residences: an apartment in New York City, an apartment in Easton, Pennsylvania and a house in Rehoboth Beach, Delaware.

The ghost was no more visible than "Kelly" but, unlike him, it did not walk. It seemed to be an altogether aerial spirit. It manifested itself by making a sound – a sound not audible to me alone, I want it understood. Anybody who was near me could hear it and a number of people did. But nobody could find an explanation.

The sound was like the snapping of fingers three times in succession. But the snaps followed each other faster than any human fingers could have made them. I always heard it in front of me and a little to the left. It did not come often: days would pass between its occurrences.

I did not like the idea of being haunted and so, when this noise continued, I undertook to find a sensible cause for it. I had a plumber in to look at the steam and water pipes. I questioned the landlord about termites and mice and other fauna that might be lurking in the walls. No sensible cause could be discovered.

When I moved to the second apartment the "phantom fingers" moved with me. The snapping sounds continued, but I just got on with my life and stopped trying to explain them. When I moved again to Delaware, I think I would have been almost disappointed if my ghost had not come, too!

More recently, I have had a ghost that whistles. It began to live with me when I was renting a farmhouse in Silver Hill, Maryland. Once again it accompanied me – or followed me – to my present home on South River, also in Maryland.

This ghost is also aerial. It makes a high, fairly musical little toot, which lasts for about two seconds. The sound is not loud, but it is perfectly audible. Other people have heard it, too.

The finger-snapper, I should perhaps just record, had taken his leave before the whistler came.

THE GLOWING CHEST

By Chapman Pincher

This distinguished Science Correspondent and expert on espionage of the Daily Express *provided the newspaper with a lifetime of exclusive stories from his well-placed sources in all areas of scientific and political life. As might be expected of a man with such a highly developed instinct in solving mysteries, Chapman Pincher set out to find a solution to his own ghostly experience which he wrote about in an Afterword to* Ghosts Over England *in 1953.*

I can best explain this theory and the new evidence for it by first describing a recent "Supernatural" experience.

I was sleeping in the attic bedroom of an old country inn. Opening my eyes around midnight I was astonished to see a huge wooden chest on the floor beside the bed. There had been no chest in the room when I went to sleep.

Only the vague outlines of the familiar furniture – the bedside chair, the old-fashioned dressing table, and the grotesque wardrobe – were visible in the darkness. But the intricate carvings which covered the chest were glowing with a green fluorescent light.

To reassure myself that the phantom was just an hallucination, I carried out a couple of quick experiments.

First, I shut my eyes. The chest disappeared. When I opened them I saw it again. This proved that the phantom was something more than a purely mental picture.

Then I turned over and peered into the darkness of the other side of the bed. The chest suddenly materialised there. Then it vanished, and I could not conjure it up again.

This eerie experience might have been frightening but for the fact that it fell into line with a ghost theory which I had put forward in the *Daily Express* several Christmases ago to explain a phantom I had seen.

According to this theory, seeing a ghost is simply due to a reversal of the process of ordinary vision, which happens in certain abnormal circumstances.

In normal vision light from an object falls on to the sensitive screen of your eye – the retina – and makes an image there. This image is then converted into nervous signals which pass along the optic nerve to the back of your brain, where they combine to form the picture you "see."

What would happen if this process suddenly backfired? Any imaginary picture in your brain at the time would be broken down into nervous signals which would then run forwards to the eye and make an image on the retina.

If this image then surged back to your brain to make a mental picture there in the normal way you would have no means of knowing whether you were seeing something real or unreal.

This is the important point to grasp. A purely imaginary object "seen" by this process would look as real as reality itself.

How could this explain the phantom chest? In this way: I was dreaming about such a chest immediately before I woke, and the image of it in my subconscious mind was projected on to the retina of my eyes.

Immediately I awoke light from real objects also fell on my retina. So I saw not only the phantom chest but the real furniture too. Then, as the false image faded, the phantom vanished.

This sort of explanation could cover all those ghost reports which begin: "I awoke with a start and there, standing at the foot of the bed . . ." It could also account for the realistic hallucinations experienced by alcoholics and sick people.

So far there has been one overriding scientific objection to the theory. The backfiring of nervous signals from brain to eye is theoretically impossible because of a series of one-way valves in the optic nerves.

But now there is hard experimental evidence that it can occur. Dr Larry Weiskrants, a young American scientist, discovered it accidentally while working at the Institute of Experimental Psychology in Oxford.

To understand his experiments, first look for ninety seconds at a picture having a clear black and white groundwork. Then switch your gaze to the ceiling. You will see a negative "after-image" – white where there was black and vice versa. You have probably done it many times as a party trick.

This illusion is due to the fact that the image of any object seen by the eye remains on the retina for a short time before fading.

While Weiskrants was carrying out experiments on this "image persistence" he asked several men and women to imagine a black square on a white background and to concentrate on this purely mental picture.

To his astonishment one woman, 24-year-old Mrs Ann Batchelor, reported that, after doing this, she could see a definite after-image before her eyes – a white square on a black background.

Mrs Batchelor's claim was repeatedly proved in tests which ruled out any possibility of trickery. In one case the false after-image lasted for 55 seconds.

In my view this can only mean that a flow of nervous signals backfired from Mrs Batchelor's brain to her eyes, in spite of the one-way valves.

The false after-image seen by Mrs Batchelor were always negatives of the pictures she visualised. Some of the fleeting phantoms reported by waking people may also be negative after-images – which would explain why so many ghosts are described as "misty wraiths."

But, if reversed vision does occur, positive false images in full colour could also be projected.

Our theory may therefore explain every type of ghost, banshee, and hallucination – except one. It would not account for a case where the same ghost was seen by two or more people at the same time.

But after four years of search I have been unable to find any really convincing evidence that this has ever happened.

THE GREENWICH VILLAGE GHOST

By Elizabeth Byrd

An American journalist and novelist, Byrd experienced a number of instances of supernatural phenomena during research for her articles and books. The accounts in The Ghosts In My Life *(1968) have been praised for "making Byrd's ghosts come to everyday life as vividly as the historical figures in her novels". The following tale from the New York paper,* The Villager, *of 30 April 1964, is typical of her skill with the delightful and the eerie.*

I walked along Gay Street last week, that tiny curving street that cuddles in the heart of Greenwich Village (New York). Little has changed since I lived there twenty-one years ago. The rows of small houses built in the early nineteenth century are still curtained in organdy frills or primly shuttered. There is an aura of age as subtle as the scent of woodruff. Cars rarely pass on this secretive little street, but when they do, you envision coaches on cobblestones. And on frosty nights, you smell oak and applewood from the still-burning fireplaces of long ago.

But it was spring when I passed by. An old horse pulled a flower cart. There were geraniums, mimosa – and great bunches of lilac.

Because of the lilac, I thought of Dandy and the ghost and wondered if the present tenants of Number Thirteen Gay Street were mischiefed by a little French poodle or had found lilacs in the garden where no lilacs grew. Of course, I couldn't barge in on strangers and ask such absurd questions; but I lingered outside my old home and remembered how it had all happened. . . .

I had moved into the basement apartment when my husband went to war in 1943. My floor-through included a rear garden which I shared with Virginia Copeland, the girl above. By the unwritten code of New York neighbors, we didn't intrude on one another. Months went by before we met.

From the desk at my window, I could see Virginia in the garden with a miniature French poodle whom she called "Dandy." I thought the name suited him, for he was a cocky, prancy, elegant little dog in a curly black coat that was fashionably trimmed. He had a black button nose, plump whiskers, and velvety brown eyes. Often he clowned with blown leaves or played with sun shadows, but I noticed he never barked except to welcome Virginia home. He never even barked when her doorbell or telephone rang – which wasn't often. She was blonde, beautiful, sad-looking, solitary.

One night, Dandy scratched on my garden door and summoned me up to her apartment. He didn't bark but his anxiety was evident. She met me at the garden steps – our first meeting – and I saw that she had been crying. It is difficult for a reticent person to pour out the story of an unhappy marriage and a divorce, yet Virginia needed someone to talk to. So we became close friends, she and Dandy and I.

Two years passed. One windy April night, just for fun, Virginia brought up her old Ouija board from the basement, and we began to ask it questions. Dandy watched us intently and his concentration was so comic that we both laughed.

I asked Ouija, "Will Virginia marry again?"

Under our fingers the planchette moved to YES. "What's the man's name?" she asked. The planchette moved to CAP. "Are those his initials?" I asked. No answer.

We varied the question but nothing happened. Finally, relinquishing Cap, Virginia asked if she would stay in New York.

The planchette moved firmly to NO. PHIL.

We asked if she would live in Philadelphia. NO. Where, then? "Man – PHIL," Ouija answered.

So the man is named Phil?" I asked.

No reply.

Virginia laughed. "It's clear as mud," she said. "I'm going to marry Cap and live with Phil. A wicked life, but *busy*."

So we joked and had coffee and talked about other matters. The wind rose to a gale, unusual for April, and the little house shuddered and creaked. Dandy put his paw onto the garden door and Virginia let him out, leaving the door open. Suddenly we heard him bark and he ran in to us, still barking – the exultant, welcoming sort of bark with which he greeted her when she'd been away. He seemed to be urging something – someone – into the room. Just as he had urged me to follow him two years before. His guest had apparently followed him over to the fireplace and was standing there. Dandy reared up on his hind legs and placed his front paws on its – what? Trousers, I thought. Dandy's pink tongue seemed to lick an outstretched hand.

"He must see a bug or a fly," Virginia said. But there were no insects on this windy April night. Later we agreed we both had the strongest illusion that a man was standing by the fireplace, relaxed, at ease, at home.

Then Dandy escorted his guest out the door, returned to Virginia and fluffed at her feet. There were shreds of blossoms on his curly coat and at the garden door – undoubtedly lilac.

But it was impossible, for lilac did not grow anywhere on Gay Street; and neither of us had lilac in our vases. The mystery charmed us but we soon forgot it. In May, we gave a cocktail party in the garden, and Dandy officiated as host, extending his usual silent welcome, offering a paw to friends. Suddenly he tore past us and made a flying leap onto a young man, who dropped a parcel and caught Dandy in his arms. For a moment two dark heads lay together, two faces pressed. The man's face was wet with kisses.

Virginia, startled by the bark, stared incredulously at Dandy in the man's arms, and then at the fallen parcel. It had broken, and a huge bunch of lilacs spilled out. A friend introduced the young man as Major Capotosto.

"Everyone calls me Cappy," he said, and gave Virginia the lilacs.

Virginia moved through the party in a radiant daze. Later she dined with Cappy and much later that night she knocked on my door. "Guess where he plans to live?"

"Philadelphia," I said.

"Manila. Philippines. Remember what Ouija said? MAN – PHIL."

So Cappy was the Gay Street ghost. He and Virginia have been married seventeen happy years. She wrote me: "Dandy lies buried here in our garden where wild orchids trail over his grave. But lilacs would be more suitable. I wish I could grow them here in Manila . . . ."

So last week, as I passed down Gay Street and saw lilacs on a flower cart, I remembered Dandy and the "ghost" and I paused outside number thirteen, tempted to ring my old doorbell. But what could I say to strangers, to whom the story would probably be ridiculous? Yet, impulsively, I rang the bell. Florence Mitchel, a dark, attractive young actress answered, accompanied by Misty, her French poodle. She was gracious when I explained my pilgrimage into the past and asked me in. Mindful of Virginia I asked who lived upstairs, and she took me to meet Alice Mulligan.

"How is the garden doing?" I asked Mrs Mulligan. "Can you grow lilacs now?"

"You can't grow anything," she said. "Not inside, either."

She showed me a row of lifeless plants on her potting table in the kitchen. "Except this."

She pointed to a miniature orange tree. "It's supposed to be perishable but it blooms on, year after year. It's called Calamondin. And it's native only to the Philippines."

EXPOSING GEORGE THE GHOST

By Ken Gardner

Chief reporter of The People, *Gardner led a team of newspapermen on several ghost hunts in the 1960s and 1970s exposing fraudulent hauntings. A resourceful and dedicated reporter, Gardner unmasked dozens of people in the pages of his newspaper from vice bosses to criminal masterminds. He was equally expert at solving suspicious cases of the supernatural like this one on 10 May 1964 – a story which predates the far more notorious "Enfield Poltergeist" in 1977.*

One of the world's most publicised ghosts was unmasked last week. For 18 months George, as he was known to his fans, has haunted a stone cottage in the old-world village of Stow-on-the-Wold, Glos.

Stories and articles about him appeared all over the world. A TV programme was devoted to his activities. Priests were called in to advise on the best methods of dealing with him.

But I can now reveal that "George" was really 14-year-old David Pethrick, who lives in the cottage with his parents.

The truth came out two nights ago, at a séance to which a team of "People" investigators had been invited.

As "George" went through his eerie routine I suddenly shone a torch on young David, who was sitting in a corner of the living-room.

And I caught him doing a daring ventriloquist act behind a handkerchief.

George the Ghost first appeared during the big freeze-up of 1963, when pools of water appeared on the floor of the cottage.

One night soon afterwards, as David and his parents, Mr Stanley Pethrick, 59, a carpenter, and his wife Nancy, 49, sat in the firelight they heard tapping noises.

A high-pitched voice, apparently from nowhere, started singing "Pop Goes the Weasel."

Later, crude drawings and messages appeared on the wall of Mr and Mrs Pethrick's bedroom. Furniture moved of its own accord. Paper was ripped from the walls.

Once, when Mrs Pethrick was tucking up David in bed, a stick appeared from beneath the blanket and struck her on the wrist.

Messages scrawled in spooky writing on odd scraps of paper were found in the cottage.

Mr and Mrs Pethrick sought the advice of a local clergyman, the Rev. Henry Cheales, who called at the cottage to hear George for himself.

Afterwards he said: "There is definitely a 'presence' here. I have advised the Pethricks to be kind to him, otherwise he might get violent."

When the "People" team went along accompanied by Brigadier Frank Spedding, an authority on the supernatural, George was too shy to appear at first.

But photographer Pat Scott felt something rubbing his leg, fired a photographic flash – and saw David's foot disappearing under the table.

Then David suggested he should move to a seat on the far side of the room. He also suggested that the room was too crowded, and that some of us, including Brigadier Spedding, should leave.

Almost at once George began to speak.

Mrs Pethrick invited him to sing, and he obliged with "Pat-a-cake." At this point I switched on my torch.

David stopped singing immediately, and stuffed his handkerchief into his pocket.

"It wasn't me – honest," he stammered.

But a few minutes later, when I took David to one side, he admitted the voice was his.

"I don't know why I do it," he said. "Most of the time I hardly realise myself that the voice is mine. Sometimes I feel that a ghost is inside me."

David denied that he was responsible for moving furniture or writing messages.

But Brigadier Spedding, who listened to David's performance through a window, and later questioned David and his parents, said:

"From all the evidence I do not feel there is anything supernatural in this house."

Said the Rev. Mr Cheales: "To be blunt, I now think that David is responsible for many of the things which were attributed to George."

Mr Pethrick said: "At first I was convinced that George was a spirit. Now I am not so sure. But if it is my son I shall be greatly surprised."

Mrs Nancy Pethrick said: "George really does exist. Nothing will shake me from that conviction."

THE SIX O'CLOCK VISITOR

By Gerard Fairlie

A correspondent for The Times *and the* News of the World, *Fairlie shared Ken Gardner's scepticism about the supernatural until he encountered what he believed to be a real event. Fairlie's war work as a correspondent and intelligence officer – not to mention an escape from the Germans – made him the inspiration for his friend, HC McNeil's famous character, Bulldog Drummond, and after the author's death, Fairlie wrote several more of the Bulldog books. In this report for the* News of the World, *20 December 1964, Fairlie describes how his disbelief in ghosts was dramatically changed.*

Do you believe in ghosts? If you don't, you're crackers. I was crackers until about a couple of years after Joan and I were married.

We then moved into a little house in a small square just south of Hyde Park in London.

We thought that it was a lovely little house, perhaps partly because it was our first home of our own. It had a cosy little sitting-room with a small open fire.

Everything was wonderful for a few weeks. Then, at six o'clock on a Friday, I was relaxing with the first drink of the evening when I nearly dropped the glass. Some silly joker had abruptly crumpled up a large newspaper just behind my chair. It makes an alarming noise.

Some silly joker hadn't. When I whipped round, already uttering my vivid protest, there was nobody there.

Now, believe it or not, this went on happening every Friday evening at six o'clock and I was not the only one who heard it.

I made sure that others, unwarned, were in the room at that hour, and they all heard it. It frightened no one but it startled everyone.

And our dog, about a minute before the hour, would jump to his feet with his hair on end, growling.

We stayed several years in that house. After a few months the noise ceased to be regular, but it went on happening occasionally, always at six on a Friday.

No, I never found any possible explanation.

But one afternoon, while we were still in that house, Joan was returning from shopping when, on entering the small square, she saw a little old lady dressed entirely in grey approaching our door.

In fact our front door was the only one in the square with steps up to it. The little old lady went up the steps and rang the bell.

Joan has never been much of a one for callers. So when she saw the door opened, and the visitor disappear through it, she circled the square hoping that, since the little old lady was bound to be told that Joan was out, she might leave.

But nothing happened. So Joan faced the inevitable, and went into the house.

She found no visitor inside. She questioned the help, who had been alone in the house. The help said that she had admitted nobody, that no bell had rung.

Joan never saw the little grey lady again.

THE EMPTY HOUSE

By Gordon Honeycombe

The actor-turned-broadcaster Gordon Honeycombe was several times voted the most popular newscaster on British television in the 1980s. Apart from newsreading, he was also the commentator on many documentaries that revealed his passion for research and investigation into the abormal. His interest in the supernatural was evident in the first of his subsequent string of novels, Dragon

Under The Hill (1972), *which was based on an experience of his own while he was still a child – as he explained in the* Sunday People, *15 December 1974.*

I used the story of *my* ghost in my first book, *Dragon Under The Sea.* It happened in India near Karachi where I was born.

As a boy I used to play a game with a friend. I stood on the verandah of this empty old house and sang. I sang any old song I could think of. And as I sang my friend and I would hear footsteps pacing about inside the empty house.

But as soon as I stopped singing, the footsteps stopped. When I started again, so did the footsteps.

Finally, the front door would open – very slowly. My friend and I never waited to see what happened. Our nerves just went and we fled.

I never found out an explanation for what happened. But it happened every time we had enough courage to go to that empty old house.

A MESSAGE FOR GEORGINA

By Brian Inglis

Brian Inglis was a journalist, television presenter and unquestionably the most important investigator of the paranormal in the second half of the twentieth century. An Irishman by birth, he joined the staff of the Spectator *in 1954 where his interest in the supernatural was formed and began the exhaustive research that would result in his masterwork,* Natural and Supernatural (1978). *This was followed by a second landmark volume,* Science and Parascience (1984), *investigating the development of psychic research. Inglis also enjoyed great popularity as a presenter on TV, especially with the series* All Our Yesterdays. *His life ended on a curious note. One of Inglis' closest colleagues, Bill Grundy, died on 9 February 1993 – and he had just finished writing his friend's obituary when he, too, died.*

In 1979 I was asked by the Features Editor of the "new, swinging *Tatler*" if I would review the autobiography of a medium, Doris Stokes. Doris was then better known in Australia than in Britain. She had just filled the Sydney Opera House three nights running, and to accommodate an interview with her on TV, Starsky and Hutch had been shifted to another slot. I had met her only once, on a TV programme in Newcastle. Still, the book proved to be rather endearing, and I agreed to bring the Features Editor – Georgina Howell – to Doris's flat in Fulham, to introduce them, so that an interview could accompany my review.

I was just about to leave them to it, after coffee, when Doris announced that she was receiving a message for Georgina from the spirit world. Doris is "clairaudient"; she "hears" what the spirits have to say. In this case the message came from "Clive", who had just "passed on". Georgina could think of nobody she knew of that name, in this world or the next. "Clive", however, was insistent. He wanted his girl-friend, Tracy, to know he was all right. She was not to worry, but to get on with her own life. Still, Georgina shook her head. She knew nobody of that name.

At this point the photographer who had come with her, who had been silent, said he felt he had to interrupt. He had a friend called Clive, he said, who had died at three o'clock that morning. Tracy was his fiancée.

There was no way in which Doris could have known about Clive and Tracy, and the long arm of coincidence would have to be dislocated to accommodate the episode. Somehow, the information must have been fed into her mind through . . . Clive, communicating with her? Or telepathic pick-up from the mind of the photographer? Either way, it was affected by what the parapsychologists call "displacement-effect", which is one of the nuisances confronting psychical researchers.

But either way, it was surely ESP?

5

Haunted Stars

Show Business and the Supernatural

There is little argument that **Marlon Brando** was one of the most famous and influential films stars of the twentieth century. Like a number of other well-known actors and actress of the last century, he was also very interested in the supernatural and towards the end of his life came to believe that he was haunted by the ghost of a man that one of his sons had killed in 1990. However, unlike some of his iconic contemporaries including Marilyn Monroe who haunts Forest Lawn Cemetery and Elvis Presley in Memphis there have been no reports, as yet, of his ghost being seen in Hollywood.

Much of the evidence for Brando's interest in the spirit world came to light after his death when the home on Mulholland Drive, where he had lived the life of a recluse for many years until his death aged 80 on 2 July 2004, was cleared to settle his affairs. In the bedroom were found books on the occult and New Age philosophy as well as a recessed shelf crowded with little figures and fertility statues that a member of the staff taking away the items for auction described as "looking like a shrine". Of course, mystery, like notoriety, had surrounded Brando for many years – he had helped to earn the street where he lived the epitaph "Bad Boy's Drive" with the eager compliance of hell-raiser Jack Nicholson who lived next door and Warren Beatty just up the road – but his fascination with the supernatural and psychic experiences were not generally known because of his obsessive desire for privacy.

During Brando's career, which had been launched with his "Method Acting" on the stage in *A Streetcar Named Desire* (1947) and iconic screen performances in 1954 in *The Wild One*, he had pursued an interest in the uncanny and apparently met a number of psychic investigators. Never a man to be duped or easily convinced, on one occasion he challenged the famous Dutch psychic Peter Hurkos to prove his ability. Brando showed him two locked wooden boxes and asked the Dutchman to tell him what was inside. Hurkos held the first box for several moments and said, "I see fire or an explosion on the sea. You have here a golden spike, a nail from a ship." Picking up the second box, Hurkos repeated the process and then added, "I see a letter and I'm sorry to tell you, sir, that the spelling is lousy!"

Brando opened the boxes and agreed that the Dutchman had been correct on both counts. The first box contained a golden spike that had come from the ship HMS *Bounty*, which had featured in his classic movie, *Mutiny on the Bounty* (1962), while the second contained a letter written by Brando in which a number of words were misspelt.

The story of the haunting of Marlon Brando began in May 1990 when his notorious and troubled life hit a new low. Christian Brando, his oldest son by his first wife, Anna Kashfi, shot and killed Dag Drollet, the Tahitian lover of his half-sister, Cheyenne. The subsequent trial made international headlines, and after a dramatic testimony in the courtroom by Brando in which he admitted the failings of himself and his wife as parents and told the Drollet family that he "would trade places with Dag if I could", Christian Brando was sentenced to ten years' imprisonment. Five years after the trial, Cheyenne, who was said to have never recovered from her lover's death, committed suicide by hanging herself in Tahiti, aged just twenty-five.

As time passed and he remained closeted behind the walls of the house in Mulholland Drive, friends of Marlon Brando came to believe he was constantly on the verge of a nervous breakdown. Anna Kashfi later claimed that the situation was even more traumatic for her former husband:

"After Dag's death, Marlon said he was being haunted. He talked about sheets that were suddenly flung off his bed. He said he heard ghostly lips that whispered to him while he was out in his car, 'I should not have died.' Marlon became convinced it was the ghost of Dag Drollet. He admitted, 'It's terrifying. I know it Dag's angry spirit.' "

A further rather more curious supernatural story emerged during the final decade of Brando's life. He apparently became intrigued by the legend of the Angel of Mons and at the turn of the new century was involved in a project to make a film utilizing the theme. A cache of personal papers and what was said to be actual footage of a mysterious apparition taken in Mons had come to light and he was involved in their purchase with a long-time associate, Hollywood director Tony Kaye. The collection had been started in 1914 by William Dodge, a West Countryman who had enlisted in the British Army and been posted to Belgium that same year.

The documents and footage had lain forgotten for years in a military trunk discovered at the Bonita Junk Shop in Monmouth. They revealed Dodge's love for a Belgian woman, identified only as Marie, and how, when he had lost her during the confusion of war, he embarked on a mystical, forty-year quest in the pursuit of an angel. According to Dodge's notes, he had seen a vision and managed to film it:

> "The whole thing took on the shape of what I can only describe as an angel. I could see what looked like long white robes. It had no feet and there were shapes like wings behind its shoulders. I found out that the spook we'd seen had been floating over the place where some men had died."

Talking to the *Sunday Times* in March 2001, Tony Kaye said he hoped that Brando would play the veteran soldier in the movie version of events. William Dodge's footage of the apparition, which he hoped to include in the film, would be "a spine-tingling moment" he said, adding: "It is the closest we have on film to proof of an angel. I've spent much of my life looking at special visual effects, and this is an effect for which I have no explanation."

The death of Marlon Brando three years later, however, brought an end to this plan. His ashes were appropriately divided: half being scattered in Tahiti and the remainder in Death Valley.

Charlie Chaplin, one of Hollywood's first superstars in the early years of the twentieth century, was also fascinated by the macabre and the occult and credited himself with extrasensory perception. He also loved telling ghost stories to his sons and Charlie Chaplin Jr remembered him acting out "chilling" scenes from Charles Dickens' famous supernatural tales. Writing in *My Father, Charlie Chaplin* (1968), of his childhood, he says:

> "We were at an age to enter wholeheartedly into the macabre world introduced to us through our father's ghost stories and we couldn't get enough of blood and violence and ghoulish horrors of all descriptions."

The Chaplin boys especially remembered their father telling them about a real haunted house close to the family's holiday home at Pebble Beach. It had been vacant for a number of years and nobody seemed willing to rent it for summer vacations. Chaplin Jr explained:

"Dad told us about this house and the weird things that went on in it. He said that someone had been murdered there and a severed head had been found in the centre of the marble floor. We decided to go and see it in daylight and knock the ghosts out. Self-appointed exorcizers, we picked up rocks and began hurling them at the big plate-glass windows. It was fun and we did a thorough job. We broke practically every window in the house before we hurried off to catch our train. Only on the way back did we begin to wonder if the place *had* been haunted – or if we'd been taken in by one of Dad's ghost stories!"

A curious story of the impact of Charlie Chaplin's success, which had psychic implications, occurred in the winter of 1916 when the star was "simultaneously paged in hundreds of hotels across the United States." This phenomenon, which was reported right across the country from the Atlantic to the Pacific coasts and from the Canadian border to the Gulf of Mexico, came to the attention of the Boston Society for Psychical Research who assigned one of their most experienced members, Professor Bamfylde More, to investigate. In February 1917 he produced a report on the extraordinary event and concluded:

"We find beyond peradventure that on the date mentioned, 12 November, there existed for some inexplicable reason a Chaplin "impulse" which extended through the length and breadth of the continent. In more than 800 of the principal hotels Mr Chaplin was being paged at the same hour. In hundreds of smaller towns people were waiting at stations to see him disembark from trains upon which he was supposed to arrive.

"There is no reason to doubt the correctness of scientific proof that constant reiteration of a certain fact or idea will or may precipitate precisely such a phenomenon as that which has resulted from the wide display of Chaplin absurdities in motion picture theatres – a sudden mental impulse manifesting itself simultaneously practically throughout the length and breadth of the land. It is therefore important, though the incident in itself appears trivial, to establish the exact extent of the Chaplin wave and, so far as it may be traced, local causerie."

In the opinion of Professor More, the "Chaplin impulse wave" deserved scientific study of the same kind that the Boston SPR had been devoting to the paranormal and the supernatural. The subject himself was apparently both intrigued and amused by the phenomenon.

Another actor with a similarly legendary status in Hollywood's Golden Era was **James Cagney**. The man who would become famous for his gangster roles after starring in the groundbreaking Prohibition story, *The Public Enemy* (1931), began his career in revue as a female impersonator. Later, he proved his versatility in such diverse roles as Bottom in *A Midsummer Night's Dream* (1935) and his song and dance routines in *Yankee Doodle Dandy* (1942) for which he won an Oscar. Unlike Chaplin, though, Cagney had no interest or belief in the supernatural, which makes his account of what happened to him and his wife in 1964 all the more extraordinary. The fact that it took place in a car gives it an uncanny resonance with the story of Marlon Brando.

"My wife and I were driving to San Francisco. We had to be there at a certain time. It was late at night and I was doing between 80 and 85 miles per hour, speeding along with nothing on our minds but getting there and having a good dinner. Then I heard a voice in my ear say, 'Take it easy, kid!' I took my foot off the accelerator, thinking at first that Billie, my wife, was imitating me. But as I turned to face her, she asked, 'Did you hear it too?'"

Cagney said that he was initially sceptical about having heard anything untoward and intended to take no notice of the command. He put his foot down on the accelerator again:

"I had no sooner touched 85 than I heard the voice again, this time shouting loudly, 'Take it easy, kid!' I was stunned. I said to Billie, 'That's my father's voice!' And she thought it was his voice, too. Some hundred yards ahead of us was a broken-down trailer lying across the road. It had evidently come loose from a car a few moments before. I saw it in time and detoured. If we had been going 85 we would have taken the last mile into eternity."

For a man who had never believed in ghosts it was a traumatic moment – for his father, an Irish bartender, had been dead for years. To Cagney it seemed that the voice had crossed the life-death boundary to save him and his wife from death.

Another American actor who had a ghostly experience in a car was **Telly Savalas,** the Greek-born star who was nominated for an Oscar for his role in *The Birdman of Alcatraz* (1962) and became an iconic figure in the TV detective series, *Kojak*. He was driving home on Long Island at 3 a.m. on a summer morning in 1954 when he ran out of petrol and decided to walk to a freeway where he knew there would be a petrol station still open. He recalled:

"I decided to walk through a wooded park as a short cut when a guy called out, 'I'll give you a lift.' I was shaken because I hadn't heard this big black Cadillac pull up, but the man who was all dressed in white looked okay and he took me to the service station. There, to my embarrassment, I found I didn't have enough money for the petrol – but the stranger just handed over some notes and said it was OK, I could pay him back later. While we were driving back to the car, the guy, out of the blue, mentioned that he knew Harry Agannis. I asked who he was and the man explained he was a baseball player with the Boston Red Sox. I had never heard of him. That was the extent of our conversation and he dropped me back at my car."

The following day Telly Savalas was in for a big surprise when he opened a newspaper and found that the baseball player Agannis had died suddenly at the age of twenty-four. It seemed he had died at just about the time his name had been mentioned by the stranger in the car. Savalas picks up his strange story again:

"I felt it was just a horrible coincidence until I tried to phone the guy to give him his money back. A woman answered and I explained why I was ringing. She sounded a little strange and asked what car the guy had been driving and what he had been wearing. When I told her, she began crying hysterically saying that I'd described her husband who'd died *three years earlier*. I've thought of all kinds of explanations, but it was a phenomenon I'll just have to accept. All I do know is that it seems I took a ride in a car with a dead man."

The British classical actor **Sir Alec Guinness** has told his story of an encounter with the supernatural, which also took place before he became a household name in films such as *The Bridge on the River Kwai* (1957), *Lawrence of Arabia* (1962) and *Star Wars* (1977).

In 1941, the Second World War interrupted Guinness's burgeoning career as a Shakespearean actor on the London stage when he was recruited into the Royal Navy. A year later, he was commissioned and put in charge of a 200-ton landing craft based at Barletta on the Adriatic coast of Italy that was employed primarily for transporting troops or civilians from danger areas. On 31 December he was ordered to the island of Vis, off the coast of Yugoslavia. Taking advantage of what looked like being a smooth journey to the island and taking on board 400 woman and children in anticipation of a German invasion, Guinness went to his cabin for a rest. What happened next he described in an essay published in 1945:

> "I slept for nearly two hours. When I woke it was with the strangest notion I have ever had in my life. I suppose I believe in ghosts. Certainly in good and evil spirits. It is difficult to describe what happened to me at six o'clock that evening. I woke up with a start, the sweat pouring off me. I trembled. The cabin was filled with an evil presence and it was concentrated twelve to eighteen inches from my left ear. Fully awake, I heard with my ear, or so it seemed to me, the word, *TO-MORROW*. It was spoken clearly and quite loudly. Then the evil thing withdrew. Never have I felt so relieved at the departure of an unwanted guest as I was by that one."

Alec Guinness believed that a mountain of evil intent had been condensed into that one word. It seemed to be telling him that soon he was going to die an unpleasant death. He did not have to wait long. Within half an hour the ship was struck by a hurricane with winds up to 120 miles per hour and an electrical storm bathed the vessel in the awful St Elmo's Fire. For the next few hours – well into 1 January 1943 – no matter what the crew did, the ship was battered by enormous waves and finally wrecked on the Italian shore. As it broke up on the rocks, Guinness and all his crew managed to scramble desperately to safety. Although the fateful warning did not come true – Sir Alec lived a triumphant career until 2000 – the implications about the day were never far from his thoughts:

> "Since then New Year's Eve has been an unlucky one for me. Disasters and near-disasters, large and small, have often struck on

that night. Family misfortunes, pipes bursting throughout the house and parties spoiled by bad weather have dogged us. It could have been my own fears making themselves manifest – but it was a very real and very sinister experience."

Anthony Quinn, the American actor who co-starred with Guinness in *Lawrence of Arabia*, was similarly unnerved by a mystery voice that spoke to him while he was making that film. A man of mixed Irish-Mexican parentage, Quinn had several brushes with the supernatural during his life and, after his biggest success in *Zorba the Greek* (1964), often favoured accepting roles in which he could appear as a mystic life force such as *The Magus* (1968) and *Mohammed Messenger of God* (1976). He recounted his brush with the unearthly to Sally Francis of *Photoplay* in March 1970:

"When I was filming *Lawrence of Arabia* in the desert, I decided one day to take a walk. I was still wearing my robes and just wandered off on my own. Suddenly I found myself to be in an open vast expanse of nothing. I felt another presence was watching me. A horrifying fear overcame me. I sank to my knees. I was aware that a voice was trying to say something to me. I put my hands over my ears to prevent myself hearing for I was sure that if I heard the voice I would die. I suppose I have regretted ever since not letting the voice speak to me. I've always wanted to know what it would have said to me. It was one of the most frightening experiences of my life."

A supernatural experience actually changed the career of **Vincent Price**, the actor who spent years of his screen career giving audiences some of the best frights of their lives. Price, who is probably best remembered for his roles in horror movies like *House of Wax* (1953), and the series of films by Roger Corman based on the stories of Edgar Allan Poe, had a privileged upbringing and obtained a degree in art history and English when, literally overnight, he opted for a creative rather than academic life. He explained:

"I was at Yale studying for my degree. I was having a problem with what I wanted to do and was discussing this with a room-mate. My friend advised me not to go into the arts, as it was such a precarious existence. Suddenly, as we were talking, he turned into an absolute flaming bush. To me he seemed to be on fire to the point where I had to back out of the room. I went out and walked for about an hour preceded by this sort of flame. It was an extraordinary and wonderful experience. Like most manifestations it was symbolic. I knew that if I did as my friend suggested it would burn me up. After that I knew I had to go into something which would give me an artistic outlet."

Opting for a career on the stage, Price crossed the Atlantic to London and managed to get a small part in *Chicago* starring John Gielgud. He followed this with bigger parts in West End productions until he broke into films as Sir Walter Raleigh in *The Private Lives of Elizabeth and Essex* in 1938. After the war ended, he rapidly established himself as a master of the screen thriller. Then in November 1958 he had another chilling moment that he never forgot.

"On 15 November while I was on a flight between Hollywood and New York I had an extraordinary glimpse of the unknown. I was immersed in a book for most of the journey, but at one point glanced idly out of the window. To my horror I saw huge, brilliant letters emblazoned across a cloudbank, spelling out the message, *TYRONE POWER DEAD*. It was a terrific shock. I began to doubt my senses when I realized that nobody else on the plane appeared to have seen them. But for a few seconds they were definitely there, like huge Teletype, lit up with blinding light from within the clouds. I was even more shocked when we finally landed and saw the newspaper headlines. Tyrone Power had suffered a heart attack and died a couple of hours earlier."

In attempting to find an explanation for his experience, Vincent Price took part in several séances and consulted a number of psychic investigators. But no one was able to give him a definitive answer. The whole thing seemed even stranger when he learned that someone else had had a premonition about Tyrone Power's death. The voluptuous Swedish actress, **Anita Ekberg**, had come to America to represent her country in the Miss World contest and stayed to become an iconic sex symbol in pictures like *La Dolce Vita* (1960). She was actually working in London in 1958 on a picture called *The Man Inside* when the supernatural intruded into her life:

"I have had prophetic dreams about my family and friends all my life – but there was something really supernatural about this one. When I got to the studio to begin work I asked first to see a newspaper. I leafed through it – but there was nothing there I was looking for. The next two days I did the same thing and there was still nothing. But on the third morning there on the front page was what I had seen so vividly. Tyrone Power had died suddenly."

Another actor who received a single word warning from the unknown was **Alan Alda**, the star of the hit television series *M*A*S*H*, who has admitted to being a firm believer in ESP after experiencing a number of unusual events during his life. The most extraordinary of these was "seeing" a disaster happen in a remote part of the world. Talking in 1984 he explained:

"At the time I was having dinner in a New York restaurant. Suddenly these vivid images flashed through my head. The word *ERUPTION* kept running through my mind. Later I discovered that during the time I was having these thoughts Mount Batur on the island of Bali had erupted violently forcing over 1,000 people to evacuate their homes. After that I never made fun of the supernatural."

That same year, Vincent Price put into words what he, Anita Ekberg and Alan Alda had felt during their experiences: "Investigations are going on all the time into the whole subject of ESP. The truth is there's a vast unexplored area of man's mind and no one knows what goes on there."

Similar sentiments were shared by the great Hollywood screen comedy actor **Jack Lemmon** who also had two inexplicable encounters with the unknown that were anything but amusing. Lemon, like Vincent Price, came from a wealthy background and was educated at several prep schools before going to Harvard where he first acted in the Dramatic Club. Determined on an acting career, he worked for years in radio and television developing his ability to play every kind of role from serious drama to slapstick before earning worldwide acclaim in 1959 with Marilyn Monroe and Tony Curtis in *Some Like It Hot*. The same year, while working on the occult thriller, *Bell, Book and Candle* he revealed his own exposure to ESP:

"I was fifteen at the time and attending the Andover Prep School in Massachusetts. I was playing tennis with a classmate, Jerry. Just as he was about to hit a serve, he suddenly doubled up as if he was in great pain and fell to the ground. I ran around the court and asked him what was wrong. He didn't know – except that he knew something terrible had happened."

Lemmon said the two boys finished the game, but his friend's mind was clearly on something else. They went back to their room and puzzled over what had happened.

"Jerry said that it had been an almost physical pain – an over-whelming realization so intense he could virtually feel it, that something terrible had happened to someone he loved. An hour later he was called to the principal's office. There he was told the sad news that his mother had died. Almost exactly *one hour earlier*."

Almost fifty years later, while appearing on stage in London, Jack Lemmon encountered another element of the supernatural at the Haymarket Theatre, starring in the anti-war play, *Veterans' Day*, with Michael Gambon. In July 1989, he saw a spirit *three times* in less than a week, as told Steve Absalom of the *Daily Mail*:

"It has scared me to death. I've been in my dressing room alone with the windows shut and three times the door has opened and slammed when there's nobody outside. At first I thought somebody might be playing a practical joke on me, which is not a wise thing to do for a guy of my age. But now I'm sure it was a ghost. It's terrifying thinking that somebody or something is watching you."

To long-serving members of the theatre staff there was little doubt that Lemmon had encountered the ghost who had been reported on a number of occasions during the past half-century. It was believed to be the spirit of a former stage manager, George Buxton, who had died on the premises some fifty years earlier and had been a stickler about keeping the theatre tidy and always keeping doors shut.

The beautiful actress **Kim Novak** who appeared with Jack Lemmon in *Bell, Book and Candle* playing a witch, was very interested in her co-star's childhood brush with ESP – and five years later had her own frightening encounter during filming of the classic period romp, *The Amorous Adventures of Moll Flanders*, at the appropriately named Chilham Castle near Canterbury in Kent. The castle, parts of which date back to the twelfth century, had been modernized in some sections and as the star, Kim was assigned to the best accommodation in an apartment in the keep, right in the centre of the building.

Kim had become interested in the occult after her earlier role, but was still not prepared for what happened one night in the apartment. Later she told her story to the *Daily Express* of a bruising encounter with the unknown after a long day's shooting:

> "I had dinner then went to my room to go over my lines for the next day. I settled in a big comfortable chair and decided to put on the television and watch a musical variety programme. After a bit I fell under the spell of the music, kicked off my shoes and began to dance. Suddenly I felt as though I wasn't dancing alone; some powerful force had grabbed hold of me. It was like strong arms around me, whirling me around the room. The music changed to a slower bit, but I was thrown around faster and faster and then the supporting arms were no longer there. I was thrown violently against the wall and I fell and struck my head and back. Fortunately, I was only dazed."

Initially, she told no one about her "invisible" dancing partner. But during the next three weeks of shooting the ghost – or "it" as she came to refer to him – began playing other tricks: turning lights on and off, moving things around in the apartment and rustling the curtains and tugging the bedclothes. All the time the windows were tightly shut. One night, the actress even felt her bottom being patted. As she was leaving Chilham Castle, Kim Novak mentioned her experiences to her British co-star, Richard Johnson. Not altogether surprised, he told her the building was known to be haunted by the ghost of King John who had stayed there on 11 October 1210 – the night before he had drowned in the North Sea:

> "Richard said the king was believed to have slept that last night in the keep. Ever since then he had been haunting the place – but no one wanted to tell me so as not to worry me. Well, if it *was* his ghost I'm glad that at least it was a royal one."

Kim might well have had a second experience two years later when she was due to make another supernatural thriller, *The Eye of the Devil*, with **David Niven**. As it was, she fell ill and her role was recast. The suave actor turned bestselling author, Niven faced the unknown on his own. He later recalled the events surrounding the film – and an even stranger event that occurred subsequently – while promoting his amusing autobiography, *The Moon's A Balloon* in 1971.

"There were so many strange things while we were making *The Eye of the Devil*. Several members of the cast were involved in accidents. The original director was taken ill with stomach trouble and Deborah Kerr also eventually replaced Kim Novak, due to illness. I was injured after being thrown from a horse while filming."

But, he explained, that was nothing to the fear that enveloped him and his wife, Hjördis, during a weekend break. They were nearly killed in an accident on their way to visit friends in Switzerland. Niven recalled:

"We were up in the mountains when the car suddenly stalled. When we looked out of the window, we discovered the vehicle was hanging over the side of a 400-feet drop. We had not been driving on a road at all, but on a hard snow ledge, which was hanging out over a valley. Hjördis was on the sheer side and she slid very cautiously out of the car with me just praying that it wouldn't tip over before we got out. It just seemed like another uncanny episode in the making of that haunting film."

A few years later, the supernatural intervened again in the lives of the Nivens while playing a benevolent old ghost in the television version of Oscar Wilde's story *The Canterville Ghost*, about an American family taking over a haunted stately home in England, which he recounted in 1974:

"It happened when Hjördis and I went on a pheasant shoot with some friends on Rhode Island. My wife is Swedish and you know how they are. Rather spooky. On the day of the shoot Hjördis refused to go. I tried my best to persuade her but she kept saying no. I asked her why and she said, 'Don't laugh at me – I will not go because someone is going to shoot me.' I didn't laugh, but went on trying to convince her. Finally, our host said, 'Look, I'll lend you a coat – it's heavy enough to stop any shotgun pellet.'"

According to Niven, his wife was still reluctant to go, but at last relented. He concluded his story with a typical flourish:

"Twenty minutes later, someone took aim at a pheasant, pulled the trigger – and the shotgun pellets struck Hjördis in the face, the arm and the side. In fact one of the pellets is still embedded in the

bone, right next to her eye. There were twelve witnesses who
heard her prediction only a short while earlier. I told you Swedes
were spooky . . ."

Films about the supernatural have had a tendency to generate
mysterious occurrences, although some have clearly been the work
of publicists attempting to get column inches in the papers about
their movies. One story that has with stood investigation took place
in Southern Italy where the exotic Israeli, Daliah Lavi was filming in
1963. The smouldering beauty who had trained as a dancer and
completed her compulsory military service brought a resilience to a
number of occult movies including *The Return of Doctor Mabuse*
(1961) and *Night is the Phantom* (1962) before going on location in
the south of Italy. She recalled the events later that year:

"I played the part of a girl possessed by demons and the devil. I
was completely possessed myself, in a way. At nights after filming
I couldn't sleep. I used to have terrible nightmares. I can remember
playing one scene dressed only in a nightgown on a freezing cold
night. Everyone else wore heavy coats, but I simply didn't feel the
cold! For another scene I had to go through a barbed wire fence.
My body was scratched to pieces yet I felt no pain."

The crew working on the picture apparently became increasingly
interested in its theme and even began holding séances themselves
through a mixture of boredom and curiosity. Daliah felt compelled
to go along.

"I just wanted to see what would happen, if anything. And the
most amazing things happened. Once we watched the mouthpiece
of a telephone rise into the air, hang in space, and then drop back.
Another night we got in touch with Mussolini and King David.
The king sent one of us into a trance. One man started to hum the
tune of an ancient Biblical melody that dated back to the time of
King David. I became so fascinated by all this, I started practising
things. Then I stopped because it was so frightening."

Five years later Daliah Lavi appeared in John Huston's James Bond
film *Casino Royale* with David Niven as Sir James Bond and Peter
Sellers as the enigmatic Evelyn Tremble. Cast as the exotic The
Detainer, she had the opportunity to share supernatural experiences
with Niven and **Peter Sellers**, who was already well-known for his

interest in psychic matters. Sellers, in particular, was always anxious to discuss this side of his life after becoming an international star via BBC Radio's famous *Goon Show* and hugely successful films including *The Ladykillers* (1955), *Dr Strangelove* (1964) and *The Pink Panther* (1964). In an interview with Bill Neech he explained:

"I'm psychic. A medium. I don't know why. I never studied it. I've believed in psychic powers a long time because I've had incredible proof. At sittings with the famous London medium, Estelle Roberts, I made contact with my mother a year after her passing. I knew it was her because we always had a very close bond. When she died it left a great void and the following months were the loneliest I have ever lived through. She came through loud and clear. Contacting her gave me a lovely warm feeling because you then know that those people you have loved in this life are really with you all the time although we cannot see them."

Sellers also believed that the old Victorian music hall star, Dan Leno, who had been one of his inspirations since childhood, helped his career. He told his biographer Peter Evans in 1969: "I've had a strange thing that has followed me all my life. Some special person in another world who takes an interest in me and guards over me. It is very weird."

He claimed to be clairaudient: that is, able to receive premonitions or warnings of impending trouble. One incident concerned his son, Michael, and the time he was going riding with a friend. The star continued:

"Somebody, I don't know who it was, said as clear as a bell in my head, 'Don't let him go – he'll have a bad accident.' But I felt I couldn't spoil his enjoyment, though I did my best to warn him and asked him to promise to be particularly careful that afternoon. Soon after the boys left the stable, a dog startled the horses and both of them were thrown. Michael, very fortunately, was guided down and fell correctly, but his friend was kicked and quite badly hurt. I felt terrible."

Despite his psychic abilities, Sellers' premonition that he would "live until he was seventy-five" fell exactly twenty years short of this time when he died in 1980.

Roger Moore, who was a friend of Sellers and took on the role of James Bond in 1973 in *Live and Let Die* after perfecting the role of the dashing and handsome leading man in a series of modest film and

TV series, has also confessed to an enduring fascination with psychic phenomena. He had actually revealed this interest in the supernatural several years earlier while filming the aptly titled *The Man Who Haunted Himself* (1970) at Elstree Studios.

"I had a couple of visitations about ten years ago when I was staying in a hotel. One night I woke up sweating. It was about 2 a.m. I remember vividly what happened and the unearthly smell in the room. I saw a mist coming streaming through the window and across the bed and form up on the right side of me. I was absolutely petrified. Then something told me not to be silly. This was not of flesh, nothing psychical. I asked it, 'What do you want?' Then suddenly the mist was gone and I felt very calm and at peace and went off to sleep."

The following night the mist appeared and disappeared at precisely the same time. Moore was understandably full of apprehension when he went to bed on the third night.

"On that third night I noticed that the Bible next to my bed had been opened at the twenty-third Psalm, 'Yea, though I walk through the valley of the shadow of death I will fear no evil for Thou are with me.' I hadn't touched it since I'd booked in. However, that night the mist didn't come. The next morning, the maid, who said she was a Jehovah's Witness, asked me if I'd seen the mist. When I replied in amazement, 'No!' she said, 'I didn't think you would.' She explained she had put the Bible beside the bed. But whether it had anything to do with keeping whatever it was away from me, I just don't know."

Sean Connery, the Scottish actor who launched the legend that is now James Bond in 1962 with *Dr No* and – significantly from his point of view, *You Only Live Twice* (1973) – is one of a group of leading actors who believe they have had previous existences. Apparently, though, he needed some convincing about psychic regression before his first session with the American psychic, Kebrina Kinkade, in 1980. Connery learned he had had earlier lives in his native Scotland and another in Africa. He talked about the second session to Douglas Thompson of the *News of the World*:

"I saw myself standing on a railway platform in Africa watching labourers work. I felt like I belonged with the *kaffirs* and black women in this community. I've gone native, sharing two separate women. They've both given birth to my sons. Then I saw myself lying on the floor of a hut. I think I have just died. I can feel the ground. I see one of my women by me. I think I died from drinking a lot of liquor. Then they burned me. I can see two men putting me on a pile and setting me on fire. People come by and have a look at me and wander off and . . . that's that."

The veteran Italian-American actor **Ernest Borgnine** who made a career from playing "heavies" like the sadistic sergeant in *From Here To Eternity* (1953), yet was capable of winning an Oscar as the kind, lonely butcher in *Marty* (1955), believed avidly in reincarnation and claimed to have experienced several previous existences. Talking about this during the making of *The Day The World Ended* in 1979 he explained in a very matter-of-fact interview:

"I was just a kid of nine in the fourth grade of Pine Street Elementary School in Hamden, Connecticut when I got the first clue. I was dreaming one day in class and I sketched a scene that kept going through my mind. A lone Roman soldier was standing at one end of a bridge. He seemed to be holding off a horde of enemy soldiers single-handedly. Years later when I made it to High School I had to read 'Horatio at the Bridge' and that's when everything clicked. I suddenly realized I'd sketched a picture of that legendary Roman hero who held the Etruscan hordes at bay, single-handedly holding the bridge over the River Tiber. An eerie tingle went right up my spine – because I knew I'd made that drawing years and years before I'd ever heard of Horatio."

Years later, when Borgnine was an established actor, the subject of reincarnation came dramatically back into his life again. He was talking to a psychic medium when she suddenly looked him straight in the eyes:

"She told me she could see me in the uniform of Roman soldier. But not any old soldier – it was Horatio at the bridge. You can say I was shocked rigid and you would still be making an understatement. You see she *couldn't* have known about that sketch and the dreams I'd been having about being Horatio."

Glenn Ford who made something of a speciality of playing amiable but tough and introspective heroes in dramas such as *The Black-*

board Jungle (1955) and classic Westerns including *3.10 To Yuma* (1957) was in his private life a serious student of ESP. During several hypnotic regression sessions he learned about two previous lives he felt sure he had led. At Ford's insistence, these experiments were held at the University of California in Los Angeles and conducted under rigorous scientific controls – and every word he spoke was recorded.

"In the first experiment I was regressed back to eighteenth-century France and the Court of King Louis XIV. Let me tell you I would have been very suspicious if I had been told I was the king. In fact I was just a minor member of the court, I remembered the smell of the swamps at Versailles – a smell that could only have existed at that time because the palace had only just been built. I was also able to describe the stables in their exact location. I apparently got caught up in a court intrigue and died in a duel with the king's best swordsman run through the chest. For many years I've had a pain in my own chest at that precise spot. No doctor could ever explain those pains. Now I know."

Ford's regression was also remarkable in that he spoke in a patois of Parisian French faithfully recorded on tape. He had never spoken a word of French previously. A second session had him speaking with an English accent about a bachelor life in the nineteenth century.

"This time I spoke about a lonely existence in a small city in the north of Scotland where I had taught the piano and died of consumption in 1892. On the tape I gave specific details of where I was buried and who was interred in the adjoining plots. The hypnotist then asked if I would play something. There happened to be a piano in the room and apparently I sat down and played a work by Beethoven. I have to tell you that I cannot play a note."

Christopher Lee, the versatile British actor, who has played many of the leading characters in literature from Dracula to Sherlock Holmes, is also fascinated by the supernatural and has told an interesting story of his regression to the fifteenth century. He explained to Lee Bury in Hollywood in 1980:

"I took part in a psychic regression session with Kebrina Kinkade and saw myself as a man of seventy lying on my deathbed. I didn't see my burial, but I saw a plain stone with a coat of arms on it and the inscription, 'He Served God and Man'. I saw my name:

Francesco di Sarsanio, Duke. This is extraordinary because my grandfather's name – in this present life – was Francesco and he was the Marquis of Sarsanio."

The ghost that haunted hell-raising actor **Oliver Reed** while he lived in a large mansion in Dorking, Surrey during the 1970s had the unique distinction of being seen by the star and caught on camera by a newspaper photographer. Reed, a powerfully built, burly man ran away from home as a teenager and worked as a nightclub bouncer, boxer and taxi driver before getting parts as an extra in British films and then starring in *The Curse of the Werewolf* in 1961. Later roles in *Night Creatures* (1962), *The Shuttered Room* (1967) and *The Devils* (1971) awakened his interest in the supernatural as well as more diverse parts in *Oliver!* (1968) and *The Three Musketeers* (1974). That year he found there was another occupant of the house and its extensive gardens as he told the *Sunday People*:

"The house was a monastery for about one hundred years before I bought it. Locals in *The Cricketers* [pub] told me that a ghost had been seen roaming about the place. It was said to be the ghost of an Irish sea captain who claimed the monks had cheated him. I've actually seen things happen and felt an icy chill. I once saw a book floating in mid-air as it went across the room. More than once, too, I've noticed a heavy armchair has been moved nearer to the fireplace. I was told the monks had also seen the ghost. One of them fainted when he saw a pair of boots moving from a chair by the fire to the liquor cabinet and then return with a bottle held by a hand . . . *Just the hand*."

Reed's reputation as a heavy drinker – he once boasted of sinking 106 pints in a two-day binge – made some people doubtful about this story. But a photograph taken in the garden on 27 April 1975 and reprinted in the *Sunday People* prompted dozens of letters from readers claiming to be able to see a ghostly face in the trees. But the figure through the branches of a tree was not that of the Irish sea captain but a female. June Hilliard of Hatfield, Hertfordshire said she could clearly see "the face of a young woman in the background", while Edna Urquhart of Sutton Coldfield thought the ghostly shape looked like that of "a real lady with refined and dignified looks". Leslie Newbold of Tarporley, Cheshire disagreed, however. He thought the figure in the undergrowth was a "horse's head".

An actor who appeared twice with Reed, **Donald Pleasence**, whose name belied the kind of evil roles he specialized in – from the title role in *Dr Crippen* (1962), Himmler in *The Eagle Has Landed* (1976) to the scene-stealing Ernst Stavro Blofeld in the Bond film, *You Only Live Twice* (1967) – also lived in a haunted seventeenth-century house at Strand-on-the-Green in west London, which he purchased in 1971. The man with the fixed gaze and unblinking eyes who always seemed to fear nothing on the screen told his story a decade later in *Weekend* magazine:

"There was actually another house adjoining it, so we bought that one, too, and knocked down the wall between them to make one large living room. That's when the fun started. We began hearing strange noises – thumping sounds. There was no explanation. We checked throughout the house on many occasions but could not find their source. At first, naturally, I was frightened. I began to worry about what I had unleashed by changing the nature of the old house – had I disturbed something or someone? Gradually, my wife, Meira, and I came to realize that the sounds were distinctly those of children running about – just children. When we'd knocked down the adjoining wall, we'd allowed the spirits of the children who'd once lived there to run through the house again as they'd probably done many years before when it was all one big house. Now that we believe we know what the once-mysterious sounds are, we just treat them as sounds of joy. We can feel the happiness of the children; it seems they're happy to have a free run of the place after all those years, probably centuries. So what harm is that? A happy house is a haunted house!"

Dirk Bogarde, a contemporary of Reed and Pleasence, who made a quite different reputation for himself on the screen as a subtle and sensitive actor with a variety of roles from the hapless young medic *Doctor in the House* (1954) to the groundbreaking homosexual in distress in *Victim* (1961), also lived in a haunted house. The former scenic designer and commercial artist, who became a leading figure in the British film industry and, latterly, a bestselling author, owned Bendrose House, an old farmhouse on Amersham Common, Buckinghamshire. Talking to ghost hunter Peter Underwood in 1971, he said:

"The oldest bedroom in the house, a gloomy, timbered chamber was reputed to be haunted. While I was there, seven people slept in the room at different times and, without previously being aware of the others' experiences, all discovered themselves waking suddenly between three and four in the morning with the feeling that an electric shock was passing through their bodies. The experience seemed to last about four minutes. Some mysterious footsteps were also heard in one particular corridor of the house. While I was living there, I learned that Oliver Cromwell was reputed to have stayed there and some local people believed it was his spirit that infested the farmhouse."

Bob Hoskins, another pillar of the British cinema industry, who has made an international reputation from playing a diversity of roles from the Fascist dictator, Mussolini, in *Mussolini and I* (1985) to the straight man to a group of cartoon characters in *Who Framed Roger Rabbit?* (1988) also came to the screen after a variety of jobs including filing clerk, accountant, labourer and picking mangoes and bananas in Israel. One provided him with an experience he has never forgotten – as he told Jim Crace of the *Sunday Telegraph*:

"When I was a lad I took a job as a porter at the old Covent Garden market. I was shifting some vegetables one evening when I saw a shadowy figure. It was a ghost – the ghost of a nun from the convent that the market was built on. I told this old porter about it, but he didn't laugh at me. He said, 'You're privileged, son. You've seen the lady – you're going to have a lucky life.' He was dead right, wasn't he? I've seen the lady and I'm leading a lucky life."

Experiences with the supernatural in old houses are not exclusive to male actors. The beautiful **Susannah York**, who came to public notice exuding sexuality in *Tom Jones* (1963) and participated in a controversial nude lesbian scene in *The Killing of Sister George* (1968), physically bumped into the supernatural while playing Margaret More in *A Man For All Seasons* in 1966. She explained:

"My husband, Michael Wells and I were looking for a new home. One of our friends owned a rambling, sixteenth-century mansion in Essex. He wanted to sell it and invited us to go and look over it with him and, if necessary, stay a few days to get the feel of the place. So Michael and I went there after a day's filming and arrived at about eleven at night. It looked marvellous, just the sort of home we were looking for. One of the most attractive features was a moat surrounding the house – on which some black swans were swimming – and a drawbridge that provided the only access to it."

When Susannah and Michael went to bed that night they were convinced they had found their dream home. Somewhere they could literally pull up the drawbridge and keep the world at bay. But at about 3 a.m. Susannah sat bolt upright in bed:

> "I had no idea what had awakened me, but I felt so wide awake that I got up and went out into the long corridor off which all the bedrooms led. Suddenly this awful feeling crept over me. I couldn't see anything or anyone, but I had the feeling that some other force was present. I was unable to move. I just stood there scared out of my wits. I tried to scream for Michael, but I fainted. I learned later that as I fell I knocked over a vase and the clatter awoke my husband. He carried me back to our room, but it took him over half an hour to revive me."

By the following morning Susannah had decided she must have had a bad dream. She and her husband were still keen on buying the house and decided they would return during the next break from filming. Again they returned at night – and once more Susannah grew edgy and irritable:

> "Suddenly, I knew what was bothering me. It was the moat. I realized the drawbridge was the only way in and out. I had a horrible thought of being trapped in the house with the draw-bridge not working – and having to jump from the window into the moat with the black swans. We left the place immediately and later Michael telephoned the owner to tell him we did not want to buy it. When he explained why, the owner said, 'Susannah must have met the ghost. It's the ghost of a girl who was trapped in the house when the drawbridge wouldn't work. *She* jumped from a window into the moat and was drowned . . .'"

Two other leading actresses have had encounters with spirits in their homes – although both properties were rather more modern. **Elke Sommer,** the sexy German actress less well known for her sharp intelligence and fluency in seven languages than her starring roles in *Love Italian Style* (1960), *The Art of Love* (1965) and *Deadlier Than The Male* (1966), shared a terrifying brush with evil spirits in her home in Benedict Canyon in 1966. Her writer husband, Joe Hyams, in the *Saturday Evening Post* of 2 July 1966, later described the events in detail.

The couple had bought the house in the summer of 1964 and thought nothing was untoward about the spacious property until a German newspaper reporter doing an interview saw an unidentifiable man walking from the house to the swimming pool. According to the journalist, the figure was about fifty years old and wore a white shirt, dark tie and black suit. Two weeks after this, Elke's mother, who was visiting the couple, woke up and found a man staring at her – but he vanished before she could scream. From then on, people in the house kept hearing unusual sounds in the dining room – in particular the noise of chairs being pushed back and forwards.

The Hyams decided to call in specialists to investigate the mystery and learned that the previous owners had had similar unnerving experiences and reached the conclusion it was haunted. In his article, Joe Hyams concluded:

"Whoever or whatever the ghost is, we do not intend to be frightened out of our house. But a few nights ago, after locking the downstairs doors and checking all the windows carefully, I went to bed anticipating a quiet night. Just as I was falling asleep, Elke nudged me and said, 'Listen!' I sat up in bed and listened. The dining room chairs were moving again."

The story took another strange turn in the autumn when an English clairvoyant, Jacqueline Easthund, was quoted in *Reveille* magazine warning Elke and Joe, "I see your dining room in flames next year; be careful." In the spring of 1967, the prediction came true, as Elke Sommer told reporter Sally Francis:

"Joe wrote a long article about the haunting. It was a strange but true story. He brought in all this photographic apparatus hoping to get some pictures of the ghost but he never did. Then, one night, just after we had agreed to sell the house, it caught fire. The fire started near the dining table where the ghost had been seen. If we had not been awakened by a mysterious knock on the door we might have been killed by the fire if it had spread beyond the room. It was all quite incredible."

A similar sense of unease awaited lovely **Charlotte Rampling** and her husband, Brian Southcombe, when they returned from honeymoon to a Kensington flat after their wedding in February 1972. She had already played a series of provocative leading ladies in *The Knack* (1965), *The Damned* (1969) and *'Tis Pity She's A Whore* (1971) and had just completed work on her ultra-sensual role in *The Night Porter* when she talked to Barbara Jeffrey of the *Sunday People* in December 1974:

"When we returned to the flat we found there was another woman in the flat – a lady ghost. We used to see her at least once a week. We never got to see her face – it was just a board creaking, then a flash like the hem of her nightdress disappearing as she flitted along the passageway. There was a very odd incident one night. Brian's dressing gown fell down behind the bathroom door. I didn't bother to pick it up – but in the morning I found it folded very neatly over the end of our bed. Brian would never have bothered to do that. I knew straight away who had, though – our ghost."

The couple grew to know when the figure would appear. There would be a strange, tense feeling in the air. A number of visitors to the flat also saw the ghost. Then, says Charlotte, the spirit disappeared as suddenly as she had appeared. The actress has a theory as to *why* this happened:

"Brian had lived in the flat for about a year before we were married and always felt uneasy about the place. I think the spirit was that of an old lady who had lived in our flat for twenty years before she died in hospital. Maybe she came back because she wanted to die at home. She must have been about all the time. I believe that when I moved in she came to have a look at me. Perhaps after she'd seen a woman's influence here again she felt she could leave her home in safe keeping and rest at last."

Probably one of most enduring rock 'n roll stars of the twentieth century, **Tommy Steele** also tells one of the most fascinating stories to come from the ranks of popular musicians. He related the facts to Innes Gray of *TV Times* in August 1974:

"When I was sixteen I was paralysed from the waist down – the result of an attack of peritonitis – and taken to Guy's Hospital in London. They thought I'd be dead by the morning and I was taken into a room full of old people. Behind the screen round my bed I could hear a child's voice giggling, then a coloured ball landed on my bed. I could move my arm so I threw it back. I went back to sleep and next morning, when they took the screens away, I was cured. I had a brother, Rodney, who died when I was three. The two of us were inseparable until then. And, although I didn't remember it at the time, my mother told me that his favourite game was throwing a ball to me."

Every bit as well known on the British music scene is the jazz duo of **Cleo Laine** and Johnny Dankworth. In 1982, she gave a remarkable account to Richard Maino of her haunted home, a 150-year-old Gothic-style rectory set in seventeen acres in Wavendon, Buckinghamshire, where the couple lived:

"I think our ghost must be a nice ghost. If he objected to us or our way of life he could have frightened the wits out of us by now. I'm not the only one to have seen him so that shows it's not just my imagination. Somebody else saw him in the dining room, but just won't believe that he is a spirit although the only other person in the house was right on the top floor."

Cleo believes the ghost has very good taste and loves music. Unfortunately, though, there is no real clue to his identity. She added:

"It's hard to describe what he looks like. He is more of a vision, a faint impression rather than a clear form. He looks as if he lived in the last century, possibly earlier. He seems restless about something – that's what I feel about the manner in which he behaves. John used to laugh at my stories about the spirit going around in the grounds, but that was until many of our friends reported similar strange incidents. I have never tried to make contact with the vision. I can only presume that he was happy at the old rectory in this life and likes to return from time to time – perhaps because it is still a happy place."

Possibly one of the most haunted of modern singers is **Lynsey De Paul**, who has lived in a haunted house and recorded one of her best-known songs in a studio where something very supernatural occurred. She told the first of her stories to Jill Evans of the *News of the World*:

"It was in 1977 when I was recording 'Rock Bottom' for the Eurovision Song Contest. With me were my manager, Mike

Moran, and a sound engineer. Just after 3 a.m. we began to hear what is known as 'white noise' – the kind of crackling sound you hear when there is interference on a radio. It gradually became so loud that I had to take my earphones off. The engineer was baffled, finding nothing wrong with the equipment. When the sound became louder we all got alarmed. Then suddenly this enormous triangle of white light appeared in the middle of the room. I felt pressure on me from head to foot as though someone had place an enormous hand on me. I was terrified and burst out crying."

Lynsey said that the two men were also scared at seeing the light, but only she experienced the feeling of pressure. The light then disappeared. She went on:

"When I recovered I said, 'Have we got a ghost?' The engineer gave me a strange look and told us about strange happenings in the men's lavatories at the studio. Apparently people kept complaining of sharp jabs in the back when they went into the loo, although there never appeared to be anyone there. Some time later I met Michael Bentine who is an expert on the paranormal. He explained to me that the white light was a friendly thing – a manifestation of energy that went back as far as the Druids."

Shortly after this Lynsey moved into a very Gothic-looking house overlooking London's famous Highgate Cemetery, a place that with its mixture of ornate mausoleums and huge tombs has prompted reports of grave robbing, horror stories and even vampire attacks for many years. Talking in 1982, she said:

"I suppose if any house looks as it should be haunted it's this one. And since I've been here, there have been lots of strange forces at work. Doors in the servant's cottage have opened and closed mysteriously and one of the stained-glass windows and a heavy metal mirror fell to the ground. I have also seen bits of electric flex bursting into flame and whenever my keys go missing they turn up in the strangest places – like the freezer, for instance. Whatever causes all this isn't necessarily evil or an evil force – although I'm sure there is only one force. It's people who make it a good or bad force."

A strange force was also reported to be at work in the Elizabethan manor house at Little Gaddesden in Hertfordshire used as a home and recording studio by the former Rolling Stones' lead guitarist,

Mick Taylor, in 1977. According to Valerie Jarvis, Taylor's partner, lights being flicked on and off and noises intruding without any apparent cause had interrupted a number of sessions. She told the *Observer:* 'None of the guitars and recording equipment have been touched, but the ghost has made recording a struggle."

Mick Taylor himself commented: "I did hear voices in the kitchen the other day and when I went in no one was there, but it didn't really worry me. We've been told a spectral churchwarden called Jerman who committed suicide over an unrequited love haunts the house. None of us think he is malevolent, though."

In September 1985, **Sting** told John Blake of the *Daily Mirror* that two ghosts – a mother and child – haunted his house in Hampstead where he often wrote and made recordings. He had staged a séance with a top spiritualist to try and communicate with the couple. He explained:

"The house is definitely haunted. Ever since I moved in there other people have said things happen. Like they're lying in bed and voices start to talk to them or things go missing. I was very sceptical until one night after Mickey, my daughter, was born. She was disturbed and I went to see her. Her room was full of mobiles and they were going berserk. I thought there must be a window open. But the windows were dead shut. And this baby was lying there with her eyes open. About two days later I woke up and looked into the corner of my bedroom and, clear as day, there was a woman and child standing in the corner. And I heard Trudie, my girlfriend, say, 'Sting, what's that in the corner?' I just went totally cold, icy cold."

Rod Stewart has admitted that he is a firm believer in ESP. Journalist Lee Bury of the *News of the World* reported in November 1980 that three years earlier, Stewart had a premonition that his friend Elton John was about to have a heart attack. Lee wrote:

"Rod told his wife Alana, who regularly consults a Hollywood psychic. A week later Elton collapsed. Doctors at first thought it was a heart attack, but later diagnosed exhaustion through overwork."

The spirits of two of the most famous rock stars of the twentieth century, Marc Bolan and John Lennon, have allegedly been in contact with people close to them according to recent reports. **Marc**

Bolan, the T-Rex front man who died in a car crash in 1977, and whose work is now enjoying a huge renaissance of interest, spoke to his former manager, Mick O'Halloran, through medium Ronald Hearn in 1980 during a public demonstration at Ryde on the Isle of Wight. O'Halloran said:

> "The most fantastic thing was the stance adopted by Mr Hearn while Marc was communicating through him. It was exactly the way Marc used to stand on stage. Mr Hearn told me of things which in no way could have been public knowledge. He spoke of one incident when I arrived in an American hotel wearing a huge pink wig and Marc fell about laughing. And he recalled two occasions when Marc narrowly missed being electrocuted and crushed to death. But the most conclusive evidence was the fact that Marc was writing a new song just before his death. I didn't know that – but when I mentioned it to a fan she said that Marc's father told her the police recovered a half-finished tape after his death."

John Lennon is claimed to have made contact with Robin Givens, the former wife of heavyweight champion Mike Tyson, who lives in a Hollywood home once occupied by the legendary Beatle while the group were on the west coast of America. Robin says that she has heard Lennon "singing in the house late at night or talking quietly out by the swimming pool". This story of the musician speaking from beyond the grave is one of several reported by Linda Domnitz in her book, *The John Lennon Conversations*. According to the medium, Lennon contacted her just four days after being shot and killed in New York. She says, "I had been meditating with a friend when John came through to me. He is such a warm and friendly spirit and has been passing on a lifetime of wisdom to me."

There have been ghostly experiences among the latest group of media celebrities, too – the television soap stars. A few of the most interesting will suffice for a great many more among this group of actors and actresses who are mostly usually being "haunted" by the press and paparazzi. One of the earliest superstars of the small screen was **Patricia Phoenix** who played the legendary Elsie Tanner in *Coronation Street*. Pat spotted the spectre of an old lady who subsequently appeared several times at her home in Sale, Cheshire in the 1960s:

"I was alone in one of the rooms when my dog suddenly pricked up his ears. I looked around and saw the woman – she was holding something. It could have been a candle or a bowl of some kind. She walked out of the door. I went after her, but she'd vanished. Even after I moved from that house to one in Salford, she would visit me from time to time. Eventually I found out who she was – or is. My old home had been owned by Madame Muelier who is believed to have been an actress of the 1800s. She died there alone – but for her dog."

Stratford Johns who played the brusque Chief Inspector Barlow in the phenomenally successful series *Z-Cars*, spent much of his screen career battling villains and hard men. Unbeknown to the public, he also had to use all his renowned toughness in a struggle with a very dark force in his home, an old coaching house in Suffolk. He talked about how this clash became a test of strength – literally:

"I have this instinct which tells me when something is about to happen. Call it a gut feeling and it's usually right. Often it's something slight like stubbing my toe – but other times it can be far more serious and unpleasant. I feel as if I've suddenly become hollow and am being filled with ice-cold water from my feet up. It's quite horrible."

Of the various experiences Stratford Johns had with the unwelcome phantom in his house, one amounted to a violent battle, which could have been fatal when he was in danger of being pushed down some stairs. Fortunately, he had had the foresight to install heavy hand-rails. The encounter happened one day when he suddenly sensed a presence in one of the bedrooms:

"I walked in and the room was like a cold store, that strange icy feeling again. There was nothing visible, but I felt I had to be forceful. I bellowed at it to leave my house. That seemed to work for a while. The room's temperature became normal. I went into the next room and it was there, but it seemed to leave again. I walked out on to the landing and as I was standing there, a massive blow on my back sent me flying headlong down the stairs. I just managed to grab the handrail and stop myself hurtling down the entire flight. The fall could have easily broken my neck – thank God I had replaced the old rail. Far from making me cower with fear, although it was frightening, it just made me very angry. I went berserk. I ranted and raved. The spirit didn't hang about that time. It did return later, though, and we had to have it exorcized."

The machinations and plotting in the famous American TV series *Dallas* gathered huge ratings as well as many stories in the media. The only one with a supernatural angle concerned the tiny actress **Charlene Tilton**, who played the role of Lucy Ewing, frequently referred to as "the poison dwarf". Off-screen, Charlene was a delightful raconteur and on several occasions told the story of being haunted by the ghost of her grandfather.

"When I was little I lived with my mom and grandfather in a little flat in Hollywood. I was six years old when he died and I often had to be left alone when my mother went out to work. One day, my mother came home from work and found me crouching on the doorstep, shivering with fright. I told her there was 'something scary' in the flat. Without a moment's hesitation, my mom told me that my grandfather's spirit was still there."

Strange things continued to happen as Charlene grew up. She was always conscious of her grandfather's presence.

"I remember very clearly something incredibly scary when I was a teenager. One day a neighbour called in and asked if I would turn down the radio, which was blaring out pop music. In a teenage tantrum I refused. Then things began to happen. The plug jerked out of the wall without anyone being near it. When I pushed it back into the socket it was jerked out again so violently that sparks flew. The neighbour stood there with her mouth open, struck dumb by what she had seen. But we knew it was the ghost again."

When Charlene left home to live in another district of Hollywood and pursue her career as a model and actress, she hoped she had left the spirit behind. When she settled down with a boyfriend in a new apartment she thought no more of the past – until her man started to complain that the place was "spooky". Charlene agreed with him – and also suspected she knew the reason why:

"You could sense something or someone invisible when you walked into an empty room. There were pockets of cold air and nearly every door would open silently and close again.

Eventually I could stand it no more and moved again hoping the presence would grow tired of following me. Thanks to the success of *Dallas* I was able to buy a beautiful place overlooking a canyon. There were no more problems with the ghost. I like to think that if he *was* my grandfather he had at last found peace."

Even stars of science fiction series have not been exempted from supernatural occurrences. **William Shatner**, the original intrepid Captain Kirk of *Star Trek* fame, who has "boldly gone" where others have feared to tread, walked into an inexplicable incident that could have come from an episode of the show while on a motorcycle trip with three friends in desert country outside Los Angeles. Speaking in 1989 he explained:

"We'd just stopped for a drink when we saw this other bike rider approaching us. In that kind of country it's not advisable to ride alone. What would happen if you came off your bike? Anyhow, the guy tagged along with us. The moment I looked into his face, though, I felt an odd vibration humming through the air. Nobody else noticed anything. Then somehow I fell behind the others and shortly afterwards my bike hit a rock and overturned. I fell on the exhaust pipe, injuring my leg and badly burning my face."

Lying on the ground, Shatner realized that the others were too far ahead to notice his accident. He called out, but no one returned. He struggled to his feet and tried without success to restart his motorcycle.

"I knew I was in trouble. My leg, face, everything seemed to be giving me pain. But I knew I couldn't just stay there under the burning sun. So I began dragging and pushing the bike. When I reached a small hill I thought I could force-start the machine if I could roll it down the slope. But by the time I reached the brow, the effort caused me to black out. I wasn't unconscious very long and when I came to I could hear that weird humming again. Strangely, too, I suddenly felt totally fit. My limp had gone, the burn had disappeared, and now the bike seemed to have a mind of its own. It wanted to go its own way, not mine. I couldn't fight it, so I just trailed along. I didn't know where I was heading – until I suddenly came over the brow of a hill and there was a gas station in the distance."

Shatner hurried to the station and asked the attendant if he could repair the bike. The man gave one push of the pedal and the machine roared back into life. At that moment, his three friends also appeared:

"I asked them what had happened to the stranger and they said he'd just vanished shortly after I fell behind. I heard the strange humming again and saw the stranger on a far hill. He was waving at us, but I was the only one who could see him. I didn't care – I waved back my thanks to whoever – or *whatever* – it was that had saved my life."

Gillian Anderson, who played FBI Agent Scully in the *X-Files*, has investigated every kind of supernatural event from UFOs to Alien abductions on the small screen. But she was forced to ask for help when eerie spirits beset her own home in Vancouver in 1995. Talking to Liz Hodgson of the *Sunday Mirror*, she recalled:

"It was really creepy. When my husband Clyde and our daughter, Piper, moved into the house weird things began to happen. Lights going on and off, noises at night and after a while it seemed there was something attached to me. I knew we would have to get help."

Gillian's knowledge of the supernatural had been carefully cultivated by all the reading and study she had done for her role as Agent Scully. She knew the best source of help would be a local expert:

"I contacted a Native American who visited the house and told us we were living near an Indian burial ground and they were still in a state of unrest after dying in a plague. He then performed a ritual called 'Smudging' in which herbs were burned to purify the space. It was amazing what happened. Once it was over we felt that whatever had been there had gone."

Indeed, ghosts have not bothered Gillian Anderson again. But after another century of haunting can there by any doubt that the next generation of stars of films, music and television will not find themselves – when they least expect it – thrust into incidents very like those described in these pages?

6

Supernatural Tales

True Ghost Stories by Famous Authors

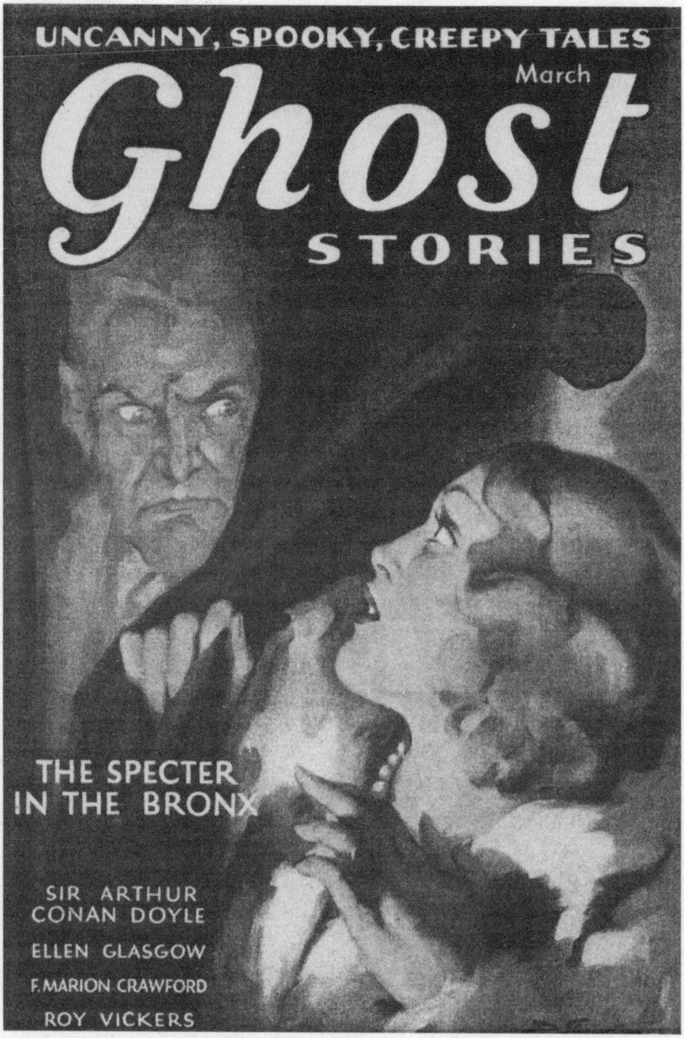
UNCANNY, SPOOKY, CREEPY TALES
March
Ghost
STORIES
THE SPECTER
IN THE BRONX
SIR ARTHUR
CONAN DOYLE
ELLEN GLASGOW
F. MARION CRAWFORD
ROY VICKERS

A substantial number of twentieth-century authors have written novels with ghost story themes, not all of them writers associated with the genre, the best of which I listed in my companion volume, *The Mammoth Book of Modern Ghost Stories*. The American writer **Stephen King** naturally features prominently in the list, notably with *The Shining* (1977) and *Bag of Bones* (1998). With this in mind I was interested to discover that King had actually come looking for a supernatural encounter for one of his books by staying in England in 1977 – a precedent that had worked for him earlier in the decade.

In the early 1970s, Stephen and his wife, Tabitha, had been forced by bad weather while travelling to seek shelter in the palatial old Stanley Hotel near Estes Park in Colorado. He was already mulling over an idea for a story about a family trapped in a haunted locality and when he discovered that the hotel, built in 1909, had a reputation for being full of mysterious sounds, phantom footsteps, doors that opened and closed of their own accord, and even a few guests who had disappeared on the premises and never been seen again, he realized he had the concept that would ultimately become the terrifying Overlook Hotel in *The Shining*.

King was hoping for the same kind of inspiration in 1977 when he came to England to work and rented a house at Fleet near Aldershot. If, however, he had done any research before crossing the Atlantic, he would have discovered that the nearest haunted building was Bramshill House about twelve miles away (as the raven flies) near Basingstoke. At this fourteenth-century mansion, the ghost of a young bride who died on the eve of her wedding is said to walk the Long Gallery in a white, ankle-length gown, while the apparition of a "Green Man" – supposed to be the Black Prince who died at Bramshill in mysterious circumstances – slinks around near a lake in the grounds. Perhaps appropriately, considering its history of suspected murder and death, the house is now a police training college. In any event, Stephen King arrived full of optimism, as he recalled in an interview with *The Times* on 21 October 2006:

"I came to write a book. I thought that England is the home of the ghost story; I'll come over here and I'll get a ghost story. But I never did. I was totally flat when I got overseas. It was like my umbilical cord had been cut. But I had a wonderful relationship with everybody while I was over here. I didn't drink too much, didn't get into any fights with anyone, but I didn't find any ghosts. I think that if I had to do it over again and maybe if we found some new place – who knows?"

Not long after his return to America, however, Stephen King did utilize another authentic ghost story as the basis for an original television mini-series, *Rose Red*, shown on ABC TV in January 2002. The story concerned a psychology college professor, Dr Joyce Reardon (played by Nancy Travis), who coerces a group of psychics to spend a weekend in a turn-of-the-century Seattle mansion that has long been abandoned. According to tradition a menagerie of spirits haunts it and the number of rooms in the labyrinth interior are forever increasing. The group are soon trapped and terrified as they struggle to uncover the horrifying secret of *how* all those who lived there died and the haunting began. Talking before the programme was shown, King – who made a brief appearance as a pizza delivery man – admitted to *TV Guide* his inspiration had been the very curious Winchester Mansion in San Jose, California:

"I first saw the story of the house in one of the *Ripley's Believe It or Not* comics when I was a kid and remembered it for years after. According to Ripley, Oliver Winchester, who invented the famous repeating rifle that won the west, left a daughter-in-law with a belief in Spiritualism when he went to his reward. At one séance, Sarah Winchester asked the medium, 'When will I die?' And the medium replied, 'When your house is done.' Well, the Winchester house was never really completed and construction went on around the clock until Sarah Winchester died. She continued to add rooms, hallways and entire wings, claiming to receive blueprints and ideas from the spirits on a nightly basis. After reading up on Winchester House, the idea of a 'never ending mansion' stuck with me and I decided to work on a screenplay."

Initially, it was hoped to shoot *Rose Red* on location in Winchester House, but all the rooms proved too small to accommodate the filmmakers. Instead, a luxurious bed and breakfast hotel, Thornewood Castle near Tacoma, Washington was chosen. Built in 1911 for Chester Thorne, one of the founders of Tacoma, the castle is actually a 400-year-old Elizabethan manor house that was dismantled and shipped across the Atlantic from England and reassembled at a cost in excess of $1 million. Over the years, a legend has developed that brides-to-be staying at the castle have seen the apparition of a woman in a mirror as they prepare for their wedding. Shades of Bramshill House here!

Stephen King has had no more brushes with the supernatural, but an old man supposedly haunts his home in Bangor, Maine. He explains: "I've never seen the old duffer, but sometimes when I'm working late at night, I get a distinctly uneasy feeling that I'm not alone."

James Herbert, Britain's most successful answer to Stephen King, also featured in my list with two novels about ghost hunter David Ash, *Haunted* (1988) and *The Ghosts of Sleath* (1994) and has returned to the theme in *The Secret of Crickley Hall* (2006) about a couple trying to start a new life after a terrible accident in which their five-year-old son has disappeared. They chose "a tomb-like place, a mausoleum" in Devil's Cleave in Devonshire and are soon beset and almost overwhelmed by paranormal phenomena even with the aid of a Spiritualist. Herbert himself lives in a huge house in West Sussex near Brighton, but it is quite free of ghosts. He said recently:

"Yes, I do believe in ghosts. Life after death is too important to trivialize. I'm a Catholic, so naturally I believe in the afterlife. I've talked to a lot of people involved in the occult while writing my books – psychics, ghost hunters and psychic researchers. One psychic told me it's not me who writes these books. It's an ancient spirit that possesses me and wills me to write. It's funny, because when I do sit down, it's as though I'm taken over. The story flows, it tells itself, like someone else is writing it . . ."

These tales are, of course, by writers immediately associated with the supernatural. But there have been plenty of others working in quite different genres who have found themselves in mysterious situations they would probably not have dared to invent – and later recalled what they *saw* and how they *felt*. The following selection of the best of their stories is, I believe, not without its surprises and, even, genuine shocks.

1900: The gloomy mansion known as Renishaw Hall in Derbyshire was the home of the Sitwell family: the eccentric Sir George Sitwell

and his famous trio of literary offspring, Osbert, Edith and Sache-
verell, all of whom were aware that the building was haunted.
SACHEVERELL SITWELL (1897–1988) in particular became
interested in the supernatural and wrote one of the best studies of
this in Poltergeists *(1940) in which he described another spirit that*
troubled the family at the turn of the century and became known
as . . .

THE TOADPOOL POLTERGEIST

There is never far to look to find the Poltergeist. A case occurred so
near home as to be upon a farm belonging to my brother, in
Derbyshire, not further, indeed, than a mile or a mile and a half
from our home. The hauntings were some forty years ago, but I have
been told of them all my life.

The scene, we can say this, had a name as good as Malking Tower.
It was a lonely farm, which has to be reached across the fields and
does not lie upon any road. The name of it is Toadpool Farm. And
this name, already sinister enough, is, perhaps, bettered if the first
syllable, as has been suggested, is the Saxon "tod" or death, in fact, a
suicide pool, or a pool in which someone was drowned. All round the
farm, in the fields, there are the mysterious mushroom rings. It is, or
was, enchanted ground, but with an evil meaning.

The hauntings took place during two successive tenancies; the
earlier of the tenant farmers being dead, long since, and his successor
still alive, but in an asylum. The usual stone-throwing took place;
showers of pebbles fell from the roof, or rattled against the windows.
There were tappings and rappings. And, for greater mystery, in the
time of both tenants, the cart-horses in the stables were found in the
morning ready harnessed, or ready saddled.

The odd point in this story is the continuance of the hauntings
under two successive tenants. The same children, therefore, or
maidservants, cannot have been in the house. But, unfortunately,
it was forty years ago and it is too late, now, to discover further
details.

The background is a little similar to that of Willington Mill in the
sense that it is rural or bucolic, but with railway lines and coal mines
near by. The great slag heaps, or clinker, as it is known locally, raise
their artificial hills in every direction, covered, in summer, with the
pink flowering flax. The great Staveley Ironworks are in the distance.

Near by is Foxton Wood, with a dam one hundred feet deep, a
favourite place for suicides, and, beyond the wood, a fine Jacobean

manor house, now become a farmhouse, but once the dower house of Lady Frescheville, the wife of the Cavalier. This manor house, which, too, in its remoteness should be haunted, has the name of Hagge Hall. Toadpool Farm and Hagge Hall, what better or more appropriate names could there be!

1910: Some old boarding schools have a reputation among former pupils for generating the most terrible fear by night – whether factual or fanciful. DENNIS WHEATLEY (1897–1977), one of the last century's most popular writers of historical, high adventure and Black Magic fiction, notably The Devil Rides Out *(1935), delighted in telling the story of "the most terrifying experience of my life" when he was a boarder at a school in Broadstairs in 1910 and came face to face with . . .*

THE CROUCHING FIGURE

This true story took place when I was at a boarding school in Broadstairs run by a Mr and Mrs Hester and their assistant, Milly Evans. The event had such an effect on me that I never forgot it and later used it in my novel, *The Haunting of Toby Jugg*, which I published in 1948. I have to admit that I learned very little at that boarding school and it always seemed to be perishingly cold in the winter.

The school had a front door that opened onto a narrow hall. This led to a flight of stairs that went up to the first and second floors where our bedrooms were situated. One night I was going to bed up these stairs rather later than usual with my friend, Bernie Amendt. We were dawdling as usual and I was peering between each banister as we climbed up.

Suddenly, as I was looking through one of the gaps, I found myself staring straight into another face. It was only inches away from me on the other side and perfectly horrible in appearance. It was very white and bloated. There was also a hand grasping the rail of the banister and I could just make out the outline of the crouching figure of a man.

I was struck dumb with fear. For several seconds I could not move.

My friend Bernie had reached the top of the stairs and was staring out of a window. I heard him whisper, "Oh, what a lovely moon!" His voice seemed to bring me back to reality and I screamed and ran back down the stairs.

I looked back once as I fled. The figure on the other side of the banisters had moved, swiftly and noiselessly, and was gliding up the stairs. It went straight past Bernie, who was now looking down to see what had happened to me.

As soon as he heard my cry, he ran down the stairs, too, and asked what was going on. I shouted that there was a burglar in the school.

Within moments Mr and Mrs Hester, Milly Evans and a man they had been entertaining to dinner appeared from the ground-floor sitting room. Mrs Hester tried to calm Bernie and I, while her husband and their guest set off up the stairs to catch the intruder.

We all knew there was no way out of the building. No back stairs, no fire escape, no barred windows – and there was a 30-foot drop from the upper floor. Everywhere was searched for the mysterious intruder – but there was no sign of him. Nothing had been touched, nothing had been stolen and nothing had even been damaged.

The Hesters told me that my imagination must have been playing tricks – and they ticked us both off for not having been in bed and fast asleep by that time. It took us both a long time to get to sleep that night and although there was never a repeat, the episode was so vivid that it never left my mind.

Fate has a habit of playing tricks – and quite by chance the mystery of that intruder was solved a few years later during the First World War. I was serving in France at the time as a gunner officer with the 36th Ulster Division. One morning I was walking along a road behind the front line when an ambulance suddenly pulled up beside me.

As I stood there puzzled, the door opened and a young woman driver got down. She smiled at me and said, "You're Dennis Wheatley aren't you? Do you remember me? I'm Milly Evans."

I was delighted to see her and we stood chatting for some time about the old boarding school days. During this conversation she asked me if I remembered the figure I had seen on the stairs. I replied that I had never forgotten it and asked if the burglar had been caught. The look on Milly's face became serious then and she shook her head.

"*You* thought it was a burglar – but it wasn't," she said. "We let you think that because we didn't want to frighten you. In fact, it was some sort of supernatural manifestation – and a pretty nasty one, at that. The Hesters were interested in spiritualism, you see, and two or three times a week we used to hold a séance – trying to raise a spirit, practise table-turning and all that sort of thing.

"There was never any doubt in my mind – and I don't think theirs either – about what happened that night. Our séances had somehow attracted some sort of elemental, which materialized and began to haunt the place. After that the Hesters were so scared of what they had done that they never held a séance again!"

1916: Family holidays to Trebetherick near Polzeath in Cornwall, gave the poet and writer, JOHN BETJEMAN (1906–84), a profound love of the area, which is reflected in several of his poems and his blank verse autobiography, Summoned By Bells *(1960). Supporting himself by journalism and satirical light verse, he rose in public affection until ultimately he became Poet Laureate in 1972. Betjeman loved ghost stories – in particular those of MR James – and claimed that it was a weird experience he had as a child in 1916 which fostered his interest in the supernatural when he was dared to enter the foul and dank world of . . .*

THE WRECKER'S CAVE

I must have been about ten years old when this happened. That is to say it was about 1916, and summer holidays in North Cornwall. It was a remote place then – oil lamps, farmhouse teas, few motor cars, and the London and South Western Railway crawling along its single line through Launceston to Wadebridge and Padstow. A wet silence hung over the nights, and legends survived as yet uncommercialised, and we were young enough to believe them. One of these was about a smuggler called Cruel Coppinger – Baring Gould writes of him in his romance *In The Roar of the Sea*. Coppinger lured ships to their doom on our great slate cliffs. When a ship was sighted he would wave a lantern so that her captain thought she was approaching harbour, but instead she was approaching a hostile cove near Port Isaac full of rocks. Coppinger arrived in the district mysteriously. It was said he was a Dane. Like another famous wrecker, Gilbert Mawgan, he is said to have left the sailors thrown up not quite dead, to die on the rocks. Mawgan even went so far as to bury alive the captain of a vessel whom he found exhausted on the strand. When Coppinger was dying – as when Mawgan died – there was a tremendous sea and a strange vessel came up channel from nowhere. On the wrecker's death it stood out to sea and disappeared.

Between two bays to which we used to make day-expeditions on foot there ran a tunnel. At high tide, and even at half tide, if you had been in this tunnel you would have been trapped. It was said that there was a way out of the tunnel by a shaft to the open air. Certainly, from the cliff path above, a dank cavern with luminous moss in it was said to lead down to the tunnel between the two bays. I never liked going down it myself because of the sense that it might fall in behind me and I would suffocate. This was the hole said to have been used by Cruel Coppinger for bringing up his plunder from the sea caves below.

One day bolder children than I, with me in their wake, explored the sea cave at a low spring tide in order to find the way through to the other bay. We wore bathing dresses. At first there was the usual scrambling over boulders and avoiding a slippery kind of green seaweed until it was too dark to know what sort of weeds, pools, or rocks were at our feet. The cave narrowed and I hoped it would peter out altogether so that we should have to turn back. But no. There was a pool in total darkness and the water came up to my chin. The others had gone ahead. I could still hear their voices. Then there was a sudden change in the air. Instead of the salt, seaweedy, iodine smell, it was as though I was in a stuffy much-breathed-in room. I had a distinct feeling, though I saw nothing, that there was someone else behind me who was not of our party. The rather sinister caress of what might have been ribbon weed, or a sea spider's legs, around my ankles made me swim forward, breast stroke, as hard as I could. Then there was the light from the other bay, the air changed back to its sea-freshness and we were all safely through.

That afternoon someone photographed us on the rocks below the entrance to the cave. When we were shown the photograph there appeared in the black entrance to the cave a face with a big moustache and a tricorn hat. This was not an illusion created by the rock formation because it was in the black darkness of the cave aperture. I can think of four people alive today who must remember that photograph.

When I go to the scene now it looks small and used and there is litter about and always people, instead of the desertion we remember. And of course I cannot be certain now, for it is 50 years ago, whether I didn't imagine that presence in the middle blackness *after* I had seen the photograph. All I am certain of is that the face I saw in the photograph was there, and that it was nobody we knew and rather larger than life.

1916: Ghosts have played an integral part in both the working and private life of BARBARA CARTLAND (1901–2000), one of the most successful romantic novelists of all time. Her home, Camfield Place, Hatfield was reputedly haunted and in 1983 she reported that her dead brother, Ronald, and friend, the late Lord Louis Mountbatten had "acted as ghost writers" on a number of her books. In fact, her interest in the supernatural, which was reflected in books such as The Ghost Who Fell in Love *(1979), can be traced back to a paranormal experience when she was a teenager and first heard the sound of . . .*

THE WOUNDED CAVALIER

In 1916 I lived in a haunted house, Nailsea Court in Somerset. There was always someone going up the stairs ahead of me or coming up behind; yet they could not be seen. The house was very old and filled with the panelling and furniture of Judge Jeffreys – the Hanging Judge. Had his bitterness and cruelty still survived? I was never alone.

One night I heard footsteps dragging their way upstairs, and the tick of the clock like the beat of a heart sounded loudly in my ears. I was terrified and could only pray desperately: "Lighten our darkness, we beseech Thee, O Lord and by Thy great mercy defend us from all perils and dangers of the night . . ."

The footsteps stopped at my door. Later I learnt that a Cavalier who had been wounded by the Roundheads came back there to die.

1917: Asham House, a Regency-Gothic house in the village of Beddingham near Lewes in East Sussex was the home for several years of VIRGINIA WOOLF (1882–1941), the famous English novelist. Here from 1912–17 she wrote her books including To The Lighthouse, *entertained members of the Bloomsbury Group and experienced the ghostly couple that, according to local legend, had been restlessly opening and shutting doorways for years in the yellow-washed property that was said to be . . .*

A HAUNTED HOUSE

Whatever hour you woke there was a door shutting. From room to room they went, hand in hand, lifting here, opening there, making sure – a ghostly couple.

"Here we left it," she said. And he added, "Oh, but here too!" "It's upstairs," she murmured. "And in the garden," he whispered. "Quietly," they said, "or we shall wake them."

But it wasn't that you woke us. Oh, no. "They're looking for it; they're drawing the curtain," one might say, and so read on a page or two. "Now they've found it," one would be certain, stopping the pencil on the margin. And then, tired of reading, one might rise and see for oneself, the house all empty, the doors standing open, only the wood pigeons bubbling with content and the hum of the threshing machine sounding from the farm. "What did I come in here for? What did I want to find?" My hands were empty. "Perhaps it's upstairs then?" The apples were in the loft. And so down again, the garden still as ever, only the book had slipped into the grass.

But they had found it in the drawing-room. Not that one could ever see them. The window panes reflected apples, reflected roses; all the leaves were green in the glass. If they moved in the drawing-room, the apple only turned its yellow side. Yet, the moment after, if the door was opened, spread about the floor, hung upon the walls, pendant from the ceiling – what? My hands were empty. The shadow of a thrush crossed the carpet; from the deepest wells of silence the wood pigeon drew its bubble of sound. "Safe, safe, safe," the pulse of the house beat softly. "The treasure buried; the room . . ." the pulse stopped short. Oh, was that the buried treasure?

A moment later the light had faded. Out in the garden then? But the trees spun darkness for a wandering beam of sun. So fine, so rare, coolly sunk beneath the surface the beam I sought always burnt behind the glass. Death was the glass; death was between us; coming to the woman first, hundreds of years ago, leaving the house, sealing all the windows; the rooms were darkened. He left it, left her, went North, went East, saw the stars turned in the Southern sky; sought the house, found it dropped beneath the Downs. "Safe, safe, safe," the pulse of the house beat gladly. "The Treasure yours."

The wind roars up the avenue. Trees stoop and bend this way and that. Moonbeams splash and spill wildly in the rain. But the beam of the lamp falls straight from the window. The candle burns stiff and still. Wandering through the house, opening the windows, whispering not to wake us, the ghostly couple seek their joy.

"Here we slept," she says. And he adds, "Kisses without number." "Waking in the morning –" "Silver between the trees –" "Upstairs –" "In the garden –" "When summer came –" "In winter snowtime –" The doors go shutting far in the distance, gently knocking like the pulse of a heart.

Nearer they come; cease at the doorway. The wind falls, the rain slides silver down the glass. Our eyes darken; we hear no steps beside us; we see no lady spread her ghostly cloak. His hands shield the lantern. "Look," he breathes. "Sound asleep. Love upon their lips."

Stooping, holding their silver lamp above us, long they look and deeply. Long they pause. The wind drives straightly; the flame stoops slightly. Wild beams of moonlight cross both floor and wall, and, meeting, stain the faces bent; the faces pondering; the faces that search the sleepers and seek their hidden joy.

"Safe, safe, safe," the heart of the house beats proudly. "Long years –" he sighs. "Again you found me." "Here," she murmurs, "sleeping; in the garden reading; laughing, rolling apples in the loft. Here we left our treasure –" Stooping, their light lifts the lids upon my eyes. "Safe! safe! safe!" the pulse of the house beats wildly. Waking, I cry "Oh, is this *your* buried treasure? The light in the heart."

1920: Bath is one of England's ancient cities with a long history of hauntings. The notorious cleric and expert on demonology and occult lore, MONTAGUE SUMMERS (1880–1948) lived and worked there for years on a number of his exhaustively researched works including The Vampire: His Kith and Kin *(1928). Despite his enquiries into the supernatural, it was not until after his death that he revealed in his posthumously published autobiography* The Galanty Show *(1980) about his meeting with a dishevelled-looking creature known as . . .*

THE BELLE OF BATH

Many years ago, when I was living in Queen's Square, Bath, one morning, in plain daylight, there passed me in the hall a lady powered and patched, in sacque and hoop. As I stood aside to let her go by in her tempestuous petticoat she dropped me a pretty little curtsy with a piquant wave of her fan, and I smelled the sweet fragrance of neroli. Bath was very full of visitors just then because of the Grand Pageant, and I merely thought how admirably this nymph had dressed herself for her part – doubtless she was wearing the gown of an ancestress to grace her role. That evening I casually observed to my good landlady, "I see, Mrs Norris, that we have pageant-guests staying in the house. How beautifully dressed that lady was whom I met in the hall. She will surely be the belle of the show." Mrs Norris stared at me for a moment, and I noticed that she turned white. "A lady! I assure you there's nobody staying here but yourself. What was she like?" As best I could, I described the Sylvia or Araminta or Dorinda whom I had seen. Mrs Norris dropped the salver she was holding, and exclaimed: "Oh, whatever shall I do? She's come back!" "Who's come back?" I asked. "Oh dear, oh dear!" and she began to sob in a subdued hopeless kind of way. "Whatever is the matter?" I queried. "I've lost visitors through her in past years, and now you'll go. I did think we were free of her at last. And the lease won't run out for another couple of years. Oh dear, oh dear, what can I do?" Eventually I succeeded in discovering that the lady in the eighteenth-century dress had several times been seen in the hall and on the stairs. Apparently, two or three years had elapsed since she last appeared, and Mrs Norris, poor good soul, had made sure that she was gone for ever. "I can't think what she wants. Why can't she rest and leave us alone? They say she lived here once, and was the Belle of Bath. I don't know her name, or why she could return. She never speaks or does anyone any harm, but there she is! And now *you'll* go." I soon reassured the frightened housewife, and convinced her that so far from intending to leave, I was most interested. But I never saw the lady in the sacque again, and I could never find out anything about her.

1922: The Magic Mountain *written in 1924 by THOMAS MANN (1875–1955), probably the greatest German novelist of the century, contains several vivid and realistic descriptions of séances that have convinced experts that the author must have been an eyewitness to parapsychical events. After his death, a little-known essay entitled simply, "Occult Experiences", confirmed this fact. In it, Mann describes sitting in on a séance in Munich in 1922 conducted by Dr Albert von Schrenck-Notzing with the physical medium Rudi Schneider, and the remarkable events that took place in . . .*

THE ROOM OF APPARITIONS

During my lifetime I have remained rather distant from questions of occultism. I was only interested in them in a theoretically sympathetic way, leaving – with a good will – things to take care of themselves. Then one day I was invited to a séance organised by von Schrenck-

Notzing, with the famous Rudi as medium. I was given the task of holding the control. In an uncomfortable position, bent over, without a backrest, but unconscious of these inconveniences, I held on to Rudi's wrists and was moved by his painful efforts.

Soon the young man had fallen into a trance between my hands. I had never before witnessed such a state; and, persuaded that here was a remarkably significant set of circumstances, I gave them rapt attention. There followed a long period of waiting for the manifestations. During this time the participants were supposed to chat for a while and then become quiet again. A zoology professor played the accordion, an old music box was set in motion, all this to help bring on the apparitions.

Finally the thing that from all evidence was not possible nevertheless took place! May I be struck by lightning if I'm lying! Before my eyes, which were free of any kind of influence and were equally disposed to see nothing if there weren't anything to see, the thing occurred; not once but repeatedly: as soon as it was lowered the drapery rose again toward the light, quicker this time than before; and there I saw with indisputable clarity, coming from the inside, intermingled and clutched together, the members of a hooked organ which was thinner than a human hand, like a claw, sinking, then rising. . . . When it had risen up there for the third time, the drapery was violently shaken by something invisible. . . . Several times the Baron asked me if I saw, if I could see everything clearly.

Of course, how could I not see? I would have had to close my eyes, whereas I had never before opened them so intensely. I have seen on this earth things more grandiose, more beautiful, more imposing; but that the impossible, in spite of its impossibility, should take place, that I had never yet seen.

And so I kept repeating, overwhelmed: "Very good! Very good!" . . . all the while feeling a certain uneasiness. I was holding the wrists of Rudi, which were covered by his sweater sleeves, and right next to me I could see his knees firmly held by the Polish man. It was impossible (there was not even the shadow of a possibility) to think that this sleeping boy could have done *here* what was going on up *there*. Who, then? Nobody! There was no one present who could have done it; and nevertheless it was done. Again I felt a vague uneasiness."

The seance went on. The little hand bell has just been grasped and it is impossible that a hand did it. By what other than a hand, then, can the handle of a bell be grasped? It is lifted up, held at an angle, high up, and rings loudly; then, in a circle, carried across part of the room, rings once again; then, in a loud clamor it is thrown in one swoop under the chair of a participant!

And that sort of thing goes on. As soon as the Baron has taken the bell out of the basket, the latter begins to waddle, is pushed, wavers, turns upside down and, in that position, is seized and lifted very high in the air; in a half-vertical position it hovers up there for four or five seconds, in a space dazzling with luminous, opaque red rays, then falls to the floor."

On my word of honor, our ears are hearing the tapping of the typewriter which had been set some distance away on the floor. This is all crazy! After what has just happened, it is ridiculous, stupefying, revolting in its very absurdity, extremely attractive in its extravagance.

Who is typing on the machine? Nobody. Nobody is stretched out on the carpet over there and nobody is using the machine in the darkness. And yet it is being used! It is operating as if under the hands of a capable typist; when a line is finished the little warning bell rings, the carriage is brusquely pushed back, a new line is begun."

In front of the curtain there appears, fleetingly, an oblong, immaterial thing, casting a pale whitish light; it is of the size and approximately the form of a section of forearm with a closed hand, not precisely identifiable. Hurriedly, the thing rises and sinks several times demonstratively, lights up, while, coming from its right flank, a white flash completely blots out its shape, and everything disappears. The séance is then declared over.

After having seen for myself, I consider it my duty to testify that, by any human estimation, all possibility of mechanical fraud, prestidigitation or illusionism must be excluded from the experiences in which I participated."

What, in sum, did I see? Two-thirds of my readers will reply: "Charlatanism, sleight of hand, hoax." Some day, however, when our knowledge of these things will have progressed, when this realm becomes broadly known, they will deny having uttered such a judgment; right now, even if they consider me as a hysterical person easily duped and played upon, they ought to have been impressed by the testimony of experimenters like the French scientist Gustave Geley, who finished his report with this categorical declaration: *I don't say that during this séance there wasn't a hoax; but that the very possibility of a hoax did not exist.* My position is identical. . . .

1924: *Few authors have written of nature with more knowledge and understanding than HENRY WILLIAMSON (1895–1977) whose* Tarka The Otter *(1927) has become a classic and, tragically, was on the first day of filming when he died. To escape the horrors of life in the army in the trenches during the First World War, Williamson moved to Devon and the countryside there provided him with the inspiration for many of his novels. The events which he describes enveloping him in this essay written for the* Daily Telegraph *also occurred in Devon, but were not imaginary and their implication provided him with a rare insight into . . .*

THE UNSEEN WORLD

One evening, forty and more years ago, while I was exploring a sunken lane in North Devon, the sky clouded over and soon rain was falling, as they said locally, "like aught out of sieve". Wide streams of water were pouring down the narrow gulley past me. There was nothing for it but to keep going and hope to find shelter. Near the top of the hill I came upon a ruinous thatched cottage. Entry was through a porch nearly obscured by withering bines of wild clematis.

I got through a broken casement window, followed by my spaniel. There was the usual one room, the kitchen downstairs, with its open hearth and cloam ovens on either side. Now for a fire. As soon as the downpour stopped I searched for wood outside, and noticed something white in the weeds of the garden. It was the skull of a dog; some of the teeth had gone from a long narrow jaw – greyhound or lurcher. Usually there was a lurcher, for silent rabbiting at night, in every hamlet at that time – the early twenties.

The few sticks I had picked up were wet, so I went up a narrow staircase, to where two small bedrooms were divided by the usual laths, nailed to upright studs, to hold the plaster. The dividing wall had partly fallen, and with an armful of trailing laths I went downstairs, broke them up, and lit a fire.

My spaniel, all this time, had shown uneasiness. Now he was whimpering, keeping close to me, as I knelt to blow under pale flame rising tenuously out of wavering smoke. By means of continually breathing upon the damp mass I got the fire going; and to keep it going with lengths of dry-rotted floorboards. At last ruddy flames were flickering on the walls, and limewashed ceiling.

The fire sank, I made it up. It consumed itself twice again, while rain outside fell steadily. We were in for a night of it. I lay down contentedly to sleep, secure with thoughts of no more Flanders trenches. And then I became aware of moonlight, wasted by low vapour everywhere, while the dog was pressed against my side, shivering. The change from sleep to that state of mind known as wide-awake seemed to have been instant. One was filled by a mournful feeling, as though one were turning to stone. The spaniel was trembling against one, suspended in pallid gloom; the spaniel was clawing my jacket, trying to get away from a grey movement on the floor under the window. I saw it divide into several parts, which moved away and then drew together again, coming towards where I was lying. The dog, with a howl of fear, leapt at the window space, and crashed through glass and rotten wooden frame.

The noise woke me up. I had been dreaming. I knew that with immense relief. Yet the spaniel was gone, the casement shattered. When I went outside, the south-west rains had blown inland, the night was starry. *But there was no moon.*

Later, the landlord of the village inn told me about the last tenant of the cottage. He was an old pensioner who lived alone with several dogs, two of them lurchers, which regularly brought him rabbits at night. One Friday he didn't turn up at the post office for his five-shilling pension, and when he didn't appear the next day the constable went up to his cottage. Both door and casement being fastened from within, where the dogs were barking, he returned for the sergeant, and pushed in a pane of glass in the casement in order to unhasp the fastening. Such was the ferocity of the lurchers, one actually thrusting its bared teeth through the small opening, that they decided to throw in poisoned meat.

The old soldier had died in his bed; the dogs had been faithful to the last. Their master was laid in consecrated ground, the dogs in the garden. The cottage became ruinous, for no one cared to occupy it after what had happened. Indeed, it was said to be haunted. I wonder . . . No! I do not wonder. There is a phrase in the Bible which expresses what one feels about the unseen world which surely is all about us. *The very stones cry out . . .*

1928: *As an advocate of the theory of reincarnation and ancestral memory, JOAN GRANT (1907–89) caused a sensation when publicizing her groundbreaking novel,* Winged Pharaoh *(1937), a first-person account of life in Ancient Egypt, by declaring she had lived there in the first of her thirty-one lives. Her other books have also revealed a profound knowledge of the supernatural and she un-*

doubtedly experienced some very unusual phenomena during her lifetime, including this account of an encounter in 1928 with . . .

SOMETHING UTTERLY MALIGN

On one of our Sundays off my husband Leslie and I went to Rothiemurchus intending to climb towards the Cairngorms. It was a beautiful day and we had it to ourselves. Basking naked in the sun, we ate sandwiches beside a burn. It was far too hot and peaceful for serious walking, so we decided to wander on for another mile or so, and then go for dinner to the hotel in Aviemore. Nothing could have been farther from my mind than spooks when suddenly I was seized with such terror that I turned and in panic fled back along the path. Leslie ran after me, imploring me to tell him what was wrong. I could only spare breath enough to tell him to run faster, faster. Something – utterly malign, four-legged and yet obscenely human, invisible and yet solid enough for me to hear the pounding of its hooves, was trying to reach me. If it did I should die, for I was far too frightened to know how to defend myself. I had run about half a mile when I burst through an invisible barrier behind which I was safe. I knew I was safe now, though a second before I had been in mortal danger; knew it as certainly as though I were a *torero* who has jumped the barrier in front of a charging bull.

A year later one of Father's professors described an almost exactly similar experience he had had when bug-hunting in the Cairngorms. He was a materialist, but had been so profoundly startled that he wrote to *The Times* – and received a letter from a reader who had also been pursued by the "Thing." Some years later, when I was living at Muckerach, the doctor told me that two hikers, for whom search-parties had been out three days, had been found dead. He showed me the exact spot on the map. It was the place of my terror. Both men were under thirty. One came from Grantown, the other from Aviemore. The weather was fine. They had spent a good night under the shelter-stone on the highest ridge, for they had written to that effect in the book which is kept up there. They were found within a hundred yards of each other, sprawled face downward as though they had fallen headlong when in flight. "I did a post-mortem on them both," said the doctor gravely. "Never in my life have I seen healthier corpses: not a thing wrong with either of the poor chaps except that their hearts stopped. I put 'heart failure' on the chit, but it is my considered opinion that they died of fright."

1941: The tradition of telling ghost stories at Christmas is a long one and owes much to Charles Dickens and the stories he wrote for magazines for the festive season. The poet and novelist ROBERT GRAVES (1895–1985), author of the imaginative reconstruction of the Roman way of life, I Claudius *(1934), was fascinated by the supernatural and in a special Christmas article for* Picture Post *on 27 December 1941, described what he had felt and heard and seen in haunted places which had led him to some remarkable conclusions on . . .*

WHAT I BELIEVE ABOUT GHOSTS

One may look at ghosts from either the religious, or the scientific, or the commonsense point of view.

John Wesley argued that, since it is a Christian's duty to believe the Bible, and since if he believes the Bible he must believe that the Witch of Endor raised the ghost of Samuel at the request of King Saul, therefore there are ghosts.

The scientific view is that one cannot deny that ghosts exist, in the same positive way that one denies, on zoological grounds, the existence of centaurs or mermaids. A great many people claim to have seen ghosts, and the duty of scientists is to interpret in scientific language, if possible, what they mean by this. The interpretation is difficult, partly because scientists no longer agree on the old distinction between subjective and objective experience, partly because ghosts are not good subjects for laboratory experiment. Sir Henry Head, the neurologist, told me some years ago that only a single type of ghost had so far proved amenable to scientific treatment. This was the tall, glowering ghost that stands silent and immovable by one's sickbed. He said that this ghost, which appears in Japanese prints as well as in clinical reports from European hospitals, corresponds with a particular kind of brain lesion and can be moved round with the bed. But he added that it was too much to hope that all ghosts could be simply explained as "phantas-magorial projections of a traumatic neurosis."

Far too much. The commonsense view is, I think, that one should accept ghosts very much as one accepts fire – a more common but equally mysterious phenomenon. What is fire? It is not really an element, not a principle of motion, not a living creature – not even a disease, though a house can catch it from its neighbours. It is an event rather than a thing or a creature. Ghosts, similarly, seem to be events rather than things or creatures – and nearly always disagreeable events.

I reckon among ghosts the nameless and disembodied hauntings of particular stretches of road, clearings in forests, bare hill-tops. I have twice met with powerful examples of this phenomenon. The first occasion was in 1921 on a hill-top near Cwmbychan in North Wales, where there was an ancient British earthwork; the second was in the Spanish island of Majorca, in 1932, on the lonely coast road near Deyá, where it is said there was once a temple of Diana. On each occasion it was dusk with a waxing moon, and I felt that sudden inexplicable dread that makes the hair of one's head rise like the fur of an angry cat and the legs run with no sense of effort, as if one were skating. Previously, I had thought that when Shakespeare wrote about the haunted ship in *The Tempest*:

> Not a soul
> But felt a fever of the mad and played
> Some trick of desperation . . . Ferdinand
> With hair upstaring – then like reeds, not hair –
> Cried "Hell is empty and all the devils are here!"

he was writing poetical nonsense. Now I know that he was giving a not exaggerated account of a disagreeable physical fact. The Greeks had a word for this sort of dread – "Panic" – meaning the fear that suddenly struck them in woods or on hills when the god Pan was about. I conclude that the spots where it is experienced have once been the scene of religious rites in which horror has been conjured up among the worshippers, and that the rocks and stones still occasionally sweat out that horror.

Haunted houses seem to enclose sharp individual horror centred in a particular room, or else a general feeling of misery, sorrow, boredom or vice which pervades the whole building. Sensitive people can tell the difference between a happy house and an unhappy one as soon as they cross the threshold. But most of them would be ashamed to tell the house agent or caretaker: "I'd rather pay a thousand pounds than rent this place – it has an evil atmosphere." They say instead: "I'm afraid, you know, that my husband would find that dressing room far too small, and there isn't enough space for his books in the sitting-room. And the garden is much too large for just the two of us."

The Chinese are a more practical nation. I am told that the house-hunter there can usually choose between "a modest residence with a good *feng-sui*" (personal atmosphere) and "a palatial mansion with a bad *feng-sui*" – both offered at the same price in dollars. If he is a man of virtue and industry, with a large, virtuous and industrious family, he may be wise to invest in the bad house and restore its original value by the irreproachable emanations of his household. A house, near Braintree in Essex, where I often stay, and which originally belonged to Wm Benlowes, Sergeant-at-Law in the reign of Mary I, used to have an extremely bad *feng-sui*, and had passed through a succession of unpleasant hands before my friends bought it. They have now reclaimed all but the spare bedroom, where there is something that wakes one up with a start nearly every night at a quarter to two – it was a quarter to four when I was there last, because of Double Summer Time – the distinct presence of someone, it seems to be a woman, in great terror. This is evidently a ghost of long standing, because three years ago, when the beams were scraped, a small piece of parchment – which I have examined – was found in a bolt hole. It was a Latin prayer in Tudor handwriting, the conventional charm against evil spirits:

O mitis Jesu, libera nos (Sweet Jesus, deliver us!)

Haunting of the disembodied sort is a matter of degree. Every house that has had a previous occupant is, in a sense, haunted. For my part I would rather live in an ordinary moated grange where a Grey Lady or Headless Monk walks regularly than in a house that has been used as a reformatory, a lunatic asylum, or a Victorian boarding school. The walls are usually so soaked with miserable brooding that only fire could cleanse them.

Of houses in which I have stayed for a time the two most unpleasant were the ancient stone-built house of Maesyneuadd, in the hills near Talsarnau in N. Wales; and a top flat in a modern block, built by a Belgian company, in the main street of Heliopolis, near Cairo.

At Maesyneuadd, when I was staying there with friends soon after the last war, uncomfortable things were continually happening. Doors opened and shut without a draught, quite stiff ones, too. There were rappings on the walls of empty rooms, and one evening I saw a shade jump off a reading-lamp in poltergeist fashion. There was a long tradition there of owners who had drunk themselves to death from boredom, and one had hanged himself in the garret. On New Year's Eve of 1919–20 we were all sitting round the fire in the drawing-room, mulling claret. I was on the right of the semi-circle and put my tumbler to cool on the side-table at the corner of the fireplace. When I reached for it again, two or three minutes later, it had been drained dry. Nobody had moved from the semi-circle of chairs and nobody had come into the room. I don't say that the ghost had drained it – but certainly I had not, and a horror descended on us that the warm wine and the pleasant smell of nutmeg and lemon-peel could not disperse.

The Heliopolis flat was far worse. I rented it for a month in 1926 from an Assyrian widow, because it was the only vacant one in the town, and I had to find temporary lodgings for my young family. It was full of gaudy furniture in bamboo and red plush and I remember a locked glass bookcase containing Hebrew books and a small French legal library. My Sudanese servants said at once that they didn't like the place, and later, complained that there were *afreets* (evil spirits) about. I told them that it was only for a month, so they did not give notice. The sense of evil grew thicker and thicker as the days passed. Soon the *afreets* were almost visible, coming as apparitions between waking and sleeping, and as little black creatures, seen only from the corner of one's eye, doing nasty things in the shadow of the sofa or bookcase. The most alarming phenomenon was the sudden whiff of burning that constantly spread through the flat even when there was no fire in the kitchen. The servants afterwards told us – I don't know how truly – that the Assyrian husband had been burned to death in the flat some months before, and it had since been used as a disorderly house. But even this was not enough to account for the strength of our impressions. Perhaps someone had been monkeying about with black magic there; black magic is a means of reviving and focusing ancient evil, and anyone sufficiently idle, cruel and curious can achieve horrible results without much difficulty. But since it was not worth while to attempt a reclamation of the flat we cleared out after ten days and took rooms in a hotel.

On the whole, I consider ghosts an unimportant and far less mysterious phenomenon than many others – for example, poetry and love. People who manage their lives well leave only gracious emanations behind them. It is the wastrels, the bores and the deliberately evil who give a place a bad name. The ghosts they leave behind should be sternly disregarded, as one disregards drunks who stop one in the street and begin a rambling hard-luck tale mixed with threats and hiccoughs. One should show neither sympathy, embarrassment nor alarm.

Another sort of ghost, which since J W Dunne's *Experiment With Time* has scientific as well as commonsense justification, is what may be called the "cosmic accident." In 1938, three friends and myself rented a chateau, La Chevrie, a few miles from Rennes, in Brittany. Five of the chimneys were full of bees, there were crickets behind the library fire, bats in the attics, rats in the cellar, but the *feng-sui* was excellent. One day I found, in a box of rubbish, an ancient sheet of cooking recipes, and began deciphering and translating them. There was one for *Blanc-Manger*, which began: "On the evening before, put two pieces of fish-glue as big as your thumb (or else gelatine) to melt on the embers. The next morning bring it to the boil. Take one and a half *quintons* of sweet almonds and half a *quinton* of bitter almonds . . ." Late that night I was crouching at the kitchen fire, blowing up the embers with the bellows to heat a coffee-pot. I was thinking to myself: "Melt the fish-glue on the embers . . . but I think gelatine would taste nicer . . . I wonder how much a *quinton* of almonds is. . . ."

Suddenly a woman's voice behind me called out sharply: "Marthe!"

"*Oui, Madame*," I answered automatically.

But of course no one was there. As I did not believe in the absolutely reality of time I was not greatly surprised. I told myself afterwards: "It was cosmic coincidence. Somehow, by thinking about the fish-glue and the embers and the almonds, I strayed into another region of time. Marthe's mistress, seeing me squatting over the embers in the half-light with my back turned, naturally mistook me for Marthe. She must have got a shock when I stood up and she saw a tall, dark man in black corduroy trousers: In fact, probably I was her ghost, not she mine."

Madame's voice, by the way, did not sound in my outer ear, so to speak, but in my inner ear as voices do when one is just waking up.

I have only once seen a daylight ghost. That was in France, in June, 1915, when I was with the B.E.F. A soldier called Private Challoner had been in my company at Wrexham when I was serving with the Royal Welch Fusiliers. When he went out with a draft to join the 1st Battalion he shook my hand and said "I'll meet you again in France, sir." I was sent out myself a month or two later, but I got posted to another regiment, the Welsh. One evening in June, while it was still light, my company mess, in billets at Béthune, were celebrating a safe return from Cuinchy trenches. We had fresh fish, new potatoes, green peas, asparagus, mutton chops, strawberries and cream and three bottles of Pommard. While we were singing very noisily – a medley of church anthems and drinking songs – Challoner looked in at the open window, saluted, grinned and passed on. There was no mistaking him or his cap-badge. No Royal Welch Fusiliers were billeted within miles of Béthune at the time. I jumped up and rushed to the window, but saw nothing except a fag-end smoking on the pavement. Challoner had been killed at Festubert, a few miles away, in the futile May 16 offensive.

I don't know how to account for this, but since Challoner's battalion had been in Béthune shortly before his death, there may have been a slight cosmic accident, assisted by my memory of his last words to me and (if you insist) by three or four glasses of Pommard.

1945: *Cornwall is again the setting for an uncanny story by one of last century's great female novelists, DAPHNE DU MAURIER (1907–89), who lived for most of her life on the south coast and featured it in several of her most popular books, notably* Rebecca *(1939) with its immortal opening line, "Last night I dreamt I went to Manderlay again." In an area steeped with legends, it is not surprising that Daphne du Maurier should have woven supernatural elements into a number of her plots. An event that occurred not long after she moved into her famous home at Menabilly caused her to wonder if she herself had been part of a "vision of the future" as she explains in . . .*

THE LADY IN BLUE

It was in 1945 when I moved to my house, Menabilly, at Par in Cornwall that I had a very strange experience. The house was a seventeenth-century mansion overlooking the sea and St Austell Bay and seemed like the ideal setting for the book I was writing, *The King's General*, about a family riven by war and haunted by a grisly discovery.

I was told that the house was haunted. That a "lady in blue" – late Victorian or even Edwardian – had been seen looking out of a bedroom window. But I was quite unable to find who it was that had actually seen this lady in blue.

Ever since then it has amused me to imagine that the lady in blue was not a phantom of the past, but a peep into the future. For when I was writing *The King's General*, I wrote it in the room where the lady was supposed to appear. I also frequently looked out of the window for inspiration and invariably wore a blue smock while I was working.

So perhaps the Victorian or Edwardian person walking across the lawn in 1910 had looked up and seen somebody of 1945 at the window!

1948: *An unfurnished house in Brighton had become impossible to let because of its reputation of being haunted when the novelist and broadcaster ALGERNON BLACKWOOD (1869–1951) decided to spend a night there in 1948. The author, who had become known as "The Ghost Man" because of his supernatural experiences in Canada, America and Britain, which he had turned into numerous short stories, was not daunted by the task – but admitted later to being quite unprepared for what happened that night at . . .*

THE MIDNIGHT HOUR

In the distant days when I was so eager to *see* a ghost with my own eyes. I recall a singular example of the strange effects of terror; and I don't mean the terror of meeting a tiger, or a burglar face to face with a pistol raised; I mean spiritual or ghostly terror, whichever you prefer.

I've always felt a psychological interest in these alleged effects of terror: paralysis of movement, speechlessness, hair turning white (apparently quite unsubstantiated) and the rest. With regard to the latter, you may know the delightful tale of the old lady who was so terrified by a ghost that her wig, carefully draped on the dressing-table, was white next morning.

But coming back to my own personal experiences, I once came across a result of terror that was quite new to me. If you don't want to hear about it, just turn over the page to the enchanting pictures you will find. If you care to listen, however, may I add, before my little tale, that it was only years later I came across a reference to this particular effect of ghostly terror in Kipling. It is the only reference I know. Kipling, you must admit, was a prince of accurate observations. He mentions it. All right. If you're still reading, here's what happened.

Eager to see a ghost with my own eyes, I was lucky enough to get advance notice of haunted houses the Psychical Research Society considered worth investigating, cases, that is, with good evidence behind them. Among these was a certain unfurnished house in a Brighton square. The story was horrible. A manservant in the household, crazily in love with a housemaid, had crashed the girl over the banisters to her death. The evidence of the crime, as also the evidence supporting its alleged re-enactment in ghostly terms, was overwhelming.

Rather by subterfuge, I got the keys of the empty house from the Brighton agents, and I well recall the agent's admission, when I pressed him, that the house was said to be haunted. That admission (from a house agent) took some getting, but I got it. And I planned to spend a night in this unfurnished, empty haunted house.

I had arranged to take a sister with me, but at the last moment she got "cold feet". She just couldn't face it. Nor did I blame her. In the daylight of the sunny Brighton front it was easy; when the dusk fell and shadows began to creep, it was different. It so happened that our hostess exclaimed suddenly. "Oh, I'll come, if you want a companion. I don't believe in this ghostly stuff and, anyhow, I don't care a damn!"

We went together. It was about 11.30 p.m. The night was still. No wind. And the sound of the surf fell booming through the deserted square as we made our quiet way, not talking much, I noticed. A moon, almost at the full, silvered the empty square and silent streets. Everybody seemed in bed. My companion, my hostess, whom I knew slightly, was a youngish woman, gay, cheery, chatty. But as we entered the square and approached the house, her chatty volubility, I noticed, died away. It was all so silent, so deserted. The bright moonlight, the booming of the surf, these alone struck our senses. We padded on together then in silence towards the empty house. I recall wishing I had been alone. I didn't quite like her increasing silence.

And then we reached the house in the corner of the square. It looked menacing to me in that blaze of moonlight. I had brought with me a thermos, candles, matches, food, and a rug. First making sure there was no one in sight, above all a wandering bobby, we mounted the steps and I put the key in. Once inside, I closed the front door behind me and took out my matchbox. For this was before the days of electric torches. I must mention. And as I opened the box, there was a sound of someone coughing close beside me. There, standing in the darkness of the entrance hall, someone coughed. It was a man's cough, I swear.

It gave me a nasty turn, I admit. There was someone else in the empty house besides our two selves. There was no possible doubt in my mind about that cough. It was close beside me as I stood in that darkened hall. It was a natural, not a premeditated cough. A shiver ran up my back. Yet, that strange thing, as later interrogation proved, was that my companion had *not* heard it. It came to my ears only. Now, please remember that of seeing a ghost I had no faintest fear. I was burning to see one. I had no fear of that kind, for my interest was far stronger than any superstitious terror. But that cough, close against my ears in the darkness – well, it gave me a nasty turn as I've said. And, to make things worse. I had opened my matchbox upside-down, so that its contents scattered on to the stone floor – and had to be picked up. A rat, a mouse even, anything might start a fire. Laboriously, while my friend said nothing, I picked them up – and lit my candle.

So, here and now, was the immediate problem. Somebody else besides ourselves was in this empty, unfurnished house. They might be crooks, using a haunted house as their hiding place. A dozen explanations flashed through my mind. But, at any rate, we must first search the house from floor to ceiling.

Persuading my companion with some difficulty that this was first necessary, we carried it out faithfully from the kitchen and scullery to the servants' rooms on the top floor. A nasty, creepy business, I admit it was, expecting any minute to see a face in the shadows or a figure slinking round a door. I think the servants' attics were the worst. It was here of course, the murderer had found his victim before he crashed her over the banisters to her death. We found – we saw – nothing; and eventually, we sat up to wait for events in a small room at the top of the stairs leading from the attics to the lower floors. We sat on the large boards, a lit candle shining through the door of a half-open cupboard . . . waiting, waiting, waiting, and listening, listening, listening. We spoke little, and for some reason in whispers only. The moonlight fell in slantingly across the floor. We just heard the distant booming of the surf at the end of the square. Otherwise there was silence, silence broken only by our rare whispered remarks.

I was expectant, keyed up, hopeful. I admit it. But I had no sense of fear. If, by any lucky chance, as the hours wore on, there came a voice, step, or some evidence of anybody moving. I was ready, on the instant, to jump up and investigate. I *might*, God knows, see the terrified housemaid in full flight down the stairs, I *might* see the love-crazed man full tilt at her heels, hunting her down to her terrible death, I *might*, with any luck, see a ghost at last!

For my companion, so eagerly did I sit there waiting as the hours passed, I admit I had little thought; and then – suddenly – it struck me: "Does she feel the same? Is she perhaps a bit scared? Could she jump up and come with me?" I think her prolonged silence made me suddenly ask these questions. And I imagine an unwelcome doubt about her state of mind caused them.

We were sitting, as I said, side by side on the bare boards of the little room at the top of the stairs. The candlelight through the opened door of the cupboard made her face plainly visible. I glanced down at her sideways.

"If we hear a step or a voice," I whispered, "we ought to go out and investigate it at once. Are you all right?"

But the sight of her face froze me stiff. She did not answer. Her face, not uncomely, had somehow gone back to the face of childhood. It was the face of a girl, lines and wrinkles all ironed out. It was a face masked by utter terror, its youthfulness somehow terrible.

My own reactions were immediate. I must get her out of the house. My mind worked quickly at that moment. If a step or a voice had come outside on the stairs or landing, she could not have moved for terror. I realised that. Her terror had been growing, increasing for hours evidently, but I had not noticed it. Had anything "ghostly" intervened just then, she would simply have passed out. I knew it. I felt sure of it. I must get her out of the house at once. To be caught in an empty house with an unconscious young woman on my hands at 2 a.m., with police and press inquisitive, publicity and the rest, would have been an unenviable situation.

And so it was. Explaining as convincingly as I could that nothing was now likely to happen – it was almost early morning and we had sat waiting for hours – I took her arm and we crawled together, side by side down the long stairs and so out into the street and the fresh keen air blowing from the sea. And she told me frankly that for hours, she had been too scared to move or speak, not even whisper.

And, as I mentioned, it was only years later that I came across a short story of Kipling's where he mentions this strange effect of real terror that blots out the adult face and masks with the innocence of childhood. My experience at least can claim this backing from a close observer. An unusual thrill had certainly come my way though it was not, after all, the thrill I had hoped for, the thrill of seeing a ghost at last.

1953: *Children feature in quite a number of ghost stories – usually tragic little figures who have died young or been brutally murdered, leaving their spirits to haunt the locality where they passed away. NICHOLAS MONSARRAT (1910–79) was a freelance writer who served with distinction in the Royal Navy during the Second World War and later wrote one of the classic books of the era,* The Cruel Sea *(1951). He had a deep interest in the traumas of the young, too – one of his first novels was* This Is The Schoolroom *(1937) – and never*

forgot an experience in Quebec in 1953 which he later described in
an unsettling portrait of . . .

THE HAUNTED CHILD

This story was told me by a man who was a stranger, and an actor as
well, so it may well have been a pack of lies. But the circumstances of
its telling – near midnight, in a shooting-lodge in northern Quebec,
with the first snowfall lying two feet deep outside, and the bare pine
forest sighing all round us, and the wind howling authentically in the
huge stone chimney – the circumstances were so eerie that belief was
easy, and a prickling fear even easier.

Here is what the stranger – call him George – told me, on that
memorable night. I think he told it to me because I had said something about his son, a boy of eight or nine, who was also staying at
the lodge, though now safely in his bunk upstairs.

The boy had the most astonishing eyes I had ever seen – really
enormous, bright blue, staring at the universe as if he did not believe
any of it. When he had first looked at me, I felt as if I were myself
gazing through a window into unfathomable depths, into a different
world altogether.

Now, when I said something about this George answered: "He's
always looked like that." Then he told me his story.

George was originally Hungarian, though he had lived in Canada
nearly all his adult life, and had become thoroughly "Canadianised"
– so much so that he played Canadian parts on television. He had
married a Canadian girl, and as soon as a baby – the boy upstairs –
was on the way, his mother had come from Hungary to help at the
birth of her first grandchild, and then to stay on with the family.

She was an old woman, of peasant stock, who spoke no English;
and she was very shocked at what Canada had done to her son – the
different customs, the different language, the smart wife, the urban
gloss over everything. She seemed to have a morbid fear that this
would happen to her grandson, that he would know nothing of his
forebears and lose all trace of his true homeland. She begged to be
allowed to bring him up in her own way.

"Let me have four years," she said, again and again. "Just a little
time – enough for the language and some of the old customs. Then he
will be yours again."

For the sake of peace and quiet – and also, George inferred,
because his mother would probably make a better job of the
upbringing than his wife – they agreed.

But just after the baby was born, the old lady died.

The boy grew up good-looking, healthy and obedient; and absolutely normal except for one thing. He never spoke a word: not at 18 months, not at two years, not at three. He just stared at his surroundings with those huge blue eyes, without uttering a syllable or making a sound. Neither doctors nor specialists could do anything, nor suggest anything to reassure the worried parents. The boy was perfectly healthy. Perhaps he was a late developer.

One night, when the boy was about three years old, George and his wife returned home late from a party. They heard a voice from an upstairs room – a voice which could not have been the maid's. They went up to their son's bedroom, and there they found him. He was standing up in his cot, staring fixedly at one corner of the room, and talking sixteen to the dozen. It was a language unknown to his mother, familiar though half-forgotten by his father. It was Hungarian.

Next day, said George, the child was silent again, and he remained silent for another whole year. Then, when he was four years old, he suddenly became perfectly normal – except for those astonishing eyes, and a strong Hungarian accent as soon as he started, quite confidently, to speak English.

1955: *Ghosts are found all over the world, of course, and though they have different traditions are essentially alike in the emotions they generate among eyewitnesses. ANTHONY BURGESS (1917–93), author of the cult novel about the exploitation of evil, A Clockwork Orange (1962), worked for several years as a teacher in Malaya where he became steeped in the culture and superstitions of the people and underwent an experience that was stranger than any fiction when he came face to face with a . . .*

HANTU

The malay word for "ghost" is *hantu*, which, being so like the English "haunt", suggests an ultimate tie-up somewhere in a pre-Sanskrit language. *Hantu-hantu* means "ghosts of all kinds," which Malaya certainly has – the graveyard *hantu*, for instance, which gets out of the grave in its winding sheet and rolls rapidly around; the *hantu* of the kitchen, which throws things about until appeased with an invitation to a party; the female *hantu* which is mostly floating entrails and a cry of "*Su su su*," a great feeder on the blood of new-born infants. For the *hantu* which my wife and I met there is no particular name: it was one of the forlorn spirits let violently loose by the Japanese during their occupation of Malaya.

We lived in King's Pavilion, the old Residency of Kuala Kangsar, which is the royal town of the state of Perak. The bigger of the two bathrooms was a fine Hollywood affair with mosaic tiles, but it had been desecrated by being turned into a Japanese torture-chamber – highly convenient, since there were drains set in the floor for easy swabbing-out, and blood could flow down these as well as water. There were, however, great dried blood-pools all over the mosaic, and these could not be cleaned off. The little *amah* tried hard enough when she could be persuaded to enter the bathroom, but she hated it – indeed, she hated the whole house. "This bad place," she said, "in Japanese time."

That the bathroom was haunted there could be no doubt. My wife and I always found it cold, even in all that heat, but not pleasantly cold. The chill was somehow obscene, as though it were trying to turn itself into a bad smell. We used the other bathroom instead, and this was neutral, too small anyway ever to have been useful as an interrogation chamber. But it was not possible to ignore the major bathroom: it was next to the master bedroom, and its very door seemed to radiate cold. It was an inescapable presence.

It erupted into an active presence when Yusof, the cook, went screaming round the verandah one day with cries about a *hantu*. Calmer, he told a confused story about going into the bedroom to collect *tuan's* shoes for cleaning (a sideline job) and finding the bathroom door half-open. He went to shut it and then saw something horrible. From the bathroom floor a strip of congealed black blood rose in the form of a miniature man and sailed towards Yusof. He banged the door shut and ran yelling.

Whether this apparition really appeared was never the point. The point was not to have servants rushing round the verandah screaming and possibly breaking crockery. To quieten Yusof we performed a mock exorcism ceremony, straight out of the *Rituale Romanum*, complete with a candle and bell, though we were dubious as to whether Oriental ghosts could be exorcized by a Western liturgy.

The next thing that happened was that Yusof (the cook) and the *amah* (whose name was Mas, which means "gold") began, hearing a phantom voice. The voice seemed to be perched, like an invisible transistor radio, on one of the ventilator grilles that brought air into the bathroom from the verandah. This time, for some reason, they were not frightened. The voice was gentle, they said, and it seemed to complain a good deal, though never in anger, and they swore that it spoke Chinese – a language which they didn't understand. One evening they came to us in the sitting-room and said, without fear, that the voice had just started up: would we ourselves listen?

We went with them to the verandah. Sure enough, a voice was quacking quietly and monotonously away from the ventilator grille. It was not possible to put a sex to the voice, but it was certainly there, and it was certainly not explicable in rational terms. I thought of the usual things – the metal grille acting as a sort of loudspeaker and picking up the news in Cantonese or Mandarin from somebody's radio; a quirky echo from somewhere – but the *hantu* explanation seemed the easiest and hence the best. It was strange that four of us should be standing there and listening – interested, wonderstruck, but not frightened. But what was the voice saying?

It was difficult to persuade one of my Chinese colleagues – whose name I have forgotten but whom I will call Guan Moh-chan – to come in as interpreter for a *hantu*, but he eventually humorously consented, though he had many fruitless, though not whiskyless, evenings of waiting before the voice started again from the grille.

It's still all so clear; the single bare bulb on the verandah ceiling, with flying ants thudding about it; a loud radio from the town; the last *waktu* called from the mosque by the *bilal*; the five hours of standing around, listening to the tinny voice from three feet above our heads. Guan spoke courteously to the *hantu*, asked and answered questions. "It is Hakka it speaks," he told us. And then he gave a long speech to it, garnished with courtly hand-movements and deferential smiles. "Very simple," he then said to us. "It has forgotten its name and its family but it remembers what the Japanese did to it in that room there. All it wishes to do is to go on complaining. I have said that it ought not to interfere with people's lives by continually complaining, and it ought to go and live out there among the banyans in the Residency Gardens. I have told it to try to be a bird."

Guan's counsel must have got home. There was no further quacking and twittering from the ventilator grille, but in the garden, if one walked there at night, the voice could be heard complaining in the air. The complaints were gentle and conventionalised into a kind of bird-chatter. There is a bird called the *burong hantu*, which ought to mean "ghost-bird" but only means "owl". For this kind of garden-ghost there seems to be no term: ours merely became the *hantu King's Pabilion*, Malay possessing no "v". The ghost must still be there.

The bathroom lost its obscene chilliness, and Mas could now be persuaded to enter it and have another try at cleaning the floor. The blood-stains yielded easily to soap and water. Twice, and in the daytime too, the ghost-voice did some good. It cried out when a child went too near a cobra's nest, and it scared two drunken fighting Tamil gardeners and made them desist.

I'm a professional fiction-writer, but none of this is fiction.

1956: *The American writer MIRIAM ALLEN DeFORD (1888– 1975) was a reporter by training and a writer of mystery stories and science fiction by inclination. Her interest in the paranormal developed during her time as contributing editor to* The Humanist *where she remained sceptical about the claims of mediums and certain accounts of haunted houses. This was despite the "jarring phenomena" that beset Miriam and her husband when they bought a cottage in Mill Valley. As she explains in this article for* True Experiences With Ghosts *(1956) it was not possible to explain in "normal" terms what happened in . . .*

THE LITTLE HOUSE ON THE HILL

When the owner showed me the little cottage on a hill in Mill Valley, California, nearly forty years ago, she made a strange remark.

We were on the sun porch, which had big glass windows around three sides. "If these windows ever break," she said, "you will have to pay to have them replaced."

I assured her that it was very unlikely we would ever open them. But a few weeks later I understood what she meant. The windows had heavy hasps, almost beyond my strength to move. On the windiest days they stood firm. But often, on calm, clear days, one of them would suddenly fly open and bang against the trees outside.

Finally, my husband, Maynard Shipley, tried an experiment. He went out on the sun porch and spoke aloud.

"If this is a demonstration of some sort of extrasensory power," he said, "please find another way to demonstrate. We can't afford to have these big windows replaced if you break them."

They never opened again.

But that was not the first "manifestation" to occur in the little house, furnished with the owner's own belongings.

One Saturday afternoon I brought home a bag of fruit. My

husband picked out a pear, then observed that it was too pretty to eat, polished it, and laid it on the bare center table in the living room.

We were both sitting near the table, reading, he facing it and I with my back turned to it, when I heard a strange bumping sound. Subconsciously I counted; there were twelve bumps in all, in rhythmic pairs. I thought he was kicking a table leg, and asked him to stop. He did not answer, and I turned around to see his eyes fixed on the pear.

I was just in time to see its last two vibrations; it was jumping up and down, rising about two inches each time.

Perhaps this is the place to explain that neither my husband nor I believed (nor do I now; he died in 1934) in occult phenomena. He was a writer and lecturer on scientific subjects, I was and am a freelance writer and a labor journalist. We were both agnostics, with no faith in survival of the personality after death. But we both had open minds and we could not deny the evidence of our senses – though the experiences we underwent made neither of us a Spiritualist convert.

In fact, my husband's first thought was that the pear was abnormal – perhaps that some parasite was in it. He cut it open, and it was perfectly sound. As he lifted it from the table there was a tinkle like that of a silver bell, and a tiny whiff of white smoke arose from below the table and was dissipated in the air.

That was the first peculiar phenomenon we witnessed in the cottage. Here are some of the others; I am not including any that were not seen by at least two persons.

There was a whirring, metallic sound sometimes that we tried in vain to locate. Finally we went into the bedroom, the doors and windows of which were closed, so that there was no breeze. Hanging on a nail on one of the doors was a metal coathanger, which was vibrating like mad.

In the bathroom was an old-fashioned bureau with drawers which had brass pulls, so stiff that they stayed in any position in which they were placed. Twice, when my husband entered the room, all the brass pulls began to dance up and down.

In the kitchen was a wooden gadget fastened to the wall, on whose arms we hung various utensils – basting spoons, can openers, spatulas, things of that sort. Frequently when Maynard approached them, all of these started to vibrate.

A door led from the kitchen to the bedroom. It was always closed at night. Every night, precisely at eleven, there would be a sound like that of a wet mop striking the kitchen side of this door. When it was opened, nothing was there.

We brought home a trailing piece of wild blackberry vine and put it in a hanging vase on the living room wall. It started to swing back and forth like a pendulum and kept it up for forty-eight hours. Maynard tried to account for this on scientific grounds, and in fact had an article published in *The Scientific American* in which he discussed the movement as a possible effect of radiant energy on a living plant, since it happened to be halfway between a window into which the sun poured, and a wall light which was on at night. But later, when we tried the experiment with many other plants, the vase did not swing at all.

We heard constant raps, day and night, and nearly every evening small bluish-green lights, like faint electric bulbs, used to move horizontally across the room, about four feet from the floor, and then vanish; this happened in both the living room and the bedroom.

In the living room was an old-fashioned Franklin stove – all the furniture was of turn-of-the-century vintage – which burned wood. In its lid was fixed a common iron stove-lifter. One night, in full electric glare, we saw this lifter raise itself about three inches from the lid and sail horizontally across the room, dropping with a thud on the floor at the other end of the living room. Another time we saw a large china bowl on the top shelf of an open china closet in the kitchen lifted as if somebody had hold of it, and deposited gently on the floor beneath; it was not even cracked.

But the prize exhibit was the folding bed. For those who have never seen such an object, it is a bygone piece of furniture which when closed is just like a big closet door against the wall. This one was in the living room, and we never thought of using it until I was ill with the flu, and my husband tried to sleep in it. (It opened out into a regular double bed.) I say "tried," because every time he got into it he had the distinct impression that he was not alone – that somebody else he couldn't see was in the bed, somebody who didn't want him in it. He stuck it out for three nights, and then he said, "Well, if you want the bed you can have it," and got out and spent the rest of the night in a chair.

After I was well we decided to try an experiment with a weekend guest. Our visitor told everybody that she was "a natural medium" and a devout believer in Spiritualism. So without mentioning anything about the bed we put Genevieve in it. About two o'clock in the morning there was a knock on the bedroom door. Genevieve said she couldn't sleep in that bed because somebody else was in it! We fixed her up on the sun porch, but we never told her why we had given her the folding bed.

We found our Mill Valley "ghosts" extremely interesting, and we hated to leave them when the owner decided to sell the house and we had to move. Later the house was destroyed in a fire which burned all that part of the town.

We never had anything again approaching the crowding phenomena of our "haunted house," but perhaps the "ghosts" did follow us for a while in San Francisco and later in Sausalito, where we lived until my husband's death.

One day I received a letter telling me of the death of a very dear old friend. That evening Maynard and I were washing and drying dishes together in the kitchen of another rented cottage. We were facing the window and it was very dark outside. I was talking to Maynard about my friend, whom he had never known, when suddenly there was a crashing blow at the window – enough, one would think, to have broken it. "Cats," Maynard said, and went outside to look. No cats, no anything. He came in again and we started to talk it over. It came again, just the same as before. This time we didn't even look.

Almost the same thing happened later in another house. This time we were in the dining room. I was seated with my back to the front window, which looked on the porch; my husband sat opposite me, facing it. Again we were talking about somebody recently dead. And again there was a smashing blow at the window. This time Maynard caught a momentary glimpse of something round and white that had struck the blow. But when we both dashed out on the porch, seconds afterward, there was nothing whatsoever there.

In the apartment in which we first lived in Sausalito, there was a big bare kitchen with wooden walls. On a nail on one of the walls hung several big paper shopping bags. We had a close friend whose husband had one day taken a train for a short business journey and had never been seen again; no trace was ever found of him, and nobody knows to this day whether he is alive or dead, though it is probable that he is dead.

One morning at breakfast we were talking about our friend's dilemma; after searching and waiting for several years, she had decided to get a divorce to remedy her anomalous position.

"My own belief is that Charlie is dead," my husband said.

At which moment, suddenly, with no breeze anywhere, all the paper shopping bags on that nail raised themselves slowly to a horizontal position and then as slowly fell back again.

If either of us could be considered a "physical medium" – whatever that really is – it was not I, but my husband, in whose presence metallic objects shook and danced. After he died, I would have given anything, including my life, for some evidence that something of him still lived and could communicate with me – as we had often promised each other to try to do, if it were possible – but it never came. There was just one slight and unexplained happening.

About a week after his death, while I was still living alone in our Sausalito home, preparing to leave it, one of our friends came to visit me. We were sitting before the fireplace, and I was saying to her what I have just said above. There was a silence. And then we both distinctly heard a strange sound. It was like a large, soft, heavy object falling to the ground from a short height – the nearest analogy I could think of was a bag of laundry.

We searched the house systematically, from cellar to attic. Nothing was disturbed nor was there anything out of position that in the least resembled what we both had heard.

Nothing of the sort ever happened to me again. It was not enough evidence.

Only twice in my life, before I met Maynard, have I had inexplicable experiences. Once, in 1917 in Hollywood, I saw a "phantom of the living" – *so distinct that I took it for granted it was the man himself, and spoke to him* – when he vanished. And later that same year, in Spokane, a friend whom I was visiting and I both heard heavy footsteps climbing the cellar stairs to the locked kitchen door, and then cross the floor. We not only searched the house but we called a policeman, who searched again for us with a bored air that we soon understood when a week later, at precisely the same hour, the whole thing happened over again – and several times more. This too was a rented house, and apparently the police had often been called to find the phantom burglar.

I never heard any story to account for this. In our Mill Valley house I made inquiries, and discovered that the owner had lived in the cottage with her old father until he died, and that he slept in the folding bed; that was all. I might add that after we left, she was unable to sell the house after all, and rented it again. I was told by neighbors that it was rented three or four times before the fire, but that nobody every stayed more than a month or two.

As for my husband, he had one other strange experience during our years in Sausalito, though it did not occur there. I tell it to complete the record, though he had only a quasi-witness.

In the course of a lecture tour in northern California, he had a speaking engagement in the town of Woodland. He could not get a hotel room, and had to take a room for the night in an apartment over a grocery store. All night he was kept awake by constant sawing and hammering downstairs; apparently the grocery store was being repaired or remodeled, and the workmen for some reason were doing the job at night. He was very much annoyed when he paid the landlady in the morning, and was about to make some caustic comment when she said, with a queer mixture of bravado and timidity, "Were you able to get any sleep in that room?"

Puzzled, he glanced in at the store when he got outside. It was precisely as he had seen it the night before when he went there after his lecture. There was no sign that any carpentry had been done on it.

Just how and why we should have had that intensive period of unexplained phenomena for the year and a half in Mill Valley, gradually tapering off for three or four years more, and then never recurring, neither of us ever knew. The last thing I can remember of this nature that we experienced was also in our last Sausalito house. One moonlit night I happened to glance from a front window, and saw on the steps leading to the front porch a curious thing – a sort of cone of light, about two feet tall and about a foot at the base, milky and solid-looking in texture. We both went out and stood directly above it; there it sat, looking like crystallized soapsuds, but with the line of the steps visible through it. It glowed faintly as if with its own light; no moonlight struck anywhere near it.

Maynard was all for stooping down and touching it, but I held him back; I had a foolish nervous feeling that it might give him an electric shock, or be in some other way unpleasant to touch. Just then an automobile passed the house, down our hilly street, and instantly the cone vanished. If it had been some trick of light which the auto's headlights had reversed, it should have reappeared when the car had passed. It did not return, and we never saw anything like it again. It was some time later that it occurred to us that the thing, whatever it was, resembled pictures we had seen of ectoplasm.

If my husband was one of those people somehow in tune with so-called parapsychic phenomena, it seems peculiar that he had not had similar experiences in the past, instead of just during this limited period. It may have been that for some reason he was in a particularly receptive condition in those years; or it may have been that I, though not myself a "medium," in some way supplemented his receptivity. The whole question is one which was beyond our powers of explanation. "There can be no such thing as the supernatural," he used to say. "Everything that occurs is a part of nature. All we can say is that these things occurred, that they were not subjective, and that therefore they will be susceptible to scientific explanation some day, even though they are not now."

In an attempt to secure some informed outside judgment of the phenomena, we wrote an account of them and sent it to Dr Walter Franklin Prince, of the Boston Society for Psychic Research. He was extremely interested (though no better able than we to explain our experiences), and intended to publish the account in a forthcoming volume in his series of *Human Experiences*, based on an extensive questionnaire sent out by the Society; but he died before another volume could be compiled.

After Maynard's death I again wrote a statement of what had happened in the Mill Valley house and sent it to Harry Price, the well-known English psychic researcher. He too was both interested and baffled.

About all one can say at the present stage of our comprehension is that the house was "haunted" – whatever that word really means – and that we, and especially my husband, were susceptible media through whom the haunting became objectified. Any more satisfactory elucidation will have to come – for me, at least – as a result of further objective investigation on a purely scientific basis. I offer this detailed description, minus dubious or very minor phenomena and those witnessed by only one person, as a document for such research.

1959: A second seasonal article from The Illustrated London News, Christmas Number, 1959 *challenged readers with a thought about the ghosts of England that, "the more seriously you take them, the more irritating they prove to be". The author ROBERT AICKMAN (1914–81) has been declared "one of the best ghost story writers ever to take pen in hand" yet also had a variety of other interests including the theatre, travel and inland waterways. Interestingly, he believed the human psychological reaction to ghosts was more important than the spirits themselves, as he demonstrates when confronting such entities as . . .*

THE ELEMENTALS

Particularly restricting is the law, in my experience, when we wish to deal with what are known as Elementals. Elementals are, it is thought, exceedingly primitive entities: they squat in a single place, and to stare full at one, even in the dusk (though it seems that occasionally they appear also in the fullest horror of daylight), is instant insanity. For this reason, no one knows exactly what an

Elemental looks like. A prominent British statesman who had a great interest in psychics (many will know who he was) went with others to visit the Elemental that occasionally materialises in the cellar of a Somerset manor (which I must not name): one of the party looked too long, and was never at all the same man. The statesman never visited another Elemental.

When, during the late war, I used to visit Hertfordshire's Art Colony at Chipperfield, and buses were few and early (though not so few and early as today), the girls of the village were complaining that there was a place on the road from King's Langley where they felt cold and frightened. Only years later did an authority on Elementals mention to me quite by chance that the nearest one to London stood beside the Chipperfield – King's Langley road. He defined the precise spot. Of course, it was the same spot. I could point to it now, but I smell the faint, stale odour of the Law Courts. I shall risk the simple statement that the spot is nearer to King's Langley; much nearer.

There is a major Elemental infestation in a churchyard about five miles from Northampton; though the thing only appears in the small hours of the morning. Not far from the village there are always gipsies: the spiteful persecution of gipsies by local authorities is another good reason for changing the subject. But the rule is this: when you think you see an Elemental, look away *at once*. To meet, in particular, its eyes, is spiritual suicide.

1962: *There are a number of stories of biographers being haunted by their subjects after they became immersed in the minutiae of that person's life. CONSTANTINE FITZGIBBON (1919–83), the American-born writer who became famous for his novels, including* When The Kissing Had To Stop *(1961), also wrote several biographies. The most critically acclaimed was* Life of Dylan Thomas *(1965) which produced a moment Fitzgibbon recalled thereafter as a . . .*

THE GHOST OVER MY SHOULDER

For some years I owned and lived in a house called Waterston Manor, in Dorset. It is a most handsome house, of immense antiquity but no particular period. An Elizabethan thug called Lord Thomas Howard built a fine, Renaissance, carved stone western front in 1586. Another front is Jacobean. The rest is principally Victorian for the house was burned out – though not burned down – on Christmas night, 1862. Only a well-panelled corner room, which I used as my study, remained from the old interior. And of course the house was said to be haunted, though neither I nor any member of my family ever saw the ghost of the eighteenth-century girl who is said to have jumped to her death from an upper window. For me it was a beautiful house, and not at all a spooky one: save for two incidents.

The first occurred on Christmas night, 1962. I had installed oil-fired central heating, and the large house was well warmed. But as I, my wife and the children ate our simple evening meal – we had gorged ourselves at lunchtime – I noticed that the dining room was rapidly growing cold. The radiators, I found, were chilly. I therefore fetched a torch and went to the small cellar under the house where the heating mechanism was. I found that the floor was deep in oil, and the furnace red hot. I waded through hot oil to the main switch, and turned it off. I then rang the heating engineer in Blandford, who was miraculously at home, and who came at once. He told me that had I not acted as I had done, in a matter of minutes the house would have burned. A safety device had failed, inexplicably, to function. This was one hundred years to the day, perhaps almost to the minute, since old Waterston had burned. Whoever shall own that beautiful house in the year 2062 had better watch out, on Christmas night.

Thomas Hardy knew the house well, both inside and out, in the years before the fire when he was a very young man. It is Bathsheba Everdene's house in *Far from the Madding Crowd*. Before 1862 it was lived in and farmed by a tenant of Lord Ilchester's named Genge. There were daughters and young Hardy was very fond of girls. He had been born, and was again living, a mere mile or so away, and may well have fallen for one of them. Was she perhaps the *Lizbie Browne* of his famous, beautiful poem, the girl to whom the shy young poet never dared declare his love? *Dear Lizbie Browne . . . sweet Lizbie Browne . . .* was she perhaps a Miss Genge?

For in late 1964 I was finishing my *Life of Dylan Thomas*. One stormy winter's night I telephoned John Betjeman to ask him about poets' incomes in the 1930s. Betjeman recalled how beautifully Dylan had once read *To Lizbie Browne* when they were both dining with the A.J.P. Taylors in Oxford. This reminded me of Dylan reading that same poem, in my house in Chelsea, in 1944. Later that night I reread the poem to myself in my darkly panelled work-room. The fire was burning low, the only light that of my desk lamp.

And then this happened. I was quite certain that somebody was standing behind my left shoulder, and that this person was also reading the poem in the open book before me. Furthermore I had a physical sensation – which I had read about but never experienced before or since: my hair was slowly rising from my scalp. It was, as they say, standing on end. How long this sensation, which was terrifying, lasted I do not know. A fraction of a second? Longer? I forced myself to turn my head. This required courage. And there was no one there, and my hair settled, and I went and poured a nightcap.

Which ghost had been reading, over my shoulder, that lovely poem written so long ago? Dylan Thomas? Thomas Hardy? I prefer to think that it was Lizbie Browne, *sweet* Lizbie Browne, herself.

1969: *This is another ghostly experience in a far-flung corner of the world by a journalist turned bestselling novelist, FREDERICK FORSYTH (1938–), famous for* The Day of the Jackal *(1971) and one of the best sequels to a classic,* The Phantom of Manhattan *(1999) in which Gaston Leroux's mysterious character achieves his dream of a great opera house in New York. Forsyth covered several stories with paranormal elements as a young reporter, but had his eeriest personal experience in Nigeria in 1969 working for the BBC when . . .*

SOMEONE STARED

In 1969, as a war correspondent covering the Biafran side of the Nigerian civil war, I found myself accompanying a group of Biafran commandos led by a mercenary on a foray deep into the bush behind Nigerian lines. We had come across a deserted village and while the Biafran soldiers rootled through it for signs of life, I was leaning against a doorpost doing nothing in particular and, as is my wont, doing it rather well.

I became aware of the sensation that someone was staring at me with considerable intensity. I could see nothing but the wall of forest fifty yards away, and the Biafrans were out of sight. Within my range of vision, from extreme left to extreme right, nothing moved. And yet I was convinced I was being stared at.

Quite suddenly there was a flicker of movement to my left. I turned my head sharply to see who it was. In fact it was a timber post, standing upright twenty yards away and the movement occurred when it just wobbled and toppled over. I later discovered termites (white ants that abound in those parts) had been nibbling at the base of the post and must have been chewing for weeks. At that moment one termite must have given the last nibble that separated the last strand of wood and the post just fell over.

As I turned my head I felt the "whump" of a passing bullet slamming into the doorpost then the "whack" of the sound. Jerking my head to the left had stopped it going through my forehead; instead, it went past my ear and buried itself in the door-jamb. I had indeed been stared at – by a Nigerian sniper in the forest fifty yards away. The shot proved the first of quite a brisk fire-fight during which I made like a tent-peg.

I never did find my friendly termite, but when it was over I dug the bullet out of the soft wood and now, on the end of a thin gold chain, I occasionally wear it for fun. Also, I am very kind to ants.

1987: *Domestic ghosts hovering in ordinary kitchens, dining rooms and lounges have been a theme in the work of BERYL BAIN-BRIDGE (1934–), rightly acknowledged as one of the greatest living British novelists. The years of her youth in Liverpool feature in many of her novels such as* An Awfully Big Adventure *(1970), while the London that became her adopted home after her success has also thrown up its own surprises like the events of . . .*

THE SOUND OF MUSIC

Last week I had a sudden urge to learn to play the piano, and I saw a ghost. The ghost sighting came after the urge and in broad daylight. It was downright spooky, though hardly frightening. Let me set the scene.

I had just returned from the BBC in Portland Place and was standing looking out of the back window of my laboratory at the top of the house.

On the way home my cab had stopped at some traffic lights and I distinctly heard through the wound-down window – I was smoking you see, so I had to put up with the fresh air – the sound of a piano playing something difficult, one of those pieces full of F sharps and B minors.

Immediately I made up my mind to take it up, the piano, that is. I would start with less classical stuff, Roses of Picardy for instance, and work my way upwards.

Anyway, there I was in the laboratory mentally flexing my fingers when I saw the ghost. Actually, the "laboratory" is really the spare bedroom where I keep my word processor, an instrument which the cleaner thinks of as a fiendish crucible of language, hence the posh name.

The view, now that it is winter, is somewhat bleak – the backs of houses, a few stripped trees, various clumps of dusty ivy.

In the distance, pink and white, rise the turrets of the building that is now the home of the theatrical costumiers, Nathan and Bermans.

To the right, painted a severe cream and piled like the super-structure of an ocean liner sails the superb bridgehead of the old 'Craven A' factory in Mornington Crescent.

I could see my bit of yard and the next, concrete covered and featuring a bottle bank and a bicycle, and the one beyond that. The sky was grey all over and fitted like a pan lid.

As you may have gathered my part of town does not go in for landscape gardening, though we try, oh, how we try. Next-door nurtures roses, man-sized cabbages, boy-sized Michaelmas daisies and family-size washing.

On the other side we have a tasteful display of unpruned rubble, late flowering piping, rampant old iron, and, until recently, set plumb in the middle of a squashed lawn a rather rare specimen of a toilet bowl with seat.

I myself have plastic poppies twined about the branches of a mountain ash, but I always bring them indoors at the first sign of frost.

You can therefore understand my astonishment the other morning when I saw a piano stool, a round one on three legs in the yard beyond the bottle bank, and a lady wearing a shady hat and white gloves sauntering among the fallen leaves towards it.

Even as I watched she sat down and raised her gloved hands and began pumping her elbows up and down like bellows. She didn't have a piano so I didn't bother to open the window, but she did have a halo round her head.

As you may imagine I fairly raced downstairs to the kitchen where my daughter and the cleaner were shaking rugs out of the back window and arguing about men. "There's no middle road," my daughter was complaining, "they either wear kid gloves or boxing gloves."

"Ah, how sweet," exclaimed the cleaner (she often gets the wrong end of the stick) when I'd described what I had just seen.

"So?" demanded my daughter, "are you trying to make out you've seen a ghost?" She ran upstairs to see the apparition for herself, but, of course, the woman had disappeared.

There followed a heated discussion both on the state of my mind and my lack of musical aptitude. My daughter also brought up the unfortunate time I arrived "half-seas-over" to collect her from a piano lesson and insisted on playing the *Fairy Wedding Waltz*, during which rendering I collapsed face downwards over the ivories.

Oh, I never, little lamb, I protested, which is what I always call her when I feel I'm being sacrificed.

It did however remind me of the cautionary tale of my son's nursery school teacher, a lady named Miss Smith who was referred to as Mith Mith by her lisping charges.

It's a true story, albeit tragic. A group of infants on a Tuesday morning just before Christmas in a house in Ullet Road, Liverpool, were discovered at home time marching up and down swigging bottles of milk in an abandoned manner while Mith Mith lay slumped across the piano.

She had been dead for a quarter of an hour and had apparently passed on in the middle of *The Grand Old Duke of York*.

This shocking incident has remained fresh as a daisy in the memory because I hadn't got round to paying the fees whereas the rest of the mothers had stumped up the three guineas a term in advance.

Neither the cleaner nor my daughter would believe a word of it. As I could no more prove the existence of that ghost of Christmas past than I could produce the lady in the back yard, I went upstairs in a huff to consult the *Oxford Companion to the Mind*, an excellent work of scholarship edited by Richard Gregory which no girl should be without.

It didn't say much about ghosts except that they're manifestations of dead persons in human form, and that sometimes the person who sees one is in a state of fear or guilt.

I'm now quite satisfied I saw Mith Mith, summoned up by that snatch of music heard at the traffic lights – for what it's worth. The taxi fare plus tip came to the equivalent of three guineas.

I'm thinking of slipping out tonight and throwing a cheque over the garden wall so that the poor soul can rest in peace.

7

Phantom Lovers

Sexual Encounters with Ghosts

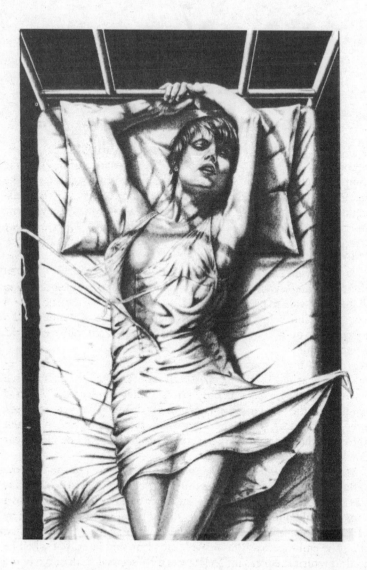

One of the great rarities of the supernatural world is *nude* ghosts, although accounts of sexual interference by spirits have become comparatively commonplace during the past century. While in the majority of cases apparitions have been described as wearing garments of some kind or other, it has long puzzled researchers why the undead rarely appear naked. Sceptical columnist George Riley bemoaned this fact in an article in the *News of the World* in January 1980:

"I cannot understand why most sightings of ghosts are so often blood-curdling events. Headless spectres or ghastly nuns rattling chains and vanishing through walls. Surely ghosts can be fun? I wouldn't mind being haunted by a glamorous nude blonde with a good sense of humour. If that happened I might believe in the supernatural!"

In fact, it might interest George Riley to know that a number of naked or near-naked ghosts have been reported over the years: some bewitching, as he hoped, but others rather unpleasant. A good example of the former appeared in the bedroom of a vicar in Essex only a few years ago. The clergyman himself, Reverend Ernest Merryweather, who saw the beautiful spirit in Langenhoe Hall, near Colchester, attests the story.

Merryweather was standing admiring the view from the window of the historic house when something caused him to turn around. He was conscious of someone else in the room and walked straight into a body he could not properly see. He found himself being embraced by what felt like a naked young girl pressing her shapely figure against him. The embrace was "fantastic", the vicar said later, but when he tried to return the pleasant feeling the girl "seemed to dissolve in my grasp".

The story of this naked spirit attracted the attention of the Ghost Club who sent a team down from London to investigate in 1980.

Locals were soon telling them that the story was well-known and Reverend Merryweather had recorded several more personal encounters with the ghost. The unusual phantom had also been seen in the vicinity of the church. A legend claimed she was the girlfriend of a rector of Langenhoe and when she became pregnant, he murdered her. It was suggested that she was seen in the nude because she was enacting one of the happier moments in her life.

Peter Wormell, the owner of the hall, told the investigators that although Merryweather was considered a bit eccentric, he was much loved by his parishioners and not the sort of man to be easily fooled. He added, "I've always understood that the sighting occurs in the best bedroom. Some people believe that the girl was Arabella Waldegrave. The name came up at séances in the church and the Waldegraves were the ancient owners of the village. The vicar was never in any doubt about what he had seen and felt."

Another church property not far from Langenhoe, Rattlesden Rectory, just outside Ipswich, is also said to be haunted by a naked phantom, although *it* is male and rather gruesome in appearance. A Stowmarket carpenter first publicly reported the spectre in June 1953 while he was working on some alterations in the rambling old house. Bill Smith told the *East Anglian Daily Times*:

"I was doing some work on the ancient panelling when I suddenly became conscious of a musty smell. The next thing I knew was when one of my white dust sheets came through the pantry with a head seemingly on it. I thought at first it must be my assistant playing a joke and I shouted at him to stop his nonsense. At this, the figure dropped the sheet, revealing a naked apparition with blotchy skin the colour of old parchment."

Subsequent enquiries established that the ghost was in all probability that of a parson who had once lived in Rattlesden and – for a reason that no one could explain – had been buried under the house instead of in an ordinary grave. A suggestion that the man had been involved in a scandal with one of his female parishioners, and as punishment was interred without his clerical garments, remains the best explanation of this curious haunting.

A second naked apparition as memorable as the beguiling spirit of Langenhoe Hall was reported two years later by James Mann, a chartered accountant practising in Moray, Scotland. The female ghost materialized in his old family home near Aberdeen. Visiting the house one summer day, James found the place full of relatives from India. As there was not a free bedroom for him, he was offered a small room on the ground floor of the big stone building. It had rarely been used in recent years and was not even wired up with electric lights or heating. In a later account given to the ghost hunter Dennis Bardens, Mann explained:

"Because these was no lighting, I had to read by the light of an oil lamp before going to sleep. Very soon I sensed an unpleasant atmosphere about the room. I also experienced a strange but distinct tension and became convinced that I was not alone. This feeling quickly developed into real fear.

"Then, through the wall, the ghost of a young girl in her twenties appeared. She wore only a petticoat and was otherwise naked to the waist. She was almost transparent and, gliding to the end of the bed, seemed to say, 'What are you doing here?' Then she smiled and disappeared. Talking to one of my relatives the following morning, I learned that the girl had been seen before in the house and the other versions of her appearances tallied exactly with mine. I can assure you that no one had told me about the existence of a half-naked ghost before that night and I am quite satisfied that I really saw her and she was not an hallucination."

In the 1980s, the *Sun* newspaper commissioned the social historian Jeremy Sandford, famous for his book *Cathy Come Home* (1967), to search the countryside for a series of articles on "Haunting Beauties". The paper, famous for its topless page three beauties, was delighted when he turned up several reports of scantily dressed phantoms. Sandford located one voluptuous beauty in Scotland: a young girl who had been seen on several occasions preening herself before a mirror in a bedroom at Muchalls Castle near Stonehaven in Grampian. The owner of the castle, Geraldine Simpson, provided him with the facts:

"There used to be a secret underground passage from the room where the girl is seen that leads to a cave by the sea. The story goes that the girl had a smuggler boyfriend and when she heard one night that his boat had put into the bay, she did not stop to put much on but ran straight down the tunnel to meet him. The man was just rowing into the cave when she fell into the sea and was washed away by the tide."

Sandford found a bevy of lovely ghostly maidens who had similarly become involved in illicit activities over the border in Wales. They were said to appear combing their long hair to hide their modesty on the shore of Llyn Morwynion. A local ghost hunter, Chris Barber, told him the story:

"Legend tells how these lively lasses were victims of a pirate raid by a party of young men from a more distant part of Wales and were carried off to be their wives. But before the men with their captives got very far, the young men hereabouts gave chase. A terrific scrimmage took place and all the raiders were killed. But the girls had fallen in love with the strangers and were so bored with the idea of going back home with the local young men that they threw themselves in the lake and drowned. Sometimes the girls emerge from the lake at dawn combing their hair."

At Bramshill House at Hartley Wintney, near Basingstoke in Hampshire, Sandford heard the story of a pretty young apparition wearing only a veil who appeared in 1944 to a footman of King Michael and Queen Marie of Rumania, who were residents in the house during the Second World War. The ghost was believed to be that of a young girl who had died horribly on her wedding day while taking part in a game of hide-and-seek and become trapped inside an old trunk. Her skeleton, still in the remnants of her wedding gown, was not found for years and then inspired a famous Victorian ballad, "The Bridal Chest of Bramshill". A member of the staff at the mansion explained to the man from the *Sun*:

"She appeared so vividly to this footman that he tried to give her a cuddle. But she dissolved in his arms as he tried to embrace her. All that she left behind was a strong smell of beautiful flowers. The scent of the tragic bride has since been smelt by a number of visitors to Bramshill."

Perhaps, though, the most remarkable story that Jeremy Sandford unearthed concerned a devout young nun, Sister Maude, who fell in love with a good-looking monk from a monastery close to her nunnery at Weston-on-the-Green near Oxford. Although like all those who had taken holy orders, the couple were forbidden to have sex, the couple met in secret to spend nights of lovemaking in the monk's cell. Their trysts were finally discovered, however, and the lovers were seized one night while in bed together. Sister Maude was sentenced to death for breaking her vow of chastity. Years later, the monastery was turned into a hotel – and guests have repeatedly told stories of a ghostly female appearing in one particular bedroom. Nicholas Price, the proprietor, elaborated to Sandford:

"Sometimes they have a feeling of dread which may be connected with the nun's terror at the moment she and her lover were discovered. Maude was apparently chained to a stake and burned to death in what are now the grounds of the hotel. But her ghost is a very friendly soul, and guests who have been haunted always remark on that, no matter how frightened they are. I have even hung around in the bedroom sometimes in the hope that she will make a pass – so far she hasn't. There are apparently other, less well-known versions of the story. One says that Maude was the girlfriend of quite a few monks . . . not just one."

Maybe the man from Weston-on-the-Green should try a night at the eighteenth-century Old Vic public house in Winchester Street, Basingstoke, where a "sexy spirit" was said to be sharing the bed of landlord Bob William. A report in the *Sunday People* of February 1979 quoted Bob: "My beauty sleep is being ruined by this ghost. It's as though there is a woman lying next to me making love. She sounds a very passionate sort of woman. Her sighs and heavy breathing often keep me awake until all hours of the night. I've always been a bit sceptical about ghosts, but this has really got me thinking . . ."

A not dissimilar story made news in America in April 1989. A young Hollywood actress – who remained anonymous – found herself sharing a bed with the amorous ghost of the great movie heart-throb of the Silent Era, Rudolf Valentino. She told her story to Sherry Hansen-Steiger, author of *Hollywood and the Supernatural* (1990):

"She felt a heavy weight press down on the edge of her bed as she was drifting off to sleep one night in the old apartment building known as Valentino Place which, according to Hollywood tradition, was once an elegant party site favoured by the actor and his intimates. For several minutes the 28-year-old actress was too paralysed by fear to move. A body of what she assumed to be a man then stretched out bedside her; she was covered only by a thin sheet. As he pressed up to her and began breathing heavily, she at last had the courage to open her eyes. 'I saw the handsome face of Valentino lying on my pillow,' she said. 'I was so terrified the man was actually Valentino's ghost that I fainted.' When she recovered, the young actress was relieved to see that although the ghost had left the bed sheets and pillow in complete disarray, it had returned to whatever dimension of reality it now called home."

The concept of sex between humans and spirits is, in fact, a very ancient one. Works by the Greek philosophers and early Christian fathers refer to men and woman "being visited in the night by supernatural beings". These phantoms were referred to as an *Incubus* for the handsome spirit that seduces women and *Succubus* for the nocturnal beguilers of men. Opinion for a time varied between supposing these spirits were capable of manufacturing a body out of air, to assuming that they stole the body of a dead person. A third school of thought maintained they were the Devil in disguise. Indeed, it is a theme that has intrigued writers and filmmakers for years as exemplified in films such as *Blithe Spirit* (1945), *The Ghost and Mrs Muir* with Rex Harrison and Gene Tierney (1947) and the Daryl Hannah/Steve Gutenberg comedy, *High Spirits* (1988).

However, a substantial number of medieval writers dismissed such stories as fantasies brought about by sexual repression – pointing out that from most accounts widows and virgins were more frequently troubled by *Incubi* than married women. Nuns, though, suffered the most of all, for – as one writer put it – "*Incubi* infest cloisters".

The famous *Malleus Maleficarum* first printed in 1486, which deals with a whole range of supernatural topics, cites almost fifty cases of women who admitted to sexual intercourse with spirits as well as about half that number of men. Two cases will suffice for many similar accounts:

"There is in the town of Coblenz, a poor man who is bewitched in this way. In the presence of his wife he is in the habit of acting after the manner of men with women and he continues to do this repeatedly; nor have the cries and urgent appeal of his wife any effect in making him desist. And after he has fornicated thus two or three times, he bawls out, 'We are going to start all over again,' when actually there is no person visible in sight lying with him . . ."

"There is in Scotland at Moray Firth a highly born girl of great beauty who refused several noblemen in marriage. When her parents commanded her to know the reason, she said that a marvellously beautiful youth had frequent intercourse with her by night, and sometimes by day, and she had no need of a husband. She did not know whence he came or whither he went . . ."

The ghost hunter, Dr E J Dingwall, devoted several years of study to this aspect of sex and the supernatural and in 1952 reported two particular cases he had investigated of people being "persecuted" by *Incubi* and *Succubi*. One was a young man who complained that phantoms in the shape of beautiful young boys came in through his window and sexually seduced him. Dingwall wrote:

"He was able for a short while to ward off the attacks by sleeping with his window fast shut. But after a few days the spirits demater- ialized themselves outside, passed through the glass in incorporeal form, and rematerialized within. The other case is a woman who, as she lies in bed, see a hand gradually take form in the air above her body, which hand then sexually assaults her."

My own files indicate that there have been an increasing number of cases of young girls molested by "supernatural hands" in recent years. I have selected a few typical examples here.

In May 1970, for instance, the *Daily Mirror* reported that a friendly ghost who "regularly slaps my wife's bottom" was haunting the converted stable home of George Meyer in Iver, Buckinghamshire. Another apparition at the Albion Arms Hotel in Bolton, Lancashire, made even more intimate attacks on the landlady, Barbara Barnes, whenever she was taking a bath. She told the *Sunday Mirror*, "I was just getting into the bath when I felt a hand caressing my bottom. At first I thought it was my husband, but I looked around and there was no one there. Since then the ghost has played tricks in the cellar and even dried up the beer in the pumps one night."

Leila Mudd, the former Miss Great Britain, also had trouble with a ghost in her husband's pub, The Liverpool Arms in Kingston, Surrey. She told the paper, "He's a kinky Peeping Tom who keeps spying on me when I'm having a bath. Other strange things have happened. He was seen standing beside my teenage daughter's bed on one occasion and even chased my mother-in-law down the stairs on another."

As she was getting ready for bed, another attractive landlady, Peggy Edwards, at the 200-year-old New Inn at Rosebush, Pembrokeshire in west Wales, found herself being bothered by spirits, she told the *News of the World* that same year: "Often when I'm undressing I hear the sound of giggling. There must be more than one because I hear the cheeky things calling out and flirting with me as I strip for bed. In the morning I find that my undies have mysteriously been scattered around the room. It's one thing to have admirers, but *supernatural* ones!"

Five years after these reports, two more public houses were being subjected to attacks by pinching ghosts. The apparition at the twelfth-century Belper Arms in Newton Burgoland, Leicestershire only targeted females, a staff member, Edith White, told the *News of the World* in December 1975: "If the girls are young and pretty the ghost always goes for their behinds. If they're older and more settled, he touches them on the shoulder to make them turn round – presumably to see whether they are worth his further attention." The same month the *Sunday Mirror* reported that a ghost who had been nicknamed "George" was pinching the bottoms of barmaids working at the Black Horse at Windsor, Berkshire.

Phantom fondlers also appeared regularly in the 1980s. In October 1981, the eighteenth-century Blue Bell pub at Warrington in Cheshire was forced to hang a notice in the bar, "Don't blame the lads, ladies – it's only our ghost!" according to a report in the *Sunday People*. It appeared that the ghost had groped three barmaids, the landlady and a number of female customers. The landlady, Lynda Wrench, told the paper, "No one has ever seen the ghost, but a few of us have felt his presence. He just grabs your behind and then pats it. Often the nearest man gets the blame. But it's happened too often when there was no one else around. We've also had a few glasses flying off the shelf – but he's really a friendly ghost."

Suggestions that the "spirits" to be found behind the bars of public houses might be the explanation for such events continued to be put forward when the *News of the World* ran another typical story in November 1983 that "the ghost of a naughty knight is causing chaos at the Knight's Lodge Inn on the outskirts of Corby in North-amptonshire". The apparition was lifting ladies' skirts, tickling the tops of their legs and pinching their bottoms. The owners had called in psychic investigator Jean Cooksley, who spent several nights on the premises and reported, "I've seen him and he's a big robust chap – a cavalier who carries an ostrich feather with him. He uses the feather to lift the ladies' skirts and tickle them. He must have been a real Casanova when he was alive."

In December 1984, the *News of the World* sent a pair of ghost hunters, Roy Stockdill and Michael Parker, with medium Shirley Waterman to investigate the "grouping ghoul" of Lee House, a 700-year-old manor house near Barnstaple in Devon. Williams spent a night in the old panelled bedroom, which was said to be the centre of the haunting. She was knocked out of the four-poster bed and told her colleagues, "I was thrown to the floor and felt a ghostly hand groping my legs. I have a strong feeling that this is a very happy room where a lot of love and lust went on."

The *Sun* returned to the theme again in December 1993 with accounts of a scantily-clad female ghost who was making a habit of haunting courting couples in Hertfordshire, whisking away under-clothes they had discarded; a nude male spectre wearing women's undies seen in a Kensington, London flat; and an undressed phantom nicknamed the "Peeping Tom of Pendle" who had been targeting young lovers in Blackburn, Lancashire at a spot once the haunt of witches. Ghost hunter Colin Waters, a forty-seven-old history lec-turer from Whitby, North Yorkshire who helped the newspaper compile its report commented: "Sex ranks with fear and love as the strongest emotion. It is no wonder a wide variety of hauntings are sexual."

One man who was in no doubt that ghosts have a sex life was American clairvoyant and author, Stanley Wojcik of New Jersey. He believes that spirits engage in lovemaking and some come to the beds of the living as "astral lovers". Writing in 1981, he claimed:

"Women who are unattached, unmarried or divorced often attract the amorous activities of male spooks for some unaccountable reason. I have investigated numerous cases where women told me that they had actually felt possessed by ghosts. They said that they felt all the excitement of lovemaking. I also believe spirits are just like human beings. They are the astral counterparts of their former mortal selves. Sex after death is not biological. Spirits *do* make love, but it is an all-cellular love – a blending of their energies."

It is not only single men and women who have been haunted by seductive spirits. There are also a number of stories on record about young couples who have been subjected to ghostly phenomena at some of the most intimate moments of their lives. Consider the story of newlyweds Steve and Debbie Mikloz of Raunds, Northampton-shire reported by the *Daily Star* in August 1979. They had just moved into a new flat on their wedding night when a day of joy turned into a night of terror:

"They got into bed, put out the lights . . . and Debbie, 17, suddenly realized they were not alone. Seconds later so did Steve. Someone grabbed him by the throat and dragged him out of bed, gasping for breath. Debbie was pinned to the bed and felt hands all over her body. She screamed and moments later struggled free. The terrified couple grabbed their clothes and fled from the flat. 'The place was haunted by something evil,' said Steve. 'We are never going back.'"

Airline steward Nigel Savage and his girlfriend, Angela Styles, a dancer with the *Young Generation* group, were also subjected to a number of terrifying attacks by a ghost that tried to take possession of the beautiful young girl's body, according to Alec Snobel in the account of their lives he wrote for the *News of the World* in March 1980. The spirit was that of an evil, curly-haired man named Edward Cadagan who had hanged himself over half a century earlier after brutally murdering a young girl. The conviction Angela was being taken over by him emerged after the pair had been together for several years. Her sudden mood swings, terrible rages and attacks on Nigel – including biting him – when they were in bed and of which she had no knowledge afterwards, convinced the pair something was dreadfully wrong. The disturbances climaxed one night in 1980 when the young dancer suddenly shook her partner awake:

"Angela edged closer to him. 'I'm scared,' she whispered. 'I just had the feeling someone walked over my grave.' Then Nigel felt it, too, an eerie presence in the room, a sense of invisible danger close by. His own heart pounded as the evil atmosphere thickened and then he shouted, 'Oh, God, Angela – I *know* it's him.' Immediately an appalling scream filled the room, high-pitched and almost choking, like a man being tortured. Angela, shaking uncontrollably, sank her nails deep into Nigel's arm, drawing blood. But he felt no pain.

"Seconds later, the screaming was joined by the sound of rushing air, very loud, like someone expelling breath noisily. It seemed to come from Angela's chest. After several seconds the scream and the noise stopped and the two of them, paralysed with fear, stared into the darkness. Just a couple of feet over their heads hung a huge, black shape. It was so overpoweringly threatening that they felt it was about to destroy them. Desperately, Nigel began saying the Lord's Prayer out loud. The black shape immediately began to dwindle. By the time he reached "Amen", the apparition had gone completely. After a moment, Nigel spoke again, 'Angela, that could only be Edward Cadagan – I'm sure the scream was his and that rush of air was him leaving your body'."

After contacting a medium and holding a séance, which satisfied the couple that the ghost was that of Cadagan, they contacted an exorcist to remove the malevolent spirit threatening to dominate the couple's life together. Alec Snobel was happy to tell his readers that the "possession" of Angela Styles was now over.

Perhaps the most unusual case of this kind I have heard was told to me by actress Debbie Watling who grew up in Loughton, Essex where I began my career as a journalist in the 1960s. Debbie followed in the footsteps of her actor father, Jack, graduating from child parts to TV drama series including *Danger UXB* and movies including *That'll Be The Day* in which she co-starred with David Essex. She told me that she had had her first taste of the supernatural while still a child growing up in the Watling family's rambling sixteenth-century home, Alderton Hall, in Loughton:

"I was about eight at the time. I was woken up one night by a face peering intently at me and I felt my hand being held by another hand. I sat up in amazement and saw the figure of a girl slowly dissolving into the wall."

Jack Watling was initially sceptical about his daughter's story. But when he investigated the history of Alderton Hall he learned that a servant girl who had occupied the same room about a hundred years before had been seduced by the squire and then turned out when she gave birth to a child. The hapless girl drowned herself and the baby in a nearby pool – and it was her ghost that was now roaming the premises. Debbie encountered the ghost again – and each time it seemed to become more intimate with her, she said:

"It was in the middle of the night. I was asleep. Then I suddenly felt a cold hand beneath the bedclothes taking hold of my hand. It gripped me and then tugged and tugged. It seemed to be trying to pull me out of the bed onto the floor. I was frightened to death."

On another occasion, Debbie awoke to find her heavy oak bed being moved unaided across the room. As she sat up in horror, books began to spill from the shelves and she briefly saw a pretty face appear on one wall. On yet another occasion she awoke in bed to feel a heavy pressure bearing down on her, but no one in sight. These incidents, though, were nothing to the horror that almost overwhelmed her in 1985:

"At first I thought it was just a ghastly dream. But then I woke up and saw a creature bending over my bed. Its top half was a goat and the bottom half a man. I've also seen it with the animal half in the shape of a wolf. Once I put my arms out and felt the middle of its body, it was definitely a man's body, but with that horrible animal head. Its presence was unbearable."

Debbie said that she always knew when something weird was going to happen. She saw strange lights moving around the room which experts told her were "spirits visible only to psychics like myself". These lights manifested themselves particularly strongly after her marriage to Nick Field, son of the famous comedian Sid Field:

"We were just about to make love when Nick shuddered and said, 'Look at your chest!' I looked down and found my breasts were covered in black hairs. I suggested that Nick must have had his hair cut recently and the clippings had fallen on me. But he hadn't had a haircut for weeks. Then the hairs started to come away and part of the room started to light up again with one of those peculiar lights."

Debbie Watling helped to rid herself of these terrifying visitations thanks to a psychic group run by Lee Everett, widow of the comedian Kenny Everett. Later, she was even able to make a joke about the unwelcome visitor to her bed:

"For a time I thought the experiences could have been a sexy practical joke by Nick's father, who died in 1950. I feel I know him and he absolutely adores me. I'd go so far as to say that he says, 'Hm. I'd like a bit of that!' when he saw me in bed!"

Reports by a number of doctors and psychiatrists reveal that ever since the 1970s there has been an increasing number of accounts of people in Britain and America – mostly women – suffering attempted rape by ghosts. There have also been dozens of accounts in the press of woman claiming to have been "assaulted" by phantoms – and although some have been rightly dismissed as sexual fantasies, the evidence of the remainder points to the fact that the phenomenon known as "Spectral Sex" might just be a reality after all. What has made some of the reports particularly intriguing has not just been the victim's story, but the physical evidence of bruises, scratches and even bite marks on their bodies that examination has shown would be extremely difficult to self-inflict. Again, I have selected a few of the more authentic cases as well as one unique personal account which must rank as the most detailed case of the sexual rape of a woman by a ghost on record.

What became a flurry of reports of sexual assaults by supernatural beings began in the 1970s with cases like that of the so-called "Smurl Poltergeist Haunting" in Pennsylvania. Accounts in the media told of a young female being sexually molested by what was compared by a local clergyman to an *Incubus*. The girl's father had also been pinned down, paralysed and then raped by a female demon the churchman referred to as a *Succubus*. The tabloid press preferred the term "randy ghosts" and the story was soon the inspiration of the film, *The Entity* (1981) about a woman who is subjected to a series of sexual assaults by an invisible ghost.

In Britain, the early examples of similar stories were a little lower key such as "The Ghost That Left Love Bites", which appeared in the *Sunday People in* March 1975. According to the paper's reporter, an amorous ghost wearing miner's boots was haunting the home of the Gladwin family in Worksop, Nottinghamshire. His attentions were particularly directed at eighteen-year-old Beryl Gladwyn who told the *People*:

"He visits me between 4 a.m. and 6 a.m. and gets into bed with me. First he tugs at the bedclothes and then I feel him next to me in bed. It holds my hand and starts kissing me and biting my neck. I've never been so frightened in my life."

Len Gladwin, Beryl's father, decided to call in a clairvoyant, Simon Alexander, to observe the dangerous spirit. His report confirmed the family's fears:

"After sitting in the room as Beryl lay in bed during the 'haunting hours', I sensed a presence outside the door. It was a malevolent spirit and first of all it tried to get me to leave by making me feel ill. I had to fight really hard to stay. Then it materialized in the room. It was trying to dodge me and was very difficult to get in focus. But I could clearly see pit boots and a miner's baggy, herringbone trousers held up by a belt with a big buckle. It tried to get into bed with Beryl and kiss her. She was trembling with fear. I am sure he will make love to Beryl unless something is done soon."

A lustful ghost with a more violent approach was featured in the *Daily Mirror* in March 1978. The spirit first manifested itself to Lorraine Price of Weoley Castle, Birmingham, but apparently quickly shifted its attention to her twenty-year-old younger sister, Jenny. The frightened girl told the newspaper:

"It first touched Lorraine about three years ago, but no one told me. Then I was sitting up in bed one night when I felt invisible hands round my neck. They had great strength and tried to push me down on the bed. I was frightened and I tried to scream. I thought the ghost was going to strangle me, but then I realized it had other intentions. A week later, the ghost returned. I realized it meant no harm and I began looking forward to his visits. Sometimes they occurred as often as three times a week."

According to the *Mirror*, as time passed the biggest problem the Price family had was getting Jenny out of bed. She seemed intent on staying there waiting for her invisible lover to return. Jenny confessed:

"It begins with a kiss on my shoulder. Then hands come under the covers and caress me before he gets into bed beside me. I just let him do what he wants and he does it beautifully. He can certainly love!"

Jenny Price offered little indication as to the appearance of her phantom lover unlike nineteen-year-old Margaret Hardie of Stockton-on-Tees who told her story to Sydney Foxcroft of the *Sunday People* five months later. He was a bald-headed Victorian gentleman who announced his arrival by slipping his hands under the bedclothes during his regular visits. Margaret revealed his "regular visits" in an interview in August 1978:

"I was lying awake in my bed one summer night when the apparition first appeared. It was some time after midnight. I heard a thumping on the landing and then the bedroom door flew open. The bed shook and the bedclothes were slowly lifted. A hand slid slowly down the outside of my nightdress from my shoulders to my legs. The hand rested on my legs. I felt paralysed."

As Jenny lay shivering, half-exposed and wondering what was going to happen next, she got a clear look at her spectral seducer.

"I saw a bald-headed man, in a Victorian cape. He kept his face hidden from me. He then spoke, 'Come to the bathroom, Margaret.' He said it four or five times. I didn't move – I couldn't. I don't know what he wanted me to go to the bathroom for. Eventually, I let out a scream and my mother ran into the bedroom and found me wringing with perspiration. After that experience, I slept downstairs – but the ghost just kept following me. I never believed in ghosts until now and I'm hoping we can persuade this Victorian gentleman to leave."

A ghost who returned to the same house after a gap of a quarter of a century with seduction in mind made headline news in June 1979. The story was told by Denise Dyke, a seventeen-year-old living in a council house in Cannock, Staffordshire to William Daniels of the *Daily Mirror*. She was lying in bed when the figure of a man she thought looked like a poacher materialized from a wardrobe and came towards her:

"He grabbed my arm and touched my leg and then seemed to pin me down on the bed. He ran his hands all over my body. He had broad shoulders and black, greasy hair and was wearing baggy trousers. A few months later he came back again. I was asleep and awoke to find him standing by the bedside. He pulled back the covers, breathing heavily. I tried to move, tried to scream, but I couldn't do either. Then he was on top of me, laughing."

Denise's mother, Flo, told the *Mirror* that she heard the sounds from the bedroom and rushed in to her daughter just in time to see the figure beginning to dissolve. Mrs Dyke continues the story:

"It doesn't need much imagination to see what he's after when he starts pinning my daughter to the bed. But I saw enough to recognize it was the same ghost who had attacked my eldest daughter twenty-six years before, just after her seventeenth birthday. He even materialized from the same wardrobe to attack my middle daughter when she was seventeen, too."

The story attracted widespread attention because of the three sisters having exactly the same supernatural experience at the same age. Suggestions that it might have been a case of a sexual fantasy repeating itself were difficult to justify because of the time lapse between the experiences of the three girls and the fact the attacks ceased as soon as each of them reached the age of eighteen. The consensus of opinion was that the visitations were real.

An ex-nurse from Liverpool, Gill Philipson, was also absolutely certain that a ghost sexually molested her for over ten years from

1984 to 1994. She told *The People* in June 1996 that she had regularly been awoken in the middle of the night to find a hooded figure with grey wrinkled skin on top of her:

"Every time I felt the figure pressing down on me. I was paralysed and unable to scream to attract the attention of my husband who was sleeping next to me. On the advice of two paranormal investigators I took a relaxation course and the attacks have become less frequent. I hope they have now disappeared forever."

The same newspaper ran a similar story about Jill Cook of Blackpool who had been raped repeatedly by an invisible entity for about four months in 1994. She explained that the entity would wake her up, speak to her and then push down on top of her. It would then fondle her genitals before raping her. Again Miss Cook was told that her attacker was probably an *Incubus*. The *People* reported that she had been advised to fill her room with electrical goods as these would block out the "mental signals" being given off by the ghost.

Which brings me to probably the most authentic case of spectral rape on record. The facts were gathered by researcher Lee Allane and published in *Forum: The International Journal of Human Relations*. The events occurred on 9 August 1980 and describe what happened to a twenty-six-year-old South London woman – whose anonymity was preserved for reasons that will become apparent – as she was getting undressed ready for bed. As she slipped off her skirt she was aware that someone was calling her name. She was a little puzzled as she knew her parents were asleep upstairs and there was no one else in the house. She takes up the story here in her own words:

"The voice was faint and taunting, as if someone close by was whispering. It was definitely a man's voice so I automatically assumed that my father must have woken up and was asking for something. But when I went upstairs to find out what he wanted, both he and my mother were asleep. Now I'd got used to the eccentricities in my parents' house – creaking doors and unidentifiable groans occurred all the time – so I dismissed the voice and returned downstairs to continue getting ready for bed."

It was a warm and humid night and the young woman was conscious that her clothes were damp with perspiration and were sticking to her body. She began to unbutton her blouse when a series of sensations changed her attitude to the supernatural and ghosts forever.

"The cool evening air which was drifting in from the open window moved affectionately between the fabric of my clothes and my flesh.

It felt good. Then it became intense as if I was actually being touched – as if there was a hand inside my blouse. I'd had a very strict Catholic upbringing and always felt uneasy about sex. I've only slept with a man twice in my entire life and both times were a total disaster. I know in my mind that there's nothing evil about making love to someone you care about – but it's hard to shake off your upbringing. Masturbation is even worse. So when I felt my body reacting, it was like getting something I wanted without being held responsible for my actions."

The young woman's first impression was that the whole thing happening to her was just a fantasy. The combination of the night, the humidity and the wind arousing her body. But as soon as she moved any such illusion was shattered.

"When I touched my breast, my hand was pushed away. 'No,' I heard someone say, 'let me, my pretty. Let me.' I was terrified. Someone was talking to me, touching me, pulling at my blouse. It wasn't fantasy – it was real. I tried to move, but I couldn't. I felt this incredibly strong arm around my waist and this hand inside my blouse, fondling my breasts. I tried to scream, but my screams were drowned by this voice whispering, 'Pretty little face, pretty little tits, pretty little pretty.'

"I don't remember what happened then, except that I was undressed. My blouse and skirt were on the floor. And someone, something was pressing me down beside them. I could feel his hands all over me, squeezing my nipples, running up and down my thigh – toying with the elastic of my panties. My body seemed to be alive with hands. And then tongues. A tongue was in my mouth and in my ear, prodding me, licking me, I couldn't see his face, but I could feel him all over me, crushing me. And his voice – I could hear his voice whispering, taunting. "A good fuck, my pretty. You'll feel better after a good fuck."

The girl admitted later that at that moment she was no longer afraid. She no longer felt she was going to be hurt. When she felt the spirit's hands inside her panties she let him slide them off her. She no longer resisted. She let whatever was going to happen . . . happen. She was conscious of nothing else until she awoke next morning.

"I found my body was covered in scratches. My vagina was sore and there were traces of blood on both my clothes and the carpet. When a doctor examined me he put the incident down to 'hysteria' caused by repressed sexuality. And the local priest who was called in by my parents said I had been the victim of an *Incubus*. But the doctor could not explain how someone who had bitten her fingernails, as I had done since I was a child, could have left deep scratches in the middle of my back. Nor could our priest understand how any demon could have ignored the crucifix I always wear around my neck . . ."

The evidence of these pages, I think, clearly indicates that "Spectral Sex" in any of its various forms is a phenomenon that deserves further study. The suggestion that it is "all in the mind" will not convince any of the men and women quoted here that their experiences with the unknown were pure fantasy. For them, amorous ghosts are an undeniable *fact*.

I have just one last story of a sexual ghost to tell. But *it* had a rather different purpose. It was told to me by an American writer, William F Nolan, author of *Logan's Run* (1967) and a skilled writer of ghost stories. In 1969, he says, director Martin Ritt was filming *The Molly Maguires* about a secret society trying to improve the lot of miners in the coalmines of Pennsylvania during the 1870s. Location shooting took place at Eckley, unflatteringly described as "the ugliest town in America", which did nothing to improve the temperaments of the three stars, Richard Harris, Sean Connery and Samantha Eggar. The filming in such an inhospitable location resulted in a number of delays, says Nolan, and the notorious womanizer Harris took every opportunity to pick up any spare women. But he had not bargained on a prudish resident ghost who, unlike his fellow spirits, *objected* to sexual shenanigans. Nolan explains:

"Another actor who was there said that Harris pursued skirts relentlessly. However, whenever he managed to get a girl into his motel room and was about to make out with her he was rudely interrupted. A ghost would appear and scare the hell out of the girl. There was nothing Harris could do to stop these visitations and it completely ruined his love life for the entire making of the movie!"

SEXY GHOSTS SEARCH FOR LOVE

WELL, 'pon my soul — there's love and sex after death!

Spirits engage in love-making like ordinary mortals, says "ghost hunter" Stanley Wojcik.

Some of them even come to the beds of the living as astral lovers, he claims.

From JOSEPH BOND
In New York

Seventy - year - old Stanley, from New Jersey, says that ghosts also go to the cinema, ride in cars and aeroplanes and even enjoy parties as a prelude to their spectral love-making.

Blending

"Spirits are just like human beings," he says. "They are the astral counterparts of their former mortal selves."

Stanley uses a pendulum and ouija board to communicate with the spirit world.

He says: "Sex after death is not biological. Spirits do make love but it's an all-cellular love — a blending of their energies."

Stanley, who has written several books on the subject of ghosts, says that not only do spirits make love to one another, they also haunt the beds of real people.

"Women who are unattached, unmarried or divorced attract the amorous activities of male spooks for some unaccountable reason," he says.

He added: "I have investigated numerous cases where women told me that they had actually felt possessed by ghosts.

"They said that they felt all the excitement of love-making."

Stanley claims that he works with a dozen spirit "controls".

They are, he says, spirits he has attracted during a lifetime of clairvoyance.

Sunday People, 25 January 1981

Go-Go ghost gives dancer the shake

By DAVID LESLIE

D A N C E R Maggie Walker and the other go-go girls at the Disco pub carry on shaking even after the music has stopped.

For the pub's ghost gets go-going when the flashing spotlights are dimmed.

His long hair and red coat might be the envy of teenagers who girated hours earlier on the floor he now trudges. But his strange outfit is centuries old.

The ghost seems to have moved into the pub in Westgate Road, Newcastle upon Tyne, since his old haunt, a 103-year-old theatre next door, shut down.

"I'm horrified about going into the changing room on my own," said Maggie (pictured right) "When I get undressed I'm always looking over my shoulder.

"I'd hate to see the ghost because I know I'd just run out of the place, clothes or not."

Staff at the old theatre said they often showed a tall, shadowy figure in a red coat to a seat, especially after the theatre was con-

Dancer Maggie : I'm horrified

verted to a cinema specialising in sexy films.

The Disco manager, 34-year-old Mr Terry Goldfingle, said: "The ghost seems to have come back to life since we opened eight months ago."

When the spirit made his last appearance, 21-

year - old b a r m a n Michael Broatch was just locking up.

He said: "The figure was wearing a long red coat, with long hair tied at the back and white breeches.

"He walked straight through me and disappeared. I got the shock of my life."

Bottom-pinch ghost nips in the inn

THE girls at the Blue Bell pub are feeling the pinch ... from a phantom fondler. Three barmaids, the landlady and female customers have all suffered the ghostly groper's advances.

Now to avoid any misunderstanding they're planning to pin a notice in the bar saying: "Don't blame the lads, ladies—it's only our ghost."

One previous landlady left for good after meeting the bottom-pinching poltergeist in the kitchen of the 18th-century pub at Warrington, Cheshire.

New landlady Lynda Wrench, an attractive 32-year-old blonde, said: "No one has ever seen the ghost but a few of us have felt his presence.

"He just grabs your behind and then pats it. Often, the nearest fella gets the blame. But it's happened too often when there was no one else around.

"We've also had a few glasses flying off the shelves, but he's really a friendly ghost.

"The previous landlady

Sunday People Reporter

told me that she was afraid to be alone in the place, but I'm not worried. It's not as if he goes bump in the night."

Barmaid Karen Asquith, 21, has also met the sexy spook.

"I was down in the cellar picking up some ice when I felt a tap on the bottom," she said.

"I ran straight up the cellar steps and I haven't been down there since."

The only one who's safe from the creepy caresses is Lynda's husband Bill.

He said: "I reckon I'm not his type. He only goes for good-looking women."

Former landlady Kathy Mitchell said: "A few times in the kitchen I felt the ghost sort of brush against me."

Sunday People, 25 October 1981

'WIVES FLEE SEXY GHOST'

Husbands blame split-ups on the ouija board

TWO husbands made an astonishing claim yesterday — that their wives walked out on them because of a frightening encounter with a sexy ghost.

They say that next-door neighbours Christine Preston, 25, and 26-year-old Janet Townsend left home after dabbling in the occult with a ouija board.

By RICHARD MOORE

Then I spoke to the runaway wives near their secret address, and they gave a different reason for leaving.

Mrs. Preston said: "It's simply a question of falling out of love with our husbands."

The women have also left their five children behind at their homes in Gillingham, Kent.

Mrs. Preston claimed she and Mrs. Townsend had contacted the spirit world through an ouija board.

According to Mr. Malcolm Preston, his wife was obsessed with the game.

And Mr. David Townsend, a 28-year-old electrician said: "That damned game is to blame for everything."

Mr. Preston said: "My wife played it for hours at a time every day with Jan.

"Their main spirit contact was an old German. Christine would hold a pen and produce strange writing.

"Once she asked the German what he wanted. She spelled out SEX. She dropped the pen immediately."

Mr. Preston, a 29-year-old motor mechanic, also told of the time he found his wife bent double.

He said: "She looked like an old man, with gnarled hands. I tried to shake her out of it. But she was convinced she was possessed and wanted to continue."

The Rev. Cecil Elliott said he had blessed the two women and their houses.

He said: "They were very disturbed, and I'm certain they were genuine."

Staff at the Britannia pub in Gillingham where the two women worked as barmaids, said they appeared to be miserable just before they disappeared eleven days ago.

But the two wives yesterday denied the claims.

Mrs. Preston, a mother of two children aged six and 18 months said: "The ouija board didn't change us. We are two bored housewives who couldn't go on living the way we were."

Mrs. Townsend, who has three children aged three to seven, has sent a letter to her husband saying that she will not be coming back.

CHRISTINE PRESTON: "We couldn't go on living the way we were."

Sunday Mirror, 23 September 1979

Groped .. by a sex-mad spook!

A PASSIONATE poltergeist has fixed his ghostly eye on teenager Denise Dyke.

His improper advances have forced her to flee from her home.

The sexy spook looks like a poacher . . . but 17-year-old Denise is definitely not game for his frolics in her bedroom.

She said last night: "Recently he grabbed my arm and touched my leg, and then he seemed to pin me down on the bed.

"He has broad shoulders and black greasy hair, and he wears baggy trousers."

Denise's mother, divorcee Flo Dyke, said: "It doesn't need much imagination to see what he's after when he starts pinning my daughter to the bed."

By WILLIAM DANIELS

The groping ghoul has haunted the council house in Laburnum Road, Cannock, Staffs, for twenty-six years.

He has always had an eye for the girls, according to mother-of-four Flo.

Before her older daughter left home the ghost regularly popped out of a wardrobe to stand looking at them as they lay in bed.

Flo said: "He has become more daring recently, and we can't take any more of it."

Flo and her daughter are now staying with relatives.

But they hope to move back into their home later this week after an exorcism ceremony by local vicar Reginald Woodall.

Last night the vicar said: "There's definitely an evil presence in the bedroom. You can sense it."

Mr. Woodall vowed: "I shall do all I can to banish this evil from the house."

Daily Mirror, 11 June 1979

8

What *Are* Ghosts?

The Theories of the Experts

In an article for the London *Evening News* on 17 April 1931, M R James, the master of the ghost story, discussed the genre and picked some of his personal favourites including Charles Dickens, Sheridan Le Fanu, Algernon Blackwood, Walter de la Mare and his friend, E F Benson. He explained how he first became fascinated by ghosts – watching the cut-out cardboard figure of "The Ghost" in a Punch and Judy Show as a child – and in response to the question as to whether they existed, added, "I am quite prepared to believe they do."

A great many of the contributors to this book share James' opinion, although there are almost as many opinions as to what ghosts *are* as there are opinion makers. By definition a ghost is a dead person who appears to the living. Yet a living person can also appear to another person – perhaps across a very great distance – which has allowed the ghost of earlier times to become the apparition of the modern day.

Ghosts have, of course, been reported by people from all walks of life, every degree of intelligence and literacy, and in every country of the world. Yet, if they are a "mental aberration", as some have claimed, then the aberration is common to a very large number of people. Just as puzzling as the idea of accepting that ghosts *exist*, is the question as to *why* particular places acquire a reputation for being haunted, regardless of whether they are old or new. And why should people who have no connection with one another and may visit a place weeks, months, and even years apart have the same uncanny experience?

What does seem to be true is that ghosts should not be dismissed as nonsense because they cannot be observed at will and no one knows precisely what they might be. Their appearances are due to factors about which we cannot be certain; and no one knows the criteria for a place to become haunted. However, there has been a tendency for spirits to appear at times of great stress, perhaps even the moment of death, giving rise to the term, "crisis apparitions". Some experts have also looked for clues in the fact that ghosts have frequently been seen during the course of buildings being demolished.

As a result of all the human interest in the supernatural over many centuries a certain number of truths have been established all over the world. Ghosts can be almost transparent, for example, or look as substantial as living people. They can materialize when people are awake or dreaming and usually appear around midnight. They may be seen by one person and completely unnoticed by others close-by. They can appear or vanish in an instant, hover, pass through solid walls and cause the temperature in a room to drop dramatically. Their purpose may be to warn, to seek revenge or simply to terrify. It is said that ghosts may also be people who are reluctant to leave the living – or simply do not realize they are dead.

Such conclusions have been reached after generations of haphazard folklore and garbled personal tales. In the twentieth century, though, with the rapid advance of science, a number of serious theories have been advanced about the various types of supernatural phenomena from haunted houses to apparitions and poltergeists. Those that follow are by no means all, but they have caught my interest during many years of research and are, I think, worthy of consideration as representative of changing and developing ideas.

Sir Oliver Lodge (1851–1940) was one of the foremost scientists at the dawn of the last century and had made great contributions in pioneering wireless communication, X-rays and electronic theory. He was also deeply interested in psychic research and joined the Society for Psychical Research (SPR) – the first body specifically formed to scientifically investigate such phenomena – where he put forward the theory that ghosts were "records of events". He suggested that strong emotions could be unconsciously recorded in matter and ghosts were a "personification of tragic moments in time". In his book, *Man and the Universe* (1925) he explained:

> "There may be a room in a haunted house wherein is the scene of a ghastly representation of some long past tragedy. On the psychometric hypnothesis, the original tragedy has been literally photographed on its material surroundings, nay, even on the ether itself."

The great scientist was also fascinated by the concept of communicating with the dead through spiritualism and argued that it was feasible to tap into this "unseen world". He explained his belief in a second book, *Phantom Walls* (1929):

"I, and many others, are growing aware that the communication between intelligent beings is not limited to the familiar methods, by voice and writing, telegraphy, and other methods we have invented – but occasionally we have telepathic communication with each other. By our study we have gradually become convinced that those who have departed are not really isolated from us. Can we prove that memory and character do survive? We have to prove it by psychic means and by employing proper means of communication you find that the person you knew is still there, that he remembers that things that happened, that his character is unchanged. My thesis is that the spiritual world is the reality and this life only a temporary episode."

A contemporary of Sir Oliver in the SPR, **Frank Podmore** (1856–1910) was, however, much less convinced about spiritualism after exposing as frauds a number of mediums who claimed to be in touch with the other side. However, the thorough and exemplary investigations by this man – who became known as "the prosecuting attorney of the SPR" – led him to propose his own theory about haunted houses – especially those beset by poltergeist phenomena. His conviction that children were usually to blame got him labelled as the exponent of the "naughty little girl" theory.

Podmore investigated many famous cases of the time and decided that for *proof* it was vital to have good, sound evidence from intelligent witnesses, plus phenomena of a kind that only a paranormal interpretation was possible. He found neither element together in the vast majority of the enquiries he pursued – but a child present in most of them. But there might be another explanation, as researchers EJ Dingwall and Trevor Hall wrote in their case history *Four Modern Ghosts* (1958):

"It was thought by some that to suppose all the phenomena in the cases examined by Podmore were due to the tricks of naughty children, to the folly of mal-observation, faulty reporting or actual hallucination of the witnesses went too far. It seems likely that much of the confusion with which the whole subject of poltergeists and hauntings is beset is due to the fact that a clear distinction had not been made between what are called 'haunted house' phenomena and 'poltergeist' phenomena. In so-called haunted houses the principal phenomena are usually unexplained noises, apparitions and various sensory effects such as the feeling of unseen presences. Poltergeist phenomena, however, usual consist of noises, mysterious stone-throwing and movement and breakage of household objects. Part of the confusion may be due to the fact that it has been common to speak of a house being 'haunted' by a poltergeist, but it is essential that a clear distinction be made between haunting and poltergeists before any explanations of the various phenomena can be discussed. It seems clear that Podmore's 'naughty child' theory was meant by him to apply to those cases where breakages and other disturbances were thought to be caused by a mischievous entity and not to other cases where few of the boisterous pranks occurred."

In 1911, **Sir William Barrett** (1844–1925), a leading figure in the foundation of the SPR, published a list of four theories that had emerged as a result of all the society's research in his book, *Psychical Research*. They are worth quoting verbatim as an indication of the conclusions being reached about hauntings from the first application of scientific experiments and after centuries of guesswork:

1. The popular view that the apparition belongs to the external world like ordinary matter and would be there whether the percipient was present or not. Some cases appear to support this view in which the phantom was followed from place to place and seen by different independent observers at successive points. This theory, however, has insuperable difficulties, among others that of accounting for the clothes of the ghost and it may be dismissed.
2. That the phantom was projected from the mind of the perci-pient and was, therefore, a hallucination; not a baseless one, but created by a telepathic impact from the mind of a deceased person. Here we have the difficulty of explaining why the phantasm should be dependent on a particular locality, although with our present knowledge this theory appears the most plausible.
3. That the phantom was due merely to expectancy and tele-pathically transferred from one mind to another. This may account for some cases that have been cited, but not all.
4. That some subtle physical influence is left in the building or locality that affects certain brains and creates the hallucination.

Sir William summarized: "To these we may add an extension of the second theory that hauntings are due to dreams of the deceased, telepathically projecting scenes of their life on earth to some persons there present. Finally, those who have *not* made a study of the subject will have their own theory that all the alleged phenomena are due to delusion or fraud."

Another person who had also been carefully studying ghosts at this time was the American psychologist and philosopher, **William James** (1842–1910). Under the auspices of Barrett, he had founded the American Society for Psychical Research and from his base at Harvard University instituted wide-ranging enquiries into mediums and hauntings in America that would ultimately make him one of the most influential figures of his day. James would, indeed, encourage many others on both sides of the Atlantic to consider the subject a field worthy of research. In an article written shortly before his death, the American took up the lead of his mentor about ghosts and hallucinations, declaring:

"Apparitions, I believe, are *objective* hallucinations, lying dormant in the invisible segments of our minds – vide Jung's 'collective' – which are susceptible to an interaction from the minds of others, even total strangers. When this interaction takes place, a hallucination emerges."

There were those, though, who argued that if a "solitary percipient" saw an apparition miles away from a possible "interacting incarnate" – across woodland, for instance – how could this argument be true? Whatever the views of William James' theory, he stimulated ideas from other like minds such as the French physiologist and Nobel Prize winner, **Charles Richet** (1850–1935). A cautious, careful and sceptical investigator who strongly criticized many reports of paranormal phenomena during the early decades of the century, Richet undertook his own studies and became one of the leading figures in European psychical research. In his thought-provoking memoirs, *Thirty Years of Psychical Research* (1923), he posed three questions about ghosts – and then proceeded to answer them:

1. Is it an impression left on things, an emanation from them?
2. Is it the astral body of a deceased human being?
3. Is it an intelligent but non-human force that comes to notify its presence?

Taking the first point, Richet wondered if there was a mysterious energy stored in things that might awaken images in sensitives – like a magnet seeming inert until a piece of iron is placed near it. If this was so, the principal cases of haunting might be explained. This did not amount to an explanation, he said, "but a verbal expression given to a phenomenon that is not understood."

Turning to the second point that phantoms might be those of deceased persons, Richet found the explanation full of contradictions:

"Why those persons only and not others? For millions of tragic events occur continually, everywhere, without causing any haunting whatsoever. Often insignificant causes would seem to have decided the ghost to return. And this ghost seems to have a very curious mentality: he throws stones, breaks bottles and opens doors with violence. He is frankly inept and shows an ineptitude that belongs to the animal more than to man. Since intelligence has vanished with the brain, and the body has undergone putrefaction, how can the dead man live again, even under a nebulous phantasmal form."

The third hypothesis, the Frenchman said, asked if there were spirits who are intelligent powers, entirely different from humanity, able to do anything objectively or subjectively. Again he revealed himself strongly opinionated:

"This hypothesis is convenient, even much too convenient – for to admit all-powerful and omniscient beings is much the same as to admit our entire ignorance. I prefer to suppose a human energy similar to the ectoplasm coinciding with a certain degree of lucidity, causing such and such forms to appear. But this, too, is unsatisfactory; even ridiculous. Nevertheless, being unable to see any cause, I would accept this opinion provisionally as a working hypothesis such as one is obliged to use in a dawning science."

"Dawning science" was an apt description of the widening search for an explanation into the mystery of ghosts and hauntings after the horrors of the First World War had subsided Now, though, ideas began to be put forward from often unlikely sources. One such was J W Dunne (1875–1949), an aeronautical engineer who startled the public with his book *An Experiment With Time* in 1927. In this he described how a number of precognitive dreams he had experienced led him to formulate a theory that Time was not a lineal flow but a sort of geography accessible to the dreaming mind. The book was to intrigue a large number of readers and prove influential on other writers such as E F Benson and J B Priestley. The success of the work prompted several sequels including *The New Immortality* (1938) in which Dunne discussed the paranormal and offered his own explanation for ghosts:

> "Everything which has established its existence *remains in existence*. A rose, which has bloomed once, blooms forever. As for man, he is not accorded distinctive treatment: he merely remains with the rest."

It was to be a theory that would resonate with the public and challenge members of the SPR and other groups studying the paranormal as scientific enquiry delved into time travel, dreams of the future, precognition and extra-sensory perception (ESP). The discussion soon found its way into the new medium of radio opening up even wider public debate. **Professor C E M Joad** (1891–1953), for years one of the most popular panellists on the weekly BBC radio programme, *The Brains Trust*, was a friend of Harry Price and investigated with him a number of the most famous hauntings of the time. Joad was an unorthodox man who liked to be provocative on and off the air. He suggested that a ghost might be a hybrid being, created by the disembodied spirit of a dead person, combining with some substance or "piece of matter" in the spiritual universe, to produce a temporary, though very elementary intelligence. Writing in *The Listener* in 1938, Joad explained:

> "The human being is not all body. In addition, most of us would claim that as well as a body we have minds or souls. But the mind or soul may not be a simple thing like an element: it may be a complex like a chemical compound resulting from a mixture of the elements. One the body; the other – for want of a better name – is sometimes called the "psychic factor". At death the compound is broken up and the mind, therefore, goes out of existence. But what of the elements of the compound? We know what happens to the psychic factor. It may persist; it may, for example, combine with the body of a medium in a trance to form the temporary mind, which sends "spirit" messages. It may even combine with pieces of matter other than human bodies to produce the moving of small

objects, the rapping of tables, the ringing of bells, and the phenomena usually ascribed to poltergeists."

Another voice that became familiar to radio listeners was that of **Sir Ernest Bennett** (1867–1947), a government minister who urged serious consideration of the paranormal in parliament. Apart from sitting as MP for Central Cardiff, Bennett was also Assistant Post-master-General and the first politician to join the SPR, serving as its President from 1932–5. In a broadcast entitled "What I Believe About Apparitions" in June 1939 he outlined the SPR's four con-clusions about ghosts and then continued:

"My conviction, after a careful study of the available evidence for many years, is that, in general, apparitions of the dead may be, and frequently are, caused by telepathy from the dead. In other words, that beyond the portals of death a discarnate mind persists still capable of the conscious transference of thought to a living percipient. This theory fits the facts best in the case of those recognized apparitions that carry with them indications of identity and exhibit some knowledge of earthly affairs. It is at first sight less appropriate to those unrecognized and unrelated phantasms which might be mere dream-fantasies of the dead. How closely do they resemble certain phenomena of somnambulism!"

Sir Ernest went on to discuss what he referred to as "the time limit" of apparitions:

"Identification of ghosts can, of course, supply a clue as to date, but personal recollection of an individual's features – apart from the aid of photographs or pictures – becomes less and less reliable as the years advance and may almost fade out towards the close of a long life. The apparition, therefore, of a person who died some fifty to a hundred years ago would be in nearly every instance unrecognized. On the other hand, we may regard some phantasms as dated by the clothing which they appear to wear. In summary, one may suggest that while recognized apparitions of the dead normally occur within a year or so of death, telepathic activity may survive the grave for an indefinite period and, in rare and sporadic cases become effec-tive after long intervals of time, in accordance with laws of which we know nothing."

Bennett also added his own contribution to the "perplexing phenomena of haunted houses and localities" and the difficulty of explaining how many well-attested ghosts had become associated with certain houses, rooms and even roads. He told his listeners:

"If we accept the view that apparitions of the dead are due to the post-mortem agency of the deceased, the local character of the haunting might be explained as due to the deceased man's personal attachment to the house, or the association of the house with certain outstanding experiences of happiness or misery during his occupation of the building. Several well-supported local cases are on record where phantasms of living persons who have left their homes are repeatedly seen in familiar surroundings of their earlier days; and if knowledge of terrain survives the grave, it may been that the spirits of the dead 'delight to dwell amid the scenes in life they loved so well'. Post-mortem agency fits the facts best, and to me it seems that in some inscrutable fashion the woodwork and masonry of a house may exert some physical or mental influences which cause certain individuals to see the phantasmal figure of a former resident."

The engineer, mathematician and radio pioneer **George Nugent Tyrell** (1879–1952) devoted some forty energetic years of his life to psychical research. He became a leader in experimental work and constructed a number of devices that obtained highly significant statistical evidence for telepathy and precognition. Tyrell had an acutely original mind and probably penetrated more deeply into the spectral world than anyone else since the founding of the SPR. He was responsible for coining the phrase of ghosts as "footprints in the sands of time" and declared in 1941:

"Apparitions are the sensory expression of dramatic constructs created in regions of the personality outside the field of normal consciousness . . . They are the proof of the existence of personality after death, the imprints, as it were, made by once-living forces."

Other experts in Britain and America were soon agreeing with Tyrell's suggestion that a ghost was not so much the physical manifestation of a dead person as the dramatization of a telepathic impulse transmitted before, during or after death. As Martin Ebon, one of these experts, later explained:

"In other words, if a son strongly wishes to contact his mother at the moment of death, this impulse may be communicated to her telepathically – and, by means as yet unknown, is transformed by her into sights, sounds or other sensory impressions. These moment-of-death or just-after-death apparitions belong in the 'crisis telepath' category."

In October 1942, Tyrell gave a landmark lecture in London – later published in book form as *Apparitions* – based on his exhaustive enquiries. In this he stated that the existence of ghosts had been proved by "overwhelming evidence" and outlined what was described in the press as the "first level-headed theory" to explain them. In a nutshell, he said that ghosts were non-physical, just as an image in a mirror had no physical properties. They were "seen" and "heard" and sometimes "smelt" by the sense organs of normal people in a temporary state of hallucination. He elaborated his thoughts to the packed audience:

"A ghost is not physically present in space – but a ghost *is* a visual solid present in physical space. There is no difference in existential status between one part of an apparition and another. In whatever sense the central figure is 'there', the auxiliary objects, the additional figures and the environment are 'there', too. That is to say that a ghost may be riding a horse through a gate in a farmyard and yet the horse, gate and farmyard may all be ghosts accompanying this phantom rider."

A decade later, just prior his death, Tyrell was asked by his friend, Robert Thurston Hopkins, for his summation of apparitions. His answer was a model of objectivity:

"Many people find it hard to grasp what is usually called an 'hallucination of the senses.' It frequently occurs. For example, I was on one occasion waiting in London for a number 14 bus. I got in. The conductor said it was not going where I wanted to go. It was a number 74. My expectation had turned the '7' into a '1'. That I was a 'ghost' if you like to call it so. I had created it *as a subjective experience of my own*. What I find people do not realize is that *all* we see, feel, hear, smell and taste is similarly created by ourselves, in so far as it is our *own experience*. Nearly always we create it so that it corresponds with our emotions or expectations or with some telepathic link with another person. The latter are called hallucinatory creations. If the cause is unknown we are apt to call them ghosts."

Following the groundbreaking research by G N Tyrell, the middle of the twentieth century saw a surge of theories about the nature of ghosts. The proponents were urged on by the new attempt to define what a ghost might be in a pamphlet, *Six Theories About Apparitions* written by the American **Professor Hornell Hart** (1888–1967) and published in 1956. A sociologist and psychic researcher, he was a member of the faculty at Duke University and conducted experiments into apparitions and out-of-body experiences which added significantly to the current knowledge of the paranormal. Perhaps, though, his "Theory" was his most important contribution and remained required reading for many years. Hart's hypothesis took the conclusions of earlier groundwork by the SPR and others and elaborated on them with more precision:

1. Apparitions are mental hallucinations created by individual percipients in response to telepathic impulses directly or indirectly received from the appearer.
2. Apparitions are idea-patterns produced currently or very recently by the subconscious levels of the percipient, with or without the co-operative assistance of the unconscious of the appearer.
3. Apparitions are etheric images, created currently, or in the past, by some mental act.
4. The Occultist theory that apparitions consist of the astral or etheric bodies of the appearers, with clothing and accessories created *ad hoc*.
5. The Spiritualist theory which assumes that apparitions of the dead are the spirits of the departed.
6. Apparitions are a combination of all or any of the other theories which can be validated by operation or experiment.

Among those with fresh ideas was the distinguished Oxford scholar, **Professor H H Price** (1899–1984), the Wykenham Professor of Logic, who had been taking a keen interest in telepathy, mediumship and the survival issue for some years. He also delivered a memorable quote in April 1953 that quickly became familiar with members of the public who shared his interest:

"The tea-party question, 'Do you believe in ghosts?' is one of the most ambiguous which can be asked. But if we take it to mean,

'Do you believe that people sometimes experience apparitions?' the answer is that they certainly do. No one who examines the evidence can come to any other conclusion. Instead of disputing the facts, we must try to explain them. But whatever explanation we offer, we soon find ourselves in very deep waters indeed."

The language was that of a man with an open and enquiring mind who, before long, was delivering challenging conclusions from his research. He looked at all the possible forms "survival" could conceivably take and argued that a "bodiless" survival was unthinkable because of the human need for personal identity, social acceptance and love. All of which, he said, were dependent upon some type of bodily recognition. However, Price suggested that images might exist – "persistent and dynamic entities" he called them – endowed with causal properties which, once formed, might persist with a kind of independent life of their own. He explained in a second essay:

"Such images, I suppose, could be originated by a mental act, but not to be themselves mental. These images, being neither mental nor material, might be endowed with telepathic charges. If we apply this logic to a haunting, such a persistent image might be tied down in some particular way to a physical place or object, and act telepathically on a percipient near this place causing him to see an apparition."

Price was also very interested in stories of poltergeists and made full use of the SPR archives and those of similar bodies to offer some ideas. He examined the evidence and having decided the facts were "complicated and difficult" to interpret wrote in February 1966:

"The German word *Poltergeist* literally means 'noisy spirit', but there is very little reason to think that a 'spirit' (i.e. a discarnate intelligent being) has much to do with the phenomena. It is often found that there is a boy or girl in the family who is at or near the age of puberty and it looks as if this young person was somehow responsible, unconsciously, for some of the mysterious movements of household objects. He or she has to be present when these movements occur, but does not cause them in any normal manner, for example by picking the objects up and throwing them, or by means of concealed strings or other physical devices. In that case, *some* poltergeist phenomena are indeed paranormal.

Presumably they are examples of telekinesis – literally 'causing movements at a distance' – and are akin to the phenomenon of physical mediumship. We need much more investigation both 'in the field' and in the laboratory."

There were, in fact, others hard at work in both locations, in particular **Nandor Fodor** (1895–1964), a colourful psychical researcher and writer who was very interested in the relationship between psychoanalysis and the paranormal. He had made something of a speciality of studying the "racketing spirit", vide *The Poltergeist Down The Centuries* (1951). In this he wrote that one of the poltergeists he had been studying could be "a fragment of a living personality".

"It is possible that this fragment has broken free in some mysterious way of some of the three-dimensional limitations of the mind of the main personality. In other words that poltergeist activity can arise consciously or unconsciously from the angers, resentments and even sexual frustrations of people. It is possible that they are loosened with conscious malice or quite uncontrolled by the person from which the forces emanate, often female adolescents. In this way poltergeists might be related to the psychic warfare reported between some mediums who must find ways of turning aside the evil to protect themselves."

A far more controversial theory was offered by retired civil servant, **G W Lambert** (1889–1983), a man with an insatiable curiosity and a lover of alternative theories for paranormal causation. He investigated several important poltergeist cases that had occurred since the Second World War and in June 1955 offered a unique "geophysical theory" as the explanation for such disturbances. According to his interpretation, poltergeist activity was brought about by the action of underground water coupled with the escape of compressed air due to pressure from water, accumulated for various reasons such as heavy rainfall and coastal weather. In his paper, *Poltergeists: A Physical Theory*, Lambert explained:

"We want to find a force that is able to tilt a house enough to spill crockery off the kitchen dresser, to make sofas and chairs slide about in the drawing room, to tilt beds so that the people in them think they are being pushed out of them, to distort windows so that panes are broken (supposedly by stones) and wrench door-frames so that locked doors fly open and, generally, to strain the timbers of the house in a way that causes them to groan and creak at almost every joint. The force, moreover, must be more often available in winter than in summer and, comparing one area with another, more likely to show itself nearer the coast than inland. So far as I am aware, the only force which answers to that specification is flood water, and as the water has never been actually seen 'at work' it must be moving in an unsuspected subterranean stream underneath the building that is affected. I have assembled the evidence to show that earth tremors can cause disturbances in houses in some parts of Britain and these have given rise to stories of poltergeists and hauntings."

Nor surprisingly, the Lambert theory stirred up a controversy, dividing those who thought the idea was brilliantly original to those who thought it was nonsense. In *Four Modern Ghosts* by Dingwall and Hall, for instance, the authors said they found it difficult to accept the theory because "Our experience leads us to suspect that *if* the movement of a house could be sufficiently violent to cause spectacular manifestations of this sort, the building could almost certainly fall into ruins during the outbreak." Two other members of the SPR, Dr Alan Gauld and A D Cornell, were also critical: "It does not seem likely that even a strongly built house could survive the vibrations necessary to throw an object into the air." Yet, despite all the differences of opinion – and other subsequent attempts to discredit Lambert's theory – all investigators of poltergeist outbreaks ever since have satisfied themselves there is *no* underground water before proceeding.

Water was also at the centre of another idea about ghosts put forward at this time by **T C Lethbridge** (1901–71), the remarkable Cambridge antiquarian and paranormal investigator. In 1961, he and his wife were on holiday in Ladram Bay in Devon collecting seaweed for their garden. Lethbridge noticed that as the couple stepped onto the beach, they passed into a kind of blanket, or fog, of depression and fear. Mrs Lethbridge soon insisted she "could not stand the place" and the pair left. The following week, however, they felt bold enough to return to Ladram Bay and again experienced the "bank of depression". Lethbridge's interest was now fully aroused. From enquiries locally, he discovered that a man had died there not long before during a quarrel. He could not help wondering if the event had "somehow imprinted itself on the atmosphere". He wrote later:

"I remembered something else, too. That the blanket had a quite definite limit – it was possible to step into it, and then step out of it again, as if it was a kind of invisible wall. It reminded me of a tingling sensation I once had alongside a rivulet when I had been waiting for a ghost to appear. Could it be that such phenomena were something to do with water – or with the electrical field that surrounds running water? Was it possible that the electrical field of water could somehow record the emotions of human beings – and even their appearance? Could the electrical field of water be the 'tape' that recorded ghosts?"

Later that year, when Lethbridge published his book, *Ghost and Ghoul*, he was feeling confident he had stumbled onto an explanation for ghosts. He elaborated:

"I feel reasonably convinced about these [ghosts]. They are pictures produced by human minds. They are not spirits of departed persons from another world. That some of them are produced by persons living on another plane of existence seems to be reasonable enough, but it also seems clear that the vast majority of ghosts must be produced by minds which are still using human bodies on this plane where we are now living. To me they appear to be no more and no less than television pictures. The television picture is a man-made ghost."

Another investigator who saw validity in the "tape recorder theory" was **Andrew Mackenzie** (1929–) author of a series of comprehensive and well-argued books starting with *The Unexplained: Some Strange Cases in Psychical Research* (1966). He believed it might be an explanation of the famous "Haunting at Versailles" in 1901. This curious event, when two young English ladies, Charlotte Moberley and Elinor Jourdain "saw" several persons, including Marie-Antoinette, dead for more than a century, while walking in the Trianons, was described by them ten years later in *An Adventure*. Nor was this to be the only such occurrence in Versailles. Visitors witnessed the retro-cognitive experience again in 1908, 1928 and 1955, thus ruling out the original story as a recreated pageant, a hallucination or a hoax. With the passage of time the story had continued to baffle one researcher after another, but then Mackenzie discovered that in all four experiences, the participants "felt unaccountably depressed" and heard a curious hissing sound that came when things were about to appear "possibly suggesting some electrical condition". He concluded from all this:

"The clues are here and it is for us to apply them. The common factors are complaints about sudden feelings of depression for which no reason can be given or oppressive weather at the time of these strange experiences. It seems that unusual atmospheric conditions at Versailles in the vicinity of the Trianons cause certain people to hallucinate the landscape and figures, or just the figures of the past. There is a theory in psychical research that cases of the appearance of apparitions involve an agent and percipient or agent percipient. If this is so, who was the long-dead agent who presumably left some influence on the Trianons which could, in certain atmospheric conditions "trigger off" the hallucinatory experiences of certain visitors to the gardens in modern times? We do not know and, in all probability, we shall never know."

The early 1960s saw the arrival on the research scene of the man destined to become one of America's most high-profile ghost hunters, **Hans Holzer** (1933–). Born in Vienna, he became interested in psychic research while at university and later crossed the Atlantic where he was invited by the American Parapsychological Foundation to investigate a number of haunted houses in the Eastern United States. The articles and books that followed, notably *Ghost Hunter* (1963), soon established him as an important and conscientious enquirer. As a result of his investigations, Holzer became convinced that ghosts were a surviving emotional memory of people who have died tragically but are unaware of their own passing. He explained in his first book:

"A ghost is a split-off personality that remains behind in the environment of the person's previous existence, whether a home or place of work, but closely tied to the spot where the person actually died. Ghosts do not travel, do not follow people around, and they rarely leave the immediate vicinity of their tragedy. Once in a while a ghost will roam a house from top to bottom, or may be observed in a garden or adjacent field. They are *free* spirits who are able to reason for themselves and to attempt communication with the living."

Also in *Ghost Hunter*, Holzer has a warning for any of his readers that they have no chance of seeing an apparition if they are out-rightly sceptical or insensitive to the possibility:

"Ghosts are people, or part of people, anyway, and thus governed by emotional stimuli. They do not perform like trained circus animals, just to please a group of sceptics or sensation seekers. Then, too, one should remember that an apparition is really a re-enactment of an earlier emotional experience and a rather personal matter. A sympathetic visitor would encourage it; a hostile onlooker inhibits it. Sometimes an 'ordinary' person does manage to see or hear a ghost in an allegedly haunted location, be it a building or open space. Such a person is, of course, sensitive or mediumistic, without knowing it, and this is less unusual than one might think."

Two years later, in an article, "Ghosts – Fact or Fantasy?" Holzer discussed the support being given by a number of American parapsychologists to a theory of ghosts as "molecules of light". This, they claimed, was the reason for the apparent reluctance of apparitions to show themselves and was based on the scientific concept of light as a molecular stream:

"They maintain that the spirits of the dead 'exist' in a sort of half-dimension. They exist as 'flows' of molecules that 'travel' the same wavelengths of light. Thus, these theorists say, light will 'blot out' or 'overwhelm' the less intense 'ghost-molecules'. They add that most ghosts are 'bound' to the rooms, houses or locales with which they have the closest associations, or where they physically died. Why? Because the majority of ghosts are spirits of persons who were murdered or grievously wronged just before their deaths. They return – or perhaps never leave – the scene of their death or sorrow. One school of thought holds that the wraith's last, and overpoweringly concentrated thought, at the very moment of death, was to remain on earth until he could be avenged or the wrong done to him righted."

The idea of ghostly molecules was taken a step further by two British writers, **Phoebe Daphne Payne** and **Laurence J Bendit** in their book, *This World and That: An Analytical Study of Psychic Communication* (1969). In it they proposed the theory of the *psychom* – "a particle of the mind shed in a haunted house which possesses and retains sufficient energy to generate the recreation of an event." Namely a haunting. The pair had reached their conclusion after years of study of the human mind, its powers and potential.

Payne and Bendit cite as their strongest evidence for the theory a very well documented case in America in 1887 when an elderly, bedridden widow, known as Granny Osborne, died during a tremendous thunderstorm in her village of Ooltewah in Tennessee. The old lady had apparently lifted herself up to the window to watch the raging weather and had died when a huge bolt of lightning struck a pine tree in the garden. When neighbours entered her house the following morning they found the body of Granny Osborne lying peacefully on her bed – but etched on the bedroom window was a perfect likeness of the old lady staring out into the garden. The etching remained clearly visible on the glass for several years as evidence of the "ghost" and then gradually faded and disappeared.

Peter Underwood (1923–) one of the pre-eminent British ghost hunters and for years chairman of the Ghost Club, has written dozens of articles and over thirty books, in the main dealing with the supernatural. He claims to have witnessed two ghosts. At the age of nine he saw the ghost of his father on the night he died – his mother also saw it – and in 1971 he spoke with a railwayman whom he subsequently discovered had died a traumatic death several hours earlier. Although Underwood believes there is as yet "no overall explanation for ghosts and ghostly activity", he agrees that "there are certain climactic or atmospheric conditions under which they appear". He does have his own theory, which he explains in these words:

"I have long been of the opinion that concentrated thought – a single-minded preoccupation – is linked to ghostly activity, which would explain why places of learning and concentration, such as churches, universities and libraries, have all been common locations for hauntings. However, there are no hard and fast rules and we are forever finding exceptions to our hypotheses and ideas. In the Ghost Club we always try to keep an open mind and acknowledge that in a world of mechanization, standardization and automation there are still some things we cannot explain."

Similarly original thought on the subject of ghosts has been forthcoming from **Dr Lyall Watson** (1939–), known as the "scientist of the supernatural" whose book *Supernature* (1973) was an international bestseller and undoubtedly changed many prejudices towards the paranormal. Born in South Africa, he became aware of the paranormal from an old Malay shaman and subsequently used his training as a zoologist, anthropologist and ethnologist to firm up a number of convictions and write his landmark book.

Watson was particularly impressed with the experiments of Dr Nicholas Seeds at the University of Colorado who, he said, had "taken mouse brains and teased them apart into their component cells". Seeds then left these in a culture solution and several days later, the cells had reassembled and were showing their usual biochemical reactions. Watson summarized:

"Somehow cells are capable of recreating past patterns; they have a molecular memory which is passed on from one cell to another so that a new one can reproduce the behaviour of its parents. If a change, or mutation occurs, this, too, is faithfully duplicated by the descendants. The dead live again in defiance of time."

This cyclical pattern of life indicated to Watson that matter is never destroyed but goes back into the system to re-emerge sometime later. It made him wonder whether the same behaviour pattern could be applied to ghosts. He explained his thinking:

"Souls or spirits that occur without benefit of body are a separate kind of phenomenon, but can be considered in much the same way. For the sake of argument, it is worth considering the possibility that man can produce an 'astral projection' or part of himself that can exist without his normal physical body and perhaps even survive his death. These spirits are said to wander at will and there are countless records of their having been seen, in whole or in part, in a great variety of situations."

Lyall Watson admitted he was puzzled by the fact that all the ghosts he had heard of wore clothes. He was, he said, prepared to admit the possible existence of an astral body, but "could not bring myself to believe in astral shoes and shirts and hats". He added: "The fact that people see ghosts as they or somebody else remembers them, fully dressed in period costume, seems to indicate that the visions are part of a mental rather than a supernatural process. In those cases in which several people see the same apparition, it could be broadcast telepathically by one of them. And where a similar ghost is seen by separate people on separate occasions, I assume that the mental picture is held by someone associated with the site."

Colin Wilson (1931–), who became famous as the author of *The Outsider* (1957), is now acknowledged as a philosopher and his interest in the supernatural has inspired a host of articles, books and even a handful of novels. His grandmother was apparently a spiritualist, he says, and his mother claimed to have seen an angel when she was ill who told her "her time had not yet come". She lived another thirty-six years. Wilson offered his own particular take on ghosts in his critically acclaimed volume, *The Occult*, published in 1979:

"It is certain that human beings possess latent powers of which they are only dimly aware and that these latent powers produce a variety of phenomena from poltergeist activity to 'thought photography' and spontaneous combustion. These 'positive' powers are connected to, but not identical with, the power of precognition and 'seeing' ghosts."

Like Lyall Watson, Wilson has reservations about the reported behaviour of some ghosts. He explains:

"Apart from man's own 'latent powers', there seems to be strong evidence that ghosts have an independent existence. Their chief characteristic appears to be a certain stupidity, since a tendency to hang around the places they knew in life would appear to be the spirit-world's equivalent of feeble-mindedness. I suggest that the state of mind of ghosts may be similar to that of someone in delirium or high fever: a disconnection of the will and inability to distinguish between reality and dreams. It must also be admitted – although for me personally, it goes against the grain to do so – that it is not improbable that the dead may be around us a great deal of the time, and that the premonitions of danger, precognition and so on, may be due to them rather than to our own psychic alarm system."

The last quarter of the twentieth century saw the emergence of a whole new group of psychic researchers who would once more throw up new and often controversial theories about the nature of ghosts. One of the most prominent of these men was **Dr Michael Shallis** (1940–), whose interest had been awakened as a small boy of ten when he saw what he was convinced was a ghost in an old Abbey in Sussex. After taking a PhD in astrophysics at Oxford, he taught physical sciences at the Department for External Studies and then began to study astrology when his wife became fascinated by the subject. Shallis came to realize that – like his childhood experience – there was still much in the world that was a mystery to science, especially time and space. In 1981, having joined the SPR and conducted a number of his own enquiries, he wrote *On Time* in which he suggested that ghosts might be the result of "time slips"!

"As the idea of ghosts is more familiar than the notion that people we see may not really be here and now all the time, but just visiting us from the future, [my] ghost idea is perhaps more acceptable. For leaving aside the spiritualistic aspects of ghosts and hauntings, ghosts are in a clear sense caught in some from of time slip. When a ghost is seen, it is seen as an apparition of someone who was in another time. Communication with such apparitions raises some problems, but if the event is considered as a 'time slip' the ghost is here and now although displaced from his proper time."

The second important figure is **Carl Sargeant** (1952–), who had the distinction of being the first person to get a PhD in parapsychology at Cambridge in 1979. The degree was a vindication for all those who had been trying to get research into the supernatural acknowledged as a respectable science – although not everyone was to agree that the ambitious, outspoken and independently minded Sargeant spoke for all of them. He famously declared, "There are scientists who wouldn't believe paranormal phenomena if they saw them with their own eyes." The Welsh-born firebrand was soon carrying out experiments at Cambridge and writing controversial articles such as "PSI, Science and the Future" in which he claimed that phenomena "has nothing to do with the evidence". In his book, *Explaining the Unexplained* (1982), co-authored with the equally outspoken psychologist, Dr Hans Eysenck, he argued:

"If we accept, for the sake of argument, that apparitions may not be explicable solely in the terms of hallucinations, visual illusions and coincidence, does this favour some kind of 'survivalist' interpretation? Or could 'Super-ESP' explain the results observed? After all, a crisis apparition could be a telepathic awareness of someone's death *plus* a strong hallucination generated in response to that stressful telepathic understanding. This is a fairly tenuous, but not logically absurd, hypothesis and some researchers have advanced it."

Although Sargeant subsequently gave up science to work in computer software – where he designed a number of popular role-playing games for *Dungeons and Dragons* – his influence has been evident in the work of other young paranormal researchers and much debated on the Internet.

The final decade of the twentieth century saw two more significant theories advanced about the nature of ghosts. The first was proposed by **Vic Tandy** (1946–), a trained engineer and expert in computer-assisted learning at Coventry University. As a result of an extra-ordinary sequence of events in 1998, he became convinced that the cause of ghosts could be "very low frequency sound waves trapped inside buildings". Tandy, previously sceptical about hauntings, had a traumatic night when he was working alone late one night in the laboratory of a medical manufacturing company in the Midlands. He had been told the building was haunted, but laughed off the idea, as he explained in June 1998:

"As I sat at a desk writing, I began to feel increasingly uncom-fortable. I was sweating but cold and the feeling of depression was noticeable – but there was also something else. It was as though *something* was in the room with me. Then I became aware that I was being watched and a figure slowly emerged to my left. It was indistinct and on the periphery of my vision, but it moved just as I would expect a person to. It was grey and made no sound. The hair was standing up on the back of my neck – I was terrified."

Tandy nerved himself to look at the apparition face on, only to see it fade and then vanish. He decided he must be ill and went home. The following morning after a good night's sleep, an explanation as to what had happened to him occurred to him when he was in the laboratory. He was in the process of modifying the blade of one of his foils that he used in his hobby of fencing:

"I left the blade clamped in the vice while I went in search of some oil. When I returned I noticed the free end of the blade was frantically vibrating up and down. I realized that the blade might be receiving energy from very low frequency sound waves filling the laboratory – so low that they could not be heard. I did some tests and these revealed the existence of a 'standing wave' trapped in the laboratory, which reached a peak in intensity next to my desk. It turned out to be caused by a new extraction fan, which was making the air vibrate at about nineteen cycles per second. When the fan's mounting was altered, the ghost left with the standing wave."

Tandy's further research established that the low frequency sound waves were capable of being triggered by nothing stronger than the wind passing over walls. The sound waves were not audible, but they could still have the effect on the human body that could account for wraith-like appearances – even the feelings of cold and terror that accompanied them. Vic Tandy was convinced he had the explanation for the ghost that materialized in the laboratory.

Although this explanation has been disputed by several authorities – in particular Professor David Fontana, of the University of Cardiff and a former president of the SPR, who believes it "does not explain those cases where there is one interaction between the person and the apparition" – Vic Tandy has received support from an unexpected source, NASA, the American space agency. Research by their scientists has shown that the human eyeball has a resonant frequency of eighteen cycles a second, at which it vibrates in sympathy to infrasound that would "cause a serious smearing of vision" and a host of physiological effects including breathlessness, shivering and feelings of fear.

The effect of electromagnetic pollution from natural and man-made sources on the brain was also put forward by an American scientist, Albert Budden, as a theory to explain both ghosts and Unidentified Flying Objects (UFOs). However, his suggestion that Flying Saucers might be just another form of the supernatural was not, in fact, new. An English writer, Joseph R Ledger, had put the idea forward in an article "Saucers or Ghosts?" in 1962, in which he listed the points of similarity between legends of ghostly nightriders and UFO phenomenon:

- A curious, broad-brimmed hat shape.
- Nocturnal visibility.
- Rapid movement through the air.
- The central object followed by a trailing appendage.

Ledger's call that the link between old ghost legends and the UFO phenomena was worth further investigation did not fall on deaf ears. In 1971, the American writer and UFO researcher, John A Keel, argued in his book, *UFOs – Operation Trojan Horse* (1971) that the space ships and their crews were visitors from an alien, possibly psychic dimension. Being independent of our world, Keel said, they could manipulate the form of their machines at will. He continued:

"In psychic phenomena and demonology we find that seemingly solid physical objects are materialized and dematerialized or apported, just as the UFOs and their splendid occupants appear and disappear, walk through walls and perform other super-natural feats. UFOlogists have constructed elaborate theories about flying saucer propulsion and anti-gravity. But we cannot exclude the possibility that these wondrous 'machines' are made of the same stuff as our disappearing psychic phenomena and they don't fly – they levitate. They are merely temporary intrusions into our reality or space-time continuum, momentary manipulations of electro-magnetic energy."

In his book, Keel cities numerous cases where UFOs have suddenly materialized from "nowhere" and numerous instances where alleged ufonauts have appeared to earth people "coming and going with the suddenness of the ghosts of antiquity". He continues:

"UFOs do not appear to exist as tangible fabricated objects. They do not conform to the natural laws with which we are familiar. They seem only to be metamorphoses, transformations that are able to adapt themselves to the capacities of our intelligence. Thousands of contacts with these beings lead us to the conclusion that they are deliberately making fools of us."

Fools or not, the mystery of ghosts and what precisely they are, is certainly going to continue to tax our intelligence in this century, as ever more sophisticated science and technology are brought to bear. Whenever this debate comes up, I am always reminded of a story that William Oliver Stevens told in his excellent book, *Unbidden Guests* (1949), a copy of which was given to me when I was an inquisitive schoolboy. In it, Stevens writes:

"A friend of mine, Head of a Department at a famous eastern college, once had a ghostly experience. His wife was with him at the time and she saw the vision at the same time he did. It happened outdoors in the middle of the forenoon, and there was no possibility of illusion. He told his colleague, the Professor of Psychology, what he and his wife had seen. 'Very simple,' replied the pundit. 'You had in your stomach, let us say, a bit of undigested bacon from your breakfast. That set up some distur-bances in your blood stream which resulted in a queer image in your brain. Your wife, as she glanced at you, caught the same picture from you by a sort of mental infection, so she thought she saw the same thing.'"

The story is, of course, a mixture of the fanciful and the factual as are all the best ghost stories. When I am asked for my own beliefs about ghosts I reply that I have met and talked to too many honest and sincere men and woman completely convinced of their paranormal encounter with the unknown for me to possibly deny their existence. If pressed for what I think ghosts *are*, I fall back on the definition of Robert Graves, which seems to embody both the desire to solve the matter but at the same time preserve the mystery:

> "The commonsense view is, I think, that one should accept ghosts very much as one accepts fire – a more common but equally mysterious phenomenon. What is fire? It is not really an element, not a principle of motion, not a living creature – not even a disease though a house can catch fire from its neighbour. It is an event rather than a living thing or a creature. Ghosts, similarly, seem to be events rather than things or creatures."

9

An A-Z of Ghosts

Phantoms of the World

A

AFRIT (Arabian)

According to Arabic folklore, the *Afrit* is the ghost of a murdered person rising to avenge their death. It is believed that the spirit materializes from the blood of the victim when it drips onto the ground and appears rather like smoke from a fire. The only way one of these apparitions can be laid to rest is by driving a nail into the ground where the blood fell. This practice is said to have given rise to the expression "nailing down the ghost".

ANKOU (European)

Also known as "The Graveyard Watcher", the *Ankou* is found all over Europe and is the spirit that guards cemeteries. The spirit originated from an ancient tradition that whenever a new cemetery was opened a selected victim would be buried alive to provide the place with a "ghostly guardian". In Great Britain, the *Ankou* is said to be the origin of the phrase used by people whenever they are struck by an involuntary shiver, "Someone is walking over my grave."

AUNGA (Malayan)

In Malaya it is believed that every human soul has two parts – and at death these break into two parts, the *Aunga*, or good ghost, and the *Adaro*, or evil ghost. According to tradition, the *Aunga* is immortal and will live on forever, watching over people, as long as it is treated with honour. The evil *Adaro*, however, can be dangerous but has only a limited time span and will eventually die.

B

BAKA (Haitian)

The *Baka* is a cannibalistic spirit that rises from graveyards at night and preys on the living. Compared in some texts as being rather like a ghoul or zombie, the phantom is almost invisible and its teeth are more often sensed than felt. Legend has it that the *Baka* is the restless ghost of someone who belonged to a Haitian secret society, which initiates followers while they are alive into the way they must behave after death.

BANSHEE (Irish)

Many ancient Irish families claim to be haunted by the "Lady of Death" as the *Banshee*, or *Bean Si*, is known in the nation. The ghost appears at night just before a member of the family is about to die and wails and cries within view of the house. Legend states that the spirit is invariably female, can be young or old, with long hair, red eyes from crying and speaks in an unknown language. The Banshee may appear more than once before a family member dies. There are on record accounts of members of old Irish families dying thousands of miles away from their home with a *Bean Si* heard wailing in Ireland. Some experts have claimed that the ghost is that of an earlier member of the family who has been selected to be the "harbinger of death".

BEAN-NIGHE (Scottish)

Another herald of death, the "Little washer by the Ford" as this ghost is known in Scotland materializes as a female carrying the recently washed grave clothes of the person about to die. The *Bean-Nighe* is invariably ugly and is said to have large, protruding teeth, one nostril and huge, pendulous breasts. The ghost is believed to be that of a woman who died in childbirth and like the Irish Banshee *(see above)* has been known to appear to exiled Scots as far away from home as Canada and Australia.

BERGMONK (German)

As its name indicates, this ghost bears a striking resemblance to a monk. According to German tradition, it is a towering figure intent on frightening people away from buried treasure. They are most frequently found in the vicinity of mines and are believed to be similar to the phantom guardians found in a number of other European countries with a similar purpose of scaring off fortune hunters – though why they should wish to do this is unclear.

BHUT (Indian)

According to Indian tradition, the *Bhut* is any angry ghost that is unhappy in the spirit world and sets out to bother the living. There are several different types of this phantom, the most feared being the *Airi*, which is apparently the spirit of a man who was killed while hunting. These ghosts are usually seen with packs of dogs and are considered an omen of death. They can, however, be driven off by burning a dish of turmeric, because they hate the smell given off by the spice.

BOGGART (English)

A disturbing and unpleasant type of ghost found in the North of England – in Lancashire, especially – where it targets farms and isolated properties. They can upset households in a manner similar to poltergeists, but are mostly prone to invading bedrooms at night, pulling the bedclothes off the sleepers and occasionally placing a "clammy" hand onto their faces. According to tradition, it is possible to prevent a *Boggart* from invading your home by hanging a horseshoe on the door or gate.

BOGIE (Scottish)

A terrifying ghost, the Bogie has the ability to change shape and can make a wailing sound that some experts have claimed imitates the phrase, "I want my bones". According to ancient tradition these ghosts once served the devil during his evil missions among mankind, but now content themselves by materializing as dark, squat figures with ugly faces that particularly like attacking the young. This facility is believed to have been the origin of the expression used by parents over many generations to quieten a fractious child, "Stop that or the Bogie man will get you!" It is claimed they can be made to vanish by holding open a copy of the Bible in front of them.

BRAHMADAITYA (Indian)

Generally regarded as the most benign of Indian ghosts, the *Brahmadaitya* lives in trees and acts as a good luck symbol to surrounding villages. The spirit is believed to be the ghost of a Brahmin who died unmarried and is now committed to looking after his "family" on earth. The spirit apparently does not like his domain to be trespassed upon and has the power to break the necks of those who are foolish enough to do so.

BUGABOO (Indian)

Another Indian ghost that is said to be kindly disposed towards human beings. The spirits appear at nightfall and will not interfere with life unless they are threatened. Some experts have claimed that Indians do not actually believe in the existence of these ghosts, but they have become familiar in family life as the spirits used by mothers to quieten noisy or difficult children.

C

CHAGRIN (European)

The *Chagrin* is an old gypsy word for a prophetic ghost, which can appear in many forms. The spirit is also referred to as a *Cogrino* or *Harginn* and is an omen of some kind of disaster that is about to happen. In some parts of Europe, it is said to appear in the form of a large, yellow hedgehog.

CORPSE CANDLE (Welsh)

Known as the *Canhywallen Cyrth*, this is the best known of Welsh phantoms and they are so named because of their resemblance to a candle flame. Like the Irish *Banshee*, the Corpse Candle will materialize near to a home where someone is about to die. The light of the phantom will indicate whether the victim is young or old: a small, blue flame for a child, while a large, red flame points to an adult. There are also numerous accounts in Welsh folklore of white lights being seen hovering over old bedridden men and woman before they pass away.

CO-WALKER (Scottish)

Another prophetic ghost, the *Co-Walker* has been described as similar to the better-known German *Doppelganger (see below)*. They are identical spirits – "in every way like the man, as a twin-brother, haunting him as his shadow", to quote one source – and appear to that person not long before they are due to die. According to accounts from the last three centuries, *Co-Walkers* have been seen at a number of funerals where their likeness to the dead person has had a horrifying effect on the mourners.

D

DOMOVOY (Russian)

The *Domovoy* is the most famous of Russia's ghosts. They are said to be invisible, but make their presence known by loud noises, throwing objects about and disturbing entire families. The similarity with *Poltergeists (see p.505)* has been much commented upon. Some old accounts of this spirit claim that those that have been treated with respect will find their household chores done when they awake in the morning.

DOPPELGANGER (German)

Sometimes referred to as the "ghost soul", the *Doppelganger* is a German term for a ghost that is the exact likeness or "double" of the person they are haunting. These spirits are said to be harbingers of death and materialize with ever-greater frequency as the person concerned nears his or her end. The term was popularized by the German writer, E T A Hoffman, and made famous in Edgar Allan Poe's story of "William Wilson" (1839) and Dostoyevsky's novel *The Double* (1846).

DRUDE (English)

The *Drude* is a ghost associated with witchcraft. According to tradition, a young witch had the ability to become one of these night phantoms when she reached the age of forty. The spirit possesses the power to haunt her victims by inflicting terrible visions on them and in some parts of the country is actually referred to as "the nightmare fiend".

DUPPY (West Indian)

A frightening phantom that is said to be only able to appear at night, the *Duppy* is believed to be the personification of evil and must depart before dawn breaks. These spirits have a long tradition in the Caribbean and it is claimed that they can be summoned from tombs by placing a glass of rum and some gold coins on the grave. West Indians believe that if a *Duppy* exhales over a person they will become ill. The ghost can be prevented from entering a house by placing tobacco seeds around the doors and windows and if one of them is prevented from returning to the grave, it will never be able to haunt anyone again.

E

ELEMENTAL (European)

Unlike most ghosts that are the spirits of the dead, *Elementals* are believed to be supernatural beings that have never been human. They are said to take the form of glowing human-shaped lights that materialize where tragic events have occurred. Stories of these strange phantoms have been recorded for centuries – a number of famous folk legends are based on them – and their favourite places for haunting are said to be treacherous marshes and shifting sands along the coast.

F

FETCH (English)

A ghost similar to the German *Doppelganger* or Scottish *Co-Walker* in that it closely resembles the person it confronts. Believed to be an omen of death, the *Fetch* has been reported appearing before people in the open countryside and in houses – and in one case materialized as a corpse on a bed before its horrified living double who died a few days later.

FOSSEGRIM (European)

A water phantom, the *Fossegrim* or *Neck*, usually resembles a young man and haunts rivers and streams. According to European tradition, the phantom is very alluring to young girls who have been fickle with their affections. Generally believed to be harmless despite his name, the *Fossegrim* can be driven off by unsheathing a knife in the ghost's presence as this will "Bind the Neck" in the words of an old saying.

G

GALLEYTROT (English)

This is an animal ghost that resembles a large dog and has been mostly seen in East Anglia where it is said to move around country lanes "like an evil whisper". The name is believed to be a corruption of the French *gardez le trésor* or "guardian of the treasure" and the majority have been seen close to old burial grounds. Some *Galleytrots* are stated to be black in colour with flaming eyes, while one of the most famous that is said to haunt the wilds of Suffolk resembles an enormous hound with the head of a monk.

GHOUL (Indian)

The *Ghoul* or *Gul* is sometimes compared to the vampire, although it does not attempt to bite those it encounters, but simply passes straight through bodies and buildings as if they were not there. According to various local traditions throughout the Indian subcontinent, the spirit has a hideous face and is mostly found in any area used for burying the dead or where soldiers have been killed in battle. There are stories that the *Ghoul* will steal corpses and has been known to prey on unwary travellers – although no one has survived such encounters to tell the tale.

H

HAG OF THE DRIBBLE (Welsh)

Known in Wales as the *Gwrach-y-rhibyn,* this ghost is notoriously ugly, appearing as an old woman with long, matted hair, a hooked nose, piercing eyes and long arms with claw-like hands. Some reports of the phantom have stated that she looks as if she has scaly black wings, and all of them screech in a voice that is claimed to be an omen of death. According to tradition, the original hags were Welsh goddesses and are mostly to be found in the vicinity of old castles. "She is as ugly as the *Gwrach-y-rhibyn!*" has been a form of abuse in Wales for many years.

HARPY (Greek)

One of the oldest ghosts on record – the *Harpy* is a phantom creature with the face of a female and the wings of a bird. Ancient Greek tradition claimed she was a "wind spirit" who could play havoc in the affairs of human beings unless she was regularly propitiated. The activities of the *Harpy* were particularly feared around harvest time when she might call up gales to ruin the crops. She is also believed to have the power to capture the souls of men and women when they die.

I

INCUBUS (European)

An evil spirit that materializes during the night in the bedroom of young girls with the intention of seducing them. According to medieval European folklore, the *Incubus* appears in the form of a handsome young man – who is referred to as "Demon Lover" – intent on turning their victims into wantons and whores. The only sure method of protection from their seductions is to hang herbs such as St John's Wort around the bed. See also *Succubus*.

IGNUS FATUUS (European)

Ghostly dancing lights that are said to be omens of death when seen by travellers have been given various names throughout Europe, but are grouped under the term, *Ignus Fatuus* or "Foolish Fire". Jack-o-Lantern and Will-o'-the-Wisp are just two terms applied to these phenomena that are said to appear where someone is going to die – and, indeed, they have a history of leading the curious into treacherous marshland as they most often appear near water. Recent research has suggested that these "ghosts" may well be caused by the spontaneous combustion of marsh gases.

J

JAK (Indian)

Jaks are male ghosts that are often reported with female partners – known as *Jakni* – and seen together in rural villages. Their mission is to guard the local population from the myriad evil spirits that can make human life so difficult. However, according to some local traditions, *Jak* and *Jakni* have been known to remove household items to which they have taken a fancy and present them to their partners.

JINN (Arabian)

Sometimes pronounced "Genie", these ancient Arab spirits have the form and substance of a ghost and are traditionally kept confined in a bottle from which they can be summoned by those knowing the secret commands, According to tradition, the *Jinns* are believed to have been created from a man's shadow and can stretch and elongate themselves into any shape whether they are intent on helping or harming people. They have, of course, become the subject of many popular fairy stories.

K

KELPIE (Scottish)

The *Kelpie* is a water-spirit that can materialize as a wild-looking man or a horse, both of which are planning to lure the unwary into the river and death by drowning. It is probably Scotland's best-known ghost and is usually reported during storms when it makes a strange, wailing sound and often jumps into a river with its tail striking the water with a sound like thunder. An old Highland legend claims that anyone who can put a bridle on a *Kelpie* can keep it – but if this is ever removed the owner and his family will be accursed.

KHU (Egyptian)

The Ancient Egyptians believed that as soon as the soul left a dying person's body, it would turn into a *Khu* or ghost. Those who had led evil lives, been executed for a crime or committed suicide would become a malevolent spirit and bring much harm on their family and relatives. In order to prevent years of haunting, the ghost would be placated with offerings. Those who had led good lives would return as benevolent spirits to watch over their families and had the power to take possession of the bodies of animals.

KIKIMORA (Russian)

Although the *Kikimora* is generally regarded as a Russian ghost, it has, in fact, been reported among the traditions of all the Slavonic-speaking peoples – including the Poles, Czechs, Serbians and Bulgarians. It is said that the spirit, which appears in an indistinct form, attaches itself to certain households and if treated with courtesy will protect the family from misfortune.

KIRKGRIM (Danish)

The *Kirkgrim* is associated with old Danish churches where it is said to live in the church tower and protect the building from vandalism. It is believed to be a similar ghost to that recorded in certain Scottish churches where an animal has been killed and buried in the churchyard to serve as a "haunting spectre" and similarly guard the building from sacrilege.

KNOCKER (English)

The *Knocker* is a ghost that dwells in mines, and for many years they were said to be quite common in the tin mines of Cornwall. It is believed they got their name from knocking on the walls of the shafts to give an indication where iron ore might be found. They also warn the miners of danger. In other parts of Britain a similar spirit, the *Kobold* has been reported, but they are apparently evil and cause rock falls and other small accidents.

KUEI (Chinese)

The Chinese have at least twenty distinct varieties of ghosts that are not always easy to distinguish from one another, although they are divided into two categories. The *Kuei* are associated with darkness, misfortune and death, while the *Shen (see p.507)* are ancestral ghosts to be revered. According to tradition, the Chinese do not fear the *Kuei* and will simply keep them away from their homes by hanging up iron or steel symbols.

L

LAR (Italian)

The *Lares Domestici* were the household ghosts of Ancient Rome. According to tradition they were the spirits of people who had led virtuous lives – although they could be troublesome, throwing objects around and interfering physically with families. Reports of them describe the *Lares* as "so ugly that nurses used the mention of them to frighten children". Some experts have compared these ghosts to *Poltergeists* and belief in them still persists in certain rural districts of Italy.

LEMURE (Italian)

Another phantom first recorded by the Romans and said to be an evil spirit of the dead that returns to haunt its family and relatives. According to tradition, the *Lemure* is very active during the month of May and so festivals are held every year to propitiate them with offerings known as *religiousae*. It has been claimed that the way of preventing the return of someone who was thought might become one of these ghosts was to burn black beans around the tomb of the deceased as the spirits are unable withstand the awful smell.

LIEKKIO (Finland)

The *Liekkio* – the word means "Flaming One" – resembles a small flame that is seen hovering in any locality where a death is believed to be imminent. In appearance, the phantom is said to be similar to the British Jack-'o-Lantern, but it is not caused by igniting marsh gas as they appear all over the countryside. One tradition claims they are the souls of dead children who have been laid to rest in unmarked graves in forests.

LORELEI (German)

The German *Lorelei* is the beautiful, beguiling creature that haunts the River Rhine singing melodies so spellbinding they can cause anyone sailing by to lose their sense of direction and wreck their boat on the river's treacherous rocks. The legend featured in Heinrich Heine's poem *The Lorelei,* and a rock at Hesse-Nassau, known as the "Nymph's Perch", is now a tourist attraction drawing thousands of visitors every year. The rock formation is such that it causes echoes which the more impressionable believe to be the spirit singing.

M

MARA (Scandinavian)

According to Scandinavian tradition, the *Mara* is an evil spirit that materializes at night with the intention of tormenting people. It appears in a misty, human shape and can settle on sleepers, giving them nightmares – from whence its name was derived. In Jutland, the *Mara* is said to take on the form of a naked woman and will target men, giving them erotic dreams. Belief in this ghost has also been reported throughout the north and west of France.

MATEBO (Angolan)

The *Matebo* – an outcast dwarf ghost – is one of the most curious spirits to be found among the large ghost population of Angola and neighbouring Zaire. All along the Congo, traditional tales state, phantoms like the *Mizimi* of the Bantu people lurk to prey on hunters and many of these like the taste of blood. However, the *Matebo* are considered to be far worse as they actually consume human flesh in order to fill their white skeleton-like appearance. It is believed that these ghosts can be placated with offerings of food.

MUMIAI (Indian)

One of the strangest ghosts recorded in India, the *Mumiai* is said to haunt members of the lower Indian castes who are lazy or have criminal tendencies. It acts rather like a *Poltergeist*, never being seen, but throwing objects around and attacking people. According to reports, the weird spirit can make its presence felt both during the daytime and at night.

MURA-MURA (Australian)

These phenomena are regarded as "ancestral spirits" who demand respect or they will prevent rain from falling. The *Mura-Mura* can be propitiated by placing small stones covered with drops of blood on the highest branches of trees. According to tradition, the stones represent clouds, the blood signifies rain and once the spirits see these representations they will respond by sending a downpour.

N

NIXIE (German)

Another water spirit, the *Nixie* is usually invisible but can appear with a human body and fish tail which has led to claims that they were the original mermaids and mermen They haunt any large stretch of water – particularly near the coast of Germany – and have been known to lure humans to their death. For generations it was believed in certain coastal parts of the country that children born with large heads were the result of a union between a *Nixie* and a human girl.

O

OLD SHUCK (English)

A phantom dog about the size of a small calf with huge eyes that glow in the dark, *Old Shuck* has been haunting East Anglia for centuries. The big black creature is said to be an ill omen, for anyone who sees him will be dead within a year. It has been argued that he is the ghost of a giant hound brought to England by Viking raiders, although his name appears to derive from the Anglo-Saxon *succa* meaning Satan. Experts have suggested that the sightings of mysterious creatures as big as panthers in Southern England may have been inspired by tales of *Old Shuck*.

P

PAISACHI (Indian)

The *Paisachi* is a ghost found all over India that materializes in a human form and is often recognized by those who see it as someone from their district that they once knew. The spirit is generally regarded as an omen of death, though not in the immediate future. It is another Indian spirit that can be propitiated with gifts of food. Families troubled by ghosts in this part of the world can call on the services of a *shaycana*, usually a village elder who has inherited powers to drive off worrying phantoms.

PERFUME GHOSTS (British)

Since the seventeenth century, it has been claimed that some ghosts materialize in the form of a scent or aroma. Although nothing can be seen, numbers of people have described being suddenly conscious of the smell of someone to whom they were very familiar in life – usually in the home or another environment where they spent a lot of time together. A nationwide survey in 1978 produced reports of "Perfume Ghosts" from as far apart as Ross-shire in Scotland to Cornwall.

PHANTOM COACH (European)

In France and Germany a number of accounts can be found of huge, black, silent coaches pulled by headless horses and driven by a solitary figure in black. According to tradition, the cortege has come to collect a dying person and to see one is an ill omen. England also has a famous phantom coach in Dorset that runs at dusk from Woodbridge Manor to Bere Regis. The story was immortalized by Thomas Hardy in *Tess of the d'Urbervilles* (1891) in which it was stated that the coach owed its origin to a terrible murder and was a sign of imminent death to anyone who saw it passing.

PHANTOM HEADS (American)

America has a tradition of stories about phantom heads. The most famous of these originates from San Francisco where one of these heads with long, matted hair and bloodstains on the forehead was reported to be haunting Oakville in 1891. This terrifying vision, like a number of the others, materializes as a spherical, eerie light that gradually forms into a head. It is said to be extremely dangerous to approach one, as they are invariably accompanied by the sensation of icy fingers gripping the throat of the eyewitness.

PHANTOM SHIPS (South African)

Although the legend of the *Flying Dutchman*, forever sailing around the Cape of Good Hope since 1641, is the most famous phantom ship, similar vessels have been reported off the coasts of England, Scotland, Ireland, France, Germany, Denmark, Canada, America and even China. Like the Dutch ship captained by Hendrik Vanderdecken, cursed for his blasphemy during a storm off the Cape to sail without ever reaching land, all such boats are believed to bring misfortune to any other ships and crews that cross their path. There are numerous accounts of these ghostly ships in both fact and fiction, perhaps most famously in the classic novel, *The Phantom Ship* by Captain Frederick Marryat (1839). The *Flying Dutchman* was also seen by Prince George (later King George V) while on a world cruise in 1881.

PHOUKA (Irish)

Another famous Irish spirit that usually appears in the shape of a horse and is said to carry off unsuspecting victims for a wild ride across the countryside. The name is said to derive from the word *Poc*, a male goat, and is believed to be the inspiration for Shakespeare's Puck. The phantom lives in isolated mountains or old ruins and there are a number of locations in Ireland, notably in County Wicklow, with localities that have become known as "The Hole of the *Phouka*". In some parts of the country, the spirit is believed to be more mischievous than dangerous.

POLTERGEIST (German)

It was the Germans who first named the "racketing spirit" that has caused such fright and chaos in homes all over the world – the verb *Polter* to make a noise by knocking things about, and the noun *Geist*, for a ghost. The complex nature of *Poltergeist* phenomena has lead to various suggestions about their origins, notably that they are often associated with unruly young adolescents. There is also an English description for the spirit as a "Polter-Ghost" deriving from the word to knock, thrash or beat but this is rarely used in preference to the German term. It has been suggested by some experts that the difference between ghosts and *Poltergeists* is that while one *haunts*, the other *infests*.

Q

QUINNS LIGHT (Australian)

This phenomenon, which appears as a phosphorescent light about the size of a large bird, is most often reported in the Bush areas of Australia. The eerie light goes round in circles before disappearing as mysteriously as it appeared – and apparently does no harm to anyone who sees it. Experts have drawn comparisons between Quinns Lights and the *Corpse Candles (see p.496)* encountered in the British Isles, which it has been suggested are caused by escaping marsh gas. Quite unique to Australia is the *MinMin*, which gives off a ghostly glow and is usually seen in cemeteries dancing on gravestones.

R

REVENANT (American)

The best reports of *Revenants* – which are not traditional ghosts, as is sometimes suggested, but spirits that have returned from the dead after a very long absence – occur in the traditions of the North American Native Indians. These phantoms are often re-ported appearing in groups such as the Ojibwa Indians who had died more than a century earlier and were sighted again in the 1970s. *Revenants* invariably appear in the clothes in which they died. There have also been accounts of their being seen in Europe, notably as recounted by Ernest Rhys in "The Altheim Revenant" in 1921.

RUDRA (Indian)

The *Rudra* is a "leader" among Indian ghosts and said to be the commander of battalions of phantoms that can be sent out to haunt the living – usually in localities where he has not been shown the necessary respect. This ghost is usually seen at different places over a large area and can travel at great speed. Because the *Rudra* and his minions are said to gather at crossroads before under-taking any haunting, the people of India have a long tradition of leaving offerings at these junctions to propitiate them.

S

SCREAMING SKULLS (English)

Accounts of ancient skulls that are believed to be haunted by the ghosts of their former owners, is a largely English tradition. There are numerous stories from places as far apart as Somerset, Lake Windermere, Manchester and Yorkshire about skulls that have uttered the most hideous screams when attempts have been made to move them from their accustomed place. In most cases, it is claimed that the owner had left specific instructions about his burial and then "objected" when his or her wishes were not carried out. The most famous "Screaming Skull" resides at Bettiscomb Manor in Dorset and is said to be that of a Negro slave who promised to haunt the house if his body was not returned to the West Indies. When his master took no notice, it seems, the haunted skull extracted its own revenge by defying any attempts to move it with such alarming noises that it has never been moved again.

SHEN (Chinese)

The *Shen* are the ancestral ghosts of the Chinese and are regarded with great respect and honoured with annual feasts. There are more than twenty different types divided into two categories of which the *Shen* (sometimes *Shin*) are one; the others being the *Kuei* (*see p.501*) who are associated with darkness, bad luck and death. For centuries the Chinese have been making contact with the *Shen* for prophecies about their future using the art of divination and a v-shaped "speaking" twig. A crayon is fixed in the point of the vee at right angles so that it is vertical and when placed on a piece of paper will write out the letters of a message – as long as the holder is "sensitive" to the *Shen*.

SHOJO (Japanese)

The *Shojo* are Japanese sea ghosts. Although they are said to be the spirits of dead sailors, they live under the surface of the ocean and are recognizable by their vivid red hair. According to tradition they intend no harm to the living and devote their time to drinking and making merry. Old tales claim that the *Shojo* particularly like saki and the way to catch one is to lure it on land with a bowl of the drink.

SILKY (Scottish)

The *Silky* is reputed to be one of the most attractive ghosts in the world. Found predominantly in the Border Counties, the spirit is female in appearance and has been named after the rustling clothes that it wears. According to tradition, these ghosts have always been welcome in Scottish homes because they are keen to carry out domestic chores and will hassle any lazy servant or person who does not do their share of work. The most famous *Silky* is said to haunt an area of North Shields and is believed to have been the ghost of a mistress of the Duke of Argyll who was murdered by a jealous lover at the beginning of the seventeenth century.

SPECTRE (European)

The *Spectre* is not just another word for a ghost, but the term now generally applied to a haunting for which there is an explanation or one proved to be deliberately fraudulent. In Victorian England, for example, there were numerous instances during the infancy of photography when apparent "spectres" were caught on camera but later proved to have been added during the development of the photographer's glass plates. Probably the most famous explanation for one of these phenomena occurred in Germany with "The Spectre of the Brocken" in the Harz Mountains, which had been regarded for centuries as a meeting place for witches and demons. Finally, in 1818, after terrifying generations of travellers, the towering figure looming overhead was proved to be a trick of the light caused by the setting sun reflecting on mist swirling around the 3,300-ft high mountain.

SPOOK (American)

Spooks are the traditional ghosts of the American Indians and are believed to have the power of taking control of the body of a living person. It is believed they can haunt a person without them being aware of the fact – absorbing themselves into the body unnoticed – although their intentions are said to be helpful rather than intended to cause harm. In several of the Eastern States of America, there are stories of people who believed their lives were heading for failure until a *Spook* took them over. The term is, of course, now also familiar referring to those who work for government surveillance agencies.

SPUNKIE (British)

The *Spunkie* is found in England and Scotland, often in the countryside and occasionally just off the coast. They are particularly sad ghosts being the spirits of unbaptized children who have died in infancy. According to tradition they can be seen in isolated lanes "looking for someone to give them a name" or appearing to the crews of coastal vessels where their plaintive cries can be very unsettling. In Scotland it is believed that *Spunkies* sometimes gather together to avoid loneliness, while in England they often foregather at Halloween. It is generally thought that the sad little spirits are doomed to wander "until Judgment Day".

SUCCUBUS (European)

These are beautiful, beguiling and apparently scantily dressed young female phantoms that come by night to seduce impressionable young men and turn them onto evil ways. Recorded since the days of medieval European folklore, the *Succubus* is the female equivalent of the *Incubus (see p.499)* who fixes his attentions on young girls. In some traditions the spirits are said to be androgynous, changing their sex at will to suit their intended victims.

T

TANWEDD (Welsh)

Another of the category of ghosts seen in the shape of a small spherical light that hovers over a house as an omen. The *Tanwedd* has been reported for centuries throughout the nation and it is believed that if one remains stationary over the building then a member of the family will shortly meet with an accident. More ominous still, if one of these lights descends onto the house then a death can be expected within the week.

TASH (Irish)

These curious little Irish ghosts can appear either as human beings or animals. Referred to as a *Tash* or *Thevshi*, the phantoms are believed to be the spirits of people who died violent deaths – either having been murdered or committed suicide. They are said to be anxious to bring to the attention of those who live in the same vicinity the folly of their actions. In some Irish country districts it is still held to be foolish to mourn too long for anyone "or else they will be kept from their rest and return as a *Tash*".

TOH (Borneo)

The headhunters of Borneo long believed that the heads of their victims contained the *Toh* or ghost of the person they had killed. They believed it had magical qualities and would place it in a position of honour so that the phantom could circulate and bring prosperity to the community. The *Toh* was widely regarded as a good luck symbol and to lose a head won in battle could well bring misfortune to the owner, his family and the whole tribe.

TOKOLOSH (South Africa)

The *Tokolosh* is a strange-looking phantom that lives in the rivers and watercourses of South Africa. Semi-human in appearance, it is said to be not much bigger than a baboon with a body covered in black hair. According to reports, the creature appears at night and carries out revengeful and spiteful acts. It makes no sound, but can become invisible in an instant. Some experts have suggested that there is a certain similarity in the actions of the *Tokolosh* to the European *Poltergeist*.

TRICKSTER SPIRIT (American)

For all its light-hearted name, the *Trickster* is an eerie phantom that appears either in human shape or as a "dancing light" that can lure the unwary to their death. Found mainly in the Florida Everglades, the ghosts are said to be the spirits of Native Indians who were killed during the Seminole Indian Wars in 1852 and have spent the years ever since seeking revenge on the white man by luring them into the treacherous swamplands.

U

UNDINE (European)

Known throughout Europe, the beautiful and beguiling *Undine* is a female spirit that haunts stretches of water reproaching unfaithful lovers. According to tradition, the spirits are those of young women who died by drowning – usually having killed themselves after a broken love affair. These ghosts – who have been celebrated in stories and poems for generations – apparently intend no harm to anyone who sees them, beyond serving as a warning to those who are being untrue to their partners.

UTUKKU (Assyrian)

Records indicate that the Ancient Assyrians were among the first people to take ghosts seriously and named the spirits they believed arose from the dead, the *Utukku*. They believed these phantoms had evil intentions and would lay in wait for unwary travellers. The *Utukku* were also said to have the power to make anyone who crosses their path fall ill. The Assyrians identified two other types of ghost: the *Alu*, a hideous-looking spirit, usually with one or more of its limbs missing, that tried to grab its victims in a "clammy embrace" and the *Ekimmu*, that appeared outside homes wailing that a death was imminent. Furthermore, the Assyrians believed that all three types of ghost resulted from either failing to observe the proper rites when burying a dead person or leaving a body unburied.

V

VERRE (Nigerian)

A traditional ghost in that it assumes human form, appears and disappears in a moment and usually haunts at night, the *Verre* of Nigeria is unusual in that the people have a special address directed to it that is read over a dead body before burial. The words declare: "You have lived long. Go now to the sun and declare that you are the last of living men and it is useless to send any more [ghosts] to us. And do not bear us malice. Return not to earth to interfere with our crops or prevent our women being childless."

VIRIKA (Indian)

The *Virika* is sometimes referred to as the "Vampire Ghost" because of its ability to leave bite marks on the flesh of its victims – although they are completely unaware of its presence. The spirits are said to have small, red-coloured bodies, long pointed teeth and roam the countryside at night making harsh, gibbering sounds. In certain parts of India little shrines can be seen at the roadside in which offerings of bloody meat have been placed in the hope of assuaging the *Virika's* appetite.

W

WATER WRAITH (Scottish)

People in Scotland are divided in their opinions about the *Water Wraith*, which has been recorded in tradition for several hundred years. The ghost is said to resemble a skinny, withered old woman who dresses all in green. She is invariably scowling and is said to be intent on luring her victims to their death by drowning. Some authorities have cast doubts on the actuality of this ghost as by far the majority of accounts of seeing the *Water Wraith* have been made by men on their way home and very much the worse for a night's drinking.

WENDIGO (Canadian)

Belief in the *Wendigo* goes back to some of the country's earliest legends and describes it as half-phantom and half-beast. According to these stories, the creature lives in forests and seizes human beings, particularly children, and eats their flesh. It is said that the *Wendigo* originally entered into a pact with evil spirits to gain their immortality. Furthermore, the spirit can be either male or female, and is occasionally found in the same vicinity as other Canadian "wood horrors" including the whimpus, the hodag and the bizarrely named filamaloo.

WHITE LADY (French)

The *White Lady* is a familiar figure in French folklore, where they are usually said to be strikingly beautiful and found in the vicinity of old bridges. According to tradition, the reason for this location is that it was once the custom to offer young women as human sacrifices to rivers over which a new bridge had been erected so that the waters would allow people to cross in safety. *White Ladies* have also been reported in a number of other European countries, where they tend to haunt the castles and old houses where they once lived and ended their lives in tragic or murderous circumstances.

WILL-O'-THE-WISP (European)

The *Will-o'-the-wisp* is just one of many names used throughout Europe to describe the ghostly lights which hover over marshland or old graveyards – *Jack-o'-Lantern, Corpse Candle, William with the Little Flame*, are just three of many more. Traditionally they have been described as the souls of dead people predicting a death, or alternately lost souls that cannot enter heaven and are condemned to lure the foolish into danger. The lights are now more likely supposed to be the igniting of gases escaping from rotting plant matter.

WOLHAARHOND (South African)

Another of the world's disturbing animal phantoms, the *Wolhaarhond* is a large, furry dog that glows in the darkness and is ill-omened. According to accounts over many years, the phantom initially appears as a red light and only begins to change into a dog when it nears a potential victim. It also bears striking similarities to the famous English hound, *Old Shuck (see p.503)*.

WOTAN (French)

Associated with terrible storms, *Wotan* is the name of the Wild Huntsman who has ridden across the skies of France with his spectral hounds in search of human souls for many centuries. In rural districts of the country, people still lock their doors very carefully at night if there is the chance of a storm brewing up, afraid that the phantom huntsman might spot them and carry them off as he did their forebears in the past.

WRAITH (European)

The *Wraith* is an exact likeness of a man or woman presenting itself at the moment of that person's death There are numerous accounts of people seeing their own likeness, notably the poet Percy Bysshe Shelley who, in 1822, saw his own *Wraith* as he was about to board the ship across the Bay of Spezia in Italy which would carry him to his death by drowning. In other instances, the phantom has presented itself to family or relatives of a person about to die many miles away. The tradition of the *Wraith* has apparently evolved from an ancient belief that a person's soul is an exact duplicate of their living body and must escape from it when death is imminent.

X Y Z

YURI (Japanese)

The Japanese have a long tradition of *Yuri* or *Kaidan* (ghosts) and even a number of "ghost gods" of varying degrees of ugliness, according to ancient documents. They all vary in temperament, the females less fierce than the males who are often deformed, with snake-like necks, elongated tongues, and either one or three eyes. They mostly haunt cemeteries and old houses, and among their number are the "Water Bogie", "The Storm Fiend" and the curious "Chink and Crevice Bogie". The ghosts of famous samurai warriors have also been reported in the localities where they died and there are occasional sightings, too, of the *Koi-Teno*, or "Fox Spirit" – a female ghost in long, flowing white robes who has the power to bewitch unwary men.

Bibliography

Alexander, Marc, *Haunted Inns*, Frederick Muller, 1973.

Archer, Fred, *Exploring The Psychic World*, W H Allen, 1966.

Bardens, Denis, *Ghosts and Hauntings*, Zeus Press, 1965.

——*Mysterious Worlds*, W H Allen, 1970.

Barrett, Sir William F, *On The Threshold of the Unseen*, Keegan Paul, 1917.

Bayless, Raymond, *Animal Ghosts*, University Books, 1970.

Bennett, Sir Ernest, *Apparitions and Haunted Houses*, Faber & Faber, 1939.

Bird, J. Malcolm, *My Psychic Adventures*, George Allen & Unwin, 1923.

Braddock, Joseph, *Haunted Houses*, B T Batsford, 1956.

Byrd, Elizabeth, *The Ghosts in My Life*, Ballantine Books, 1968.

Carrington, Hereward, *Haunted People*, E P Dutton, 1951.

——*Invisible World*, Rider & Co., 1947.

——*Psychical Phenomena and the War*, T Werner Laurie, 1918.

Cohen, Daniel, *Encyclopaedia of Ghosts*, Michael O'Mara, 1989.

Crowe, Catherine, *The Night Side of Nature*, George Routledge & Sons, 1848.

Day, James Wentworth, *Ghosts and Witches*, B T Batsford, 1954.

Dingwall, Eric J and Hall, Trevor, *Four Modern Ghosts*, Duckworth, 1958.

——& John Langdon Davies, *The Unknown: Is It Nearer?* Cassell, 1956.

Douglas, Alfred, *Extra Sensory Powers*, Victor Gollancz Ltd., 1976.

Doyle, Arthur Conan, *History of Spiritualism*, Cassell & Co., 1926.

——*The New Revelation*, Hodder & Stoughton, 1918.

——*The Vital Message*, Hodder & Stoughton, 1919.

Ebon, Martin, *Exorcism: Fact Not Fiction*, New American Library, 1974.

——*The Psychic Reader*, New American Library, 1969.

——*True Experiences with Ghosts*, New American Library, 1968.

Finucane, R C, *Appearance of the Dead*, Junction Books, 1983.

Flammarion, Camille, *Haunted Houses*, T Fisher Unwin, 1924.

Fodor, Nandor, *Between Two Worlds*, Prentice Hall, 1964.

——*Haunted People: The Poltergeist Down the Ages*, Dutton, 1951.

——*On The Trail of the Poltergeist*, Citadel Press, 1958.

——*The Haunted Mind*, Garrett Publications, 1959.

Forman, Joan, *Haunted East Anglia*, Robert Hale, 1974.

Garrett, Eileen G, *Adventures in the Supernormal*, Paperback Library, 1968.

Gauld, Alan and Cornell, A D, *Poltergeists*, Routledge & Kegan Paul, 1979.

Gooch, Stan, *The Paranormal*, Wildwood House, 1978.

Green, Andrew, *Ghost Hunting: A Practical Guide*, Garnstone Press, 1973.

——*Our Haunted Kingdom*, Wolfe Publishing, 1973.

Green, Celia and McCreery, *Apparitions*, Hamish Hamilton, 1975.

Haining, Peter, *A Dictionary of Ghosts*, Robert Hale, 1982.

——*Ghosts: The Illustrated History*, Sidgwick & Jackson, 1975.

Hall, Trevor H, *New Light on Old Ghosts*, Gerald Duckworth, 1965.

——*Search for Harry Price*, Gerald Duckworth, 1978.

Harper, Charles G, *Haunted Houses*, Chapman & Hall, 1907.

Harries, John, *The Ghost Hunter's Road Book*, Frederick Muller, 1968.

Hole, Christina, *Haunted England*, Batsford, 1940.

Holzer, Hans, *Ghost Hunter*, Bobbs-Merrill, 1963.

——*Great British Ghost Hunt*, W H Allen, 1976.

——*In Search of Ghosts*, Manor Books, 1980.

Hopkins, R Thurston, *Cavalcade of Ghosts*, World's Work, 1956.

——*Ghosts Over England*, Meridian Books, 1953.

Houdini, Harry, *A Magician Among the Spirits*, Harper & Brothers, 1924.

Inglis, Brian, *Natural and Supernatural*, Hodder & Stoughton, 1977.

Iremonger, Lucille, *The Ghosts of Versailles*, Faber, 1957.

Koestler, Arthur, *The Roots of Coincidence*, Hutchinson, 1972.

Knight, David C, *The ESP Reader*, Grosset & Dunlap, 1969.

Lambert, R S, *Exploring the Supernatural*, Arthur Barker, 1955.

Leslie, Shane, *Ghost Book*, Hollis & Carter, 1955.

Lethbridge, T C, *Ghost and the Divining Rod*, Routledge & Keegan Paul, 1963.

——*Ghost and Ghoul*, Routledge & Keegan Paul, 1961.

Lodge, Sir Oliver, *The Survival of Man*, Methuen, 1909.

——*Why I Believe in Personal Immortality*, Cassell & Co., 1928.

Lombroso, Cesare, *After Death – What?*, T Fisher Unwin, 1909.

Lorenzen, Coral E, *The Shadow of the Unknown*, New American Library, 1970.

MacGregor, Alasdair Alpine, *Ghost Book*, Robert Hale, 1955.

——*Phantom Footsteps*, Robert Hale, 1959.

MacKenzie, Andrew, *Adventures in Time*, Athlone Press, 1977.

——*Apparitions and Ghosts: A Modern Study*, Arthur Barker, 1971.

——*Frontiers of the Unknown*, Arthur Barker, 1968.

——*Hauntings and Apparitions*, Heinemann, 1982.

——*The Unexplained*, Arthur Barker, 1966.

Manning, Matthew, *The Strangers*, W H Allen, 1978.

Maple, Eric, *The Realm of Ghosts*, Robert Hale, 1964.

Myers, F W H, *Human Personality & Its Survival of Bodily Death*, Longmans, 1903.

O'Donnell, Elliott, *Animal Ghosts*, Rider & Sons, 1913.

——*Byways of Ghostland*, Rider & Sons, 1911.

——*Family Ghosts*, Philip Allen, 1933.

——*Haunted Britain*, Rider & Co., 1948.

——*Twenty Years as a Ghost Hunter*, Heath Cranton Ltd., 1916.

Pike, James A, *The Other Side*, Doubleday, 1968.

Playfair, Guy Lyon, *This House is Haunted*, Souvenir Press, 1980.

Podmore, Frank, *Modern Spiritualism*, Methuen, 1902.

——*The Newer Spiritualism*, T Fisher Unwin, 1920.

Price, Harry, *Confessions of a Ghost Hunter*, Putnam, 1936.

——*Fifty Years of Psychical Research*, Longmans Green, 1939.

——*The Most Haunted House in England*, Longmans Green, 1940.

——*Poltergeist Over England*, Country Life, 1945.

——*The End of Borley Rectory*, George G Harrap & Co., 1946.

Reynolds, James, *Ghosts in Irish Houses*, Paperback Library, 1968.

Rhine, J B, *Extrasensory Perception*, Bruce Humphries, 1964.

Richet, Charles, *Thirty Years of Psychical Research*, W Collins Sons & Co., 1923.

Rosenthal, Eric, *They Walk By Night*, Howard B Timmins, 1949.

Salter, W H, *Ghosts and Apparitions*, G Bell & Sons, 1938.

Saltzman, Pauline, *Ghosts and Other Strangers*, Lancer Books, 1970.

——*The Strange and the Supernatural*, Paperback Library. 1968.

Schrenck-Notzing, Baron von, *Phenomena of Materialisation*, Reinhardt, 1914.

Sitwell, Sacheverell, *Poltergeists*, Faber, 1940.

Smith, Susy, *ESP*, Pyramid Books, 1962.

——*Prominent American Ghosts*, Dell Books, 1967.

Stevens, William Oliver, *Unbidden Guests*, Allen & Unwin, 1949.

Swaffer, Hannen, *My Greatest Story*, W H Allen, 1945.

Tabori, Paul, *Harry Price: The Biography of a Ghost Hunter*, Athenaeum Press, 1950.

Thurston, Herbert, *Ghosts and Poltergeists*, Burns Oates & Washbourne, 1953.

Tyrrel, G N M, *Science and Psychical Phenomena*, University Books, 1961.

——*Apparitions*, Gerald Duckworth, 1943.

Underwood, Peter, *Gazetteer of British Ghosts*, Souvenir Press, 1971.

——*Hauntings*, J M Dent & Sons, 1977.

Wilson, Colin, *The Occult*, Hodder & Stoughton, 1971.

——*Mysteries*, Hodder & Stoughton, 1978.

Research Organizations

Great Britain

The Society for Psychical Research
49 Marloes Road,
Kensington,
London W8 6LA.

Institute of Psychophysical Research
118 Banbury Road,
Oxford,
Oxfordshire OX2 6JU.

The Churches' Fellowship for Psychical & Spiritual Studies
The Rural Workshop,
South Road,
North Somercotes,
Nr. Louth,
Lincolnshire LN11 7PT.

The Ghost Club
PO Box 160,
St Leonards-on-Sea,
East Sussex TN38 8WA.

Scottish Society for Psychical Research
45 Glen Shee Avenue,
Neilston,
Glasgow G78 3QF.

Northern Ireland

Belfast Psychical Society
Gateway House,
57 Dublin Road,
Belfast
BT2 7HE.

Australia

Australasian Society for Psychical Research
PO Box 2001,
Kardinya,
6163 Perth,
Western Australia.

France

Institut Metapsychique International
51 Rue de l'Aqueduc,
75010 Paris,
France.

Germany

Institut fur Grenzgebiete der Psychologie
Wilhelmstrasse 3a,
D-79098 Freiburg i.Br.
Germany.

Italy

Societa Italiana di Parapsicologia
Via dei Montecatini 7,
00186 Roma,
Italy.

New Zealand

Auckland Psychic Research Society
PO Box 5894,
Wellesley Street,
Auckland,
New Zealand.

United States of America

American Society for Psychical Research
5 West 73rd Street,
New York,
NY 10023.

International Society for the Study of Ghosts & Apparitions
Penthouse North,
29 Washington Square West,
New York,
NY 10011-9180.

Parapsychological Research Group
3101 Washington Street,
San Francisco,
California CA 94511.

Center for Scientific Anomalies Research
PO Box 1002,
Ann Arbour,
Michigan MI 48103.

Department of Parapsychology
PO Box 102,
Medical Centre,
University of Virginia,
Charlottesville VA 22908.

California Society for Psychical Study
PO Box 844,
Berkeley,
California 94701.

Psychical Research Foundation
Duke Station,
Durham,
North Carolina 27708.

There are numerous other groups, societies and organizations around the world that study the paranormal, the supernatural and ghosts; for current details the best source of information is the Internet.

Acknowledgments

This book is the result of almost half a century of research into incidents of true hauntings: collecting personal stories, newspaper reports and extracting accounts from books about the supernatural and the paranormal. As a result I owe a great deal of thanks to many individuals, publishers and organizations. I can only include those who have been most helpful here and trust that any I have overlooked or inadvertently left out will forgive me.

First, I would like to acknowledge the following people who have provided me with their stories of hauntings either in oral or written form: Robert Aickman, Marc Alexander, Fred Archer, Beryl Bainbridge, Maurice Barbanell, Dennis Bardens, Michael Bentine, Sir John Betjeman, James Braddock, Anthony Burgess, Eddie Burks, Elizabeth Byrd, Hereward Carrington, Dame Barbara Cartland, James Wentworth Day, Alan Dent, Shaw Desmond, Eric Dingwall, Mia Doran, Gerald Fairlie, Thomas Fletcher, Benny Fisz, Nandor Fodor, Miriam Allen de Ford, Joan Forman, Frederick Forsyth, Ken Gardner, Eileen Garrett, Robert Graves, Andrew Green, Arthur Guirdham, John Harries, Professor John Hasted, Hans Holzer, Gordon Honeycombe, Robert Thurston Hopkins, Brian Inglis, John A Keel, Frederick Knaggs, Arthur Koestler, G W Lambert, Shane Leslie, T C Lethbridge, Coral Lorenzen, Alasdair Alpin MacGregor, Andrew MacKenzie, Matthew Manning, Daphne du Maurier, Nicholas Monsarrat, William F. Nolan, Elliott O'Donnell, Canon John Pearce-Higgins, Dom Robert Petitpierre, Bishop James Pike, Chapman Pincher, Professor H H Price, James Reynolds, Mary Carter Roberts, D Scott Rogo, Professor Archie Roy, Charles Sampson, Jeremy Sandford, Carl Sargeant, Dr Michael Shallis, Susy Smith, John Gay Stevens, Doris Stokes, Hannen Swaffer, Vic Tandy, Paul Tabori, G N Tyrell, Ena Twigg, Peter Underwood, Debbie Watling, Lyall Watson, Dr Caroline Watt, Dennis Wheatley, Henry Williamson and Colin Wilson.

Secondly, my gratitude is extended to the following newspapers and magazines for allowing me to quote from their pages, in particular: *Autocar, Baltimore Sun, Cape Times, Chicago Daily News, Country Life, Daily Express, Daily Mail, Daily Mirror, Daily Star, Daily Telegraph, Dallas Morning Herald, East Anglian Daily Times, East Anglian Magazine, Evening Standard, Forum, Guardian, Halifax Courier, Harper's Magazine, Illustrated London News, Kent Messenger, Lancashire Echo, Lancashire Evening Post, Listener, Liverpool Echo, Los Angeles Examiner, Mail on Sunday, Memphis Commercial Appeal, News of the World, New York Post, New York Daily News, New York Times, New Yorker, New Zealand Herald, Northern Echo, Northwest Evening Mail, Observer, Oxford Mail, People, Perth Weekend Mail, Psychic News, Radio Times, Scientific American, Scotsman, South Wales Echo, The Spectator, Sun, Sunday Express, Sunday Mirror, Sunday Telegraph, Sunday Times, Sydney Morning Herald, The Times, Village Voice, Warwickshire Advertiser, West Essex Gazette, Western Daily Press.*

Finally, a word of thanks to the following publishers for permission to quote passages from their books which are cited in the text: W H Allen, Arrow Books, Batsford & Co., Dell Books, J M Dent & Sons, Duckworth, Faber, Fontana Books, Robert Hale, Charles Letts & Co, Rider & Co., Paperback Library, Manor Books, New American Library, Routledge & Keegan Paul and Souvenir Press Ltd.